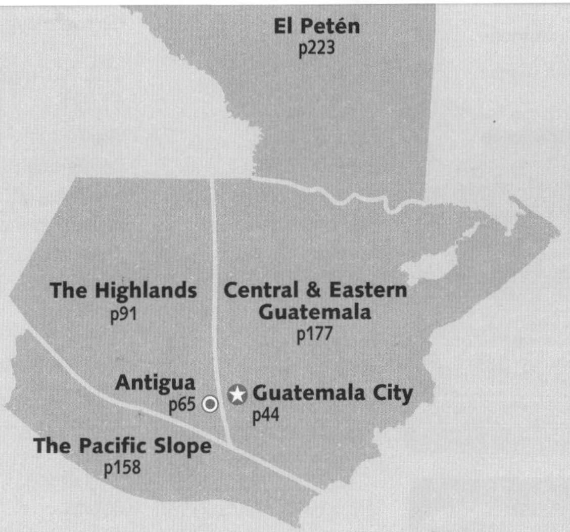
El Petén
p223
The Highlands
p91
Central & Eastern Guatemala
p177
Antigua
p65
Guatemala City
p44
The Pacific Slope
p158

PLAN YOUR TRIP

COLORFUL BUS, PANAJACHEL P93

PUPUSAS (THICK CORN TORTILLAS STUFFED WITH A SAVORY FILLING)

ON THE ROAD

Contents

LOCA4MOTION/SHUTTERSTOCK ©

SEMANA SANTA (HOLY WEEK) CELEBRATIONS, ANTIGUA P77

UNDERSTAND

SURVIVAL GUIDE

SPECIAL FEATURES

Welcome to Guatemala

Central America's most diverse country captivates travelers with its extraordinary landscapes and a civilization-spanning culture that reaches back centuries.

Land of the Maya

The dizzying pyramids of Tikal are Guatemala's most famous tourist drawcard. And what's not to love about this mighty monument to Central America's greatest civilization? But those who stop to ask whatever happened to the Maya are sometimes surprised by the simple answer: nothing. Maya culture continues to evolve today.

The Maya villages in the highlands, where locals still wear traditional dress, are the most visible indicators of this centuries-old culture. But look closely when you're visiting an archaeological site and you'll see altars with modern offerings to ancient spirits.

Colonial Influences

The Spanish left behind plenty of footprints from their colonial conquest of Guatemala, the most visible being the frequently stunning architecture. The best are dotted around Antigua, the old capital, with its neat plazas and crumbling ruins. From the grandiose coffee-boom buildings of Quetzaltenango, to Guatemala City's stately cathedral, to the churches and municipal buildings clustering around central squares in even the smallest towns, Guatemala bears the marks of its European encounters in vivid brick and tile.

Natural Highs

With barely 2% of its landmass urbanized, it's not surprising that Guatemala offers some superb natural scenery. National parks are few but impressive, particularly in the Petén region, and the lush canyons of the Río Dulce make for an unforgettable boat ride. The natural beauty of the volcano-ringed Lago de Atitlán has been captivating travelers for centuries, and you can get high in the Cuchumatanes mountains or below ground in the cave-riddled Verapaces. The swimming hole that launched a thousand postcards, Semuc Champey, has to be seen to be believed, and you can dip your toes in both the Pacific Ocean and the Caribbean Sea.

Adventure Awaits

Active souls tend to find their agenda very full once they get to Guatemala. Stunning trekking routes through the jungles and up volcanoes, world-class white-water rafting, miles of caves to explore, and what seems like a zipline strung between every two trees in the country are just the beginning. Like to take things up a notch? How about paragliding around the high-altitude Lago de Atitlán? You might even luck onto some good swell on the surfer-friendly Pacific coast. Or you could just find a hammock and languidly consider your options. Your call.

Why I Love Guatemala

By Paul Clammer, Writer

It's the smallest moments that leave the deepest impression. A friend took me to San Andrés Xequl and showed me a church built on top of an old Maya temple. Next to it, three locals stood at a blackened altar burning incense and reciting prayers in K'iche'. The offerings were to the old Maya gods, and the prayers told the conquistadors, 'We are still here.' And as they finished, crossing themselves and checking their cell phones, they reminded us how Guatemala's culture has deep roots and will always assimilate what it needs to take its people into the future.

For more about our writers, see p320

Above: The Río Cahabón flows through Semuc Champey (p189)

Guatemala

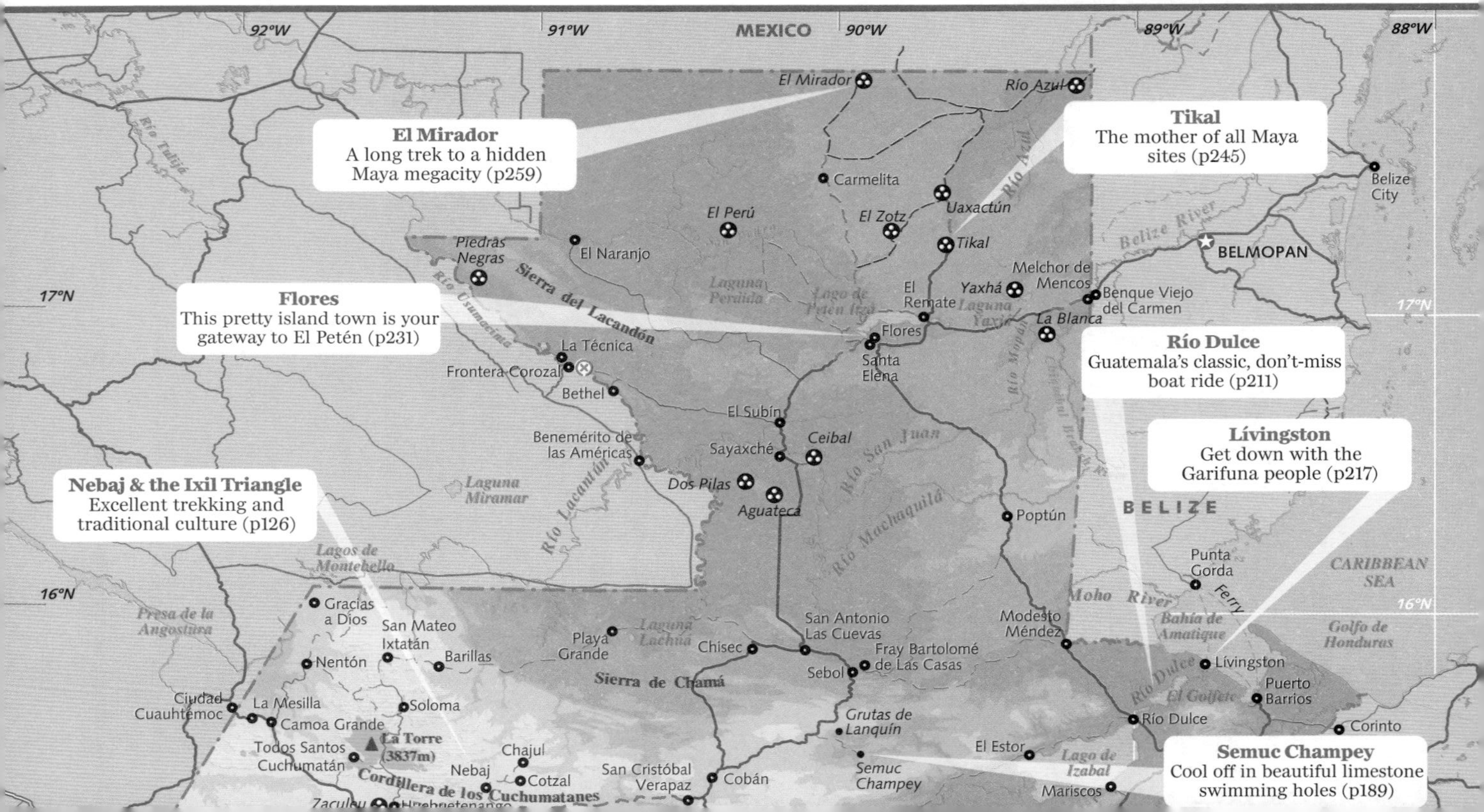

El Mirador
A long trek to a hidden Maya megacity (p259)
Tikal
The mother of all Maya sites (p245)
Flores
This pretty island town is your gateway to El Petén (p231)
Río Dulce
Guatemala's classic, don't-miss boat ride (p211)
Lívingston
Get down with the Garifuna people (p217)
Nebaj & the Ixil Triangle
Excellent trekking and traditional culture (p126)
Semuc Champey
Cool off in beautiful limestone swimming holes (p189)
0 100 km
0 50 miles
MEXICO
BELIZE
BELMOPAN
Belize City
CARIBBEAN SEA
Golfo de Honduras
Bahía de Amatique
92°W
91°W
90°W
89°W
88°W
17°N
16°N
El Mirador
Río Azul
Carmelita
Uaxactún
El Perú
El Zotz
Tikal
Piedras Negras
El Naranjo
Sierra del Lacandón
Yaxhá
Melchor de Mencos
Benque Viejo del Carmen
El Remate
La Blanca
Flores
Santa Elena
La Técnica
Frontera Corozal
Bethel
El Subín
Ceibal
Sayaxché
Benemérito de las Américas
Dos Pilas
Aguateca
Poptún
Punta Gorda
Ferry
Modesto Méndez
Lívingston
Puerto Barrios
Río Dulce
Corinto
El Estor
Mariscos
Lago de Izabal
El Golfete
Semuc Champey
Grutas de Lanquín
Fray Bartolomé de Las Casas
San Antonio Las Cuevas
Sebol
Chisec
Playa Grande
Sierra de Chamá
Cobán
San Cristóbal Verapaz
Chajul
Cotzal
Nebaj
Cordillera de los Cuchumatanes
La Torre (3837m)
Todos Santos Cuchumatán
Soloma
Barillas
San Mateo Ixtatán
Gracias a Dios
Nentón
La Mesilla
Camoa Grande
Ciudad Cuauhtémoc
Lagos de Montebello
Presa de la Angostura
Laguna Miramar
Laguna Perdida
Lago de Petén Itzá
Laguna Yaxjá
Laguna Lachuá
Río Usumacinta
Río Lacantún
Río San Juan
Río Machaquilá
Río Mopán
Río Azul
Belize River
Moho River
Río Tulijá

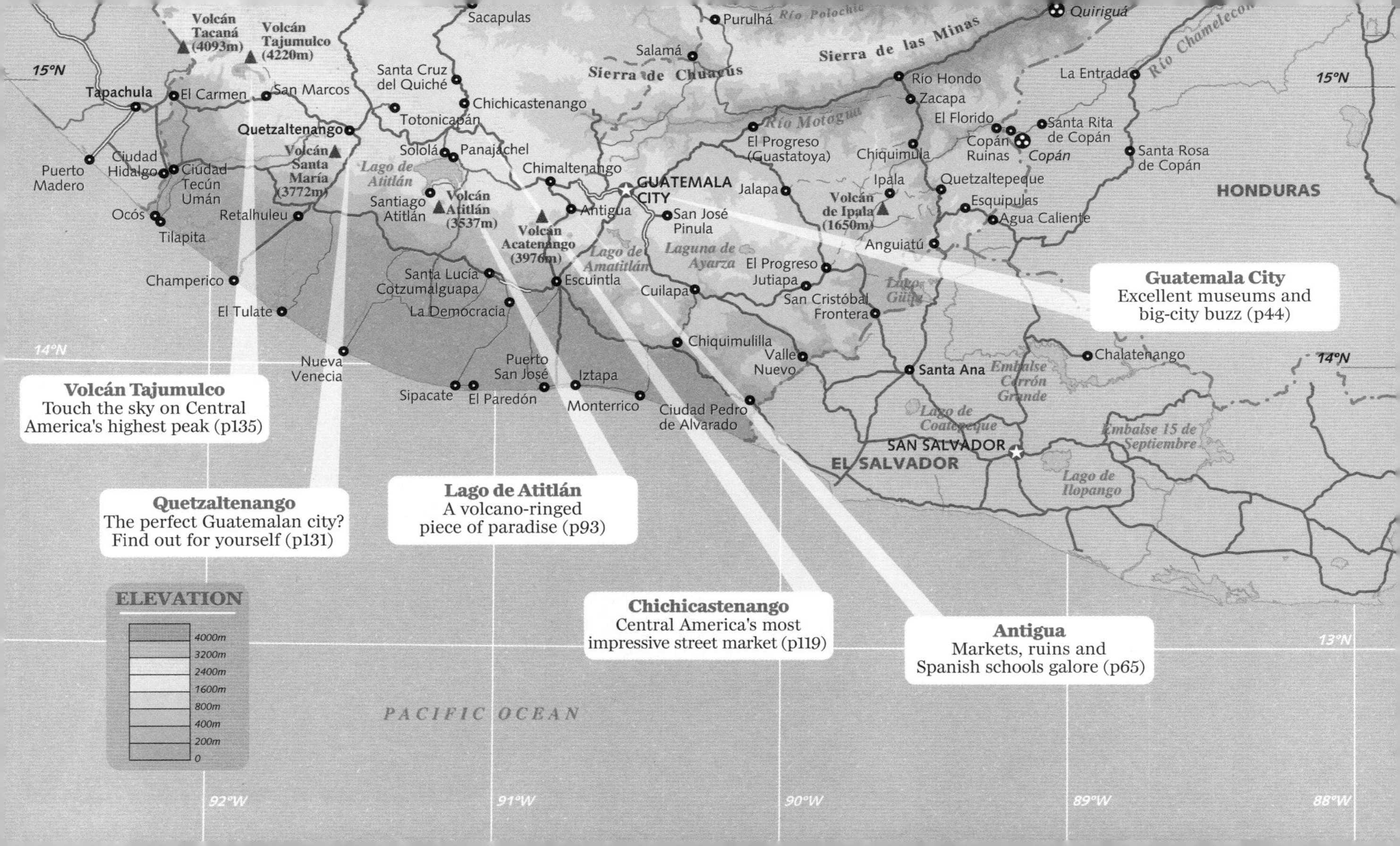
Volcán Tajumulco
Touch the sky on Central America's highest peak (p135)
Quetzaltenango
The perfect Guatemalan city? Find out for yourself (p131)
Lago de Atitlán
A volcano-ringed piece of paradise (p93)
Chichicastenango
Central America's most impressive street market (p119)
Antigua
Markets, ruins and Spanish schools galore (p65)
Guatemala City
Excellent museums and big-city buzz (p44)
ELEVATION
4000m
3200m
2400m
1600m
800m
400m
200m
0
PACIFIC OCEAN
HONDURAS
EL SALVADOR
GUATEMALA CITY
SAN SALVADOR
Sierra de las Minas
Sierra de Chuacús
Río Polochic
Río Motagua
Río Chamelecón
Volcán Tacaná (4093m)
Volcán Tajumulco (4220m)
Volcán Santa María (3772m)
Volcán Atitlán (3537m)
Volcán Acatenango (3976m)
Volcán de Ipala (1650m)
Lago de Atitlán
Lago de Amatitlán
Laguna de Ayarza
Lago Güija
Embalse Cerrón Grande
Lago de Coatepeque
Embalse 15 de Septiembre
Lago de Ilopango
Tapachula
El Carmen
San Marcos
Puerto Madero
Ciudad Hidalgo
Ciudad Tecún Umán
Ocós
Tilapita
Retalhuleu
Quetzaltenango
Champerico
El Tulate
Nueva Venecia
Santa Cruz del Quiché
Sacapulas
Chichicastenango
Totonicapán
Sololá
Panajachel
Santiago Atitlán
Chimaltenango
Antigua
Santa Lucía Cotzumalguapa
La Democracia
Escuintla
Sipacate
El Paredón
Puerto San José
Iztapa
Monterrico
Salamá
Purulhá
San José Pinula
Cuilapa
Chiquimulilla
Ciudad Pedro de Alvarado
El Progreso (Guastatoya)
Jalapa
El Progreso Jutiapa
San Cristóbal Frontera
Valle Nuevo
Río Hondo
Zacapa
Chiquimula
Ipala
Anguiatú
Quetzaltepeque
Esquipulas
Agua Caliente
El Florido
Copán Ruinas
Copán
Santa Rita de Copán
Quiriguá
La Entrada
Santa Rosa de Copán
Santa Ana
Chalatenango
15°N
14°N
13°N
92°W
91°W
90°W
89°W
88°W

Guatemala's Top 15

1

Tikal

1 The remarkably restored Maya temples (p245) that stand in this partially cleared corner of the jungle astonish for both their monumental size and architectural brilliance – as an early morning arrival at the Gran Plaza proves. Occupied for some 16 centuries, they're an amazing testament to the cultural and artistic heights scaled by this jungle civilization. A highlight is the helicopter-like vantage from towering Temple IV on the west edge of the precinct. Equally compelling is the abundance of wildlife, which can be appreciated as you stroll ancient causeways between ceremonial centers.

Antigua

2 With mammoth volcanic peaks and coffee-covered slopes as a backdrop for the scattered remnants of Spanish occupation, the former capital of Guatemala makes an appealing setting for learning Spanish, and a globally varied population comes to Antigua (p65) to study at one of the many quality institutes. Nowhere else in the country packs in such a great culinary and nightlife scene, along with fabulous souvenir shopping in the markets, a sweet little central plaza replete with bubbling fountain, and picture-postcard vistas around every corner.

ROB CRANDALL/SHUTTERSTOCK ©

2

ELADIO RODRÍGUEZ MARTÍN/500PX ©

Chichicastenango

3 'Chichi' (p119) is a vivid window on indigenous tradition, an ancient crossroads for the area's K'iche' Maya–speaking inhabitants, and a spiritually charged site. At Santo Tomás church in the center of town and the hill of Pascual Abaj on its southern edge, Maya rituals blend with Christian iconography to the point where it's hard to tell where one ends and the other begins. The enormous and colorful twice-weekly market is a fabulous place for souvenir hunting, though – particularly if you're after finely woven textiles or carved wooden masks. Top: Market (p121)

Lago de Atitlán

4 Possibly the most beautiful destination in Guatemala, Atitlán (p93) elicits poetic outbursts from even the most seasoned traveler. This blue mirrored lake is ringed by volcanoes and its shores are studded with villages such as Santiago Atitlán, with its thriving indigenous culture, and San Marcos, a haven for seekers who plug into the lake's 'cosmic energy.' Plus there are enough activities – from paragliding and kayaking to hiking the glorious lakeshore trails – to make a longer stay highly attractive. Bottom: View of Volcán San Pedro from Lago de Atitlán

Volcanoes

5 Sacred to the Maya and integral to the country's history, Guatemala's volcanoes dominate the skylines of the country's west, and are one of its emblematic features. You can gaze upon their domed beauty from the comfort of a cafe in Antigua or on Lago de Atitlán, or get up close and personal by climbing (at least) one. Favorites include the lava-spewing Pacaya, Tajumulco – Central America's highest point – and San Pedro, with its sweeping views over picturesque Lago de Atitlán.

Top: Volcán Pacaya (p73)

Sweet River

6 The Río Dulce (p211; literally, 'sweet river') connects Guatemala's largest lake with the Caribbean coast, and winding along it, through a steep-walled valley, surrounded by lush vegetation, bird calls and the (very occasional) manatee is Guatemala's classic, don't-miss-it boat ride. This is no tourist cruise – the river is a way of life and a means of transportation around here – but you get to stop at a couple of places to visit river-dwelling communities and natural hot springs, making for a magical, unforgettable experience.

ANDY KRAMER/ALAMY STOCK PHOTO ©

Quetzaltenango & Around

7 Its blend of mountain scenery, highlands indigenous life, handsome architecture and urban sophistication attracts plenty of visitors to Quetzaltenango (p131) – 'Xela' to most everyone. Come here to study Spanish at the numerous language institutes, or make it a base for excursions to such excellent high-altitude destinations as Laguna Chicabal, a crater lake/Maya pilgrimage site, or the Fuentes Georginas, a natural hot-springs resort ensconced in a verdant valley, and the mysterious Maya deity of San Simón who resides at Zunil. Top left: Iglesia San Andrés Xecul (p145)

Semuc Champey

8 Turquoise-colored water cascades down a series of limestone pools at jungle-shrouded oasis Semuc Champey (p189), creating an idyllic setting that many consider the loveliest spot in the country. You can make it out here on a rushed day tour, but you'd be mad to – Semuc and the nearby village of Lanquín are rural Guatemala at its finest.

Handicrafts & Textiles

9 Inextricably woven into the country's heritage, Guatemalan fabrics are much more than tourist tat. The designs tell the stories of the wearer's community and beliefs. Likewise, handicraft production has always been a part of local life. Fine examples of craftwork and weaving can be seen on the streets all over the country, but if you're looking to take some home (or even to just get some priceless pics), you'll find the best selections in the markets in Guatemala City (p60), Antigua, Panajachel and Chichicastenango.

CLAUDE LETIEN/GETTY IMAGES ©

Guatemala City

10 Vibrant and raw, often confronting and occasionally surprising, the nation's capital (p44) is something of a love it or leave it proposition. Don't blindly listen to the naysayers who'd give it a wide berth, though – those who choose to embrace it look behind its scruffy edges to find a city teeming with life. For culture vultures and museum fans, fine diners, mall rats, live-music lovers and city people in general, the capital has a buzz that's unmatched in the rest of the country.

MARIO RÍOS/EYEEM/GETTY IMAGES ©

El Mirador

11 For true adventurers, the trek to El Mirador (p259) is a thrilling chance to explore the origins of Maya history; it is still being uncovered by archaeologists whom you're likely to meet at the site. Among the hundreds of vegetation-shrouded temples is the tallest pyramid in the Maya world, La Danta, which can be climbed for panoramic views of the jungle canopy. It's at least a six-day hike here and back through the mud and mosquitoes, unless you hire a chopper to the site.

Top: Detail of a stucco frieze

Garifuna Culture in Lívingston

12 Descended from Carib, Arawak and West Africans, the Garifuna are probably the most strikingly different of Guatemala's 23 indigenous language groups. They have their own religion, cuisine, dance and music styles, and a strong cultural identity that has survived despite direct and indirect attempts to quash it. The Garifuna are historically coastal dwellers – their heritage is strongly linked to the Caribbean – and the best place in Guatemala to immerse yourself in Garifuna culture is in the accessible-by-boat-only enclave of Lívingston (p217).

11

EDDIE GERALD/GETTY IMAGES ©

12

SVETLANA BYKOVA/SHUTTERSTOCK ©

TRAVEL INK/GETTY IMAGES ©

ONDREJ PROSICKY/SHUTTERSTOCK ©

PXHIDALGO/GETTY IMAGES ©

Nebaj & the Ixil Triangle

13 A pocket of indigenous culture in a remote (though easily accessed) alpine setting, Nebaj (p126) is little visited, yet it is essential Guatemala. Homeland of the resilient Ixil Maya people, whose language and vivid culture survived the harshest persecutions during the civil-war era, it's also a starting point for hikes through the spectacular Cuchumatanes mountain range, with dozens of intensely traditional villages, such as Cocop and Chajul, where community-run lodgings offer locals much-needed extra income and visitors a glimpse into this fascinating corner of the world.

Wildlife-Watching

14 There are several species worth keeping an eye out for in Guatemala's jungles, rivers, oceans and mountains. The Pacific coast is popular for whale-watching and turtle-spotting and there are manatees around the Río Dulce region. The Verapaces are a popular birding destination – you might even spot an endangered quetzal in Biotopo del Quetzal (p181) – as are the jungles of the Petén region, where you also stand a chance of spotting jaguars, howler monkeys, armadillos and agoutis, among others. Top right: A quetzal (Guatemala's national bird)

Flores

15 An isle of calm at the threshold of a vast jungle reserve, Flores (p231) is both a base for exploring El Petén and a stunning spot to recharge your rambling batteries. Unwinding at the numerous dining and drinking terraces that look across Lago de Petén Ixtá, or cruising in a weathered longboat to even smaller islets, you're likely to find companions for forays to Tikal or more remote places. But the picturesqueness of the town, with its captivating tableau of distant villages, is reason enough to head here.

Need to Know

For more information, see Survival Guide (p291)

Currency
Quetzal (Q)

Languages
Spanish (official), Maya languages (K'iche', Kaqchiquel and Mam most widespread), Garifuna

Visas
Many nationalities do not require tourist visas and will be given a 90-day stay upon entry, though citizens of some countries do need visas.

Money
Banks change cash but *casas de cambio* (currency-exchange offices) are usually quicker and may offer better rates. ATMs widely available.

Cell Phones
Roaming is expensive in Guatemala. Most travelers buy a local SIM card (if you have an unlocked phone) or a local prepaid phone on arrival. ID is required to buy both. 4G is increasingly available.

Time
Central Standard Time (GMT/UTC minus six hours)

When to Go

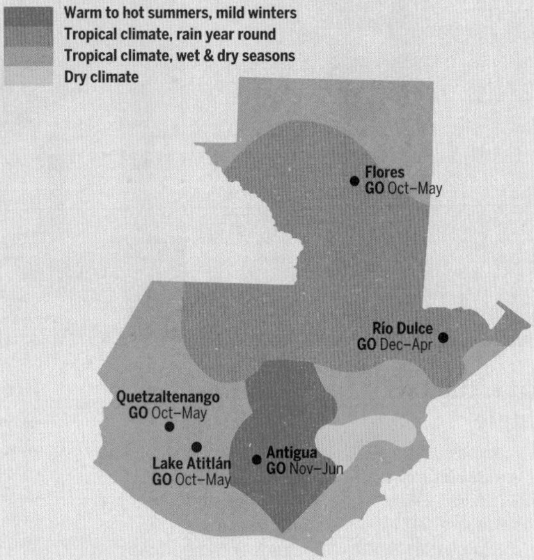
Warm to hot summers, mild winters
Tropical climate, rain year round
Tropical climate, wet & dry seasons
Dry climate
Flores
GO Oct–May
Río Dulce
GO Dec–Apr
Quetzaltenango
GO Oct–May
Lake Atitlán
GO Oct–May
Antigua
GO Nov–Jun

High Season
(Dec–Apr, Jun & Jul)

➡ Around key times (Christmas, New Year, Easter) hotel prices rise significantly.

➡ Book well in advance for Easter in Antigua.

Shoulder
(Oct & Nov)

➡ Rains begin to ease up, but October is peak hurricane season.

➡ Mild temperatures and clear days make this a good time to travel and hike in the highlands.

Low Season
(Apr–Sep)

➡ Prices drop, crowds thin out at archaeological sites, and booking accommodations is rarely necessary.

➡ Daily afternoon rains can make traveling chilly in the highlands and muddy in the jungle.

Useful Websites

Entre Mundos (www.entremundos.org) Guatemalan social and political issues and NGO volunteer database.

Lonely Planet (www.lonelyplanet.com/guatemala) Destination information, hotel bookings, traveler forum and more.

Xela Pages (www.xelapages.com) Information on the highlands and coast, plus blog.

Pacunam (www.pacunam.org) Guatemalan foundation focusing on Maya archaeology, conservation and sustainable tourism to provide context for your trip.

Important Numbers

Guatemala has no regional, area or city codes; just dial the eight-digit number from anywhere in the country.

Guatemala country code	☎502
International access code	☎00
Police	☎120
Proatur (24hr tourist information & assistance)	☎1500
Ambulance	☎125

Exchange Rates

Australia	A$1	Q5.55
Canada	C$1	Q6.00
Euro zone	€1	Q8.92
Japan	¥100	Q.067
New Zealand	NZ$1	Q5.07
UK	UK£1	Q10.05
US	US$1	Q7.67

For current exchange rates, see www.xe.com.

Daily Costs

Budget: Less than Q400

- Dorm bed: Q60–100
- Budget hotel double room: Q130–200
- Set meal in a *comedor* (cheap eatery): Q30–45
- 'Chicken-bus' ride (3hrs): Q20

Midrange: Q400–Q1000

- Hotel double room: Q200–550
- À la carte meal in a local restaurant: Q100–130
- Archaeological site admission: Q50–150
- Three-hour shuttle-bus ride: Q150

Top End: More than Q1000

- Superior hotel double room: Q550 or more
- Meal in an elegant restaurant: Q150 or more
- Guide at archaeological site: up to Q450
- 4WD car-hire per day: Q650

Opening Hours

Hours provided are general guidelines, but there are many variations. Restaurant times, in particular, can vary by up to two hours either way.

The *Ley Seca* (dry law) stipulates that bars and *discotecas* must close by 1am, except on nights before public holidays; it is rigidly followed in large cities and universally mocked in smaller towns.

Banks 9am–5pm Monday to Friday, 9am–1pm Saturday

Bars 11am–1am

Cafes & Restaurants 7am–9pm

Government offices 8am–4pm Monday to Friday

Shops 8am–noon and 2–6pm Monday to Saturday

Arriving in Guatemala

Aeropuerto Internacional La Aurora (p62; Guatemala City) Authorized taxis wait out the front of departures. Buy a coupon (Q80 for Zona 1, Q70 for Zona 10 or 13) at the booth before the exit. Shuttle buses to Antigua (Q80) wait out the front, too – just listen for someone yelling 'Antigua, Antigua.'

Aeropuerto Internacional Mundo Maya (p238) Taxis wait outside, charging Q30 to Flores or Santa Elena. For Tikal or El Remate, go out to the main road and hail a passing minibus.

Getting Around

Pullman Bus Running only on major highways, these are the most comfortable choice. Seats are numbered and they run either semidirect or direct.

Shuttle Minibus Booked through travel agents, hotels etc, these nonstop minibuses run between major tourist destinations, offering door-to-door service.

Chicken Bus Recycled US school buses, these are cheap, go everywhere, stop for everybody and have no maximum capacity.

Pick-up Truck In areas where there is no bus service this is a common way to get around. Flag one down wherever, climb into the back and hang on. Fares are equivalent to chicken buses.

Car If you're accustomed to crazy Latino traffic, driving is a great way to get off the beaten track.

Tuk-tuk These little three-wheelers are great for short hops around town at a fraction of a taxi fare.

For much more on **getting around**, see p302

First Time Guatemala

For more information, see Survival Guide (p291)

Checklist

- Make sure your passport is valid for at least six months past your arrival date
- Check visa requirements
- Arrange for appropriate travel insurance
- Inform your debit-/credit-card company that you'll be making foreign transactions
- Organize necessary immunizations
- Read up on your government's Guatemala travel advisories

What to Pack

- International plug adapter (for non-US appliances)
- Spanish phrasebook
- Small medical kit
- Flashlight (torch)
- Money belt
- Good walking shoes
- Warm clothes if going to the highlands
- Padlock (if staying in dorms)
- Driver's license (if driving)
- Sunscreen and insect repellent
- Pocketknife
- Antibacterial hand gel

Top Tips for Your Trip

- If possible, learn some Spanish before you arrive and some more when you get here – Guatemalans are extremely patient and will love you for just giving it a go.
- Pack as lightly as possible. Anything that locals use on a day-to-day basis can be bought cheaply. Anything remotely luxurious (electronics, imported goods etc) will be cheaper at home.
- Be aware of your surroundings (but not paranoid). If your gut tells you something is not right, it probably isn't.
- Be realistic in your planning. Sure you'd like to see everything, but it's better to focus on quality time in a few places rather than rushing from place to place and spending most of your time on a bus.

What to Wear

Regardless of their economic status, Guatemalans do their best to look neat at all times, and you should do the same. This goes double when dealing with officialdom. The general look is neat-casual – pants and jeans are fine for both sexes, skirts should be (at least) below the knee. The only places you're really going to want to dress up for are fancy restaurants or Guatemala City *discotecas*.

Shorts and sleeveless tops are OK for the beach and coastal towns. In the highlands people tend to cover up more – a sensible move, considering the climate.

Dress conservatively when entering churches and visiting rural communities.

Sleeping

Guatemala has a wide variety of good accommodations options, from tried-and-trusted backpacker hostels to boutique hotels and international chains. It's generally not necessary to book your accommodations in advance. If, however, you're planning on being in Antigua or down at the beach during Semana Santa, the sooner you book the better.

Money

Banks change cash but *casas de cambio* (currency-exchange offices) are usually quicker and may offer better rates. ATMs widely available. Credit cards accepted in many hostels and most midrange and above hotels and restaurants.

For more information, see p297.

Bargaining

Haggling is pretty much a national pastime in Guatemala. Treat it as a game, and if you feel you're getting ripped off, just walk away. Don't haggle in small stores and restaurants; always haggle in markets and with taxi drivers.

Tipping

A 10% tip is expected in restaurants (often automatically added to your bill in tourist towns such as Antigua). In small *comedores* (basic, cheap eateries) tipping is optional, but follow local practice and leave some spare change.

Homestays Better to buy a gift than give cash.

Hotels Q10 per bag.

Restaurants 10% maximum (if not already included).

Taxis Not customary.

Trekking & tour guides Q50 per person per day (optional).

Maya women cooking tortillas, Sacatepéquez

Etiquette

Dress General standards of modesty in dress have relaxed somewhat. Coastal dwellers tend to show a lot more skin than highland types, but not all locals appreciate this type of attire.

Entering a room In public places such as a restaurant or waiting room, make a general greeting to everyone – *buenos días* or *buenas tardes* will do.

Greetings When meeting someone personally, men shake hands with men, women air-kiss women, and men and women may air-kiss or shake – wait to see if the woman offers her hand.

Maya women Many Maya women avoid contact with foreign men. As a general rule, male travelers in need of information should ask another man.

Photos Understandably, the Maya can be very sensitive about being photographed. Always ask for permission before taking pictures.

Eating

Comedores Found everywhere but particularly around bus stops and markets, these simple diners dish out set meals at low prices.

Restaurantes A more formal dining experience than the *comedor*, you'll get a wider menu, maybe a tablecloth, and probably a selection of wines and beers.

Carritos Mobile food vendors deal out tacos, hot dogs, *churrascos* (barbecued meat), *pupusas* (gilled corn meal with cheese or bean filling), barbecued corn, and other street foods.

What's New

Franja Trasversal del Norte

Work continues apace on this long-delayed route, which will offer 337km of highway from southwest Mexico to the Guatemala-Belize border. It's the only sane way to cross the country without backtracking through Guatemala City, When finished it should bring new development and tourism opportunities to neglected corners of Alta Verapaz, Huehuetenango and Quiché – all areas that still carry deep scars from the civil war.

Guatemala City Zona 1

This once-gritty area is gaining ground as the go-to spot for local 20- and 30-somethings who want to chill or party. (p46)

Crater Azul

This rival to Samuc Champey near Sayaxché is a great swimming spot in sublimely clear water at the head of a spring-fed tributary. (p228)

Tikal

Old is the new new at this amazing ruin, which has been at the heart of new 'laser radar' LIDAR exploration that's reshaping our entire understanding of the ancient Maya. (p245)

Flores

Enjoy Japanese excellence at Posada de Quiriguá (p200) near one of the area's most interesting and out-of-the-way ruins, and drop in on Maple y Tocino (p235) to enjoy great donut-topped milkshakes, breakfast treats, and hot sandwiches, overlooking Lago de Petén Itzá.

Zaculeu Museum, Huehuetenango

The brilliant museum at this heavily restored Maya site in the highlands gives a perfect presentation on the region's ancient history. (p149)

Boutique Hostels, Antigua

Flashpacking has arrived in the old colonial capital, allowing you to bed down in fashionably upmarket dorms at the Maya Papaya (p78), Adra (p78) and Cucuruchos hostels (p77).

Surf Guatemala, El Paredón

Guatemala's Pacific 'surf coast' moves beyond backpackers with the stylish new Surf House (p171) and Swell (p171) guesthouses, along with ecotourism operator La Choza Chula (p170).

Quetzaltenango

The capital of the highlands finally gets the rooftop bar with a view that travelers were waiting for with new hostel Kasa Kiwi (p138), plus smart Asian cuisine at its nearby sister restaurant Esquina Asiatica (p140).

El Hato

Make like Frodo and Bilbo at the Middle Earth-themed mountain lodge of Hobbitenango. (p88)

For more recommendations and reviews, see **lonelyplanet.com/guatemala**

If You Like...

Colonial Architecture

Antigua Guatemala's colonial show pony is a riot of gorgeous cobblestoned streetscapes, crumbling ruins and noble churches. (p65)

Iglesia San Andrés Xecul Colonial/indigenous fusion at its wildest, this small church features a phantasmagoric facade laced with Maya imagery. (p145)

Guatemala City While most of the city is fabulously ugly, there are some definite gems here, particularly in the Centro Historico. (p44)

Cobán This cute hilltop town has a couple of real lookers, some of which have been converted into charming hotels. (p182)

Quetzaltenango The country's second city has some great old buildings, especially around the Parque Central. (p131)

Volcanoes

Tajumulco Central America's highest point is a relatively easy climb, particularly if you take two days and camp overnight. (p135)

Pacaya An easy day trip from Antigua, this smoking, lava-dribbling peak is an all-time favorite for hikers. (p73)

Santa María Get an early start and catch the sunrise and views that stretch from Mexico to Antigua and out to the Pacific. (p135)

San Pedro A moderate half-day hike rewards you with gorgeous views of Lago de Atitlán and surrounds. (p109)

Ruins

Tikal This regional superstar is well on the tourist trail, but totally worth the visit for its soaring, jungle-shrouded temples. (p245)

El Mirador A little hard to get to (unless you pony up for the helicopter ride), you can watch archaeologists at work at this former megacity. (p259)

Copán Just over the border in Honduras, this site hosts some of the finest carvings and stonework in the region. (p201)

Aguateca Impressive clifftop Maya site with walls and chasm defenses and tremendous views, accessible by river trip only. (p228)

Takalik Abaj The only really impressive set of ruins on the Pacific Coast shows evidence of some of the earliest links between Olmec and Maya cultures. (p164)

Off-the-Beaten-Track Places

Chajul Step back in time and experience life as it has been lived for hundreds of years in this very traditional town. (p129)

San Mateo Ixtatán Up near the Mexican border, this cute village is surrounded by spectacular scenery. (p155)

Tilapita This classic one-hotel beach town is a great place to take a breather and watch the world go (slowly) by. (p159)

Wildlife

Monterrico Save a turtle, spot a whale or go birdwatching in the mangroves from this Pacific coast village. (p172)

Biotopo del Quetzal The cloud forest of this reserve near Cobán is home to a plethora of bird species, including the national bird, the resplendent quetzal. (p181)

Río Dulce If you're very quiet and very lucky, you might just spot a manatee or a crocodile near the banks of this jungle-shrouded river. (p211)

Estación Biológica Las Guacamayas Biologists travel to this research station in a protected jungle reserve to study jaguars, crocodiles, turtles and exotic scarlet macaws. (p258)

Handicrafts & Textiles

Chichicastenango Central America's oldest and largest handicrafts market is a visual feast and souvenir heaven. (p121)

Antigua For a tourist-town market, prices are reasonable and shopping is reasonably hassle-free with a country-wide selection of goods. (p84)

Santiago Atitlán Maya women weave textiles as they have for centuries in this Tz'utujil community on Lago de Atitlán's southern shore. See the work and the process at the excellent Cojolya Association of Maya Women Weavers museum. (p106)

Panajachel Sure, they're pushy, but the street vendors and roadside stalls in this lakeside town have some of the best collections of textiles, at very reasonable prices. (p102)

Doing Nothing

San Marcos La Laguna Taking it easy is pretty much a way of life in Guatemala's lakeside yoga and wellness hub. (p114)

Lanquín Sure there are caves to explore and rivers to tube... tomorrow... (p187)

El Paredón You can hit the surf at this Pacific village, but there are some equally important beach hammocks to test out for an afternoon or three. (p170)

Río Dulce Kick back riverside for a few days in a secluded jungle lodge. (p211)

Earth Lodge Chill out on an avocado farm in the hills above Antigua. (p88)

Top: Maya woman selling handmade textiles, Panajachel (p102)

Bottom: Volcán Agua (p73) looms behind the Santa Catalina arch, Antigua (p65)

Month by Month

TOP EVENTS

Desfile de Bufos, March

Semana Santa, April

Día de Todos los Santos, November

Garifuna Day, November

Quema del Diablo, December

January

Generally cooler temperatures make this a good time to be traveling. In the first couple of weeks you're bound to meet plenty of Guatemalan families taking advantage of school holidays.

El Cristo Negro de Esquipulas

Pilgrims in their thousands flock to the town of Esquipulas in the days leading up to January 15 to pay homage to the Black Christ.

Rabinal Achí

In the highly traditional Baja Verapaz town of Rabinal, pre-Columbian dances are performed during the Fiesta de San Pedro from the 19th to the 25th.

March

The European spring break sees a mini high season – nothing books out, but things start to get a little more lively.

Desfile de Bufos (The Parade of Fools)

On the Friday before Good Friday, this 100+ year-old tradition sees thousands of hooded Guatemala City university students take to the streets in floats and costumes to mock the government.

April

On average the warmest month. All the foreigners want to be in Antigua and all the Guatemalans want to be at the beach – accommodations for both places should be booked well in advance.

Semana Santa

While there are Easter processions all over the country, the most atmospheric are in Antigua and the most elaborate floats are in Guatemala City.

May

The semi-official start of the rainy season (although this is starting to vary wildly) sees afternoon showers across the country until the end of October (or thereabouts).

Día del Trabajo (Labor Day)

On the first day of May there are celebrations, parades and protests throughout the country, the largest being in Guatemala City.

June

The end of the US college year sees a large influx of students arriving to study Spanish, volunteer and travel. The rainy season continues.

Turtle Nesting Season

Running until November, the main nesting season on the Pacific coast sees thousands of turtles come ashore to lay eggs. The best place to spot them is around Monterrico. (p173)

July

The college break continues, with many Spanish students finishing their studies and starting to travel. This is the depths of the rainy season, with the most rain and least sunshine.

Fiesta de Cubulco

The small town of Cubulco is one of the few places left in the country to keep the Palo Volador (literally, 'flying pole') tradition alive. It happens on the last day of its five-day festival, on July 25.

Rabin Ajau

In the last week of July Cobán hosts this festival that showcases pre-Columbian traditions, including Maya ceremonies, traditional handicrafts, and plenty of music and dance.

August

Crowds start to thin out as college students return home. Often in this month there is a phenomenon called the *canicula* ('dog days' in English), which sees a warm, sunny break in the rains.

Fiesta de la Virgen de la Asunción

Peaking on August 15, this fiesta is celebrated with folk dances and parades in Sololá, Guatemala City and Jocotenango.

September

Temperatures start to cool and rains begin to ease up. This is the start of the real low season, and if you're into haggling on accommodations, now's a good time to start.

Independence Day

September 15 marks Guatemala's anniversary of independence. There are celebrations all over the country, but because it coincides with Quetzaltenango's week-long festival, you'll find the most activity there, with loads of concerts and other cultural activities.

October

As the rains peter out, this month marks the start of volcano-trekking season, with spectacular cloud formations until mid-November.

Fiesta de San José Petén

On the night of the 31st a very curious ceremony takes place, as one of three skulls (thought to be of the village's founding fathers) is removed from the town church and paraded through this small town.

November

This is the peak of the volcano-trekking season, which runs until the end of January, with clear skies and cool, moderate temperatures.

Día de Todos los Santos

All Saint's Day (November 1) is celebrated with particular rigor in Santiago Sacatepéquez and Sumpango, where celebrations include the flying of huge, technicolor kites.

Todos Santos Cuchumatán

On All Saints Day, this tiny highlands town hosts drunken horse races through the main streets. Some love it, others find it a rather disturbing spectacle.

Garifuna Day

The Garifuna enclave of Lívingston celebrates its heritage on November 26 with live music, dancing, parades, traditional food and other lively celebrations.

December

Seriously chilly temperatures hit the highlands – bring warm clothes or plan on buying some here. There's a little spike in vacationing Guatemalans, but most wait until after Christmas before they start traveling.

Orchid Festival

The misty hill country around Cobán makes for a perfect orchid habitat and this annual festival, held in the first week of December, showcases the variety of species that can be found in the area.

Quema del Diablo

All over the country (but particularly in the highlands) people haul their trash out into the street on December 7 and make huge bonfires while men dressed as devils run and dance amid the smoke.

Whale-Watching Season

From mid-December until the end of May, humpback and sperm whales can be seen migrating along the Pacific coast.

Itineraries

1 WEEK Greatest Hits

On a short break and want to see it all? Well, that's not going to happen, but with a week you can at least see Guatemala's Big Three – Antigua, Lago de Atitlán and Tikal.

Flying into Guatemala City, shuttle or taxi directly to **Antigua**. If you don't arrive too late, grab dinner at one of the city's many fabulous restaurants and maybe a nightcap in a cozy bar. The next morning, take a walk around town – cut corners if you like, but don't miss the **Arco de Santa Catalina** and **Iglesia Merced**. You'll probably want an early night because the next day you'll be climbing a volcano – check with the locals to see which one is safe/recommended to climb at the moment. Back in town, catch dinner at the wonderfully atmospheric Mesón Panza Verde.

The next day it's on to **Lago de Atitlán**. Panajachel is great for shopping and eating, but read up on the other villages around the lake – each is different and has its own appeal. Regardless of where you end up, spend half a day exploring 'your' village and the next day exploring the rest of the lake.

Next it's off to **Tikal**, so shuttle back to Guatemala City and then on to **Flores**. Head straight for the site, spend the day exploring and then return to Guatemala City for your flight home.

10 DAYS

Highland Fling

Guatemala's most spectacular scenery and strongest Maya traditions await along this well-traveled route. It could easily take a few months if you stop off to learn some Spanish or to take advantage of the great sightseeing and hiking possibilities along the way.

From the capital head first to picturesque **Antigua**, enjoying the country's finest colonial architecture, the great restaurants and the traveler and language-student scene. Several volcanoes wait to be climbed here including the fiery Volcán Fuego – but ask around for current conditions before planning anything. From Antigua move on to Panajachel on volcano-ringed **Lago de Atitlán**. Hop in a boat to check out some of the quieter, more traditional Maya villages around the lake such as Santiago Atitlán, where the curious deity Maximón awaits, or San Pedro La Laguna, a party town with a certain fame countrywide. San Marcos La Laguna is much more laid-back and a magnet for yoga and natural-healing types. Santa Cruz La Laguna, meanwhile, is just plain tiny and gorgeous. From the lake, hop a shuttle or 'chicken bus' north to **Chichicastenango** for its huge Thursday or Sunday market and, if you're lucky, a religious ceremony where it's hard to tell where the Maya-ism ends and the Catholicism starts.

From Chichicastenango you can follow the Interamerican Hwy west along the mountain ridges to **Quetzaltenango**, Guatemala's clean, orderly second city, with a host of intriguing villages, markets and natural wonders waiting within short bus rides away. From Quetzaltenango it's possible to go further into the hills to **Todos Santos Cuchumatán**, a fascinating Maya mountain town with great walking possibilities.

If you have extra time, consider pushing east to explore **Nebaj** and the Ixil Triangle, where you'll find great hiking opportunities and a strong Maya way of life amid stunning scenery. A rough but passable road leads further eastward from here, passing Uspantan and providing a back-door route to Alta Verapaz, where you can check out the divine waters of **Semuc Champey** or head further north toward the famous Maya ruins of **Tikal**.

2 WEEKS Guatemala Circuit

With two weeks to play with you can work your way around the best that Guatemala has to offer without breaking too much of a sweat – unless you count the jungle heat of Tikal, of course.

After taking in the museums and restaurants of **Guatemala City**, head northeast to the hot and sticky Caribbean coast and the beaches and Garifuna culture of **Lívingston**. From here you can take the spectacular boat trip upriver to **Río Dulce** and its hot springs.

From Río Dulce town, head north to traveler-friendly **Flores** on Lago de Petén Itzá. You'll use this town as your base to visit the extraordinary ruins at **Tikal**, where you can spend as much time spotting monkeys as Maya ruins.

When you've had your fill of ancient culture, travel south to **Cobán**, the springboard to the gorgeous jungle waterfalls and swimming holes of **Semuc Champey**. It's one of the prettiest corners of the entire country.

Bypass the capital on the second half of your trip to take stock in the old colonial capital of **Antigua**, with its beautiful buildings, great food and lively traveler scene. It's a short hop from here to **Chichicastenango**: time your visit to take in the twice-weekly market, which is one of the largest and most colorful in Central America.

Continue to volcano-fringed **Lago de Atitlán**, where you have a wide choice of lakeside towns and villages to stay in according to your taste. You might choose busy **Panajachel**, the yoga-chilling **San Marcos La Laguna**, backpacker party hub **San Pedro La Laguna** or ecofriendly **Tzununá**. As ferries zip constantly between them, there's time to visit more than one, and still squeeze in a quick volcano hike.

Finish your adventure with a dash down the Pacific coast to the up-and-coming town of **El Paredón**, where you can grab a surf board, do a wildlife tour of the mangroves or simply laze in a hammock. When you're done, pack up your souvenirs and take a shuttle back to Guatemala City for your flight home.

FREDY ESTUARDO MALDONADO/GETTY IMAGES ©

Top: Traditional festival, Chichicastenango (p122)

Bottom: Playa Blanca (p217), Lívingston

29

3 WEEKS The Maya Loop

This 1900km round trip takes you to the best of Guatemala's Maya ruins, into its dense jungles and to some of its spectacular natural marvels, covering the center, east and north of the country. Really pushing, you might do it in two weeks; if you have four, you'll enjoy it even more.

Start out northeastward from **Guatemala City**, where you can enjoy great food, nightlife and culture and then detour south into Honduras to see the great Maya site of **Copán**. Don't just make it a flying visit, though – Copán is a great town and there's plenty to do in the surrounding countryside. Return to Guatemala and continue northeastward to another fine Maya site, **Quiriguá**, where you can marvel at the 10m-plus carved stelae and you may just have the place to yourself. From here move on to the curious Garifuna enclave of **Lívingston** on the sweaty Caribbean coast. Soak up the atmosphere in this entirely different corner of Guatemala and get in some beach time on the country's finest beaches. Take a boat up the jungle-lined **Río Dulce**, stopping for a dip in the hot springs along the way before reaching **Río Dulce town**. Head north up Hwy 13 to chill out at **Finca Ixobel** before continuing to **Flores**, a quaint small town on an island in the Lago de Petén Itzá. From Flores, head for **Tikal**, the most majestic of all Maya sites. Spend a night at Tikal itself or nearby El Remate. While in the Flores/Tikal area, you should have time to take in further impressive Maya sites such as **Yaxhá** and **Uaxactún**.

From Flores head southwest to the relaxed riverside town of **Sayaxché**, which is at the center of another group of intriguing Maya sites – **Ceibal**, **Aguateca** and **Dos Pilas**. The road south from Sayaxché is now paved all the way to **Chisec** and **Cobán**, jumping-off points for a whole series of pristine natural wonders, such as jungle-ringed **Laguna Lachuá**, the **Grutas de Lanquín** and the turquoise lagoons and waterfalls of **Semuc Champey**. Finally, make your way back to Guatemala City for your flight home.

Guatemala: Off the Beaten Track

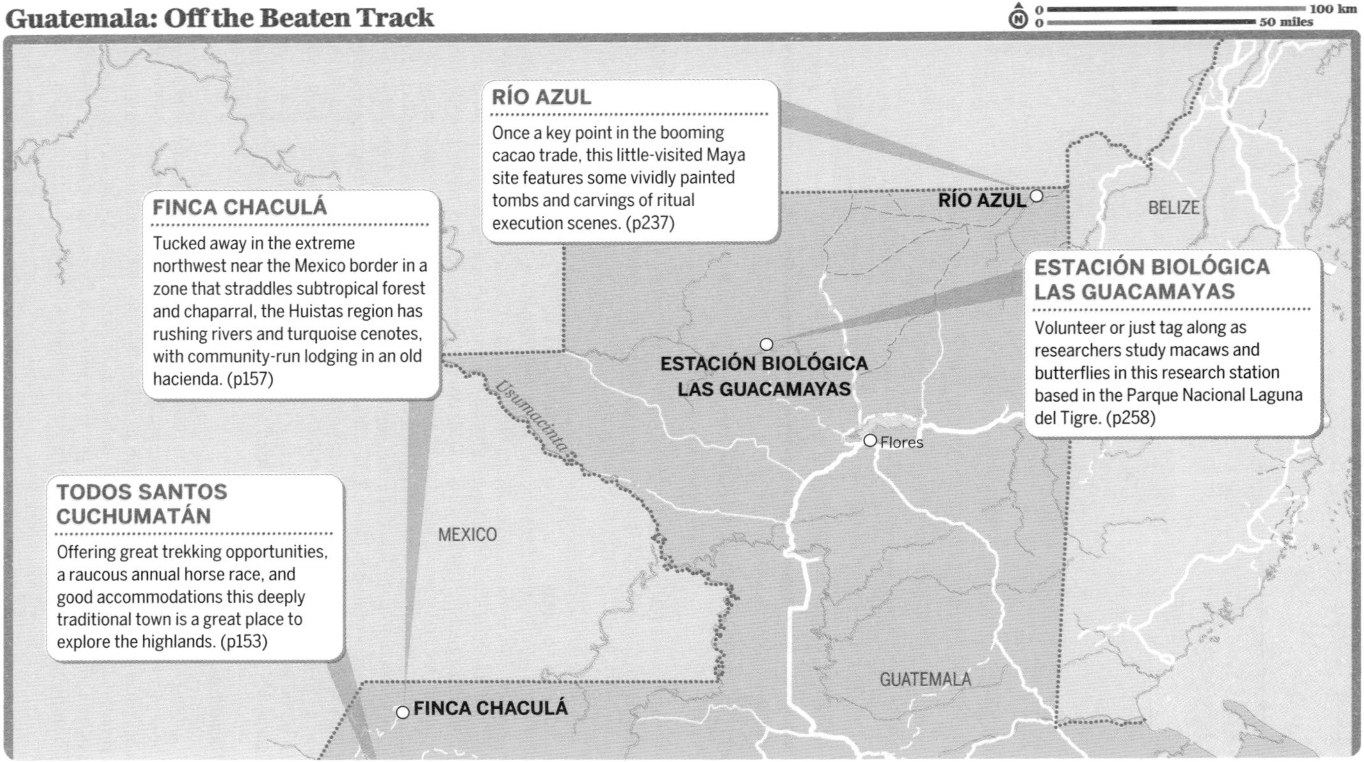
0 100 km
0 50 miles
RÍO AZUL
Once a key point in the booming cacao trade, this little-visited Maya site features some vividly painted tombs and carvings of ritual execution scenes. (p237)
FINCA CHACULÁ
Tucked away in the extreme northwest near the Mexico border in a zone that straddles subtropical forest and chaparral, the Huistas region has rushing rivers and turquoise cenotes, with community-run lodging in an old hacienda. (p157)
ESTACIÓN BIOLÓGICA LAS GUACAMAYAS
Volunteer or just tag along as researchers study macaws and butterflies in this research station based in the Parque Nacional Laguna del Tigre. (p258)
TODOS SANTOS CUCHUMATÁN
Offering great trekking opportunities, a raucous annual horse race, and good accommodations this deeply traditional town is a great place to explore the highlands. (p153)
RÍO AZUL
BELIZE
ESTACIÓN BIOLÓGICA LAS GUACAMAYAS
Flores
Usumacinta
MEXICO
GUATEMALA
FINCA CHACULÁ

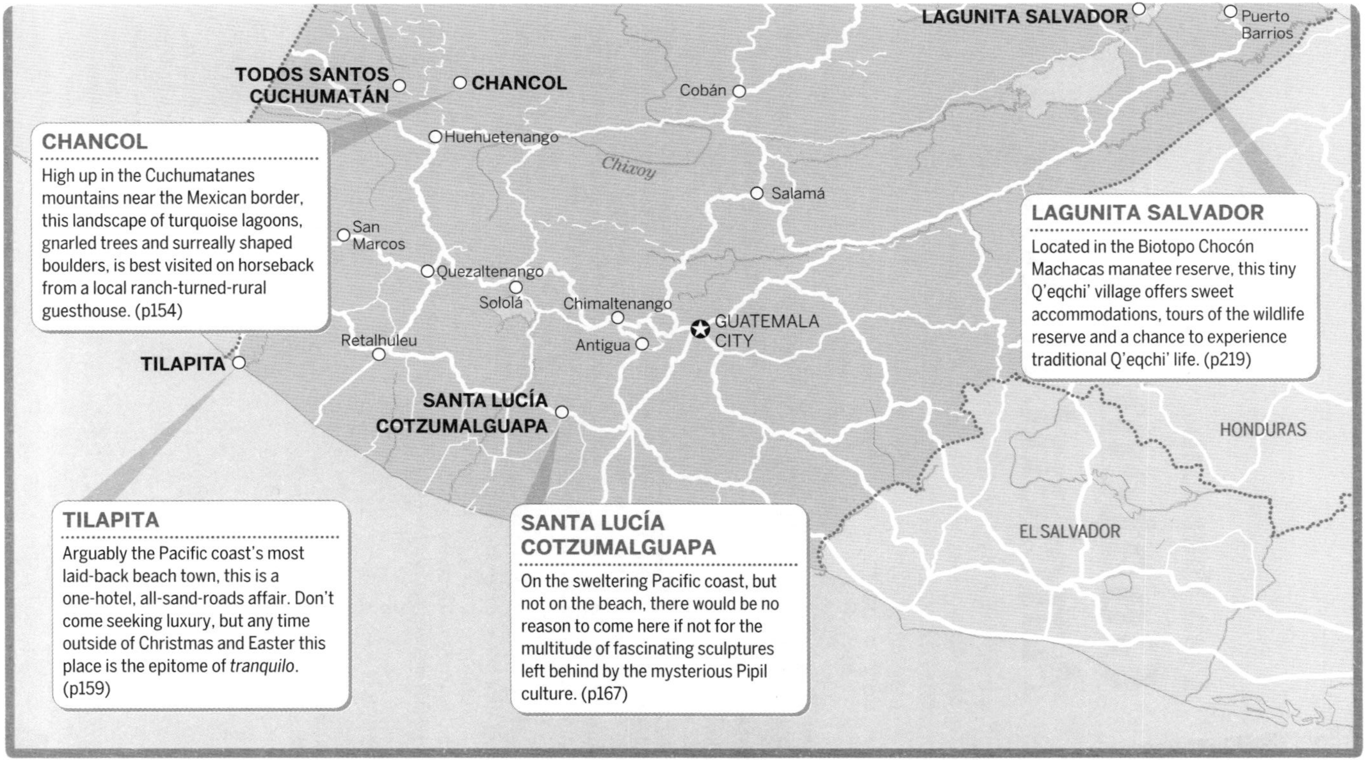

CHANCOL

High up in the Cuchumatanes mountains near the Mexican border, this landscape of turquoise lagoons, gnarled trees and surreally shaped boulders, is best visited on horseback from a local ranch-turned-rural guesthouse. (p154)

LAGUNITA SALVADOR

Located in the Biotopo Chocón Machacas manatee reserve, this tiny Q'eqchi' village offers sweet accommodations, tours of the wildlife reserve and a chance to experience traditional Q'eqchi' life. (p219)

TILAPITA

Arguably the Pacific coast's most laid-back beach town, this is a one-hotel, all-sand-roads affair. Don't come seeking luxury, but any time outside of Christmas and Easter this place is the epitome of *tranquilo*. (p159)

SANTA LUCÍA COTZUMALGUAPA

On the sweltering Pacific coast, but not on the beach, there would be no reason to come here if not for the multitude of fascinating sculptures left behind by the mysterious Pipil culture. (p167)

Plan Your Trip

Guatemala's Ancient Ruins

Stretching at its peak from northern El Salvador to the Gulf of Mexico, the Maya empire during its Classic period was arguably pre-Hispanic America's most brilliant civilization. The huge ceremonial center of Tikal is undoubtedly Guatemala's greatest visitor attraction, but there are plenty of lesser known sites worth exploring.

Need to Know

Where

The majority of Maya sites are in El Petén region, in the country's flat north. The other major grouping is in the southwest, roughly centered on Lago de Atitlán.

When

The ideal months to visit archaeological sites are outside of the rainy season. In El Petén you want to avoid the heat, while in the highlands seriously cold nighttime temperatures can make travel uncomfortable. Roughly speaking, the better times to visit El Petén are from November to April, while the highlands are best from February to May.

Opening Hours

Most sites are open from 8am to 4pm daily, but check times ahead of your visit. For the more popular sites, the best time to go is soon after opening time, thereby beating the tour bus crowds and the midday sun.

Visiting the Ruins

Maya achievement during this period rivaled anything that was going on in Europe at the time, boasting an advanced writing system, awe-inspiring engineering feats, advanced mathematics and astrology, and stone-working skills that remain impressive to this day.

Many legacies of the Maya have disappeared over time. Archaeological pieces have been carried off either by tomb raiders or foreign governments and much cultural heritage has been lost over the centuries due to government and church campaigns to assimilate the Maya into mainstream Hispanic culture. However, the current use of the revolutionary LIDAR ground survey technique (think radar, but with lasers) is currently revealing thousands of previously unknown Maya structures otherwise hidden by jungle or other vegetation, making today an exciting and radical time for Mayan archaeology.

Outside of Guatemala City's fantastic selection of museums, the best way to get a feel for the achievements of this unique culture is to visit archaeological sites.

Visiting a Maya ruin can be a powerful experience, a true step back in time. While some sites are little more than a pile of

Guatemala's Ancient Ruins

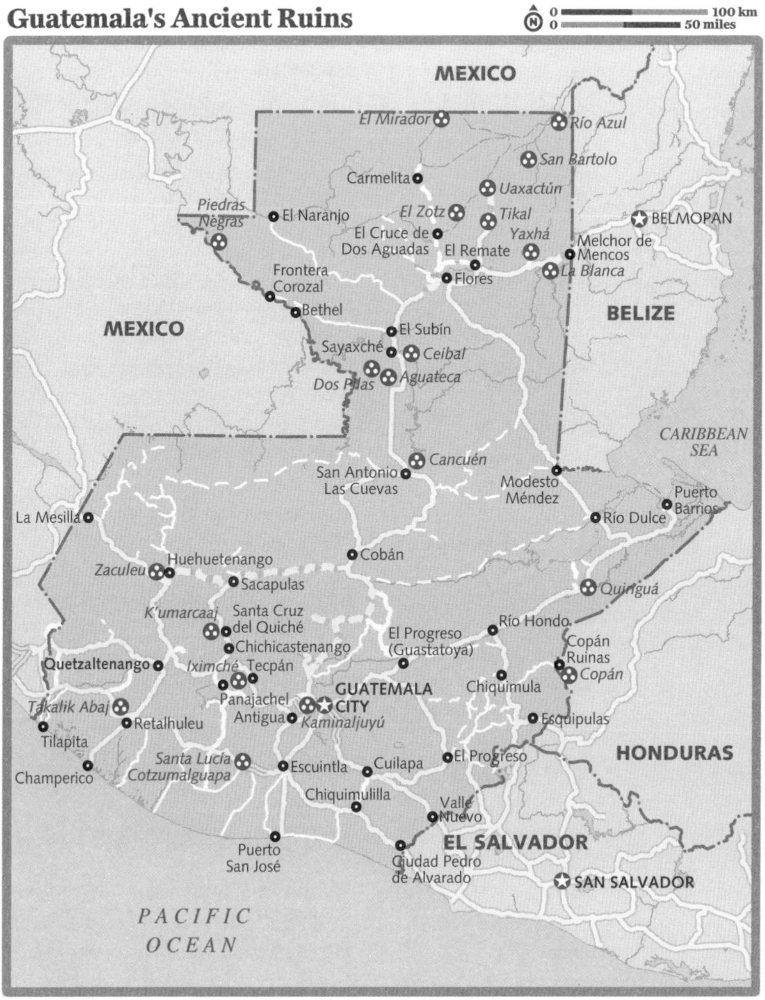

rubble or some grassy mounds, others (such as Tikal and Copán) have been extensively restored, and the temples, plazas and ballcourts give an excellent insight into what life must have been like in these places.

The most famous sites are generally thronged with visitors. Others are hidden away in thick jungle, reachable only by multiday treks or helicopter – for those with a sense of adventure, these can be the most exciting and rewarding to visit.

Site Practicalities

- Admission to sites costs between nothing (rare) and Q150 (also rare; generally reserved for top sites such as Tikal and Copán). Most sites charge around Q80.
- Protect yourself against the sun and, at jungle sites, mosquitoes.
- Sites such as Tikal and Copán have restaurants, bookstores, toilets and authorized guides.

ANCIENT MAYA SITES

REGION	SITE	DESCRIPTION
El Petén	Tikal (p245)	Most famous of all Guatemalan Maya sites, with as many as 10,000 structures
El Petén	El Mirador (p259)	Late Preclassic site with the largest cluster of buildings in the Maya world
El Petén	San Bartolo (p237)	Over 100 structures in 1 sq km 'discovered' in 2003 after looters began sacking the site
El Petén	Piedras Negras (p237)	One of Guatemala's most extensive, least-accessible sites
El Petén	La Blanca (p237)	Late Classic period trading center with impressively preserved walls
El Petén	El Zotz (p237)	A sprawling, largely unexcavated site occupying its own *biotopo* abutting Tikal National Park
El Petén	Río Azul (p237)	Key trading post for cacao from the Caribbean in the early Classic period
El Petén	Ceibal (p228)	Ceremonial site featuring impressive stelae
El Petén	Aguateca (p228)	Easily accessible lakeside walled city
El Petén	Dos Pilas (p228)	Breakaway city from the Tikal group
Guatemala City	Kaminaljuyú (p47)	Important Preclassic site a few kilometers from downtown area
Highlands	Iximché (p104)	Naturally fortified ex-Kaqchiquel capital
Highlands	K'umarcaaj (p124)	Former K'iche' capital surrounded by ravines
Highlands	Zaculeu (p149)	Postclassic Mam religious center
Pacific Slope	Takalik Abaj (p164)	Important late Preclassic trading center
Pacific Slope	Santa Lucía Cotzumalguapa (p167)	Various small sites dotted around a modest town
Eastern Guatemala	Quiriguá (p199)	Important ceremonial center with strong links to nearby Copán
Honduras	Copán (p201)	Religious and political capital rivaling Tikal for importance

HIGHLIGHTS	LOCATION	TRANSPORTATION
Towering temples, including the 65m-high Templo IV	60km northeast of Flores	Public transport or tour
La Danta, the largest Maya pyramid yet discovered	7km south of Mexican border	82km by bus from Carmelita, Guatemala, plus two days' walking (or direct helicopter)
Features one of the best-preserved Maya murals with a depiction of the creation myth from the Popol Vuh	Approximately 40km northeast of Uaxactún	Tours from Uaxactún or Flores
Impressive carvings and a sizable acropolis complex	40km downstream from Yaxchilán	Tours from Flores or river cruises from Bethel
'Graffiti' dating back to the Early Postclassic era	On the Río Mopan near the Belize border	Tours from Flores or Melchor de Mencos
Views all the way to Tikal from the top of the Pirámide del Diablo	25km southwest of Uaxactún	Tours from Uaxactún or Flores; guide cooperative leads walks from Cruce de Dos Aguadas
Tombs featuring vibrant painted glyphs	Near the corner where the Belize, Guatemala and Mexico borders meet	Tours from Uaxactún
Intricate carvings, atmospheric river-boat ride to get there	17km from Sayaxché	Boat tour or bus from Sayaxché to 8km from site, then walk or hitch
Maya world's only bridge, intricate carvings	Southern tip of Laguna Petexbatún	Boat tour from Sayaxché
Heiroglyphic stairway, impressive carvings	16km from Sayaxché	Pick-up truck to Nacimiento followed by 20-minute hike
Ongoing excavations open to public	Guatemala City suburbs	Bus or taxi
Important ceremonial site for modern Maya	1km from Tecpán	Walk, bus or tours from Panajachel/Antigua
Sacred tunnel still used for Maya ceremonies	3km west of Santa Cruz del Quiché	Minibus
Spectacular restored setting, park-like grounds	4km west of Huehuetenango	Bus or taxi
Sculptures, ceremonial baths and broad stone causeway	19km north of Retalhuleu	Bus, taxi and pick-up
Stone sculptures, links with Mexican Olmec culture	29km west of Escuintla	Frequent buses
10m-plus stelae	45km south of Río Dulce	Frequent buses
Excellent sculpture museum, hieroglyphic staircase with longest-known Maya hieroglyphic carving	5km from the Guatemala–Honduras border, in Honduras	Bus; tours from Antigua

PETER MAERKY/SHUTTERSTOCK ©

Top: Man dressed as a priest performs at Parque Arqueológico Takalik Abaj (p164)

Bottom: Zaculeu (p149)

- Little-visited sites may have no food or water available.
- Guided tours to many sites are usually available from nearby towns, although most (but not all) are accessible independently.
- Explanatory signs may be in Spanish only; Spanish and English; Spanish, English and the local Maya dialect; or completely nonexistent.
- Many sites are still used for traditional Maya religious ceremonies such as burning offerings to the deities. Look for signs indicating sacrificial areas and behave in a respectful manner around them.

Resources

- Mesoweb (www.mesoweb.com). A great, diverse resource on ancient Mesoamerican cultures, especially the Maya.
- *The Maya* by Michael D. Coe and Stephen Houston. Currently the best history and guide to ancient Maya civilization, including the latest scholarship.
- *Archaeology of Ancient Mexico and Central America: An Encyclopedia,* by Susan Toby Evans and David L Webster. A bit big for a backpack, but this encyclopedia is an essential resource.
- *Maya Art and Architecture*, by Mary Ellen Miller. Gorgeously illustrated and paints the full picture, from gigantic temples to intricately painted ceramics.

Don't Miss Sites

Tikal (p245) – Guatemala's most famous, and spectacular, Maya ruins.

Copán (p201) – Across the border in Honduras, one of the most outstanding achievements of the Maya.

El Mirador (p259) – Late-Preclassic metropolis buried in the deepest jungle.

Ceibal (p228) – Memorable river journey to low, ruined temples.

Santa Lucía Cotzumalguapa (p167) – Great stone heads carved with grotesque faces and fine relief scenes.

VLADIMIR KOROSTYSHEVSKIY/SHUTTERSTOCK ©

Ancient Maya hieroglyphs, Quiriguá (p199)

Top Museums

Some sites have their own museums – the ones at Tikal and Copán are well worth the extra admission fee – but there are also important city and regional museums that hold many of the most valuable and impressive pre-Hispanic artifacts.

Museo Nacional de Arqueología y Etnología, Guatemala City (p50) By far the most impressive collection of ancient Maya artifacts, with pieces from all the important ceremonial areas, including an impressive throne from the Piedras Negras site.

Museo Popol Vuh, Guatemala City (p49) A wealth of smaller pieces, including figurines, wooden masks, textiles and a faithful copy of the *Dresden Codex*.

Colección Dr Juan Antonio Valdés, Uaxactún (p253) Housed in the Hotel El Chiclero, this private collection holds a remarkable wealth of Maya pottery from Uaxactún, Yaxhá, and as far away as Oaxaca, Mexico.

Plan Your Trip

Guatemala Outdoors

Guatemala's relatively compact size, and vast and varied natural beauty make it a perfect place to get out and get active. Any town where there are things to do will have at least one tour operator offering trips.

Best of Guatemala Outdoors

Best Hikes

Nebaj to Todos Santos Cuchumatán, Quetzaltenango to Lago Atitlán

Best Volcano Climbs

Tajumulco, Santa María, Pacaya and San Pedro

Best Paragliding

Lake Atitlán

Best Surfing

El Paredón

Best Birdwatching

Tikal, Biotopo del Quetzal, Estación Biológica Las Guacamayas

Best Spelunking

Lanquín, B'ombi'l Pek, Rey Marcos

Best White-Water Rafting

Río Cahabón (Lanquín)

Climbing, Trekking & Hiking

Guatemala's many volcanoes are irresistible challenges, and many of them can be done in one day from Antigua or Quetzaltenango. There's further great hill country in the Ixil Triangle and the Cuchumatanes mountains to the north of Huehuetenango, especially around Todos Santos Cuchumatán and Nebaj (the multiday hike between these two is possibly the country's best long walk). The Lago de Atitlán is likewise surrounded by spectacular trails, and the three-day hike from Quetzaltenango to the lake is deservedly popular.

Treks of several days are perfectly feasible, and agencies in Antigua, Quetzaltenango and Nebaj can guide you.

In the Petén jungles of the lowlands, treks to remote archaeological sites such as El Mirador and El Perú offer an exciting challenge.

Cycling

There's probably no better way to experience the Guatemalan highlands than by bicycle. Panajachel, San Pedro La Laguna, Quetzaltenango and Antigua in particular are the best launch points, with local agencies offering trips and equipment.

Horseback Riding

Opportunities for a gallop, a trot or even a horse trek are on the increase in Guatemala. There are stables in Antigua, Laguna Brava and Nakum. Unicornio Azul (p152), north of Huehuetenango, offers horse trekking in the sublime Cuchumatanes.

Paragliding

Paragliding remains relatively undeveloped in Guatemala, but its mountains and volcanoes make excellent launch points and the views are superb. There are reliable, experienced operators in Panajachel that can take you flying over Lago de Atitlán.

Spelunking

Guatemala attracts cavers from all around the world. The limestone area around Cobán is particularly riddled with cave systems, the full extents of which remain largely unknown. The caves of Lanquín, B'ombi'l Pek, Candelaria and Rey Marcos are all open for tourist visits. There are also exciting caves to visit from Finca Ixobel, near Poptún, and some near Flores.

Water Sports

There are varied activities for getting on the water: rafting the white waters of the Río Cahabón near Lanquín, or surfing the Pacific at El Paredón. You can also canoe or kayak the waterways of Monterrico, Lago de Atitlán and Lago de Petén Itzá, Lívingston, the Bocas del Polochic or Punta de Manabique, or sail from the yachtie haven of Río Dulce.

Mayan Whitewater

Mayan Whitewater Guatemala by Greg Schwendinger is your ultimate guide to the waterways of Guatemala, packed with tips on how to explore the country afloat.

ANTHONY PAPPONE/GETTY IMAGES ©

Collared aracari toucan

Wildlife-Watching

National parks and nature reserves offer lots of wildlife-watching opportunities, while generally having few tourist facilities. Fine locations in the Petén jungles for birdwatching include Tikal, El Mirador, Cerro Cahuí, Laguna Petexbatún and (for scarlet macaws) the Estación Biológica Las Guacamayas and the Macaw Mountain Bird Park. Elsewhere, the wetlands of Bocas del Polochic, Punta de Manabique and Monterrico, and the Río Dulce and Laguna Lachuá national parks provide lots of avian variety, as does the Biotopo del Quetzal – where you can search for the quetzal, Guatemala's national bird.

Mammals tend to prove more elusive, but you should see several species at Tikal. Monkey fans will also be happy at the Reserva Natural Atitlán, the Bocas del Polochic and Cerro Cahuí.

Regions at a Glance

Guatemala is so diverse the six regions outlined here could just as easily be six separate countries. Travel 100km or so and everything changes, from the scenery down to the food and the way people talk and dress. The capital is all big-city buzz, while it's hard to imagine things getting any more laid-back than they do in the little beach towns down on the coast. Antigua is the epitome of stately colonial charm, whereas the temple-laden jungles and small towns of El Petén have a very rough-and-ready frontier atmosphere. The highlands of the center and west are probably the most similar, but where the volcano-studded west gets chilly and starkly beautiful, the cloud forest–covered center is much milder and more lush.

Guatemala City

Art & Archaeology
Nightlife
Urban Buzz

Museums & Galleries

Don't be tempted to dodge the capital – if you're at all interested in art and archaeology, you need to spend some time here. All the best pieces end up here, often in world-class, superbly curated spaces.

The Big Night Out

The capital's massive population of students, the live-music scene and burgeoning nightlife district just off the Parque Central make it the best place to go out in the country, hands down.

That Feeling...

For all its craziness and stress, you're not going to get that big-city kick anywhere else in the country. Just walking down the street will show you murals, architecture, markets and more that the city has to offer.

p44

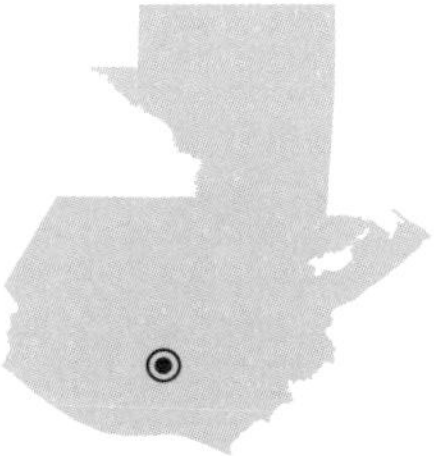

Antigua

Colonial Architecture
Language Lessons
Food

Colonial Charms

Though much of the Spanish legacy in the former capital lies in ruins, the remaining fragments add allure to the streetscapes, offering picture-postcard views at every corner and a chance to scramble through history.

Back to School

Despite some tough competition, Antigua remains the capital of Spanish-language study in Latin America. Dozens of small, affably run institutes offer personalized instruction in charming surrounds at bargain prices.

Gourmet Traveling

Owing to its globally varied visitor profile, Antigua rivals much loftier destinations as a cuisine capital. Here you can enjoy everything from French fine dining to Argentine empanadas at restaurants run by transplants from their culinary places of origin.

p65

The Highlands

Indigenous Attire
Volcanoes
Festivals

Maya Costume

From the pom-pommed headdresses of women in Chajul to the flamboyant red-and-white striped trousers of men in Todos Santos Cuchumatán, traditional Maya clothing is a dazzling display of identity throughout the highlands.

Peaking Out

With a chain of 33 volcanoes, four of them active, climbers, geology buffs and landscape painters find plenty to inspire them here. An early-morning hike up the Santa María volcano leads to a mesmerizing view of the periodically erupting Santiaguito.

Party Time

Every highlands town likes to let its hair down at an annual fest, and outsiders are always welcome. Good bets include Quetzaltenango's late September toast to its Virgen del Rosario and Todos Santos Cuchumatán's patron saint's day on November 1 with madcap horse racing and drunken marimba dancing.

p91

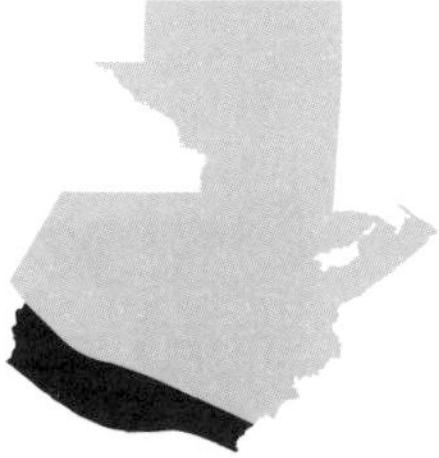

The Pacific Slope

Beaches
Food
Wildlife

Sun, Sand & Surf

If you've been up in the hills or traveling hard, the Pacific coast is dotted with little beach towns where you can dial it back a notch or two and get in some quality do-nothing time.

Catch of the Day

With so much coastline it's no surprise that the seafood here is excellent – fried fish and shrimp are staples, but don't miss out on the *caldo de mariscos* (seafood stew) if you see it on a menu.

Animal Magic

With whales and turtles in the waters off the beaches and the mangroves buzzing with birdlife, this region is a wildlife-watcher's paradise.

p158

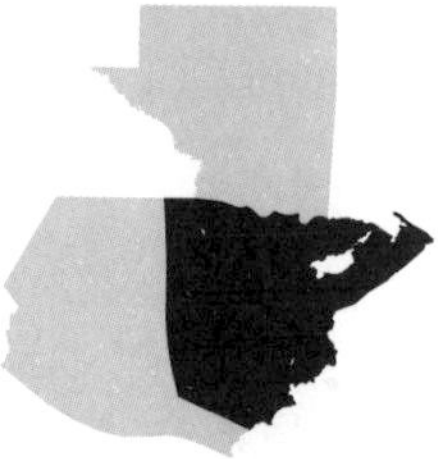

Central & Eastern Guatemala

Nature
Culture
Caves

Natural Paradise

From the lush cloud forests of the Verapaz and the pools of Semuc Champey to the verdant landscapes of Lago de Izabal and the Río Dulce, the rivers, lakes, canyons, waterfalls and jungles of this region showcase Guatemala at its natural best.

Cultural Mosaic

Ethnically diverse and at times intensely traditional, the center and east of the country are home to Achi', Poqomchi', Ch'ortí and Q'eqchi' Maya, many of who maintain traditional customs. Over on the Caribbean, the culturally distinct Garifuna represent one more ingredient in Guatemala's ethnic stew.

Going Underground

The limestone crags, particularly north of Cobán, play host to a network of caves and caverns, making for great photo opportunities and fascinating forays for casual strollers and serious spelunkers alike.

p177

El Petén

Classic Maya Sites
Wildlife
Trekking

Site Seeing

With literally hundreds of sites sprinkled across the jungle lowlands, you may delve as deeply as you choose into the mysteries of Classic Maya civilization, from the fabulously dramatic temples of Tikal to the seldom-seen astronomical observatory of Uaxactún.

Animal Planet

Rare and endangered creatures still roam the protected expanses of the Maya Biosphere Reserve, and guides from *petenera* communities can help you track them down, whether it's nocturnal crocodile cruising at the Estación Biológica Las Guacamayas or awakening to howler monkeys at Biotopo Cerro Cahuí.

Going Bush

Seasoned guides at places such as Ni'tun Ecolodge on Lago de Petén Itzá or Aldana's Lodge in Uaxactún accompany you on multiday odysseys through the mud and mosquitoes to such remote Maya sites as El Zotz and El Mirador.

p223

On the Road

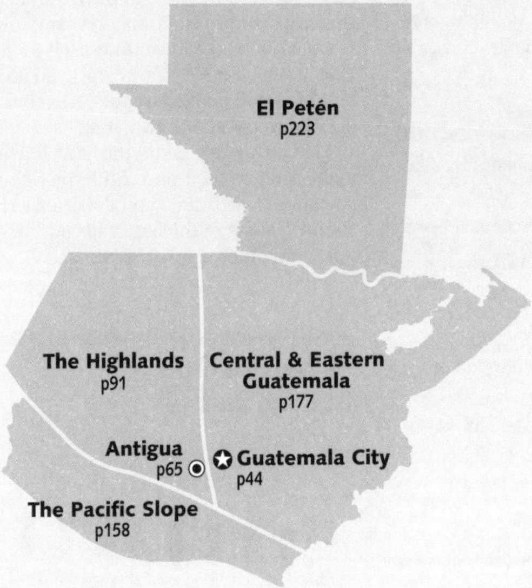
El Petén
p223
The Highlands
p91
Central & Eastern
Guatemala
p177
Antigua
p65
Guatemala City
p44
The Pacific Slope
p158

Guatemala City

POP 3.5 MILLION

Includes ➡

Best Places to Eat

- Ambia (p58)
- Bistro Tamarindos (p58)
- La Cocina de Señora Pu (p57)
- Café de Imeri (p56)
- Kacao (p58)

Best Places to Stay

- Dai Nonni Hotel (p55)
- Hotel Royal Palace (p54)
- Quetzalroo (p55)
- Eco Suites Uxlabil (p55)
- Posada Belen (p51)

Why Go?

Depending on who you talk to, Guatemala City (or Guate as it's also known) is either big, dirty, dangerous and utterly forgettable, or big, dirty, dangerous and utterly fascinating. Either way, there's no doubt there's an energy here unlike anywhere else in Guatemala. It's a place where dilapidated buses belch fumes next to BMWs and Hummers, and where skyscrapers drop shadows on shantytowns.

Guate is busy reinventing itself as a people-friendly city. Downtown Zona 1, for years a no-go zone of abandoned buildings and crime hot spots, is leading the way with the pedestrianized 6a Calle attracting bars, cafes and restaurants.

Many travelers skip the city altogether, preferring to make Antigua their base. Still, you may want, or need, to get acquainted with the capital, because this is the hub of the country, home to the best museums and galleries, transport hubs and other traveler services.

When to Go

Guatemala City

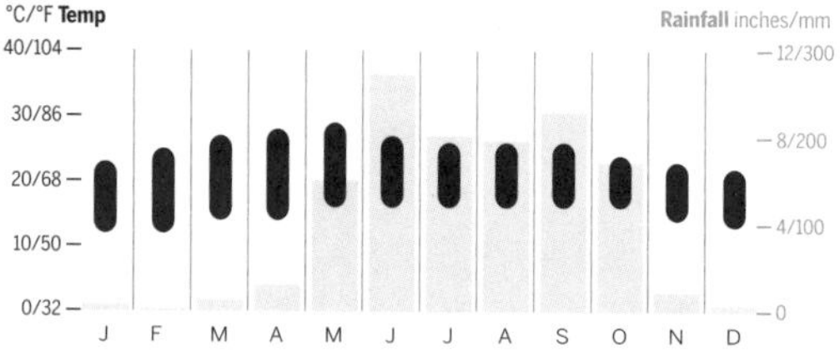

Mar & Apr The capital makes a good base for day trips to over-crowded Antigua during Easter.

Aug The Fiesta de la Virgen de la Asunción on the 15th features fireworks, parades and folk dancing.

Nov–Mar The drier, cooler months are a perfect time to visit the otherwise muggy city.

Guatemala City Highlights

❶ **La Aurora Zoo** (p51) Visiting the capital's surprisingly leafy and animal-friendly zoo.

❷ **Nightlife** (p59) Heading straight for the rejuvenated Zona 1 for the best night out on the town.

❸ **Mapa en Relieve** (p47) Being oddly mesmerized by this 3D representation of the country – part engineering marvel, part tourist curio.

❹ **Pasos y Pedales** (p51) Joining pretty much everybody else in town for a stroll/bike ride/dog walk through leafy Zona 10.

❺ **Parque Central** (p46) Catching buskers, wandering preachers, free concerts and other random stuff in the always-bustling plaza, or just stopping by to feed the pigeons.

❻ **Museo Ixchel** (p49) Taking a journey through Guatemala's rich cultural heritage in this museum devoted to indigenous textiles.

History

Kaminaljuyú (kah-mih-nahl-huh-yuh), one of the first important cities in the Maya region, flourished two millennia ago in what is now the western part of Guatemala City. By the time Spanish conquistadors arrived in the 16th century, only overgrown mounds were left. The site remained insignificant until the earthquake of July 29, 1773, razed much of the then Spanish colonial capital, Antigua. The authorities decided to move their headquarters to La Ermita valley, hoping to escape further destruction, and on September 27, 1775, King Carlos III of Spain signed a royal charter for the founding of La Nueva Guatemala de la Asunción. Guatemala City was officially born, and construction began the next year.

Unfortunately, the colonial powers didn't quite move the capital far enough, for earthquakes in 1917, 1918 and 1976 rocked the capital and beyond, reducing buildings to rubble. The 1976 quake killed nearly 23,000, injured another 75,000 and left an estimated one million people homeless. An eruption of Mt Fuego in 2018, though far from Guatemala City, forced the closure of the airport for several days.

Sights

The major sights are in Zona 1 (the historic center, where the plaza is) and Zonas 10 and 13, where the museums are grouped.

Zona 1

The main sights in Zona 1 are grouped around **Parque Central** (Plaza de la Constitución; Map p48; Zona 1). Back in the day, standard colonial urban planning required every town in the New World to have a large plaza for military exercises and ceremonies: on the north side of the plaza was usually the *palacio de gobierno* (colonial government headquarters); on another side, preferably the east, would be a church or cathedral; and the remaining sides of the square would feature additional civic buildings or the imposing mansions of wealthy citizens. Guatemala City's Parque Central is a classic example of the plan.

Parque Central and the adjoining Parque Centenario are never empty during daylight hours, with shoeshine kids, ice-cream vendors and sometimes open-air political meetings and concerts adding to the general bustle.

★Casa MIMA MUSEUM
(Map p48; ☎2253-4020; www.casamima.org; 8a Av 14-12, Zona 1; Q20; ⏲10am-5pm Mon-Sat) A wonderfully presented museum and cultural center set in a house dating from the late 19th century. The owners of the house were collectors with eclectic tastes ranging from French neo-rococo, Chinese and art deco to indigenous artifacts. The place is set up like a functioning house, filled with curios and furniture spanning the centuries, such as top hats, an Underwood typewriter and a vintage Sunbeam blender.

Palacio Nacional de la Cultura HISTORIC BUILDING
(Map p48; ☎2253-0748; cnr 6a Av & 6a Calle, Zona 1; Q40; ⏲9am-4pm Mon-Fri, 10am-3pm Sat) On the north side of Parque Central is this imposing presidential palace, which was built between 1936 and 1943 during the dictatorial rule of General Jorge Ubico at enormous cost to the lives of the prisoners who were forced to labor here. It's the third palace to stand on the site.

Despite its tragic background, architecturally the palace is one of the country's most interesting constructions, a mélange of multiple earlier styles from Spanish Renaissance to neoclassical. Today, most government offices have been removed from here, and it's open as a museum and for a few ceremonial events.

Visits are by guided tour (available in English). You pass through a labyrinth of gleaming brass, polished wood, carved stone and frescoed arches. Features include a mural of Guatemalan history by Alberto Gálvez Suárez above the main stairway, and a two-ton gold, bronze and Bohemian-crystal chandelier in the reception hall. The banqueting hall sports stained-glass panels depicting – with delicious irony – the virtues of good government. From here your guide will probably take you out onto the presidential balcony, where you can imagine yourself a banana-republic dictator reviewing your troops.

In the western courtyard, the **Patio de la Paz**, a monument depicting two hands, stands where Guatemala's Peace Accords were signed in 1996; each day at 11am the rose held by the hands is changed by a military guard and the one from the previous day is tossed to a woman among the spectators.

Catedral Metropolitana CATHEDRAL
(Map p48; 7a Av, Zona 1; ⏲6am-noon & 2-7pm) Facing Parque Central, this cathedral was

constructed between 1782 and 1815 (the towers were finished in 1867). It has survived earthquake and fire, though the earthquakes of 1917 and 1976 did substantial damage. Its heavy proportions and sparse ornamentation don't make for a particularly beautiful building, but it has a certain stateliness, and the altars are worth a look.

Museo del Ferrocarril MUSEUM

(Railway Museum; Map p48; ☎2208-4747; www.museofegua.com; 9a Av 18-03, Zona 1; Q2; ⏲9am-4pm Tue-Fri, 10am-4pm Sat & Sun) This is one of the city's more intriguing museums, with lots of photos and interesting memorabilia from the train days of old. Documented here are the glory days of the troubled Guatemalan rail system, along with some quirky artifacts, such as hand-drawn diagrams of derailments and a kitchen set up with items used in dining cars. You can climb around in the passenger carriages, but not the locomotives. There's even a room displaying the administrative office, replete with bored-looking bureaucrat.

Locals make an afternoon out of it by bringing along a picnic lunch to eat inside the train cars.

Centro Cultural Metropolitano CULTURAL CENTER

(Map p48; 7a Av 11-67, Zona 1; ⏲7am-6pm Mon-Fri, to 4pm Sat) To the rear of the ground floor of the *palacio de correos* (post office), you'll find a surprisingly avant-garde cultural center, hosting art exhibitions, book launches, handicraft workshops and film nights. Well worth a peek if you have time.

Museo Nacional de Historia MUSEUM

(Map p48; ☎2253-6149; 9a Calle 9-70, Zona 1; Q50; ⏲9am-5pm Mon-Fri, to noon & 1-4pm Sat & Sun) This museum hosts a jumble of historical relics with an emphasis on photography and portraits. Check out the carefully coiffed hairstyles of the 19th-century generals and politicos.

Banco de Guatemala NOTABLE BUILDING

(Map p48; 7a Av, Zona 1; ⏲9am-5pm Mon-Fri) It's interesting to visit this bank building, which bears relief sculptures by Dagoberto Vásquez depicting his country's history.

Municipalidad de Guatemala NOTABLE BUILDING

(City Hall; Map p48; 22a Calle, Zona 1) The city hall contains a huge mosaic by Carlos Mérida, completed in 1959.

Zona 2

Mapa en Relieve MONUMENT

(Relief Map; ☎3525-0397; www.mapaenrelieve.org; Av Simeón Cañas Final, Zona 2; Q25; ⏲9am-5pm) North of Zona 1, Zona 2 is mostly a middle-class residential district, but it's worth venturing along to Parque Minerva to see this huge open-air map of Guatemala showing the country at a scale of 1:10,000. The vertical scale is exaggerated to 1:2000 to make the volcanoes and mountains appear dramatically higher and steeper than they really are.

Constructed in 1905 under the direction of Francisco Vela, it was fully restored and repainted in 1999. Viewing towers afford a panoramic view. This is an odd but fun place, and it's curious to observe that Belize is still represented as part of Guatemala. It's an easy walk (or short cab ride) from Parque Central.

Parque Minerva PARK

(Av Simeón Cañas Final, Zona 2) Minerva, the Roman goddess of wisdom, technical skill and invention, was a favorite of President Manuel Estrada Cabrera. Her park is a placid place, good for walking among the eucalyptus trees and sipping a cool drink. Watch out, however, for pickpockets and purse-snatchers.

Zona 4

Centro Cívico ARCHITECTURE

(Map p48; Zona 4) Pride of Zona 4 (actually straddling its borders with Zonas 1 and 5) is the Centro Cívico, a set of large government and institutional buildings constructed during the 1950s and '60s. One is the headquarters of INGUAT (Guatemalan tourist institute), housing the city's main tourist office (p62).

Zona 7

Parque Arqueológico Kaminaljuyú ARCHAEOLOGICAL SITE

(11a Calle 25-50 & 24a Av, Zona 7; Q50; ⏲8am-4pm) Containing remnants of one of the first important cities in the Maya region, this park is just west of 23a Av and is some 4km west of the city center. At its peak, from about 400 BC to AD 100, ancient Kaminaljuyú had thousands of inhabitants and scores of temples, and probably dominated much of highland Guatemala.

Guatemala City North

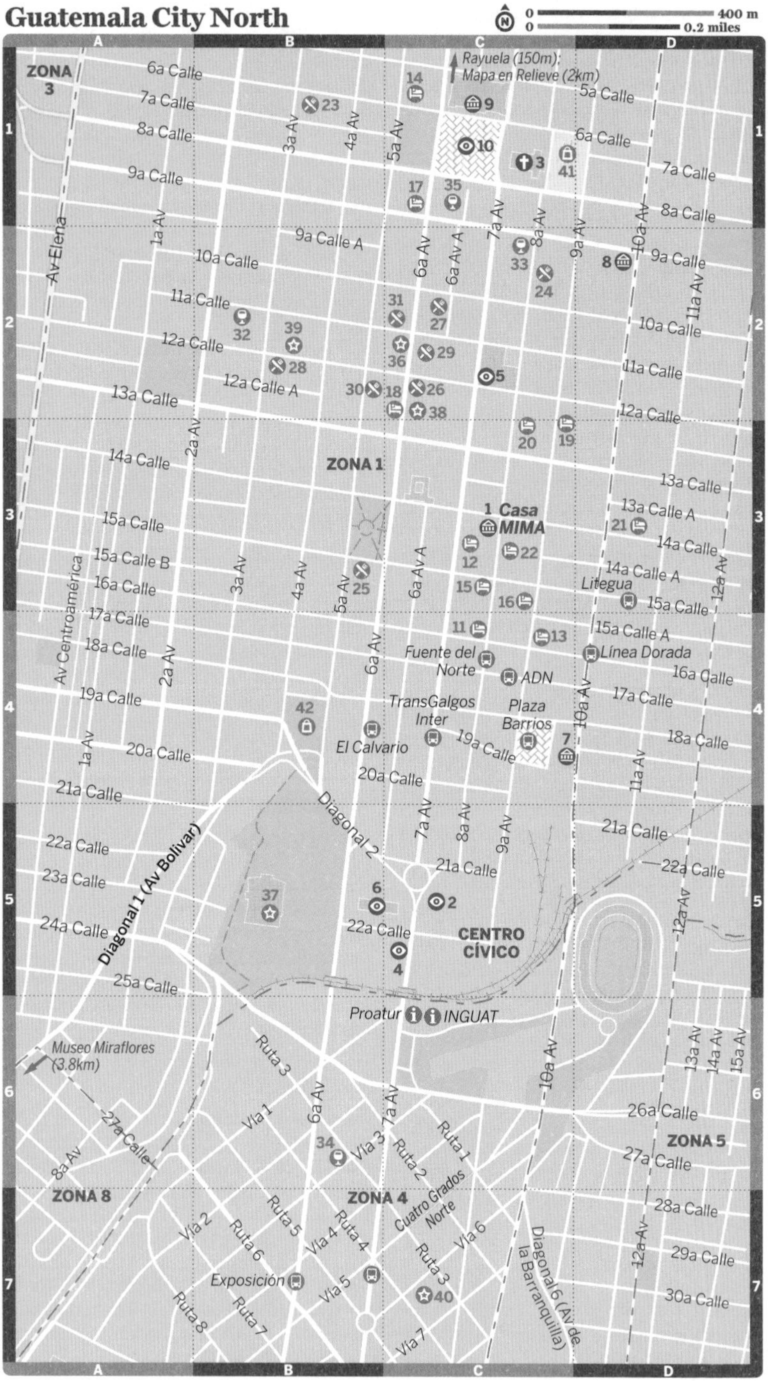

Guatemala City North

Top Sights

1 Casa MIMA ... C3

Sights

2 Banco de Guatemala ... C5
3 Catedral Metropolitana ... C1
4 Centro Cívico ... C5
5 Centro Cultural Metropolitano ... C2
6 Municipalidad de Guatemala ... B5
7 Museo del Ferrocarril ... C4
8 Museo Nacional de Historia ... D2
9 Palacio Nacional de la Cultura ... C1
10 Parque Central ... C1

Sleeping

11 Hotel Ajau ... C4
12 Hotel Ajau Colonial ... C3
13 Hotel Capri ... C4
14 Hotel Centenario ... C1
15 Hotel Clariss ... C3
16 Hotel Excel ... C3
17 Hotel Pan American ... C1
18 Hotel Royal Palace ... C2
19 Hotel Sevilla ... C3
20 Hotel Spring ... C3
21 Posada Belen ... D3
22 Theatre International Hostel ... C3

Eating

23 Café de Imeri ... B1
24 Café Leon ... C2
25 Café-Restaurante Hamburgo ... B3
26 Fu Lu Sho ... C2
Hotel Pan American ... (see 17)
27 La Cocina de Señora Pu ... C2
28 La Majo ... B2
29 Picadilly ... C2
30 Restaurante Altuna ... B2
31 Restaurante Rey Sol ... C2

Drinking & Nightlife

32 Black ... B2
33 El Gran Hotel ... C2
34 Genetic ... B6
35 Las Cien Puertas ... C1

Entertainment

36 Centro Cultural de España ... C2
37 Centro Cultural Miguel Ángel Asturias ... B5
38 Cine Capitol Royal ... C2
39 La Bodeguita del Centro ... B2
40 TrovaJazz ... C7

Shopping

41 Mercado Central ... C1
42 Plaza El Amate ... B4

Large-scale carvings found here were the forerunners of Classic Maya carving, and Kaminaljuyú had a literate elite before anywhere else in the Maya world. The city fell into ruin before being reoccupied around AD 400 by invaders from Teotihuacán in central Mexico, who rebuilt it in Teotihuacán's *talud-tablero* style, with buildings stepped in alternating vertical *(tablero)* and sloping *(talud)* sections. Unfortunately, most of Kaminaljuyú has been covered by urban sprawl: the archaeological park is but a small portion of the ancient city, and even here the remnants consist chiefly of grassy mounds. To the left from the entrance is **La Acrópolis**, where you can inspect excavations of a ball court and *talud-tablero* buildings from AD 450 to 550.

A couple of hundred meters south of the entrance and across the road are **two burial statues** from the Late Preclassic era. They're badly deteriorated, but are the only examples of carving left at the site – the best examples have been moved to the Museo Nacional de Arqueología y Etnología (p50).

A taxi from Zona 1 costs around Q50.

Zona 10

Two of the country's best museums are housed in large, modern buildings at the Universidad Francisco Marroquín, 1km east of Av La Reforma.

Museo Ixchel MUSEUM

(Map p52; 2361-8081; www.museoixchel.org; 6a Calle Final, Zona 10; Q45; 9am-5pm Mon-Fri, to 1pm Sat) This museum is named for the Maya goddess of the moon, women, reproduction and textiles. Photographs and exhibits of indigenous costumes and other crafts show the incredible richness of traditional arts in Guatemala's highland towns. Guided tours are available in English (with prior reservation) or Spanish.

If you enjoy Guatemalan textiles at all, you must visit this museum. It has access for travelers with disabilities, a section for children, a cafe, a shop and a library.

Museo Popol Vuh MUSEUM

(Map p52; 2338-7896; www.popolvuh.ufm.edu; 6a Calle Final, Zona 10; adult/child Q45/15; 9am-5pm Mon-Fri, to 1pm Sat) Inside Museo

BONJOUR, AMIGO

It's been a long time since anybody called Guatemala City the Paris of anywhere, which makes it all the more remarkable to find a replica of the Eiffel Tower straddling a busy downtown intersection. The **Torre del Reformador** (Map p52; cnr 7a Av & 2a Calle, Zona 9), originally named the 'Torre Conmemorativa del 19 del Julio,' was completed in 1935 to celebrate the 100th anniversary of the birth of former president and reformer Justo Rufino Barrios.

Popol Vuh you'll find well-displayed pre-Hispanic figurines, incense burners and burial urns, plus carved wooden masks and traditional textiles filling several rooms of this museum. Other rooms hold colonial paintings and gilded wood and silver artifacts. A faithful copy of the *Dresden Codex*, one of the precious 'painted books' of the Maya, is among the most interesting pieces.

Also here is a colorful display of animals in Maya art.

Jardín Botánico GARDENS
(Map p52; ☎2334-6065; Calle Mariscal Cruz 1-56, Zona 10; Q10; ⊙8am-3pm Mon-Fri) The Universidad de San Carlos has a large, lush botanical garden on the northern edge of Zona 10. The admission includes the university's Museo de Historia Natural at the site.

Museo de Historia Natural MUSEUM
(Natural History Museum; Map p52; ☎2334-6065; Calle Mariscal Cruz 1-56, Zona 10; Q10; ⊙8am-3pm Mon-Fri) The university's small yet packed Museo de Historia Natural is at the same site as the Universidad de San Carlos' botanical garden, which is also included in the admission price. The museum has a well-arranged collection of flora and fauna specimens from around the country – it's packed with gems (one room literally!) and has displays on history, archaeology, fauna, fossils and more.

Zona 11

Museo Miraflores MUSEUM
(☎2208-0550; www.museomiraflores.org.gt; 7a Calle 21-55, Zona 11; Q25; ⊙9am-7pm Tue-Sun) This excellent modern museum is inauspiciously jammed between two shopping malls a few kilometers out of town. Downstairs focuses on objects found at Kaminaljuyú (p47), with fascinating trade-route maps showing the site's importance. Upstairs there are displays on textiles and indigenous clothing, separated by region, from around the country.

Signs are in Spanish and (for the most part) English. Out back is a pleasant grassy area with paths and seating – a good place to take a breather.

To get here, catch any bus from the center going to Centro Comercial Tikal Futura. The museum is 250m down the road between it and the Miraflores shopping center.

Zona 13

The attractions here in the city's southern reaches are all ranged along 5a Calle in the Finca Aurora area, northwest of the airport. While here you can also drop into the Mercado de Artesanías (p60).

Museo Nacional de Arqueología y Etnología MUSEUM
(Map p52; ☎2475-4399, 2475-7010; www.munae.gob.gt; 6a Calle, Sala 5, Finca La Aurora, Zona 13; Q60; ⊙9am-4pm Tue-Fri, to noon & 1:30-4pm Sat & Sun) This museum has the country's biggest collection of ancient Maya artifacts, but explanatory information is very sparse. There's a great wealth of monumental stone sculpture, including Classic-period stelae from Tikal, Uaxactún and Piedras Negras; a superb throne from Piedras Negras; and animal representations from Preclassic Kaminaljuyú.

Also here are rare wooden lintels from temples at Tikal and El Zotz, and a room with beautiful jade necklaces and masks. Don't miss the large-scale model of Tikal. The ethnology section has displays on the languages, costumes, dances, masks and homes of Guatemala's indigenous peoples.

Museo Nacional de Arte Moderno GALLERY
(Map p52; ☎2472-0467; 6a Calle, Sala 6, Finca La Aurora, Zona 13; Q50; ⊙9am-4pm Tue-Fri, 9am-noon & 1:30-4pm Sat & Sun) Here you'll find a collection of 20th-century Guatemalan art including works by well-known Guatemalan artists such as Carlos Mérida, Carlos Valente and Humberto Gavarito.

Museo de los Niños MUSEUM
(Children's Museum; Map p52; ☎2475-5076; www.museodelosninos.com.gt; 5a Calle 10-00, Zona 13; Q40; ⊙8:30am-noon & 1-4:30pm Tue-Fri, 9:30am-1:30pm & 2:30-6pm Sat & Sun) Almost opposite the zoo entrance is this hands-on

affair that is a sure success if you have kids to keep happy. The fun ranges from a giant jigsaw-map of Guatemala to an earthquake simulator and, most popular of all, a room of original and entertaining ball games.

La Aurora Zoo ZOO

(Map p52; ☎2463-0463; www.aurorazoo.org.gt; 5a Calle, Zona 13; adult/child Q33/16; ⏱9am-5pm Tue-Sun) This is not badly kept as far as zoos in this part of the world go, and the lovely, parklike grounds alone are worth the admission fee.

Museo Nacional de Historia Natural Jorge Ibarra MUSEUM

(Map p52; ☎2472-0468; 6a Calle 7-30, Zona 13; Q50; ⏱9am-4pm Tue-Fri, to noon & 2-4pm Sat & Sun) This natural-history museum, located behind the Museo Nacional de Arqueología y Etnología, has a large collection of dissected animals.

Activities

Pasos y Pedales WALKING

(Map p52; ⏱10am-2pm Sun) If you're here on a Sunday, check out a wonderful municipal initiative that sees the Av de las Americas in Zona 10, and its continuation, Av La Reforma in Zona 13, blocked off to traffic for 3km and taken over by jugglers, clowns, in-line skaters, dog walkers, food vendors, tai chi classes, skate parks and playgrounds for kids.

It's a great place to go for a walk (or you can hire bikes or in-line skates on the street) and check out a very relaxed, sociable side of the city that otherwise is rarely seen.

X-Park ADVENTURE SPORTS

(☎2380-2080; www.xpark.net; Av Hincapié, Km 11.5; entry Q10, activities Q10-Q50; ⏱10am-5pm Mon-Fri, to 6pm Sat & Sun) About 10 minutes' drive south of the airport is this very well constructed 'adventure sports' park. Attractions (X-Park prefers to call them 'challenges') cost Q20 to Q50 each and include bouldering and climbing walls, reverse bungees, mechanical bulls, a rope course, ziplines and a playground for kids. A fairly limited range of fast food is available at the cafeteria. A taxi here from Zona 10 should cost you around Q35.

Tours

Clark Tours BUS

(Map p52; ☎2412-4700; www.clarktours.com.gt; 7a Av 14-76, Zona 9; ⏱9am-7pm Mon-Fri, to 1pm Sat) Guatemala's longest-established tour operator offers morning and full-day city tours. The morning tour (available Saturday to Wednesday) visits the Palacio Nacional de la Cultura, cathedral and Centro Cívico. The day tour adds the Ixchel and Popul Vuh museums. Clark Tours also has branches in the **Westin Camino Real** (Map p52; ☎2363-3920; www.clarktours.com.gt; cnr 14a Calle & Av La Reforma, Zona 10; ⏱7:30am-7pm Mon-Fri) and the **Hotel Barceló Guatemala** (Map p52; ☎2362-9716; 7a Av 15-45, Zona 9; ⏱7:30am-7pm Mon-Fri).

Maya Expeditions ADVENTURE

(Map p52; ☎2366-9950; www.mayaexpeditions.com; 13a Av 14-70, Zona 10) One of Guatemala's respected adventure-tourism companies, Maya Expeditions specializes in white-water rafting and trekking, but also offers archaeological trips, wildlife-watching expeditions and a whole lot more, mostly in the Alta Verapaz and Petén regions.

Sleeping

For budget and many midrange hotels, make a beeline for Zona 1. If you have just flown in or are about to fly out, there are a number of convenient guesthouses near the airport. Top-end hotels are mostly located around Zona 10.

Zona 1

Theatre International Hostel HOSTEL $

(Map p48; ☎4202-5112; www.theatreihostel.com; 8a Av 14-17, Zona 1; dm incl breakfast Q55-80, s/d/tr without bathroom Q140/170/180; wifi) Zona 1 is the key reason (and the only reason) to stay here, but keep expectations low because this place is in need of major TLC. Spotty wifi, long waits for bathrooms, and cluttered courtyard are downers, as is the lack of mosquito screening on the windows. Staff are helpful and the free breakfast is welcome, but that's about it.

★ **Posada Belen** BOUTIQUE HOTEL $$

(Map p48; ☎2253-4530; www.posadabelen.com; 13a Calle A 10-30, Zona 1; s/d Q322/411; nonsmoking, wifi) One of Zona 1's most stylish options, this boutique hotel has just 10 rooms, arranged around a couple of lush patios. Rooms are well decorated with *típico* (traditional) furnishings and there's a good restaurant onsite (reservations required).

Hotel Spring HOTEL $$

(Map p48; ☎2230-2858; www.hotelspring.com; 8a Av 12-65, Zona 1; s/d from Q200/250, without bathroom Q150/195; P nonsmoking, @ wifi) With a beautiful courtyard setting, the Spring has a lot more

Guatemala City South

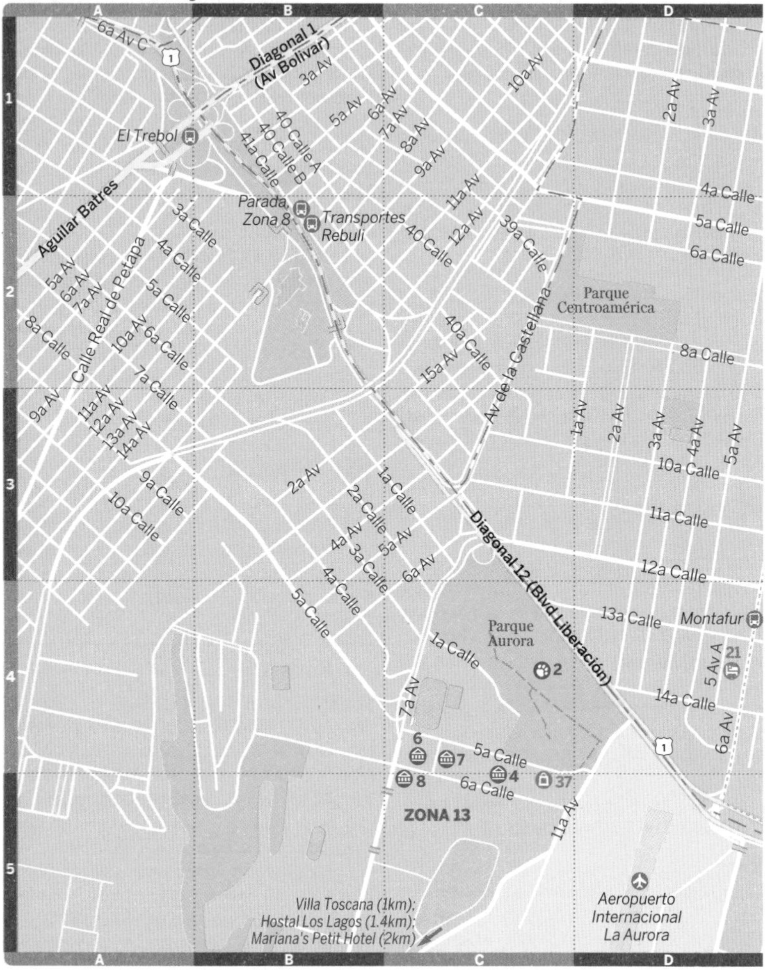

Guatemala City South

Sights

1 Jardín Botánico F1
2 La Aurora Zoo C4
3 Museo de Historia Natural F1
4 Museo de los Niños C5
5 Museo Ixchel G2
6 Museo Nacional de Arqueología y Etnología C4
7 Museo Nacional de Arte Moderno C4
8 Museo Nacional de Historia Natural Jorge Ibarra C5
9 Museo Popol Vuh H2
10 Torre del Reformador E1

Activities, Courses & Tours

11 Clark Tours E5
12 Clark Tours E4
Clark Tours .... (see 15)
13 Maya Expeditions H5
14 Pasos y Pedales F2

Sleeping

15 Barceló Guatemala E4
16 Eco Suites Uxlabil H4
17 Hotel Ciudad Vieja F3
18 Hotel San Carlos F3
19 Hotel Villa Española E1
20 La Inmaculada G4

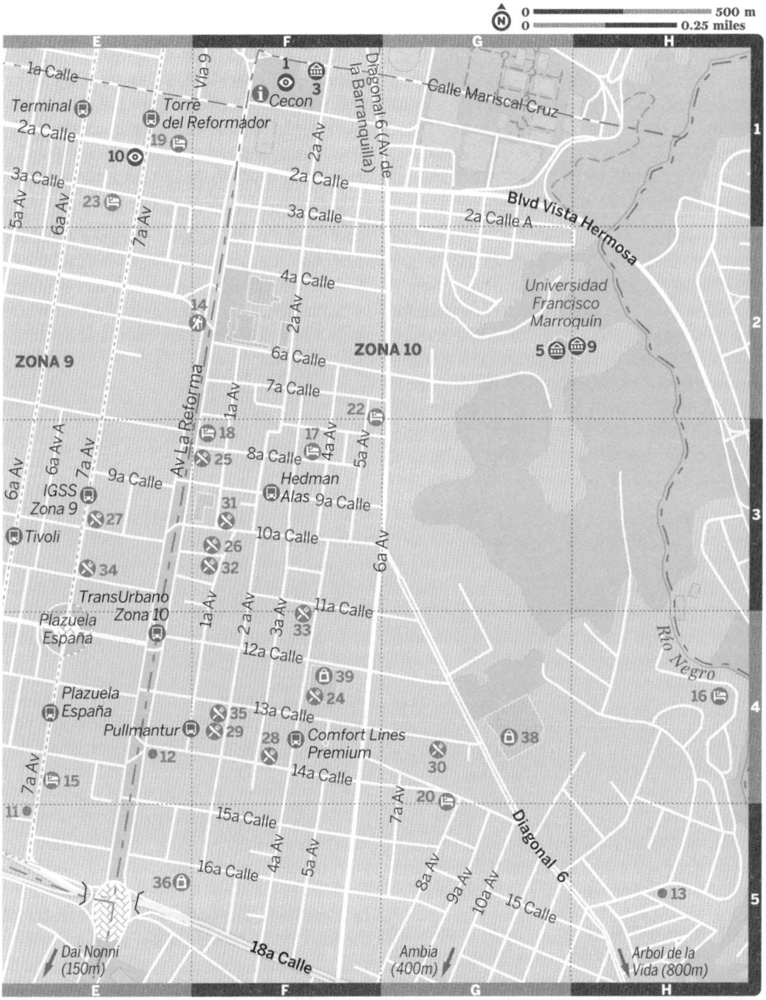

21 Mi Casa ... D4
22 Quetzalroo ... F2
23 Residencia del Sol ... E1

Eating

24 Bistro Tamarindos ... F4
25 Cafetería Patsy ... F3
26 Casa Chapina ... F3
27 Celeste Imperio ... E3
28 Donde la Tía ... F4
29 Kacao ... F4
30 La Maison de France ... G4
31 Los Alpes ... F3
Nais Aquarium ... (see 38)
32 Paco's Café ... F3
33 Pecorino ... F4
34 Puerto Barrios ... E3
35 San Martín & Company ... F4

Entertainment

Cinépolis Oakland Mall ... (see 38)

Shopping

36 Centro Comercial Los Próceres ... E5
37 Mercado de Artesanías ... C5
38 Oakland Mall ... G4
39 Sophos ... F4

style than other Zona 1 joints. It has central but quiet sunny patios. The 43 rooms vary greatly, but most are spacious and clean with high ceilings. Have a look around if you can. All rooms have cable TV; some of the more expensive ones are wheelchair accessible. It's worth booking ahead. A cafeteria serves meals from 6:30am to 11:30am. Rooms have neither a fan nor air-con.

Hotel Sevilla HOTEL **$$**
(Map p48; ☎2230-6538; 9a Av 12-29, Zona 1; s/d Q197/247; P ⊖ ≋) A step up from most hotels in this price range, the Sevilla doesn't quite live up to its self-awarded three-star status, but it still does a pretty good job, and there's an onsite restaurant. The location is supercentral and the somewhat aging rooms are spacious and light. Front rooms get some street noise. Rooms have neither a fan nor air-con.

Hotel Clariss HOTEL **$$**
(Map p48; ☎2232-1113; 8a Av 15-14, Zona 1; dm/s/d Q100/250/355; P ⊖ ≋) This friendly place is set in a modern building with some good-sized rooms (and other, smaller ones). Those at the front get more air and light, but also the bulk of the street noise.

Hotel Ajau HOTEL **$$**
(Map p48; ☎2232-0488; www.hotelajau.net; 8a Av 15-62, Zona 1; s/d Q190/265, without bathroom Q110/180; P ⊖ @ ≋) One of the few cheaper hotels in Guate with any tangible sense of style, the Ajau is a pretty good deal, with lovely polished floor tiles and cool, clean rooms. Room sizes vary, and those at the front can get very noisy. Fans only here, no air-con.

Hotel Ajau Colonial HOTEL **$$**
(Map p48; ☎2232-2955; www.hotelajaucolonial.com; 7a Av 14-19, Zona 1; s/d Q215/305, without bathroom Q135/220; P ⊖ @ ≋) This large converted house has spacious communal areas and heavy, dark, colonial decor. It's a very well-run establishment, with 35 clean, good-sized and adequately furnished fan-cooled rooms. All but two have a private bathroom and TV.

Hotel Capri HOTEL **$$**
(Map p48; ☎2232-8191; 9a Av 15-63, Zona 1; s/d Q175/250; P ⊖ ≋) This modern four-story number is in a decent location and rooms are set back from the street, so they're quiet. Big windows looking onto patios and light wells keep the place sunny and airy.

Hotel Centenario HOTEL **$$**
(Map p48; ☎2338-0381; www.hotelcentenario.wordpress.com; 6a Calle 5-33, Zona 1; s/d/tr Q185/250/330; P ⊖ ≋) Although it's looking a bit worn around the edges, the Centenario offers a pretty good deal, right on the park. Rooms are basic and unrenovated, with TV and hot shower. Wi-fi is in the lobby only.

Hotel Excel HOTEL **$$**
(Map p48; ☎2253-2709; www.hotelexcel.amawebs.com; 9a Av 15-12, Zona 1; s/d Q200/260; P ⊖ ≋) The Excel's modern motel style may be a bit bland for some, but the rooms are spotless and the showers blast hot water.

Hotel Royal Palace HOTEL **$$$**
(Map p48; ☎2416-4400; www.hotelroyalpalace.com; 6a Av 12-66, Zona 1; s/d Q580/670; P ⊖ ❄ ≋) A little island of glamor amid the rough and tumble of 6a Av, this place offers most comforts. The style is modern-reconstruction, with plenty of dark woods and fancy tiling around the place. Rooms are large, sparkling clean and wheelchair accessible. Those at the front have balconies overlooking the street – a fascinating, if noisy, spectacle. Facilities include a restaurant, a bar, and airport transfers with two-day notice.

Hotel Pan American HOTEL **$$$**
(Map p48; ☎2244-0850; www.hotelpanamerican.com.gt; 9a Calle 5-63, Zona 1; s/d Q700/760; P ⊖ ≋) Guatemala City's only luxury hotel before WWII, the Pan American is one of the few hotels in the city with any air of history. There's a fine, art-deco lobby that's filled with plants and a not-too-shabby restaurant. Rooms are simple but large, often with three or more beds. The bathrooms are stylish and modern. Avoid rooms facing the noisy street.

Zona 9

Hotel Villa Española HOTEL **$$**
(Map p52; ☎2205-0200; www.hotelvillaespanola.com; 2a Calle 7-51, Zona 9; s/d Q443/546; P ⊖ ❄ ≋) One of the very few options with colonial stylings in this part of town, the Villa Española has some beautiful touches. It's on a busy road, but rooms are set well back, so there's little noise. There's a good restaurant on the premises, and you're right near the Torre del Reformador (p50).

Mi Casa HOTEL **$$**
(Map p52; ☎2339-2247; www.hotelmicasa.com; 5a Av A 13-51, Zona 9; s/d incl breakfast Q350/450; P ⊖ ❄ ≋) Set in a family house on a quiet

street, Mi Casa offers big and sunny rooms with bathrooms, lino floors, standard acrylic paintings, fans and reading lamps. Breakfast is served in a leafy little patio out back. Call ahead for airport pickup.

Residencia del Sol HOTEL $$$
(Map p52; ☎2360-4823; www.residenciadelsol.com; 3a Calle 6-42, Zona 9; s/d Q500/580; P ⊖ ≋) The spacious, good-looking rooms here make up for the slightly out-of-the-way location. Some rooms have wooden floorboards and a balcony. There's a restaurant onsite.

Barceló Guatemala BUSINESS HOTEL $$$
(Map p52; ☎2378-4000; www.barceloguatemalacity.com; 7a Av 15-45, Zona 9; r from Q900; P ⊖ ❄ @ ≋ ≈) For that big, corporate, somewhat bland hotel experience, it's hard to go past the local outlet of the Spanish Barceló hotel chain.

Zona 10

Quetzalroo HOSTEL $
(Map p52; ☎5746-0830; www.quetzalroo.com; 6a Av 7-84, Zona 10; dm/s/d without bathroom Q147/275/360; P ⊖ @ ≋) Guatemala City's best downtown hostel has nine private rooms and 14 beds in four different dorms, a cramped kitchen area and a great rooftop terrace. The location's handy for the Zona Viva eating and nightlife scene. Simple breakfast is included and it sells craft beers well into the night. Call for free pickup from the airport or bus terminal.

★ **Eco Suites Uxlabil** APARTMENT $$
(Map p52; ☎2366-9555; www.uxlabil.com; 11a Calle 12-53, Zona 10; s/d incl breakfast Q389/479; ⊖ ❄ ≋) If you're planning on being in town for a while (or even if you're not), you could do a lot worse than these sweet little apartments decked out in indigenous motifs and tucked away in a leafy corner of Zona 10. Weekly discounts apply.

Hotel Ciudad Vieja HOTEL $$$
(Map p52; ☎2210-7900; www.hotelciudadvieja.com; 8a Calle 3-67, Zona 10; s/d incl breakfast Q817/885; P ⊖ ❄ @ ≋) A modern construction decked out superbly with old-world touches, the Ciudad Vieja is one of the few truly atmospheric hotels in this part of town. The rooms are good (although the singles can be a bit cramped), and the lovely, shady patio-atrium is perfect for taking a midday breather or enjoying a long and lazy breakfast.

La Inmaculada HOTEL $$$
(Map p52; ☎2314-5100; www.inmaculadahotel.com; 14a Calle 7-88, Zona 10; r Q961-1052, ste Q1281; P ⊖ ❄ @ ≋) In a quiet corner of Zona 10, this chic and sleek 22-room hotel goes out of its way to please, with rainforest showers and Egyptian cotton bedding. Balconies overlook the lush gardens.

Hotel San Carlos HOTEL $$$
(Map p52; ☎2247-3000; www.hsancarlos.com; Av La Reforma 7-89, Zona 10; s/d incl breakfast Q779/875, apt from Q1445; P @ ≋ ≈) OK, so it goes a little heavy on the baroque furnishings, but this place is still a good deal. Set well back from the busy street, it's quiet, and the well-appointed rooms and apartments are spacious and comfortable. Rates include airport pickup.

Zona 13

The middle-class residential area around the airport in Zona 13 is filling up with guesthouses catering to arriving and departing travelers. All the room rates include breakfast and airport transfers (call from the airport on arrival). There are no restaurants out here, but hotel staff have the complete lowdown on fast-food home-delivery options.

Hostal Los Lagos HOSTEL $
(☎2261-2809; www.loslagoshostal.com; 8a Av 15-85 Aurora 1, Zona 13; dm/s/d Q140/243/372; P ⊖ ≋) This is the most hostel-like of the near-the-airport options. Rooms are mostly set aside for dorms, which are airy and spacious, but there are a couple of reasonable-value private rooms. The whole place is extremely comfortable, with big indoor and outdoor sitting areas.

★ **Dai Nonni Hotel** HOTEL $$
(☎2362-5458; www.dainonnihotel.com; 15 Av A 5-30, Zona 13; s/d/tr incl breakfast Q456/522/608; P ⊖ @ ≋) Just south of the Zona 10 action, this hotel wins points for its eclectic decorations, backyard hangout areas and big rooms.

Villa Toscana HOTEL $$
(☎2261-2854; www.hostalvillatoscana.com; 16 Calle 8-20 Aurora 1, Zona 13; s/d incl breakfast Q368/492; P ⊖ @ ≋) One of the 'new breed' of airport hotels, Toscana features big, comfortable rooms, LCD TVs, a tranquil atmosphere, a kitchen for guest use and a lovely backyard. Free airport transfers are only available from 5am to 9:30pm – outside those hours, you pay less than the taxi.

GUATEMALA CITY FOR CHILDREN

Guatemala City has enough child-friendly attractions to make it worth considering as an outing from Antigua if you have kids to please. The Museo de los Niños (p50) and La Aurora Zoo (p51), conveniently over the road from each other in Zona 13, top the list. Kids might also relish the dead animals in various states of preservation at the nearby Museo Nacional de Historia Natural Jorge Ibarra (p51).

The Mapa en Relieve (p47), north of the center, amuses most ages, and there are a few swings and climbing frames in the adjacent park.

On Sundays, kids and adults will enjoy the relaxed atmosphere and abundant free entertainment on offer at Pasos y Pedales (p51).

It shouldn't be too hard to find some food that the little 'uns are willing to eat at the food courts in the Centro Comercial Los Próceres (p60) or Oakland Mall (p60), where everyone can also enjoy a little air-con and shopping (window or otherwise). At Oakland Mall you'll find the restaurant Nais Aquarium (p58) – a winner with the kids for its huge aquarium filled with tropical fish (a scuba diver swims through periodically, cleaning the tank and feeding the inhabitants).

Facilities for families in Guatemala City are not easily found – change rooms and child car seats are pretty rare, although with some advance notice a rental-car company could probably come up with one. For pram-pushers, sidewalks tend to be reasonably level and wide, but can get awfully crowded – consider bringing a baby carrier if you've got a really little one along.

Patricia's Bed & Breakfast GUESTHOUSE $$
(☎5402-3256; www.patriciashotel.com; 19 Calle 10-65, Aurora 2, Zona 13; s/d/tr without bathroom incl breakfast Q135/270/405; P ⊖ @ 📶) This family house is a relaxed and comfortable airport-region option with a sweet little backyard where guests can hang out. It also offers private transport around the city and shuttles to bus stations. Rooms are fan cooled.

Mariana's Petit Hotel GUESTHOUSE $$
(☎2261-4144, 2212-9320; www.marianaspetithotel.com; 20 Calle 10-17 Aurora 2, Zona 13; s/d incl breakfast Q270/340; P ⊖ 📶) One of the better airport hotels, Mariana's features spacious rooms, a good breakfast and a range of hotel services and amenities.

Eating

For cheap eats head to Zona 1 – there are little *comedores* around the Mercado Central, and the cheapest of all are inside the market, on the lower floor. Zonas 10 and 14 have the lion's share of upscale restaurants, with a good selection of international cuisines.

American fast-food chains are sprinkled liberally throughout Zona 1 and across the city. Pollo Campero is Guatemala's KFC clone.

Zona 1

Cheap eats are easy to find in Zona 1 – dozens of restaurants and fast-food shops are strung along, and just off, 6a Av between 8a and 15a Calles.

Coffee culture is just beginning to hit Zona 1, and a number of cool little cafes have sprung up where you can enjoy good coffee, sandwiches and snacks. Even the older, more venerable cafes are able to pump out a drinkable espresso or cappuccino.

★ **Café de Imeri** CAFE $
(Map p48; ☎2232-3722; 6a Calle 3-34, Zona 1; mains Q40-70; ⏲7am-7pm Mon-Fri, to 6:30pm Sat; 📶) Interesting breakfasts, soups and pastas. The list of sandwiches is impressive and there's a beautiful little courtyard area out the back.

Café Leon CAFE $
(Map p48; ☎2232-7526; 8a Av 9-15, Zona 1; breakfast Q30-50; ⏲7am-6pm Mon-Thu, to 6:30pm Fri, 8am-5pm Sat; 📶) Hugely popular and atmospheric, with some great old photos of the city on the walls. Some good breakfasts and sandwiches are on offer, but the coffee is the drawcard.

Café-Restaurante Hamburgo GUATEMALAN $
(Delicadezas Guatemaltecas; Map p48; ☎2238-4029; 15a Calle 5-34, Zona 1; mains Q22-44; ⏲7:30am-9:15pm Mon-Sat, to 8:30pm Sun) This bustling spot facing the south side of Parque Concordia serves good Guatemalan food, with chefs at work along one side and

aproned waitstaff scurrying about. At weekends a marimba band adds atmosphere.

Restaurante Rey Sol VEGETARIAN $
(Map p48; ☎2232-3516; www.restaurantereysol.com; 11a Calle 5-51, Zona 1; mains Q20-35; ⏰7am-7pm Mon-Sat, to 4pm Sun; ✎) The good, fresh ingredients and some innovative cooking keep this strictly vegetarian restaurant busy at lunchtime. It's across from the Teatro Lux theater complex. You can't miss the spring green and yellow decor.

Fu Lu Sho CHINESE $
(Map p48; 6a Av 12-09, Zona 1; mains Q40-70; ⏰7:30am-11:30pm) This classic Zona 1 Chinese eatery has been going for years and is a reliable if somewhat unexciting choice. It's straight-up Chinese with a few Guatemalan staples thrown in, but for late-night cheap eats, it's hard to beat.

★**La Cocina de Señora Pu** GUATEMALAN $$
(Map p48; ☎5055-6480; www.senorapu.com; 6a Av A 10-16, Zona 1; mains Q75-125; ⏰noon-3pm & 6-9pm Mon-Fri, noon-9pm Sat) This tiny hole-in-the-wall eatery serves up excellent 'modernized' versions of classic Maya dishes. The menu is impressively wide – featuring beef, chicken, pork, duck, turkey, pigeon, rabbit, fish and shrimp – considering it's all done on a four-burner stove in front of your eyes. The flavors are delicious and sometimes surprising.

La Majo GUATEMALAN $$
(Map p48; 12a Calle 3-08, Zona 1; mains Q50-80; ⏰2-11:30pm Wed-Sat; ✎) Downtown Guatemala City's cultural renaissance continues in this pleasing little boho cafe set in a crumbling colonial house. There's some OK food on offer and a couple of vegetarian and vegan dishes, but the big draw is the events calendar, featuring live music, theater and other local acts.

Casa Chapina GUATEMALAN $$
(Map p52; ☎2367-6688; www.restaurantecasachapina.com; 1a Av 10-24, Zona 10; mains Q85-200; ⏰noon-10pm Mon-Fri, 8am-10pm Sat & Sun) Down-home Guatemalan food served in more or less formal surrounds can be hard to come by in Zona 10, but this place does it well at good prices. Tables out front on the shady terrace are cool and breezy.

Hotel Pan American INTERNATIONAL $$
(Map p48; ☎2232-6807; 9a Calle 5-63, Zona 1; breakfast Q40-76, mains Q95-143; ⏰7am-9pm; ☰) The restaurant at this venerable hotel is high on ambience. It has notably experienced and polished waitstaff sporting traditional Maya regalia. The food (Guatemalan, Italian and North American) is fine, although it is a little on the expensive side.

Picadilly INTERNATIONAL $$
(Map p48; ☎2253-4522; 6a Av 11-01, Zona 1; mains Q40-80; ⏰7am-9pm Sun-Thu, to 10pm Fri & Sat) Right in the thick of the 6a Av action, this bustling restaurant does pizzas, pastas, good steak dishes and serves good espressos and lattes. The place is clean and street views out of the big front windows are mesmerizing.

Restaurante Altuna SPANISH $$$
(Map p48; ☎2232-0669; www.restaurantealtuna.com; 5a Av 12-31, Zona 1; mains Q112-239; ⏰noon-10pm Tue-Sat, to 5pm Sun & Mon; 👪) This large and classy restaurant has the atmosphere of a private club. It has tables in several rooms that open to a skylit patio. The specialties are seafood and Spanish dishes; service is both professional and welcoming. A kiddie bounce house fills one of the side rooms on weekends.

Zona 9

Celeste Imperio CHINESE $$
(Map p52; www.celesteimperio.com; 7a Av 9-99, Zona 9; mains Q65-150; ⏰11am-10pm) One of the city's many Chinese restaurants, this one gets the thumbs-up from locals. All your favorites are here, plus some unusual options, such as baked pigeon (Q85).

Puerto Barrios SEAFOOD $$
(Map p52; ☎2334-1302; 7a Av 10-65, Zona 9; mains Q100-200; ⏰11am-4pm & 6-11pm Mon-Fri, 11am-11pm Sat & Sun) Puerto Barrios specializes in prawn and fish dishes and is awash in nautical themes: paintings of buccaneers, portholes for windows and a large compass by the door. If you're having trouble finding it, just look for the big pirate ship in which it is housed. Ahoy!

Zona 10

Zona 10's upmarket ambience is matched by its range of restaurant choices – prices are higher here, but you're bound to find more variety on the menus and more comfortable surroundings.

Arbol de la Vida VEGETARIAN $
(☎2368-2124; 17 Calle A 19-60, Zona 10; mains around Q35-60; ⏰7am-6pm Mon-Fri, 7:30am-4pm

LOCAL KNOWLEDGE

ZONA 10 CHEAP EATS

A cheap lunch in GC's hoity-toity Zona 10? These places are nothing fancy, but they are popular with local office workers.

Paco's Café (Map p52; ☎2360-6419; 1a Av 10-50, Zona 10; mains Q15-25; ⏰7am-4pm Mon-Sat) Down-home Guatemalan food served in an eatery at the side of a *kiosko* (small store).

Donde la Tía (Map p52; ☎2337-1045; 14a Calle, btwn 3a & 4a Avs, Zona 10; mains Q10-20; ⏰7:30am-3pm Mon-Fri) Good-value breakfasts and smoothies.

Cafetería Patsy (Map p52; ☎2383-6565; Av La Reforma 8-01, Zona 10; set lunch Q40-60; ⏰7:30am-8pm) A bright, cheerful place offering subs, sandwiches and good-value set lunches.

Sat & Sun; P 📶 ✍) Zona 10's best vegetarian restaurant opens up for early breakfasts and offers a wide menu with tasty soups and mains featuring veg-friendly goodies such as tofu and quinoa.

San Martín & Company CAFE, BAKERY $
(Map p52; ☎2420-9916; 13a Calle 1-62, Zona 10; light meals Q40-60; ⏰6am-10pm Mon-Sat, 7am-8pm Sun; 📶) Cool and clean, with ceiling fans inside and a small terrace outside, this Zona Viva cafe and bakery is great at any time of the day. For breakfast try a scrumptious omelet and croissant (the former arrives inside the latter); later there are tempting and original sandwiches, soups and salads.

Los Alpes CAFE, BAKERY $
(Map p52; ☎2331-4606; 10a Calle 1-09, Zona 10; breakfast Q40-60; ⏰7am-7pm Mon-Sat, 9am-6pm Sun) This relaxing garden restaurant-bakery is set well back from the road, behind a wall of vegetation, giving it a feeling of deep seclusion. The freshly made sandwiches and cakes really hit the spot.

★**Kacao** GUATEMALAN $$
(Map p52; ☎2337-4188; 2a Av 13-44, Zona 10; mains Q90-160; ⏰noon-10:30pm Mon-Sat, to 9:30pm Sun) Set under a thatched *palapa* roof with a soft marimba soundtrack, this is Zona 10's best *comida típica* (regional food) restaurant. The atmosphere and food are both outstanding.

La Maison de France FRENCH $$
(Map p52; ☎2337-4029; 13a Calle 7-98, Zona 10; mains Q65-100; ⏰noon-10pm Mon-Sat) French-Guatemalan probably isn't a combination you were expecting, but this little place does it well, with some good French dishes, such as garlic snails (Q60), imported wines and live music on Fridays.

Nais Aquarium INTERNATIONAL $$
(Map p52; ☎2234-6009; www.gruponais.com; Diagonal 6 13-01, Oakland Mall, Zona 10; mains Q60-100; ⏰7am-11pm) The food's just OK here, but as gimmicks go, this one is pretty good: kids will love the massive aquarium that forms the central wall of this restaurant, especially when the scuba diver comes swimming through, feeding the fish and manta rays. There's even a little crawl space that you can go into and look at the fish up close.

★**Bistro Tamarindos** FUSION $$$
(Map p52; ☎2336-7364; Plaza Fontabella, 2F, Zona 10; mains Q130-300; ⏰7am-10:30pm Mon-Thu & Sat, to 11pm Fri, to 5pm Sun; 📶) This upscale bistro is in one of Guate's ritziest shopping malls. It has an inspiring range of salads on offer and some very good Japanese and Thai-inspired dishes. The decor is stylish and the service prompt but friendly.

Pecorino ITALIAN $$$
(Map p52; ☎2360-3035; 11a Calle 3-36, Zona 10; mains Q89-192; ⏰noon-11pm; 📶) With a beautiful courtyard setting, this is widely regarded as the city's best Italian restaurant. The menu features a huge selection of antipasto, pizza, pasta, meat and seafood dishes. Real flowers grace the white-linen-covered tables.

Zona 14

★**Ambia** FUSION $$$
(☎2312-4666; http://ambia.com.gt; 10a Av 5-49, Zona 14; mains Q115-510; ⏰noon-midnight Mon-Sat, to 3:30pm Sun) As the prices may suggest, this is some of the city's finest dining, with a wide-ranging menu offering some good fusion dishes, leaning heavily on influences as far ranging as Asia and Peru. The presentation is fantastic and the ambience superb. On balmy nights, the outdoor courtyard-lounge area is the place to be.

Cocktail lovers, you're in for a treat, as many of the specialties include a bit of dry ice, making your beverage bubble like a witch's potion. Lots of fun.

Drinking & Nightlife

Zona 1 has a clutch of good drinking places, including some Latin music and dance venues, all advantageously within half a block of each other just south of Parque Central.

Zona 10 has a few electronic dance clubs, but many of these have now moved further south to the outskirts of town. Check flyers around town for special nights.

★Rayuela BAR
(2221-2453; www.facebook.com/rayuelagt; 6a Av 3-61, Zona 1; 11am-1am) This small spot for craft beers and cocktails is dedicated to the author Julio Cortázar, as aficionados will know from the name *Rayuela* (one of the author's novels). Inside, you'll find a red-walled montage of photos, quotes and trivia all connected somehow to one of Latin America's greatest literary minds, with friendly 20- and 30-somethings and decent food as well.

El Gran Hotel PUB
(Map p48; www.facebook.com/ElGranhotel; 9a Calle 7-64, Zona 1; 6pm-1am Tue-Sun) You can't actually stay here, but the downmarket renovated lobby of this classic hotel is one of Zona 1's better-looking bars. It also hosts one of the area's more reliable dance floors, alternating between Latin and electronic music.

Las Cien Puertas BAR
(Map p48; 9a Calle 6-45, Pasaje Aycinena 8-44, Zona 1; 4pm-1am Mon-Sat) This superhip (but not studiously so) little watering hole is set in a colonial arcade that's said to have a hundred doors (hence the name) and is sometimes closed off for live bands.

The bar and the alley are both called Las Cien Puertas. Little bars spring up in this area all the time – it's one of the few places in Zona 1 you can really go bar-hopping, with dozens to choose from in this alley alone.

Entertainment

Guatemala City is home to nearly half the country's population, so it's no surprise that there are entertainment options to spare. The city's various cultural centers are the place to catch music and art shows, and there's live music most nights in the bars around Parque Central, and in the park itself most Sundays.

Live Music

★La Bodeguita del Centro LIVE MUSIC
(Map p48; 2230-2976; 12a Calle 3-55, Zona 1; 9pm-1am Tue-Sat) There's a hopping, creative local scene in Guatemala City, and this large, bohemian hangout is one of the best places to connect with it. There's live music of some kind almost every night from Thursday to Saturday, usually starting at 9pm, plus occasional poetry readings, films or forums. Entry is usually free Tuesday to Thursday, with a charge of Q25 to Q60 on Friday and Saturday nights; food and drinks are served.

TrovaJazz LIVE MUSIC
(Map p48; 2267-9388; www.trovajazz.com; Vía 6 3-55, Zona 4; noon-6pm Mon-Wed, to 1am Thu-Sat) Jazz, blues and folk fans should look into what's happening here.

Cinema

Various multiscreen cinema complexes show Hollywood blockbusters, often in English with Spanish subtitles (unless it's a kids' movie, in which case it will most likely be dubbed into Spanish). Most convenient are **Cine Capitol Royal** (Centro Comercial Capitol; Map p48; 2251-8733; 6a Av 12-51, Zona 1) or **Cinépolis Oakland Mall** (Map p52; 2378-2300; www.cinepolis.com.gt; Diagonal 6 13-01, Zona 10). Tickets cost around Q35. Movie listings can be found in the *Prensa Libre* newspaper.

Cultural Centers

The English-language magazine *Revue* (www.revuemag.com) has events details, although it focuses more on Antigua. Your hotel should have a copy or know where to get one. Free events mags in Spanish come and go. At the time of writing, *El Azar* (www.elazarcultural.blogspot.com) had the best info. Pick up a copy at the city's cultural centers.

Centro Cultural Miguel Ángel Asturias PERFORMING ARTS
(Map p48; 2332-4041; 24a Calle 3-81, Zona 1) Cultural events are held at this outdoor amphitheater.

Centro Cultural de España PERFORMING ARTS
(Map p48; 2377-2200; www.cceguatemala.org; 6a Av 11-02, Zona 1; 9am-7pm Tue-Fri, 10am-2pm Sat) The Spanish Cultural Center hosts an excellent range of events, including live music, film nights and art exhibitions, mostly with free admission. See the website for current details.

LGBT GUATEMALA CITY

The gay and lesbian scene in Guatemala City is not comparable to San Francisco (not by a long shot), but there are several places worthy of mention.

Black (Map p48; ☎5904-1758; www.blackclubgt.com; 11a Calle 2-54, Zona 1; ⌚7pm-1am Thu-Sat) A well-established gay disco-bar in a former private house near the city center with drag shows and theme parties most weekends. Once called Black & White Bar, it's now known as Black.

Genetic (Map p48; Ruta 3 3-08, Zona 4; from Q30, often Q100-150; ⌚9pm-1am Fri & Sat) Genetic has been hosting Guatemala's gay crowd since the '70s, although these days it gets a mixed crowd and is one of the best places in town to go for trance/dance music. It has two dance floors, a runway, a rooftop patio and a relaxed atmosphere.

Shopping

For fashion boutiques, electronics and other goods, head for large shopping malls such as Centro Comercial Los Próceres or Oakland Mall in and around Zona 10. Zona 1's 6a Av is a fun window-shopping experience – half the city turns out to check out the shops, eat ice cream and just cruise the pedestrian mall.

Mercado Central MARKET
(Map p48; cnr 8a Av & 8a Calle, Zona 1; ⌚9am-6pm Mon-Sat, to 2pm Sun) Until the quake of 1976, Mercado Central, behind the cathedral, was where locals shopped for food and other necessities. Reconstructed after the earthquake, it now deals in colorful Guatemalan handicrafts such as textiles, carved wood, metalwork, pottery, leather goods and basketry. It's a pretty good place to shop for these kinds of things, with reasonable prices.

Sophos BOOKS
(Map p52; ☎2419-7070; www.sophosenlinea.com; 4a Av 12-59, Plaza Fontabella, Zona 10; ⌚10am-9pm Mon-Sat, to 7pm Sun) A relaxed place to read while in the Zona Viva, with a good selection of books in English on Guatemala and the Maya, including Lonely Planet guides, and maps. Also stocks books in French.

Oakland Mall MALL
(Map p52; www.oaklandmall.com.gt; Diagonal 6 13-01, Zona 10; ⌚8am-8pm) One of Guatemala City's fancier shopping malls.

Mercado de Artesanías MARKET
(Crafts Market; Map p52; ☎2475-5915; cnr 5a Calle & 11a Av, Zona 13; ⌚9am-6pm) This sleepy market near the museums and zoo sells fabrics, clothes and other standard souvenirs without the crowds of the other markets.

Plaza El Amate MARKET
(Map p48; cnr 18a Calle & 4a Av, Zona 1; ⌚8am-7:30pm) Less hectic than the central market, the Plaza El Amate features a satisfying jumble of everyday items, clothes, CDs and DVDs mixed in with souvenirs and food stalls. There is also a Cajero 5B ATM for withdrawing cash.

Centro Comercial Los Próceres MALL
(Map p52; www.proceres.com; 16a Calle, Zona 10; ⌚8am-8pm) One of the first malls in Guatemala, this has been surpassed by many others, but is still a standby for fashion boutiques, electronic goods and other things.

Orientation

Guatemala City is quite spread out, with the airport to the south, the two major bus terminals to the southwest and northeast, the majority of interesting sights in the downtown Zona 1, and museums and higher-end accommodations clustered around Zona 10. None of these are really within walking distance of each other, but taxis are plentiful and cheap, and two relatively safe bus networks connect various parts of the city.

Information

DANGERS & ANNOYANCES

- Street crime, including armed robbery, happens. Use normal urban caution (behaving as you would in, say, Manhattan or Rome). Keep valuables such as smartphones out of sight when walking.
- It's safe to walk downtown in the early evening, as long as you stick to streets with plenty of lighting and people. Stay alert, leave your valuables in your hotel and catch a taxi after dark.
- The more affluent sections of the city – Zonas 9, 10 and 14, for example – are safer, but crimes against tourists are not unknown.
- The Zona Viva, in Zona 10, has police patrols at night.
- Never try to resist if you are confronted by a robber.

➡ Hustling also happens, particularly in bus stations where a panicked 'priest' needing money for a ticket to get his wife's lost medicines bilks you for as much as you're willing to give.

EMERGENCY

Guatemala City (and, in fact, all of Guatemala) has no area codes – just dial the number as you see it.

INGUAT Tourist Information	☎2421-2854
Tourist Police Liaison (24hr)	☎1500

MEDICAL SERVICES

Guatemala City has many private hospitals and clinics. Public hospitals and clinics provide free consultations but can be busy; to reduce waiting time, get there before 7am.

Hospital Centro Médico (☎2279-4949; 6a Av 3-47, Zona 10; ⏱24hr) Recommended. This private hospital has some English-speaking doctors.

Hospital General San Juan de Dios (☎2321-9191; 1a Av 10-50, Zona 1; ⏱24hr) One of the city's best public hospitals.

MONEY

Card skimming is rife in Guatemala City – try to use ATMs that are under some sort of watch at all times, such as those inside stores or shopping malls, rather than those accessible 24 hours on the street.

American Express (☎2331-7422; 12a Calle 0-93, Centro Comercial Montufar, Zona 9; ⏱8am-5pm Mon-Fri, to noon Sat) In an office of Clark Tours.

Banco Agromercantil (7a Av 9-11, Zona 1; ⏱9am-7pm Mon-Fri, to 1pm Sat) Changes US dollars (cash, not traveler's checks).

Banrural (Aeropuerto Internacional La Aurora; ⏱7am-6pm) Located on the airport departures level, this bank offers currency-exchange services.

Visa/MasterCard ATMs, Zona 10 (16a Calle, Zona 10; ⏱10am-8pm Mon-Sat, to 7pm Sun) Inside Los Próceres Mall.

TOURIST INFORMATION

Cecon (Centro de Estudios Conservacionistas de la Universidad de San Carlos; Map p52; ☎2334-7662; www.cecon.usac.edu.gt; Av La Reforma 0-63, Zona 10; ⏱7:30am-3:30pm Mon-Fri) Administers several protected areas and can arrange stays in them.

Disetur (Tourist Police; ☎3033-7759, 4063-9567; 11a Calle 16-53, Zona 1; ⏱24hr) Guatemala's tourist police; travelers are advised to contact its liaison, **Proatur** (Map p48; ☎toll-free, in English 1500; 7a Av 1-17, Zona 4; ⏱24hr).

SECOND-CLASS ('CHICKEN BUS') SERVICES

DESTINATION	COST (Q)	TIME (HR)	FREQUENCY	DEPARTS
Amatitlán	5	30min	every 4-10min, 7am-8:45pm	CentraSur, Zona 12
Antigua	10	1	every 5min, 7am-8pm	El Trebol
Chichicastenango	30	3	hourly, 5am-6pm	Parada, 41a Calle, Zona 8
Ciudad Pedro de Alvarado	50	2½-3	15min, 4am-5pm	CentraSur, Zona 12
Escuintla	10-15	1	half hourly, 3:30am-7:30pm	CentraSur, Zona 12
Huehuetenango	70	5	half hourly, 7am-5pm	Parada, 41a Calle, Zona 8
La Democracia	30	2	half hourly, 6am-4:30pm	CentraSur, Zona 12
La Mesilla	100	8	hourly, 8am-4pm	Parada, 41a Calle, Zona 8
Monterrico	60	3	3 daily	CentraSur, Zona 12
Panajachel	60-80	3	half hourly, 7am-5pm	El Trebol
Puerto San José	25	2	every 30min, 5am-5pm	CentraSur, Zona 12
Salamá	35-50	3	half hourly, 5am-5pm	17a Calle 11-32, Zona 1
San Pedro La Laguna	60	4	few, 2am-2pm	Parada, 41a Calle, Zona 8
Santa Cruz del Quiché	35	4	10min, 5am-5pm	Parada, 41a Calle, Zona 8
Santiago Atitlán	45	4	half hourly, 4am-5pm	CentraSur, Zona 12
Tecpán	15	2	every 15min, 5:30am-7pm	El Trebol

Fundación Defensores de la Naturaleza (☎2310-2929; www.defensores.org.gt; 4a Av 23-01, Zona 14; ⌚7:30am-4:30pm Mon-Thu, to noon Fri) Administers several protected areas and can arrange stays in them.

INGUAT (Map p48; ☎2290-2800; www.visitguatemala.com; 7a Av 1-17, Zona 4; ⌚8am-4pm Mon-Fri) Main office of the Guatemalan tourism department; has limited handout material, but staff are extremely helpful. There's also a **branch** (☎3128-6900; Aeropuerto Internacional La Aurora; ⌚6am-9pm) at the airport.

Getting There & Away

AIR

Guatemala City's **Aeropuerto Internacional La Aurora** (Map p52; ☎2260-6257) is the country's major airport. All international flights to Guatemala City land and take off here. The arrivals hall has a sometimes-working ATM, sometimes-attended tourist information booth and currency-exchange desks. Travelers have complained about the rates given at the exchange booth inside arrivals. There is also a reliable ATM in the departures hall, helpfully hidden behind the stairs leading up to the mezzanine.

At the time of writing, the country's only *scheduled* domestic flights were between Guatemala City and Santa Elena with **Avianca** (☎2279-8222; www.avianca.com), leaving Guatemala City at 6am and 7:30pm, and **TAG** (☎2380-9494; http://tag.com.gt; Aeropuerto Internacional La Aurora; ⌚7am-7pm), which departs at 6:30am and 5:15pm. Domestic flights *may* leave from the domestic terminal, a 15-minute cab ride from the international terminal.

Fourteen international airlines also serve Guatemala, flying direct from North, Central and South America and Europe.

BUS

Buses from Guatemala City run all over Guatemala and into Mexico, Belize, Honduras, El Salvador and beyond. Many bus companies have their own terminals, some of which are in Zona 1. The city council has been on a campaign to get long-distance bus companies out of the city center, so it may be wise to double-check with INGUAT or staff at your hotel about the office location before heading out.

Buses for the Pacific coast mostly leave from the **CentraSur** terminal in the southern outskirts of town. Departures for Central and Eastern Guatemala and El Petén mostly leave from **CentraNorte** (☎2500-9800; http://centranorte.com.gt; Carretera 9; ⌚6am-8pm) in the city's northeast. Second-class buses for the Western Highlands leave from a series of roadside **paradas** (Map p52), **El Trebol** (Map p52), or bus stops, on 41a Calle between 6a and 7a Avs in Zona 8.

International Bus Service

The following companies offer 1st-class bus services to international destinations.

Comfort Lines Premium (Map p52; ☎2501-1000; www.king-qualityca.com; 4a Av 13-60, Zona 10) Serves most Central American capitals.

Hedman Alas (Map p52; ☎2362-5072; www.hedmanalas.com; 2a Av 8-73, Zona 10) Serves multiple destinations in Honduras.

Línea Dorada (Map p48; ☎2415-8900; www.lineadorada.com.gt; cnr 10a Av & 16a Calle, Zona 1; ⌚5:30am-10pm) Has a service to Tapachula, Mexico.

INTERNATIONAL BUS DEPARTURES FROM GUATEMALA CITY

DESTINATION	COST (Q)	TIME (HR)	FREQUENCY (DAILY)	COMPANY
San José, Costa Rica	692-714	40-60	3	Tica Bus
San Salvador, El Salvador	168-390	5	6	Comfort Lines Premium, Pullmantur, Tica Bus
Copán, Honduras	278-520	5	1	Hedman Alas
La Ceiba, Honduras	442-690	12	1	Hedman Alas
San Pedro Sula, Honduras	405-645	8	1	Comfort Lines Premium, Hedman Alas
Tegucigalpa, Honduras	336-697	10-35	6	Hedman Alas, Comfort Lines Premium, Pullmantur, Tica Bus
Tapachula, Mexico	175-228	5-7	2	Tica Bus, Transportes Galgos Inter
Managua, Nicaragua	462-545	16-35	2	Comfort Lines Premium, Tica Bus
Panama City, Panama	1034-1176	76	2	Tica Bus

Pullmantur (Map p52; ☎2495-7000; www.pullmantur.com; 1a Av 13-22, Holiday Inn, Zona 10) Covers El Salvador and Honduras.

Tica Bus (☎2473-3737; www.ticabus.com; Calz Aguilar Batres 18-35, Zona 12; ⏲5am-6pm) Covers all of Central America and Mexico.

TransGalgos Inter (Map p48; ☎2230-5058, 2232-3661; www.transgalgosintergt.com; 7a Av 19-44, Zona 1; ⏲5am-5pm) Can book connections to Tapachula, Mexico. Also goes to El Salvador.

National Pullman Buses

The following bus companies have services to Guatemalan destinations.

ADN (Map p48; ☎2251-0610; www.adnautobusesdelnorte.com; 8a Av 16-41, Zona 1) Connects Guatemala City to Flores, Santa Elena, and points in between.

Fortaleza del Sur (☎2230-3390; CentraSur, Zona 12) Covers the Pacific coast.

Fuente del Norte (Map p48; ☎2251-3817; 17a Calle 8-46, Zona 1) Covers the whole country.

Hedman Alas Daily departures between Guatemala City and Antigua.

Línea Dorada Luxury buses to El Petén, Quetzaltenango, Huehuetenango etc.

Litegua (Map p48; ☎2220-8840; www.litegua.com; 15a Calle 10-40, Zona 1; ⏲3:30am-7pm) Covers the east and Antigua.

Los Halcones (☎2439-4911; Calz Roosevelt 37-47, Zona 11) For Huehuetenango.

Monja Blanca (CentraNorte, Zona 18; ⏲3am-6pm) For Cobán and points in between.

Rapidos del Sur (☎2232-7025; CentraSur, Zona 12) For the Pacific coast.

Rutas Orientales (☎2503-3100; CentraNorte, Zona 18) Covers the east.

Transportes Álamo (☎2471-8646; 12a Av A 0-65, Zona 7) For Quetzaltenango.

Transportes Rebuli (Map p52; ☎2230-2748; 41a Calle btwn 6a & 7a Av, Zona 8) For Panajachel.

CAR

Most major rental companies have offices both at La Aurora airport (in the arrivals area) and in Zona 9 or 10. Companies include the following:

Avis Airport (☎2324-9000; www.avis.com.gt; Aeropuerto Internacional La Aurora; per day from Q500; ⏲6am-midnight)

Avis Downtown (☎2324-9000; www.avis.com; 6a Calle 7-64, Zona 9; ⏲8am-5pm Mon-Fri, to noon Sat)

Guatemala Rent a Car Airport (☎2208-9000; www.guatemalarentacar.com; Aeropuerto Internacional La Aurora; per day from Q256; ⏲5:30am-9:30pm)

Guatemala Rent a Car Downtown (☎2329-9020; www.guatemalarentacar.com; 12a Calle 5-54, Oficina 15, Zona 9; ⏲8am-6pm Mon-Fri, to 1pm Sat)

Tabarini Airport (☎2322-5088; www.tabarini.com; Aeropuerto Internacional La Aurora; ⏲8am-9pm)

Tabarini Downtown (☎2444-4200; www.tabarini.com; 2a Calle A 7-30, Zona 10; ⏲8am-6pm Mon-Fri, 9am-1pm Sat)

NATIONAL BUS DEPARTURES FROM GUATEMALA CITY

DESTINATION	COST (Q)	TIME (HR)	FREQUENCY	COMPANY
Antigua	50-70	1	7 daily	Hedman Alas, Litegua
Chiquimula	40-50	3-4	half hourly, 5am-6:30pm	Rutas Orientales
Cobán	50-80	5	hourly, 4am-5pm	Monja Blanca
El Carmen	90	7	hourly, 4am-5pm	Fortaleza del Sur
Esquipulas	65-75	4-5	half hourly, 4:30am-7pm	Rutas Orientales
Flores & Santa Elena	130-205	8-10	6-8 daily	ADN, Fuente del Norte, Línea Dorada
Huehuetenango	90-100	5	4 daily	Línea Dorada, Los Halcones
Poptún	120-200	8	3 daily	Línea Dorada, Fuente del Norte
Puerto Barrios	100-150	5-6	hourly, 3:45am-7pm	Litegua
Quetzaltenango	70	4	10 daily	Álamo, Fuente del Norte, Línea Dorada
Retalhuleu	85	3	5 daily	Fuente del Norte
Río Dulce	80-100	5	hourly, 5:30am-5pm	Litegua
Tecún Umán	75	6	4 daily	Fortaleza del Sur

Tally Renta Autos Airport (☎2261-2526; www.tallyrentaautos.com; 7a Av 13-74 Zona 13; per day from Q180; ⏰4:30am-10pm)

Tally Renta Autos Downtown (☎2261-2579; www.tallyrentaautos.com; 7a Av 14-60, Zona 1; per day from Q180; ⏰8:30am-5pm Mon-Fri)

SHUTTLE MINIBUS

Shuttle services from Guatemala City to popular destinations such as Panajachel and Chichicastenango (via Antigua; both around Q260) are offered by travel agencies in Antigua. Quetzaltenango-based travel agents also have shuttles to and from Guatemala City.

Getting Around

TO/FROM THE AIRPORT

Aeropuerto Internacional La Aurora Guatemala City's international airport is in Zona 13, a Q80 taxi ride from Zona 1 and Q70 from Zona 10 or 13. If you're arriving late at night, a popular option is to spend the night in one of the guesthouses close to the airport and get a fresh start the next day.

BUS

Arriving from other parts of the country, you'll most likely be coming in on a bus. Guatemala City's bus stations are scattered all over town. Wherever you're going, if it's more than a few blocks away it's a good idea to grab a taxi. Taxis are plentiful (especially around bus stations) and a whole lot cheaper than getting mugged while lugging your backpack around.

Due to an increase in (sometimes violent) crime on Guatemala City's red city buses, it is pretty much universally accepted that tourists should only use them in case of dire emergency. The major exceptions are the TransMetro and TransUrbano buses, which are most useful for getting to the CentraSur and CentraNorte bus terminals, respectively.

We've listed the most useful red-bus routes. Buses will stop anywhere they see a passenger, but street corners and traffic lights are your best bet for hailing them – just hold out your hand. Buses should cost Q1 per ride in the daytime (but this can as much as quadruple on public holidays or at the driver's whim). You pay the driver or the driver's helper as you get on. Don't catch these buses at night.

Airport to Zona 1 (Bus No 82) Travels via Zonas 9 and 4.

Zona 1 to Airport (Bus No 82) Travels via 10a Av in Zona 1 then down 6a Av in Zonas 4 and 9.

Zona 1 to Zona 10 (Bus No 82 or 101) Travels via 10a Av, Zona 1, then 6a Av and Ruta 6 in Zona 4 and Av La Reforma.

Zona 10 to Zona 1 (Bus No 82 or 101) Travels via Av La Reforma then 7a Av in Zona 4 and 9a Av, Zona 1.

TransMetro

In early 2007, in answer to growing concerns about traffic congestion and security on urban buses, the city inaugurated the TransMetro system (www.muniguate.com/muni/transmetro). TransMetro buses differ from regular old, red urban buses because they are prepaid (the driver carries no money, thus reducing the risk of robberies), travel in their own lanes (not getting caught in traffic jams), only stop at designated stops and are new, comfortable and bright green.

There are currently seven routes in operation, each named for the zone they reach: thus, Línea 13 takes you out to Zona 13. Among the routes, one connects Zona 1's Plaza Barrios with the CentraSur bus terminal, from where the majority of buses for the Pacific coast now depart. Another runs south from Plaza Barrios through Zonas 9 and 10.

Crime has increased so much on regular red buses that travelers are advised not to use them, but TransMetro buses are safe, fast and comfortable. All rides cost Q1, payable with a Q1 coin at the bus stop before boarding.

TransUrbano

TransUrbano is a much wider network of buses that aren't quite as slick as TransMetro but are still safe, reliable and comfortable. They're slower because they don't have a dedicated lane, but safer than the old red buses because to board you need a magnetic rechargeable card (card and first ride free), which can only be obtained by showing your passport or Guatemalan ID card. The rechargeable cards are available from special booths, the most useful for travelers being in Zona 1's Plaza Barrios, the CentraNorte bus terminal and the **Zona 10 TransUrbano office** (Map p52; cnr Av Reforma & 12a Calle, Zona 10).

TAXI

Plenty of taxis cruise most parts of the city. Fares are negotiable; always establish your destination and fare before getting in. Zona 1 to Zona 10, or vice-versa, costs around Q50. If you want to phone for a taxi, **Taxi Amarillo Express** (☎1766) has metered cabs (figure on Q5 per kilometer) that often work out cheaper than others, although true *capitaleños* (capital city residents) will tell you that taxi meters are all rigged and you get a better deal bargaining for a flat price.

Antigua

POP 46,700

Includes ➡

Best Places to Eat

➡ Casa Troccoli (p82)
➡ Fridas (p82)
➡ Luna de Miel (p81)
➡ Mesón Panza Verde (p83)
➡ Rincón Típico (p82)

Best Places to Stay

➡ Cucuruchos Boutique Hostel (p77)
➡ Earth Lodge (El Hato; p88)
➡ Posada del Ángel (p80)
➡ Hotel Quinta de las Flores (p80)
➡ Lo de Bernal (p79)

Why Go?

Antigua's beguiling beauty starts to seduce the moment you arrive. Once capital of Guatemala, its streetscapes of pastel facades unfold beneath the gaze of three volcanoes, and beautifully restored colonial buildings sit next to picturesque ruins in park-like surroundings. The city's World-Heritage listed status means that even fast-food chains have to hide themselves behind traditional building facades.

While Antigua's churches, plazas and markets throb with activity, the town is also a global hot spot with a laid-back vibe, thanks to the dozens of Spanish-language schools that operate here. Outside the city, Maya communities, coffee plantations and volcanoes offer ample opportunities for exploration.

Through the course of its history, this city has suffered earthquakes, floods, volcanic eruptions and virtual abandonment. But in recent decades it has re-emerged with a vengeance, buoyed by the pride of its inhabitants. No wonder Antigua remains Guatemala's most visited destination.

When to Go

Antigua

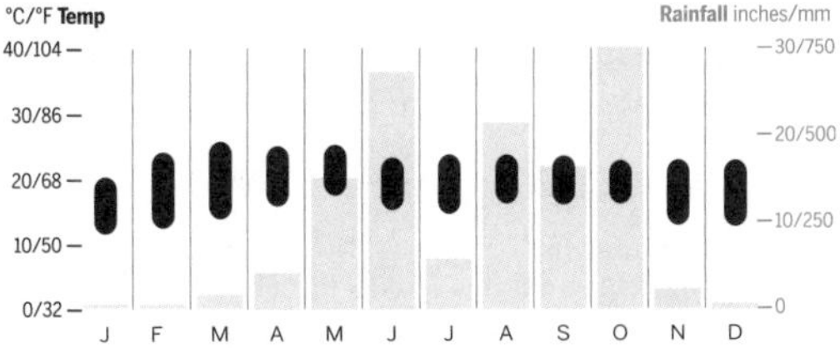

May–Oct The cooler months to visit, but with afternoon rain showers the norm.

Jul–Aug The busiest times for Antigua language schools

Holy Week Religious processions enliven the streets in the run-up to Easter. Hotels book up quickly.

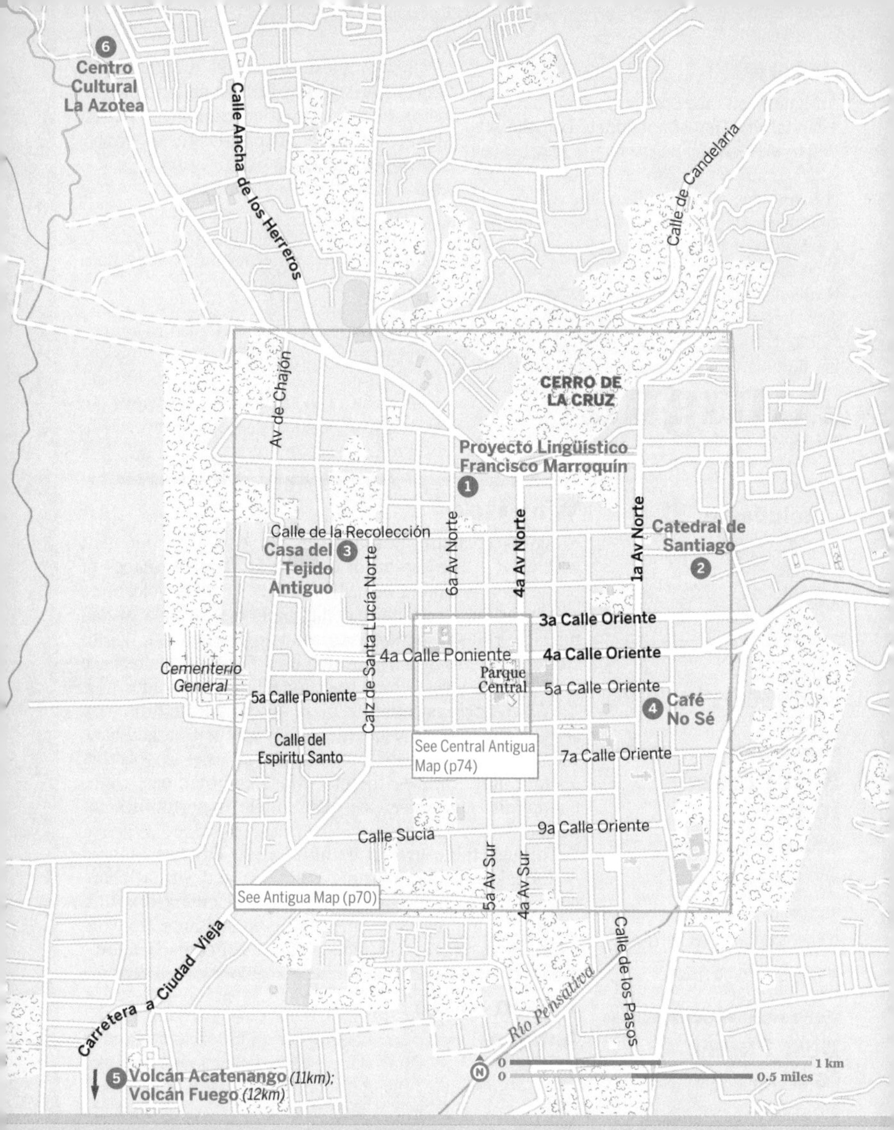

Antigua Highlights

1 **Language lessons** (p75) Resurrecting your high-school Spanish at such highly regarded language schools as Proyecto Lingüístico Francisco Marroquín.

2 **Ruins** (p67) Witnessing scattered slabs of masonry, such as at Catedral de Santiago, that display mute evidence of Antigua's quake-ridden history.

3 **Casa del Tejido Antiguora** (p88) Admiring and acquiring traditional Maya wear at this seminal collection of *huipiles* and *cortes*.

4 **Café No Sé** (p84) Sampling a clandestine mescal at this low-lit lair of choice for Antigua's expats.

5 **Volcanoes** (p73) Scaling Acatenango for jaw-dropping views of its sister volcanoes, including fire-spewing Fuego.

6 **Centro Cultural La Azotea** (p87) Savoring volcanic coffee beans at this coffee plantation.

History

Antigua wasn't the Spaniards' first choice for a capital city. That honor goes to Iximché, settled in 1524 to keep an eye on the Kaqchiquel, with whom they had an uneasy truce. Things got uneasier when the Kaqchiquel rebelled, so the city was moved in 1527 to present-day Ciudad Vieja on the flanks of Volcán Agua. That didn't work out, either – the town practically disappeared under a mudslide in 1541. And so it was that on March 10, 1543, La muy Noble y muy Leal Ciudad de Santiago de los Caballeros de Goathemala, the Spanish colonial capital of Guatemala, was founded. The long-winded title attests to the founders' reverence for St James (Santiago in Spanish), to whom their early military victories were attributed.

Antigua was Spain's epicenter of power throughout Central America, and during the 17th and 18th centuries little expense was spared on the city's architecture, despite the regular ominous rumbles from the ground below. Indigenous labor was marshaled to erect schools, hospitals, churches and monasteries, their grandeur only rivaled by the houses of the upper clergy and the politically connected.

At its peak Antigua had no fewer than 38 churches, as well as a university, printing presses, a newspaper and a lively cultural and political scene. Those rumblings never stopped, though, and for a year the city was shaken by earthquakes and tremors until the devastating earthquake of July 29, 1773. A few years later, the capital was transferred again, this time to Guatemala City. Antigua was evacuated and plundered for building materials, and orders were given for its inhabitants to relocate and for the city to be systematically dismantled. Despite this, however, it was never completely abandoned. Fueled by a coffee boom early in the next century, the town, by then known as La Antigua Guatemala (Old Guatemala), began to grow again. Ongoing renovation of battered buildings helped maintain the city's colonial character despite an official lack of interest, but lobbying by Antigua's citizens led to President Ubico's 1944 declaration of the city as a national monument, and restoration ensued in earnest. Just as serious efforts were being made to return the city to its former splendor, however, disaster struck again with another major quake in February 1976, leaving thousands dead and undoing much of the restoration work.

Unesco's designation of Antigua as a World Heritage site in 1979 added new impetus to the restoration campaign. Within this new climate, Spanish-language schools began popping up, pulling in droves of foreign students and leading to a genuine cultural renaissance. In recent years, Antigua has become an enormously popular wedding destination for Latin American couples, adding to its visitor numbers.

Antigua's current mayor, Susana Asencio, elected in 2015, has worked hard to control traffic and to start to tackle the city's notoriously bad drains – an important if unglamorous measure to improve the quality of life for Antigua's residents as the resurgent city continues to surf its tourism boom.

Sights

Parque Central & Around

Parque Central PLAZA

(Map p74; btwn 4a Calle & 5a Calle) Surrounded by superb colonial structures, this broad and beautiful plaza is the gathering place for *antigüeños* and visitors alike – a fine, verdant place to sit or stroll and observe the goings-on, from hawkers and shoeshiners to school kids and groups of tourists. The buxom mermaids in the central fountain are a reconstruction of the original 1738 version, which was trashed early in the 20th century.

Catedral de Santiago CATHEDRAL

(Map p74; cnr 4a Av Norte & 5a Calle Oriente; ruins Q8; ruins 9am-5pm, parish 6:30am-noon & 3-6:30pm Mon, Tue, Thu & Fri, 8am-noon & 3-7pm Sat, 5:30am-1pm & 3-7:30pm Sun) Antigua's cathedral was begun in 1545, wrecked by the quake of 1773, and only partially rebuilt over the next century. The present sliver of a church – the parish of San José – occupies only the entrance hall of the original edifice. Behind it are the roofless **ruins** of the main part of the cathedral, which are entered from 5a Calle Oriente.

The ruin is a haunting place, with massive chunks of pillars strewn beneath sweeping brick archways and vegetation sprouting from cracks in the walls. Reproductions of the intricate plasterwork figures and moldings between the arches seem all that more impressive against the ruined backdrop. Behind the main altar, steps lead down to a former crypt, now serving as a chapel, with a smoke-blackened Christ.

The main part of the cathedral was built in the 17th century by Joseph de Porres, an architect of mixed African-Maya descent.

Palacio de los Capitanes Generales HISTORIC BUILDING
(Palace of the Captains General; Map p74; ☎7832-2868; www.centroculturalrealpalacio.org.gt; 5a Calle Poniente; ⊙9am-4:30pm Wed-Sun) FREE Dating from 1549, the palace was colonial headquarters for all of Central America, from Chiapas to Costa Rica, until the capital was relocated in 1776. The stately double-arcaded facade that anchors the south side of the plaza is all that remains of the original complex. Following extensive renovations, the palace now hosts occasional art exhibits and performances.

Antiguo Colegio de la Compañía de Jesús HISTORIC BUILDING
(Map p74; ☎7932-3838; www.aecid-cf.org.gt; 6a Av Norte; ⊙9am-6pm) FREE Established in 1626, the Jesuit monastery and college was a vital component of Antigua life until the order was expelled in 1767; just six years later, the great earthquake left it in ruins. Rescued from the rubble by the Spanish government, the complex has been reborn as a cultural center, the **Centro de Formación de la Cooperación Española**.

The former offices, classrooms and refectories now contain lecture halls, exhibit spaces, a fashionable cafe and an excellent library. The three cloisters have been made over with fine wood columns and balconies, a brilliant setting for photo exhibits, concerts, films and festivals. One component remains respectfully unrestored, though: the Compañía de Jesús church, the grand facade of which stands to the left of the main entrance of the complex.

Palacio del Ayuntamiento HISTORIC BUILDING
(City Hall Palace; Map p74; 4a Calle Poniente) This double-decker structure on the north side of the park dates from the 18th century. Besides town offices, the palace houses the **Museo del Libro Antiguo** (Old Book Museum; Map p74; ☎7832-5511; 4a Calle Poniente, Palacio del Ayuntamiento; Q30; ⊙9am-4pm Tue-Fri, 9am-noon & 2-4pm Sat & Sun), showcasing the early days of Guatemalan printing. The stone benches looking over to the park from beneath the lower arcade make a fine people-watching perch.

West of Parque Central

★Arco de Santa Catalina ARCHITECTURE
(Map p70; 5a Av Norte) The Arco de Santa Catalina is Antigua's most iconic monument, and an early-morning or late-afternoon photo opportunity framing Volcán Agua through its arch is an essential part of any visit to the town. It was built in 1694 to enable nuns from the Santa Catalina convent to cross the street without being seen; the clock tower is a 19th-century add-on.

★Iglesia Merced CHURCH, MONASTERY
(Iglesia y Convento de Nuestra Señora de la Merced; Map p70; cnr 1a Calle Poniente & 6a Av Norte; monastery ruins Q15; ⊙church 6am-noon & 3-8pm, ruins 8:30am-5:30pm) At the northern end of 5a Av is La Merced – a striking yellow building trimmed with white plaster filigree. Its facade is one of the most beautiful in Guatemala The squat, thick-walled structure was built to withstand earthquakes, and three centuries after its construction it remains in good shape. Only the church is still in use; a candlelit procession, accompanied by bell ringing and firecrackers, starts and ends here on the last Thursday evening of each month.

Inside the monastery ruins is a fountain 27m in diameter, said to be the largest in Hispanic America. It's in the shape of a water lily (traditionally a symbol of power for the Maya), and lily motifs also appear on the church's entrance arch. Go upstairs for a bird's-eye view of the fountain and the town.

Iglesia y Convento de la Recolección RUINS
(Map p70; Av de la Recolección; Q40; ⊙9am-5pm) A serene air pervades the remains of the monastery of La Recolección, which stands well west of the center. Erected in the early 18th century by the Récollets (a French branch of the Franciscan order), its church was one of the largest in Antigua at the time. The earthquake of 1773 toppled the structure, of which only the great arched doorway remains intact.

Beyond are strewn the massive chunks of masonry that formed the original walls. The adjoining cloisters, laid out on an equally grand scale, have been cleared of debris and have variously served as fairgrounds and swimming pool following the complex's short life as a monastery.

Colegio de San Jerónimo RUINS

(Real Aduana; Map p70; cnr Calz de Santa Lucía Norte & Calle de la Recolección; Q40; ⏲9am-5pm) Completed in 1757, the Colegio de San Jerónimo was used as a school by friars of the Merced order, but because it did not have royal authorization, it was taken over by Spain's Carlos III and, in 1765, designated for use as the Royal Customs House. Today it's a tranquil, mostly open-air, site in an excellent state of preservation.

The handsome cloister centers upon an octagonal fountain, an evocative setting for occasional dance and other cultural performances. Head upstairs for great photo angles of Volcán Agua through stone archways.

East of Parque Central

★ Iglesia y Convento de Santo Domingo MONASTERY

(Map p70; ☎7820-1220; 3a Calle Oriente 28; Q42; ⏲9am-6pm Mon-Sat, 11:45am-6pm Sun) Founded by Dominican friars in 1542, Santo Domingo became the biggest and richest monastery in Antigua. Following three 18th-century earthquakes, the buildings were pillaged for construction material. The site was acquired as a private residence in 1970 by a North American archaeologist, who performed extensive excavations before it was taken over by the Casa Santo Domingo Hotel (p80). The archaeological zone has been innovatively restored as a 'cultural route.'

The zone includes the picturesque ruined monastery church, the adjacent cloister with a replica of the original fountain, workshops for candle and pottery makers, and two underground crypts that were discovered during the church excavations. One of these, the **Calvary Crypt**, contains a well-preserved mural of the Crucifixion dating from 1683.

Also part of the archaeological zone are six museums, with extraordinarily rich collections presented in top-class exhibitions. All can be visited with one admission ticket. This museum route may be entered either through the hotel or the Universidad de San Carlos extension on 1a Av Norte. Starting from the hotel side, the route includes the following museums: the **Museo de la Platería**, with silverwork masterpieces including incense burners, candelabras and crowns; the **Museo Colonial**, with canvases and wooden sculpture on religious themes from the 16th to 18th centuries; the **Museo Arqueológico**, with ceramic and stone objects from the Maya Classic period; the cleverly curated **Museo de Arte Precolombino y Vidrio Moderno**, with Mayan sculpture and ceramics shown as art pieces alongside glass works by modern artists; the **Museo de Artes y Artesanías Populares de Sacatepéquez**, with exhibits on traditional handicrafts from the Antigua region; and the **Museo de la Farmacia**, a restored version of a 19th-century apothecary's shop from Guatemala City.

La Antigua Galería de Arte GALLERY

(Map p70; ☎7832-2124; www.facebook.com/LaAntiguaGaleria; 5a Avenida Norte 29; ⏲10am-7pm Mon-Sat, noon-6pm Sun) FREE Displaying works by more than 70 Guatemalan artists in the halls and patio of a colonial mansion, Antigua's premier art gallery merits an extended visit. There are regular expositions of new and old artists.

Convento de Capuchinas CONVENT

(Iglesia y Convento de Nuestra Señora del Pilar de Zaragoza; Map p70; cnr 2a Av Norte & 2a Calle Oriente; adult/student Q40/20; ⏲9am-5pm) Inaugurated in 1736 by nuns from Madrid, the convent of Las Capuchinas was seriously damaged by the 1773 earthquake and thereafter abandoned. Thanks to meticulous renovations in recent decades, it's possible to get a sense of the life experienced by those cloistered nuns, who ran an orphanage and women's hospital.

Wander round to admire the fine cloister with its stout columns and high arched passageways, remarkably restored washbasins and well-tended gardens. At the rear you'll find the convent's most unique feature, a towerlike structure of 18 nuns' cells built around a circular patio.

Iglesia de San Francisco CHURCH, MONASTERY

(Map p70; ☎7882-4438; cnr 7a Calle Oriente & Calle de los Pasos; museum & monastery adult/child Q6/3; ⏲9am-5:30pm) This church is imbued with the spirit of Hermano Pedro de San José de Bethancourt, a Franciscan monk who founded a hospital for the poor in Antigua and earned the gratitude of generations. On the south side are the ruins of the adjoining monastery, with some vivid frescoes still visible amid its earthquake rubble.

Hermano Pedro's intercession is still sought by the ill, who pray fervently by his tomb, housed in an elaborate pavilion since his canonization in 2002. Devotees may enter via a garden north of the church. A

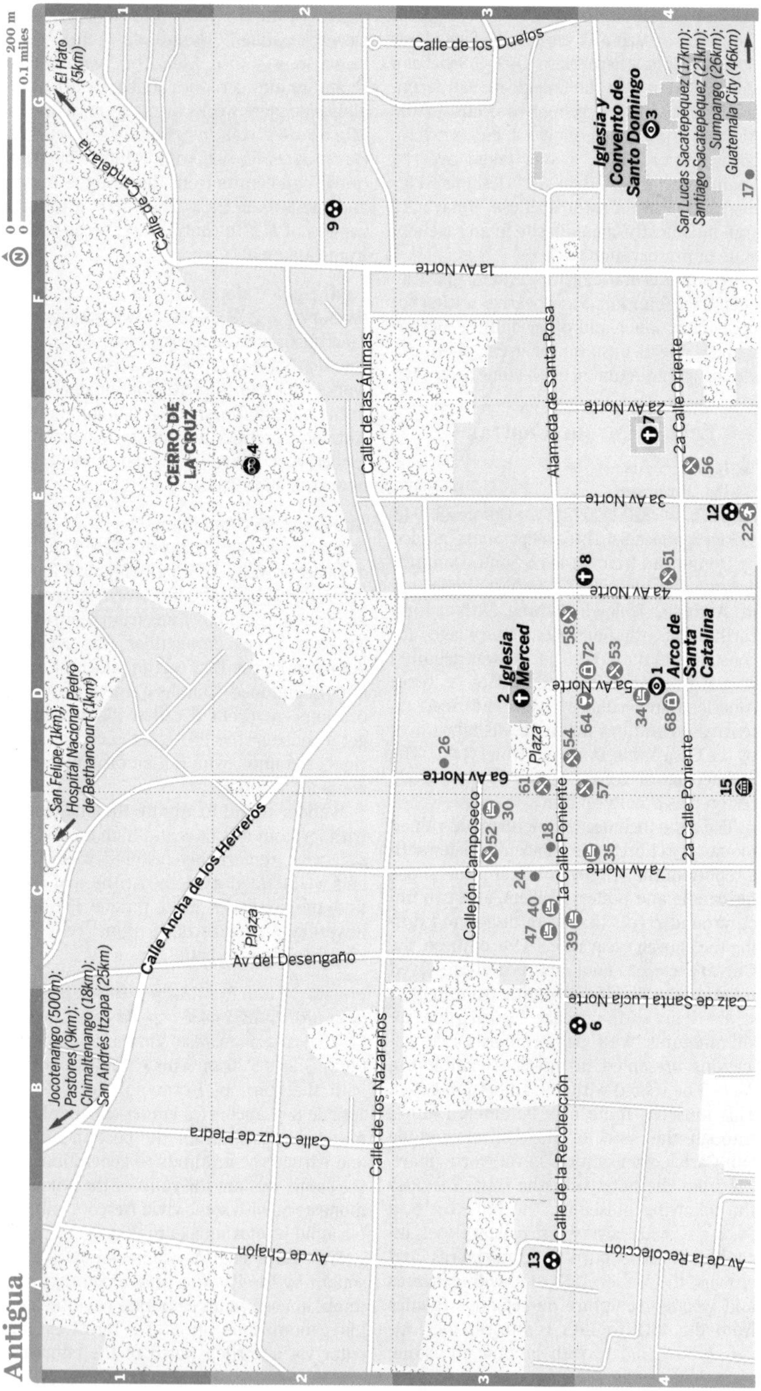
Antigua
200 m
0.1 miles
El Hato (5km)
San Felipe (1km); Hospital Nacional Pedro de Bethancourt (1km)
Jocotenango (500m); Pastores (9km); Chimaltenango (18km); San Andrés Itzapa (25km)
San Lucas Sacatepéquez (17km); Santiago Sacatepéquez (21km); Sumpango (26km); Guatemala City (46km)
CERRO DE LA CRUZ
Iglesia y Convento de Santo Domingo
2 Iglesia Merced
Arco de Santa Catalina
Calle de los Duelos
Calle de Candelaria
1a Av Norte
Calle de las Ánimas
Alameda de Santa Rosa
2a Av Norte
2a Calle Oriente
3a Av Norte
4a Av Norte
5a Av Norte
6a Av Norte
7a Av Norte
Calle Ancha de los Herreros
Callejón Camposeco
1a Calle Poniente
2a Calle Poniente
Plaza
Av del Desengaño
Calz de Santa Lucía Norte
Calle de los Nazareños
Calle Cruz de Piedra
Calle de la Recolección
Av de Chajón
Av de la Recolección

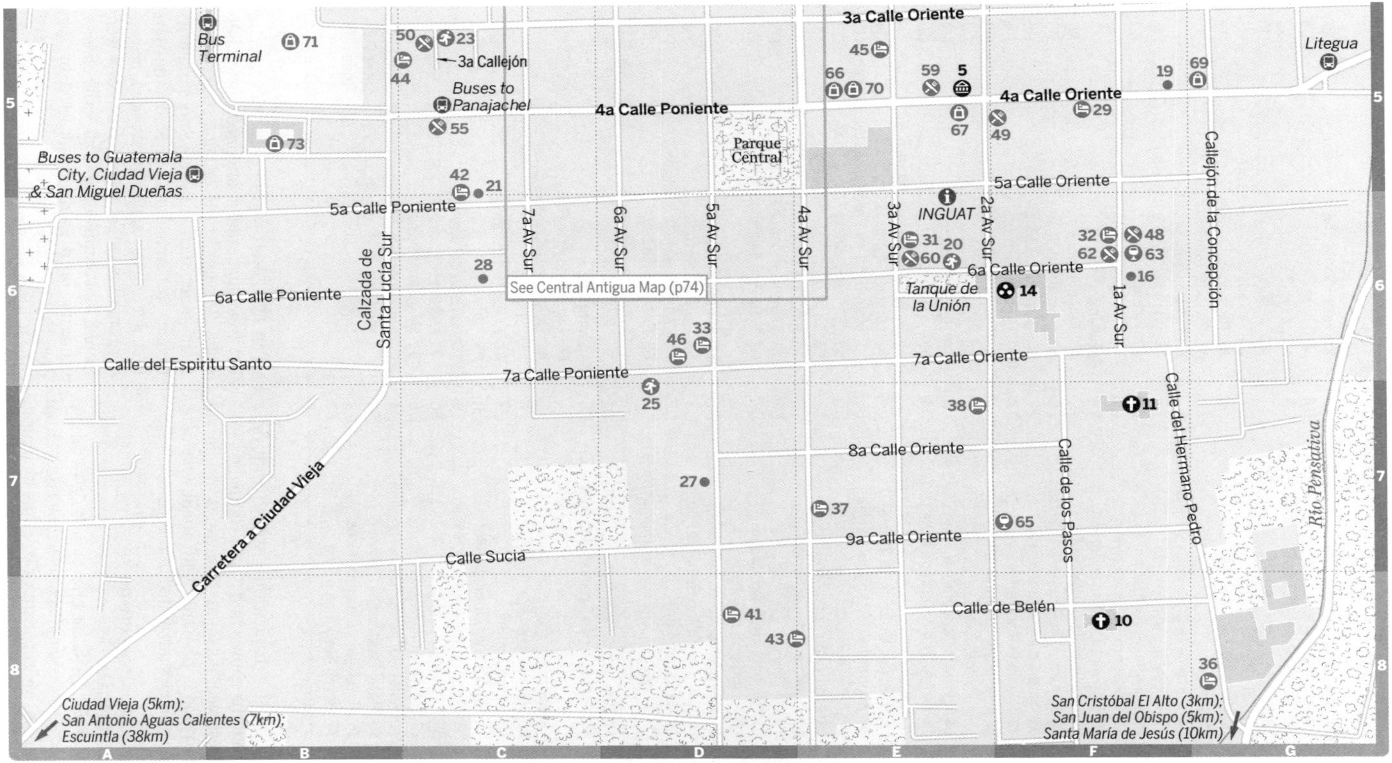
3a Calle Oriente
Bus Terminal
71
50
23
3a Callejón
44
Buses to Panajachel
55
73
Buses to Guatemala City, Ciudad Vieja & San Miguel Dueñas
42
21
5a Calle Poniente
4a Calle Poniente
Parque Central
45
66
70
59
5
67
49
4a Calle Oriente
29
19
69
Litegua
5a Calle Oriente
INGUAT
Callejón de la Concepción
7a Av Sur
6a Av Sur
5a Av Sur
4a Av Sur
3a Av Sur
2a Av Sur
31
20
60
32
48
62
63
16
6a Calle Oriente
Tanque de la Unión
14
1a Av Sur
28
See Central Antigua Map (p74)
6a Calle Poniente
Calzada de Santa Lucía Sur
46
33
Calle del Espiritu Santo
7a Calle Poniente
25
7a Calle Oriente
38
11
Calle del Hermano Pedro
Río Pensativa
8a Calle Oriente
Calle de los Pasos
27
37
65
9a Calle Oriente
Calle Sucia
Carretera a Ciudad Vieja
Calle de Belén
10
41
43
36
Ciudad Vieja (5km); San Antonio Aguas Calientes (7km); Escuintla (38km)
San Cristóbal El Alto (3km); San Juan del Obispo (5km); Santa María de Jesús (10km)
A
B
C
D
E
F
G
5
6
7
8

Antigua

Top Sights

1 Arco de Santa Catalina D4
2 Iglesia Merced D3
3 Iglesia y Convento de Santo Domingo G4

Sights

4 Cerro de la Cruz E2
5 Choco Museo E5
6 Colegio de San Jerónimo B4
7 Convento de Capuchinas E4
8 Convento de Santa Teresa E4
9 Iglesia de la Candelaria F2
10 Iglesia de la Escuela de Cristo F8
11 Iglesia de San Francisco F7
12 Iglesia El Carmen E4
13 Iglesia y Convento de la Recolección A3
14 Iglesia y Convento de Santa Clara F6
15 La Antigua Galería de Arte D4

Activities, Courses & Tours

16 Academia de Español Sevilla F6
17 Antigua Tours G4
18 Antigüeña Spanish Academy C3
19 Cambio Spanish School F5
20 CATours E6
21 Centro Lingüístico Maya C5
22 La Antigua City Tour E4
23 La Tortilla C5
24 New Sensation Salsa Studio C3
25 Ox Expeditions D7
26 Proyecto Lingüístico Francisco Marroquín D3
27 Spanish School San José el Viejo D7
28 Tecún Umán Spanish School C6

Sleeping

29 Adra Hostel F5
30 Casa Cristina C3
Casa Santo Domingo Hotel .... (see 3)
31 Cucuruchos Boutique Hostel E6
32 El Hostal F6
33 Hostal Antigua D6
34 Hotel Convento Santa Catalina D4
35 Hotel Posada San Pedro II C4
36 Hotel Quinta de las Flores G8
37 Hotel San Jorge E7
38 Hotel Santa Clara E7
39 Lo de Bernal C3
40 Maya Papaya C3
41 Mesón Panza Verde D8
42 Posada de Don Valentino C5
43 Posada del Ángel D8
44 Posada Juma Ocag C5
45 Posada San Sebastián E5
46 Wicho & Charlie's Hostel D6
47 Yellow House C3

Eating

48 Angie Angie F6
49 Bistrot Cinq F5
50 Casa de las Mixtas C5
51 El Papaturro E4
52 Fernando's Kaffee C3
53 Fridas D4
54 Hector's Bistro D3
55 La Bodegona C5
56 La Cuevita de Los Urquizú E4
57 Luna de Miel D4
Mesón Panza Verde .... (see 41)
58 Quesos y Vino D3
59 Restaurante Doña Luisa E5
60 Rincón Típico E6
61 Tienda La Canche D3
62 Y Tu Piña También F6

Drinking & Nightlife

63 Café No Sé F6
64 Las Vibras de la Casbah D4
65 Por Qué No? F7
Tabacos y Vinos .... (see 34)

Shopping

66 Centro de Arte Popular E5
67 Doña María Gordillo Dulces Típicos E5
68 El Reino del Jade D4
69 Jade Maya G5
70 La Casa del Jade E5
71 Market B5
72 Maya Arte Nativo D4
73 Mercado de Artesanías B5
Mercado del Carmen .... (see 22)
Nim Po't .... (see 53)

museum is haphazardly strewn with relics from the church and Santo Hermano's well-preserved personal belongings, while the corridor is plastered with thank-you notes for miracles attributed to the saint.

Iglesia y Convento de Santa Clara — RUINS

(Map p70; 2a Av Sur, btwn 6a & 7a Calles Oriente; Q40; 9am-5pm) Established by sisters from Puebla, Mexico, Santa Clara was inaugurated in 1734, destroyed four decades later by the great quake and abandoned. Fortunately some elements of the original structure remain intact, such as the church's stonework facade, the arched niches along the nave that served as confessionals, and an underground chamber where provisions were stored. Most captivating of all is the cloister, centering on a fountain bordered by gardens, though only one side of the upper-level arcade remains in place.

Choco Museo MUSEUM

(Map p70; ☎7832-4520; www.chocomuseo.com; 4a Calle Oriente 14; ⏲10am-6:30pm Sun-Thu, to 7:30pm Fri & Sat; 👪) FREE It was the Maya who discovered the culinary uses of the cacao bean, which later became a form of currency for the Aztec empire. These are a few of the things you'll learn at this kid-friendly expo, the Antigua branch of a hemisphere-wide project. The museum also offers 'bean to bar' chocolate-making workshops (Q150) and cacao plantation tours.

Activities

Antigua has any number of activities to fill your days, and a seemingly endless number of schools and tour agencies offering to sell you their services. Take your time to visit their offices and choose what's right for you.

Old Town Outfitters ADVENTURE SPORTS

(Map p74; ☎5399-0440; www.adventureguatemala.com; 5a Av Sur 12C) Mountain-biking, rock-climbing, kayaking and trekking are among the high-energy activities offered by this respected and highly responsible operator, which works with guides from local communities.

Ox Expeditions ADVENTURE SPORTS

(Map p70; ☎5801-4301; www.oxexpeditions.com; 7a Calle Poniente 17) Offers rigorous climbing opportunities in the area, plus such adrenaline-fueled activities as mountain-biking, kayaking, surfing and ziplining, as well as volcano hikes. Many of its easier bike tours are designed for families with children.

Ravenscroft Riding Stables HORSEBACK RIDING

(☎7830-6669; www.facebook.com/ravenscroftstables; 2a Av Sur 3, San Juan del Obispo; per hour beginner/experienced riders Q200/240) This outfit, 3km south of Antigua on the road to Santa María de Jesús, offers English-style riding, with scenic rides of two to three hours around the foothills of Volcán Agua. There are horses for beginners and for more experienced riders.

Volcano Ascents

All three volcanoes overlooking Antigua – **Agua**, **Acatenango** and **Fuego** – are tempting challenges, but after Fuego's deadly 2018 eruption, hikes here are likely to be curtailed for some time. In many ways the twin-peaked Acatenango (3975m) is the most exhilarating summit. For an active-volcano experience many people take tours to **Pacaya** (2552m), 25km southeast of Antigua (a 1½-hour drive).

The strenuous hike up Volcán Acatenango traverses four ecosystems to reach the summit. Typical agency prices are around Q1100, including lunch and 5am transport to the trailhead in the village of La Soledad. Overnight hikes are another option, camping just below the treeline, then ascending to the summit the following morning (Q1300 per person with two people).

Ascents of Volcán Agua (3766m) take off from the village of Santa María de Jesús (Q3.50 from Antigua bus terminal) on the volcano's northeast slopes. You can hire INGUAT-authorized guides (one day/overnight Q200/250 per person, plus park entry fee of Q40) from the tourist office just off Santa María's Parque Central. Don't attempt this without a guide, as assaults on the slopes have been known to take place, so take trusted advice before climbing.

Most agencies run seven-hour Pacaya trips daily for Q90 (leaving Antigua at 6am and 2pm), but food and drinks are not included, nor is the Q50 admission to the Pacaya protected area. It takes about 1½ hours to make the steep ascent to the simmering black cone. (If you're out of breath, you can rent horses on the way up.) From the summit there are stupendous views northwest to Agua and northeast to Lago de Atitlán. The descent is quicker as you slide down the powdery slope.

Courses

Antigua's Spanish-language schools attract students from around the world. There are dozens of schools to choose from. The INGUAT tourist office (p86) has a list of authorized schools, but price, teaching quality and student satisfaction can vary greatly. The most popular classes are for conversational Spanish, but if you want to focus on your grammar, or learn for a specific purpose (such as for medicine, business or law), you'll find the class to suit you in Antigua.

Classes start every Monday at most schools, though you can usually be placed with a teacher any day of the week. Most schools cater for all levels and allow you to stay as long as you like. Three or four weeks is typical, though it's perfectly OK to do just one week. The busiest seasons are during January and from April to August, and some schools request advance reservations for these times.

Central Antigua

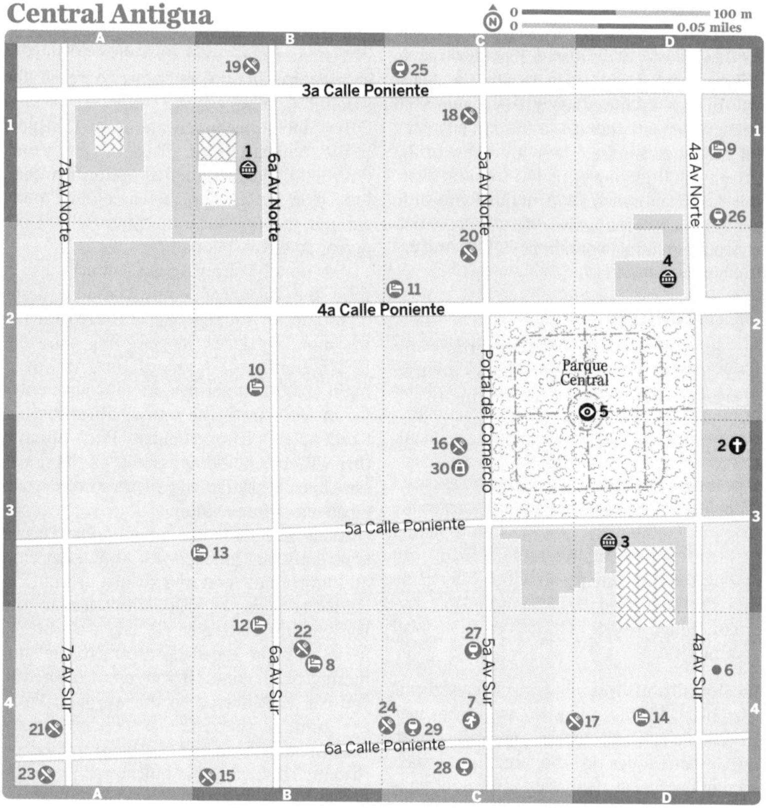

Central Antigua

Sights

1 Antiguo Colegio de la Compañía de Jesús....B1
2 Catedral de Santiago....D3
Museo del Libro Antiguo....(see 4)
3 Palacio de los Capitanes Generales....D3
4 Palacio del Ayuntamiento....D2
5 Parque Central....D2

Activities, Courses & Tours

6 El Frijol Feliz....D4
7 Old Town Outfitters....C4

Sleeping

8 Bigfoot Hostel....B4
9 Hotel Casa del Parque....D1
10 Hotel Casa Rústica....B2
11 Hotel Euro Maya....C2
12 Hotel Posada San Vicente....B4
13 Posada de San Carlos....B3
14 Tropicana Hostel....D4

Eating

15 Cactus Taco Bar....B4
16 Café Condesa....C3
17 Caffé Mediterráneo....D4
18 Casa Troccoli....C1
19 El Viejo Café....B1
20 La Fonda de la Calle Real....C2
21 Rainbow Café....A4
22 Saberico....B4
23 Samsara....A4
24 Travel Menu....C4

Drinking & Nightlife

25 Antigua Brewing Company....C1
26 El Barrio....D1
27 La Sin Ventura....C4
28 Reilly's en la Esquina....C4
29 Snug....C4

Shopping

30 Librería La Casa del Conde....C3

Instruction is nearly always one-on-one and costs Q900 to Q1200 per week for four hours of classes daily, five days a week. Most schools offer to arrange room and board with local families, usually with your own room and three meals daily (except Sunday), for around Q850 per week (a bit more with private bathroom). Most schools also offer lessons by Skype if you want to continue your study or start lessons before you arrive.

Homestays are meant to promote the total immersion concept of language learning, but this becomes tricky where there are several foreigners staying with one family or separate mealtimes for students and the family. Indeed, there are so many foreigners about Antigua, it can take discipline to converse in Spanish rather than your native tongue. Many enjoy this social scene, but if you think it may deter you, consider studying in Quetzaltenango, El Petén or elsewhere, where there are fewer foreign students.

Cambio Spanish School LANGUAGE
(Map p70; ☎7832-8033; www.cambiolanguageschool.com; 4a Calle Oriente 28) All profits from this school support Niños de Guatemala, a local educational program for underprivileged kids. Teachers use the curriculum devised by the Spanish Instituto Cervantes.

Proyecto Lingüístico Francisco Marroquín LANGUAGE
(Map p70; ☎7832-1422; www.spanishschoolplfm.com; 6a Av Norte 43) Antigua's oldest Spanish school, founded in 1969, is run by a nonprofit foundation to preserve indigenous languages and culture, with capacity to teach K'iche', Mam, Kaqchiquel and other Maya tongues (advance booking needed to arrange local teachers).

Antigüeña Spanish Academy LANGUAGE
(Map p70; ☎5735-4638; www.spanishacademyantiguena.com; 1a Calle Poniente 10) Regularly recommended school, and authorized by the Ministry of Education. Lessons take place in a leafy hacienda, and the school has two student apartments as well as homestay options.

Academia de Español Sevilla LANGUAGE
(Map p70; ☎7832-5101; www.facebook.com/SpanishSchoolAntigua; 1a Av Sur 17C) This well-managed institute offers plenty of free activities, and it can arrange volunteer work in local community projects. One-on-one classes are conducted amid the remnants of a colonial monastery. Shared student housing is offered as an accommodations option.

Spanish School San José el Viejo LANGUAGE
(Map p70; ☎7832-3028; www.sanjoseelviejo.com; 5a Av Sur 34) Long-standing school with park-like study environment, complete with its own accommodations and pool. Students switch teacher every week unless requested. Accredited by the Guatemalan Ministry of Education.

Tecún Umán Spanish School LANGUAGE
(Map p70; ☎5513-4349; www.tecunumanschool.edu.gt; 6a Calle Poniente 34A) Long-standing Guatemalan-run outfit with university-trained staff who mostly have more than two decades of teaching experience each. Classes are held on the pleasant rooftop terrace of a nearby cafe.

Centro Lingüístico Maya LANGUAGE
(Map p70; ☎7832-0656; www.centrolinguisticomaya.com; 5a Calle Poniente 20) One of the pricier schools, but with over 30 years of experience and well respected by embassy staff and foreign journalists.

New Sensation Salsa Studio DANCING
(Map p70; ☎5033-0921; www.facebook.com/salseandosevivemejor; 7a Av Norte 78; per hour Q85) If you want to get your dancing shoes on, try the free salsa group classes every Monday and Tuesday from 5pm to 6pm. The studio also offers one-on-one instruction in salsa and *bachata* (a style of dance originating in the Dominican Republic) – either by the hour or in extended packages.

La Tortilla COOKING
(Map p70; ☎4181-8227; www.latortillacookingschools.com; 3 Calle Poniente 25; lessons Q225-375; from 2 to 6 dishes) This excellent cooking school runs classes twice a day at 10:30am and 4:30pm. The personable instructors guide you through classes from a 90-minute one covering two dishes, to a three-hour lesson with six dishes from mains and sides to dessert (and unlimited wine).

El Frijol Feliz COOKING
(Map p74; ☎7832-5274; www.frijolfeliz.com; 4a Av Sur 1; 3hr class Q365) Hands-on instruction preparing Guatemalan meals; students may choose their own menu to cook and eat – you'll prepare one main dish, two secondary dishes and a dessert. For Q465 you can make a day of it with a foodie tour of local markets as well as a cooking class at the end.

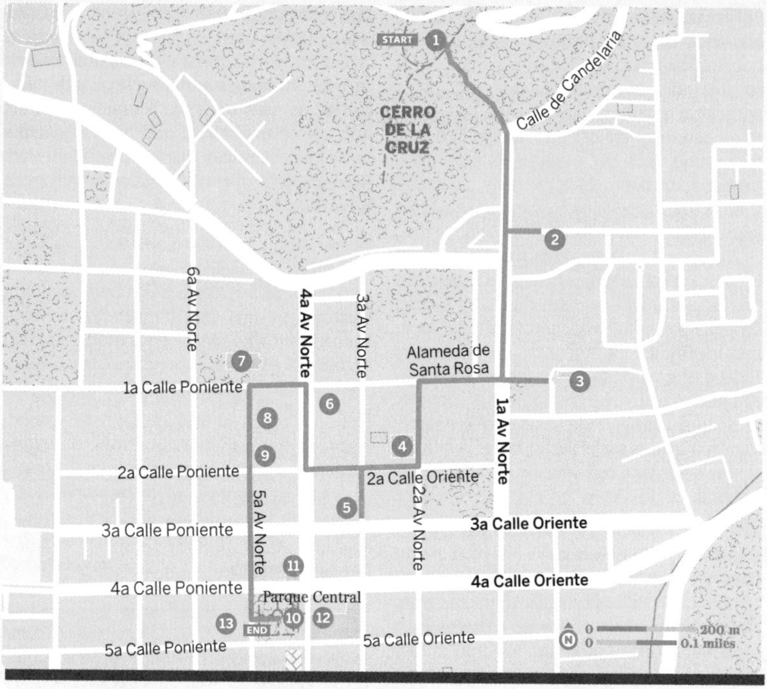

City Walk
Walking Colonial Antigua

START CERRO DE LA CRUZ
END CAFÉ CONDESA
LENGTH 2.3KM; 2½ HOURS

For the big picture, take a taxi up 1 **Cerro de la Cruz** (p78), north of town. Beyond the stone cross that gives the hill its name, Antigua spreads out, with the majestic Volcán Agua as a backdrop. Descend the wooded slopes via the path to the left. At the bottom, turn right down a cobblestone street. You'll come to a basketball court backed by the swirly columns of the ruined 2 **Iglesia de la Candelaria** (Map p70). Proceed one block south to a small plaza, then head left alongside a high yellow wall to glimpse the 3 **Templo de Santa Rosa de Lima**, a small church with an elaborate facade that stands on a private estate. Turn around and head west along jacaranda-lined Alameda de Santa Rosa. Take the first left, onto 2a Av Norte, past an ironworks shop. At the next corner on the right are the ruins of the 4 **Convento de Capuchinas** (p69), with its unique tower. Go right on 2a Calle Oriente. Passing 3a Av Norte, look down to your left to see the multicolumned facade of 5 **Iglesia El Carmen** (Map p70) and the adjacent handicrafts market. Continue another block west and turn right on 4a Av Norte. Near the next corner on the right is the old 6 **Convento de Santa Teresa** (Map p70), which until recently served as the men's prison. Turn left into 1a Calle Poniente, from where you'll see the yellow bell tower of the 7 **Iglesia Merced** (p68). Turn left down 5a Av Norte, jam-packed with tourist-friendly locales, including the handicrafts center, 8 **Nim Po't** (p85). Proceed beneath the 9 **Arco de Santa Catalina** (p68); a remnant of the 17th-century convent that stood here (now occupied by a luxury hotel and B&B), the enclosed arch enabled nuns to cross the street unseen. Continue down 5a Av Norte to 10 **Parque Central** (p67). Ascend to the balcony of the 11 **Palacio del Ayuntamiento** (p68) for photo ops of the square and nearby 12 **Catedral de Santiago** (p67). Finally, stop at the 13 **Café Condesa** (p81), on the square's west side, for a well-deserved cappuccino and wedge of pie.

Tours

INGUAT-authorized guides around Parque Central offer city walking tours, with visits to convents, ruins and museums, for around Q80 per person. Similar guided walks are offered daily by Antigua travel agencies such as **Atitrans** (7832-3371; www.atitrans.net; 6a Av Sur 8; 8am-9pm). Also on offer are trips to the surrounding villages and coffee plantations.

Antigua Tours (Map p70; 7832-5821; www.antiguatours.net; 3a Calle Oriente 22; tour incl museum fees Q190), run by Elizabeth Bell, a noted scholar of Antigua history, leads three-hour cultural walking tours of the town (in English and/or Spanish) on Tuesday, Wednesday, Friday and Saturday mornings. Groups congregate at the park's fountain at the appointed hour. Bell's book, *Antigua Guatemala: The City and its Heritage,* is well worth picking up. It has extensive descriptions of all the monuments, and neatly encapsulates the city's history and fiestas. Bell and company also offer tours to the nearby villages of San Antonio Aguas Calientes and San Andrés Itzapa to investigate weaving workshops and Maya shrines, respectively.

La Antigua City Tour (Map p70; 7832-6151; www.antiguacitytour.com; 2½-hr tour Q200; 9am-5pm) runs a little bus around town, hitting all the key sites from Cerro de la Cruz to Parque Central.

De la Gente (5585-4450; www.dlgcoffee.org; tour per person (min 2 people) Q200) offers tours of coffee plantations around San Miguel Escobar, a suburb of Ciudad Vieja, with local growers demonstrating cultivation, harvesting and processing techniques. At the end, participants are guided through traditional roasting methods and share a cup with the family. Tours (three to five hours) depart at 9am or 1pm and should be booked at least a day in advance.

Art Tours Antigua (4149-4663; http://artintheamericas.net/art-tours-antigua-guatemala/; Q375) offers specialized gallery tours to learn more about contemporary Guatemalan art.

CATours (Map p70; 7832-9638; www.catours.co.uk; 6a Calle Oriente 14; 9am-5pm Tue-Sun) offers motorbike day tours around Volcán Agua, as well two day trips to Lago de Atitlán or Monterrico from Q1400.

Festivals & Events

The most exciting time to be in Antigua is **Semana Santa** (Holy Week; Easter week), when hundreds of devotees garbed in deep purple robes bear revered icons from their churches in daily street processions in remembrance of Christ's crucifixion and the events surrounding it. Dense clouds of incense envelop the parades and the streets are covered in elaborate *alfombras* (carpets) of colored sawdust and flower petals. These fragile works of art are destroyed as the processions shuffle over them, but are re-created each morning for another day of parades.

The fervor and the crowds peak on Good Friday, when an early-morning procession departs from La Merced (p68), and a late afternoon one leaves from the **Escuela de Cristo** (Map p70; cnr Calles de los Pasos & de Belén; 9am-1pm & 3-7pm Thu-Tue). There may also be an enactment of the crucifixion in Parque Central (p67). Have ironclad Antigua room reservations well in advance of Semana Santa, or plan to stay in Guatemala City or elsewhere and commute to the festivities.

Processions, *velaciones* (vigils) and other events actually go on every weekend through Lent, the 40-day period prior to Semana Santa. Antigua's tourist office has schedules of everything, and the booklet *Lent and Holy Week in Antigua* by Elizabeth Bell gives explanations.

Sleeping

With around 150 hotels, *posadas* (guesthouses) and hostels, Antigua has a wide range of accommodations to suit any traveler's style or budget, including some of the best places in the country. Some of Antigua's midrange hotels allow you to wallow in colonial charm for a moderate outlay of cash.

Room rates vary: midweek stays can often be 20% cheaper than Friday and Saturday nights (hostels tend to be the exception to this rule). Prices double during Semana Santa and demand surges – book as far ahead as you possibly can.

★**Cucuruchos Boutique Hostel** HOSTEL
(Map p70; 7832-1479; www.facebook.com/hostelcucuruchos; 3a Ave Sur 1A; d Q100-125, r Q435;) This hostel hits stylish heights without the need to break the budget. Bunk bed dorms are spacious and very well appointed, sleeping four, six and 12 people (prices vary according to which place you take) with excellent bathrooms. There's a cute courtyard and a roof terrace and one of the nicest communal kitchens we've ever seen.

ANTIGUA FOR KIDS

With gaudily painted buses roving around town, rainbow candles burning in the churches and gigantic volcanoes in the background, Antigua holds an innate magic that appeals to children. Within most of the monastic complexes are parklike expanses where kids can run around amid the ruined walls and fountains. The craft shop Nim Po't (p85) overflows with colorful kites and tiny replicas of those buses to look at, while the market (p84) holds many novel sights, sounds and smells.

At the Choco Museo (p73), you can make your own chocolate confections, while the amazing stuffed crepes and juices at Luna de Miel (p81) make a great lunchtime stop. For fresh air, take the kids up to **Cerro de la Cruz** (Hill of the Cross; Map p70) for mesmerizing views of the town and surrounding volcanoes; sign up with Ravenscroft Riding Stables (p73) for a bit of horseback riding; take a family-friendly bike adventure with Ox Expeditions (p73); or consider a trip to Earth Lodge (p88), a kid-friendly retreat with a playground, fanciful cabins and plenty of hiking trails.

★Maya Papaya HOSTEL $
(Map p70; ☎7832-2837; www.mayapapayaantigua.com; 1a Calle Poniente 20; dm Q100, r with/without bathroom Q460/370; @📶) Modern and well-designed, Maya Papaya knows its flashpacker market well. The hostel opens onto a modest bar area, where breakfasts are also taken, while at the rear (where it is quieter) are airy spacious dorms (one mixed, one women only) with all mod cons.

★Adra Hostel HOSTEL $
(Map p70; www.adrahostel.com; 4a Calle Oriente 15; dm Q165, incl breakfast dm/r Q165/860; 📶) The Adra is one of several upmarket hostels that have sprung up in Antigua recently. It's a gorgeous affair – Scandi-style dorms with impressively structured bunks fitted with generously sized beds, lights and power, great communal facilities and a pretty courtyard garden festooned with fairy lights. The bar shuts early so everyone sleeps well, and the cafe-restaurant serves clever French food.

The private rooms sleep eight.

Wicho & Charlie's Hostel HOSTEL $
(Map p70; ☎7832-1215; www.facebook.com/wichoandcharlies; dm Q75-120) This is a quiet hostel for outdoorsy types, particularly as it specializes in its own volcano hiking trips. It's a cute but modest place, with capsule-hotel style boxed-in bunks (each with their own light and fan), and some with double beds. There's a hot tub and a terrace, a kitchen and a mostly friendly cat and dog to welcome guests.

Tropicana Hostel HOSTEL $
(Map p74; ☎7832-0462; www.tropicanahostel.com; 6a Calle Poniente 2; dm Q80, r with/without bathroom Q300/200; 📶🏊) Check in any time you like to this party hostel and join the flock of global youth sunning by the poolside bar or soaking in the hot tub against a backdrop of bright murals. Mixed-gender dorms feature triple-decker bunks each with built-in lockers, curtains and power outlets. Don't be surprised if you're checked-in by a receptionist in a rainbow unicorn onesie.

El Hostal HOSTEL $
(Map p70; ☎7832-0442; www.elhostalbnb.com; 1a Av Sur 8; incl breakfast dm/s/d/tr without bathroom Q85/200/280/380; 📶) Within stumbling distance of plenty of cafes and restaurants, El Hostal is a super-relaxed budget option with a hint of colonial style. Set around a cheery little patio-cafe are half a dozen neatly kept private rooms and dorms with sturdy single beds or well-spaced bunks, a few sticks of furniture and creatively painted walls.

There's a sparkling guest kitchen and good gas-heated showers.

Hostal Antigua HOSTEL $
(Map p70; ☎7832-8090; www.hostalantigua.com; 5a Av Sur 22; dm/r Q60/300; 📶🐾) Just a block and a half from Parque Central, this low-key hostel favors cleanliness and comfort over frenetic socializing. Roomy 12- and four-bed dorms and private rooms, featuring sturdy wood beds and ceiling fans, line up along a pretty leafy corridor. Up above is a roof terrace with guest kitchen and tiled tables.

Bigfoot Hostel HOSTEL $
(Map p74; ☎7832-0489; www.bigfoothostelantigua.com; 6a Av Sur; dm/d/tr/q Q75/250/300/350; ❄📶) This place is always hopping, both as a hostel and a bar. It's cramped and the dorm beds have you stacked like sardines, but the social scene and mellow

courtyard are a big draw for its youthful clientele. The beer pong table made from the donated bras of former guests gives an idea of the in-house party scene.

Yellow House HOSTEL $

(Map p70; ☎7832-6646; yellowhouseantigua@hotmail.com; 1a Calle Poniente 24; dm/r without bathroom Q70/200; @) This is a fine budget choice. Rooms vary in style and size, but comfy beds, recessed lighting and screened windows are the norm. It can get crowded with just three bathrooms downstairs, but they're all kept clean. The plant-filled terrace is perfect for enjoying the huge, healthy breakfast served each morning, or sleeping it off in a hammock.

★ **Lo de Bernal** B&B $$

(Map p70; ☎7832-3242; www.lodebernal.com; 1a Calle Poniente 23; r Q530;) Don't be intimidated by the full suit of armour at this small new bed and breakfast; service here comes with a warm and personal touch. Rooms are comfortable with lovely bedsteads, and breakfast is taken in a cosy lounge area near a rippling fountain.

Posada de San Carlos HOTEL $$

(Map p74; ☎7832-4698; www.posadadesancarlos.com; 5a Calle Poniente 11; dm/s/d Q70/400/500;) A global inn with an emphasis on comfort, the San Carlos features spacious rooms along a corridor that opens onto a neat patio with fountain. Both private rooms and the seven-bed dorm have colonial flair, with carved wood beds and chests. The front cafe whips up tasty natural fare and there are bikes available for exploring.

Posada San Sebastián GUESTHOUSE $$

(Map p70; ☎7832-2621; www.posadasansebastian.com; 3a Av Norte 4; s/d Q490/570;) What do you show for a lifetime of collecting? San Sebastián's auteur-owner has the answer – a guesthouse packed to the gunwales with curios and museum pieces, from old phones and abandoned statues of saints to restored antique furniture. Each of the nine rooms is like a gallery, with big bathrooms including tub a bonus, along with the roof terrace and pretty little courtyard garden.

Casa Cristina HOTEL $$

(Map p70; ☎7832-0623; www.casa-cristina.com; Callejón Camposeco 3A; s/d Q300/400;) There are just a dozen rooms at this hotel on a pretty backstreet near La Merced. Though compact, all are quaintly appointed with *típico* (traditional) bedspreads, brushed-on pastels and wood-stained furniture, and the plant-laden roof terrace makes a nice retreat. Discounts are sometime available for the downstairs rooms with internal windows only. *Muy tranquilo.*

Posada Juma Ocag HOTEL $$

(Map p70; ☎7832-3109; www.posadajumaocag.com; Calz Santa Lucia Norte 13; r Q180-200;) Juma Ocag's seven spotless, comfortable rooms have quality mattresses and traditional appointments including wrought-iron bedsteads, armoires and mirrors crafted in-house, and there's a kitchen for guests. Despite the hectic location opposite the market, it remains peaceful – especially the upstairs rooms – with a rooftop patio and well-tended little garden.

Hotel San Jorge HOTEL $$

(Map p70; ☎7832-3132; www.hotelsanjorgeantigua.com; 4a Av Sur 13; s/d Q390/510;) This low hacienda-style hotel arranges itself around a beautiful flower-filled garden, with each room having a small bench outside to enjoy the setting. The rooms vary quite a bit in size, but they're all done out with neat local fabrics and art, and have good bathrooms. The quiet setting reflects its position slightly outside the immediate bustle of the main tourist areas.

Hotel Euro Maya HOTEL $$

(Map p74; ☎7832-6298; www.hoteleuromaya.com; 4a Calle Poniente 22A; s/d incl breakfast Q300-450;) Half a block west of Parque Central, this colonial confection has big bright rooms reached by a cool staircase and a wall of carnival masks. There's a leafy courtyard to relax in, and the reception has its own travel agency for arranging tours, shuttles and the like.

Hotel Posada San Pedro II HOTEL $$

(Map p70; ☎7832-4122; www.posadasanpedro.net; 7a Av Norte 29; s/d/tr Q280/360/400; P) Somebody has restored this place with a whole lot of love and attention to detail. Rooms are spacious and if they're a little on the plain side, they do look out onto two lush patios surrounded by hanging plants, and the whole place is very tranquil.

Hotel Casa Rústica HOTEL $$

(Map p74; ☎7832-3709; www.casarusticagt.com; 6a Av Norte 8; s/d Q350/425, without bathroom Q280/340; @) Everything about the 'rustic house' feels right, from the lily-shaped fountain in the patio to the tiled tables on the top deck. It's also one of the few hotels in this price range to offer guests full kitchen access, not to mention a pool table and entertainment lounge. Attractively done up with regional textiles, the 14 rooms occupy two buildings.

Hotel Posada San Vicente HOTEL **$$**
(Map p74; ☎7832-3311; www.posadasanvicente.com; 6a Av Sur 6; s/d/tr Q280/360/440; P 📶) One of eight Antigua lodgings under the stewardship of a former resident of Tennessee, this long-standing lodging a block west of Parque Central is done up in contemporary colonial style. Sporting *típico* bedspreads and plenty of exposed brick and stone, the 23 rooms wrap around a lovely lily-shaped fountain; above it all, there's an inviting roof terrace.

Hotel Santa Clara HOTEL **$$**
(Map p70; ☎7832-0342; www.hotelsantaclaraantigua.com; 2a Av Sur 20; s/d/tr Q290/400/480; P 📶) A little south of the center, the Santa Clara has brilliantly restored antique chambers alongside a small courtyard, with carved-wood bedsteads and skylights set into the roof beams. Toward the rear are two levels of newer, mostly brighter rooms, with glimpses of the Iglesia de San Francisco from the upper level.

Posada de Don Valentino HOTEL **$$**
(Map p70; ☎7832-0384; www.posadadonvalentino.com; 5a Calle Poniente 28; s/d/tr Q300/380/450; @ 📶) This friendly little guesthouse has spacious, cheerfully decorated rooms of varying brightness. There's a kitchen for guests to use, and the dining lounge opens onto a courtyard terrace with lots of pot plants.

★ **Mesón Panza Verde** BOUTIQUE HOTEL **$$$**
(Map p70; ☎7955-8282; www.panzaverde.com; 5a Av Sur 19; r/ste from Q950/1700; P @ 📶 🏊) Antigua's original luxury boutique hotel, the Panza Verde is cloistered in a serene compound south of the center. The three doubles and nine lavishly appointed suites open onto private terraces amid gardens overflowing with orchids, ferns and bamboo. Along with its renowned restaurant (p83), the hotel also features its own art gallery.

★ **Posada del Ángel** BOUTIQUE HOTEL **$$$**
(Map p70; ☎7832-0260; www.posadadelangel.com; 4a Av Sur 24A; r/ste from Q1600/2400; P 📶 🏊) Hidden behind a very unassuming door, the luxury at this *posada* just keeps unfolding. The five rooms and two suites all have fireplaces, fresh flowers, four-poster beds and highly polished tile floors. There's a hint of the Marrakesh townhouse happening here, including the utterly delightful minipool.

★ **Hotel Quinta de las Flores** HOTEL **$$$**
(Map p70; ☎7832-3721; www.quintadelasflores.com; Calle del Hermano Pedro 6; r from Q715, cottages Q1200; P 📶 🏊) More a village than a hotel, this property on the southeastern edge of town is bursting with charms. Pebbly paths weave through and around parklike lawns and stands of aspidistras and birds-of-paradise, cobblestoned plazas with weathered fountains, a pool and an open-air restaurant. There are eight luxurious rooms in the main building, most with fireplaces, and five more 'garden rooms' with private terraces.

There are also two-story *casitas* (cottages), each with two bedrooms, a kitchen and living room. Considerable discounts are offered for stays by the week.

Casa Santo Domingo Hotel HOTEL **$$$**
(Map p70; ☎7820-1220; www.casasantodomingo.com.gt; 3a Calle Oriente 28A; r from Q1400; P @ 📶 🏊) 🍃 Innovatively created from the remains of the sprawling Santo Domingo monastery, this is Antigua's premier lodging. The 128 rooms and suites are of an international five-star standard, while the grounds retain their colonial splendor, dotted with archaeological relics and featuring a large swimming pool, several fine restaurants, five museums and lots of art. The Dominican friars never had it so good.

Hotel Casa del Parque BOUTIQUE HOTEL **$$$**
(Map p74; ☎7832-0961; www.hotelcasadelparque.com; 4a Av Norte 5; s/d Q490/560; P 📶 🏊) One of Antigua's original boutique hotels, this little place near Parque Central combines a designer's eye with colonial charms. Each room has a unique layout, but all are picture perfect. Those upstairs are spectacular, with sweeping views, luxurious baths and minibars. Cheaper downstairs rooms lack views but give easier access to the charming and hidden pool, spa and sauna.

Hotel Convento Santa Catalina HISTORIC HOTEL **$$$**
(Map p70; ☎7832-3080; www.hotelconventosantacatalina.com; 5a Av Norte 28; s/d/tr Q610/725/800; P @ 📶) This impressively restored property echoes Antigua's past: the city's signature arch is outside the front door, built

for the nuns of the convent the hotel now occupies. Though the front colonial section has more panache, the modern addition is quieter, with picture windows facing the old convent walls across a lawn; rooms in this section have good kitchenettes.

Eating

Antigua has possibly the widest range of eating options in Guatemala. All major international cuisines are represented here, as well as plenty of good local and Central American food, at all price points.

On Saturday and Sunday, tables are set up in front of Convento La Merced (p68), serving, among other snacks, chicken salad sandwiches, *rellenitos* (mashed plantian balls), *enchiladas* (pastry with spiced meat), tamales and their Guatemalan variant *chuchitos* laced with hot sauce and pickled cabbage, along with bowls of *atol blanco* (a corn-based hot beverage). Talk about comfort food!

A quick word about taxes: most formal restaurants don't include VAT and service charges on their menus, but happily add them to the bill. This can add more than 20% to what you might have expected, so be prepared.

★Luna de Miel CRÊPES $
(Map p70; 7882-4559; www.lunademielantigua.com; 6a Av Norte 40; crepes Q34-55; 10am-9:30pm Mon & Tue, 9am-9:30pm Wed-Sun;) Loungey Luna de Miel offers dozens of savoury and sweet variations on the classic crepe – try the *chapín* version stuffed with avocado, cheese and fried tomatoes – plus fabulous tropical smoothies. Eat on the roof deck, amid murals depicting Marilyn Monroe, Yoda and Maradona all enjoying the same fare. Be prepared for long queues on weekends.

Restaurante Doña Luisa CAFE $
(Map p70; 7832-2578; 4a Calle Oriente 12; sandwiches & breakfast mains Q20-45; 7am-9:30pm) Refreshingly local in character, this cafe is a place to enjoy the colonial patio ambience over breakfast or a light meal. It's hard to beat the selection of pastries from the attached bakery; banana bread comes hot from the oven around 2pm daily.

Samsara VEGETARIAN $
(Map p74; 7832-2200; 6a Calle Poniente 33; breakfast Q26-38, salads around Q40; 7am-10pm;) At this small veggie cafe – sitting just the right side of hippie-dom – fresh organic ingredients are excitingly combined in soups, salads and drinks. How about a kale, peanut butter and avocado smoothie? For breakfast there's quinoa porridge or banana and amaranth-seed pancakes, along with French-press coffee and numerous tea blends.

Tienda La Canche GUATEMALAN $
(Map p70; 6a Av Norte 42; set lunch Q25; 7am-8pm) A hole in the wall if there ever was one, this eatery behind a 'mom and pop' store consists of two tables and a dining room behind the counter. Just a couple of traditional options are prepared daily, such as *pepián de pollo* (a hearty chicken stew), accompanied by thick tortillas. *Frescos,* home-squeezed fruit beverages, are served alongside.

Y Tu Piña También SANDWICHES $
(Map p70; 1a Av Sur 10B; sandwiches & salads Q40-50; 7am-7pm;) An international crossroads, this natural-foods cafe does healthy fare for foreign students on the go. There's a tempting array of sandwiches (served on whole wheat, pita or bagel) and salads. It opens early and makes a good breakfast stop, with omelets, abundant fruit salads and banana pancakes, plus excellent coffee.

Café Condesa CAFE $
(Map p74; 7832-0038; www.cafecondesa.com.gt; Portal del Comercio 4; cakes & pies Q20-26; 7am-8pm Sun-Thu, to 9pm Fri & Sat;) Baked goods – pies, cakes, quiches and house-baked whole-wheat sandwich bread – are the strong suit at this grand old cafe set around the patio of a 16th-century mansion off the main square. You can also enjoy big healthy salads or just a cold beer in the courtyard. The lavish Sunday buffet (Q85), from 9am to 1pm, is an Antigua institution.

Fernando's Kaffee CAFE $
(Map p70; 7832-6953; www.fernandoskaffee.com; cnr 7a Av Norte & Callejón Camposeco; cinnamon rolls Q10, empanadas Q40; 7am-7pm Mon-Sat, noon-7pm Sun;) Long a draw for coffee and chocolate mavens, this friendly corner cafe also bakes an array of fine pastries, including some delightfully gooey cinnamon rolls. Beyond the counter is an inviting patio courtyard ideal for a low-key lazy breakfast. We're not sure if the house cat ever moves from the counter, but it's good at collecting tips and cuddles.

Casa de las Mixtas GUATEMALAN $

(Map p70; 3a Callejón; mixtas Q20; ⌚8am-9pm Mon-Sat) For very down-home Guatemalan fare, try this family-run operation on a quiet backstreet across from the market. Aside from its namesake snack (*mixtas* are Guatemalan-style hot dogs, wrapped in tortillas with lots of fillings), it also serves a range of set breakfasts. Regulars make for the little terrace upstairs.

★**Casa Troccoli** INTERNATIONAL $$

(Map p74; ☎7832-0516; cnr 3a Calle Poniente & 5a Av Norte; mains Q90-175; ⌚11:45am-10pm) Front of house at this restaurant looks just like the early 20th-century general store it once was, but with the walls racked with a rather more impressive collection of wine bottles. Amid the period photos and bistro furniture, enjoy superior seafood and meat dishes, including good racks of lamb and local rabbit stew – all washed down with a good glass, of course.

The clientele is well heeled, but the extensive kitchen behind also served as a base for an NGO feeding program after the 2018 eruption of nearby Volcán Fuego, helping to feed over 10,000 displaced locals daily.

★**Cactus Taco Bar** MEXICAN $$

(Map p74; ☎7832-2163; 6a Calle Poniente 21; tacos Q45-60; ⌚11am-11pm) The bright 'Andy Warhol does Zapata' wall mural at Cactus gives an idea of how it mixes up traditional and new-wave Mexican food, with superb salsas served in clay bowls. The shrimp and bacon tacos are heartily recommended. It's along the nightlife corridor; start the evening with a chili-fringed margarita or a bottle of good craft beer.

★**Rincón Típico** GUATEMALAN $$

(Map p70; 3a Av Sur 3; breakfast Q20, mains Q30; ⌚7am-8pm) This courtyard restaurant is always packed with locals who know a good thing when they see it. If you don't come for the huge Guatemalan breakfast, make it for the chicken cooked over coals with garlicky potatoes or pork *adobado* (pork marinated with paprika and pepper), served up at simple bench tables by never-stopping waitstaff.

★**Fridas** MEXICAN $$

(Map p70; ☎7832-1296; 5a Av Norte 29; mains Q75-140; ⌚noon-midnight) Dedicated to the eponymous artist, this brightly colored and ever-busy bar-restaurant has an enormous range of tasty Mexican fare, including some of the best soups and tacos in town. There's live music on Thursday and Friday evenings, and a lively, LGBT-friendly, bar upstairs. The restaurant's Frida Kahlo-meets-Patti Smith poster art is inspired.

★**El Papaturro** SALVADORAN $$

(Map p70; ☎7832-0445; 2a Calle Oriente 4; pupusas Q30, mains Q70-85; ⌚noon-10pm Tue-Sun) This homey spot run by natives of El Salvador serves authentic *pupusas* – thick tortillas stuffed with cheese or *chicharrónes* (fried pork fat) and garnished with *curtido* (marinated cabbage) – and other snacks from Guatemala's southern neighbor in a relaxed courtyard setting. The obvious accompaniment is *horchata,* a beverage blend of cacao, ice, cinnamon, cashews and more.

★**Hector's Bistro** FRENCH $$

(Map p70; ☎7832-9867; 1a Calle Poniente 9A; mains Q80-175; ⌚noon-10pm) This intimate, candlelit salon across the way from La Merced has just a few tables, with the kitchen behind the bar. Hector, who hails from Guatemala City, has garnered acclaim for his versions of *bœuf bourguignon,* grilled duck breast and so on. There's no proper menu: check the chalkboard for daily specials and the quiche of the week.

El Viejo Café CAFE $$

(Map p74; ☎7832-1576; www.elviejocafe.com; 3a Calle Poniente 12; breakfasts from Q25, mains from Q50; ⌚7am-9pm; 📶🐾) Popular with tourists and *chapínes* (Guatemalans) alike, this atmospheric cafe strewn with antique curios makes an ideal breakfast stop. Choose from an array of fresh-baked croissants and well-roasted Guatemalan coffees and settle into a window nook to start your day

Caffé Mediterráneo ITALIAN $$

(Map p74; ☎7882-7180; 6a Calle Poniente 6A; mains Q90-140; ⌚noon-3pm & 6-10pm Wed-Sat & Mon, noon-4:30pm & 7-9pm Sun) Here you'll find the finest, most authentic Italian food in Antigua, plus superb service, in a lovely candlelit setting. The chef does a tantalizing array of salads, homemade pasta and delicately prepared carpaccio, using seasonally available ingredients.

Travel Menu INTERNATIONAL $$

(Map p74; ☎7832-2937; 6a Calle Poniente 14; mains around Q55-70; ⌚noon-11pm; 🎵) This cosy restaurant-bar is indeed aimed at travelers, serving up hearty comfort food (lasagne, Irish stew and shepherd's pie) in a relaxed, roomy space, with live acoustic music most evenings. Weekly steak nights (the exact day varies) serve up a perfectly cooked steak with a glass of wine for Q85.

Angie Angie ARGENTINE $$
(Map p70; ☎7832-3352; 1a Av Sur 11A; empanadas 2 for Q30, mains Q65-95; ⊙noon-11pm Wed-Mon) This South American eatery, with a hint of art gallery about it, is always worth stopping at, if only to lounge around the tropically abundant back garden. Besides the great array of *empanadas,* mixed grills and homemade pastas, there's a good-value set lunch and a Spanish tapas menu. Live blues and jazz on weekends.

Quesos y Vino ITALIAN $$
(Map p70; ☎7832-7785; 5a Av Norte 32A; pizzas Q55-175, cheese platters from Q45; ⊙noon-4pm & 6-10pm Wed-Mon) This Italian-owned establishment is comprised of three rustic buildings, with a lovely outdoor patio and adjoining deli. Like the restaurant's name, the food is basic and satisfying: hearty soups, well-stuffed sandwiches on homemade bread, salads, antipasti platters and wood-fired pizzas. Good wine and cheese – what more do you really need? Enter from 1a Calle Poniente.

La Cuevita de Los Urquizú GUATEMALAN $$
(Map p70; ☎7882-4532; 2a Calle Oriente 9D; lunch combo Q80; ⊙8am-4pm Mon & Tue, to 8pm Wed-Sun) Sumptuous *típico* food is the draw here, all kept warm in great earthenware stew pots out front. Help yourself to *pepián* (chicken and vegetables in a piquant pumpkin seed sauce), *kaq'ik* (spicy turkey stew), *jocón* (herbed green stew of chicken or pork with tomatillos) and other Guatemalan favorites, and you'll get two accompaniments.

Saberico DELI $$
(Map p74; ☎7832-0648; www.saberico.com.gt; 6a Av Sur 7; sandwiches & salads Q65-80; ⊙8am-7pm Mon & Wed, to 4pm Tue, to 9pm Thu-Sat, 9am-4pm Sun) This little deli whips up tasty salads and sandwiches, using ingredients from its herb garden. It also offers fresh-baked breads and brownies, fine wines and imported foods. Eat in one of the various salons or stock up for a picnic. If you just need a refresher, the teas and fresh juices are great.

La Fonda de la Calle Real GUATEMALAN $$
(Map p74; ☎7832-0721; 5a Av Norte; mains Q70-80; ⊙noon-10pm) This attractive restaurant, with several rooms and patios done up in appealing colonial style, offers a varied menu highlighted by regional specialties from around Guatemala. The *caldo real* (Q50), a hearty chicken soup served in a traditional clay bowl, makes a good meal in itself. There are two other branches of the restaurant in Antigua.

★**Mesón Panza Verde** FUSION $$$
(Map p70; ☎7832-2925; www.panzaverde.com; 5a Av Sur 19; mains Q150-200; ⊙6-10pm Mon, noon-3pm & 6-10pm Tue-Sun) The restaurant of the exclusive B&B Mesón Panza Verde (p80) dishes up divine continental cuisine in an appealing Antiguan atmosphere. The menu features an eclectic global lineup, with the French-trained chef putting an emphasis on fresh seafood and organic ingredients. Live music (jazz, Cuban) enhances the ambience Wednesday to Saturday nights, while locals turn out for the popular Sunday brunch buffet (10am to 2pm).

Drinking & Nightlife

The bar scene jumps, especially on Friday and Saturday evenings when the hordes roll in from Guatemala City for some Antigua-style revelry. Besides the watering holes, the restaurants Fridas and **Bistrot Cinq** (Map p70; ☎7832-5510; www.bistrotcinq.com; 4a Calle Oriente 7; mains Q140-220; ⊙noon-10:30pm) are at least as popular for the cocktails as the cuisine. Start drinking early and save: *cuba libres* (rum and colas) and mojitos are half price between 5pm and 8pm at many bars.

★**Antigua Brewing Company** BAR
(Map p74; 3a Calle Poniente 4; ⊙11am-10pm Sun-Thu, 11am-1am Fri & Sat) Put your Gallo beer down for one moment and get to the forefront of Guatemala's craft-brewing revolution at the Antigua Brewing Company. Sup its signature Fuego IPA while looking out to Volcán Agua from the roof terrace, or try a flight of beers (Q75) ranging from Belgian blondes to rich coffee stouts.

Por Qué No? PUB
(Map p70; ☎4324-5407; www.porquenocafe.com; cnr 2a Av Sur & 9a Calle Oriente; ⊙6-10pm Mon-Sat) This alternative cafe is a vertically oriented space that takes up an absurdly narrow corner of an old building (grab the rope to reach the upper level). Vintage bric-a-brac hangs from the rafters and every surface is scrawled with guest-generated graffiti. The vibe is relaxed and conversational and a crowd spills out the door each evening.

LGBT ANTIGUA

Antigua has a veneer of cosmopolitanism and tolerance beyond that of other similar-size Guatemalan cities. There are Pride events here every June, and the nightlife scene embraces every persuasion. Particularly LGBT-friendly spaces include the restaurant-bar Fridas (p82), which hosts a queer dance party with DJs on the final Saturday of each month (upstairs), and the dance club Las Vibras de la Casbah.

El Barrio PUB
(Map p74; ☎5658-9028; 4a Av Norte 3; ⊙4:30pm-1am) Just off Parque Central, this sprawling bar tavern has wall-length sofas, murals of literary and sports heroes, and board games. Upstairs is a popular and lively rooftop bar. Round up a gang for the trivia nights, but take care if you overindulge: we're never too sure about a bar that has its own tattoo parlour at the back.

Café No Sé BAR
(Map p70; www.cafenose.com; 1a Av Sur 11C; ⊙2pm-1am) Something of a local institution, this downbeat little bar is a point of reference for Antigua's budding young Burroughses and Kerouacs. It's also the core of a lively music scene, with players wailing from a corner of the room most evenings. Be sure to try its home-brand Ilegal Mezcal.

Tabacos y Vinos WINE BAR
(Map p70; 5a Av Norte 28B; ⊙10am-11pm) Tucked right next to the Santa Catalina arch, is this small but perfectly formed wine bar with an extensively sourced cellar. Wine by the glass starts at Q35, but if you keep with the same bottle it gets cheaper with each refill. The bar is no smoking but it also has a wide selection of cigars, as well as local chocolates and coffee.

Reilly's en la Esquina IRISH PUB
(Map p74; ☎7832-6251; 6a Calle Poniente 7; ⊙noon-12:30am) Holding a key corner of Antigua's nightlife corridor, Reilly's packs in both Guatemalans and gringos on weekends. The sprawling pub has several bars but most of the action focuses on the central patio. Midweek it's mellower, with the billiard table, pub grub and Guinness on tap pulling in a faithful following. Particularly good when there's a big sporting event.

Snug IRISH PUB
(Map p74; ☎5838-5390; 6a Calle Poniente 14; ⊙noon-11pm) Spirits are high at the aptly dubbed Snug, a real hole-in-the-wall bar and favourite expat drinking scene. Green walls, harps and Guinness add a hint of the Irish, and somehow there's live music squeezed in on the weekends.

La Sin Ventura CLUB
(Map p74; 5a Av Sur 8; ⊙4pm-1am Tue-Fri, noon-1am Sat, noon-8pm Sun) The liveliest dance floor in town is packed with Guatemalan youth toward the weekend. DJs pump out *cumbias* (Colombian dance tunes) and reggaetón most nights, while musicians play live salsa on Tuesdays.

Las Vibras de la Casbah CLUB
(Map p70; ☎3141-5311; www.lasvibrasantigua.com; 5a Av Norte 30; ⊙5pm-1am Wed-Sat) It's quite a party most nights at this split-level disco near the Santa Catalina arch: plenty of selfies, vapor shots and EDM form the scene. To take a breather, make your way to the open-air terrace out front. The cocktails are great, and it has an LGBT-friendly reputation.

☆ Entertainment

Many bars and restaurants have live music, especially at weekends.

Café No Sé, Angie Angie (p83), the **Rainbow Café** (Map p74; ☎7832-1919; www.rainbowcafeantigua.com; 7a Av Sur 8; mains Q40-60; ⊙8am-10pm; 🖉) and Mesón Panza Verde (p83) host regular folk, rock and jazz performances.

Shopping

Woven and leather goods, ironwork, paintings and jade jewelry are some of the items to look for in Antigua's various shops and markets. For beautiful *típico* fabrics, first get educated at the Casa del Tejido Antiguo (p88), then have a look around Nim Po't or the big handicrafts markets near the bus terminal and next to Iglesia El Carmen.

Market MARKET
(Map p70; Calz de Santa Lucía Sur; ⊙6am-6pm Mon, Thu & Sat, 7am-6pm Tue, Wed & Fri, 7am-1pm Sun) Antigua's market – chaotic, colorful and always busy – sprawls north of 4a Calle Poniente. The best days are the official market days (Monday, Thursday and especially Saturday) when villagers from the vicinity roll in and spread their wares north and west of the main market building.

The entrance to the market is dominated by tourist goods, so make sure you continue past to get to the heart of the everyday commerce.

Nim Po't ARTS & CRAFTS
(Map p70; ☎7832-2681; www.nimpotexport.com; 5a Av Norte 29; ⏲9am-9pm Sun-Thu, to 10pm Fri & Sat) This brilliant, sprawling depot has a huge collection of Maya clothing, as well as hundreds of masks, wood carvings, kites, refrigerator magnets, assorted Maximón figurines and local coffee and chocolate. The *huipiles, cortes* and other garments are arranged by region, so it makes for a fascinating visit whether you're buying or not.

Maya Arte Nativo ARTS & CRAFTS
(Map p70; 5a Av Norte 35; ⏲9am-6pm) This long and narrow shop has a superior selection of bright local handicrafts and home decorations, from flocks of miniature birds to hang from Christmas trees to painted ceramics, mirror frames and quirky sculptures.

Mercado del Carmen ARTS & CRAFTS
(Map p70; cnr 3a Calle Oriente & 3a Av Norte; ⏲9am-6pm) Next to the ruins of the Iglesia El Carmen, this excellent market is a good place to browse for textiles, pottery and jade, particularly on weekends, when activity spills out onto 3a Av Norte. The inside is a warren of individual stalls, so take your time to find the treasure you're after.

La Casa del Jade JEWELRY
(Map p70; www.lacasadeljade.com; 4a Calle Oriente 10; ⏲9am-6pm) More than just a jewelry shop, the Casa has a small museum displaying dozens of pre-Hispanic jade pieces and an open workshop where you can admire the work of contemporary craftspeople. It's inside the Casa Antigua El Jaulón shopping arcade.

Mercado de Artesanías ARTS & CRAFTS
(Map p70; 4a Calle Poniente; ⏲9am-6pm) Masses of Guatemalan handicrafts fill the stalls of this building at the west end of town just below the main market. While not at the top end of the quality range, it has a variety of colorful masks, blankets, jewelry, purses and so on. Don't be afraid to bargain.

Jade Maya JEWELRY
(Map p70; www.jademaya.com; 4a Calle Oriente 34; ⏲9am-6pm) Started by a pair of North American archaeologists who were researching ancient jade quarries in the Motagua valley, this shop features a jade workshop and a worthwhile small museum (free admission) with an assortment of pre-Hispanic pieces.

El Reino del Jade JEWELRY
(Map p70; ☎7832-1593; 5a Av Norte 28; ⏲9am-6:30pm) This shop near the Santa Catalina arch specializes in designer jewelry featuring jade and other gems.

Centro de Arte Popular ART
(Map p70; 4a Calle Oriente 10; ⏲9:30am-6:30pm) Inside the courtyard shopping arcade Casa Antigua El Jaulón, this shop/museum displays Tz'utujil oil paintings, cedar figurines, masks and other crafts. The art is thematically arranged to illustrate the various aspects of indigenous life.

Doña María Gordillo Dulces Típicos FOOD
(Map p70; 4a Calle Oriente 11; ⏲10am-6pm Mon-Sat) If you want to eat your way around some toothsome traditional Guatemalan sweets and pastries, this is the place for you. Try the coconut macaroons, *dulces de leche* (vanilla and cinnamon cookies) and marzipan.

Librería La Casa del Conde BOOKS
(Map p74; ☎7832-3322; Portal del Comercio 4; ⏲9am-6pm) Bookshop with a good selection of English as well as Spanish titles, including books on Central American history and politics, plus nature guides, literature and Lonely Planet titles.

Orientation

Antigua's focal point is the broad Parque Central (p67); few places in town are more than 15 minutes' walk from here. Compass points are added to the numbered Calles and Avs, indicating whether an address is *norte* (north), *sur* (south), *poniente* (west) or *oriente* (east) of Parque Central.

Three volcanoes provide easy reference points: Volcán Agua is south of the city and visible from most points within it; Volcán Fuego and Volcán Acatenango rise to the southwest (Acatenango is the more northerly of the two).

Another useful Antigua landmark is the Arco de Santa Catalina (p68), an arch spanning 5a Av Norte, two and a half blocks north of Parque Central, on the way to La Merced church.

Information

DANGERS & ANNOYANCES

- Antigua generally feels safe to walk around, but street crime does occur, so don't let your guard down completely or flash wads of cash or smartphones. This holds doubly true after the bars close at 1am; after 10pm, consider taking a taxi back to your accommodations.

➡ Pickpockets work the busy market, doing overtime on paydays at the middle and end of the month. December (bonus time) brings a renewed wave of robberies.

➡ Some of the more remote hiking trails have seen muggings, though stepped-up police patrols have reduced the likelihood of such incidents. If you're planning on hiking independently, check with Proatur about the current situation.

EMERGENCY

Ambulance	☎125
Fire (Bomberos Voluntarios)	☎7832-0234
Police	☎120
Tourist Police	☎1500 or 2421-2810

INTERNET ACCESS

Wi-fi is widely available in restaurants, cafes and almost all accommodations.

Funky Monkey (5a Av Sur 6, Pasaje El Corregidor; per hour Q10; ⏲8am-12:30am) One of Antigua's few remaining internet cafes.

MEDIA

The free English-language *Revue Magazine* (www.revuemag.com) has reasonable information about cultural events; it's available everywhere.

MEDICAL SERVICES

Farmacia Cruz Verde Ivori (☎7832-8318; 7a Av Norte; ⏲24hr) Convenient pharmacy with some English spoken.

Hospital Nacional Pedro de Bethancourt (☎7831-1319; ⏲24hr) Public hospital in San Felipe, 2km north of the center, with emergency service.

Hospital Privado Hermano Pedro (☎7790-2000; www.hospitalhermanopedro.net; Av de la Recolección 4; ⏲24hr) Private hospital that offers 24-hour emergency service and accepts foreign insurance.

MONEY

The following banks around Parque Central all change US dollars and euros, and have Visa/Mastercard ATMs:

Bac Credomatic (Portal del Comercio, facing Parque Central)

Banco Agromercantil (4a Calle Poniente 8; ⏲9am-7pm Mon-Fri, to 5pm Sat & Sun)

Banco Industrial (5a Av Sur 4; ⏲9am-7pm Mon-Fri, to 1pm Sat)

Citibank (cnr 4a Calle Oriente & 4a Av Norte; ⏲9am-4:30pm Mon-Fri, 9:30am-1pm Sat)

TELEPHONE

Wi-fi in Antigua is mostly good enough for Skype calls. If you plan to be around a while, consider purchasing a local cell phone; you can pick one up at **La Bodegona** (Map p70; 4a Calle Poniente 27) or any number of phone shops.

TOURIST INFORMATION

INGUAT (Map p70; ☎7832-0787; info-antigua@inguat.gob.gt; 5a Calle Oriente 11; ⏲8am-4pm Mon-Fri, 9am-5pm Sat & Sun) The tourist office has free city maps, bus information and helpful, bilingual staff.

BUSES FROM ANTIGUA

DESTINATION	FARE	DURATION	FREQUENCY	SERVICE
Chimaltenango	Q5	30min	every 10min	
Ciudad Vieja	Q5	15min	every 15min	Take a San Miguel Dueñas bus.
Escuintla	Q10	1hr	every 20min	
Guatemala City	Q10	1hr	every 15min from 7am to 8pm	A Pullman service (Q60; 9:30am and 4pm) by **Litegua** (Map p86; ☎7832-9850; www.litegua.com; 4a Calle Oriente 48) also runs from its office at the east end of (p70)
Panajachel	Q45	2½hr	one bus daily at 7am	**Transportes Rebulli service** (Map p86), departing from Panadería Colombia on 4a Calle Poniente, half a block east of the (p70)
San Antonio Aguas Calientes	Q5	20min	every 10min	

Proatur (☎5578-9835; operacionesproatur@inguat.gob.gt; 6a Calle Poniente Final; ⏲24hr) The tourism assistance agency has its headquarters on the west side of town, three blocks south of the market. If you're the victim of a crime, staff will accompany you to the national police and assist with the formalities, including any translating that's needed. Given advance notice, Proatur can provide an escort for drivers heading out on potentially risky roads.

Getting There & Away

BUS

Buses (p89) from Guatemala City, Ciudad Vieja and San Miguel Dueñas arrive and depart from a street just south of the market, across from the Mercado de Artesanías.

Antigua is off the major through-highways, so for most onward travel you'll need to head to the nearby junction towns of Chimaltenango or Escuintla and change there. Buses for these depart from the main **bus terminal** (Map p70; Av de la Recolección).

For the Highlands (including Chichicastenango, Quetzaltenango and Huehuetenango) take one of the many buses to Chimaltenango, on the Interamerican Hwy, then catch an onward connection. The same station has buses to Escuintla, where you should change for all destinations along the Carretera al Pacifico Hwy.

If you're heading out to local villages, go early in the morning and return by mid-afternoon, as bus services decrease dramatically as evening approaches.

SHUTTLE MINIBUS

Antigua's many travel agencies (and every hotel and hostel) sell tickets for tourist shuttles. They cost more than buses, but are comfortable and convenient, with door-to-door pickup and drop-off. Bear in mind that if you're leaving town, shuttles can sometimes spend an hour driving around Antigua collecting passengers.

Every conceivable traveler destination is served, but some typical one-way prices include: Guatemala City (Q80, one hour), Panajachel (Q80, two hours), Quetzaltenango (Q175, four hours), San Pedro La Laguna (Q80, two hours), El Paredón (Q100, two hours), Monterrico (Q100, two hours) and Cobán (Q125, three hours), as well as to the airport (Q80, one hour).

Cross-border shuttles include to Copán (Honduras), San Cristóbal de Las Casas (Mexico) and Belize City.

CAR & MOTORCYCLE

If you're planning to drive out of town on a reportedly hijack-prone road (such as to Panajachel via Patzún), you may request an escort from Proatur by emailing them at least 72 hours in advance. There's no fee other than the escort's expenses.

CATours (p77) Rents motorbikes from Q400 per day and offers one- to seven-day motorcycle tours.

Guatemala Renta Autos (☎2329-9030; www.guatemalarentacar.com; 4a Av Norte 6; rental per day/week from Q270/1800; ⏲8am-6pm Mon-Fri, to 3pm Sat) Rents compact cars up to 4WDs. Advance online booking gets better rates.

Tabarini (☎7832-8107; www.tabarini.com; 6a Av Sur 22; rental per day/week from Q290/1800; ⏲8am-6pm) Reliable car rental; book in advance for better rates.

To park on the street in Antigua, you must have a *marbete* (label) hanging from your rearview mirror, or risk a fine. Purchase these from traffic cops stationed on the entry roads into Antigua for Q10.

Getting Around

Taxis wait where the Guatemala City buses stop and on the east side of Parque Central. An in-town taxi ride costs Q25 to Q30. *Tuk-tuks* are Q5 to Q15. Note that *tuk-tuks* are not allowed in the center of town, so you'll have to hike a few blocks out to find one; they do not operate after 8pm.

AROUND ANTIGUA

Jocotenango

This village just northwest of Antigua (but slowly being subsumed by it) opens a window on a less self-conscious, less Unesco-authorized version of Guatemalan life compared with central Antigua. Aloof from the traffic of the main thoroughfare stands the **church**, as it has for centuries, its peach facade graced by baroque columns and elaborate stucco behind elaborate gardens and a majestic ceiba tree. The town is known for its processions during Lent – or perhaps more so as the birthplace of Latin American pop star Ricardo Arjona.

A sprawling coffee plantation outside Jocotenango, **Centro Cultural La Azotea** (☎7831-1120; www.azoteaestate.com; Calle del Cementerio Final; adult/child Q50/30; ⏲8:30am-5pm Mon-Fri, 8:30am-3pm Sat) features a complex of three museums. The **Museo del Café** covers the history and process of coffee cultivation; the **Casa K'ojom** holds a superb collection of traditional Maya musical instruments, masks, paintings and other artifacts; and the **Rincón de Sacatepéquez** displays the multicolored outfits and crafts of the Antigua valley.

WORTH A TRIP

EARTH OR MIDDLE EARTH?

The village of **El Hato**, above Jocotenango, has two of the region's most idiosyncratic places to stay or just visit from Antigua for lunch.

Earth Lodge (5664-0713; www.earthlodgeguatemala.com; dm Q65, s/d cabin Q200/280;) High in the hills above Jocotenango, this extraordinary 40-acre spread is set around a working avocado farm, and the views of the Panchoy valley and volcanoes are truly mesmerizing. Developed and overseen by an affable North American couple, the ecofriendly retreat offers plenty to do: hiking trails, birdwatching, yoga sessions, a *chuj* (Maya sauna) or just hanging in a hammock.

Accommodations are in lovely A-frame cabins, an eight-bed dorm and a couple of fabulous tree houses (which book up well in advance). Lip-smacking food is served with a view, and a portion of the profits buys supplies for the village school.

To get here, your best bet is to call at least a day in advance to see if the lodge can pick you up from Antigua (Q30 per person with two passengers). Otherwise, an 'El Hato' bus leaves from behind the market in Antigua at least six times Monday, Thursday and Saturday, less often the rest of the week. From there it's a 25-minute walk downhill – any villager can give you directions – just ask for 'los gringos.' Note that it's a 10-minute walk down to the lodge even from the shuttle drop-off point (and twice that uphill with luggage).

Hobbitenango (3090-8812; www.hobbitenango.com; El Hato; lodge Q560-674) The steep ascent to Hobbitenango might make you think you're climbing Mt Doom, but this Middle Earth–styled lodge is a great place to get away from it all. Accommodations are indeed in half-buried and round-doored lodges, with turf roofs, cosy fireplaces for cool nights and everything to make a hobbit happy; they sleep four to six people.

It's a popular place for meals, with a good, rustic restaurant (mains Q50 to Q80) with tremendous views and a well-curated selection of craft beer.

The lodge runs 4WD shuttles (Q15) from a parking space 10 minutes (and 800m below) the property – call ahead.

You can roam the coffee plantation itself, which is crisscrossed by nature trails; adjacent to it is a botanical garden and nursery with an incredible variety of tropical plants. A shop sells quality coffee, local crafts and Maya instruments. Beside the estate is Establo La Ronda, a stable of 30 horses where experienced riders can join tours of the highlands.

Catch a *tuk-tuk* from Antigua to La Azotea; it costs Q10 to the *finca*, an additional Q5 to be taken the further 500m to the museum entrance.

Any bus from Antigua bound for Chimaltenango can drop you off in front of the church (Q5, five minutes); or catch a *tuk-tuk* (Q15).

Ciudad Vieja & Around

Seven kilometers southwest of Antigua along the Escuintla road is Ciudad Vieja (Old City), near the site of the first capital of the Captaincy General of Guatemala. Founded in 1527, it met its demise 14 years later when Volcán Agua let loose a flood of water that had been penned up in its crater. The water deluged the town with tons of rock and mud, leaving only the ruins of La Concepción church.

The actual site of the former capital is a bit to the east at **San Miguel Escobar**; Ciudad Vieja was populated by survivors of the flood. The pretty church on the main square has an impressive stuccowork facade, though it's about two centuries newer than the plaque by the door claims it to be.

Today, visitors come to Ciudad Vieja for its innovative community tours and macadamia plantation.

Sights & Tours

Casa del Tejido Antiguo MUSEUM

(7832-3169; www.casadeltejido.org; 0 Av 4-16, San Antonio Aguas Calientes; Q15; 9am-5pm Mon-Fri, to 4pm Sat) This space is like a museum, market and workshop all rolled into one, with exhibits on regional outfits and daily demonstrations of backstrap weaving techniques. Founder Alicia Pérez, an indigenous

Kaqchiquel woman, is an expert on the significance of designs that appear on the *tocoyales* (head coverings), *tzutes* (shawls) and *huipiles* (long embroidered tunics) displayed here. Weaving classes are offered, and the museum will pick you up at your Antigua hotel if you call ahead.

Valhalla Macadamia Farm TOUR
(☎7831-5799; www.exvalhalla.net; ⏲8am-4:30pm) Between San Antonio Aguas Calientes and Ciudad Vieja, near the village of San Miguel Dueñas, is this macadamia farm raising 300 species of the remarkable nut. You can tour this organic, sustainable agriculture project and sample nuts, oils and cosmetics made from the harvest. Be sure to try the macadamia pancakes, served in an open-air cafe surrounded by lush tropical foliage.

Niños de Guatemala CULTURAL
(☎7832-8033; www.ninosdeguatemala.org; 4a Calle 28; tours around Q200-300) The NGO Niños de Guatemala, which runs three schools for low-income kids in and around the town, leads alternative tours of Ciudad Vieja that really get beneath the surface of the community. A half-day tour takes you through the poorer section of town, then focuses on two of its principal industries: 'chicken bus' rebuilding and coffin making.

On another tour, participants visit a woodworking workshop in the outlying district of San Lorenzo el Cubo and learn how to make *quitapeñas* (worry dolls). Tour fees include transport from Antigua, guide and a snack. Prices vary according to group numbers (a private tour for two costs Q260 per person).

Getting There & Away

Frequent buses to Ciudad Vieja (Q5, 12 minutes) depart from a **lot** (Map p70; cnr 5a Calle Poniente & Calle de Recoletos) south of Antigua's main market.

San Cristóbal El Alto

Just 3km south of Antigua along the road to Santa María de Jesús, San Cristóbal El Alto sits around 300m above the city, on a perch that affords superb views of the Panchoy valley. Most people visit for the superb Cerro San Cristóbal organic farm and its restaurant. The forested slopes here are laced with trails, and members of the tight-knit community can guide you around. It's also a center for woodwork, pottery and textiles, which are displayed on the plaza every Sunday.

Sights & Activities

Cerro San Cristóbal GARDENS
(☎5941-8415; www.restcerrosancristobal.com; ⏲tours Mon-Fri by request) FREE Perched on a hillside overlooking the Panchoy valley, this is a well-managed organic farm that's packed with small pleasures. Tours are given of a medicinal plant garden, neatly arrayed plots of organic veggies and a greenhouse full of orchids. There are also demonstrations by weavers on a bicycle-powered loom, a consecrated shrine to Maximón and a traditional sauna.

Cooperativa Cosender HIKING
(☎5560-5081; per person Q150) This community guide association leads half-day hikes from San Cristóbal El Alto up into the hills, then down to a gorge that's a sacred site for the Maya community. Call ahead to made arrangements.

Sleeping & Eating

Casa Xicayá GUESTHOUSE **$$**
(☎5560-5081; www.facebook.com/xicaya/; Calle Principal 41 Oriente; r per person incl breakfast Q160) San Cristóbal El Alto's single lodging option is a supremely relaxing one, two blocks east of the main square, enjoying a tranquil setting on grounds dotted with avocado and loquat trees. There are two options, both with bathroom: three upstairs doubles with volcano views, and a nine-bed cabin in the woods. The rate includes a huge local breakfast.

★ **Restaurant Cerro San Cristóbal** VEGETARIAN **$$**
(☎5941-8145; www.restcerrosancristobal.com; Calle Principal 5; mains Q50-110; ⏲8:30am-7pm Mon-Thu, 8am-8pm Fri-Sun; ☑) Contender for the slow-food star of the Antigua area, this restaurant puts its own organically grown produce on the table. Giant salads are loaded with avocados, nasturtiums, greens and herbs from the surrounding gardens. It also serves tilapia from its own fish pond. Dine on a terrace with stupendous views of the Panchoy valley.

The restaurant has a shuttle that will pick you up at your Antigua accommodation (Q10, 15 minutes) – call ☎7832-2681 to book ahead.

Getting There & Away

Cerro San Cristóbal runs a shuttle that will pick you up at your Antigua accommodation (Q10, 15 minutes) – call ☎7832-2681 to book ahead. Alternatively, book an Antigua taxi.

OFF THE BEATEN TRACK

VILLAGE EXPLORATIONS

While Antigua itself is pretty much well-trodden territory from end to end, there are plenty of little villages just outside of town that are begging to be explored:

Santa María de Jesús At the foot of Volcán Agua; holds a major market on Sundays.

San Juan del Obispo Has a wonderful colonial church and panoramic views of Antigua.

San Felipe An artisans' village with some of the finest jade, silver and ceramic work in the area.

Pastores Ground zero for leatherwork. This is the place to come for handmade cowboy boots and stock whips – every other shop on the main street is a leather outlet.

San Juan Comalapa

Set on the side of a deep ravine, this village 16km north of Chimaltenango is best known for its tradition of primitive folk painting. Its setting is alluded to in its original Kaqchiquel name, Chixot, 'on the edge of a frying pan.' Though a bit rundown, Comalapa is worth visiting for glimpses of both the realities and artistic reflections of contemporary Kaqchiquel life, particularly on market days (Tuesday, Friday and Sunday).

Comalapa gained its reputation during the 1950s when native son Andrés Curruchich (1891–1969) rose to fame for his primitive paintings of village life, ceremonies and legends, and his works ended up on display as far away as San Francisco, Dallas and Detroit. Considered the father of Guatemalan 'primitivist' painting, he was awarded the prestigious Order of the Quetzal.

Comalapa is also known as the birthplace of Rafael Álvarez Ovalle (1858–1946), composer of Guatemala's national anthem (there's a monument to him in the main square).

Sights

Museo de Arte Maya MUSEUM
(5068-4047; www.facebook.com/musartemaya; 3a Calle 0-74, Zona 1; Q10; 8am-4pm Mon-Sat, 10:30am-4pm Sun) The museum is mostly a showcase for the work of painter Julián Gabriel, whose canvasses go beyond the usual scenes of daily life to portray an apocalyptic vision of the future. There's also a gallery of historic photos of the town, including images of the damage caused by the quake of 1976.

Galería de Arte Gabriel GALLERY
(7849-8168; 0 Av 2-88; 9am-5pm) FREE Two blocks south of the main plaza, this attractive old house contains the studio and gallery of a prominent Comalapa painter, Iván Gabriel. The artist's son, Wilder, is well versed in Comalapa's history and legends and offers tours of the town in perfect colloquial English.

Iglesia San Juan Bautista CHURCH
In 1976 a major earthquake caused widespread devastation in Comalapa and took the lives of 3500 inhabitants. The Iglesia San Juan Bautista, the town's oldest church and a survivor of four previous quakes, was mostly toppled but later rebuilt. Scenes from the earthquake and other events appear on a major set of murals – at 184m reputedly the country's longest – that cover the walls along the southern approach.

Painted by students in 2002, the panels allude to the origins of Maya culture and envision a possible future.

Sleeping & Eating

Hotel Pixcayá HOTEL $
(7849-8260; 0 Av 1-82; s/d with bathroom Q70/140, without bathroom Q40/80; P) If you want to stay the night in Comalapa, the Pixcayá, a block south of the church, is a decent bet. It has three levels of neat and simple rooms around a plant-laden courtyard.

Rinkoncito Chapin GUATEMALAN $
(0 Av 251; mains Q25-50; 7am-9pm) The best choice for food is this friendly establishment south along the main street with polished log tables and a brilliant panorama of the surrounding hills from the rear window. Grilled steaks and seafood are its specialty, and it serves Spanish wines.

Getting There & Away

Buses (Q10, 45 minutes) run roughly every half hour between San Juan Comalapa and Chimaltenango, from where there are links to Antigua and wider destinations.

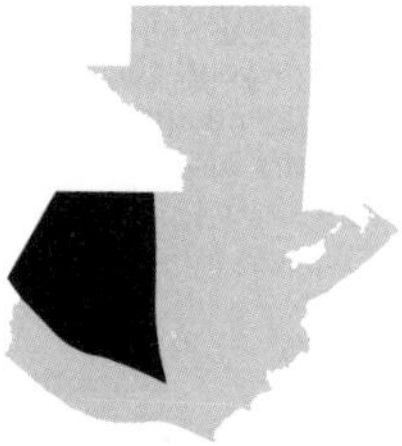

The Highlands

Includes ➡

Best Places to Eat

➡ Café El Artesano (p113)

➡ Café Sabor Cruceño (p118)

➡ Villa Cofrades (p123)

➡ Esquina Asiatica (p140)

➡ Circus Bar (p100)

Best Places to Stay

➡ La Casa del Mundo Hotel (p116)

➡ Bambu Guesthouse (p119)

➡ Unicornio Azul (p152)

➡ Kasa Kiwi (p138)

➡ Casa Morasan (p139)

Why Go?

The highlands – El Altiplano – stretch from Antigua to the Mexican border, and is Guatemala's most breathtaking region by some degree. Maya identity is stronger here than anywhere in the country and over a dozen distinct groups dwell within the region, each with its own language and clothing. Indigenous tradition blends most tantalizingly with Spanish, and it is common to see Maya rituals taking place in front of and inside colonial churches.

Most travelers spend a spell at the dizzyingly beautiful Lago de Atitlán, an azure lake dramatically ringed by volcanoes. From here it's easy to strike out to the exuberant spectacle of the weekly market at Chichicastenango. Head west to Quetzaltenango, Guatemala's laid-back second city. Northward spread the Cuchumatanes mountains, where Maya life follows its own rhythms amid picturesque villages and fantastic mountain landscapes. For hikers, this is the promised land.

When to Go

Huehuetenango

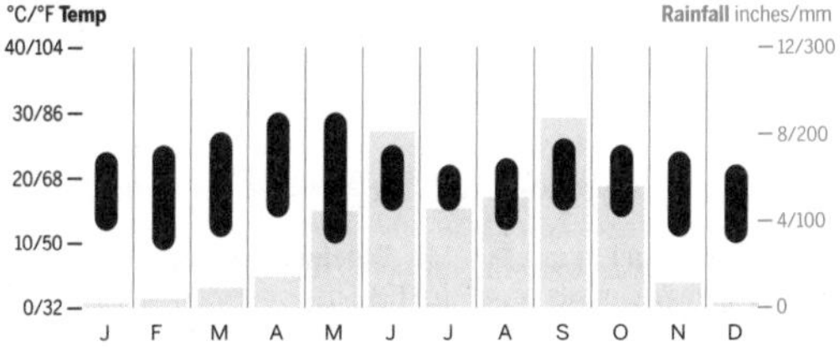

Nov–Apr Drier months are better for trekking, with clearer views in the mountains and less muddy conditions on hikes.

May–Oct Nights at altitude can be distinctly chilly, but rain tends to restrict itself to afternoons.

Late Sep/Early Oct Quetzaltenango's annual party, the raucous Feria de la Virgen des Rosario.

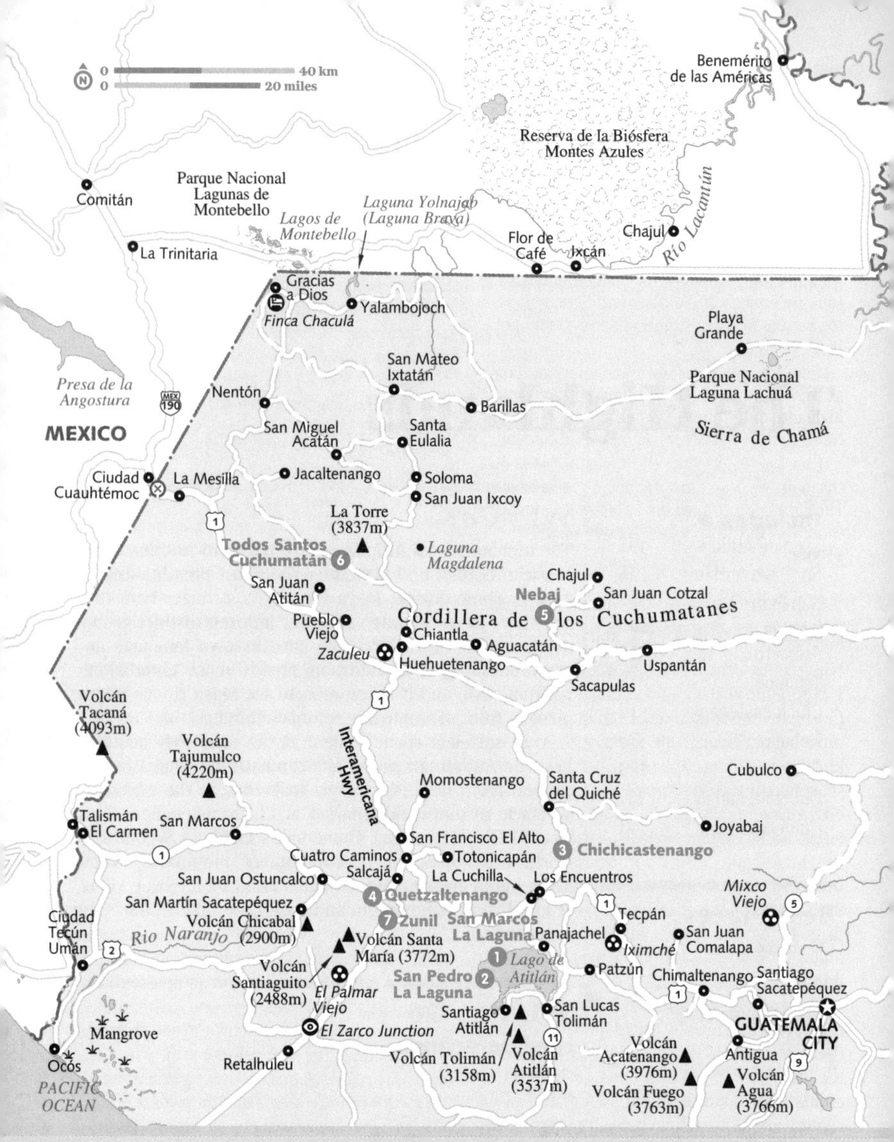

The Highlands Highlights

1. **San Marcos La Laguna** (p114) Taking yoga classes by the sublime volcano-fringed waters of Lago de Atitlán.
2. **San Pedro La Laguna** (p109) Hiking volcanoes and learning Spanish in one of Central America's backpacker hubs.
3. **Chichicastenango** (p119) Shopping for *huipiles* and a hundred other souvenirs at this colorful market.
4. **Quetzaltenango** (p131) Upgrading your Spanish and climbing volcanoes in Guatemala's second city.
5. **Nebaj** (p126) Taking in the stunning scenery and village life of the Ixil Triangle.
6. **Todos Santos Cuchumatán** (p153) Learning about traditional Maya life and festivals in the Cuchumatanes mountains.
7. **Zunil** (p144) Paying your respects to a traditional Maya deity near Quetzaltenango.

ℹ Getting Around

The meandering Interamericana (Hwy 1), running 345km along the mountain ridges between Guatemala City and the Mexican border at La Mesilla, passes close to all of the region's most important places, and countless buses roar up and down it all day, every day. Two key intersections act as major bus interchanges: Los Encuentros for Panajachel and Chichicastenango, and Cuatro Caminos for Quetzaltenango and Huehuetenango. If you can't find a bus going to your destination, simply get one to either of these points.

Microbuses – large vans that depart as soon as they fill with passengers – are popular along highland routes such as Santa Cruz del Quiché–Nebaj and Chichicastenango–Los Encuentros.

Otherwise, tourist shuttle buses zip between the major destinations of the region and beyond. They are faster, more comfortable and more expensive than buses but give door-to-door service.

LAGO DE ATITLÁN

Nineteenth-century traveler/chronicler John L Stephens, writing in *Incidents of Travel in Central America*, called Lago de Atitlán 'the most magnificent spectacle we ever saw,' and he had been around a bit. Today even seasoned travelers marvel at this incredible environment. Fishers in rustic crafts ply the lake's aquamarine surface. Fertile hills dot the landscape, and over everything loom the volcanoes, permeating the entire area with a mysterious beauty. It never looks the same twice. No wonder many outsiders have fallen in love with the place and made their homes here.

The main lakeside town is Panajachel and most people initially head here to launch their Atitlán explorations. Working around the lake, Santiago Atitlán has a strong indigenous identity, San Pedro La Laguna has a reputation as a backpacker party haven, and San Marcos La Laguna is a haven for new-agers. Santa Cruz La Laguna and Jaibalito, nearer to Panajachel, are among the lake's most idyllic, picturesque locales.

History

Though volcanic explosions have been going on here for millions of years, today's landscape has its origins in the massive eruption of 85,000 years ago, termed Los Chocoyos, which blew volcanic ash as far away as Florida and Panama. The quantity of magma expelled from below the earth's crust caused the surface terrain to collapse, forming a huge, roughly circular hollow that soon filled with water – Lago de Atitlán. Smaller volcanoes rose out of the lake's southern waters thousands of years later: Volcán San Pedro (today 3020m above sea level) about 60,000 years ago, followed by Volcán Atitlán (3537m) and Volcán Tolimán (3158m). The lake today is 8km across from north to south, 18km from east to west, and averages around 300m deep, though the water level has been on the rise since 2009.

Around 900 AD, when the Maya highland civilization was in decline, the region was settled by two groups that had migrated from the Toltec capital of Tula in Mexico, the Kaqchiquel and Tz'utujil. The latter group settled at Chuitinamit, across the way from the present-day village of Santiago Atitlán, while the former occupied the lake's northern shores; this demographic composition persists to this day. By the time the Spanish showed up in 1524, the Tz'utujil had expanded their domain to occupy most of the lakeshore. Pedro de Alvarado exploited the situation by allying with the Kaqchiquels against their Tz'utujil rivals, whom they defeated in a bloody battle at Tzanajuyú. The Kaqchiquels subsequently rebelled against the Spanish and were themselves subjugated by 1531.

Panajachel

POP 14,950 / ELEV 1584M

The busiest and most built-up lakeside town, Panajachel ('Pana') is the gateway to Lago de Atitlán for most travellers. Strolling the main street, Calle Santander, crammed with travel agencies, handicraft hawkers and rowdy bars, dodging noisy *tuk-tuks* all the way, you may be forgiven for supposing this paradise lost.

Heading to the lake, though, gives a better idea of why Pana attracts so many visitors. Aside from the astounding volcano panorama, the town's excellent transportation connections, copious accommodations, varied restaurants and thumping nightlife make it a favorite destination for weekending Guatemalans.

Pana is an unexpectedly cosmopolitan crossroads in an otherwise remote and rural vicinity. This makes for a convenient transition into the Atitlán universe – but to truly experience the beauty of the lake, most travelers venture onward soon after arrival.

Lago de Atitlán

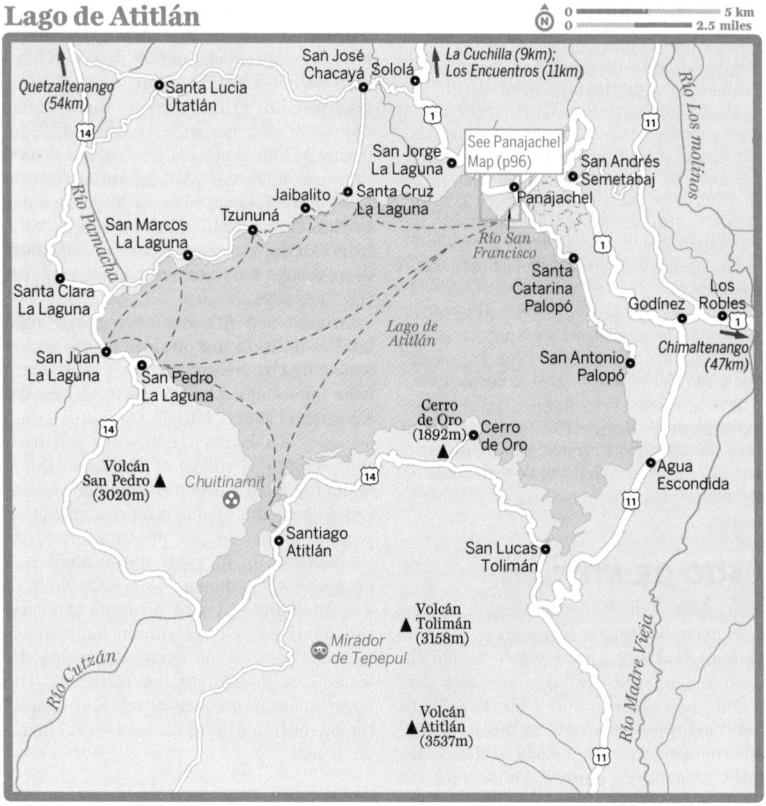

Sights

★Reserva Natural Atitlán PARK

(☎7762-2565; www.atitlanreserva.com; adult/child Q50/25; ⊙8am-5pm) A former coffee plantation being retaken by natural vegetation, this reserve is 200m past the Hotel Atitlán on the northern outskirts of town. It makes a good outing on foot or bicycle. You can leisurely walk the main trail in an hour: it leads up over swing bridges to a waterfall, then down to a platform for viewing local spider monkeys.

You should also see pisotes (coatis), relatives of the raccoon with long snouts and long, upright, furry tails. The reserve includes a butterfly enclosure and herb garden, an interpretive center, a small coffee plantation and an aviary. For more extreme thrills, there are various ziplines spanning canyons and forest, the longest of which extends nearly a kilometer.

★La Galería GALLERY

(☎7762-2432; www.galeria-panajachel.com; Calle Rancho Grande; ⊙9am-noon & 2-6pm Wed-Mon) FREE Overflowing with art by Guatemalan painters and sculptors, this gallery functions as both an exhibit space and cultural center, hosting lectures, films and occasional concerts. Started in 1971 by the German-K'iche' painter Nan Cuz, the gallery holds a number of the hallucinatory landscapes that garnered Cuz international acclaim.

Casa Cakchiquel ARTS CENTER

(☎7762-0969; Calle 14 de Febrero; ⊙7am-8pm) Pana's cultural center started life as one of the first hotels on the lake, built by a Swedish countess in 1948. Now it holds a radio station, Japanese restaurant and a tremendous little gallery of photos and postcards of Atitlán in simpler times, when steamboats plied the lake.

During its 1950s heyday, such illustrious guests as Ingrid Bergman, Aldous Huxley and Ernesto 'Che' Guevara chatted around the fireplace.

Museo Lacustre Atitlán MUSEUM
(Calle Santander; Q35; ⏲8am-6pm) Inside the Hotel Posada de Don Rodrigo, this museum has displays on the history of the Atitlán region and the volcanic eruptions that created its landscape, plus a collection of ancient artifacts recovered from the lake. A hall below the main gallery covers Samabaj, an ancient ceremonial center discovered at the bottom of the lake near Cerro de Oro.

Activities

Cycling, Hiking & Kayaking

Lago de Atitlán is a cycling and hiking wonderland, spreading across hill and dale. But before setting out for any hike or ride, make enquiries about safety with Proatur (p102), and keep asking as you go. Volcán San Pedro climbs with numerous operators in town cost around Q700 per person, including boat transportation, taxi to the trailhead, entry fees and guide. Paddleboards are available for rent from Pana Surf.

Roger's Tours ADVENTURE SPORTS
(☎7762-6060; www.rogerstours.com; Calle Santander; bike rental per hour/day Q35/170) This outfit rents quality mountain bikes and leads a variety of cycling tours (Q450 per person including helmet, guide and lunch). One tour travels by boat from Panajachel to Tzununá, then by bike west via dirt trail to San Marcos La Laguna and road to San Pedro La Laguna, finally returning to Pana by boat.

Roger's Tours also arranges volcano hikes, horse-riding and kayak tours on the lake.

Pana Surf PADDLEBOARDING
(per hour Q100) The surf aspect of this outfit's name might be a bit out of place on such a placid lake, but it will rent you a paddleboard to explore from Pana, and donate the proceeds to local health and animal welfare charities.

Paragliding

RealWorld Paragliding GLIDING
(☎5634-5699; www.realworldparagliding.jimdo.com; Calle Santander, Centro Comercial San Rafael; tandem flights Q700) The lake has become a center for paragliding enthusiasts and RealWorld Paragliding provides tandem flights, with passengers seated in a canvas chair attached to the flyer's harness so you're free to take photos or simply gaze in amazement at the panorama below.

Courses

Panajachel has a niche in the language-school scene. Two well-set-up schools are **Jardín de América** (☎7762-2637; www.jardindeamerica.com; Calle del Chalí) and **Jabel Tinamit** (☎7762-6056; www.jabeltinamit.com; cnr Avenida de Los Árboles & Callejón Las Armonías; per week Q980, homestay per week additional Q650). The former is set amid ample gardens while the latter is in the center of town. Four hours of one-on-one study five days per week, including a homestay with a local family, will cost around Q1500 per week.

Tours

Inumerable tour agencies along Calle Santander offer day trips on the lake, stopping at several villages. They cost around Q100 and are good value if you're short of time. Typical tours take in San Pedro, San Juan and Santiago Atitlán, stopping for an hour or two at each village.

Travel agencies also offer more extensive tours, which may include weaving demonstrations, visits to the shrine of Maximón in Santiago, and so on.

Posada Los Encuentros TOURS
(☎7762-2093; www.losencuentros.com; Callejón Chotzar 0-41) Offers half- and full-day educational tours to lakeside villages, focusing on such topics as Maya medicine, Tz'utujil oil painting and organic coffee cultivation. Guide Richard Morgan is a scholar of Maya history and culture, and a longtime lake resident. Hiking tours and volcano climbs are also offered.

Festivals & Events

Independence Day SPORTS
(⏲Sep) On September 14, the day before Independence Day, torch-bearing athletes run in marathons throughout the country, but the tradition is celebrated with special fervor in Panajachel, where it all started in 1957. The main event, though, is the marathon from Guatemala City to Panajachel. The runners arrive in Pana's main square around midnight, heralded by cheering crowds, marimbas and fireworks displays.

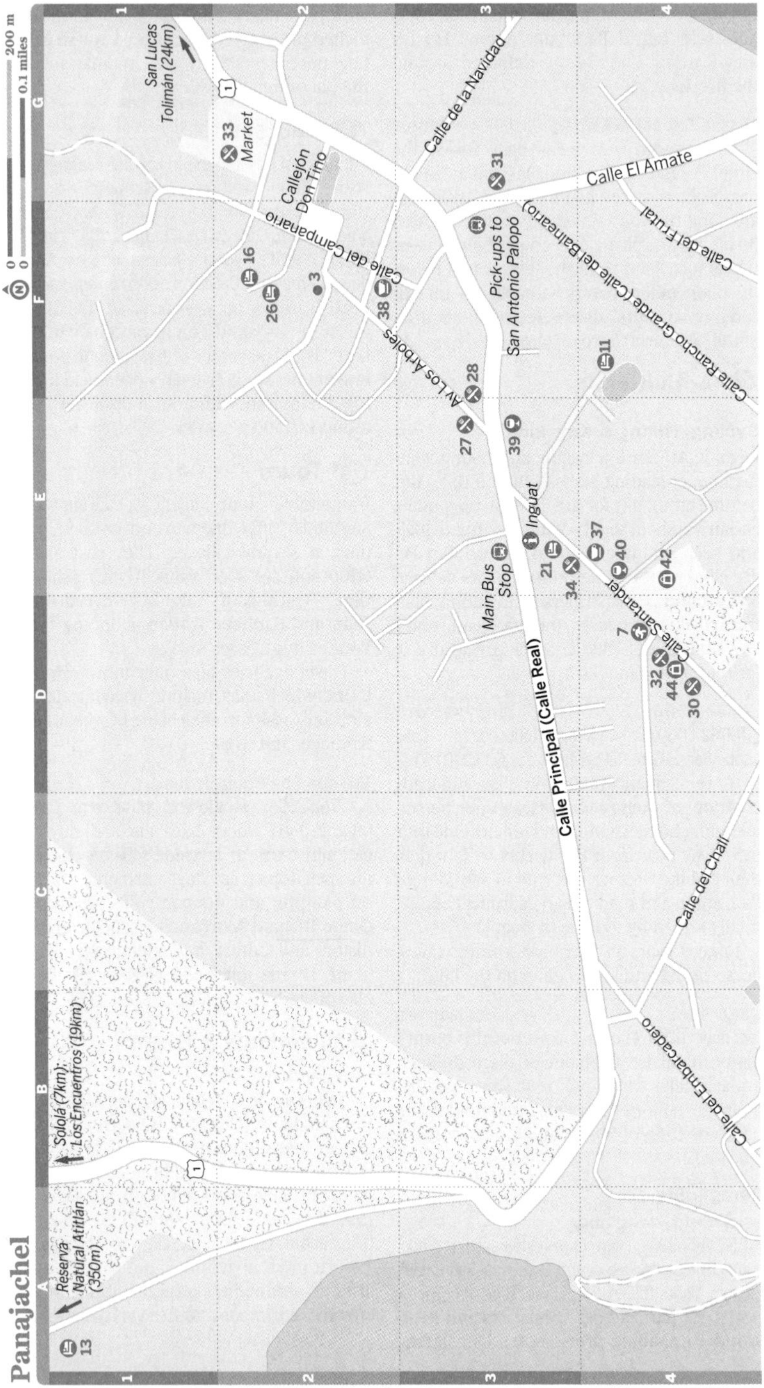
Panajachel
200 m
0.1 miles
13
Reserva Natural Atitlán (350m)
Sololá (7km); Los Encuentros (19km)
San Lucas Tolimán (24km)
33
Market
Callejón Don Tino
16
26
3
Calle del Campanario
38
Calle de la Navidad
31
Calle El Amate
Pick-ups to San Antonio Palopó
Calle Rancho Grande (Calle del Balneario)
Calle del Frutal
Av Los Árboles
27
28
39
11
Inguat
Main Bus Stop
21
34
37
40
42
Calle Santander
7
32
44
30
Calle Principal (Calle Real)
Calle del Chalí
Calle del Embarcadero

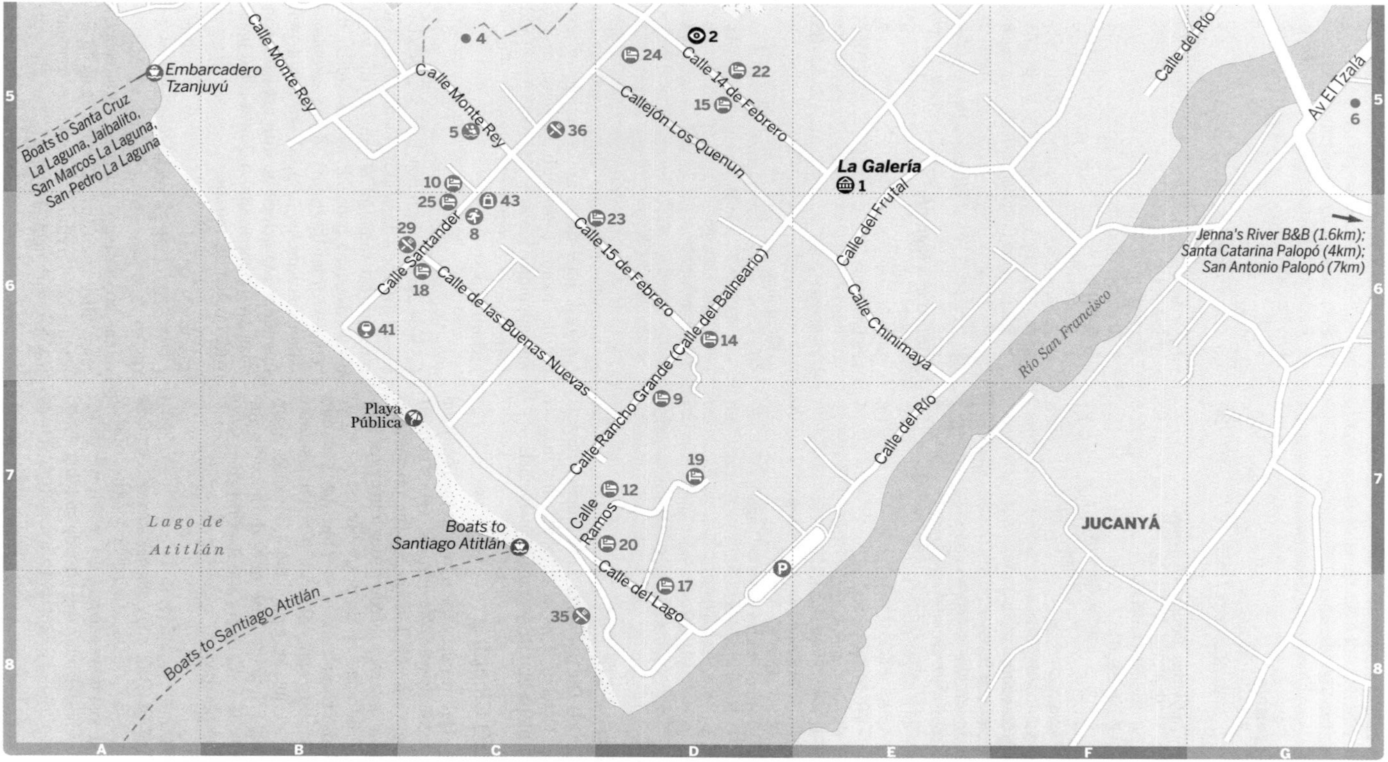
Calle Monte Rey
Embarcadero Tzanjuyú
Boats to Santa Cruz La Laguna, Jaibalito, San Marcos La Laguna, San Pedro La Laguna
4
2
24
22
Calle 14 de Febrero
15
Calle Monte Rey
5
36
Callejón Los Quenun
La Galería
1
Calle del Río
Av El Tzalá
6
10
25
43
8
29
23
Calle Santander
18
Calle 15 de Febrero
Calle del Frutal
Jenna's River B&B (1.6km); Santa Catarina Palopó (4km); San Antonio Palopó (7km)
Calle de las Buenas Nuevas
Calle Rancho Grande (Calle del Balneario)
Calle Chinimaya
41
14
Río San Francisco
9
Playa Pública
Calle del Río
19
12
Calle Ramos
20
Lago de Atitlán
Boats to Santiago Atitlán
JUCANYÁ
P
Calle del Lago
17
35
Boats to Santiago Atitlán
A
B
C
D
E
F
G
5
6
7
8

Panajachel

Top Sights
1 La Galería ... E5

Sights
2 Casa Cakchiquel ... D5
Museo Lacustre Atitlán ... (see 18)

Activities, Courses & Tours
3 Jabel Tinamit ... F2
4 Jardín de América ... C5
5 Pana Surf ... C5
6 Posada Los Encuentros ... G5
7 RealWorld Paragliding ... D4
8 Roger's Tours ... C6

Sleeping
9 Casa Texel ... D7
10 Dreamboat Hostel ... C5
11 Hospedaje Casa Linda ... F4
12 Hospedaje Sueño Real ... D7
13 Hotel Atitlán ... A1
14 Hotel Jere ... D6
15 Hotel Larry's Place ... D5
16 Hotel Montana ... F2
17 Hotel Playa Linda ... D8
18 Hotel Posada de Don Rodrigo ... C6
19 Hotel Posada K'amol B'ey ... D7
20 Hotel Posada Viñas del Lago ... D7
21 Hotel Primavera ... E3
22 Hotel Utz Rajil ... D5
23 Hotel Utz-Jay ... D6
24 Mario's Rooms ... D5
25 Posada de los Volcanes ... C6
Posada Los Encuentros ... (see 6)
26 Villa Lupita ... F2

Eating
27 Chero's Bar ... E3
Chez Alex ... (see 21)
28 Circus Bar ... F3
29 Deli Jasmín ... C6
30 Deli Llama de Fuego ... D4
31 Despensa Familiar ... G3
32 El Patio ... D4
33 Fuentes de Vida ... G2
Guajimbo's ... (see 30)
34 Mister Jon's ... E3
35 Restaurante El Atitlán ... C8
Restaurante Hana ... (see 2)
36 Ristorante La Lanterna ... C5

Drinking & Nightlife
37 Café Loco ... E4
38 Crossroads Café ... F2
39 La Palapa ... E3
40 Pana Rock Café ... E4
41 Sunset Café ... B6

Shopping
42 Comerciales de Artesanías Típicas Tinamit Maya ... E4
43 Libros del Lago ... C6
44 Oxlajuj B'atz' ... D4

Festival of San Francisco de Asís FERIA
(Oct) The festival of San Francisco de Asís, on October 4, is celebrated with massive drinking and fireworks in Panajachel.

Sleeping

Budget travelers will rejoice at the profusion of family-run *hospedajes* (guesthouses). They're simple but cheap. The pricier ones offer generous discounts for longer stays.

Midrange lodgings are busiest on weekends. From Sunday to Thursday you may get a discount; likewise if you're planning on staying for longer than four days. Many establishments raise rates during July, August, Semana Santa and the Christmas–New Year holidays.

★ **Dreamboat Hostel** HOSTEL
(7762-2530; http://dreamboathostel.com; Calle Santander; dm Q65, d without bathroom Q175-225) The paint was barely dry when we visited this hostel, but it was already building a good reputation. Bright four-bed dorms (mixed or women only) stop things getting too crowded, plus there are a couple of airy private rooms (one with balcony) and a well-appointed kitchen. The roof terrace and lounge bar are good for daytime chilling or nighttime partying.

Villa Lupita HOTEL $
(5054-2447; Callejón Don Tino; s/d Q75/150, without bathroom Q50/100) Family-run Lupita is great value for staying in the town center. Facing a plaza below the church, it's removed from the tourist drag. Accommodations are pretty stripped down but well maintained nonetheless, with art from San Juan wrapping around a flower-filled patio with broken-tile mosaic.

Mario's Rooms HOTEL $
(7762-1313; Calle Santander; s/d incl breakfast Q150/230;) On Pana's main drag, Mario's rooms are arranged on two floors facing a plant-filled courtyard. Despite being in the middle of everything it somehow remains low-key, with helpful staff.

Hospedaje Casa Linda GUESTHOUSE **$**
(☎7762-0386; Callejón El Capulin; r Q180, s/d/tr without bathroom Q80/160/180) Twenty-one spotless little rooms surround a lush garden at this tranquil family-run establishment down a lane off Calle Santander. Upstairs units get a nice breeze and the balconies are good for afternoon siestas. Basilio, the proprietor, plays a mean marimba.

Hotel Larry's Place HOTEL **$**
(☎7762-0767; www.hotellarrysplace.com; Calle 14 de Febrero; s/d/tr Q125/150/200; P) Centrally located but set back from the road behind a wall of vegetation, Larry's Place offers good-sized, cool rooms in a sylvan setting. Traditional fabric furnishings are tasteful, ceilings high and the balconies welcome. Low key but great value.

Hospedaje Sueño Real HOTEL **$**
(☎7762-0608; hotelsuenorealpana@hotmail.com; Calle Ramos; s/d from Q150/180; P @ wifi) A good budget option close to the Playa Pública, the Sueño Real has cheerfully decorated, if smallish, rooms with TV and fan. The best are the upstairs triples, opening on a plant-covered terrace with lake views.

Hotel Jere HOTEL **$**
(☎7762-2781; www.jerehotel.com; Calle Rancho Grande; s/d/tr Q100/125/180; P @) Jere's brick-walled rooms are enlivened with traditional textiles, and some open on to sun-splashed balconies (though you'll want to avoid the ones overlooking the main street). You can book shuttle buses and lake tours on the spot and rent bicycles.

Hotel Posada Viñas del Lago HOTEL **$**
(☎7930-5053; braulio.pana@hotmail.com; Playa Pública; s/d/tr Q185/250/350; P wifi pool) Steps from the lakefront, this garishly painted lodging is managed by a Kaqchiquel extended family. Cabin-like rooms enjoy great lake views, and you can walk down the lawn to the jetty or eat at the poolside restaurant-bar.

Jenna's River B&B B&B **$$**
(☎5458-1984; www.jennasriverbedandbreakfast.com; Calle Rancho; d from Q560; no smoking wifi) You'll feel right at home at Jenna's place, just outside Pana proper, with seven uniquely decked-out hard-standing 'yurts' (all with bathrooms) that are starlit by night. Jenna and pooches welcome travelers to their tropically abundant garden, gazebo and breakfast room, where the table is set with her own fresh-baked bread and homemade jams.

Those who are bowled over by the abundant art, antiques and textiles that adorn the rooms can browse for such items in the adjacent shop.

Posada Los Encuentros LODGE **$$**
(☎7762-1603; www.losencuentros.com; Callejón Chotzar 0-41; s/d incl breakfast from Q300/340; wifi) Just across the river from Pana town is this 'ecocultural B&B,' featuring seven cozy rooms in a relaxed home, plus a volcanically heated tub, medicinal plant garden, terrace and fitness center. Owner Richard Morgan is happy to share his encyclopedic knowledge of the lake and offers tours of the area.

Hotel Utz-Jay HOTEL **$$**
(☎7762-0217; www.hotelutzjay.com; Calle 15 de Febrero 2-50; s/d/tr from Q225/360/495; P wifi) These eight cottages stand amid lush gardens bursting with heliconia, orange trumpet and ferns where no fewer than 46 types of birds have been spotted. Rooms are decorated with traditional fabrics and have porches out front. Good breakfasts are available and there's a *chuj* (traditional Maya sauna).

Hotel Montana HOTEL **$$**
(☎7762-0326; atitlanhotelmontana@hotmail.com; Callejón Don Tino; s/d Q180/300; P wifi) Down a narrow street near the church, the Montana is an old-fashioned establishment with simple rooms and wonderful plant-laden balconies fronted by pot-bellied railing. Choose a room on the upper level for brilliant views of the mountainside to enjoy the greenery inside and out.

Posada de los Volcanes HOTEL **$$**
(☎7762-0244; www.posadadelosvolcanes.com; Calle Santander 5-51; s/d from Q380/450; wifi) This chalet-style lodging has lovely pine-paneled rooms. On the 4th floor, you'll be rewarded with your own private terrace, suitable for kicking back with cocktails and surveying the lake. Breakfast is included; the freshly-squeezed juice and homemade jams are a nice touch.

Hotel Posada K'amol B'ey HOTEL **$$**
(☎7762-0215; www.hotelposadakamolbey.com; Final Calle Ramos; r from Q180, bungalows Q600; P wifi) At the end of the row of hotels leading up from the Playa Pública, the 'king of the road' is about the tidiest and quietest option. Two levels of spacious units with quality beds face a clipped suburban lawn where hummingbirds flit around. At the rear are three bungalows, each with two rooms and kitchen.

Hotel Utz Rajil HOTEL $$
(7762-0303; www.facebook.com/hotelutzrajil; Calle 14 de Febrero; s/d/tr Q150/220/280;) A modern, three-story hotel with 13 large, well-maintained rooms and quality furniture, the Utz Rajil (Kaqchiquel for 'good deal') features cool balconies for photo ops of the street activity below (and unfortunately, early-morning street noise, too). Guests rave about the copious hot water in the showers – not automatically a given in this town.

Hotel Primavera HOTEL $$
(7762-2052; www.primaveraatitlan.com; Calle Santander; s/d/tr from Q225/300/375;) This stylish Norwegian-owned hotel near Pana's main intersection just feels right. Ten large rooms with plant-filled window boxes, soft lighting and handsome fabrics face a sleek wood-decked patio, making for a relaxing atmosphere. Chez Alex, the restaurant downstairs, serves foie gras, escargot *und wienerschnitzel* in a Euro-toned setting.

Hotel Playa Linda HOTEL $$
(7762-0097; www.hotelplayalinda.com.gt; 7a Calle 0-70, Playa Pública; s/d Q200/250, with view r Q300;) The rambling Playa Linda has 17 good-sized rooms with fireplaces and a cute swimming pool. Rooms 1 to 5 have the best lake views, with large balconies from which to enjoy them. The gardens out front are a fecund fantasy of blooms and squawking parrots. Guests may use the kitchen.

★ **Hotel Atitlán** HERITAGE HOTEL $$$
(7762-1441; www.hotelatitlan.com; Finca San Buenaventura; r incl breakfast from Q1400;) A coffee plantation for much of the 20th century, this estate was remade as Pana's loveliest hotel in the 1970s. Located on the lakeshore 1.5km northwest of the town center, it's a rambling, semicolonial affair surrounded by manicured tropical gardens.

The 60 rooms all have lake-facing balconies; decorations go heavy on religious imagery, wood carvings and wrought iron. A restaurant, bar and lakefront pool with killer volcano views ensure you'll never want to leave the premises, except perhaps on one of the hotel's kayaks.

Casa Texel HOTEL $$$
(7762-2076; www.casatexel.com; Calle Rancho Grande; s/d/tr incl breakfast Q480/850/1250;) This pristine hotel a block from the lakefront is a swish spread with a proper dose of indigenous style. Rooms on three levels line up along brick balconies with terraces at the end and plenty of lake views. Decor is modern with colorful bedspreads, pretty tiles, cast-iron fixtures and vintage photos. Borrow a bike to explore or relax in the spa.

Hotel Posada de Don Rodrigo HOTEL $$$
(7832-9858; www.posadadedonrodrigo.com; Calle Santander; d/ste from Q1225/1400;) Down by the lakeside, this hotel has landscaped grounds that hold many delights – squash courts, a swimming pool with waterslide, a couple of saunas and a fine museum. Large rooms are decorated in colonial style and open onto the lawn. Breakfast is served on the fabulous lake-view terrace. There's a sister *posada* in Antigua.

Eating

There are plenty of restaurants lining Calle Santander, which swell in the late afternoon and evening with taco stalls and other cheap street eats.

Near the south end of Calle del Lago, there is an agglomeration of thatched-roof restaurants crowding the lakefront. All serve the local specialties of lake *mojarra* and black bass.

★ **Circus Bar** ITALIAN
(7762-2056; Av Los Árboles; noon-midnight) Behind the swinging doors, Circus Bar has a cabaret atmosphere, with live music nightly from 7:30pm to 10:30pm. There is good pizza and even better pasta, plus a respectable wine list and imported liquors. Flamenco, folk or marimbas nicely complement the cozy atmosphere.

Chero's Bar SALVADORAN $
(Av Los Árboles; pupusas Q10; 12:30pm-1am Tue-Sat) Usefully located in the nightlife zone, Chero's can get pretty lively, with beer-drinking patrons gathering around simple wood tables as *tuk-tuks* zip by. Salvadoran staff slap out *pupusas,* either straight up or filled with such items as *güicoy* (a kind of squash) or the spinach-like herb *chipilín,* and served with the customary pickled cabbage and salsa.

Fuentes de Vida GUATEMALAN $
(Market; lunch Q20; 7:30am-4pm) This is the largest of a group of rather rustic cook stalls at the rear of the market building, near the pork vendors. It offers half a dozen menu options daily, all of which come with beans, tortillas and a fiery salsa made from dried red chilies.

Deli Jasmín CAFE $
(☎7762-2585; Calle Santander; items Q25-45; ⏰7am-6pm Wed-Mon; ✎) This tranquil garden restaurant with hummingbirds darting about the flowers serves a range of healthy foods and drinks. Breakfast is served all day, and you can buy whole-wheat or pita bread and hummus to take away.

★ **El Patio** GUATEMALAN $$
(☎7762-2041; Plaza Los Patios, Calle Santander; mains Q30-60; ⏰7am-9:30pm) This is a locally popular joint for lunch; the front terrace makes an obvious meeting place. Try to make it for Monday lunch when everyone chows down on *caldo de res* (chunky broth), served with all the trimmings.

Mister Jon's AMERICAN $$
(☎4710-8697; www.mister-jon.com; Calle Santander; breakfast Q35-50; ⏰7am-10pm Tue-Sun; 📶) All the perks of a US diner are here in abundance, including buttermilk pancakes, great omelets with hash browns or country biscuits on the side, and free coffee refills (of Guatemala's finest). But it's no gringo ghetto – *chapínes* (Guatemalans) who've been up north like it, too.

Mister John's also has more power sockets than anywhere we've been in Guatemala – perfect if you need to catch up with your laptop.

Restaurante Hana JAPANESE $$
(☎4298-1415; www.restaurantehana.com; Calle 14 de Febrero; mains Q65-85; ⏰noon-9pm Tue-Sun) Serving authentic Japanese cuisine, Hana is ensconced in the serene courtyard of the Casa Cakchiquel (p94), graced by hanging plants and a gallery of photos of old Pana. Besides preparing such classics as *nigiri* sushi, sashimi and tempura, Chef Mihoko does *uramaki* ('inside-out' sushi), *donburi* and cold udon noodles just as they're done in her native Japan.

Guajimbo's STEAK $$
(☎7762-0063; Calle Santander; mains Q55-100; ⏰7:30am-9:30pm Fri-Wed) This Uruguayan grill serves up generous helpings of steak, sausage and chicken dishes with vegetables, salad, garlic bread and rice or boiled potatoes. Vegetarians can enjoy tofu kebabs. You won't leave hungry. In the mornings there are hearty breakfasts, and there is frequently live music at night.

Deli Llama de Fuego INTERNATIONAL $$
(☎7762-2586; Calle Santander; items Q40-60; ⏰7am-9pm Thu-Tue) This groovy natural-foods haven revolves around a *llama de fuego* (African tulip) tree. Vegetarian options are well represented, along with a barrel-full of delicious fruit smoothies, as well as big burritos, tasty quesadillas, sandwiches, pasta and more.

Restaurante El Atitlán SEAFOOD $$
(Calle del Lago; black bass Q140; ⏰7am-9pm) One of a string of thatched-roof restaurants along the lakefront. The main draw, aside from the stunning setting, is the lake fish, highlighted by *mojarra* (bream) and black bass.

Ristorante La Lanterna ITALIAN $$
(Calle Santander 4-72; mains Q65-90; ⏰7am-3pm & 6-10pm) Ensconced in the gardens of Hotel Dos Mundo, La Lanterna makes its own pasta and stocks an impressive range of wines from the motherland. Bonus: you're welcome to use the hotel swimming pool if you eat here.

Chez Alex EUROPEAN $$$
(☎7762-0172; www.primaveraatitlan.com; Hotel Primavera, Calle Santander; mains Q95-180; ⏰noon-10pm) The restaurant component of the Hotel Primavera serves some of Pana's finest cuisine, with a hefty dash of European influence and a wine list to back it up. After a meal of mussels in white-wine sauce or Camembert-stuffed schnitzel, kick back with a Habana cigar.

Despensa Familiar SUPERMARKET
(Calle El Amate) Self-caterers will find all they need at this large, well-stocked supermarket.

Drinking & Nightlife

Panajachel's miniature Zona Viva (party zone) focuses on Av Los Árboles. Especially at weekends, it seems as if every other restaurant on Calle Santander has live music.

Crossroads Café CAFE
(☎5292-8439; www.crossroadscafepana.com; Calle del Campanario 0-27; ⏰9am-1pm & 2:30-6pm Tue-Sat) This cafe has made Panajachel a major crossroads for coffee aficionados. When he's not roasting beans, the Bay Area owner/head barista spends his time combing the highlands for small estate coffees to add to his roster, including the tangy Acatenango Eighth Wonder and smooth Huehue Organic.

La Palapa PUB
(Calle Principal; ⏲9am-1am) As the name suggests, this party center unfolds beneath a thatched-roof shelter (actually two), with a beachy ambience. It's popular with volunteer gringos, but all sorts crowd in for the Saturday afternoon BBQ. Other diversions include weekend live music, trivia quiz nights and sports TV at all times.

Pana Rock Café PUB
(☎7762-2194; Calle Santander 1-74; ⏲8am-midnight) Like a Hard Rock by the lake, this lively little pub hosts plugged-in bands nightly from 9pm. It's popular with Guatemala City youth, who settle in for the evening with a *cubetazo* (bucket of beer) or two.

Café Loco COFFEE
(Calle Santander; ⏲9am-8pm Tue-Sun, 3-8pm Mon) This Korean-run cafe is heaven for coffee connoisseurs. The youthful staff set up a formidable range of espresso variations, from 'Brown Cloud' (a small espresso with a bit of milk and foam) to 'Habana Blues,' with brown sugar sprinkled over espresso grounds.

Sunset Café BAR
(cnr Calles Santander & del Lago; ⏲11am-11pm) This open-air lounge at the end of Calle Santander is the place to enjoy those dream-like volcano sundowns. In high season, there's live music Friday to Sunday evenings; but midweek during the rainy season you'll have to talk to the bar staff to find any excitement.

Shopping

Calle Santander is lined with booths, stores and complexes that sell (among other things) traditional Maya clothing, colorful blankets, leather goods and wood carvings. Otherwise, head for the traditional market building in the town center, busiest on Sundays when every square meter of ground alongside is occupied by vendors in indigenous garb.

Oxlajuj B'atz' ARTS & CRAFTS
(Thirteen Threads; ☎7762-2921; www.oxlajujbatz.org.gt; Plaza Hotel Real Santander; ⏲10am-6pm) Supporting an NGO for the empowerment of indigenous women, this fair-trade shop features beautiful naturally dyed rugs, handbags, handwoven goods and beaded jewelry. Pick up a bar of locally-made chocolate while you're there.

Libros del Lago BOOKS
(Calle Santander; ⏲10am-6:30pm) Refreshingly good stock of books in English and Spanish on Guatemala, the Maya and Mesoamerica, plus maps and Latin American literature in English.

Comerciales de Artesanías Típicas Tinamit Maya ARTS & CRAFTS
(⏲8am-7pm) Be sure to browse the many stalls of this extensive handicrafts market, which has an impressive variety of bags, clothing, blankets, belts and hammocks. More booths line up along the beach end of Calle Santander.

Information

EMERGENCY

Proatur (Programa de Asistencia al Turista; ☎5874-9450; proatur.solola@gmail.com; Calle Rancho Grande; ⏲9am-5pm)

MEDICAL SERVICES

The nearest hospital is **PanaMed** (☎4224-2648; Callejon Juzgado, Zona 2) in Sololá.

Pana Medic (☎4892-3499; drzulmashalom@hotmail.com; Calle Principal 0-72) Clinic run by an English-speaking doctor.

MONEY

Banco de América Central (Calle Santander, Centro Comercial San Rafael; ⏲9am-5pm Mon-Fri, 9am-1pm Sat) ATM; Visa, American Express and MasterCard cash advances; US dollars exchanged.

Banco Industrial (Calle Santander, Comercial Los Pinos; ⏲9am-4pm Mon-Fri, 9am-1pm Sat) Visa/MasterCard ATM.

5B ATM Visa/MasterCard ATM.

TOURIST INFORMATION

INGUAT (☎2421-2953; info-pana@inguat.gob.gt; Calle Principal 1-47; ⏲9am-5pm)

TRAVEL AGENCIES

Many of Panajachel's full-service travel agencies are scattered along Calle Santander. These establishments offer trips, tours and shuttle services to other destinations around Guatemala as well as destinations such as San Cristóbal de Las Casas in Mexico.

Atitrans (☎7762-0146; www.atitranspanajachel.com; Calle Santander; ⏲8am-8pm)

Magic Travel (☎7762-0755; www.magictravel.com.gt; Calle Santander, Edificio Rincón Sai)

Eternal Spring (☎7762-6043; eternalspring_conexiones@hotmail.com; Calle Santander)

Getting There & Away

BOAT

There are two docks for passengers boats.

Boats for Santiago Atitlán (30 minutes) depart from the **Playa Públlica** (Playa Publíca) at the foot of Calle Rancho Grande. All other departures leave from the **Embarcadero Tzanjuyú**, at the foot of Calle del Embarcadero. From here, *lanchas* (small motorboats) go counterclockwise around the lake, with direct and local service to San Pedro La Laguna (Q25, 25 minutes). The local services stop in Santa Cruz La Laguna (15 minutes), Jaibalito, Tzununá, San Marcos La Laguna (30 minutes), San Juan La Laguna and San Pedro La Laguna (45 minutes). The first boat to San Pedro departs at 7am, the last around 5pm.

One-way passage to San Pedro, Santiago or San Lucas costs Q25. Closer destinations like Santa Cruz shouldn't top Q10.

Lanchas are also available for private hire from the Playa Pública or Embarcadero Tzanjuyú: expect to pay around Q400 to San Pedro La Laguna.

SHUTTLE MINIBUS

Pretty much every tourist destination you could think of is served by a shuttle minibus. You can book at a number of travel agencies on Calle Santander.

Typical one-way fares include Antigua (Q80), Chichicastenango (round trip Thursday and Sunday Q120), Guatemala City (Q160), Quetzaltenango (Q125) and San Cristóbal de Las Casas, Mexico (Q280).

Around Panajachel

Southeast of Pana, 5km and 10km respectively along a winding road, lie the lakeside hamlets of Santa Catarina Palopó and San Antonio Palopó. (The name 'Palopó' is a Spanish-Kaqchiquel amalgam referring to a type of fig tree that grows here.) Compared with nearby Pana, the Palopós feel remote, with narrow streets paved in stone blocks and adobe houses with roofs of thatch or tin. Many villagers, both men and women, go

BUSES FROM PANAJACHEL

Panajachel's **main bus stop** (Calle Real) is at the junction of Calles Santander and Principal, immediately west of the Centro Comercial El Dorado. There is a separate stop for minibuses to **San Antonio Palopó**. Departures – approximately and subject to change – are as follows:

DESTINATION	COST (Q)	DURATION	FREQUENCY	ALTERNATIVE
Antigua	45	2½hr	11am Mon-to Sat	Guatemala City bus; change at Chimaltenango
Chichicastenango	20	1½hr	Five services 6:45am- 6pm	Any bus heading to Los Encuentros (via Sololá); change buses there
Ciudad Tecún Umán (Mexican border)				By the Pacific route (via Mazatenango), bus to Cocales and change there; by the highland route, transfer at Quetzaltenango
Guatemala City	60	3½hr	Five services 4:30am- 3pm	Bus to Los Encuentros (via Sololá); change there
Huehuetenango		3½hr		Bus to Los Encuentros (via Sololá), then Huehue- or La Mesilla–bound bus. Or Quetzaltenango service, change at Cuatro Caminos
Los Encuentros	10	40min		Bus to Sololá; change there
Quetzaltenango	25	2hr	Four services 5am-1pm	Bus to Los Encuentros (via Sololá); change there
Sololá	5	15min	Every 10 min 7am-7pm	

WORTH A TRIP

IXIMCHÉ

The remnants of the Kaqchiquels' 15th-century capital stand some 15km due east of Lago de Atitlán. The 'palaces' and temples uncovered here are modest in scale but ensconced in a serene, park-like setting. Iximché remains an important ceremonial site for indigenous pilgrims, who visit the area to perform magic rituals, burning copal resin, wood or liquor in front of the pyramids to ward off illness or bring down enemies.

K'icab the Great, leader of the Kaqchiquels, relocated his capital here in 1463 from its previous location near the K'iche' Maya stronghold of K'umarcaaj. At that time, the Kaqchiquel were at war with the K'iche', and the natural defences of the new location, a flat promontory surrounded by ravines, served them well. The Spanish, who arrived in 1524, set up their first Guatemalan headquarters here, forming an alliance with the resident Kaqchiquels against their K'iche' enemies. However, the Europeans' demands for gold and other loot soon put an end to their alliance with the Kaqchiquel, who were defeated in an ensuing guerrilla war.

Entering the **archaeological site** (Q50; ⏲8am-4pm), visit the small museum (closed Monday) on the right, then continue to the four ceremonial plazas, which are surrounded by temple structures up to 10m high, and ball courts. Some structures have been uncovered; on a few the original plaster coating is still in place.

The ruins are reached from the town of Tecpán, off the Interamericana. Buses traveling east from La Cuchilla junction can drop you at the turnoff; from there it's about a 1km walk (or, if you're lucky, a short ride on an urban bus) to the center of town. 'Ruinas' microbuses to the site (Q5, 10 minutes) leave from near Tecpán's main plaza every 15 minutes till 4pm. The last bus back leaves the site no later than 4:30pm. Tour agencies in Antigua and Panajachel offer trips to Iximché.

about their daily activities clad in traditional outfits, and these are good places to look for the luminescent indigo weavings you see all around Lago de Atitlán. The villages are also known for their cream and blue pottery.

Sololá

POP 156,800

Long before the Spanish showed up, the Kaqchiquel town of Sololá held importance due to its location on trade routes between the *tierra caliente* (hot lands of the Pacific Slope) and *tierra fría* (the chilly highlands). All the traders still meet here, and Sololá's **market** (⏲Tue & Fri) is one of the most vivid in the highlands.

The sprawling Mercado Mayoreo (wholesale market), north of the central plaza, is the stage for the twice-weekly market, held Tuesday and Friday, when the building and vicinity are ablaze with the colorful costumes of people from surrounding villages and towns. Displays of meat, vegetables, fruit, homewares and clothing are neatly arranged in every available space, with tides of buyers ebbing and flowing around the vendors. Elaborate stands are stocked with brightly colored yarn used to make the traditional costumes you see around you.

Sunday mornings the officers of the traditional *cofradías* (religious brotherhoods) parade ceremoniously to the cathedral.

Sights

Museo de Sololá MUSEUM

(Q10; ⏲9am-6pm Mon-Fri, 8am-5pm Sun) Housed atop the elaborate Swiss-built clock tower that fronts the city hall, the museum is devoted to photograph exhibits and the clock mechanism itself, though the biggest thrill here is the dramatic view it affords down the slope to Lago de Atitlán.

Sleeping & Eating

Hotel Cacique Ralón HOTEL $$

(☎7762-4657; www.hotelcaciqueralon.webnode.es; 4a Calle 6-43; s/d/tr Q150/250/375; P 📶) A fair choice for lodging in Sololá is this tranquil retreat halfway between the bustling market and the central plaza. Simply adorned rooms and several terraces surround a garden studded with birds of paradise and an avocado tree, with a small cafe.

Comedor Eben Ezer GUATEMALAN $

(6a Av; set lunch Q20; ⏲7am-6:30pm) This simple lunch hall at the base of the town hall is a gathering place for the Kaqchiquel community. Expect hearty helpings of such down-home fare as *caldo de res* (broth with meat and veggies) and *carne guisado* (stewed beef) with abundant side portions of rice and veggies.

Shopping

Mercado de Artesanías ARTS & CRAFTS
(Handicrafts Market; 6a Av) This small but excellent market on the upper level of the town hall displays beautiful *huipiles* (embroidered tunics), beadwork, bags and other crafts produced by a cooperative of 30 indigenous groups from around Sololá department.

Getting There & Away

All buses between Panajachel and the junction town Los Encuentros stop at the Parque Centroamérica. It's Q5 and 20 minutes to either place from Sololá.

San Antonio Palopó

POP 14,400

San Antonio Palopó is a remote and captivating hillside village where entire families tend their terraced fields in traditional garb – women in indigo-striped *huipiles* (long embroidered tunics), dark blue *cortes* (long skirts) and sparkly headbands, and men in traditional wool skirts. At the top, a gleaming white church forms the center of activity. About 150m down the path to the right, the **Tienda Candelaria** houses a weaving cooperative where women produce shawls, *huipiles* and *tocoyales* (headdresses) on backstrap looms and get a fair price for them. Together with the nearby village of Santa Catarine Palopó, this area is also known for its cream pottery, with a distinctive blue and green decoration.

Sleeping & Eating

Hotel Terrazas del Lago HOTEL $$
(7762-0157; www.hotelterrazasdellago.com; s/d/tr Q200/250/330; P) At this delightfully affordable retreat, 15 attractive stone-walled rooms climb the hillside, with small terraces and hammocks. Good inexpensive meals (Q50 to Q80) are served on the lakefront deck with views straight across to Volcán Tolimán.

Villa Santa Catarina HOTEL $$$
(7762-1291; https://hotelvillasantacatarina.negocio.site; s/d/ste Q790/935/1400; P @) In stark contrast to its humble surroundings stands this luxury spread with elegant restaurant and pool fringed by palm trees and sumptuous gardens. The 38 spacious and simply furnished rooms sport tasteful weavings and cool adobe walls. The two suites face across the lake to Volcán San Pedro.

Getting There & Away

Pick-ups to San Antonio leave about every half hour from Calle El Amate in Panajachel, near its intersection with Calle Principal (Q5, 30 minutes). The last pick-up back to Pana leaves San Antonio about 6pm. All transport passes through Santa Catarina.

San Lucas Tolimán

POP 35,400

San Lucas Tolimán is busier and more commercial than most lakeside villages. Set at the foot of the dramatic Volcán Tolimán, it's a coffee-growing town and a transportation point on a route between the Interamericana and the Carretera al Pacífico. Market days are Sunday, Tuesday and Friday. Atypically not standing on the town's plaza but along the street to the lakefront is the 16th-century **Parroquia de San Lucas** parish church. The parish, aided by Catholic missionaries from Minnesota and volunteers from North America and Europe, has been active in redistributing coffee-plantation land, setting up a fair-trade coffee cooperative and founding a women's center, a medical clinic and a reforestation program. For visits to the cooperative and information on volunteering, contact the **parish office** (7722-0112; www.sanlucasmission.org).

Sleeping & Eating

Hotel Don Pedro HOTEL $
(7722-0028; Final de Calle Principal; s/d/tr Q70/130/190; P) Down by the lakeside, this hotel is made entirely of stone and rough-hewn timber beams around a green courtyard. The construction feels a little like a medieval inn (the good restaurant/bar sports the same motif) but the rooms thankfully have comfortable beds rather than straw pallets.

Hotel Tolimán HOTEL $$$
(7722-0033; www.hoteltoliman.com; 6a Ave; s/d incl breakfast from Q520/640; P) This is a low-key resort on the site of a former coffee-processing plant, with 20 colonial-style rooms with local textiles, plus a few cottages around a spreading *amate* tree. A terrace restaurant overlooks a fountain-fed pool on landscaped grounds leading down to the lakeshore – great views to enjoy with your meals.

Getting There & Away

Buses run roughly every hour from San Lucas Tolimán to Panajachel; there are also frequent buses to Santiago Atitlán.

Santiago Atitlán

POP 53,200

Santiago Atitlán is the largest of the lake communities, with a strong indigenous identity. Many *atitecos* (as its people are known) proudly adhere to a traditional Tz'utujil Maya lifestyle. Women wear purple-striped skirts and *huipiles* embroidered with colored birds and flowers, while older men still wear lavender or maroon striped embroidered pants. The town's *cofradías* (brotherhoods) maintain the syncretic traditions and rituals of Maya Catholicism. There's a large arts and crafts scene here, too. Boatbuilding is a local industry, and rows of rough-hewn *cayucos* (dugout canoes) are lined up along the shore. The liveliest days to visit are Friday and Sunday, the main market days, but any day will do.

Santiago is worth a trip to visit the home of the Mayan spirit **Maximón** (mah-shee-*mohn*). He changes house every year, but he's easy enough to find by asking around (would-be guides will approach you at the dock).

The Tz'utujil had been in this area for generations when the Spanish invaded, with their ceremonial capital at Chuitinamit, across the inlet. Santiago was established by Franciscan friars in 1547, as part of the colonial strategy to consolidate the indigenous population. In the 1980s left-wing guerrillas had a strong presence in the area, prompting the Guatemalan army to kill or 'disappear' hundreds of villagers.

Sights

★Cofradía Maximón RELIGIOUS SITE

(donation requested) Maximón is a traditional Maya deity who resides in Santiago Atitlán. He appears as a life-sized but broken-legged effigy in a hat, dark suit and glasses, surrounded by candles, flowers and the scent of burning incense. His *cofradía* (brotherhood) looks after him, and receives visitors who give offerings. In the syncretic way of much tradtional Maya belief, he is also associated with Judas Iscariot.

Maximón ceremonially moves to a new home every year on May 8 (after Semana Santa).

Cojolya Association of Maya Women Weavers MUSEUM

(☎7721-7268; www.cojolya.org; Calle Real, Comercial Las Máscaras, 2nd fl; donation requested; ⏰9am-5pm Mon-Fri, 9am-2pm Sat) This small

TZ'UTUJIL OIL PAINTING

Emanating primarily from the lakeside towns of Santiago Atitlán, San Pedro La Laguna and San Juan La Laguna, Tz'utujil oil painting has a distinctive primitivist style, with depictions of rural life, local traditions and landscapes in vibrant colors.

This distinctly Maya mode is generally handed down through generations of the same family, and the leading artists share surnames. In San Pedro La Laguna, the name of note is González. Legend has it that Tz'utujil art began when Rafael González y González noticed some dye that had dripped and mixed with the sap of a tree; he made a paintbrush from his hair and began creating the type of canvases still popular today. His grandson Pedro Rafael González Chavajay and Pedro's cousin Mariano González Chavajay are leading contemporary exponents of the Tz'utujil style. The artist Emilio González Morales pioneered the motif of depicting rural scenes from above – the vista del pájaro, or bird's-eye view – as well as from below, an ant's-eye view.

The granddaddy of Santiago painting was Juan Sisay; success at an international art exhibition in 1969 sparked an explosion of painters working in his style. You can even learn to paint in this style at several studios around town.

Among the leading figures in San Juan are husband and wife Antonio Vásquez Yojcom and Juana Mendoza Cholotío, whose paintings are exhibited at the **Galería Xocomeel** on the way up from the main dock.

Artists in all three communities are experimenting with new forms while continuing to explore Maya cultural themes.

If you've got more than a passing interest, consider taking the 'Maya Artists & Artisans' tour offered by Posada Los Encuentros (p95) in Panajachel.

museum and showroom is devoted to the art of backstrap loom weaving. Well-designed exhibits show the history of the craft and the process from spinning the cotton fibers to the finished textile. There's a shop, daily demonstrations of backstrap loom techniques and, if you want to really learn more, weaving lessons (Q150; book ahead).

Iglesia Parroquial Santiago Apóstol CHURCH

The formidable parish church was built by the Franciscans in the mid-16th century. A memorial plaque just inside the entrance on your right commemorates Father Stanley Francis Rother, a missionary priest from Oklahoma. Beloved by the local people, Rother was murdered by ultrarightists in the parish rectory next door in 1981; the bedroom where he slept remains open to visitors.

Along the walls of the church are wooden statues of the saints, each of whom has new clothes made by local women every year. At the front stand three colonial altarpieces that were renovated between 1976 and 1981 by brothers Diego Chávez Petzey and Nicolás Chávez Sojuel. These symbolize the three volcanoes around Santiago, which are believed to protect the town. The central one was subtly changed from a traditional European vision of heaven to a more Maya representation of a sacred mountain with two *cofradía* members climbing toward a sacred cave.

Parque de Paz MEMORIAL

(Peace Park) During the civil war, Santiago became the first village in the country to succeed in expelling the army, following a notorious massacre of 13 villagers on December 2, 1990. The site of this massacre, where troops were encamped, is now the small Parque de Paz, about 1km south of the Parque Central along the road toward San Pedro La Laguna.

Activities

There are several rewarding **day hikes** around Santiago. Most enticing of all are the three volcanoes in the vicinity: Tolimán, Atitlán and San Pedro. Before attempting a climb, enquire about the current security situation. It's best to go with a guide; the Posada de Santiago can set up a reliable one. Guided volcano climbs are about Q450 for two to five people.

Less daunting a challenge than the massive volcanoes in the vicinity, **Cerro de Oro** (1892m) still yields great views and features several Maya ceremonial sites. It's some 8km northeast, about halfway between Santiago and San Lucas Tolimán.

Another worthy destination is the **Mirador de Tepepul**, about 4km south of Santiago, near where the inlet ends (four to five hours round trip, Q250 per person). The hike goes through cloud forest populated with many birds, including parakeets, curassows, swifts, boat-tailed grackles and tucanets, and on to a lookout point with views all the way to the coast.

The pre-Hispanic Tz'utujil capital of **Chuitinamit** is across the inlet from Santiago. The hilltop archaeological site features some carved petroglyphs as well as fanciful painted carvings of more recent vintage. From the dock, it's a 20-minute hike to the top, where there are good views of Santiago. Milpas Tours can take you across the inlet by *cayuco* and accompany you up the tenuous trail to the site.

Tours

At Cojolya Association, you can join 'Meet the Weavers' tours (Q80, in Spanish). You'll visit three traditional homes where women demonstrate how to set up a backstrap loom, warp the threads and perform the *jaspe* technique, a form of Japanese tie-dye that reached Guatemala through indirect contact with Spain's Pacific trade routes.

Dolores Ratzan Pablo CULTURAL

(☎5730-4570; dolores_ratzan@yahoo.com) This English-speaking Tz'utujil woman can introduce you to the wonders of Maya birthing and healing, point out examples of Maya-Catholic syncretism at the church and *cofradías,* and describe the incidents that led to the massacre at the Parque de Paz in 1990. Tours typically last two hours and cost Q300 per person.

Milpas Tours CULTURAL TOUR

(☎5450-2381; milpastours@yahoo.es) INGUAT-authorized local guide Miguel Pablo Sicay is a personable *atiteco* who leads various fascinating tours in and around Santiago Atitlán. He'll lead you up to the observation point of Rey Tepepul (Q225), near where the inlet ends; show you the temporary shrine devoted to locally worshiped saint Maximón (Q180); or convey you by *cayuco* (wooden rowboat) to the ancient Tz'utujil capital of Chutinamit.

Sleeping

Hotel Ratzán HOTEL $
(☎7721-7840; Calle Principal; s/d Q80/160;) This budget option, near the center of town, is a family-run establishment with nice wood-beam ceilings and large, modern bathrooms. Only three of the five rooms have exterior windows but considering it's just down the street from the massive Evangelical church, with raucous nightly services, maybe that's a good thing.

Hotel La Estrella HOTEL $$
(☎7721-7814; www.hotel-laestrella.blogspot.com; Calle Campo; s/d/tr Q180/320/450; P) This good value option is a short walk north of the ferry dock along the San Lucas road. It has modern, comfortable units with handsome wood ceilings and locally woven bedspreads. Room 13, adjacent to the top terrace, takes best advantage of the hotel's lakeside position, looking straight across the inlet at Volcán San Pedro. There's a small restaurant, too.

Hotel Bambú LODGE $$$
(☎7721-7332; www.ecobambu.com; Carretera San Lucas Tolimán Km 16; s/d/tr incl breakfast Q550/700/820; P) The Bambú is an ecologically harmonious hotel on the outskirts of Santiago. Scattered around wild yet manicured grounds, the 10 spacious rooms are in grass- or bamboo-roofed buildings, with cypress fittings and earthy tile floors. A pebbly path leads to a swimming pool, hot tub and sauna in a serene, jungly setting. The restaurant and several rooms have divine lake views.

If you're arriving by boat, ask to be dropped off at the hotel's own dock or take a *tuk-tuk* from town.

Posada de Santiago LODGE $$$
(☎7721-7366; www.posadadesantiago.com; s/d Q300/400, cottages Q500-1200; P@) Somewhere between rustic and luxurious, the North American–owned *posada* makes a great retreat. Seven cottages (some sleeping six) and five suites, all with stone walls, fireplaces, porches, hammocks and folk art, are set amid rambling gardens. Across the road stretches a lakeside resort with pool and bar. The restaurant is celebrated locally for its eggs benedict with blue corn tortillas.

The *posada* is 1.5km from the town dock. Catch a *tuk-tuk* (Q10) or hire a *lancha* over to the hotel's own dock.

Eating & Drinking

Comedor Santa Rita GUATEMALAN $
(Calle de Santa Rita 88; lunch Q25-30; 7am-9pm Mon-Fri) The latest incarnation of a generations-old dining hall, this is a good place to try such Maya specialties as *pulique* (a veggie-rich stew) and *patín* (an Atitlán fish stew) served with a stack of tortillas. Half a block east of the Parque Central.

Restaurant El Gran Sol GUATEMALAN $$
(☎4271-4642; Cantón Tzanjuyú; mains Q55; 8am-7pm Mon-Sat) One block up from the dock on the left, this highly popular family-run establishment is a great bet for breakfast, lunch or snacks, with a spiffy kitchen and breezy deck over a busy junction. Thelma and clan love to cook; try the soups, pancakes or quesadillas (with homemade cheese).

Café Quila's PUB
(5-10pm Wed-Sun) Quila's is a casual gathering place where expats and lake dwellers can bond over sports TV or table tennis. Good burgers and other bar food is served in the cozy front lounge or rear patio with a mural of Santiago. Coming up from the dock, take the first right.

Shopping

Colorful textiles, wooden animals, beadwork jewelry, leather belts and paintings are produced and sold at workshops along the street leading up from the dock. For contemporary bags, clothing and accessories with Tz'utujil elements, check out the excellent Cojolya Association of Maya Women Weavers (p106).

Information

G&T Continental (8:30am-5pm Mon-Fri, 9am-1pm Sat) There's a Cajero 5B ATM at G&T Continental, on the south side of the Parque Central.

Hospitalito Atitlán (☎7721-7683; www.hospitalitoatitlan.org; Canton Ch'utch'aj) The Nuevo Hospitalito Atitlán, on the way out of town toward San Lucas Tolimán, is a modern hospital staffed by English-speaking doctors and American volunteers.

Getting There & Away

Boats leave hourly from Santiago's **dock** for San Pedro La Laguna (Q25, 30 minutes) and slightly more frequently to Panajachel (Q25, 30 minutes). Pick-ups to Cerro de Oro and San Lucas Tolimán depart from in front of the market. Buses to Guatemala City (Q40, 3½ hours) leave every half hour from 3am to 6am, then hourly until 3pm, from the main plaza.

There is a weekday tourist shuttle (Q150, three hours) to El Paredón, operated by **Pacifico Surf Transport** (www.facebook.com/pacificsurfgt).

San Pedro La Laguna

POP 12,300 / ELEV 1592M

Spreading onto a peninsula at the base of the volcano of the same name, San Pedro remains among the most visited of the lakeside villages – due as much to its reasonably priced accommodations and global social scene as to its spectacular setting. It's a backpacker haven – travelers tend to dig in here for a spell, in pursuit of (in no particular order) drinking, fire-twirling, African drumming, Spanish classes, volcano hiking, hot-tub soaking, partying and hammock swinging.

While this scene unfolds around the lakefront, up the hill San Pedro follows more traditional rhythms. Clad in indigenous outfits, the predominantly Tz'utujil *pedranos* (as the locals are called) congregate around the market zone. You'll see coffee being picked on the volcano's slopes and spread out to dry on wide platforms at the beginning of the dry season.

Sights

Museo Tz'unun 'Ya MUSEUM

(6a Av; Q35; 8am-noon & 2-5pm Mon-Fri) This museum focuses on the history of the Tz'utujil people and geology of the region, with a film on the formation of the lake and an interesting gallery of colorized photos of San Pedro in former days. As a bonus, staff will identify and interpret your *nahual* (animal counterpart), based on your birth date according to the Maya calendar.

Activities

Looming above the village, **Volcán San Pedro** (3020m) almost demands to be climbed by anyone with an adventurous spirit and a reasonable level of fitness. It is the most accessible of the three volcanoes in the zone and, classified as a municipal ecological park, it's regularly patrolled by tourism police.

Guides (required) take you up from San Pedro for around Q130, including entrance fee. Start your climb at dawn.

The ascent is through fields of maize, beans and squash, followed by primary cloud forest. It's a three- to -four-hour climb and two hours back down; take water, snacks, a hat and sunblock.

Another popular hike goes up the hill referred to as **Indian Nose** – its skyline resembles the profile of an ancient Maya dignitary. **Asoantur** (4379-4545; www.facebook.com/asoantur; 4a Av A 3-60; 7am-7pm), an association made up of 16 INGUAT-authorized guides from the local community, leads expeditions to the peak for Q100 per person. It also offers cultural tours of San Pedro and nearby coffee plantations, horseback-riding tours, and kayak, bicycle and motorbike rentals. It operates from a hut on the lane up from the Pana dock.

Geo Travel HIKING

(3168-8625; www.geotravelguatemala.com) These tours, led by a geology expert, focus on the natural environment. One popular tour ascends before dawn to the Rostro Maya (Indian Nose; Q200 per person), from which you may observe eight volcanoes, and learn how they came to stand in a line and how Lago de Atitlán was formed.

Overnight trips to Santiaguito, Fuego and Pacaya (all active volcanoes) are offered, for around Q700 per person.

Solar Pools SPA

(7a Av 2-22; Q40; 11am-5pm) After a day's hiking or cycling, it's time for a good soak in one of these spring-fed pools, near the bend in the trail between the two docks. Book ahead so that your pool is already hot when you arrive.

Courses

San Pedro is making a name for itself in the language game with ultra-economical rates at its various Spanish institutes. The standard price for four hours of one-on-one classes, five days a week, is Q900. Accommodations with a local family, with three meals daily (except Sunday) typically cost Q50. Volcano hikes, Maya culture seminars and dance classes are among the extracurricular activities offered.

Community Spanish School LANGUAGE

(5466-7177; www.communityspanishschool.com) A professionally managed school staffed by accredited local instructors, who lead one-on-one classes in thatched huts along a strip of garden running down to the lakefront.

San Pedro Spanish School LANGUAGE

(5715-4604; www.sanpedrospanishschool.org; 7a Av 2-20) Well-organized school on the street between the two docks, with consistently good reviews. Classes are held under thatched-roof huts amid an attractive garden setting. The school supports Niños del Lago, an organization that provides education, health care and nutrition for local Tz'utujil children. It has a sister school in San Marcos using the same curriculum.

Celas Maya LANGUAGE
(☎5933-1450; www.spanishschool.com.gt) The lake branch of the prestigious Quetzaltenango institute takes documentaries, TV reports and storytelling as the basis for one-on-one classes aimed at building speaking and listening skills. Classes in Tz'utujil are also offered. It's at the end of the lakefront trail from the Pana dock.

Casa Rosario LANGUAGE
(☎in US 415-282-7684; www.casarosario.com) Classes at San Pedro's first Spanish school are held in little huts amid gardens near the lake. Weaving classes and *huipil* appreciation (from the owner's voluminous collection) are among the extracurricular activities. In addition to homestays, language learners may stay in one of the primitive elevated shelters on the premises.

Sleeping

San Pedro does not lack for accommodations, particularly at the budget end of the spectrum. Most hotels charge a slight premium for rooms with a lake view. Deals are there to be had for long stays or during low season, along with rooms and houses to rent – ask around.

Mr Mullet's Hostel HOSTEL $
(☎4419-0566; www.mrmullets.com; incl breakfast dm Q60, r with/without bathroom Q140/95;) This party point in lakeside San Pedro overflows with fun seekers who pile into the four-bed dorms and cell-like private rooms on two levels or crowd the hammocks in the patio/bar at rear, which shuts at 11pm for those who actually want to sleep. From the Pana dock, it's a five-minute walk to the left.

Hostel Fe HOSTEL $
(☎3486-7027; www.hostelfe.com; incl breakfast dm Q75, r Q200;) Fe's flag-draped front is unmissable if you arrive in San Pedro by boat. It's a massive concrete block 100m south of the Pana dock. It's a destination of choice for global youth, who come more for the lively waterfront cafe and sundeck bar (with waterslide) than the sparsely furnished steel-doored rooms and dorms.

Zoola HOSTEL $
(☎5847-4857; dm Q60, r with/without bathroom Q170/140;) 'Ultra-laid-back' best describes this Israeli-run establishment. It's reached down a long, jungly boardwalk opposite the Museo Tz'unun 'Ya. Behind the cafe/chill-out lounge, low adobe blocks of dorms extend to the lake, where a canopied swimming pool is the focus of nightly parties. Two-night minimum stay.

Hotel Peneleu HOTEL $
(☎7721-8182; 5a Av 2-20, Zona 2; s/d Q50/100, without bathroom Q40/80;) One of several ultra-budget options along a side street, this concrete tower offers modestly furnished rooms with frayed curtains and wayward electric showers. It's all about the views, however; fly a kite from the amazing top terrace looking down on the lake. To find it, walk 500m up from the dock and turn left; or take a *tuk-tuk* up the steep approach.

Hotel Gran Sueño HOTEL $
(☎7721-8110; 8a Calle 4-40, Zona 2; s/d Q100/175;) Though certainly not in the prettiest part of town, beyond its plant-draped entryway and up a spiral staircase are bright rooms with colorful abstract designs, comfortable beds and uniquely designed bathrooms. Rooms 9 and 11 are fantastic lake-view perches. From the Pana dock, it's a few doors left of the first crossing.

Hotel Mansión del Lago HOTEL $
(☎7721-8124; www.hotelmansiondellago.com; 3a Vía & 4a Av, Zona 2; s/d/tr Q100/150/225;) This massive L-shaped property is high above the Santiago dock and is brilliant value. Sparkling clean rooms are done up in cloud or dove motifs, with rockers on wide balconies looking right at Indian Nose. There'a nice cafe out front, and an in-house laundry.

Hotel María Elena HOTEL $
(☎4771-0508; s/d/tr Q150/250/350;) No more than 200m northeast of the Pana dock, this yellow block stands perpendicular to the lakefront – locals bathe and wash their clothing off the rocks nearby. Though the rooms lack views, they are spacious and well maintained, and you can enjoy the breeze swinging on a hammock along the broad terrace.

Hotel Sak'cari El Amanecer HOTEL $$
(☎7721-8096; www.hotel-sakcari.com; 7a Av 2-12, Zona 2; s/d/tr Q275/305/385; P) About midway along the trail between the two

docks, the Sak'cari (Tz'utujil for 'sunrise') has 20 clean wood-paneled rooms with lots of shelves. Rooms at the rear are best (and priciest), with big balconies overlooking the lake past a landscaped lawn that's a splendid place for hammock swinging. More active guests can grab a kayak and navigate the lake.

Hotel Mikaso HOTEL **$$**
(☎7721-8232; www.mikasohotel.com; 4a Callejon A-88; dm Q60, s/d/tr from Q150/180/300; 📶) The Mikaso stands proudly at Atitlán's shores, surrounded by local kitchen gardens. Big rooms with carved wood furniture and ceiling fans ring a garden bursting with birds of paradise; a few have private patios. The rooftop bar/restaurant has fantastic lake views and a baby grand piano, plus there's a deck/lounge that features a Jacuzzi and pool table.

Eating

Blue Parrot BURGERS
(7a Avenida; burgers from Q50) Airy sports bar that does a wicked line in over two dozen different gourmet burgers, plus chilli dogs and seriously filled sandwiches to go down with its extensive range of craft beers. Friday night is seafood night, and there's always a scene when there's a big match on.

Smokin Joe's BARBECUE
(☎7721-8381; ⏲7am-5pm Sun-Fri; 📶) The pool on the grounds of campground/cafe Chuasinayi is a global gathering place, particularly on Sundays when a character known as Smokin' Joe barbecues baby back ribs by the dozen and other meaty treats. Coming from the Santiago dock, take the first right and go along 100m or so.

Shanti Shanti ISRAELI **$**
(6a Av; mains Q20-30; ⏲7am-11pm; 🌱) With terraced seating cascading down to the lakeside, this makes a pleasant perch for Mideast staples such as falafel, baba ghanoush and hummus, plus hearty soups.

Hummus-Ya MIDDLE EASTERN **$$**
(6 Av A, Zona 2; platters Q25-50; ⏲11am-10pm Mon-Sun) *Sabich*, an Israeli sandwich lovingly stuffed with hard-boiled eggs, hummus, and fried eggplant, is just one highlight on the menu at this cheerful Mideast eatery upstairs, midway between the Pana and Santiago docks. Order rounds of hummus, baba ghanoush, Moroccan lentils and Iraqi filo pastry rolls stuffed with ground beef and feta.

Drinking & Nightlife

San Pedro has something of a hard-partying reputation, and while authorities have regular clean-ups of backpacker excesses, there are still plenty of bars. Many *pedranos* steer well clear and prefer to spend their evenings shouting the Lord's praises at evangelical congregations.

D'Juice Girls JUICE BAR
(juices from Q20; ⏲7am-11pm) D'Juice Girls are young Hebrew-speaking Tz'utujil women who squeeze the tropical fruits of Guatemala into supernutritious combos, such as carrot-ginger-beet. This popular stand is a five-minute walk east of the Pana dock.

Café Las Cristalinas CAFE
(⏲7am-9pm; 📶) To savor a shot of the coffee grown on the surrounding slopes (and roasted here), head for this thatched-roof structure on the way up from the Pana dock to the center of town. Come for breakfast and be sure as well to try the excellent banana bread, which you may enjoy on various inviting terraces.

Bar Sublime BAR
(⏲noon-1am) Bar Sublime is the current epicenter of San Pedro's party scene. During the day its lakefront terraces are pretty relaxed and you can enjoy good sandwiches, pasta and salads, but things ramp up as the sun starts to dip. Expect cheap mixers, thumping music and crowds of the young, the beautiful and the slightly disheveled.

El Barrio PUB
(7a Av 2-07, Zona 2; ⏲5pm-1am) This boisterous pub on the path between the two docks has one of the most happening happy hours in town (5pm to 8pm). Every night has a different theme; we particularly liked the curry night on Saturdays.

Shopping

Grupo Ecológico Teixchel CLOTHING
(☎5932-0000; www.teixchel.org; ⏲8:30am-noon & 2-6pm) This is a Tz'utujil women's collective that sells fair-trade woven goods and offers weaving classes for Q30 per hour (not including materials). It's about 150m uphill from the Pana dock toward the center of town.

Information

ATM There's a Cajero 5B ATM just up from the Panajachel dock on the left.

Banrural (8:30am-5pm Mon-Fri, 9am-1pm Sat) You can change cash US dollars and euros here, two blocks east of the market in the town center; has a Visa ATM.

Clínica Los Volcanes (7823-7656; www.clinicalosvolcanes.com) A private clinic providing medical and dental services, with English-speaking staff. It's near the Pana dock.

Getting There & Away

San Pedro has two docks, one for Panajachel and villages on the northern shore, and another for Santiago Atitlán.

From **Pana Dock**, boats to Panajachel (Q25) run every half hour or so from 6am to 5pm. Some go direct; others make stops at San Juan (though it's quicker to take a *tuk-tuk* direct), San Marcos (Q10) and Jaibalito/Santa Cruz (Q20) en route.

From **Santiago Dock**, boats to Santiago (Q25, 25 minutes) run hourly from 6am to 4pm.

San Pedro's main **bus stop** is outside the Catholic church. Buses leave hourly from 3am to 2pm for Guatemala City (Q60, four hours) and seven buses leave for Quetzaltenango (Q40, three hours) between 4:45am and 1:30pm Monday to Saturday. Buses to both destinations travel via Santiago, and have reduced services on Sunday.

San Pedro's myriad travel agencies can sell tickets for the twice-daily tourist shuttle to Antigua (Q80, two hours) and onward connections.

San Juan La Laguna

POP 12,400 / ELEV 1605M

San Juan La Laguna is just 2km east by road from busy San Pedro, on a rise above a spectacular bay, but this neat, mellow village has escaped many of the excesses of its neighbor, and some travelers find it a more tranquil setting in which to study Spanish or experience local life. San Juan is special: the Tz'utujil inhabitants take pride in their craft traditions – particularly painting and weaving – and have developed their own tourism infrastructure to highlight their culture to outsiders.

Perhaps part of what makes it all run so well is the communal spirit: coffee growers, fishers, organic farmers, natural dyers and widows are among the like-minded groups who've formed cooperatives here.

As you wander around the village, you'll notice various murals depicting aspects of Tz'utujil life and legend.

Courses

Eco Spanish School LANGUAGE

(4727-6481; www.ecolanguages.net; 20 hrs from Q900) Located on a coffee plantation with views of the lake, this school offers one-on-one classes based on an immersion methodology with opportunities to experience Tz'utujil culture. It can arrange homestays with local families. A path to the school is signed near the Catholic church.

Tours

Rupalaj K'istalin TOURS

(5930-4773; www.rupalajkistalin.com; 8am-5pm) The association offers a worthwhile tour of San Juan La Laguna's points of interest, led by indigenous guides (Q110 per person), in Spanish. You'll visit two weaving cooperatives, both of which use dyes from native plants, and an art studio/gallery featuring the Tz'utujil primitivist painting style. The office is a short walk up the hill from the dock.

Other tours offered include trips with local fishers in rustic *cayucos* to learn about traditional lake fishing techniques and a demonstration of the harvesting of the lakeshore reeds, which are used as material for *petates*, the woven mats the town is known for.

The association can also set up guides for one-way walks to San Marcos La Laguna, returning by *lancha*, and hikes up Rupalaj K'istalin, the mountain that towers above San Juan and is the site of Maya religious rituals.

Sleeping

★ **Mayachik'** LODGE $

(4218-4675; www.mayachik.com; dm Q70, bungalows Q140-350; P) Immediately southwest of town, this European-managed ecoresort blends harmoniously with its surroundings. Traditional wood and stone accommodations with compost toilets and solar-powered showers include a circular bungalow, eight-bed dorm, and at the top of the hill a large adobe house with three bedrooms. A kitchen prepares vegetarian and vegan meals alongside homegrown coffee.

Spanish classes and getting involved with community development projects are options.

Hotel Pa Muelle HOTEL $

(4141-0820; hotelpamuelle@turbonett.com; Camino al Muelle; s/d Q120/200) This small but delightful hotel has a delightful setting, with

ATITLÁN RISING

At San Juan La Laguna an art gallery is half submerged, its upper floor abandoned. At Tzununá, only the roof is visible of what used to be a shelter for waiting boat passengers. And in Panajachel the public beach has been washed off the map. New docks have been built in all the lakeside villages, and in Santa Cruz, a plank walk has replaced the lakeside trail, now underwater. It may appear that a tsunami or some similar disaster has struck. But what's actually happening is that the lake level is rising, inexorably – around 5m since 2009. In the process, it keeps swallowing dwellings and businesses, most of them owned by outsiders. Foreign residents are learning the hard way why it is that almost all local towns are built well above the lakeshore. The lake's capricious behavior is well lodged in the community's collective memory. The elders of Atitlán know of its cyclical rise and fall, a phenomenon noted as far back as the 16th century by the Spanish conquistadors. The water level has been considerably higher in the past and it will no doubt drop again. In the meantime, the rising trend is the talk of the lake, with various theories proposed. Some attribute it to the deforestation of the lakeside slopes, which causes soil erosion. When Tropical Storm Agatha hit in 2010, it might have washed a great deal of this sediment into the lake, clogging the crevices in its basin that provide natural drainage. A more authoritative theory attributes the phenomenon to the lake's volcanic origins. According to this view, seismic activity heats the ground beneath the lake bed and forms a sort of subterranean 'bladder' that keeps expanding until exit vents appear. This periodic expansion causes the lake level to rise.

blue rooms along a patch of lawn high above the lake. A plant-laden lounge/restaurant provides even more fantastic views. It's near the top of the hill coming up from the dock.

Uxlabil Eco Hotel HOTEL $$

(☎5990-6016; www.uxlabil.com; N-14 Km 175; s/d incl breakfast Q350/450) The Uxlabil stands on a small coffee plantation on the southern edge of San Juan's bay. Made by local artisans from natural materials, the four-level structure blends seamlessly into the hillside gardens that are rich in birdlife. Featuring hand-carved stone trimmings, all the rooms face the lake and have excellent terraces looking straight at the Rostro Maya.

The restaurant serves organic food and coffee. You can ask to be dropped off at the dock; if arriving from the town, hike down to the lake and follow the path along the bank.

Eating

Alma de Colores VEGETARIAN $

(☎4261-2646; www.almadecolores.org; set lunch Q30; ⏱8am-5pm Mon-Fri) Bread, pizza and focaccia are baked at this pleasant open-air bakery/cafe on the way out to San Pablo, and there are two lunch options daily prepared with vegetables from a local organic farm. It's run by an Italian NGO as part of a program to integrate young adults with disabilities into the workplace.

Comedor Elenita GUATEMALAN $

(Calle al Estadio Municipal; set lunch Q35; ⏱7am-10pm) Locals crowd in for the daily specials at this no-nonsense dining hall in the center of town, where a brimming bowl of *caldo de res* (beef and vegetable soup) served with rice, avocado and tortillas, is well within anyone's budget.

★**Café El Artesano** CHEESE $$

(☎4555-4773; Salida a Guatemala; cheese or smoked meat platter Q125, sharing platters per person Q110; ⏱noon-4pm Mon-Fri) El Artesano offers one of Guatemala's best dining experiences. Let the staff guide you around the platter of two dozen cheeses (all produced in Guatemala and aged in-house), from creamy goat through blue to hard pecorino, served with fruits, nuts, jams, pickles and artisan breads. The same is on offer for some extraordinary home-smoked meats.

Everything is served under a delightful rustic arbor, with perfectly matched wines. When the food is this good, you'll understand why reservations are essential.

Getting There & Away

It's a 40 minute boat ride between San Juan and Pana (Q25), stopping at all points on the north of the lake – fun if you're not in a rush. Otherwise it can sometime be quicker to catch a *tuk-tuk* (Q10) to/from San Pedro, with its more frequent boat connections.

San Marcos La Laguna

POP 5800 / ELEV 1580M

One of the prettiest of the lakeside villages, San Marcos La Laguna lives a double life. The mostly Maya community occupies the higher ground, while expats and visitors cover a flat jungly patch toward the shoreline with paths snaking through banana, coffee and avocado trees. The two converge under the spreading *matapalo* (strangler fig) tree of the central plaza.

San Marcos has become a magnet for global seekers, who believe the place has a spiritual energy that's conducive to learning and practicing meditation, holistic therapies, massage, Reiki and other spiritually oriented activities. Whatever you're into, it's a great spot to kick back and distance the everyday world for a spell. Lago de Atitlán is beautiful and clean here, and you can swim off the rocks.

It's an outlandish melange of cultures – evangelical Christians, self-styled shamans, Kaqchiquel farmers and visionary artists – against a backdrop of incredible natural beauty.

Boats put in at a central dock below Posada Schumann. The path leading from there to the village center, and a parallel one about 100m west, are the main axes for most visitors.

Sights

Cerro Tzankujil NATURE RESERVE
(Q15; 8am-6pm) This nature reserve is on a sacred hill west of San Marcos village. Well-maintained pebbly trails lead to swimming areas with shelters by the bank and a diving platform. The water is crystal clear here. A branch off the main trail ascends to a Maya altar on the summit, while a lower spur reaches a volcano lookout.

Activities

San Marcos is the place to come if you want to spend your time refocusing your energies with yoga, meditation, Reiki and a host of alternative healing techniques.

Yoga Forest YOGA
(3301-1835; www.theyogaforest.org; yoga classes Q50) Up in the hills north of town amid lush forest, this is a blissfully secluded perch to learn and practice shamanic healing and other esoteric arts, with a magnificent yoga platform built into the hillside. A cafe prepares vegetarian food and accommodations are available in shared adobe *cabañas* with thatched roofs and magnificent lake views.

There are daily morning yoga classes, but most visitors like to take extended yoga and mediation retreats. There are other wellness offerings such as Thai massage; check the website for the current program.

East-West Center MASSAGE
(3102-4666; 1hr massage Q250) Deep tissue massage, reflexology, acupuncture and Bach flowers are among the holistic therapies offered here, along with workshops in I-Ching readings, herbal remedies and so on. It's near the top of the main trail from the dock.

Las Pirámides Meditation Center MEDITATION
(5205-7302; www.laspiramidesdelka.com; 75min yoga & meditation sessions Q50) This retreat by the lake has been providing spiritual guidance for more than two decades. Most structures on the property are pyramidal in shape and oriented to the four cardinal points, including the two temples where sessions are held. A one-month personal development course begins every full moon, with three sessions daily (Q6000).

There's also a three-month solar course running from each equinox to the following solstice (the moon course is a prerequisite). Nonguests can come for the morning meditation or Hatha yoga sessions. Accommodations are available to course participants in pyramid-shaped houses, including use of the sauna and access to the esoteric library. The center also has a vegetarian restaurant and room to wander about in the medicinal herb garden.

Courses

San Marcos Spanish School LANGUAGE COURSE
(5715-4604; www.sanmarcosspanishschool.org; 20 hrs Q1200) This small chain has three Spanish schools around the lake (the others are in San Pedro and San Juan). Homestays are available, and as a nice touch, kids' classes are available if you're travelling with children. Find it near the soccer ground.

Fé Cookery Classes COOKING
(3009-5537; pcsa1521@gmail.com; classes Q225) Restaurant Fé has two branches on opposite sides of the street – the one on the right as

you walk up from the dock hosts cookery classes. With advance notice you can learn to cook almost anything you like over three hours, but most people start with the Guatemalan basics, from tortillas and tamales to rich stews like *pepián* and *jocón*.

Festivals & Events

Cosmic Convergence CULTURAL
(www.cosmicconvergencefestival.org; festival pass Q1120; Dec/Jan) Held in San Marcos for three days over new year, Cosmic Convergence is an arts, spirit and eco festival. Expect everything from Maya religion to permaculture to new-tech.

Festival of Consciousness CULTURAL
(www.festivalofconsciousness.weebly.com; festival pass Q475; Mar) Held around the spring equinox, this weekend festival is devoted to expansion of environmental, social and spiritual awareness. A cavalcade of workshops on everything from mindfulness to holistic health takes place during the day, followed by live music at night, and to wrap things up, the obligatory fire ceremony.

Sleeping

There aren't any street signs but most lodgings have posted their own fancifully painted versions to point you in the right direction. If you're heading here for one of the festivals, book well in advance.

★ **Circles** HOSTEL $
(3327-8961; www.circles-cafe.com; dm Q100, s/d Q175/200) Near the top of the path from the dock is this casual hostel/cafe with an attached bakery and coffee roaster to provide the essentials of a good stay. Upstairs are two private rooms and a thoughtfully designed dorm with curtains on each bunk. A chill-out terrace looks over a garden with shady cushioned nooks.

Hostel San Marcos HOSTEL $
(3009-5537; www.hostelsanmarcos.com; dm Q50, r incl breakfast Q120, without bathroom Q100) This features seven rustic cabins (three log, four stone) in two separate banks with large front windows (which unfortunately cannot be opened) and a six-bed dorm in the old house at the rear. Take your complimentary breakfast at Restaurant Fe, closer to the center. To get to the hostel from the dock, take the first left.

Hotel Jinava Bay RESORT $$
(5299-3311; www.hoteljinava.com; r with/without bathroom Q380/300; P) Cobbled paths weave through gardens bursting with flowers, coffee, palms and a profusion of hummingbirds at this tropical lakeside location 300m west of the village. Bungalows are terraced down the hillside, with jaw-dropping views over the bay – though the lower ones are nicer, with stone walls and beds of tropical hardwoods. Children may not stay here.

Reception is by the lakefront restaurant, so it's best approached by boat – it's a long steep walk down from the road.

Dragon Hotel BOUTIQUE HOTEL $$
(3109-7707; www.eldragonhotel.com; r from Q470;) This lakefront spread created by a North American artist could be the wackiest of San Marcos lodgings. Signs of artistic exuberance pop up everywhere, from the dining area with its hanging spheres to the waterfront deck/bar with its trademark serpent, but not at the expense of luxury. Uniquely designed rooms feature plasma TVs, loft beds and private terraces.

The kitchen is equally inspired; the key lime pie here is legendary. To find El Dragon, head east off the main trail past Restaurante Fé and follow this lane to a football field; look for the horned monster at the far right corner.

Posada Schumann HOTEL $$
(5202-2216; www.laposadaschumann.com; s/d with breakfast from Q345/500, r without bathroom Q185) Set in gardens that stretch right to the shores of Lago de Atitlán, Posada Schumann has neat rooms in stone or wooden cottages, some with kitchens. An idyllic cafe deck looks over the water. Don't miss the igloo-shaped sauna (included in the room rate, along with kayaks). San Marcos' main dock is right outside the gate.

Hostal del Lago HOSTEL $$
(3227-9077; dm Q80, s/d Q200/250, without bathroom Q150/200) This ramshackle locale by the lakefront east of the center has a theatrical flair, with impromptu performances on a regular basis. Enthusiastically managed, it shelters legions of global drifters who settle into a series of psychedelically painted cottages. You can feed on lovely vegetarian food in the cafe (mains from Q35) or join the free daily yoga sessions on a raised platform by the water.

Lush BOUTIQUE HOTEL $$$
(www.lushatitlan.com; r Q375-1300;) Truly chic Lush seems to sprout organically from the living rock of the hillside, with recycled glass, plastic and other flotsam ingeniously incorporated as construction materials. Each of its seven suites and three rooms is unique, with handcrafted furnishings and beautiful stained-glass windows; most feature private balconies with lake or garden views.

Long-term stay rates are available and accommodations also include kitchens. There are also a few budget rooms available on a drop-in basis only (Q185). From the dock, it's a six-minute walk to the left (west) along the lakeside path.

Eating

★ **Comedor Konojel** GUATEMALAN $
(daily specials Q30) This cheerily-painted clapboard canteen serves up big healthy portions of Guatemalan food according to a changing daily menu to help support a wider feeding program and other community projects in the area around San Marcos. Doing good rarely tastes so delicious.

Moonfish HEALTH FOOD $
(sandwiches & burritos Q30; 7:30am-8pm Wed-Mon;) Along the main thoroughfare west of the square, Moonfish whips up healthy fare including tempeh sandwiches, tofu scrambles and mighty fine falafel with ingredients fresh from the garden.

Comedor Mi Marquensita Susi GUATEMALAN $
(Comedor Mi Marquensita; Parque Central; set lunch Q30; 8am-5pm Mon-Sat) This 'mom and pop' store on the central plaza is popular with expats after a cheap, home-cooked meal, which might explain why tofu dishes pop up among the chicken and pork chops.

Restaurante Fé INTERNATIONAL $$
(mains Q55-80; 7:30am-10pm;) Fé, about midway down the main trail, offers informal candlelit dining in a pleasant, open-air hall with a tree in the middle. The pastas, pan-fried fish and particularly the curries are all well worth savoring here, and the mulligatawny stew is excellent. A good place to while away the evening.

Blind Lemon's BURGERS $$
(www.blindlemons.com; mains Q55-70; noon-10pm;) This hangout brings a hint of Mississippi to Atitlán, with weekly blues jams in a colonial-style mansion. The menu features chicken platters, Cajun-blackened fish, pizza, burgers and other gringo comfort food. It's at the top of the western path.

Information

Visit San Marcos (www.visit-sanmarcos.com) A useful village information board, with directory and events listings.

Getting There & Away

Boats run throughout the day between San Marcos and Panajachel (Q20, 20 minutes). The last dependable boat to Santa Cruz La Laguna and Panajachel departs about 5pm.

A gravel road runs east from San Marcos to Tzununá and a paved one west to San Pablo, where it meets the road running from the Interamericana to San Pedro La Laguna. You can travel between San Marcos and San Pedro by pick-up, with a transfer at San Pablo.

Jaibalito

POP 750 / ELEV 1562M

This tiny Kaqchiquel hamlet is only accessible by boat (a 20-minute *lancha* ride from Panajachel or San Pedro, Q20) or on foot via a ridgeline trail from Santa Cruz La Laguna, 4km to the east (45 minutes). The hike west to San Marcos (6km) is equally picturesque. Deliciously, there are a couple of great places to stay if you really want to get away from it all.

Sleeping & Eating

Posada Jaibalito HOSTEL $
(5192-4334; dm/s/d Q40/70/100;) Jaibalito's budget choice is just up from the dock on the left. The German-owned operation is remarkable value, with dorm and a few private rooms occupying a garden flanked by coffee plants and solar panels. Authentic bratwurst and goulash (Q25) are served at the cafe, along with cold beer and shots of aged Zacapa rum.

★ **La Casa del Mundo Hotel & Café** HOTEL $$$
(5218-5332; www.lacasadelmundo.com; Q355-700) On a secluded cliff facing the volcanoes is one of Guatemala's most spectacular hotels. It features sumptuous gardens, lake swimming from Mediterranean-style terraces, and a wood-fired hot tub overhanging the lake. The best rooms seem to float above

the water, with no land visible beneath. Every room is outfitted with comfortable beds, Guatemalan fabrics and fresh flowers. Reservations are recommended.

The restaurant prepares a toothsome four-course dinner (Q85 to Q95), served family style. You can rent kayaks (Q50 per hour) for exploring the lake.

Club Ven Acá FUSION **$$**
(☎5122-6047; www.clubvenaca.com; mains Q65-130; ⏲10am-5pm Wed-Sun) Right at the dock is this trendy restaurant with a seasonally varying menu and a popular happy hour highlighted by purple-basil mojitos. Sunday brunch is a big deal with to-die-for eggs Benedict. When you're not eating, unwind in the hot tub or infinity pool.

Santa Cruz La Laguna

POP 9400

Santa Cruz fits the typically dual nature of the Atitlán villages, comprising both a waterfront resort (home of the lake's scuba-diving outfit) and an indigenous Kaqchiquel village. The village is about 600m uphill from the dock (there are *tuk-tuks* if you don't fancy the stiff walk). It's a lovely spot, with relaxing accommodations, activities on the water and a complete lack of hustle.

Activities

ATI Divers DIVING
(☎5706-4117; www.atidivers.com) Lago de Atitlán is one of the rare places in the world where you can dive at altitude without using a dry suit, and ATI Divers offers trips from Santa Cruz. These include a four-day PADI open-water diving certification course (Q220), as well as a PADI high-altitude course (Q750) and fun dives (Q480) for beginners.

Courses include accommodation at its base at La Iguana Perdida.

The lake fills a collapsed volcanic cone with bizarre geological formations and aquatic life such as cichlids, which spawn near an active fault line where hot water vents into the lake. Diving at altitude brings its own challenges – you need better control over your buoyancy, visibility is reduced and you cannot leave the lake the day of your final dive due to the change in atmospheric pressure. During the rainy season the water clouds up, so the best time to dive is between October and May.

Los Elementos Adventure Center KAYAKING
(☎5359-8328; www.kayakguatemala.com; kayak per hour Q60, 2-hr tour Q220, 2-day tour Q1250) This outfit offers kayaks and paddleboards to explore the lake, ranging from rental by the hour to fully supported and guided multi-day kayak and hiking tours around Atitlán. Its two-day paddle-and-hike tour includes a visit to Santa Catarina Palopó, followed by kayaking along the lake's northern shore and hiking along the old Maya trail through Tzununá and Jaibalito.

Its base is a 10-minute walk west of Santa Cruz along the lakeside track.

Amigos de Santa Cruz COOKING
(classes Q200) Part of same community development project as the Café Sabor Cruceño, you can take cooking classes here, and whip up a bowl of *pepián* stew, along with tortillas, *tamalitos* and *rellenitos*. Traditional weaving and beading classes are also available.

Sleeping & Eating

Free Cerveza TENTED CAMP
(☎5811-2001; www.freecerveza.com; dm tent Q75, s/d/tr tent Q120/212/254; 📶) When you go to a hostel that offers free beer, has a sign on its dock reminding guests that locals get upset by nude sunbathing, and operates a strict under-40s policy you know what you're going to get. And to be fair, Free Cerveza serves its target market well, and gets everyone together nightly for communal dinners.

The decision to make all accommodations tented is a brave one – they look great but swelter in the sun, and even when new at the start of the rainy season were already spotted with black mold.

★ **La Iguana Perdida** LODGE **$$**
(☎5706-4117; www.laiguanaperdida.com; dm Q50, s/d without bathroom Q115/150, r Q335-415; @📶) La Iguana Perdida is one of the granddaddies of Guatemala's backpacker scene, but you wouldn't know it from its ever-fresh appearance. It features a range of rooms, from basic dorm in an A-frame cabin to more decadent (an adobe structure with stylish furnishings and private balconies). Evening meals are served family style, making a stay here highly sociable.

The Iguana is a great hangout to enjoy the lake views and meet other travelers, go scuba diving or kayaking, or sweat it out in the sauna. There are regular evening events, from quiz nights to music and even barbeques where guests are encouraged to dive into the house dressing-up box.

Hotel Isla Verde GUESTHOUSE **$$**
(☎5760-2648; www.islaverdeatitlan.com; s/d cabin Q392/440, without bathroom Q296/344; 📶) This stylish, environmentally friendly lodging makes the most of its spectacular setting. A mosaic stone path winds through exuberant vegetation to the nine hillside cabins (six with private bathroom); the higher you go, the more jaw-dropping the picture-window views. Simple rooms are tastefully decorated with art and recycled elements. Bathrooms are jungle-chic affairs, and water and electricity are solar powered.

Stylish new family suites sleeping six were under construction when we visited. A lakeside terrace restaurant serves delicious cuisine, and there's a pavilion for yoga and meditation. It's a 10-minute walk west of the dock along the lakefront trail.

Casa de la Rosa GUESTHOUSE **$$**
(☎5803-2531; www.hotellacasarosa.com; s/d Q250/450, without bathroom Q200/300; 📶) Slightly east of the dock, this is a low-key lodging amid wonderfully lush gardens traversed by Gaudí-esque tiled paths. Stay in homey, pink-tinged rooms or private bungalows and dine on traditional meals with herbs from the garden. Guests may meditate in a thatched-roof hut, swing in various hammocks or sweat in a traditional Maya sauna.

La Fortuna BUNGALOW **$$$**
(☎5203-1033; www.lafortunaatitlan.com; bungalows Q670-1040) As luxurious as it is wild and remote, this ecologically outfitted retreat is at Patzisotz, a secluded bay just east of Santa Cruz around a rocky cliff. Four thatched-roof cabins are elegantly constructed of locally forested wood with Asian influences. Each features a porch and upper deck overlooking the lake, mosquito-netted beds and open-air bathrooms with rain showers.

The old coffee plantation is the creation of North American owners Kat and Steve, the latter a former guide and chef who prepares delectable meals using produce from the resort's garden. Meals are brought to your cabin or served in the stunning dining room/clubhouse, in front of which stands a wood-fired hot tub. *Lanchas* will drop you at the dock (Q10 from Santa Cruz).

★ **Café Sabor Cruceño** GUATEMALAN **$**
(www.amigosdesantacruz.org; breakfast Q32-45, lunch Q35-50; ⏰8am-5pm Mon-Sat) Up in the village, this brilliant community project *comedor* is run by local students who are learning to make traditional Guatemalan dishes to global tourism standards. Such Kaqchiquel fare as *subanik* (a tomato sauce of ground seeds and chilies accompanied by *tamalitos*) is prepared with locally grown herbs and veggies and served in the terrace restaurant with obligatory stunning lake views.

It's inside the CECAP training center, at the lower end of Santa Cruz' central plaza.

Getting There & Away

Santa Cruz is a 15-minute *lancha* ride from Panajachel (Q10) or 25 minutes from San Pedro (Q20). The last boat back to Pana passes at around 5:15pm.

Unless you have the sturdiest of 4WDs and it's the dry season, don't believe maps that suggest Santa Cruz has proper road access.

Tzununá

POP UNDER 2000

Tzununá, located 2km east of San Marcos by a paved road, has seen a bit of a gringo incursion in recent years. But this Kaqchiquel village ('Hummingbird of the Water') still retains a strong indigenous character and a lush natural beauty with year-round rivers springing from forested mountain slopes. Women in scarlet *huipiles* tread the paths between traditionally managed groves of coffee, avocados, bananas and *jocote*. Whereas foreign travelers head for San Pedro to party or San Marcos to meditate, many who come here are into sustainable agriculture, which they can study at Atitlán Organics.

Courses

Atitlán Organics COURSE
(☎4681-4697; www.atitlanorganics.com) For those who like to get dirt under their fingernails, this organic farm offers a variety of permaculture courses and volunteer opportunities. The most popular courses are the intensive week-long introduction to permaculture or natural building (both Q4300 including meals and accommodations). Volunteers get discounts at the nearby Bambu Guesthouse.

Tours of the farm are given each Friday morning (donation requested), including lunch, ending up at a set of waterfalls with swimming holes.

Sleeping & Eating

★Bambu Guesthouse GUESTHOUSE
(☎4681-4697; www.bambuguesthouse.com; dm Q100, tr Q250-300, all meals Q40; 📶) Affiliated with Atitlán Organics, Bambu is a guesthouse in splendid wood and bamboo that looks like it grew from the earth. Rooms are calming and airy, the dorms are spacious and chilled out, and everywhere there are balconies with tremendous views. The private rooms sleep up to three.

There are daily yoga classes, plus healthy meals at the farm-to-table restaurant.

Maya Moon Lodge LODGE $$
(☎5533-2433; www.mayamoonlodgeatitlan.com; dm Q80, r Q300-525; 📶) This retreat a bit west of the main dock consists of large, simply furnished cabins at various levels of a florally abundant hillside, all with hammock-slung balconies facing the lake. The lodge is stamped with the patient, generous character of its English owners. A restaurant at the lakefront serves meals with organic veggies from the garden.

Yoga on the lodge's dock is offered, along with Reiki and Thai massage.

Getting There & Away

Regular *lanchas* running between Panajachel (Q20) and San Pedro (Q15) stop at Tzununá. The last boat back to Pana passes at around 5:15pm. Alternatively, you could hike here from San Marcos La Laguna via a gravel road.

QUICHÉ

Quiché is the homeland of the K'iche' people, though other groups form the fabric of this culturally diverse region, most notably the Ixil of the eastern Cuchumatanes mountains. Most visitors who come to this largely forgotten pocket of the country are on a jaunt to the famous market at Chichicastenango. Similarly captivating commerce is conducted in the less trammeled territory of Santa Cruz del Quiché, the departmental capital to the north. On its outskirts lie the mysterious ruins of K'umarcaaj, the last capital city of the K'iche'. Adventurous souls push further north for Nebaj, heart of the culturally vibrant Ixil Triangle, with myriad hiking opportunities.

This region was at the heart of the violence of the civil war, with the Ixil people suffering greatly in reprisals from the army to such an extent that it's locally often referred to as a genocide. Be extremely circumspect about the war if it comes up in conversation.

Chichicastenango

POP 173,300 / ELEV 2172M

Surrounded by valleys with mountains serrating the horizons, Chichicastenango can seem isolated in time and space from the rest of Guatemala. When its narrow cobbled streets and red-tiled roofs are enveloped in mist, it's downright magical. The crowds of crafts vendors and tour groups who flock in for the huge Thursday and Sunday markets lend it a much worldlier, more commercial atmosphere, but Chichi retains its mystery. *Masheños* (citizens of Chichicastenango) are famous for their adherence to pre-Christian beliefs and ceremonies, and the town's various *cofradías* (religious brotherhoods) hold processions in observance of their saints around the church of Santo Tomás.

Once called Chaviar, Chichi was an important Kaqchiquel trading town long before the Spanish conquest. In the 15th century the group clashed with the K'iche' (based at K'umarcaaj, 20km north) and were forced to move their headquarters to the more defensible Iximché. When the Spanish conquered K'umarcaaj in 1524, many of its residents fled to Chaviar, which was renamed Chugüilá ('Above the Nettles') and Tziguan Tinamit ('Surrounded by Canyons'). These are the names still used by the K'iche' Maya, although everyone else calls the place Chichicastenango, a name given by the Spaniards' Mexican allies.

Today, Chichi has two religious and governmental establishments. On the one hand, the Catholic Church and the Republic of Guatemala appoint priests and town officials; on the other, the indigenous people elect their own religious and civil officers to manage local matters, with a separate council and mayor, and a court that decides cases involving only local indigenous people.

Chichicastenango

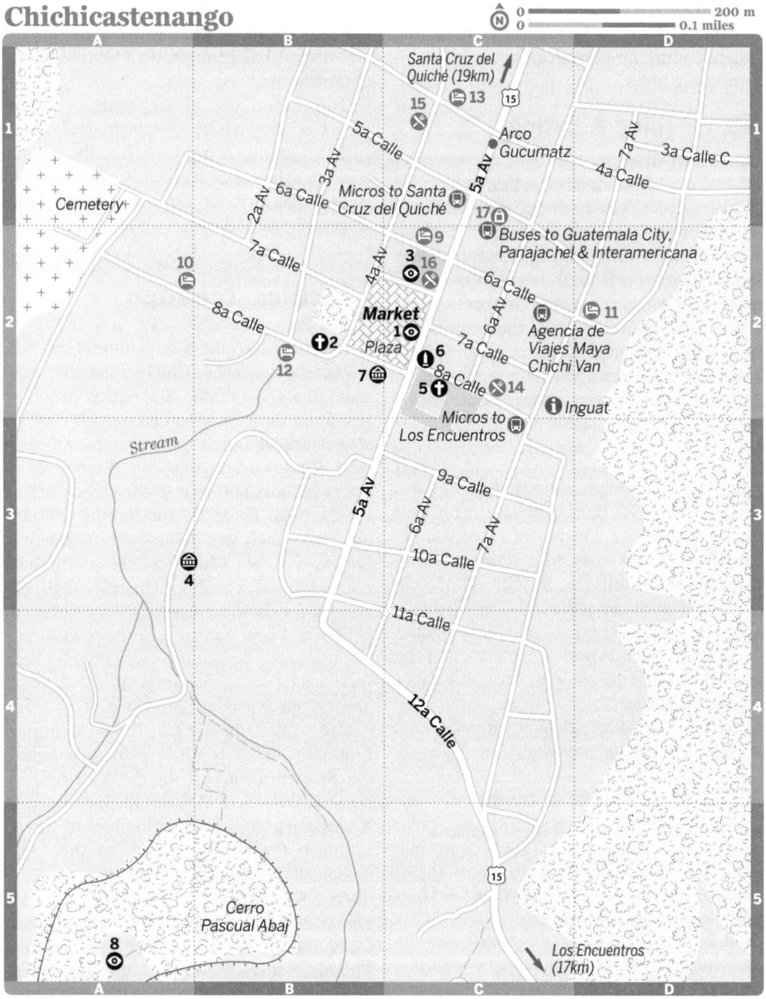

Chichicastenango

Top Sights
1 Market C2

Sights
2 Capilla del Calvario B2
3 Centro Comercial Santo Tomás C2
4 Galería Pop-Wuj A3
5 Iglesia de Santo Tomás C2
6 Mural C2
7 Museo Arqueológico Regional B2
8 Pascual Abaj A5

Sleeping
9 Hotel Girón C2
10 Hotel Mashito A2
11 Hotel Santo Tomás D2
12 Mayan Inn B2
13 Posada El Arco C1

Eating
14 Casa San Juan C2
15 Comedor Típico C1
Mayan Inn .... (see 12)
16 Villa Cofrades C2

Shopping
17 Ut'z Bat'z C1

Sights

★Market MARKET

(Plaza Principal; ⏲ Thu & Sun) Some villagers still walk for hours carrying their wares to reach Chichi's market, one of Guatemala's largest and a highlight of many people's trips to the country. It's a rich mix of the traditional and the tourist, where local women shopping for a new *huipile* rub shoulders with travellers looking for a textile souvenir. Sunday is the busier of the two market days, when Spanish school students and weekenders from Guatemala City descend en masse on Chichi.

At dawn on Thursday and Sunday vendors spread out their vegetables, chunks of chalk (ground to a powder and boiled with dried maize to soften it), handmade harnesses and other merchandise, and wait for customers. In the past vendors erected their stands of tree limbs and covered them with cotton sheeting each market day, but these days a sea of tin roofs remains a permanent fixture atop the plaza.

Tourist-oriented handicraft stalls selling masks, textiles, pottery and so on now occupy much of the plaza and the streets to the north. Things villagers need – food, soap, clothing, sewing notions, toys – cluster at the north end of the square and in the covered Centro Comercial Santo Tomás (p122) off the north side, whose upper deck offers irresistible photo opportunities of the fruit and vegetable-selling business conducted below.

Iglesia de Santo Tomás CHURCH

(5a Av) This church on the plaza's east side dates from 1540 and is often the scene of rituals that are more distinctly Maya than Catholic. Inside, the floor of the church may be dotted with offerings of maize, flowers and bottles of liquor wrapped in corn husks; candles are arranged in specific patterns along low stone platforms. Enter through the side door rather than the front entrance and note that photography is very strictly not permitted inside.

The church's front steps serve much the same purpose as the great flights of stairs leading up to Maya pyramids (there are 20 steps, for each day of the Maya calendar). For much of the day (especially Sunday), they smolder with incense of *copal* resin, while indigenous prayer leaders called *chuchkajaues* (mother-fathers) swing censers (usually tin cans poked with holes) and chant magic words marking the days of the ancient Maya calendar and in honor of ancestors. The candles and offerings inside recall those ancestors, many of whom are buried beneath the floor just as Maya kings were buried beneath pyramids.

Capilla del Calvario CHURCH

(4a Av) On the west side of the plaza, this whitewashed church is similar in form and function to Santo Tomás, but smaller. Ceremonies go on continually in front of the church, as worshippers ring a bonfire of fragrant *copal*, while within, candles are placed upon blackened stone slabs.

Mural PUBLIC ART

Be sure to admire the mural that runs alongside the wall of the town hall on the east side of the plaza – it's dedicated to the victims of the civil war and tells the story of the war using symbology from the *Popol Vuh*, the book compiled by members of the Maya nobility soon after the Spanish Conquest.

Another lengthy mural, focusing on village life, fronts the Museo Arqueológico Regional, on the plaza's south side.

Galería Pop-Wuj GALLERY

(☎4629-9327; www.galeriapopwuj.wix.com/galeriapopwuj; Casa 2-27, Calle Pascual Habaj) FREE On the way down the hill to the shrine at Pascual Abaj, you might stop into this interesting gallery. Developed as an art institute for local children with the backing of Project Guggenheim, it holds a small but unique collection of oil paintings by the artist brothers Juan and Miguel Cortéz and their pupils. K'iche' classes are sometimes offered, along with the chance to experience traditional Maya ceremonies (contact the gallery in advance).

Pascual Abaj SHRINE

On a hilltop south of town, Pascual Abaj (Sacrifice Stone) is a shrine to the Maya earth god Huyup Tak'ah (Mountain Plain). A stone-faced idol stands amid a circle of squat stone crosses in a clearing. Said to be hundreds – perhaps thousands – of years old, it has suffered numerous indignities at the hands of outsiders, but local people still revere it.

Chuchkajaues come regularly to offer incense, food, cigarettes, flowers, liquor and perhaps even a sacrificial chicken, in thanks and hope for the earth's continuing fertility. The area is littered with past offerings. The worshippers won't mind if you watch the goings on, but be sure to request permission before taking any photos. You may be asked if you want to make an offering yourself.

Even if there are no ceremonies going on, you can still see the idol and enjoy the walk up the pine-clad hill. To get there from the plaza, walk down 5a Av, turn right into 9a Calle and proceed downhill. At the bottom, bear left along a path and head up through either of the *morerías* (ceremonial mask workshops) that are signposted here; the one on the right houses a museum of local culture. Exiting at the rear, follow the path uphill through the trees to the top of the hill.

Centro Comercial Santo Tomás LANDMARK
Even on non-market days, the covered market on the north side of the square buzzes with activity. The fresh produce on display is a reflection of Guatemala's bounty, from temperate vegetables from the highlands to tropical fruit brought up from the Pacific coast. Many vendors have tired of having their photos taken so tourists are recommended to visit the upper deck, which offers irresistible photo opportunities of the business conducted below without invading their privacy.

Museo Arqueológico Regional MUSEUM
(Museo Rossbach; 5a Av 4-47; Q5; 8am-12:30pm & 2-4:30pm Tue, Wed, Fri & Sat, 8am-4pm Thu, 8am-2pm Sun) Chichi's archaeology museum holds the collection of Hugo Rossbach, a German who served as the town's Catholic priest until his death in 1944. It includes some beautiful jade necklaces and figurines, along with ceremonial masks, obsidian spearheads, incense burners, figurines and *metates* (grindstones for maize). A second hall features a portrait gallery of *cofradía* leaders.

Festivals & Events

Feast of Santo Tomás CULTURAL
(Dec) This celebration of the patron saint's day goes on for most of December, starting on the 5th with an inaugural parade and culminating on the 21st when pairs of brave (some would say mad) men fly about at high speeds suspended from a tall, vertical pole. Traditional dances, concerts and fireworks also feature.

Quema del Diablo CULTURAL
(Burning of the Devil; Dec 7) In this ceremony, residents burn their garbage in the streets and usher a statue of the Virgin Mary to the steps of the Iglesia de Santo Tomás. There are lots of incense and candles, a marimba band and a fireworks display that has observers running for cover.

Feast of the Immaculate Conception CULTURAL
(Dec 8) Don't miss the early-morning dance of the giant cartoon characters in Chichi's main plaza.

Sleeping

If you want to secure a room the night before the Thursday or Sunday market, it's a good idea to call or arrive early the day before.

Hotel Girón HOTEL **$**
(5527-1101; hotelgiron@gmail.com; 6a Calle 4-52; s/d/tr Q150/200/450; P) It won't win any prizes for decor but this motel-style place a block north of the plaza is functional and reliable. It's reached through a shopping alley, so it's slightly removed from the hubbub of the town center. Get a room on the first floor if you can. Prices include breakfast.

Hotel Mashito HOTEL **$**
(5168-7178; 8a Calle 1-72; s/d Q80/150, s/d without bathroom Q50/100) On the road to the cemetery, the family-run Mashito is built around a plant-filled patio. Though a bit frayed, at least it's colorful, with green paint framing the brick, and patchwork blankets on the beds. See a few rooms before checking in – the wood-paneled rooms up top (with shared bath) are in much better shape than those downstairs.

Posada El Arco GUESTHOUSE **$$**
(3469-1590; 4a Calle 4-36; s/d Q244/305) Near the Arco Gucumatz, this homey, solar-powered spread is one of Chichi's more original accommodations. All nine rooms are idiosyncratically appointed, with Maya weavings, colonial bedsteads and fireplaces. Rooms 3, 4, 6 and 7 have views over the tranquil rear garden and northward to the mountains. Well-read owner Pedro likes to converse in English. Reservations are a good idea.

Mayan Inn HOTEL **$$$**
(2412-4753; www.mayaninn.com.gt; 8a Calle A 1-91; s/d/tr Q630/700/1110;) Founded in 1932, the inn today encompasses several restored colonial houses on either side of 8a Calle. The courtyards are planted with tropical flora and the walls draped in indigenous textiles. Each of the 16 rooms is uniquely appointed, with carved armoires and fireplaces. Those on the south side have the best views. The restaurant here does some of Chichi's finest cuisine.

Hotel Santo Tomás HOTEL $$$
(☎5865-6453; www.hotelsantotomas.com.gt; 7a Av 5-32; s/d/tr Q725/840/1070; P ❄) Popular with tour groups, this large colonial-style hotel wraps around garden patios with tinkling fountains, squawking macaws, and lots of potted plants. All of the 75 rooms feature a tub and fireplace. There's a good bar and sumptuous dining room where marimba groups perform on market days.

Eating

There are plenty of restaurants living by the twice-weekly influx of local and foreign visitors.

The real food action in Chichicastenango is in the central plaza, where attentive *abuelitas* (grandmas) ladle chicken soup, beef stew, tamales and *chiles rellenos* from huge pots as their daughters and granddaughters minister to the throngs of country folk sitting at long tables covered with oilcloth. What are called tamales here are made of rice and laced with sauce. Sliced watermelon and papaya can be had at other stalls. On non-market evenings, you'll find enchiladas and *pupusas* in front of the cathedral, served with *atole de plátano*, a warm plantain beverage spiked with cinnamon.

★**Villa Cofrades** CAFE $
(Centro Comercial Santo Tomás; ⏰7am-7pm Wed, Thu, Sat & Sun; 📶) This charming cafe is tucked into the outside corner of Centro Comercial Santo Tomás and is a gem if you want to step back from the bustle of the market but still get a view of the action outside. It's decorated with an eccentric eye – old typewriters, prints, cutlery installations and auction house catalogues.

The decor thankfully doesn't get in the way of the food. There are breakfast pancakes, sandwiches, cheese and bacon muffins and pesto potatoes to tempt, along with good coffee and palate-cleansing fruit juices.

Comedor Típico GUATEMALAN $
(4a Av 4-23; mains Q20) One of the few non-touristy eateries in town, this locally popular lunch hall does cow's foot soup, chicken stews and other hearty fare for the traveler's soul.

Mayan Inn GUATEMALAN $$
(☎2412-4753; 8a Calle A 1-91; breakfast from Q25, mains Q70-125; ⏰7am-10pm) The three dining rooms at Chichi's classiest hotel feature colonial-style furnishings and canvases by renowned painter Humberto Garabito. Waiters wear costumes evolved from the dress of Spanish colonial farmers. The food is lavishly presented and abundantly served, with a few traditional options like *pepián* (chicken and tomato stew) and *jocón* (chicken and green tomatillo stew).

Casa San Juan GUATEMALAN $$
(☎7756-2086; 6a Av 7-30; mains Q40-65; ⏰10am-9:30pm Tue-Sun) One of the more stylish eateries, the San Juan occupies a beautiful colonial structure beside Santo Tomás with candlelit dining in various salons. Offerings range from burgers and sandwiches to more traditional fare, including good *chiles rellenos* laced with zesty salsa.

Shopping

The twice-weekly market is one of the best places for souvenir shopping in Guatemala.

Ut'z Bat'z ARTS & CRAFTS
(5a Avenida 5-24; ⏰1-5pm Wed, 10am-5pm Thu, Sat & Sun) This fair-trade shop by the plaza's southwest corner displays the work of a local women's cooperative comprising 30 weavers, including scarves, shawls, table runners, bags and pillows.

Information

DANGERS & ANNOYANCES

'Hola, amigo!' is the refrain you'll hear from the myriad vendors and touts who depend on tourism for their livelihood; it can wear you down, but try to be polite. Ignore touts offering assistance in finding a hotel; you'll have no difficulty finding lodgings on your own.

Chichi is plagued by traffic and exhaust fumes. Keep an eye out for buses tearing around corners.

MEDICAL SERVICES

Hospital El Buen Samaritano (☎7756-1163; 6a Calle 3-60) Maintains a 24-hour emergency clinic.

MONEY

Chichi's many banks all stay open on Sunday, and there are plenty of ATMs.

ATM (cnr 5a Av & 6a Calle)

Banco Industrial (6a Calle 6-05) Visa/MasterCard ATM.

TOURIST INFORMATION

INGUAT (☎5966-1162; 7a Av 7-14; ⏰8am-4pm Sun-Thu) Authorized guides can be hired here for cultural tours of the town and up to Pascual Abaj.

Getting There & Away

Buses heading to Panajachel, Quetzaltenango and all other points reached from the Interamericana arrive and depart from 5a Calle near the corner of 5a Av, one block uphill from the Arco Gucumtaz. You can also catch a micro to **Santa Cruz del Quiché** here. Buses approaching from the south go up 7a Avenida, dropping off passengers at the **gas station** two blocks east of the central plaza.

Microbuses to **Los Encuentros** leave from in front of the Telgua building on 7a Avenida.

Agencia de Viajes Maya Chichi Van (☎5007-2051; mayachichivan@yahoo.es; 6a Calle 6-45) offers shuttles to Guatemala City (Q125), Antigua (Q90) and Panajachel (Q55) on Thursday and Sunday at 2pm, plus a service to San Cristóbal de las Casas in Mexico at 7am daily. In most cases at least five passengers are needed. It also runs tours to K'umarcaaj near Santa Cruz del Quiché, Nebaj and elsewhere.

Santa Cruz Del Quiché

POP 130,300 / ELEV 1979M

Without Chichicastenango's big market and attendant tourism, Santa Cruz – or just El Quiché – presents a less self-conscious slice of regional life and is refreshingly free of competition for tourist lucre. Just 19km north of Chichi, Santa Cruz is the capital of Quiché department, drawing a diverse populace on business and administrative affairs. The main market days are Thursday and Sunday, boosting the bustle considerably. Travelers who come here usually do so to visit K'umarcaaj, the ruins of the old K'iche' Maya capital, or to change buses en route further north.

The most exciting time to be here is mid-August during the Fiestas Elenas, a week of festivities and a proud display of indigenous traditions. It all leads up to the *Convite Femenino,* when El Quiché's women don masks and dance up a storm to marimba accompaniment.

Sights

El Quiché's main draw is the ruins of K'umarcaaj just outside the town, but there are several points of interest around the central tripartite plaza. The top square is flanked on its east side by Gobernación (the departmental government palace), the middle one by the cathedral and the *municipalidad* (town hall), and the bottom one by the big domed events hall, in front of which stands a statue of K'iche' warrior Tecún Umán in a fierce posture. The main market occupies a series of buildings east of the plaza.

K'umarcaaj ARCHAEOLOGICAL SITE

(Q'um'arkaj, Utatlán; Q30; ⏲8am-4pm) The ruins of the ancient K'iche' Maya capital of K'umarcaaj remain a sacred site for the Maya, and contemporary rituals are customarily enacted here. Archaeologists have identified more than 80 large structures in 12 groups, but only limited restoration has been done. The ruins have a fine setting, shaded by tall evergreens and surrounded by ravines. Bring a flashlight.

The kingdom of K'iche' was established in late Postclassic times (about the 14th century) by a mixture of indigenous people and invaders from the Tabasco–Campeche border area in Mexico. King Ku'ucumatz founded K'umarcaaj which, owing to its naturally fortified position, commanded an extensive valley, and conquered many neighboring settlements. During the long reign of his successor, Q'uik'ab (1425–75), the K'iche' kingdom extended its borders to Huehuetenango,

BUSES FROM CHICHICASTENANGO

DESTINATION	COST (Q)	DURATION	FREQUENCY	ALTERNATIVE
Antigua	25	3½hr		Any bus to Guatemala City; change at Chimaltenango
Guatemala City	30	2½hr	Half hourly 3am to 5pm	
Los Encuentros	10	30min	frequent	
Panajachel	25	2hr		Microbus to Los Encuentros; change there
Quetzaltenango	25	2hr	Half hourly to 3pm	Microbus to Los Encuentros; change there
Santa Cruz del Quiché	10	40min	Half hourly between 7am and 8pm	

Nebaj, Rabinal and the Pacific Slope. At the same time, the Kaqchiquel, a vassal people who once fought alongside the K'iche', rebelled, establishing an independent capital at Iximché.

When Pedro de Alvarado and his Spanish conquistadors hit Guatemala in 1524, it was the K'iche', under their king Tecún Umán, who led the resistance against them. In the decisive battle fought near Quetzaltenango on February 12, 1524, Alvarado and Tecún engaged in mortal combat. Alvarado prevailed. The defeated K'iche' invited him to visit K'umarcaaj. Smelling a rat, Alvarado enlisted the aid of his Mexican auxiliaries and the anti-K'iche' Kaqchiquel, and together they captured the K'iche' leaders, burnt them alive in K'umarcaaj's main plaza and then destroyed the city.

The museum at the entrance will help orientate you. The tallest of the structures round the central plaza, the **Templo de Tohil** (a sky god), is blackened by smoke and has a niche where contemporary prayer-men regularly make offerings to Maya gods. The L-shaped ball court alongside it has been extensively restored.

Down the hillside to the right of the plaza is the entrance to a long tunnel known as the *cueva*. Legend has it that the K'iche' dug the tunnel as a refuge for their women and children in preparation for Alvarado's coming, and that a K'iche' princess was later buried in a deep shaft off this tunnel. Revered as the place where the K'iche' kingdom died, the *cueva* is sacred to highland Maya and is an important location for prayers, candle burning, offerings and chicken sacrifices.

If there's anyone around the entrance, ask permission before entering. Inside, the long tunnel (perhaps 100m long) is blackened with smoke and incense and littered with candles and flower petals. Use your flashlight and watch your footing: there are several side tunnels and at least one of them, on the right near the end, contains a deep, black shaft.

The ruins of K'umarcaaj are 3km west of El Quiché. Gray 'Ruinas' microbuses depart from in front of the cathedral in Santa Cruz every 20 minutes (Q1). The last one back is at 6:50pm.

Festivals & Events

Fiestas Elenas CULTURAL

(www.fiestaselenas.com; mid-Aug) The most exciting time to be here is mid-August, during the Fiestas Elenas, a week of festivities and a proud display of indigenous traditions. It all leads up to the *convite femenino*, when El Quiché's women don masks and dance up a storm to marimba accompaniment.

Sleeping & Eating

The hotels are located between the Parque Central and the bus terminal.

For budget grub, there's plenty of grilling action going on around and within the market.

Hotel Rey K'iche HOTEL $

(7755-0827; 8a Calle 0-39, Zona 5; s/d/tr Q160/225/290;) Between the bus station and plaza, the Rey K'iche is excellent value with well-maintained, brick-walled rooms around a quiet interior and affable staff. There's free drinking water and a decent cafe upstairs serving breakfast and dinner. All things considered, it's the best place to stay.

El Sitio Hotel HOTEL $$

(7755-3656; elsitiohotel@gmail.com; 9a Calle 0-41, Zona 5; s/d/tr Q175/300/400; P) From the outside, this business-class hotel two blocks north of the bus terminal could almost be a modern evangelical church. Though rather sterile with a cavernous lobby, rooms are modern and well maintained and have a bit of local-style decor.

BUSES FROM SANTA CRUZ DEL QUICHÉ

DESTINATION	COST (Q)	DURATION	FREQUENCY (DAILY)
Chichicastenango	10	40min	Frequent
Guatemala City	35	3hr	Every 10min 3am-5pm
Huehuetenango	25	2hr	Half hourly 5am-6pm
Nebaj	20	2hr	Half hourly 6am-7pm
Quetzaltenango	25	3hr	Hourly 5am-6pm
Uspantán	30	2-2½hr	Frequent 5:30am-7pm

Restaurant El Chalet STEAK **$$**
(☎7755-0618; 1a Calle 2-39, Zona 5; mains Q60-70; ⌚7am-9pm) The specialty here is grilled meats, served with homemade salsa. You could make a light meal of the tortilla-sized portions. Dining is beneath an arbor flanked by a strip of garden. It's part of a posh hotel/conference center a few blocks east of the big clock tower.

Getting There & Away

El Quiché is the jumping-off point for the remote reaches of northern Quiché department, which extends all the way to the Mexican border. The main **bus terminal**, a dusty lot in Zona 5, is located four blocks south and two blocks east of the plaza. Microbuses for Chichicastenango depart from the corner of 5a Calle and 2 Av, opposite Café San Miguel.

Uspantán

POP 83,400

Uspantán, a town halfway between Huehuetenango and Cobán along the 7W road, is set amid sky-high scenery. The town itself is quiet and charming, if short of actual attractions, but the setting is stunning, in a fertile valley at the base of green forested mountains over which a bank of clouds rolls in each afternoon. Women wear lacy, loose-fitting *huipiles* in bright orange or pink.

Founded by the Uspanteko Maya around the 6th century AD, it was originally dubbed Tz'unun Kaab' – place of hummingbirds. The severe repression it experienced during the armed conflict of the 1980s forged indigenous leader Rigoberta Menchú, who grew up a five-hour walk through the mountains in the village of Laj Chimel. Cardamom is grown here, and pigs and sheep are raised on the surrounding slopes.

As ever, life centres on the central plaza; the covered market streets around its edge are worth exploring.

Sleeping & Eating

Hotel Don Gabriel HOTEL **$**
(☎7951-8540; hoteldongabriel@yahoo.es; 7a Av 6-22; s/d Q90/160; P 📶) Rooms at this excellent value lodging, just around the corner from the Parque Central, have plenty of thick blankets for the evening chill. If possible, choose a room on the top level opening onto a Gaudí-esque terrace with various plant-laden gazebos and fabulous views of the mountains.

Hotel Posada Doña Leonor HOTEL **$**
(☎7951-8041; calutis54@hotmail.com; 6a Calle 4-25, Zona 1; s/d Q90/180; P 📶) This well-maintained option a block east of the plaza features 21 rooms around a courtyard with a jacaranda tree in the middle and a small restaurant for breakfast and supper. You'll find firm beds, fresh paint, and spotless bathrooms with electric shower heads.

Restaurante Mexicana MEXICAN **$**
(breakfast from Q20, mains Q25-50; ⌚7am-9.30pm) Half a block down from the church end of the main plaza, this well-signed restaurant has just one smallish room but a large menu and generous serves of Mexican and Guatemalan dishes. Breakfasts are hearty, as are the burritos, quesadillas and plates of grilled meats. With luck, you'll end up with control of the TV remote to turn the blast down.

Getting There & Away

Microbuses for Quiché (Q30, 2½ hours), via Sacapulas, leave whenever full from Uspantán's bus terminal on 6a Calle, three blocks west of the Parque Central, until 7pm. For Cobán (Q35, three hours), microbuses go hourly from 4am to 3:30pm; a 35km stretch of that journey is over a frequently poor road surface. For Nebaj, there are a couple of direct microbuses (coming from Cobán), though it's easier to get a microbus to Sacapulas where you'll find frequent connections up to the Ixil Triangle.

Nebaj

POP 106,200 / ELEV 2000M

Hidden in a remote fold of the Cuchumatanes mountains north of Sacapulas is the Triángulo Ixil (Ixil Triangle), a 2300-sq-km zone comprising the towns of Santa María Nebaj, San Juan Cotzal and San Gaspar Chajul, as well as dozens of outlying villages and hamlets. The local Ixil Maya people, though they suffered perhaps more than anybody in Guatemala's civil war, cling proudly to their traditions and speak the Ixil language. Nebaj women are celebrated for their beautiful purple, green and yellow pom-pommed hair braids, scarlet *cortes,* and their *huipiles* and *rebozos* (shawls) featuring bird and animal motifs. Nebaj is a good base for hiking – the three-day hike to Todos Santos is particularly lovely. While you're in town, visit the unexpectedly good museum dedicated to the region's history.

Nebaj

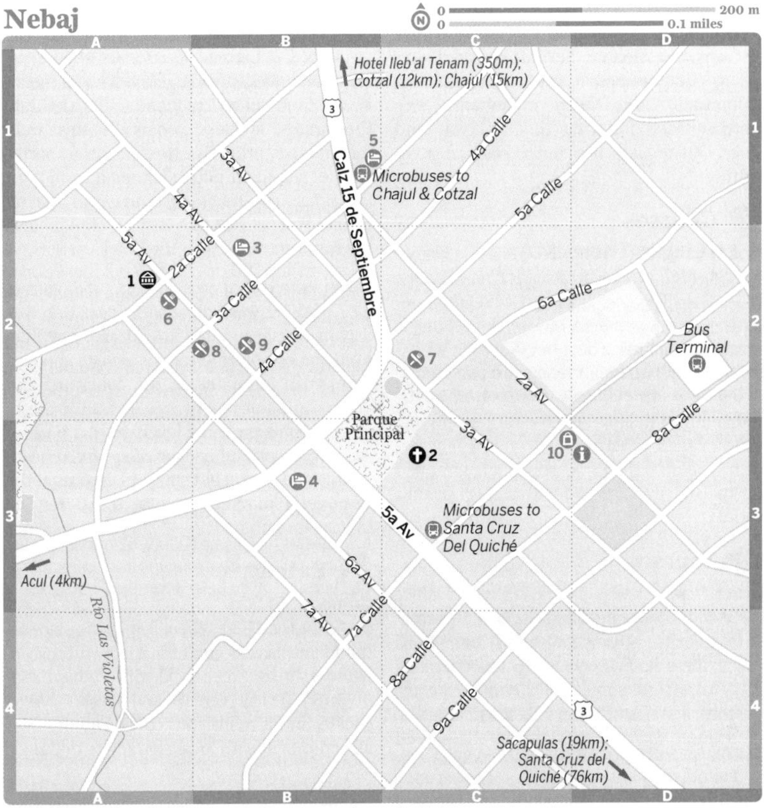

Sights

Centro Cultural Kumool MUSEUM

(5a Av 1-32; Q20; 9am-noon & 1-6pm Mon-Fri, 8am-1pm Sat) This small museum is something of an unexpected gem for a town of Nebaj's size. It displays a collection of mostly ceramic objects excavated in the Ixil region, all arranged by historical period. Among the more interesting pieces are a ceremonial ax with a skull handle and a giant funerary urn with a jaguar face, plus some well-preserved polychrome vases. If you're a Spanish-reader, the small library of books on local history and culture is excellent.

Iglesia de Nebaj CHURCH

(Parque Principal) This formidable church dominates the south side of Parque Principal. Inside, to the left of the entrance, is a memorial to Juan José Gerardi, who as bishop of Quiché witnessed widespread human

Nebaj

Sights
1 Centro Cultural Kumool A2
2 Iglesia de Nebaj C3

Activities, Courses & Tours
Guías Ixiles .... (see 8)
Nebaj Language School .... (see 8)

Sleeping
3 Hotel Santa María B2
4 Hotel Turansa B3
5 Hotel Villa Nebaj B1

Eating
6 Asados El Pasabien A2
7 Comedor El Si'm C2
8 El Descanso B2
9 Popi's Restaurant B2

Shopping
10 Mercado de Artesanías C3

rights abuses here. Soon after he released a report about these atrocities, Gerardi himself was assassinated. Several hundred simple wooden crosses around the monument memorialize the Nebaj inhabitants who were murdered during the civil war and since. Outside, a bright mural celebrates Ixil culture.

Courses

Nebaj Language School LANGUAGE
(☎5847-4747; www.nebaj.com/nls.html; 3a Calle, El Descanso Bldg, Zona 1; 1 week Q615) Offers instruction in Spanish. A one-week package is available, including accommodations with a local family, two meals a day and two guided hikes to nearby villages. Instruction in the indigenous Ixil language is another option.

You can also learn how to make regional dishes like *boxboles* (corn dough wrapped in squash leaves, served with a spicy peanut sauce).

Tours

Guías Ixiles HIKING
(☎5847-4747; www.nebaj.com; 3a Calle, El Descanso Bldg, Zona 1; ⏱8am-12:30pm & 2-5pm) Guías Ixiles offers half-day walks to Las Cascadas (Q55 for one person plus Q25 for each extra person), a series of waterfalls north of town, or around town with visits to the sacred sites of the *costumbristas* (people who still practice non-Christian Maya rites). Guías Ixiles also leads three-day treks over the Cuchumatanes to Todos Santos Cuchumatán. Some Spanish is required.

Sleeping

Hotel Ileb'al Tenam HOTEL $
(☎7755-8039; Calz 15 de Septiembre; s/d Q60/105, without bathroom Q35/65; P) This cordially managed lodging at the north edge of town features two sections: a long wooden house with simple rooms along a plank veranda; and at the rear, an 'annex' with more modern units around a tranquil patio.

Hotel Turansa HOTEL $
(☎4887-8584; cnr 5a Calle & 6a Av; s/d from Q85/150; P Wi-Fi) This friendly, central establishment – just a block from the Parque Principal – has decent-sized rooms with big comfy beds and flat-screen TVs along plant-draped balconies. Top-floor triples open onto a sunny terrace, lower rooms get noise from the courtyard parking area.

Hotel Santa María HOTEL $$
(☎4212-7927; www.hotelsantamarianebaj.com; cnr 4a Av & 2a Calle; s/d Q150/250; P Wi-Fi) Scarlet woven bedspreads, carved-wood headboards and other Ixil handicrafts decorate the bright, spotless rooms at this well-maintained property three blocks northwest of the main plaza. There's a restaurant (breakfast not included) and – on the off chance you get sick in Nebaj – a clinic shares the same entrance with the hotel.

Hotel Villa Nebaj HOTEL $$
(☎7756-0005; www.hotelvillanebaj.com; Calz 15 de Septiembre 2-37; s/d/tr Q150/250/350; P Wi-Fi) Behind the elaborate facade is a neat, modern hotel with fountains in the courtyard and elaborate paintings of *nebajenses* in fiesta wear. Rooms on three levels have a dash of style, with colorful bedspreads, carved headboards and piping hot showers. Rooms at the front get a lot of street noise, so ask for one in the rear annex.

Eating

Comedor El Si'm GUATEMALAN $
(3a Av; breakfast Q30; ⏱7am-9pm) This place off the main plaza is great for a gut-stuffing *desayuno* (breakfast), served with a bonus bowl of *mosh* (warm cereal) and freshly baked cookie, and it refills your coffee cup. It's usually crammed with local characters by 8am.

El Descanso INTERNATIONAL $
(☎5847-4747; www.nebaj.com; 3a Calle, Zona 1; mains Q25-35; ⏱6:30am-9:30pm; Wi-Fi) This cozy restaurant features a bar and lounge areas in Nebaj's most alternative ambience. A range of sandwiches, salads, pastas and soups is served, as well as western and Guatemalan breakfasts. Popular with foreign volunteers.

Asados El Pasabien STEAK $
(cnr 5a Av & 2a Calle; mains Q35-45; ⏱noon-3pm & 6-10:30pm) Steaks, chicken and shrimp are skillfully grilled and served up with heaping portions of halved potatoes, salad and nice homemade salsas at this locally popular dining hall – probably Nebaj's swankiest dining option.

Popi's Restaurant CAFE $
(☎4872-5299; 5a Av 6-74; mains Q25-40; ⏱7am-9pm) This low-key cafe/bakery/hostel/expat hangout whips up gringo comfort foods. A copious breakfast menu includes three-egg omelets, homemade granola and burritos. It also does a good line in local travel information.

CHAJUL'S HIDDEN MURALS

While renovating the kitchen of his ancient dwelling in Chajul, resident Lucas Ariscona made a momentous discovery. Removing several layers of plaster revealed a series of murals that had probably not seen light for centuries. The paintings, which cover several walls of Ariscona's home, depict some kind of procession made up of both Spaniards and Mayas. Though they're seriously faded by sudden exposure to the elements after being concealed for so long, it is still possible to make out a figure in European attire playing a drum for another character in Maya ceremonial costume as well as a caped reveler bearing a human heart in his hand. Though Ariscona has made efforts to preserve the murals, his resources are limited and in the smoke-filled environment of a typical Chajul home, the rare testament to a Euro-Maya encounter faces inevitable deterioration.

As many as four other old houses in the community harbor historically significant paintings beneath the plaster, some of them rich in Maya symbolism. Inquire at the Museo Maya Ixil to locate and visit these long-dormant works of art. A small donation is requested.

Shopping

Mercado de Artesanías ARTS & CRAFTS
(Handicrafts Market; cnr 7a Calle & 2a Av, Zona 1; 8am-6pm) The numerous vendor stalls here offer well-made *rebozos* (scarves), *cintas* (the pom-pommed braid woven into Ixil women's hair) and *huipiles*, which can cost anywhere from Q300 to Q3000, depending on quality.

Information

There is a **5B ATM** in the town hall building, opposite the park.

Banrural (8am-4:30pm Mon-Fri, 7-11am Sat) In a little shopping center underneath the Parque Principal; changes dollars and euros.

The **tourist office** (3072-4224; cnr 7a Calle & 2a Av, Zona 1; 8am-6pm Mon-Sat, 8am-noon Sun), inside the Mercado de Artesanías, can answer any question as long as it's posed in Spanish.

Getting There & Away

The bus terminal is just below the market. **Microbuses** bound for Santa Cruz del Quiché, via Sacapulas, go every half hour from 4am until 5pm (Q20, two hours), departing from behind the church at the corner of 5a Av and 7a Calle. To head west to Huehuetenango or east to Uspantán and Cobán, change at Sacapulas.

Microbuses to Chajul (Q15, 45 minutes) depart every 20 minutes or so until 6pm from in front of the Hotel Villa Nebaj, on Calz 15 de Septiembre.

The main **bus terminal**, behind the market, mainly serves outlying villages such as Tzalbal, Vicalama and Palop; one bus travels all the way to Guatemala City (Q50, 5½ hours) via Chichicastenango, departing around 2am.

Chajul

POP 67,900

A good paved road winds northeast through piney slopes to Chajul, an impoverished but intensely traditional Ixil village, where hundreds-of-years-old customs are still widely practiced. Women stroll arm-in-arm wearing maroon *cortes* (wraparound skirts), earrings made from silver coins, and bright blue or purple *huipiles* woven with geometric patterns. Along the dirt streets, adobe structures with tile roofs propped up by carved wooden pillars are interspersed with patches of maize and squash. Tuesday and Friday are market days.

Chajul was the base for one of the main guerrilla groups during the civil war, and was consequently the site of many bloody reprisals by the army against the Ixil people. More than two decades later, the scars of the conflict still run deep.

Chajul has a notable church famous for one of the biggest pilgrimages in Guatemala during Lent. The town is also known for its woven grass baskets, which make great souvenirs.

Sights

Iglesia Católica CHURCH
(Parque Centrale) The church is home to the icon of Christ of Golgotha, which is the focus of a huge pilgrimage on the second Friday of Lent – one of the biggest pilgrimages in the country. The huge wooden doors carved with stylised animals are particularly worth noting, as is the statue of the Virgin Mary dressed entirely in local Ixil costume.

Museo Maya Ixil MUSEUM
(☎4586-8238; centroculturalmayaixil08@gmail.com; Q20; ⊙8am-6pm) The musical instruments, stone implements, weapons, indigenous outfits and archaeological finds crammed into this humble adobe home have been painstakingly selected by a local historian, along with evidence of Chajul's resistance during the armed conflict of the 1980s. From the Parque Central, turn left at the bank, then right uphill. If there's no one around, inquire at the Banrural.

Tours

Limitless Horizons Ixil CULTURAL
(☎5332-6264; www.limitlesshorizonsixil.org) This California-based NGO works to expand educational opportunities for local children. It offers 'community engagement trips', multiday excursions that involve visiting homes of local families, learning backstrap weaving, speaking the Ixil language, exploring the highlands and collaborating on community service projects.

Sleeping & Eating

Posada Vetz K'aol LODGE $
(☎5784-8802; www.asociacionchajulense.org; per person Q65; P 📶) On the edge of the village with forested views, this *posada* is a former stable, built in the local style with carved wood columns along an arcade. Most of the pine-paneled rooms have four or five bunk beds and there's one double with its own bathroom for the same price. A cozy sitting room has a large fireplace and coffee maker.

Located a 15-minute stroll from the center of Chajul, down a path off the road from Nebaj, it's owned by a local coffee growers' cooperative that offers half-day tours of the area with visits to beekeepers and a sacred hill where devotees perform ceremonies (Q50 per person). Meals are available on request.

Comedor Sarai GUATEMALAN $
(set lunch Q15; ⊙7am-9pm) Join the *chajulenses* for lunch at this humble hall next to the pharmacy. The one or two items on the menu usually consist of chicken or beef and are served at wooden tables.

Getting There & Away

From Nebaj, microbuses to Chajul (Q15, 45 minutes) depart every 20 minutes or so until 6pm from in front of the Hotel Villa Nebaj, on Calz 15 de Septiembre. The last micro back to Nebaj departs around 5pm.

Acul

POP LESS THAN 1500

Acul sits astride the bucolic Río Azul valley, at the end of a very rutted road. Its functional appearance, with stores and evangelical prayer halls along either side of a broad dirt street, speak to its relatively recent founding. It was established in 1983 as the first *polo de desarrollo* (pole of development) during the civil war. Considered 'strategic hamlets', these settlements were constructed to enable the army to keep inhabitants from having contact with the guerrillas.

These days Acul's main activities are ranching, weaving and loom building.

Just outside Acul is a pair of farms devoted to cheese making. They were started by two immigrant brothers, the Azzaris, cheese makers in their native Italian Alps who moved to Guatemala in the 1930s, perhaps choosing the Acul valley because of its alpine appearance. Older brother José gained renown as a prize wrestler before being killed in the ring.

Sleeping & Eating

Hostal Doña Magdalena HOSTEL $
(per person Q50) A rustic wooden home with garden on the edge of Acul village that has a couple of rooms turned into six-bed dorms with bunks and bathrooms with hot water. Doña Magdelena is a generous host and speaks a little English. The local Acul dishes are a highlight, with stews heavy on potatoes and *tayujos* (tortillas whose dough has been stuffed with beans and cheese).

Hacienda Mil Amores CHALET $$
(☎5704-4817; itaazzari.33@hotmail.com; r per person Q185; P) These four cozy cabins, two with fireplaces, stand on a dairy farm amid the idyllic mountains of the Acul Valley. Fine meals are served in the farmhouse kitchen or on the terrace and feature cheeses from the farm. A round of cheese made from cow's milk, goat's milk or a mix of the two (Q130) is an especially tasty souvenir.

Hacienda San Antonio FARMSTAY $$
(☎5702-1907; www.quesochancol.com; r per person Q155) Located on a dairy farm started by Italian immigrants in the 1930s, this rural retreat enjoys a superb alpine-like setting. A pair of chalet-like buildings contain seven neat, wood-floored rooms, four with private bath. Among the many activities to engage in here are horseback riding, hiking and sweating in the *temascal* (Maya sauna).

Getting There & Away

Microbuses run between Nebaj and Acul every hour (Q45, 40 minutes). Acul is also a stopping point on the popular three-day hike from Nebaj to Todos Santos; you can also hike direct with Nebaj-based Guías Ixiles (p128) and take the bus back.

WESTERN HIGHLANDS

The mountainous departments of Quetzaltenango, Totonicapán and Huehuetenango are generally less visited by tourists than regions closer to Guatemala City. But with extraordinarily dramatic scenery and vibrant indigenous culture, this part of the country presents an invariably fascinating panorama. Highlights of any visit include Quetzaltenango ('Xela' for short), Guatemala's second-largest city, with an ever-growing language school and volunteer work scene; the nearby town of Zunil, with its volcanically heated springs and Maya deity; ascents of the volcanoes around Quetzaltenango; and the remote mountain enclave of Todos Santos Cuchumatán, north of Huehuetenango, with a strong traditional culture and excellent walking possibilities.

Quetzaltenango

POP 166,700 / ELEV 2367M

Quetzaltenango is Guatemala's second city. It has a great atmosphere – not too big, not too small, enough foreigners to support a good range of hotels and restaurants, but not so many that it loses its national flavor. The Guatemalan 'layering' effect is at work in the city center – once the Spanish moved out, the Germans moved in and their architecture gives the zone a somber, even Gothic, feel.

The city's name might be a mouthful, but locals kindly shorten it to Xela (*shell*-ah), an abbreviation of the original K'iche' Maya name, Xelajú.

Xela is popular with travelers with time to settle in to a place and work on their Spanish. It also functions as a base for a range of spectacular hikes through the surrounding countryside – the ascent to the summit of Volcán Tajumulco (Central America's highest point) and the three-day trek to Lago de Atitlán, to name a few.

History

Quetzaltenango came under the sway of the K'iche' Maya of K'umarcaaj when they began their great expansion in the 14th century. Before that it had been a Mam Maya town. It was near here that the K'iche' leader Tecún Umán was defeated and killed by the Spanish conquistador Pedro de Alvarado in 1524.

The town prospered in the late-19th-century coffee boom, with brokers opening warehouses and mostly-German *finca* (plantation) owners coming to town to buy supplies. Wealthy Quetzaltenango briefly declared independence from Guatemala in 1896, during one of the country's periodic dictatorships. Its boom busted when a combined earthquake and eruption of Santa María in 1902 wreaked mass destruction. Still, the city's position at the intersection of roads to the Pacific Slope, Mexico and Guatemala City guaranteed it some degree of prosperity. Today it's again busy with commerce, of the indigenous, foreign and *ladino* (a person of mixed indigenous and European parentage) varieties.

VOLUNTEERING IN XELA

The Quetzaltenango area has many nonprofit organizations working on social projects with the K'iche' Maya that welcome volunteers. Volunteer jobs can range from designing websites for indigenous organizations to working in animal shelters. You can volunteer part-time for a week or two while also studying Spanish, or you can live and work in a close-knit indigenous village for a year. Indeed, some schools exist primarily to generate funds for social projects and can help students to participate in their free time. Skills in fields such as medicine, nursing, teaching, youth work and computers are prized. Volunteers must normally meet all their own costs and be willing to commit to a project for a specified minimum time. Three months is fairly typical for full-time posts.

EntreMundos (p142) is a trusted solidarity organisation that works with NGOs and community groups, offering skill-building workshops and computer classes to local NGO workers. Its website has details of 100 projects all over Guatemala looking for volunteers, and its free bilingual bimonthly magazine features articles about social development and human rights issues, as well as local volunteer opportunities.

Quetzaltenango

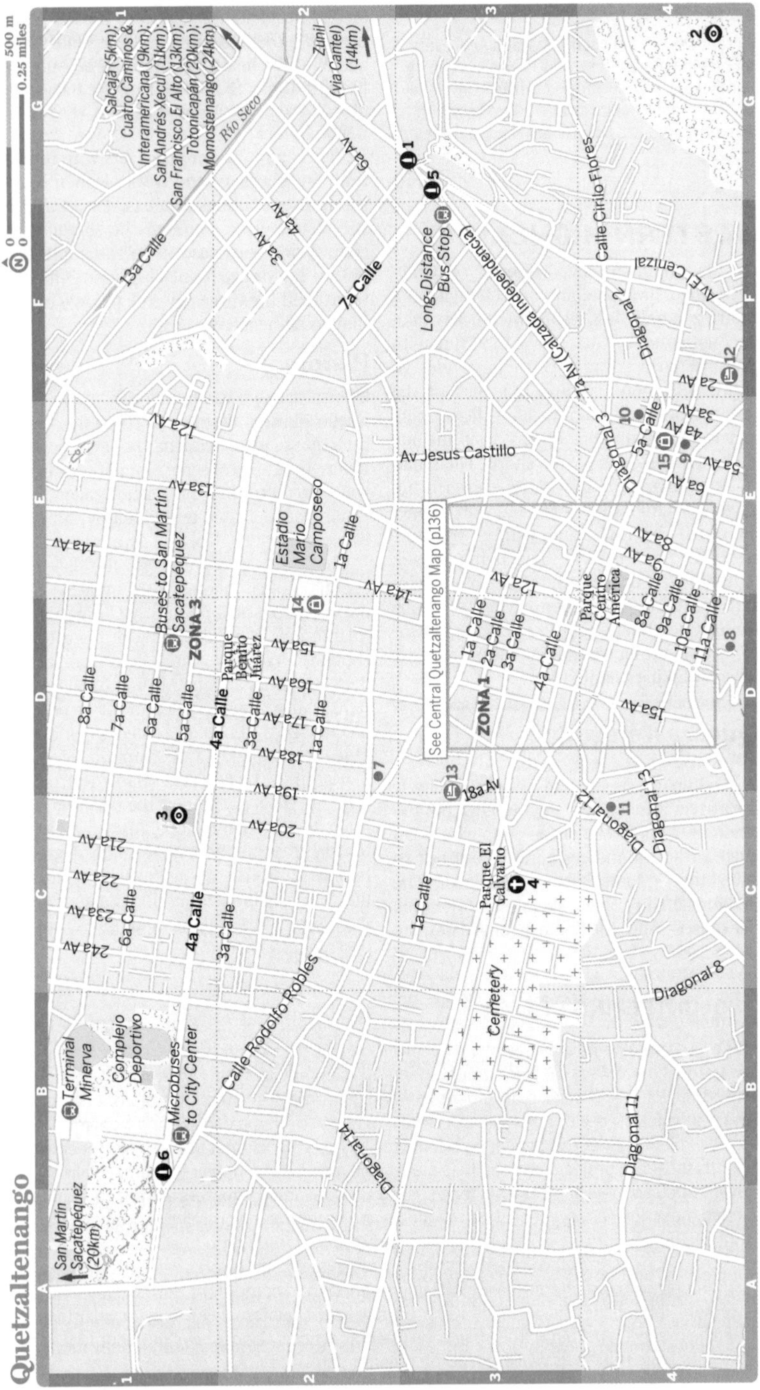

0 500 m
0 0.25 miles
N
San Martín Sacatepéquez (20km)
Terminal Minerva
Complejo Deportivo
Microbuses to City Center
Calle Rodolfo Robles
Diagonal 14
Cemetery
Parque El Calvario
Diagonal 11
Diagonal 8
Diagonal 12
Diagonal 13
1a Calle
24a Av
23a Av
22a Av
21a Av
20a Av
19a Av
18a Av
17a Av
16a Av
15a Av
14a Av
13a Av
12a Av
6a Calle
4a Calle
3a Calle
8a Calle
7a Calle
5a Calle
Buses to San Martín Sacatepéquez
ZONA 3
Parque Benito Juárez
Estadio Mario Camposeco
ZONA 1
See Central Quetzaltenango Map (p136)
2a Calle
3a Calle
4a Calle
Parque Centro América
8a Calle
9a Calle
10a Calle
11a Calle
8a Av
9a Av
6a Av
5a Av
4a Av
3a Av
2a Av
5a Calle
Diagonal 3
Diagonal 2
Av El Cenizal
Calle Cirilo Flores
7a Av (Calzada Independencia)
Long-Distance Bus Stop
Av Jesus Castillo
7a Calle
13a Calle
Río Seco
Salcajá (5km); Cuatro Caminos & Interamericana (9km); San Andrés Xecul (11km); San Francisco El Alto (13km); Totonicapán (20km); Momostenango (24km)
Zunil (via Cantel) (14km)
A
B
C
D
E
F
G
1
2
3
4

Quetzaltenango

Sights

Parque Centro América PLAZA
(Map p136) Most of Xela's sights crowd in and around the broad central plaza. It's a great place for a stroll or to sit and people watch. It was originally two separate parks, designed by Italian architect Alberto Porta in the 19th century; these were combined in a 1930s update into its current oblong shape. The most notable of the monuments scattered along its expanse is a rotunda of Ionic columns dedicated to the composer Rafael Álvarez Ovalle.

In the center of the plaza is a pillar dedicated to Justo Rufino Barrios, the 19th-century president whose 'reforms' transferred land ownership from Maya peasants to coffee-plantation owners.

Cemetery CEMETERY
(Map p132; Parque El Calvario, Zona 1; 6am-5.30pm) Quetzaltenango's enormous cemetery is a pleasant and fascinating green space for a walk. To the left of the main entrance, visit the grave of the gypsy Vanushka, spurned and shamed by her wealthy lover until she died of a broken heart. Flowers are still left at her grave by those seeking better fortune in affairs of the heart. We recommend only visiting Friday to Sunday during the day, when there are plenty of people around.

Cerro el Baúl VIEWPOINT
(Map p132) This wooded hill is a popular weekend destination for city dwellers, for its wonderful views across Xela's broad plain and to the volcanos that fringe it. There's a small cafe, some surprisingly fast and scary kids' slides and a giant obelisk with great Mayan warrior Tecún Umán carved in relief – legend claims he is buried on this spot.

Centro Intercultural de Quetzaltenango CULTURAL CENTER
(Map p132; 4a Calle & 19a Av, Zona 3) FREE Quetzaltenango's railroad station, 1km east of the Templo de Minerva along 4a Calle, lay dormant for many years until the city converted it into this center, which now houses schools of art and dance, plus three interesting museums.

The **Museo Ixkik'** (Map p132; 5653-5585; 4a Calle & 19a Av, Zona 3; donation requested Q35; 9am-5pm Mon-Fri) is devoted to Maya weaving and traditional outfits, while some 400 paintings by Guatemala's leading modernists are exhibited in the **Museo de Arte** (Map p132; 4a Calle & 19a Av, Zona 3; donation requested; 9am-1pm & 3-7pm), including works by Efraín Recinos, Juan Antonio Franco and the landscape artist José Luis Álvarez. The **Museo del Ferrocarril de los Altos** (Map p132; 4a Calle & 19a Av, Zona 3; Q6; 9:30am-1pm & 3-6pm) covers the ambitious rail project that connected Quetzaltenango to the Pacific coast but operated for just three years from 1930 to 1933.

Cathedral CATHEDRAL
(Map p136) The ornately carved facade of the Iglesia del Espíritu Santo marks the site of the original 1532 construction, which was pulverized by the quakes of 1853 and 1902. The modern Metropolitan Cathedral behind it was constructed in the 1990s.

Iglesia El Calvario CHURCH
(Map p132) The church that lends its name to the neighborhood west of the center was built four centuries ago on a rise to avoid Xela's periodic flooding. Check out the grand interior with its unusually broad single-nave design. Calvario is one of the chief way stations during Semana Santa celebrations.

Templo de Minerva MONUMENT
(Map p132) FREE Rising incongruously from an island in the middle of traffic-choked 4a Calle, this temple was erected by dictator Estrada Cabrera to honor the Roman goddess of education and to inspire Guatemalans to new heights of learning. Bizarre contrast notwithstanding, it makes a handy shelter during a rainstorm and a useful landmark for the nearby bus terminal

Arco Del Sexto Estado MONUMENT
(Map p132) This monumental arch that greets all visitors on the road into Xela commemorates the 1897 Quetzalteca Revolution, a short-lived uprising in the city against dictatorial rule from Guatemala City. A lion mounts the arch and beneath it an inscription to the revolution's dead reads 'the love of freedom made them heroes, the hatred of tyrants made them martyrs', reminding visitors that the city retains its independent spirit even today.

Museo de Historia Natural MUSEUM
(Map p136; 7761-6427; 7a Calle, Zona 1; Q6; 8am-noon & 2-6pm Mon-Fri, 9am-5pm Sat & Sun) The natural history museum holds a hodgepodge of Maya artifacts, vintage photos, dried leaves, old coins, marimbas, sports trophies, stuffed mammals and birds, all displayed in cases reminiscent of elementary school outings. Most interesting, perhaps, is the section devoted to the liberal revolution in Central American politics and the Estado de Los Altos, of which Quetzaltenango was once the capital.

Activities

Yoga House YOGA
(Map p136; www.yogahousexela.wordpress.com; 9a Av 6-68, Zona 1; per class/week Q20/50) The best place to practice yoga in Quetzaltenango. There are daily hatha yoga classes aimed at either beginner or intermediate levels, as well as Ashtanga yoga. On Saturdays there are free fitness training sessions where you 'only pay in sweat and tears'.

Los Vahos SWIMMING
(Q10; 8am-6pm) Just a short hike south of Xela are the rough-and-ready sauna/steam baths at Los Vahos (the Vapors). These natural saunas are just two dark stone rooms behind plastic curtains – occasionally the vents are carpeted with eucalyptus leaves, giving the steam a herbal quality. The baths are a 2km (1.2mi) uphill walk away, with good views of the city.

Courses

Language Courses

Quetzaltenango's many language schools attract students from around the world, and the city makes for a different, possibly more studious, scene than heavily touristed Antigua.

Standard weekly prices start at Q900/1000 for four/five hours of instruction per day, Monday to Friday. Add around Q350 to Q450 for room and board with a local family. Some places charge up to 20% more for tuition in the June to August high season, and many require nonrefundable registration fees. Extras range from movies, dance and cooking classes to talks on Guatemalan politics and culture.

★ **Proyecto Lingüístico Quetzalteco de Español** LANGUAGE
(Map p132; 7763-1061; www.plqe.org; 5a Calle 2-40, Zona 1) This collectively managed and politically minded language institute also runs the **Escuela de la Montaña**, a limited-enrolment language-learning program in a rural zone near the town of Colomba. Intensive courses in K'iche' are also offered, along with classes on Latin American history and literature.

El Quetzal Spanish School LANGUAGE
(Map p132; 7761-2784; www.elquetzalspanish.com; 7a Calle 4-24, Zona 1) One of the few indigenous-owned and run Spanish school in town, offering plenty of activities.

Centro de Estudios de Español Pop Wuj LANGUAGE
(Map p132; 7761-8286; www.pop-wuj.org; 1a Calle 17-72, Zona 1) As well as running Spanish classes, Pop Wuj's profits go to rural development projects in nearby K'iche' villages, in which students can participate.

Inepas LANGUAGE
(Instituto de Español y Participación en Ayuda Social; Map p136; 7765-1308; www.inepas.org; 15a Av 4-59) Guatemalan social issues are woven into the Spanish lessons at this Unesco-recognized NGO that promotes educational development in rural communities, and students can participate in a variety of worthy projects. The institute offers a selection of inexpensive accommodations as well as homestays.

El Portal Spanish School LANGUAGE
(Map p132; 7761-5275; www.spanishschoolelportal.com; 9a Callejón A 11-49, Zona 1) Small

WORTH A TRIP

HIKING ROUTES AROUND XELA

There are many exciting walks and climbs to be done from Xela. **Volcán Tajumulco** (4220m), 50km northwest, is the highest point in Central America, and is a challenging one-day trek from the city or two days with a night camping on the mountain. This includes about five hours of walking up from the starting point, Tuhichan (2½ hours by bus from Xela).

With early starts, **Volcán Santa María** (3772m), towering to the south of the city, and the highly active **Santiaguito** (2488m), on Santa María's southwest flank, can both be done in long mornings from Xela, though their tough, slippery trails are recommended only for seasoned hikers. You start walking to both at the village of Llanos del Pinal, 5km south of Xela (Q5 by bus), from where it's four to five hours up to the summit of Santa María. Getting too close to Santiaguito is dangerous, so people usually just look at it from a point about 1½ hours' walk from Llanos del Pinal.

Popular non-volcano hikes include the three-day walk from Xela to Lago de Atitlán, and the six-day hike from Nebaj to Todos Santos Cuchumatán.

Most tour agencies organise volcano treks, but it's worth shopping around to find the one you like best. Prices start at around Q200 for Santa María, and Q450 for the overnight Tajumulco hike. The Xela–Lago de Atitlán trek comes in at around Q700.

outfit with an enthusiastic and supportive atmosphere. Income from classes helps provide scholarships for local children of single mothers.

Other Courses

★Trama Textiles WEAVING
(Map p136; www.tramatextiles.org; 3a Calle 10-56, Zona 1) A fair-trade shop representing 17 weaving cooperatives from five different regions of Guatemala, Trama Textiles also offers backstrap-loom weaving classes, taught alongside a history of traditional Guatemalan textiles. Options range from a simple demonstration of techniques (Q40) to a one-on-one 20-hour course in which you produce an embroidered table runner (Q675).

Bakanos Dance Studio DANCING
(Map p136; ☎5651-4474; www.facebook.com/bakanosstudio; 15a Av 3-51, Zona 1; group/individual session Q35/125) Learn or improve your salsa, *merengue*, *bacchata* and *cumbia* moves at this locally recommended studio.

Tours

★Monte Verde Tours TOURS
(Map p136; ☎5729-6279; www.monte-verdetours.com; 13a Av 8-34, Zona 1) Highly recommended local trekking and cultural tourism outfit, with knowledgeable and friendly guides. Itineraries close to Xela include tours to Zunil and Fuentes Georginas, day hikes up Santa María and overnight treks on Tajumulco. It also ranges south to Takalik Abaj and its nearby coffee and rubber plantations.

Guate Guides ADVENTURE
(Map p136; ☎5195-7734; www.guateguides.com; 6a Calle 15-16, Zona 1) This small, locally run outfit offers tours to area volcanoes, villages and nature reserves, with an emphasis on quality equipment and knowledgeable commentary. Among the excursions are half-day cycling trips to San Andrés Xequl via the Samalá river valley, climbs up Santa María and Tacaná volcanoes, and photography tours to the quetzal reserve near San Marcos.

Altiplano's Tour Operator CULTURAL
(Map p136; ☎7766-9614; www.altiplanos.com.gt; 6a Calle 7-55, Zona 1; half-day tours per person Q250-350) This outfit offers some interesting half-day tours to indigenous villages and markets, colonial churches and coffee plantations around Xela, as well as volcano hikes.

Quetzaltrekkers ADVENTURE
(Map p132; ☎7765-5895; www.quetzaltrekkers.com; Diagonal 12 8-37, Zona 1) Most of the guides at this outfit are foreign volunteers (experienced trekkers can join their ranks). It offers one-day hikes to Fuentes Georginas and Santa María volcano, three-day trips to Lago de Atitlán and six-day treks from Nebaj to Todos Santos Cuchumatán run on a weekly basis; check the calendar to see when they go. Based at the rear of the Casa Argentina hotel.

Adrenalina Tours TOURS
(Map p136; ☎7761-4509; www.adrenalinatours.com; 13a Av & 4a Calle, Pasaje Enríquez, Zona 1) Provides a range of trips in the Xela area, including to Laguna de Chicabal, Fuentes

Central Quetzaltenango

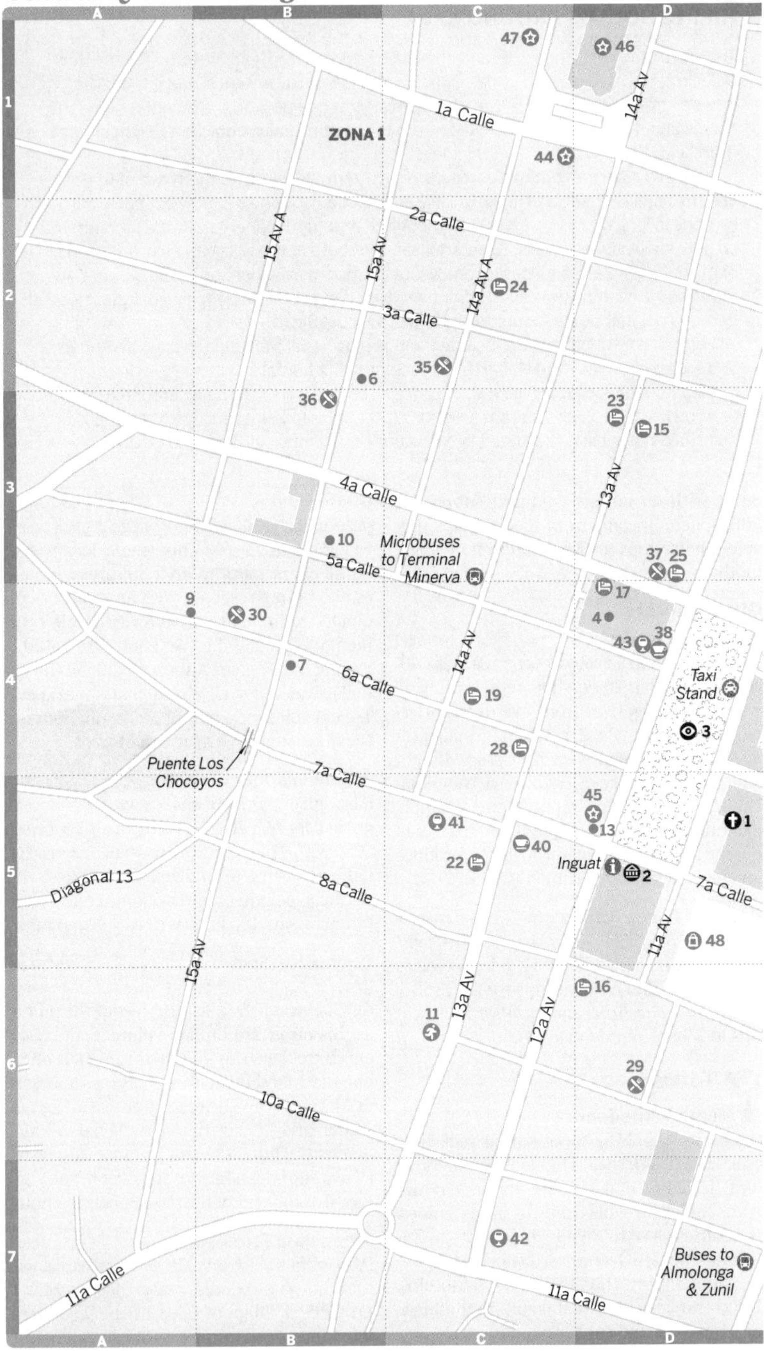

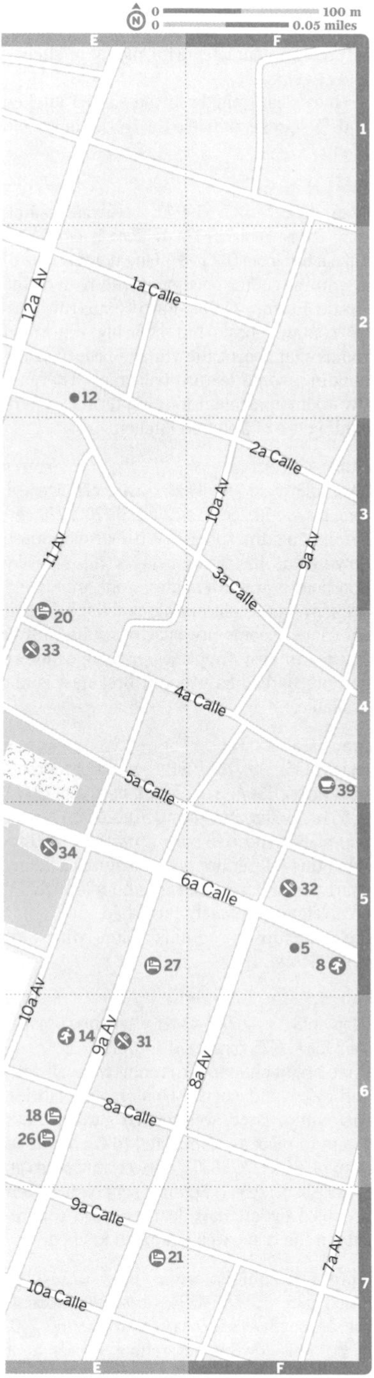

Central Quetzaltenango

Sights
1 Cathedral ... D5
2 Museo de Historia Natural ... D5
3 Parque Centro América ... D4

Activities, Courses & Tours
4 Adrenalina Tours ... D4
5 Altiplano's Tour Operator ... F5
6 Bakanos Dance Studio ... B2
7 Celas Maya ... B4
8 EntreMundos ... F5
9 Guate Guides ... A4
10 Inepas ... B3
11 Monte Verde Tours ... C6
12 Trama Textiles ... E2
13 Tranvía de los Altos ... D5
14 Yoga House ... E6

Sleeping
15 Black Cat Hostel ... D3
16 Casa Morasan ... D6
17 Casa Nativos ... D4
18 Casa Seibel ... E6
Guest House El Puente ... (see 7)
19 Hostal Casa Doña Mercedes ... C4
20 Hotel Bonifaz ... E4
21 Hotel Casa del Viajero ... E7
22 Hotel Kiktem-Ja ... C5
23 Hotel Los Olivos ... D3
24 Hotel Modelo ... C2
25 Hotel Villa Real Plaza ... D3
26 Kasa Kiwi ... E6
27 Posada Catedral Hotel ... E5
28 Villa de Don Andrés ... C4

Eating
29 Aj de Lunas ... D6
30 Café Canela ... B4
Doña Cristy ... (see 48)
31 Esquina Asiatica ... E6
32 La Red Kat ... F5
33 La Stampa Bistro ... E4
34 Panque Waffles ... E5
35 Sabe Delis ... C2
36 Sabor de la India ... B3
37 Tacorazon ... D3

Drinking & Nightlife
38 Café El Balcón del Enríquez ... D4
39 Café La Luna ... F4
40 El Cuartito ... C5
41 King & Queen ... C5
42 Pool & Beer ... C7
43 Salón Tecún ... D4

Entertainment
44 Bari ... C1
45 Casa No'j ... D5
46 Teatro Municipal ... D1
47 Teatro Roma ... C1

Shopping
48 Central Market ... D5

Georginas and El Aprisco nature reserve, plus week-long itineraries focused on Maya cosmology and Guatemala's natural attractions.

Tranvía de los Altos TOURS
(Map p136; ☎5752-8369; www.tranviadelosaltos.com; Q50) This curious pseudo-streetcar does various circuits of the city, complete with knowledgeable commentary (in Spanish) and cheesy sound effects. Two-hour tours start at 11am and 3pm, departing from the south side of the Parque Central.

Festivals & Events

Feria de la Virgen del Rosario CULTURAL
(Feria Centroamericana de Independencia; ⊙Sep/Oct) Held in late September or early October, this is Xela's big annual party. Students create colorful 'flower' carpets of sawdust upon the streets of the city, taxi drivers shoot fireworks and the sirens of the fire trucks wail. Residents kick up their heels at a fairground on the city's perimeter and there's plenty of entertainment across town, including a battle of the brass bands in the Parque Centro América.

Sleeping

With a continual influx of foreign volunteers and language students, Xela counts numerous long-term-stay options. Some guesthouses offer furnished apartments and most language institutes can set up homestays with local families. Local rentals are listed in the classified section of the publication *XelaWho*.

★**Kasa Kiwi** HOSTEL $
(Map p136; ☎7765-4251; www.kasakiwi.com; 9a Av 8-38, Zona 1; dm Q50, r with/without bathroom Q170/120; 📶) Despite its distinctly un-Guatemalan name, Kasa Kiwi has quickly established itself as a top player on Xela's hostel scene. Generously-sized dorms mean that everyone gets a bed not a bunk, and there are also a handful of private rooms, a kitchen and helpful staff. The relaxed roof terrace-bar clinches the deal, with rare views across the town to the mountains.

Casa Seibel HOSTEL $
(Map p136; ☎7765-2130; www.casaseibel.com; 9a Av 8-10, Zona 1; dm/r Q50/120; 📶) Incorporated into a late 19th-century Xela house, Casa Seibel is cozy and comfortable. Set around two plant-filled courtyards, its dorms and private rooms (sharing two bathrooms, one with tub) have attractive wood floors and painted ceilings and retain some original furniture and character with plenty of shelves and closet space.

Guests can mingle in the shared kitchen and TV lounge, or tickle the ivories of the old piano.

Casa Nativos HOSTEL $
(Map p136; ☎7765-4723; www.casanativos.com; Pasaje Enríquez, 13a Av, Zona 1; dm Q40, d without bathroom Q125; 📶) One component of a cultural center occupying the rear of the Pasaje Enríquez, this Euro/Guate-run hostel contains basic but stylishly renovated rooms that accent the vintage beauty of the building; some feature balconies. There's a two-room apartment for long-term stays, including use of a shared kitchen.

Hotel Kiktem-Ja HOTEL $
(Map p136; ☎7761-4304; www.hotelkiktem-ja.com; 13a Av 7-18, Zona 1; s/d/tr Q135/200/270; 🅿) Set in an atmospheric 100-year-old house downtown, the Kiktem-Ja is all squeaky floorboards at weird angles, stone arches and squiggly wood columns along foliage-draped corridors. Rooms are spacious with sturdy bedsteads, cosy fireplaces, arched windows and pretty tiled bathrooms. Breakfast is not available.

Black Cat Hostel HOSTEL $
(Map p136; ☎7761-2091; www.facebook.com/blackcatxela; 13a Av 3-33, Zona 1; dm incl breakfast Q55, r with/without bathroom Q170/120; 📶) A popular place to head to meet up with other travelers, this full-service hostel features a sunny courtyard, a bar-restaurant and a lounge/TV area. Though sparsely furnished, the rooms are done up in soothing colors with nice wood floors.

Guest House El Puente HOSTEL $
(Map p136; ☎7761-4342; celasmaya@gmail.com; 15a Av 6-75, Zona 1; s/d/tr Q75/150/225) The three bright and modern rooms here, all with bathroom and cheery Guatemalan fabrics, surround a large, well-tended garden that's a gem to relax in. Connected to **Celas Maya** (Map p136; ☎7765-8205; www.celasmaya.edu.gt; 6a Calle 14-55, Zona 1) Spanish school, it's often occupied by language learners who congregate in the large, well-equipped kitchen.

Hotel Casa del Viajero HOTEL $
(Map p136; ☎7761-4594; casadelviajeroxela@hotmail.com; 8a Av 9-17, Zona 1; s/d/tr Q90/160/240; 🅿📶) This low-budget refuge stands at a

high-traffic intersection, though things are thankfully calmer beyond the glassed-in reception area. A series of fluorescent-lit, brick-walled rooms of varying size and shape open onto a green interior patio. Bright paint jobs make the best of an otherwise austere building.

Posada Catedral Hotel GUESTHOUSE **$$**
(Map p136; ☎7765-2472; www.hotelposadacatedral.com; 9a Av 6-47, Zona 1; s/d incl breakfast Q300/400) A cosy guesthouse centred on the obligatory courtyard, with clean white rooms and dark-wood colonial-style furniture. The rooms on the upper level are slightly brighter and lovelier with skyline views, but it's a welcoming place across the board. There's a small bar-restaurant tucked into the courtyard corner.

Hostal Casa Doña Mercedes BOUTIQUE HOTEL **$$**
(Map p136; ☎7765-4687; 6a Calle 13-42, Zona 1; s/d Q190/300, without bathroom Q100/180; wi-fi) Two blocks west of Parque Centro América is this good-value, quiet establishment. Neat rooms have a bit of colonial flair with burnished wood floors and wicker bedsteads, and there's plenty of space to lounge around. Well-equipped guest kitchen.

Hostal 7 Orejas HOSTEL **$$**
(Map p132; ☎7768-3218; www.facebook.com/7Orejas; 2a Calle 16-92, Zona 1; dm/s/d/tr Q70/180/320/400; P @) The 'Seven Ears' (named after a nearby mountain range) is a scrupulously maintained hostel on a quiet street northwest of the center. The pseudo-colonial structure features spacious, clean rooms alongside a strip of garden. Each has three queen-size beds with carved-wood chests for storage. Breakfast (not included) is served on the rooftop terrace.

Casa San Bartolomé B&B **$$**
(Map p132; ☎7761-9511; www.casasanbartolome.com; 2a Av 7-17, Zona 1; s/d/tr Q175/225/336; P wi-fi) In the family for generations, this atmospheric old residence has been converted into a cozy B&B. All six rooms have beautiful furniture and modern art. Guests may prepare meals in a shared kitchen and take tea on the lovely and leafy upper terrace. Located in a quiet neighborhood a 15-minute walk east of the park.

Villa de Don Andrés B&B **$$**
(Map p136; ☎7761-2014; www.hotelvilladedonandres.com; 13a Av 6-16, Zona 1; s/d/tr incl breakfast Q280/400/550, without bathroom Q190/350/380; P wi-fi) This B&B in the center of town is a welcoming sort of place. Done up with antique decor, historic photos and colorful woven bedspreads, the seven large carpeted rooms are pleasantly arranged along a broad patio where a complimentary breakfast is served.

Hotel Modelo HOTEL **$$**
(Map p136; ☎7761-2529; www.hotelmodelo1892.com; 14a Av A 2-31, Zona 1; s/d from Q400/525; P @ wi-fi pets) A few blocks below the Teatro Municipal, the colonial-style Modelo offers 19 atmospheric rooms with wooden floorboards, firm beds and spacious bathrooms. These are lined up alongside pretty patios with seasonal flower arrangements and an old-fashioned dining room with cupboards of china and a relaxed bar.

Look out for the many bright paintings by the celebrated Xela artist Zipacná de León – you can tell he was one of Picasso's godsons.

Hotel Villa Real Plaza HOTEL **$$**
(Map p136; ☎7761-4045; hotelvillarealplazaventas@gmail.com; 4a Calle 12-22, Zona 1; s/d/tr Q280/380/450; P wi-fi) Beyond the frosted glass doorway, this grand old hotel, just off the main square, is the picture of faded elegance, with stone archways and sweeping staircases around a lavish courtyard. Though on the gloomy side, rooms here are quite spacious, with high ceilings and mock fireplaces.

Hotel Los Olivos HOTEL **$$**
(Map p136; ☎7765-3469; hotel.losolivos13@hotmail.com; 13a Av 3-32, Zona 1; s/d/tr incl breakfast Q140/260/360; P wi-fi) This compact lodging offers comfortable rooms with firm beds and wood slat ceilings, all opening on to plant-filled interior balconies. There's a small restaurant. It's just up the hill from Pasaje Enríquez.

★ **Casa Morasan** BOUTIQUE HOTEL **$$$**
(Map p136; ☎7765-0616; www.casamorasan.com; 12a Av 8-21, Zona 1; d/tr/ste from Q500/650/700) It's difficult not to be charmed by Casa Morasan. Set in a restored townhouse, rooms cluster around a courtyard with trickling fountain, and lots of old wooden features and tile work offset by gleaming whitewash. Rooms are a comfortable mix of traditional and contemporary design, with crisp linens and modern bathrooms.

If you fancy some self-catering, the suite has a small kitchen.

Hotel Bonifaz HOTEL $$$
(Map p136; ☎7723-1100; www.pensionbonifaz.com.gt; 4a Calle 10-50, Zona 1; s/d/tr Q695/790/950; P @ ≋) The oldest and grandest hotel in Xela looms above the Parque Centro América. Comfortable, refurbished rooms are on the top three floors; the 2nd-floor chambers surround a leafy colonial patio where breakfast is served, and there's an opulent front bar where you can drink cocktails and make like you're part of the city's cognoscenti.

Eating

Quetzaltenango has an excellent selection of places to eat in all price ranges. Cheapest are the food stalls on the lower level of the central market, where snacks and main-course plates are sold for Q10 or less. Most restaurants are just a few minutes' walk from Parque Centro América.

★ **Aj de Lunas** GUATEMALAN $
(Map p136; ☎7761-0097; 9a Calle 11-16, Zona 1; lunch combos Q25; ⏱8am-9pm Mon-Sat; 📶 ✎) This simple but cheerful dining hall is a good place to savor Xela home cooking, with daily specials like *jocón* (stew with tomatillo and cilantro) and *caldo de patas* (cow foot soup) served with a pile of tortillas and little dishes of lemons and tiny chilies. Vegetarian options are available.

★ **Esquina Asiatica** ASIAN $
(Map p136; ☎7763-0316; 9a Av 6-79, Zona 1; starters Q15-30, mains Q25-40; ⏱8am-9pm Mon-Sat, 8am-1pm Sun) This charming upstairs restaurant refreshes palates with generous plates from around Asia – Chinese dumplings, Indonesia satay, pad thai, Vietnamese spring rolls and more, against a backdrop of vintage travel posters. Early risers will enjoy delicious non-Asian breakfasts including Parmesan avocado on toast and ultra-filling fruity yogurt parfait with chia. There are regular buffet events and live music. Alcohol is served.

La Red Kat GUATEMALAN $
(Map p136; www.cafered.org; 8a Av 5-19, Zona 1; weekly specials Q50; ⏱11am-5pm Mon, 10am-10pm Tue-Sat; 📶) An alternative cultural center focusing on the economic reintegration of returning migrants, La Red Kat also provides grants for young chefs in training, which translates into gourmet meals at popular prices. Locally grown greens go into salads, soups and burritos, and there are nightly specials. Meals are served in a pretty patio and the various salons around it.

Café Canela GUATEMALAN $
(Map p136; ☎7761-6654; 6a Calle 15-16, Zona 1; lunch menus Q20; ⏱7am-3pm Mon-Fri; 📶 ✎) For breakfast and lunch on weekdays, *la nicaragüense* owner has a simple setup with a sunny patio and alternative vibe. You'll find creative variations on the essential *menú del día* (Q20), nicely dressed salads and tasty soups. There are three set lunch choices daily including a vegan option. Wash it down with a fresh juice (Q12).

Panque Waffles INTERNATIONAL $
(Map p136; 6a Calle 10-25, Zona 1; waffles from Q25, burgers from Q38; ⏱9am-9pm; 📶) A good recipe for any restaurant is to do one or two things, and do them well. Panque Waffles nails it with, um, waffles, as well as brilliant burgers. Throw in some coffee and juices, decent wi-fi and some urban shabby chic, and you can see why it's so popular with Xela hipsters tapping away on their MacBooks.

Tacorazon MEXICAN $
(Map p136; 12a Av, Zona 1; burritos Q25; ⏱noon-10pm Mon-Sat, noon-5pm Sun) Burritos lovers need go no further than Tacorazon to fill their boots. Conveniently tucked into a corner across from the main park, this bright place does deliciously stuffed burritos made to order in increasingly monstrous sizes. A plate of fries with guacamole makes the perfect side, and if you're not going for takeaway, the in-house mojitos aren't too bad either.

Doña Cristy GUATEMALAN $
(Map p136; snacks from Q10; ⏱7am-7pm) One of various snack stalls on the lower level of the central market, Doña Cristy cheerfully serves *atol de elote* (a hot maize beverage), empanadas and *chuchitos* (small tamales garnished with chopped beets and grated cheese).

Sabe Delis CRÊPES $
(Map p136; ☎7761-2635; 14a Av A 3-38; crepes Q35-50; 📶) Crepes and wood-fired pizzas are the main attractions at this upscale dining hall, which also prepares exceptionally zesty salads. Popular with both foreigners and *chapines* (Guatemalans). Eat in or order ahead to takeaway to your digs.

★ **Sabor de la India** INDIAN $$
(Map p136; ☎7765-2555; 15a Av 3-64, Zona 1; mains Q50-70; ⏱noon-10pm Tue-Sun; 📶 ✎) Authentic south Indian fare is whipped up here

by a fellow from Kerala. Servings are huge; the *thalis* – platters of curried veggies, chicken or beef – are highly recommended, and the paneer (cheese) almost as good as anything you'd find on the subcontinent itself. Perennially popular.

La Stampa Bistro INTERNATIONAL **$$**
(Map p136; 4a Calle, cnr of Parque Centro América, Zona 1; mains from Q45; ⏲8am-10pm Sun-Wed, 8am-11pm Thu-Sat) This cute bistro just off the central plaza is liberally decorated with printing paraphernalia – the owner's great-grandfather ran Xela's first printing workshop. The menu has a bit of everything – steaks, fresh pasta and salad dishes, as well a good wine menu. There's breakfast too, making it ideal for early starts as well as romantic dinners.

Drinking & Nightlife

Coffee and hot chocolate fuel much of Xela's day-to-day life, and there are plenty of places to grab a cup.

Xela's Zona Viva revolves around the Teatro Municipal, with discos and clubs popping up along 1a and 2a Calles and up 14 Av.

★ Salón Tecún PUB
(Map p136; Pasaje Enríquez, Zona 1; ⏲9:30am-12:30am) On the plaza end of the elegant Pasaje Enríquez, alive day and night with a healthy mix of Guatemalans and foreigners quaffing Cabro by the liter, the Tecún claims to be the country's longest-running bar (since 1935). It also serves good pizza and pub food, and frequently has someone picking out songs on their guitar. An essential Xela experience.

★ Café La Luna CAFE
(Map p136; ☎7761-4354; 8a Av 4-11, Zona 1; ⏲11am-9pm Mon-Fri, 4-9pm Sat; wi-fi) For chocolate aficionados, this is a shrine. Made from scratch on the premises, the chocolate is velvety smooth and served in a variety of beverages: the chocolate cappuccino is especially good. Groups of friends gather in the various salons, which are littered with vintage bric-a-brac.

El Cuartito CAFE
(Map p136; 13a Av 7-09, Zona 1; ⏲10am-11pm; wi-fi) This offbeat cafe-bar is a point of reference for travelers and language students, with quirky decor and art installations. It serves a good range of breakfasts, vegetarian snacks, herbal teas and organic coffee just about any way you want it, plus some creative cocktails – how about a raspberry mojito? There's regular live music.

King & Queen PUB
(Map p136; 7a Calle 13-27, Zona 1; ⏲6pm-1am) This tiny pub packs in a mixed crowd, so count on a bilingual evening. Whether there's live music, a heated trivia quiz (Tuesday) or karaoke (Thursday), the giant playing cards on the wall take it all in.

Café El Balcón del Enríquez CAFE
(Map p136; 12a Av 4-40, Pasaje Enríquez; ⏲8am-10pm) With specially designed viewing counters overlooking the Parque Centro América, this lively cafe-bar on the upper level of the Pasaje Enríquez makes a nice perch for morning espresso or evening cocktails; great terrace views.

Pool & Beer PUB
(Map p136; 12a Av 10-21; ⏲7:30pm-1am Thu-Sat) There's no mistaking what's on offer at this refreshingly unfashionable spot. The pool tables are worn and the cues crooked, but this ramshackle clubhouse remains a friendly place. As the evening proceeds, the DJ gets louder and the dance floor starts to jump.

☆ Entertainment

Parque Centro América is a popular place for an evening stroll.

The music scene is particularly strong in Xela. Many of the town's restaurants, cafes and bars double as performance venues between Wednesday and Saturday – to see what's on, pick up a copy of *XelaWho*.

Teatro Municipal THEATER
(Map p136; ☎7761-2218; www.teatromunicipalquetzaltenango.org; 14a Av & 1a Calle, Zona 1) Quetzaltenango's grand neoclassical theater north of the center is the main venue for plays, concerts and dance performances. An elaborate two-tiered curved wooden balcony has private boxes for prominent families. During the day, it's sometimes possible to pop in to admire the interior, which dates from 1895.

Bari LIVE MUSIC
(Map p136; 1a Calle 14-31, Zona 1; ⏲8pm-1am Wed-Sat) One of several nightspots opposite the Teatro Municipal, Bari hosts live acoustic and Latin music every Wednesday to Sunday. Performances tend to start at around 9.30pm.

Teatro Roma THEATER
(Map p136; ☎3010-0100; 14a Av A-34, Zona 1) This palace of culture is a showcase primarily for comedy revues and plays, with the occasional dance program.

Casa No'j PERFORMING ARTS
(Map p136; ☎7761-4400; www.centroculturalcasanoj.blogspot.com; 7a Calle 12-12, Zona 1; ⏱8am-6pm Mon-Fri) Just off the park's southwest corner, the 19th-century former Convent of Bethlehem now houses Xela's premier cultural center. Besides photo and art exhibits, it stages anything from poetry festivals to marimba recitals to archaeology conferences, and it occasionally hosts internationally acclaimed artists and literary figures. Regional food festivals take place here on Sundays. Check the blog for upcoming events.

Shopping

Pixan CLOTHING
(Map p132; ☎7761-6408; www.amaguate.org; 5a Av 6-17, Zona 1; ⏱9am-5pm Mon-Fri) Outlet shop for the women's empowerment association AMA (highland women's association), Pixan sells beautiful high quality textiles and clothing produced by Maya weavers, often in collaboration with international designers.

Central Market MARKET
(Map p136) Xela's central market is three floors of reasonably priced handicrafts, as well as everyday items and fresh produce. Souvenir hunters will need to bargain hard.

Mercado La Democracia MARKET
(Map p132; 1a Calle, Zona 3) For one of Xela's more intense everyday marketing experiences, hit the Mercado La Democracia, about 10 blocks north of Parque Centro América in Zona 3, with food, clothing, CDs and other necessities for city dweller and villager alike.

Information

MEDIA

English-language publications are available free in bars, restaurants and cafes around town.

XelaWho (www.xelawho.com) This monthly English-language magazine lists cultural events, has a handy map and an irreverent take on life in Xela and Guatemala as a whole.

EntreMundos (Map p136; ☎7761-2179; www.entremundos.org; 6a Calle 7-31, Zona 1; ⏱2-4pm Mon-Thu) Publishes a bimonthly magazine, which has plenty of information on political developments and volunteer projects in the region.

MEDICAL SERVICES

Rainy season brings regular floods to Xela, and with it lots of diarrhoeal sicknesses – it's very easy to succumb, so pay extra attention to hygiene and hand-washing.

Hospital Privado Quetzaltenango (☎7774-4700; www.hospitalprivadoquetzaltenango.com; Calle Rodolfo Robles 23-51, Zona 1; ⏱24hr) For 24-hour emergency and ambulance service. Usually has an English-speaking doctor on staff. Recommended but can be expensive, so check you have medical insurance.

Hospital San Rafael (☎7761-4381; 9a Calle 10-41, Zona 1; ⏱24hr) Foreign insurance policies accepted.

Clínico La Fe (☎7794 3232; www.facebook.com/LaboratorioClinicoLAFE; 12a Av C-12, Zona 1) Trusted private clinic offering the full battery of laboratory tests for diagnoses. Offers free home visits.

MONEY

There are numerous ATMs at the banks around Parque Centro América.

Banco Industrial (4a Calle 11-38, Zona 1; ⏱9am-6pm Mon-Fri, 9am-1pm Sat) Also changes US dollars.

TOURIST INFORMATION

There's a plethora of tourist maps circulating, of which Xelamap is the best. Look for it at language schools and hotels.

INGUAT (Map p136; ☎7761-4931; www.vivexela.visitguatemala.com; 7a Calle 11-35, Zona 1; ⏱9am-5pm Mon-Fri, 9am-1pm Sat) Usually staffed by an English speaker; at the southern end of Parque Centro América.

Getting There & Away

BUS

All 2nd-class buses depart from **Terminal Minerva** (Map p132; 7a Calle, Zona 3), a dusty, crowded yard in the west of town, unless otherwise noted. If you're getting here by public transport, get off at the Templo de Minerva and walk through the market to the buses.

Leaving or entering town, buses bound for Salcajá, Cuatro Caminos, San Francisco El Alto and Totonicapán make a **stop** (Map p132) east of the center at the Rotonda, a traffic circle on Calz Independencia, marked by the **Monumento a la Marimba** (Map p132). Getting off here when you're coming into Xela saves the 10 to 15 minutes it will take your bus to cross town to Terminal Minerva.

Buses for Almolonga and Zunil depart throughout the day from the **Shell station** (Map p136) at the corner of 9a Avenida and 10a Calle. Buses to San Martín Sacatepéquez (for Laguna Chicabal) leave from a **stop** (Map p132; cnr of 15a Av & 6a Calle) on the corner of 15a Avenida and 6a Calle.

SHUTTLE MINIBUS

Xela travel agencies all sell tickets for shuttle minibuses to all major destinations including Antigua (Q150), Chichicastenango (Q150), Panajachel (Q125), Guatemala City (Q225), Coban/Lanquín (Q360), Flores (Q500) and San Cristóbal de Las Casas, Mexico (Q225).

Getting Around

Terminal Minerva is linked to the city center by **microbuses** (Map p132), charging Q1.25 for the 10- to 15-minute ride. From the terminal, walk south through the market to the intersection by the Templo de Minerva, where you'll see the vehicles waiting on the south side of 4a Calle. Going from the center to the terminal, catch **microbuses** (Map p136) on 14a Av north of 5a Calle. **Taxis** (Map p136; Parque Centro América) await fares at the north end of Parque Centro América; a ride to the Terminal Minerva should not cost more than Q30 during the day.

The Rotonda bus stop on Calz Independencía is served by 'Parque' microbuses running to the center.

INGUAT (p142) has information on other city bus routes.

BUSES FROM QUETZALTENANGO

DESTINATION	COST (Q)	DURATION	FREQUENCY	ALTERNATIVE
Almolonga	5	10min	Every 15min, 6am-10pm	
Antigua				Guatemala City–bound bus via the Interamericana; change at Chimaltenango
Chichicastenango	25	2hr	Half hourly, 8am-5pm	Guatemala City–bound bus; change at Los Encuentros
Ciudad Tecún Umán (Mexican border)	40	3hr	Hourly	Coatepeque-bound bus; change for Ciudad Tecún Umán
El Carmen/ Talismán (Mexican border)				San Marcos–bound bus; change for Malacatán, then collective taxi
Guatemala City	40	3½hr	Every 15min, 2am-5pm	
Huehuetenango	25	2hr	Every 15min, 4am-6pm	Cuatro Caminos–bound bus; then Pullman service by Los Halcones and Velasquez
La Mesilla (Mexican border)	40	4hr	4 buses, 7am-2:15pm	Huehuetenango-bound bus; change there
Momostenango	10	1½hr	Every 15min, 6am-7pm	
Panajachel	30	2hr	Hourly, 9am-7pm	
Retalhuleu	15	1hr	Every 10min, 5am-7pm	
San Andrés Xequl	10	30min	Half houly, 6am-3pm	
San Pedro La Laguna	35	3hr	Hourly, 10.30am-5pm	
Zunil	5	25min	Every 15min, 6am-10pm	

Around Quetzaltenango

The beautiful volcanic country around Xela offers up numerous exciting day trips. For many, the volcanoes themselves pose irresistible challenges. You can feast your eyes and soul on the wild church at San Andrés Xequl, hike to the ceremonial shores of Laguna Chicabal or soak in the idyllic hot springs at Fuentes Georginas. Or simply hop on a bus and explore the myriad small traditional villages that pepper this part of the highlands. Market days are great opportunities to observe locals in action, so Sunday and Wednesday in Momostenango, Monday in Zunil, Tuesday and Saturday in Totonicapán and Friday in San Francisco El Alto are good days to visit.

Zunil

POP 13,600 / ELEV 2262M

As you speed downhill toward Zunil from Quetzaltenango, you'll see this pretty market town spreading across a lush valley framed by steep hills and dominated by a towering volcano. Zunil's yellow colonial church gleams above the red-tiled roofs of the low houses.

Founded in 1529, Zunil is a typical Guatemalan highland town, where traditional indigenous agriculture is practiced with irrigation canals. Traditional extends to religious matters – the town is home to San Simón, a Mayan deity who it's possible to visit.

Sights

★Cofradia San Simón RELIGIOUS SITE

(admission Q5, photo Q10) While you're in Zunil, visit the image of San Simón, the name given here to the much-venerated Mayan deity known elsewhere as Maximón. His effigy, propped up in a chair, is moved each year to a different house during the festival of San Simón, held on October 28. Ask any local where to find him.

San Simón appears as a dapper white man with hat and dark glasses, a disguise he took to help him hide from the conquistadors. He is known to be particularly fond of the pleasures in life and always has a glass of rum at his hand and a cigarette in his mouth. Candles and incense surround him.

Members of the *cofradia* that look after San Simón can also tell your fortune (Q25), counting out piles of red beans to the cardinal points to answer questions about your life.

Iglesia Zunil CHURCH

Zunil has a particularly striking old church. Its ornate yellow facade, with eight pairs of serpentine columns, is echoed inside by a richly carved gilt altar, with saints garbed in silver-embroidered robes.

Sleeping & Eating

Hotel Las Cumbres HOTEL $$

(☎5399-0029; www.lascumbres.com.gt; Carretera al Pacífico, Km 210.5; s/d incl breakfast Q350/400, s/d with sauna Q450/570; P) Located 1km south of Zunil, Las Cumbres seems like a colonial village amid a volcanic landscape where great plumes of steam emanate from the earth. The hotel is built on top of natural steam vents, and some of the 20 cozy rooms come equipped with their own sauna and/or hot spring–fed Jacuzzi.

There's a good restaurant (mains Q40 to Q80) serving organic vegetables from the hotel garden, along with a gym and a handicrafts store. Nonguests can use the public sauna (Q30 per hour, open 7am to 7pm), a modern pine-paneled installation, or spa, offering massages and facials. Any bus bound for Retalhuleu or Mazatenango from Quetzaltenango can drop you at the entrance (Q5).

Shopping

Cooperativa Santa Ana CLOTHING

(⌚8am-6pm Mon-Fri, 8am-1pm Sat) Half a block downhill from the church plaza, this handicrafts cooperative is made up of more than 600 local women. Finely woven vests, jackets and traditional *huipiles* (from Q400) are displayed and sold here. You can try them on and discuss their making with the weavers, who may sometimes be creating new items at the loom.

Getting There & Away

Buses (Q10) depart from the Shell station at the corner of 9a Av and 10a Calle in Quetzaltenango every 15 minutes from 6am to 10pm. Returning, buses depart from in front of the church.

Almolonga

POP 20,300 / ELEV 2351M

An indigenous town with a population that is more than 90% evangelical Christian, Almolonga has become relatively wealthy from vegetable growing – something locals put down to God's bounty. The market bustles daily, and you'll see piles and piles of cabbages, limes, chilis, *güisquil* (a squash-like vegetable), onions and other gorgeous

OFF THE BEATEN TRACK

EXPLORING AROUND QUETZALTENANGO

The wide-open spaces and mountainous countryside around Xela offer an almost endless array of opportunities for getting out there and doing a bit of solo exploration. Small villages dotted around the valley mean that you shouldn't ever have much trouble getting directions, and the relative safety of the area means that the biggest danger you're likely to face is that of a yapping dog (carry a stick). A few destinations to head toward:

Santiaguito lookout Get a close-up view of volcanic eruptions, going off like clockwork every 20 minutes.

Lava fields Over near Mt Candelaria, these extensive fields are a great place for a picnic and a spot of sunbathing.

San Cristóbal waterfall Halfway between Xela and San Francisco, the falls are most impressive in the wet season.

Las Mojadas The walk to this pretty flower-growing village takes you from Llanos del Pinal and past the Santiaguito volcano. You can catch a bus back.

veggies, handled by hordes of women in embroidered aprons. Don't miss the **Iglesia de San Pedro**, which has a gilded altarpiece with a backdrop of incongruous neon lights, and an inverted galleon ceiling. Almolonga celebrates its annual fair on June 27.

At the lower end of the village, the road passes through **Los Baños**, an area with natural hot sulfur springs. Several little places down here have bath installations with private tiled tubs available for Q25 an hour. **San Silvestre Spa** (pool Q20, private room per 2 hrs/overnight Q50/250) has one of the better setups, including a 27°C (80°F) pool with waterfall.

From Xela, buses depart every 15 minutes or so from the Shell station at the corner of 9a Av and 10a Calle (Q5, 10 minutes), and then continue on to Zunil.

Fuentes Georginas

A superb natural spa in a spectacular setting, **Fuentes Georginas** (☎4766-7066; info@fuentesgeorginas.com; admission Q25, towels Q10, lockers Q5; ⏲9am-6pm) is an 8km drive uphill from Zunil. It's named after the wife of 'benevolent dictator' Jorge Ubico, who customarily comandeered the installations on weekends in the 1930s and '40s for his personal use. Four pools of varying temperatures are fed by hot sulfur springs and framed by a steep, high wall of tropical vines, ferns and flowers. Though the setting is intensely tropical, the mountain air currents keep it deliciously cool through the day. There is a little 500m walk starting from beside the pool, worth doing to check out the birds and orchids. Bring a bathing suit; towels are available (Q10 plus deposit). Lockers cost Q5.

Down the valley a bit from the pools are nine rustic but cozy **cottages** (per person Q160), each with a hot tub and cold shower, BBQ and a fireplace to ward off the mountain chill at night (wood and matches provided). Included in the price of the cottages is access to the pools all day and all night, when rules are relaxed.

Besides the **restaurant/bar** (meals Q70-85; ⏲8am-7pm), which serves great grilled steaks, sausage and *papas*, there are three sheltered picnic tables with cooking grills.

Daily shuttles to Fuentes Georginas (Q130 return door-to-door, including entrance fee) are offered by most Xela agencies, leaving at 9am and 2:30pm. Shuttles return to Xela at noon and 6:30pm, respectively.

San Andrés Xecul

POP 43,500

Boxed in by fertile hills, this small town has the most bizarre, stunning church imaginable. At **Iglesia San Andrés Xecul** technicolored saints, angels, flowers and climbing vines fight for space with angels frolicking on the ledges and a pair of jaguars scratching the top column on a shocking yellow facade. The cones on the bell towers are straight from the circus big top. Inside, a carpet of candles illuminates bleeding effigies of Christ. Above the altar, 'Fisher of Men' is written in blue neon, a reference to the town's patron saint.

Take a walk of the town with visits to *huipil* embroiderers, and dyers and candle makers, continuing up to **El Calvario**, the little yellow church at the top of the hill. Maya ceremonies, with plenty of burnt offerings, are still held at the triple-cross altar alongside, and the panoramic view across the valley is phenomenal.

Friday is the big market day. The annual festival, on November 30, features tightrope walkers.

To get here, take any northbound bus from Xela, alighting at the Esso station at the Morería crossroads, and hail a pick-up or walk the 3km uphill. Buses returning to Xela line up at the edge of the plaza and make the trip until about 5pm.

Salcajá

POP 20,800

The town of Salcajá is 7km from Xela. Its most famous export is perhaps its people – on the roundabout entering town you pass a **monument** (Autopista Los Altos) to a heroic figure, the undocumented emigrant seeking a better life in the USA.

Dating from 1524, the **Iglesia de San Jacinto** (Ermita Conquistadora De La Inmaculada Concepción; 3a Calle), two blocks west on 3a Calle from the main road, was the first Christian temple in Central America. It is also known as the Ermita Conquistadora De La Inmaculada Concepción, a reference to Pedro de Alvarado, the devout Catholic who conquered the territory. The small squat structure appears quite austere from outside, but within are original paintings and a beautiful painted-wood altar.

Salcajá is famed for its traditional *ikat*-style textiles, remarkable for the hand-tied and dyed threads that are laid out in the preferred pattern on a loom. Shops selling bolts of this fabric are ubiquitous here, and you can usually visit the workshops before purchasing.

Frequent buses depart for Salcajá from Quetzaltenango's Terminal Minerva, stopping en route at the Monumento a la Marimba on the eastern side of town.

Totonicapán

POP 156,600 / ELEV 2476M

San Miguel Totonicapán ('Toto') is known for its artisans. Shoemakers, weavers, tinsmiths, potters, leather workers and carpenters all make and sell their goods here. Market days are Tuesday and Saturday; it's a locals market, not a tourist affair, and it winds down by late morning.

The ride from Cuatro Caminos is along a pine-studded valley. From Totonicapán's bus station it's a 600m hike up 3a Calle to the twin main plazas, or you can take a *tuk-tuk*. The lower plaza has a **statue of Atanasio Tzul**, leader of an indigenous rebellion that started here in 1820, while the upper one, known as Parque San Miguel, is home to the large **colonial church** and neoclassical **municipal theater**.

Activities

Sendero Ecológico El Aprisco HIKING

(☎5355-0280; Q25; ⊙8am-5pm) Encompassing some 13 hectares of old-growth forest northeast of Totonicapán, this eco-reserve makes for some delightful hiking. Well-marked trails traverse the community-run site, domain of the endangered *pinabete* tree and 29 endemic bird species, such as the amethyst-throated hummingbird and plumed quetzalillo. For overnight stays, there are adobe cabins with fireplaces, bunk beds and straw bedding, and meals are prepared.

El Aprisco is 5km up the Santa Cruz del Quiché road from Toto; microbuses bound for El Quiché can drop you at the entrance in about 20 minutes. Alternatively, Altiplano's (p135) in Xela can organize early-morning birdwatching expeditions to the reserve.

Aventura Maya K'iche' CULTURAL

(☎5696-2207; www.aventuramayakiche.org; tour Q615) This program introduces visitors to the town's traditional crafts as well as other aspects of life in Toto. A day-long cultural tour, with an English-speaking guide, includes visits to weaving and pottery workshops, a bit of sightseeing and a traditional lunch with a marimba concert and dance performance. Book at least five days in advance.

Festivals & Events

Apparition of the Archangel Michael RELIGIOUS

(⊙May 8) Features fireworks and traditional dances.

Feria Titular de San Miguel Arcángel RELIGIOUS

(Name-Day Festival of Archangel St Michael) Runs from September 24 to 30, peaking on September 29.

Eating

Restaurante Bonanza GUATEMALAN $$
(☎7766-1064; 7a Calle 7-17, Zona 4; mains Q35-60; ⏲7am-9pm; 📶) Totonicapán's most conventional restaurant (as opposed to a *comedor*) is a meat-and-tortillas sort of establishment, where bow-tied waitstaff deliver heaped helpings of steak, chicken and seafood.

Shopping

Mercado de Artesanías ARTS & CRAFTS
(Handicrafts Market; 6a Calle & 9a Av; ⏲8am-6pm) The upper level of the main market building is devoted to the town's renowned handicrafts. You'll find quality textiles, carved wood objects, ceramics and metalwork.

Getting There & Away

Toto buses from Quetzaltenango depart every 10 minutes or so (one hour) throughout the day from the **Rotonda** on Calz Independencia (passing through Cuatro Caminos). The last direct bus to Quetzaltenango leaves Toto at 6:30pm.

San Francisco el Alto

POP 33,240 / ELEV 2582M

Some 17km away from Quetzaltenango is the clothes- and fabric-producing town of San Francisco El Alto. The Friday market here is one of the biggest in the country. The large plaza in front of the 18th-century **church** is covered in goods. Stalls are crowded into neighboring streets, and the press of people and traffic is great (beware pickpockets) There's even a market area for livestock.

Panoramic views can be had from the roof of the church. On the way through, have a look at the six elaborate gilded altarpieces and remains of what must once have been very colorful frescoes.

San Francisco's big party is the **Fiesta de San Francisco de Asís**, celebrated around October 4 with traditional dances.

Sleeping & Eating

There is one recommended hotel in the thick of the market activity.

Good *chuchitos* (small tamales), *chiles rellenos* and other prepared foods are sold from stacks in the marketplace.

Hotel Real Plaza HOTEL $
(☎7738-4110; 3a Av 2-22, Zona 1; s/d Q80/150, without bathroom Q50/80) This hotel has beautiful views out over the valley to the Santa María volcano. Rooms are spacious, with balconies and (thankfully) hot showers. Thursday nights it fills up with market vendors.

Getting There & Away

Buses to San Francisco leave Quetzaltenango from the Rotonda on Calz Independencia (passing through Cuatro Caminos) frequently throughout the day (Q5, 40 minutes). Arriving on market day, get off on 4a Av at the top of the hill and walk toward the church.

Momostenango

POP 154,300 / ELEV 2259M

Beyond San Francisco El Alto, 26km from Quetzaltenango, this town ('Momos' for short), set in a pretty mountain valley along a road through pine woods, is famous for the making of *chamarras* (thick woolen blankets), as well as ponchos and other woolen garments. The best days to look for these are Wednesday and Sunday, the main market days.

Momostenango is noted for its adherence to the ancient Maya calendar and observance of traditional rites. The town's five main altars (including one opposite the church on the main plaza) are the scene of ceremonies enacted on important celestial dates, such as the summer solstice, the spring equinox, the start of the Maya solar year (known as El Mam, observed in late February), and Wajshakib' B'atz, the start of the 260-day *tzolkin* year. Should you be allowed access to these ceremonies, be sure to treat altars and participants with the utmost respect.

Tours

Takiliben May Wajshakib Batz CULTURAL
(☎7736-5537; wajshakibbaztz13@yahoo.es; 3a Av A 6-85, Zona 3) This is a Maya mission, dedicated to studying and teaching Maya culture and sacred traditions. Its director, Rigoberto Itzep Chanchavac, is a *chuchkajau* (Maya priest) responsible for advising the community on when special days of the Maya calendars fall. His full- or half-day workshops focus on customs that usually remain hidden from outsiders. Rigoberto's son can help with English translations.

The mission also leads a tour of Momostenango, with visits to the sacred hill of Paclom and the ritual hot springs of Payashú (Q100, including a homestay with a local family).

Sleeping & Eating

A few basic *comedores* provide cheap, filling meals while the restaurant of the Hotel Otoño is a classier option. The street food on market days is excellent.

Hotel Otoño HOTEL $
(7736-5313; gruvial.m@gmail.com; 3a Av A 1-48, Zona 2; r per person Q100; P) Momostenango's best lodging has 14 great value spacious rooms with glossy tile floors and huge bathrooms. Some feature balconies or picture windows taking in the surrounding hills. The hotel restaurant serves all meals.

Information

Banco Reformador (1a Av 1-13, Zona 1; 9am-5pm Mon-Fri, 8am-noon Sat & Sun) has a Cajero 5B ATM.

Getting There & Away

You can get buses to Momostenango from Quetzaltenango's Terminal Minerva (Q10, 1½ hours) or from San Francisco El Alto (45 minutes). Buses run about every 15 minutes, with the last one back to Quetzaltenango normally leaving Momostenango at 4:30pm.

Laguna Chicabal

This magical lake is nestled in the crater of Volcán Chicabal (2712m) on the edge of a cloud forest. Considered a cosmic convergence point by the Mam and K'iche' Maya, it is a sacred place and a hotbed of ceremonial activity. There are Maya altars at each of the four cardinal points along its sandy shores, and worshippers come from far and wide to perform ceremonies and make offerings here. Forty days after Easter Sunday is the observance of 13 Q'anil, when faithful farmers flock here to pray for rain. By observing the level of the lagoon and seeing if the roots of surrounding trees are submerged, they can judge whether to plant. Because the lake and grounds have great ceremonial significance, campers and hikers are asked to treat them with the utmost respect.

Birdwatchers will find plenty to keep them interested; there are reportedly quetzals in the area.

From the **visitor center** (4957-5983; lake park entrance fee Q25; 7am-3pm), a trail leads 3km uphill to the site. About two-thirds of the way up you'll reach a fork, where you can bear right to go directly to the lagoon, or left up to a *mirador* (viewpoint) and then a stamina-testing 615 steep steps down to the lake. Start early for best visibility.

Sleeping

There are good accommodations at the visitor center, (p148) which is managed by the local Mam community, including a pair of six-sided bungalows with four bunks each (per person Q50) sharing a cold-water bath house, and a two-level log cabin with private bathrooms (double per person Q75).

Bring food if you plan to stay: there's no restaurant and the one store has just the basics.

Getting There & Away

Access to Laguna Chicabal is via the community of Toj Mech, southwest of the town of San Martín Sacatepéquez (also known as Chile Verde) along the road to Colomba. Microbuses from Xela (Q5) depart every 20 minutes, Monday to Saturday, from 15a Av and 6a Calle in Zona 3. These vehicles drop you at the stop for 'la laguna' – from here it's a 45 minute walk to the visitor center. If you're lucky, there will be pick-ups offering to ferry you up for around Q75.

Huehuetenango

POP 126,000 / ELEV 1909M

Often used as a stop off on the journey to or from Mexico, or as a staging area for forays deeper into the Cuchumatanes mountain range, Huehuetenango has a welcoming if scruffy character. 'Huehue' *(way-way)* packs in plenty of eating and sleeping options along with some striking mountain scenery, and in Zaculeu has a Mayan site well worth a visit.

Huehuetenango was a Mam Maya region until the 15th century, when the K'iche', expanding from their capital K'umarcaaj (near present-day Santa Cruz del Quiché), pushed them out. But the weakness of K'iche' rule soon brought about civil war, which engulfed the highlands and provided a chance for Mam independence. The turmoil was still unresolved in 1525 when Gonzalo de Alvarado, the brother of Pedro, arrived to conquer Zaculeu, the Mam capital, for Spain.

Sights

The lively indigenous market is filled daily with traders who come down from surrounding villages. Actually, it's about the only place you'll see traditional costumes in this town, as most citizens are *ladinos* in modern garb.

Huehuetenango

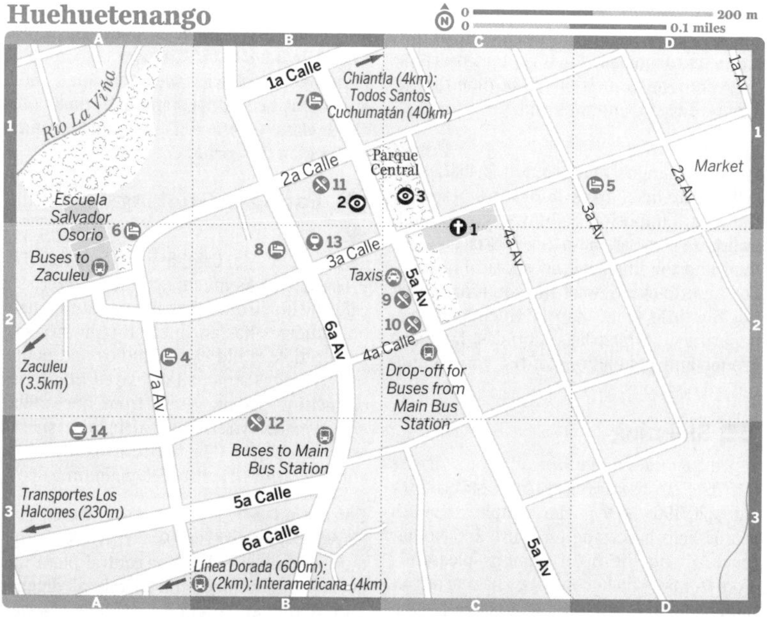

Huehuetenango

Sights
1 Catedral de Huehuetenango C2
2 Municipalidad B1
3 Parque Central C1

Sleeping
4 Hotel Casa Blanca A2
5 Hotel El Centro D1
6 Hotel San Luis de la Sierra A2
7 Hotel Zaculeu B1
8 Royal Park Hotel B2

Eating
9 Cafetería Carilo C2
10 Cafetería Las Palmeras C2
11 La Fonda de Don Juan B1
12 La Tinaja B3

Drinking & Nightlife
13 Café D'Carlo B2
14 Café Museo A3

Xela-based **Adrenalina Tours** (3355-1240; www.adrenalinatours.com; 5a Calle 6-89) has an office in Huehue and can arrange tours in the Cuchumatanes.

Zaculeu ARCHAEOLOGICAL SITE
(Q50; 8am-4pm) A remnant of the Mam capital, the Zaculeu archaeological zone was restored by the United Fruit Company in the 1940s, leaving its pyramids, ball courts and ceremonial platforms covered by a thick coat of graying plaster. It's the sort of restoration that probably makes archaeology purists scream, but for casual visitors the site, set amid pleasant lawns, goes a long way in simulating the appearance of an active religious center.

With ravines on three sides, the Postclassic religious center Zaculeu ('White Earth' in the Mam language) occupies a strategic defensive location that served its Mam Maya inhabitants well. It finally failed, however, in 1525, when Gonzalo de Alvarado, aided by Tlaxcalan and K'iche' forces, laid siege to the site for two months. It was starvation that ultimately defeated the Mam.

An excellent **museum** at the site holds, among other things, skulls and grave goods found in a tomb beneath Estructura 1, the tallest structure at the site.

Zaculeu is located 4km west of Huehuetenango center. Buses to the site (Q2.50, 15 minutes) leave about every 30 minutes between 7:30am and 6pm from in front of the **school** at the corner of 2a Calle and 7a Av. A taxi from the town center costs Q30 one way. One hour is plenty of time to look around the site and museum.

Parque Central PLAZA
Huehuetenango's main square is shaded by cylindrical ficus trees and surrounded by the town's imposing buildings: the **municipalidad** (Town Hall; with a band shell on the upper floor) and the imposing neoclassical **church**. For a bird's-eye view of the situation, check out the little relief map of Huehuetenango department, which lists altitudes, language groups and populations of the various municipal divisions.

Sleeping

Hotel San Luis de la Sierra HOTEL $
(7764-9217; hsanluis@gmail.com; 2a Calle 7-00; s/d Q120/190; P wi-fi) The simple, smallish rooms here have pine furniture and homey touches, and the hotel remains pleasantly aloof from the racket outside. The real attraction, though, is the rambling coffee plantation out back, with paths for strolling.

Hotel Zaculeu HOTEL $$
(7764-1086; www.facebook.com/HotelZaculeu; 5a Av 1-14; s/d/tr Q130/250/340; P @ wi-fi) The long-standing Zaculeu has plenty of character, and despite its advanced age it remains quite spiffy. Rooms in the 'new section' (20 years plus old) are a bit pricier but larger and more stylish. The sprawling patio area, overflowing with plants and chirping birds, is conducive to lounging, as is the bar. There's a restaurant for dinners as well as breakfast.

Hotel Casa Blanca HOTEL $$
(7769-0777; hotelcasablancahuehue@hotmail.com; 7a Av 3-41; s/d Q190/230; P wi-fi) Hanging ferns and sculpted shrubs grace the attractive courtyard here, ringed by spacious, modern rooms with arched pine ceilings and good hot showers. The patio restaurant out back serves up good-value set lunches (Q25), and its Sunday breakfast buffet (Q40) is a major deal. Given how busy the road outside it is, the rooms themselves are amazingly quiet.

Royal Park Hotel BUSINESS HOTEL $$
(7762-7775; 6a Av 2-34; s/d Q145/290; P @ wi-fi) This central business-class hotel is pretty posh as far as Huehue goes, with earth-toned bedspreads, padded headboards and jumbo flat-screen TVs – quite decent value. Rooms ending in 08 have mountain views.

Hotel El Centro HOTEL $$
(7764-8966; hotelcentro@hotmail.com; 3a Calle 2-65, Zona 1; s/d Q125/250; P wi-fi) Good value midrange hotel with well-appointed modern rooms behind its sometimes dusty blue plate glass exterior. There's underground parking on the corner entrance.

Eating & Drinking

★**La Tinaja** GUATEMALAN $
(7764-1513; 4a Calle 6-51; set menus Q25; noon-10pm) As much a cultural center as a cafe, the home of historian/gourmand Rolando Gutiérrez has an interesting library and a collection of old clocks, radios and namesake *tinajas* (urns), all displayed in a series of inviting salons. Aside from quesadillas and tamales, you'll find such local snacks as *sangüichitos* (Huehue-style sandwiches) and *rellenitos* (fried stuffed plantain balls).

Cafetería Carilo GUATEMALAN $
(5a Av 3-54; menú del día Q25; 7am-9pm) This humble dining hall on the central plaza fills quickly with families and friends, all digging into abundant portions of home-cooked stews served with avocado wedges and plenty of just-slapped tortillas.

Cafetería Las Palmeras GUATEMALAN $
(4a Calle 5-10; mains Q27-50; 7am-8:30pm; wi-fi) Popular Las Palmeras features a breezy upper level with views over the Parque Central. The *caldo de pollo criollo* (Q30) is a must, brimming with chicken, *güisquil* (a squash-like vegetable) and corn. On Saturdays there are tasty tamales.

La Fonda de Don Juan PIZZA $$
(2a Calle 5-35; pizzas Q45-75; 24hr) The place for Huehue's night owls and early risers, the red-and-white fronted La Fonda serves varied Guatemalan and international fare including good-value pizzas and breakfasts. And yes, it really is open all hours.

Café Museo CAFE
(7764-1101; 4a Calle 7-40; 7am-9:30pm Mon-Sat, 2-9:30pm Sun; wi-fi) This 'museum' serves some of Huehue's best coffee, and that's saying something. More than just a place to get a well-prepared cup, it also provides some background on this bewitching bean that has so influenced Guatemala's history. The various salons and delightful patio buzz with java hounds from early morning till late evening (for which there's a good wine list).

Besides examining antique coffee-processing paraphernalia and some diagrams demonstrating coffee production techniques, you can roast your own beans for purchase. Enquire about local coffee plantation tours between January and April.

Café D'Carlo BAR
(☎7764-2204; 6a Av 2-59) Opposite the Royal Park Hotel, this upper-level, open-air lounge has a friendly, relaxed vibe and a terrace/counter facing the street, a good spot for snacks and a bucket of chilled Gallos. Friday and Saturday nights from around 9pm there are often performances by singer-songwriters.

Information

There are plenty of ATMs in the banks close to the main plaza, including **Banco Industrial** (6a Av 1-26).

Getting There & Away

The bus terminal is in Zona 4, 2km southwest of the plaza along 6a Calle. A number of companies ply the same routes, though information is not posted in any coherent fashion. Microbuses leave from the south end of the station. Another stop, for microbuses to Cobán and Barrillas, via Soloma and San Mateo Ixtatán, is by a **gas station** at El Calvario, at the corner of 1a Av and 1a Calle, four blocks northeast of the Parque Central.

BUSES FROM HUEHUETENANGO

DESTINATION	COST (Q)	DURATION (HR)	FREQUENCY	ALTERNATIVE
Antigua				Guatemala City–bound bus; change at Chimaltenango
Barillas	50	6	Microbuses half hourly 2am-4:30pm	
Cobán	45	7	Microbus at 1pm Mon-Sat from El Calvario gas station	
Gracias a Dios (Mexican border)	60	5	Hourly 3am-1pm by Chiantlequita	
Guatemala City	70	5	5 Pullman buses by Velázquez Plus 5:30am-2:30pm	
La Mesilla	20	2	Every 15min, 3am-7pm by Transportes Los Verdes	
Nebaj				Microbus to Sacapulas for connections to Nebaj
Panajachel				Guatemala City–bound bus; change at Los Encuentros
Quetzaltenango	25	2	Every 15min, 3:30am-7pm	
Sacapulas	20	2	Frequent microbuses 5:30am-5:30pm	Via Aguacatán
Santa Cruz del Quiché	25	2	Frequent microbuses 5am-5pm	
San Pedro Soloma	25	3	Hourly microbuses 4:30am-2:30pm from El Calvario gas station	
Todos Santos Cuchumatán	20	2	Every 30min, 3am-3pm from El Calvario gas station	

OFF THE BEATEN TRACK

CHANCOL

Chancol sits high on the Cuchumatanes plateau, in a sparse landscape of thin mountain grass, low gnarled trees and trickling streams.

Most visitors come to stay at the charming **Unicornio Azul** (☎5205-9328; www.unicornioazul.com; Chancol; s/d/tr incl breakfast Q510/870/1200, lunch/dinner Q55-70), about 25km by road northeast of Huehuetenango, offering horse riding through the Cuchumatanes plateau. Unicornio Azul also functions as a thoroughly welcoming *posada rural*, with 10 simple but comfortable rooms in the estate home or a separate building. The nightly rate includes a one-hour horse ride. There's no heating and the high altitude nights are cold, so you'll be thankful for the hot water bottles and generous piles of blankets.

The *posada* also has a wonderful *mirador* (viewpoint) looking down along the breadth of the highlands – on a clear day it's possible to count the distant peaks of at least half a dozen volcanoes.

Tours are guided by Pauline Décamps, a member of the French Equestrian Federation, who manages the dozen or so robust horses stabled here. There are mounts for all abilities of rider including beginners, and the French army-style saddles are a lot more comfortable than the local alternative.

Overnight horse treks are not currently offered.

To get to Chancol by public transport, take any bus between Huehuetenango and Todos Santos or Barillas and get off in La Capellanía; the owners will come pick you up (Q45).

For Guatemala City, two lines run Pullman buses from their own private terminals: **Transportes Los Halcones** (☎7765-7985; 10a Av 9-12, Zona 1) leaves seven times a day from 1am to 3:30pm (Q77), with deluxe service (Q90) at 7am, 10:30am and 2pm; **Linea Dorada** (☎7768-1566; www.lineadorada.com.gt; 8a Calle 8-70, Zona 1) departs at 11pm (Q100).

Buses to Zaculeu (p150) leave from near the Hotel San Luis de la Sierra, or take a private **taxi**.

Getting Around

City buses circulate between the bus station and the town center from 5am to around 7:30pm. Arriving in Huehue, leave the east side of the station through the gap between the Transportes Fortaleza and El Condor offices; walk through a small covered market, then the main market building to the next street, where '**Centro**' buses depart every few minutes (Q2). To return to the bus station from the center, catch **buses** outside the Hotel La Sexta.

Around Huehuetenango

Except for picturesque and very traditional Todos Santos Cuchumatán, the mountainous far northwest of Guatemala is little visited by travelers. The adventurous few will often be a novelty to the local Maya folks they meet. Spanish skills, patience and tact will pave the way in these parts. Beyond the coffee lands of the Huistas (Santa Ana and San Antonio), the lower northwestern corner of the department is cut through by rivers and dotted with cenotes (circular pools in limestone craters).

Chiantla

POP 7700

At the foot of the Cuchumatanes beyond Huehuetenango is the village of Chiantla, the former seat of the municipality. It is famous for its silver statue of the **Virgen del Rosario** (Parque Centrale), who draws pilgrims from across the country. The main date for the pilgrimage is February 2, when the town packs out with supplicants and the infirm.

Another 4km on from Chiantla, **El Mirador** overlooks Huehuetenango from a point up in the Cuchumatanes. On a clear day it offers a truly stunning view of the entire region and many volcanoes. Mounted on plaques here is the poem, *A Los Cuchumatanes*, penned by Juan Dieguez Olaverri.

Sleeping & Eating

Chicano's Hotel HOTEL $$
(☎7764-5342; s/d Q95/250; P 📶) There's no pressing need to to stay in Chiantla, but Chicano's Hotel is a decent enough option. Rooms are compact and a little dark, as they're inward-facing with no external windows, but there's hot water and wi-fi, and ample parking at the back.

Café Del Cielo CAFE $

(El Mirador Dieguez Olaverri; mains from Q30; ⏲8am-5pm Mon-Thu, 8am-7pm Fri & Sat) This pretty wood and stone cabin cafe is tucked just below the *mirador* (viewpoint), allowing you to enjoy a coffee, beer or light meal served alongside one of Guatemala's best views. Eat inside or take refreshments on the sunny terrace.

La Fonda de Don Juan INTERNATIONAL $$

(☎7765-9031; 7a Calle 4-43; mains Q35-80; ⏲6am-9.30pm) Chiantla's best restaurant, this charming spot with a pleasant dining terrace at the rear bills itself as a pizzeria (and the pizzas are certainly good), but in reality it offers a bit of everything, from hearty Guatemalan breakfasts to filling sandwiches, pasta and steaks. The lamb, a reflection of the locally raised sheep, is worth a try. It's across from the Parque Centrale.

Getting There & Away

Any bus from Huehue heading for Todos Santos, Soloma or Barillas goes through Chiantla and past the turnoff for the *mirador*.

Chiabal

High in the Sierra de los Cuchumatanes (3400m), amid a rocky plateau dotted with maguey plants and sheep, Chiabal, 17km east of Todos Santos, welcomes visitors looking to experience rural life in a tiny **Mam community** (☎5381-0540; esteban.matias@hotmail.com). The villagers provide simple accommodations and prepare hearty local fare. A community-built 2.5km interpretive trail leads to the Piedra Cuache, an oddly shaped boulder at a 3666m lookout point. Guides can take you to various sites in the 18,000-hectare Parque Regional Municipal de Todos Santos Cuchumatán (p154), including the summit of La Torre (Q25). There is also the chance to participate in community activities such as herding llamas, weaving *huipiles* and planting potatoes while getting to know the local inhabitants.

Microbuses go directly to Chiabal (Q10) from the El Calvario gas station at the corner of 1a Av and 1a Calle in Huehuetenango. Otherwise, hop on a Todos Santos bus and get off at Chiabal, 4km west of the turnoff on the Huehue–Barillas road.

Todos Santos Cuchumatán

POP 2980 / ELEV 2470M

Way up in the highlands, the community of Todos Santos is nestled at the bottom of a deep valley and bordered by beautiful forested slopes. Todos Santos has excellent walking in the hills, and its horse-racing festival at the start of November draws thousands of visitors.

Unusually for the highlands, it's the men's dress here that is the more eye-catching. Men wear red-and-white-striped trousers, little straw hats with blue ribbons, jackets with multicolored stripes and thick woven collars. Women's *cortes* are navy with a royal blue pinstripe. It's a close-knit but friendly community, which suffered great violence during Guatemala's civil war, and although it's photogenic, people are very sensitive about tourists blithely snapping away. Saturday is the main market day; there's a smaller market on Wednesday.

If you're coming to Todos Santos in the wet season (mid-May to November), bring warm clothes, as it's cold up here, especially at night.

Sights

Museo Balam MUSEUM

(☎5787-3598; Cantón Twitnom; Q40; ⏲8am-6pm) Todos Santos' museum is on a hilly rise on the eastern edge of town. The small but fascinating collection of outfits and masks, traditional kitchen implements, archaeological finds and musical instruments comes to life when Fortunato, its creator and a community leader, is there to provide commentary.

Iglesia Todos Santos CHURCH

(Parque Centrale) Todos Santos's Catholic church is a modest whitewashed affair, but it's worth popping in to see the beautiful painted wooden ceiling, with its brightly decorated carved angels emerging from the heavens to watch over the congregation.

Tuj K'man Txun MONUMENT

This ceremonial site, just up the street beside the central plaza, consists of two wooden crosses upon a stone altar for contemporary Maya offerings. The crosses commemorate the incidents of August 1982, when the army executed hundreds of alleged guerrilla collaborators, then torched many homes.

Activities

Hiking in the Cuchumatanes is a major draw for visitors to Todos Santos. January to April are the best months for hitting the trails through the rugged countryside but you can usually walk in the morning, before the weather closes in, year-round.

Parque Regional Todos Santos Cuchumatán HIKING
The section of the Cuchumatanes range to the north and east of Todos Santos presents superb hiking opportunities through subtropical montane wet forest, much of it above 3700m. Among the unique species of vegetation found at these heights is the coniferous shrub known as *huitó*. One of the most spectacular destinations is La Torre (3837m), the highest nonvolcanic point in Central America.

Las Cuevas HIKING
The walk to Las Cuevas, a sacred cave still used for Maya rituals, starts from La Maceta, a tree growing out of rock beside a football field, 15 minutes by bus up the Huehue road from Todos Santos (Q5).

Tours

Red de Turismo Natural y Cultural de Huehuetenango HIKING
(☎4051-5597; www.turismoruralguatemala.com/roberto-jeronimo; hikes from Q250) This network of ecologically oriented guides throughout the department is locally represented by Roberto Jerónimo Bautista. He leads hikes to the isolated mountain community of San Juan Atitán, where the women wear dazzling *huipiles*, in about six hours, returning by bus to Todos Santos. The trail climbs through old-growth forest to summits that afford views all the way to the Mexican border.

Roberto also leads three-day treks to Nebaj (per person from Q700, with minimum of two), including food and lodging in community dwellings.

Mam Trekking HIKING
(☎5206-0916; rigoguiadeturismo@yahoo.com; hikes from Q100) Knowledgeable, English-speaking *todosantero* Rigoberto Pablo Cruz leads walks around the Parque Regional Todos Santos Cuchumatán, including a climb to the peak of La Torre, followed by a descent to La Maceta. In addition, Rigoberto leads walks to Tzunul, a community where men weave women's *cortes* on a loom and women weave men's shirt collars by hand.

Mam also offers the chance to relax in a traditional Maya *chuj*, a welcome option in Todos Santos' chilly climate. A *chuj* is a small adobe building with wooden boards covering the entrance. A wood fire burns in a stone hearth within, and water is sprinkled on the stones to provide steam.

Rigo also leads three- and four-day hikes to Nebaj (per person from Q700, with a minimum of two).

Festivals & Events

El Día de Todos los Santos FIESTA
(Nov 1) Todos Santos is famous for the annual horse races held during the festival of El Día de Todos los Santos. Traditional foods are served throughout the day and there are mask dances.

Sleeping

For such a small place, Todos Santos has an assortment of good, cheap accommodations, two of which are near the main plaza. If you're planning to visit for El Día de Todos los Santos, you need to book accommodations at least three months in advance.

★ **Hotel Casa Familiar** HOTEL $
(☎5737-0112; hotelyrestaurante_casafamiliar@yahoo.com; s/d Q125/200; wi-fi) This cheerfully run guesthouse uphill from the main plaza has a selection of cozy rooms with hardwood floors, traditional textile bedspreads, good hot showers and private terraces (the roof terrace has excellent hillside views). Have a breakfast bowl of *mosh* (porridge) or fresh-baked banana bread at the cafe downstairs, where lunch and dinners are also available for Q35 to Q40.

The staff are well versed in helping arrange local treks, as well as weaving their own fabrics that are on sale in the shop next door.

Hotelito Todos Santos HOTEL $
(☎3030-6950; s/d Q75/150) South of the plaza, up a side street that branches left, this trusted hotel has small and bare but well-scrubbed rooms with tile floors and firm beds. It's on several levels, and the higher you go the better the views – room 15, one of the four private bath units in the tower, has particularly good views over the valley. Breakfast is available but not included in the rate.

Eating

There are a couple of basic *comedores* in the center of town for good home-cooked fare. For a little more variety, try the dining hall at the Hotel Casa Familiar.

Comedor Evelín GUATEMALAN $
(meals Q15-40; ⏲7am-8pm) Inside this often busy eatery you'll find the menu scrawled on a styrofoam board. At lunchtime it serves such traditional fare as *pepián de pollo* (chicken in pumpkin-seed sauce) and *caldo de res* (broth with large chunks of meat and veggies). It's 100m east of the plaza, turning uphill at the bookstore.

Comedor Katy GUATEMALAN $
(meals Q20-40; ⏲7:30am-8pm) Women in traditional garb attend to great vats bubbling over glowing embers at this rustic cook shack just above the central plaza. There are tables on a terrace overlooking the market activity.

Information

Todos Santos' main street is about 500m long. Toward its west end are the church and market, with the central plaza raised above street level on the south side.

The Grupo de Mujeres weaving shop at the base of the Hotel Casa Familiar functions as a de facto information center.

BAM (Central Plaza) changes US dollars and has a Cajero 5B ATM.

Getting There & Away

Buses depart from the main street between the plaza and the church, leaving for Huehuetenango (Q20, two hours) between 4:30am and 2pm. It's a spectacular drive, though the switchbacks can be a bit nervy when you're in the hands of a chicken bus driver. Buses continue on to Guatemala City. Microbuses going as far as Tres Caminos (the junction with the Huehue–Barillas highway) leave throughout the day, whenever they fill up. A Huisteca bus heads for La Mesilla around 5am.

San Pedro Soloma & Around

North of the Todos Santos turnoff, the paved road winds up between often mist-shrouded cliffs and a precipitous gorge. Out of the mists emerges a pair of massive fingers of granite, known as the **Piedras de Captzín**. Soon after, you arrive in **San Juan Ixcoy**, where the women wear traditional white *huipiles* embroidered at the collar and hanging almost to their ankles.

Some 70km north of Huehuetenango, San Pedro Soloma fills a valley and spreads up into the hills. This agricultural town is one of the biggest in the Cuchumatanes. The Maya here speak Q'anjob'al, but some of the *ladino* cowboys may greet you in English. San Pedro Soloma's prosperity and its residents' language skills can be attributed to the migratory laborers who annually make the arduous trip to the US to work. On Sunday, market day, the town floods with people from surrounding villages. The pink-and-pastel **Hotel Don Chico** (☎7780-6087; 4a Av 3-65, San Pedro Soloma; s/d/tr Q90/180/270; P@📶), opposite the massive gold-domed **Iglesia San Pedro**, is the most comfortable lodging in town.

From San Pedro Soloma, the road cuts through a lushly wooded canyon, then climbs to the town of **Santa Eulalia**, which feels much more remote and traditional. It can get quite chilly here. This is sheep-farming territory, and you'll see shepherds wearing *capixays* (short woolen ponchos) in the fields. The town has a reputation for producing some of the finest marimbas in the country, as a little monument in front of the town hall proclaims, with locally grown hormigo trees providing the wood for the keys. A new Gothic version of Santa Eulalia's church is springing up with intricate floral motifs on its cement facade and a Maya inscription dedicated to the mother of the patron saint. There's reasonable lodging here at **Hotel Del Coronado** (☎5734-5850; Santa Eulalia; s/d Q60/120, without bathroom Q45/90), a weird modernistic structure with bright spotless rooms and wonderful views of the surrounding slopes.

From Santa Eulalia, the narrow road keeps climbing through pasture and occasional pine forest – sit on the left and you can see all the way to Mexico. After 30km you'll reach **San Mateo Ixtatán**, the logical place to break the journey if you're heading for Laguna Lachuá from Huehue. Perched on an aerie with the jagged peaks of the Cuchumatanes trailing off into the clouds, the town unfolds organically over the green slopes. (The mist can descend early here, wiping out visibility by early afternoon.) Quaint buildings with pillared verandas and painted designs on the doors line largely traffic-free paths. The women of this small Chuj town wear captivating *huipiles,* lacy white affairs with concentric floral patterns embroidered on the neckline. San Mateo's church has a primitive charm. Beyond a

OFF THE BEATEN TRACK

TODOS SANTOS' BIG DAY OUT

Todos Santos Cuchumatán is renowned for its wildly colorful horse races, the highlight of El Día de Todos los Santos (p154), a no-holds-barred annual celebration held on November 1. It's the culmination of a week of festivities and an all-night spree of male dancing to marimbas and *aguardiente* (cane liquor) drinking on the eve of the races, which are often sponsored by *todosanteros* diaspora abroad. The races are part competition, part chance for the bravado of riding up and down as fast as possible while getting progressively drunker the whole day long (with a break for lunch). Horses are brought from across the region; ironically few people in Todos Santos still keep them.

The authentically local event attracts throngs of inhabitants from surrounding communities who gather on a grassy hillside alongside the sand track or upon the rooftops opposite to observe the riders decked out in their finest traditional garb. Todos Santos, incidentally, is the only place in Guatemala where the Day of the Dead is not observed on November 1, since that day is reserved for a celebration of autonomy within Huehuetenango province. Instead, the traditional visit to the cemetery is postponed to the following day, when graves are decorated and marimbas serenade groups of mourners as they arrive to pay their respects.

rather dumpy facade is an austere interior with crude fruit motifs painted on the pillars. The real action seems to be out front in the atrium, where a smoking altar attests to the enduring Maya influence.

San Mateo holds an interesting archaeological site, **Wajxaklajunh**. It consists mostly of unexcavated mounds, with their stone foundations visible, and a large polygonal structure, whose top platform makes an ideal observation point for the surrounding hills. At the base stands a group of surprisingly intact stelae. To get there from the main plaza, go down the main street, then turn right downhill at a blue shop.

Hotel Magdalena (☎5336-2823; dfpa85@icloud.com; San Mateo Ixtatán; s/d Q65/130; 📶) is easily the best option in town and the showers are scalding hot (but ask if the heater is on beforehand). From the park, go uphill and take the first street on the right; the yellow box is adjacent to the Banco Agromercantil. Right above the turnoff is spiffy **Los Picones al Chaz Chaz** (San Mateo Ixtatán; meals Q25; ⏲6am-8pm), where you can have fresh tamales with delicious salsas in the morning, as well as tacos and burritos.

Barillas-bound buses from Huehuetenango stop in San Pedro Soloma, Santa Eulalia and San Mateo. Each town has buses to Guatemala City.

Barillas

POP 75,000 / ELEV 1450M

Leaving San Mateo, the road drops and weather becomes slightly kinder. After 28km, you'll reach Barillas, a prosperous coffee-growing town with a lowland feel, 28km east of San Mateo Ixtatán.

There's no pressing need to stop at Barillas, unless you're in transit to the Mexican border or travelling from El Petén further east.

Sleeping & Eating

Hotel Villa Virginia HOTEL $
(☎7780-2236; cnr 3a Calle & 3 Av; r per person Q80; P 📶) Barillas' most straightforward option is right on the plaza, with decent beds on clean tile floors – but get a room away from the street. Across the way is a couple of good cafes where you can grab a bite.

Restaurant La Cañada CAFE $
(2a Av; mains Q30-40; ⏲6:30am-9:30pm; 📶) This bright, clean and lively spot just up from Barillas' main square won't win any awards for originality, but makes a mean *huevos a la ranchera*, served with plenty of beans and tortillas.

Getting There & Away

Tuk-tuk drivers can take you from the **bus station** (cnr 4a Calle & 6 Ave) to the town center (Q10, five minutes).

If you're moving on to Cobán or El Petén, get an early start. Microbuses head for Playa Grande (Q50, 3½ hours) hourly from 3am to 3pm, departing from the traffic light by Mercado No 1 in the center of town. The road goes through the remote villages and forests of the Ixcán region, much of the way traveling above the landscape with vistas of vast distances. Much of the road is very poor quality until you reach Mayalán and the smoothest section of the Transversal del Norte, after which the drive accelerates tenfold.

Yalambojoch & Laguna Brava

In a lower lying, more lushly vegetated zone between the Cuchumatanes and the Mexican border, the northwest corner of Huehuetenango department has a distinctive culture where the Awakateko language is spoken. About 20km east of the border post at Gracias a Dios is the hamlet of Yalambojoch. Most of the inhabitants fled during the conflict of the 1980s and have only returned relatively recently to pick up the pieces of their lives.

West of Yalambojoch, toward the border post at Gracias a Dios, is the Finca La Trinidad junction, from where a paved road leads south to the Interamericana. Approximately 5km south of the Finca La Trinidad junction is the turnoff for **Posada Rural Finca Chaculá** (☎5780-4855; www.turismochacula.com; s/d/tr incl breakfast Q270/420/525, without bathroom Q240/360/435), a community-tourism project started by returnees from five different ethnic groups who took refuge in Mexico during the civil war. The 37-sq-km farm features a small lagoon, some Maya archaeological sites, a waterfall and abundant forest.

One of the chief attractions for visitors is the Laguna Brava (also known as Laguna Yolnajab), 6.5km to the north. There's good swimming in the crystalline waters of the lagoon, reached by a two-hour descent on foot or horseback from Yalambojoch (best attempted from March to June). There's a Q25 entry fee to the lagoon, and guides charge Q75 to take you down, plus Q75 per day for horses.

East of Yalambojoch, a series of surprisingly intact Maya pyramids dating from the 10th century stand near the site of what used to be the village of San Francisco, where one of the civil war's most atrocious massacres occurred, part of Rios Montt's scorched earth campaign in 1982.

Getting There & Away

From Huehuetenango, buses bound for Gracias a Dios (12:30pm) and Yalambojoch (1pm) traverse this region.

A bus by La Chiantlequita (Q40, six hours) departs for Yalambojoch from Huehuetenango around the middle of the day. There is also transport from San Mateo Ixtatán.

La Mesilla

Mesilla is the main border crossing along the Interamerican Hwy, connecting the highlands to San Cristóbal de las Casas in Mexico. It's a scrappy place, as border towns often are.

The strip in La Mesilla leading to the border post has a variety of services, including a police station, a post office and a bank. There are also money changers who will do the deal – at a mediocre rate, but as no banks on either side of the border will perform this exchange, it's your only option. For changing dollars, you're better off going to a bank in Huehue or Xela.

If you're stuck at the border there are a couple of straightforward places to spend the night.

Tacos stalls and a few basic *comedores* line the strip down to the border.

Getting There & Away

Entering Guatemala via La Mesilla, you'll find chicken buses leaving for Huehuetenango (Q20, two hours) every 20 minutes till 6pm, as well as transport to Quetzaltenango (Q40). Otherwise, Línea Dorada runs a Pullman to Guatemala City (Q190, eight hours) at 8pm.

From Mesilla's bus terminal, it's a hike of about 1km to the Guatemalan immigration post. Mexican immigration is at Ciudad Cuauhtémoc, 4km west of the border; taxis charge M$10 for the ride. About 30m past Mexican immigration, you'll find TAOSA buses to Comitán (M$50, every half hour), from where there are onward connections to San Cristóbal (M$55, 2¾ hours).

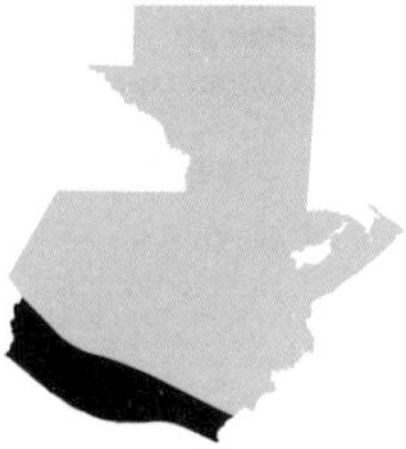

The Pacific Slope

Includes ➡

Best Places to Eat

➡ Taberna El Pelicano (p175)

➡ Soul Food Kitchen & Guesthouse (p170)

➡ Yoli's (p171)

Best Places to Stay

➡ Takalik Maya Lodge (p165)

➡ Hotel Paredon Surf House (p171)

➡ Swell (p171)

Why Go?

Separated from the highlands by a chain of volcanoes, the flatlands that run down to the Pacific are universally known as La Costa. It's a sultry region – hot and wet or hot and dry, depending on the time of year – with rich volcanic soil good for growing coffee, palm-oil seeds and sugarcane.

The culture is overwhelmingly *ladino* (mixed indigenous and European heritage), and even the biggest towns are humble affairs, with low-rise houses and the occasional palm-thatched roof.

Archaeologically, the big draws here are Takalik Abaj and the sculptures left by pre-Olmec civilizations around Santa Lucía Cotzumalguapa.

Guatemalan beach tourism has always been rather underdeveloped, but modest El Paredón is growing in popularity as a surf and backpacker destination, while a larger scene in Monterrico is helped along by a nature reserve protecting mangroves and their inhabitants.

When to Go

Retalhuleu

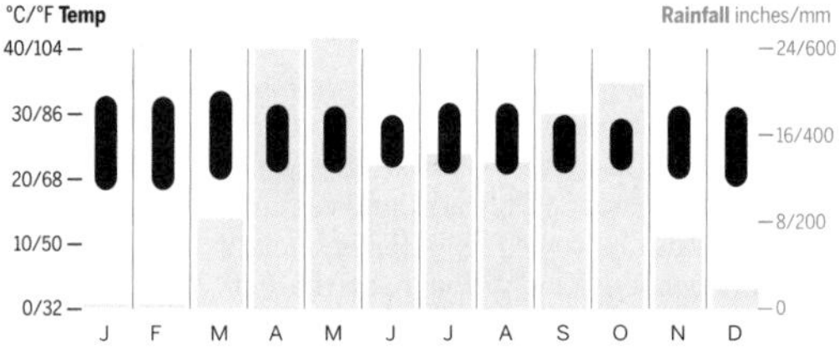

Nov–Mar Temperatures are moderate during these months. November has the best surfing.

Jul–Oct Rainy season makes the Pacific Slope sticky, while winds pick up for hurricane season.

Easter & Christmas The most popular times for Guatemalans to visit the beach; book accommodations in advance.

History

Despite it being one of the first settled areas in Guatemala, relatively little is known about the Pacific region's early history. Many archaeological sites are presumed overgrown by jungle; others have been destroyed to make way for agriculture.

What *is* known is that the Olmecs were among the first to arrive, followed by the Ocós and Iztapa, whose cultures appear to have flourished around 1500 BC.

Although these cultures were much more humble than those of their northerly counterparts, they developed a level of sophistication in stone carving and ceramics. It's also thought that the coastal region acted as a conduit, passing cultural advances (like the formation of writing and the Maya calendar) from north to south.

Between AD 400 and 900, the Pipil moved in, most likely displaced by the turmoil in the Mexican highlands, and began farming cacao, which they used to make a (rather bitter) chocolate drink. They also used cacao beans as currency.

Toward the end of the Postclassic period, the K'iche', Kaqchiquel and Tz'utujil indigenous groups began moving in as population expansion in Guatemala's highlands made food scarce and land squabbles common.

Pedro de Alvarado, the first Spaniard to land in Guatemala, arrived here in 1524, pausing briefly to fight the K'iche' as a sort of forerunner to a much larger battle around present-day Quetzaltenango.

Further agricultural projects (mostly indigo and cacao) were started around this time, but it wasn't until independence that the region became one of the country's main agricultural suppliers, with plantations of coffee, bananas, rubber and sugarcane. Towns boomed in the the late 19th century, linking these exports to the Pacific steamers.

In the languid tropical climate, not much changes, particularly the social structure. The distribution of land – a few large landholders and many poorly paid, landless farm workers – can be traced back to these early post-independence days. You'll see the outcome as you travel around the region – large mansions and opulent gated communities alongside squalid, makeshift workers' huts.

Getting There & Around

The Pacific Slope has good road connections to Mexico to the north, El Salvador to the south, Antigua, Guatemala City and the Western Highlands. The major bus hubs are at Escuintla and Retalhuleu – coming from elsewhere in the country, it's more than likely that you will be passing through (and possibly changing buses in) one of these towns.

The relatively small number of foreign tourists means few tourist shuttles, but services exist between Monterrico and Antigua/Guatemala City, and El Paredón to Antigua and Santiago Atitlán.

Tilapita

This little fishing village a seashell's throw from the Mexican border is somewhere to come for some seriously off-the-beaten-track beach time. It's a world away from the often hectic, scruffy feel of other towns along the coast.

The village, which sits on a sandbar cut off from the mainland by the Ocós estuary, is only reachable by boat from the town of Tilapa. There's some excellent swimming to be had here, although, as with all the beaches along this coast, the undertow can be quite serious and there are no lifeguards. If you're not a strong swimmer, don't go too far out.

Sleeping & Eating

The only place to eat on the island is at the Hotel Pacifico del Mar, where delicious meals (Q50 to QF90) are served in an oversized *palapa* (thatched palm-leaf shelter) and generally consist of the catch of the day. Shrimp, fish and *caldo de mariscos* (seafood stew) are always a good bet, washed down with fresh juice or a cold beer.

El Pacífico BUNGALOW

(7761-4396; www.playatilapa.com; cabin Q500) This palm-thatched beach cabin is a good option if there is a group of you, as it has four netted double beds as well as a simple kitchen (there's no fridge but several Tilapita stores sell ice). Relax in the hammocks and refresh yourself in the outdoor showers. There's a two night minimum stay.

Hotel Pacifico del Mar HOTEL $

(5914-1524; www.playatilapa.com; s/d Q75/100;) Pacifico del Mar is nothing fancy, but it has decent-sized, clean rooms with fans (though no nets). The good-sized swimming pool is a welcome addition, as things can get slightly warm here. There's a restaurant with a fishy sort of menu, and non-guests can use the pool if they eat here.

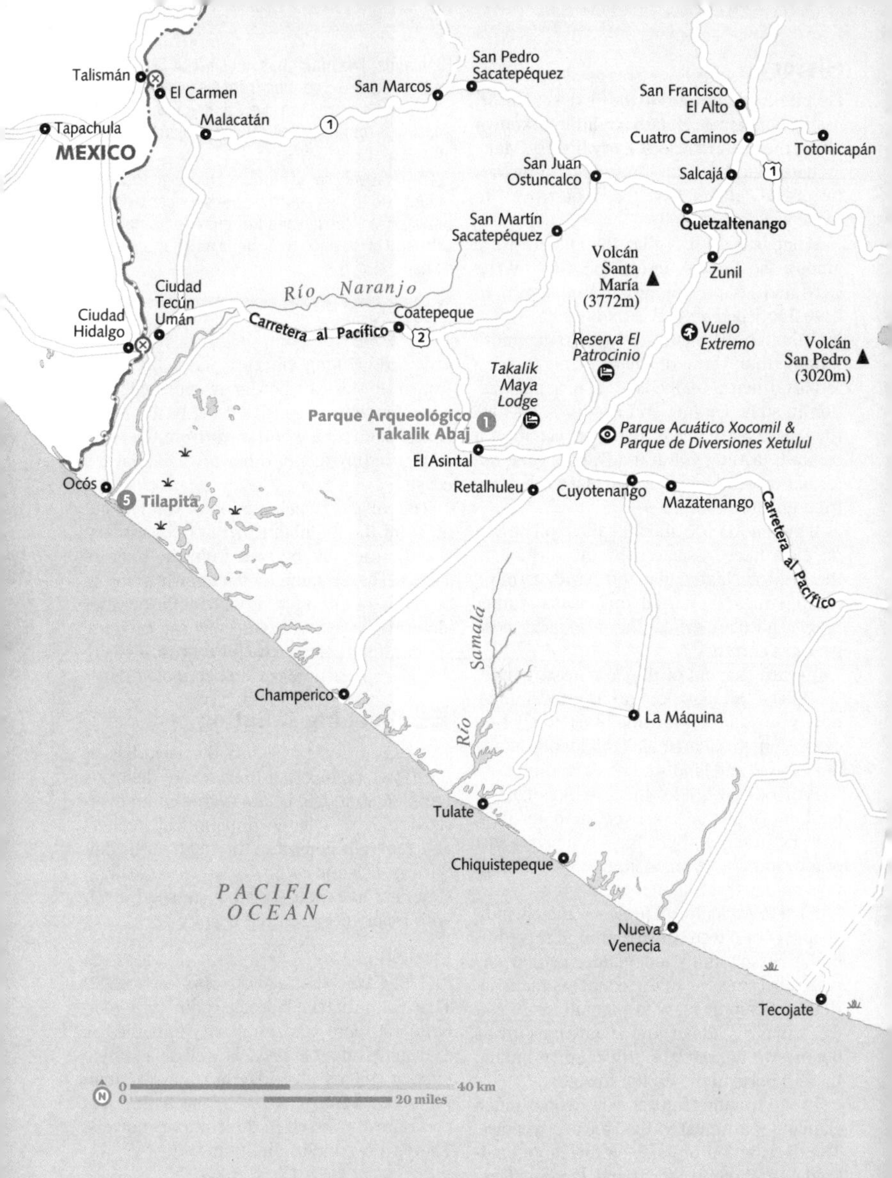

The Pacific Slope Highlights

1 **Parque Arqueológico Takalik Abaj** (p164) Investigating the bridge in history between the Olmec and the Maya while strolling this grassy archaeological site.

2 **El Paredón** (p170) Catching the surf in this up-and-coming backpacker hangout.

3 **Biotopo Monterrico-Hawaii** (p173) Spotting wildlife among the mangrove-lined canal and lagoons.

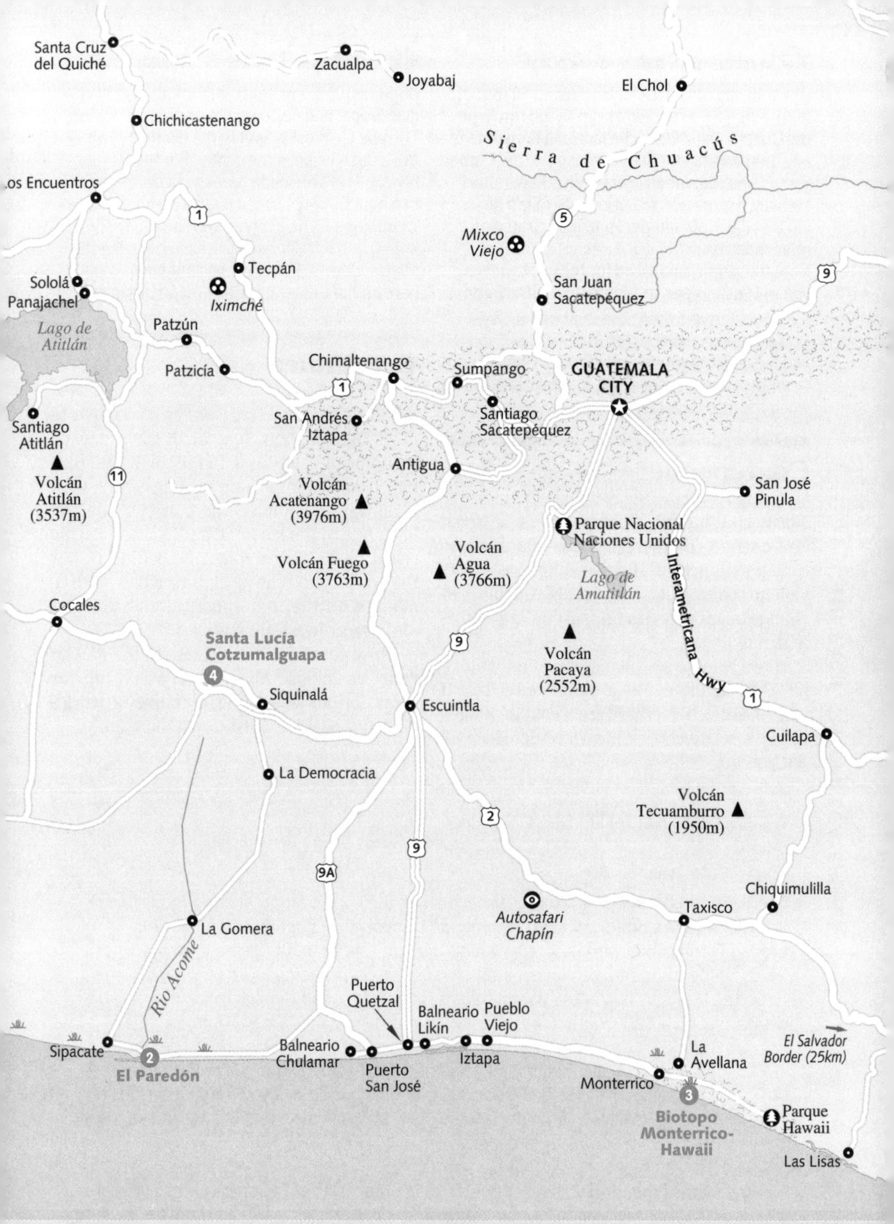

4 **Santa Lucía Cotzumalguapa** (p167) Checking out the big mysterious heads carved by members of the non-Maya Pipil culture.

5 **Tilapita** (p159) Getting away from absolutely everything in this sleepy one-horse town close to the Mexican border.

Getting There & Away

Direct buses run from Coatepeque to Tilapa (Q15, two hours). If you're come from Tecún Umán on the Guatemalan side of the Mexican border, take any bus heading out of town, get off at the Tilapa turnoff and wait for an onward bus there. Alternatively, a more scenic option is to take a bus to Ocós (Q15, 30 minutes) and a *lancha* (small motorboat; around Q40, 45 minutes) to Tilapita from there. In Tilapa, head for the dock, where you will find *lanchas* to Tilapita (Q10, 10 minutes).

Pullman drivers doing the Guatemala City–Tecún Umán run often stop in at Tilapa. If you're headed straight for the capital (Q70, four hours) or anywhere in between, ask around to find out when the next departure is.

Coatepeque

POP 155,100

Noisy and humid, Coatepeque is a brash and chaotic commercial town and a major transport junction. It's also infamous for its violent street gangs, so unless you have to change buses here, it's not particularly somewhere to linger.

If you want to see the nearby ruins at Takalik Abaj, Retalhuleu is a much better bet. If you get stuck here, there are a couple of places in the relatively quiet town center that will put you up.

Getting There & Away

Coatepeque is a major transport hub for the Pacific Slope, and bus connections here are good. The bus terminal is 2km to the north of town, but most buses stop in the center. For the Mexican border, there are departures to El Carmen (Q35, two hours), Tecún Umán (Q35, two hours), Quetzaltenango (Q40, 2½ hours), Tilapa (Q15, 1½ hours) and Retalhuleu (Q15, one hour), among others. Several Pullman bus companies stop here on the Guatemala City–Tecún Umán run.

Retalhuleu

POP 96,200

Retalhuleu, or Reu (*ray*-oo) as it's known to most Guatemalans, is a small town packed with fine old buildings. In the early 20th century it was an important trading centre, with a railway that linked the cotton-producing lowlands to the steamer trade on the Pacific coast. Its best days might be behind it, but the area around the plaza is worth exploring, along with the atmospherically abandoned and overgrown train station.

Most people visit for access to the Mayan ruins at Takalik Abaj, but if you're up for some serious downtime, a couple of world-class fun parks are just down the road.

CROSSING INTO MEXICO

Ciudad Tecún Umán

There are two border crossings for Mexico along the Pacific Slope; Ciudad Tecún Umán is busier and has better onward Guatemalan transport connections. A bridge links Ciudad Tecún Umán with Mexico's Ciudad Hidalgo. The town has all the trademarks of a seedy border outpost, with uninspiring cheapie hotels, *comedores* and money changers.

On the Mexican side of the border, buses run from Ciudad Hidalgo to the city of Tapachula (around M$20, 50 minutes) every 10 minutes from 4:30am to 10pm.

From Ciudad Tecún Umán frequent buses depart until about 6pm along the Carretera al Pacífico to Coatepeque, Retalhuleu, Escuintla and Guatemala City. There are direct buses to Quetzaltenango (Q45, 3½ hours) up until about 2pm. If you don't find a bus to your destination, take one to Coatepeque or, better, Retalhuleu, and change buses there.

El Carmen

A bridge across the Río Suchiate connects the border town of El Carmen with Talismán (Mexico). The border is open 24 hours daily. This border is generally far more hassle-free than Tecún Umán, but offers far fewer options for easy onward travel. There are few services at El Carmen, and those that are there are very basic.

On the Mexican side, minibuses run every 10 minutes between Talismán and Tapachula (M$15), from 5am to 9pm.

Most buses between here and the rest of Guatemala go via Ciudad Tecún Umán, 39km south, and then along the Carretera al Pacífico through Coatepeque, Retalhuleu and Escuintla. For Quetzaltenango, the quickest and easiest option is to change at Coatepeque (Q30, two hours from El Carmen).

Retalhuleu

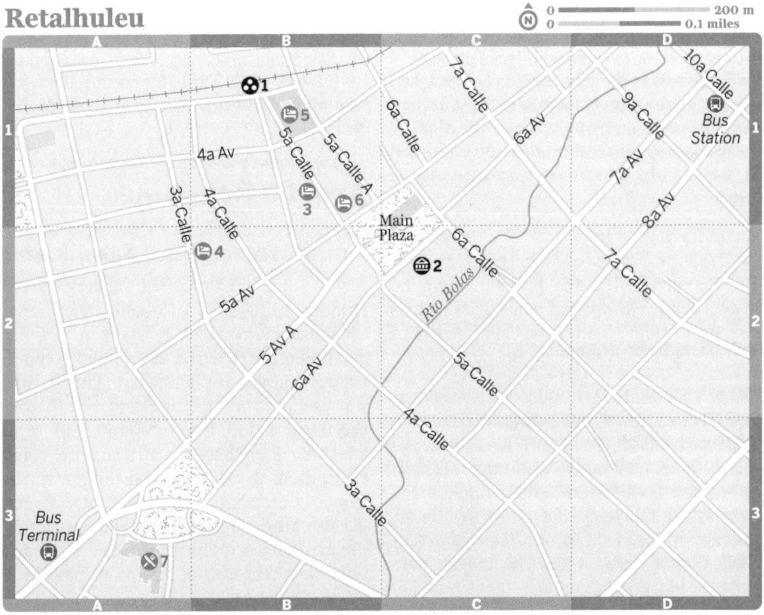

Sights

Museo de Arqueología y Etnología MUSEUM
(6a Av 5-68; Q15; ⌚8:30am-5pm Mon-Fri) Retalhuleu has a small museum of archaeological relics from local Mayan sites, as well as an interesting collection of historic photos showing the town in its heyday. The mural of the 33 archaeological sites in Retalhuleu department alone gives some hint at the great span of Guatemala's human history.

Abandoned Train Station RUINS
In the early 20th century, Retalhuleu was an important way station for cotton, coffee and sugar exports to the port at Champerico. The trains have long since stopped running, but this abandoned station, with its rusting clock and atmospherically overgrown tracks and platforms, makes for a diverting insight into the town's heyday.

Sleeping & Eating

Retalhuleu has some surprisingly good accommodations options, although it's a bit short on budget choices.

There are decent street food options around the plaza in the evening; the dining rooms of the Hotel Posada de Don José (p164) and the **Hotel Astor** (☎7771-2559; 5a Calle 4-60, Zona 1; mains Q60-120; ⌚7:30am-11pm) both offer more refined dining options. The modern **La Trinidad Mall** (5a Av) has all the chain restaurants popular in Guatemala.

Retalhuleu

Hotel Astor HOTEL $$
(☎7957-8300; www.hotelastorguatemala.com; 5a Calle 4-60, Zona 1; s/d Q285/400; P ❄ 🏊) The Astor is one of Reu's older and loveliest hotels, set in a low red building that was well located to serve the traffic from the old train line. Pretty rooms sit around a lush courtyard in old colonial style. There's a good restaurant and bar.

La Quinta HOTEL $$

(☎7771-0872; www.hotellaquintaguatemala.com; cnr 5a Avenida & 5a Calle, Zona 1; s/d incl breakfast Q235/300; P❄📶) This modern hotel just off the main square has a bit of contemporary style, once you get past the slightly industrial-looking common areas (tempered at least by the green courtyard). Service is good.

Hotel Casa y Campo HOTEL $$

(☎7771-3829; https://bit.ly/2zoLsmk; 3a Calle 4-73, Zona 2; s/d Q175/250; P❄📶) This hotel in charming yellow with terracotta floor tiles has comfortable and good-value rooms a couple of blocks north from the main plaza.

Hotel Posada de Don José HOTEL $$

(☎7771-0180; www.posadadedonjose.com; 5a Calle 3-67, Zona 1; r from Q375; P❄📶🏊) A beautiful mid-19th century hotel built around a huge swimming pool. Swan dives from the top balcony are tempting, but probably unwise. Rooms are spacious, comfortable and very slick after a recent refit. The hotel's large Guatemalan art collection – there are canvases everywhere – is a particular delight.

Orientation

The town center is 4km southwest of the Carretera al Pacífico, along Calz Las Palmas, a grand boulevard lined with towering palms. The main bus stop (p164) is northeast of the plaza. To find the plaza, look for the twin church towers and walk toward them.

Information

Both **Banco Agromercantil** (5a Av, Zona 1) and **Banco Industrial** (cnr 6a Calle & 5a Av, Zona 1) change US dollars and have ATMs.

Getting There & Away

Most buses traveling along the Carretera al Pacífico detour into Reu. Shared taxis (Q10) are the best way to get to El Asintal (for Takalik Abaj). Look for station wagons with 'Asintal' painted on the windshield around the bus stop and plaza.

Most buses make two stops in town, at the **main terminal** (5a Av, Zona 5) and a smaller **bus station** (10a Calle, Zona 1).

Around Retalhuleu

Parque Arqueológico Takalik Abaj

About 25km northwest of Retalhuleu, the Parque Arqueológico Takalik Abaj (www.takalikabajpark.com; Q50; ⏰7am-5pm) is a fascinating archaeological site set amid coffee, rubber and cacao plantations. Takalik Abaj was an important trading center in the late Preclassic period, before AD 250, and forms a historical link between Mesoamerica's first civilization, the Olmecs, and the Maya. The Olmecs flourished from about 1200 to 600 BC on Mexico's southern Gulf coast, but their influence extended far and wide, and numerous Olmec-style sculptures have been found at Takalik Abaj.

The city, which had strong connections with the town of Kaminaljuyú (in present-day Guatemala City), was sacked in about AD 300 and its great monuments, especially those in Maya style, were decapitated. Some monuments were rebuilt after AD 600 and the site retained a ceremonial and religious importance for the Maya, which it maintains to this day. Maya from the highlands regularly come here to perform ceremonies.

This 6.5-sq-km archaeological site spreads over nine natural terraces. The rainforest-like grounds boast temple mounds, ball courts and flights of steps paved with rounded river stones, along with an impressive number of stone sculptures. These works include numerous representations of animals and aquatic creatures (some in a curious pot-bellied style known as barrigón), miniature

BUSES FROM RETALHULEU

DESTINATION	COST (Q)	TIME (HR)	FREQUENCY
Champerico	15	1	every few minutes, 6am-7pm
Guatemala City	55-95	3	every 15min, 2am-8:30pm
Quetzaltenango	25	1½	every 30min, 4am-6pm
Santa Lucía Cotzumalguapa	30	2	every 15min, 2am-8:30pm
Tecún Umán (Mexican border)	25	1½	every 20min, 5am-10pm

versions of the characteristic Olmec colossal heads and early Maya-style monuments depicting finely adorned personages carrying out religious ceremonies.

Some imagination is needed to picture how the site would have looked when occupied, though there are plenty of helpful (Spanish) information boards. Archaeological work is continuing outside the kernel of the site, which is the Grupo Central on terrace No 2, where the most important ceremonial and civic buildings were located. Classic-era baths and multicolored floors were discovered here in late 2005.

The largest and tallest building is Estructura 5, a pyramid 16m high and 115m square on terrace No 3, above No 2. This may have formed one side of a ball court. Estructura 7, east of Estructura 5, is thought to have been an observatory.

Animal lovers may want to give the site's small zoo of Guatemalan rainforest animals a miss.

Tours

★Takalik Maya Lodge TOURS

(www.takalik.com; per person Q100) Takalik Maya Lodge runs fascinating tours of its plantations, which are rich in tropical produce from coffee to macadamia nuts. Highlights include sucking the sweet seeds of a just-picked cacao pod and poking the pungent elastic exudation of a freshly-tapped rubber tree. Tours are year-round but if you want to see the coffee being processed, visit between December and April.

Horse tours and a hike to a local waterfall are also possible, but for all options call ahead to book. Lunch available on request.

Sleeping & Eating

The site has a small snack shop for refreshments, but El Asintal offers basic *comedores*. Takalik Maya Lodge, nearby, has a lovely restaurant offering reasonably priced meals.

★Takalik Maya Lodge HOTEL $$

(☎2334-7693; www.takalik.com; farmhouse/bungalows Q450/600; P ⊛) Set on the grounds of a working farm 2km past the entrance to Takalik Abaj (and on top of a large, unexcavated section of it), this is by far the most comfortable place to stay in the area. Accommodations options include the old farmhouse and a gorgeously atmospheric electricity-free house amid the trees (lanterns are provided – it's a lot cosier than it sounds).

DON'T MISS

VUELO EXTREMO

If you're into the whole zipline thing, **Vuelo Extremo** (☎5908-8193; www.vueloextremo.com; Carretera a Retalhuleu, Km 198; 3/4/11 cables Q75/100/150; ⊙6am-6pm) is one of the better-value ones in the country, located almost exactly halfway between Retalhuleu and Quetzaltenango. It starts and ends with a terrifying 300m-long, 29m-high zip across the valley over the highway and then follows a circuit zigzagging down the hill on the other side.

For the fainter of heart there are some nice walking trails (Q25), crossing swinging bridges and passing by small waterfalls; and you can refresh yourself with lovely views over the valley in the cafe.

Check the website for package deals including accommodations, meals and tours of the plantations. The indoor-outdoor restaurant (mains Q55 to Q100) is excellent, but bring bug spray.

Getting There & Away

To reach Takalik Abaj by public transportation, catch a shared taxi from Retalhuleu to El Asintal (Q9, 30 minutes), which is 12km northwest of Reu and 5km north of the Carretera al Pacífico. Less frequent buses leave from a bus station on 5a Av A, 800m southwest of Reu plaza, about every half hour from 6am to 6pm. Pick-ups at El Asintal provide transportation on to Takalik Abaj (Q5), 4km further by paved road. You'll be shown around by a volunteer guide, whom you will probably want to tip (Q20 per person is a good baseline). You can also visit Takalik Abaj on tours from Quetzaltenango.

Parque Acuático Xocomil & Parque de Diversiones Xetulul

If you have children along, or your own inner child is fighting to get out, head to one of these two gigantic theme parks next door to one another on the Quetzaltenango road, about 12km north of Retalhuleu.

Both Xocomil and Xetulul are run by Irtra (Instituto de Recreación de los Trabajadores de la Empresa Privada de Guatemala; Guatemalan Private Enterprise Workers' Recreation Institute), which administers several fun sites around the country for workers and their families. Between them, the two sites comprise the most popular tourist attraction in Guatemala, with over a million visitors a year.

Activities

Parque Acuático Xocomil AMUSEMENT PARK
(☎7772-9400; www.irtra.org.gt; Carretera CITO, Km 180.5; adult/child Q100/50; ⏲9am-5pm Thu-Sun) With a distinct Guatemalan theme, this world-class water park offers aquatic diversions for all ages (under-fives must have a flotation device, but you can hire one for Q20). Among the 14 waterslides, two swimming pools and two wave pools are recreations of Maya monuments from Tikal, Copán and Quiriguá.

Visitors can bob along a river through canyons flanked with ancient temples and Maya masks. Three real volcanoes – Santiaguito, Zunil and Santa María – can be seen from the grounds.

Parque de Diversiones Xetulul AMUSEMENT PARK
(☎7722-9450; www.irtra.org.gt; Carretera CITO, Km 180.5; adult/child Q100/50; ⏲10am-5pm Fri-Sun) Xetulul is a surprisingly well organised amusement park, with first-class rides for all ages. Themed areas include representations of a Tikal pyramid, historical Guatemalan buildings and famous buildings from many European cities. An all-you-can-ride bracelet costs Q50 on top of admission.

Sleeping

Irtra Hostales HOTEL $$
(☎7722-9100; www.irtra.org.gt; Carretera CITO, Km 180; r with fan/air-con from Q250/300; P ❄ 📶 ≋) Set on lush, tropical grounds that feature swimming pools, a spa bath, various sports fields and probably the most impressive minigolf course in the country, this complex has the best accommodations for miles around. There are seven main buildings within the complex, each decorated in a different style – Colonial, Mediterranean, Polynesian, Indonesian, Thai, African, Maya – but rooms are modern and comfortable throughout.

Prices listed range wildly. It's quieter from Sunday to Wednesday; Thursday to Saturday nights (when the parks are open) the place packs out and prices rise considerably. The San Martín complex is the cheapest (rooms are often less than Q200), while the glitzier Paljunoj complex weighs in at around Q800.

Getting There & Away

Any bus heading from Retalhuleu toward Quetzaltenango will drop you at Xocomil, Xetulul or the Irtra Hostales (Q10, 30 minutes). From Quetzaltenango, any Retalhuleu-bound bus will do the same (Q15, one hour).

Champerico

POP 41,900

Built as a shipping point for coffee and cotton during the boom of the late 19th century, Champerico, 38km southwest of Retalhuleu, is a sweltering sort of spot, and the beach destination of choice for anyone based in Quetzaltenango.

It's a modest and slightly scruffy place, but presents an interesting picture of regular Guatemala at play that's a long, corrective way from a trending Instagram post.

Head to the end of the town until you hit the 'boardwalk' at the beach, where there are countless restaurants and tourist shacks. Beware of strong waves and an undertow if you go in the ocean, and stay in the clearly marked central part of the beach: muggings have been known outside this area.

Sleeping & Eating

Most beachgoers come only to spend the day, but it's possible to overnight here. Most accommodations options are scattered along the beachfront or a block or two inland; all are very basic.

All of the seaside eateries offer a similar deal – fresh seafood for around Q40 to Q80 per plate. *Camarones al ajillo* (garlic shrimp) and *caldo de mariscos* (seafood stew) are the standout items. As always, the freshest food tends to be at the busiest eateries.

Hotel Maza HOTEL $$
(☎7773-7180; s/d Q180/270; ❄) With large clean rooms just across the road from the beach, Hotel Maza is the best bet on the beach, but don't expect too many frills.

7 Mares SEAFOOD $
(mains Q40-90; ⏲8am-7pm) One of a handful of similarly styled restaurants in the beach zone, 7 Mares offers a small shaded swimming pool, dining area and upstairs deck that catches good breezes and views. Naturally, go for the fresh seafood.

Getting There & Away

Regular buses connect Champerico with other Pacific Slope towns, Quetzaltenango and Guatemala City. The bus stop is two blocks back from the beach on the road out of town. The last buses back to Quetzaltenango (Q30, 2½ hours) leave at about 6pm, and a bit later for Retalhuleu (Q15, one hour).

Tulate

Tulate is a tiny village that remains almost defiantly off the radar of most travelers. The lack of breakers means that Guatemala's surfing scene gives it a wide berth, but the gently shelving beach makes it a great place to swim and just hang around and have some fun (bodysurfers should still be able to get a ride any time of the year).

A strip of mangroves separates Tulate proper from its beach – you have to catch a boat (Q5) across the estuary. Once on the other side, the water is 500m in front of you, straight down the only paved street.

Sleeping & Eating

If you're heading toward either the Paraíso or Shamma, avoid the long hot walk along the beachfront by taking the riverfront path to the left as soon as you get off the *lancha* (small motorboat). If you don't feel like walking, a *lancha* all the way will cost you around Q60.

You can eat at your hotel but the best and most atmospheric dining is at the little shacks right on the beachfront, where good, fresh seafood meals start at around Q40.

Playa Paraíso BUNGALOW **$$**
(7872-1191; www.facebook.com/HotelPlayaParaisoTulate; bungalows Q420;) This comfortable option is about 1km down the beach to the left from the main street. The bungalows here have two double beds, a sitting room and laid-back little balconies out front. There are hammocks strung around the property, a pool practically on the beach and a good, if somewhat pricey, restaurant. Things can get a little hectic on weekends, but midweek you'll likely have the place to yourself.

Hotel Shamma HOTEL **$$**
(4477-9887; https://bit.ly/2zpnzeM; s/d Q150/250; P) The Shamma sits practically on the beach. It has a long row of rooms with shaded verandas and a pool and restaurant. Rooms are pretty stripped down and basic, but they're clean and you'll be thankful for the air-con.

Getting There & Away

Buses run direct to Tulate from Retalhuleu (Q45, two hours) and Mazatenango.

Santa Lucía Cotzumalguapa

POP 153,000

Santa Lucía Cotzumalguapa is an unremarkable sort of place, but it's an important stop for anyone interested in archaeology. In the fields and *fincas* (plantations or farms) near the town stand great stone heads carved with grotesque faces and fine relief scenes, the product of the enigmatic Pipil culture that flourished here from about AD 500 to 700.

In your explorations of the area, you may also get to see a Guatemalan sugarcane *finca* in full operation.

Sights

There are three main sites to visit, all outside town: El Baúl hilltop site, about 4.5km north; the museum at Finca El Baúl, 2.75km further north; and the Museo Cultura Cotzumalguapa, off the highway about 2km northeast of town.

Taxi drivers in Santa Lucía's main square will take you around all three sites for about Q300 without too much haggling. It won't just save you sweat in a sticky climate – muggings in the isolated locations aren't unknown.

Museo El Baúl MUSEUM
(8am-4pm Mon-Fri, to noon Sat) FREE This museum, about 2.75km on foot or 5km by vehicle from El Baúl hilltop site, comprises a very fine open-air assemblage of Pipil stone sculpture collected from around Finca El Baúl's sugarcane fields. A large stone jaguar faces you at the entrance.

Other figures include four humans or monkeys with arms folded across their chests; a grinning, blank-eyed head reminiscent of the one at the hilltop site; carvings of skulls; and, at the back, a stela showing a personage wearing an animal headdress, standing over a similarly attired figure on the ground: seemingly winner and loser of a ball game.

To get there, if driving, leave town northward on the road passing El Calvario church. From the intersection just past the church, go 2.7km to a fork in the road just beyond a bridge; take the left fork and follow the paved road 3km to the headquarters of the Finca El Baúl sugarcane plantation. Buses trundle

Santa Lucía Cotzumalguapa

along this road every few hours. (If you're on foot, you can walk from the hilltop site back to the crossroads with the paved road. Cross the road and continue along the dirt track. This will eventually bring you to the asphalt road that leads to the *finca* headquarters. When you reach the road, turn right.)

Approaching the *finca* headquarters (6km from Santa Lucía's main square), you cross a bridge at a curve. Continue uphill and you will see the entrance on the left, marked by a guard post and a sign 'Ingenio El Baúl Bienvenidos.' Tell the guards that you would like to visit the *museo,* and you should be admitted. Pass the sugar refinery buildings to arrive at the museum on the right.

El Baúl Hilltop Site ARCHAEOLOGICAL SITE

With two great carved stones, this archaeological site has the additional fascination of being an active place of pagan worship for local people. Maya people visit regularly, especially on weekends, and make offerings, light fires and candles, and sacrifice chickens. They will not mind if you visit as well, and may be happy to pose with the idols for photographs in exchange for a small contribution.

Of the two stones, the large, grotesque, half-buried head is the most striking, with its elaborate headdress, beak-like nose and 'blind' eyes with big bags underneath. The head is stained with wax from candles, splashes of liquor and other drinks, and with the smoke and ashes of incense fires, all part of worship. People have been coming here to pay homage for more than 1400 years.

The other stone is a relief carving of a figure with an elaborate headdress, possibly a fire god, surrounded by circular motifs that may be date glyphs.

To get here, leave town northward on the road passing El Calvario church. From the intersection just past the church, go 2.7km to a fork in the road just beyond a bridge; the fork is marked by the entrance to the Ciudad España housing development (signposted from the center). Buses heading out to Finca El Baúl, the plantation headquarters, pass this sign. Take the right-hand fork, passing a settlement called Colonia Maya on your right. After you have gone 1.5km from the Los Tarros sign, a dirt track crosses the road: turn right here, between two concrete posts. Ahead now is a low mound topped by three large trees: this is the hilltop site. After about 250m, fork right between two more identical concrete posts, and follow this track around in front of the mound to its end after some 150m. Then take the path up on to the mound, which is actually a great ruined temple platform that has not been restored.

Museo Cultura Cotzumalguapa MUSEUM
(☎5157-9112; Q30; ⌚8am-1pm & 2:30-4:30pm Mon-Fri, 8am-1pm Sat) At the headquarters of the Finca Las Ilusiones sugarcane plantation, you'll find this museum, which holds a collection of sculptures found around Las Ilusiones' lands. There is some explanatory material and you'll probably be shown around by caretaker René Hernández.

The museum includes a reconstruction of a sacrificial altar with the original stones, and photos of some fine stelae that were removed to the Dahlem Museum in Berlin in 1880. The most impressive exhibit, Monumento 21, is actually a fiberglass copy of a stone that still stands in the fields of Finca Bilbao (part of Las Ilusiones' plantations), depicting what may be a shaman holding a sort of puppet on the left, a ball-game player in the middle with a knife in one hand, and a king or priest on the right holding what may be a heart. Another copy of this stone, along with one of Monumento 19, lies on the ground across the street from the museum. Along the road just before the bridge to the *finca* house are copies of some of the sculptures from El Baúl museum.

To find the museum, head about 1.5km east of the town center on Carretera al Pacífico (Hwy 2). Take a left shortly before the Tecún farm supplies depot and travel about 400m north.

Sleeping & Eating

Hotel Internacional HOTEL $
(☎7882-5504; Calle los Mormones; s/d Q130/180, with air-con Q200/250; P ❄) Down a short lane (signposted) off Carretera al Pacífico is the best budget hotel in town. It has clean, good-sized en suite rooms with fan or air-con.

Hotel Santiaguito HOTEL $$
(☎7882-5435; www.hotelsantiaguito.com; Carretera al Pacífico, Km 90.4; s/d Q330/435; P ❄ ≋) On the highway on the west edge of town, the Santiaguito is fairly lavish for Guatemala's Pacific Slope, with spacious tree-shaded grounds and a nice swimming pool. The large rooms have huge, firm beds and are set around a jungly patio/parking area. There's a half-decent restaurant.

Hotel El Camino HOTEL $$
(☎7882-5316; Carretera al Pacífico, Km 90.5; s/d Q180/300; P ❄ ≋) Hotel El Camino's rooms are almost ridiculously large, with a few sticks of furniture, such as clothes racks and writing tables. You could organize a game of soccer with the rest of the floor space, but don't tell management it was our idea.

Robert's STEAK $$
(Carretera al Pacífico, Km 89; mains Q50-180; ⌚11am-10pm) This steak house with leafy outdoor seating is probably the nicest place to eat in town.

Information

Banco Industrial (cnr 4a Av & 4a Calle; ⌚9am-5pm Mon-Fri, to 1pm Sat) A block north of the plaza; changes US dollars cash and has an ATM.

Getting There & Away

There are buses throughout the day between Santa Lucía Cotzumalguapa and Guatemala City's CentraSur terminal (Q30, two hours). Many intercity buses no longer come to Santa Lucía as the Carretera al Pacifíco Hwy bypasses the city. For Antigua, take a bus to Escuintla (Q15, 30 minutes) and change there. From Cocales, 23km west of Santa Lucía, there are plenty of buses to Panajachel (Q35, 2½ hours).

La Democracia

POP 29,000

La Democracia is a modest Pacific Slope town 10km south of Siquinalá on the Carretera al Pacifíco. It's one for the archaeology buffs, as during the late Preclassic period (300 BC to AD 250), this area, like Takalik Abaj to the northwest, was home to a culture showing influence from southern Mexico – the remnants of which are on display in the town center. As you come into town from the highway, follow signs to the regional *museo*, which is on the plaza. You'll find a 5B ATM there, too.

Sights

At the archaeological site of Monte Alto, on the outskirts of La Democracia, huge basalt heads and pot-bellied sculptures have been discovered, probably dating from around 500BC. These heads resemble crude versions of the colossal heads that were carved by the Olmecs on Mexico's southern Gulf Coast some centuries previously.

Today, these great Olmecoid heads are arranged around La Democracia's renovated main **plaza** (Parque Centrale), set in their own little roofed stands and illuminated at night.

Museo Regional de Arqueología MUSEUM
(☎7880-3650; Q30; ⏰8:30am-1pm & 2-4:30pm Tue-Sat) Facing La Democracia's main plaza – along with the expected church and *palacio municipal* (city hall) – is this small modern museum that houses some fascinating local archaeological finds. The undoubted star of the show is an exquisite jade mask. Small figures, yokes used in *juego de pelota* (the Mayan ball game), relief carvings and other objects make up the rest of the collection.

Sleeping & Eating

There's very little here to hold the average visitor's attention for more than a day, which is lucky as there aren't any sleeping options.

Totitos Pizza FAST FOOD $
(mains Q25-45; ⏰8am-9pm) Just off the square, this is as close as the town gets to a restaurant.

Getting There & Away

There are buses to La Democracia throughout the day from the CentraSur terminal in Guatemala City to La Democracia (Q25, two hours) via Escuintla. From Santa Lucía Cotzumalguapa, catch a bus 8km east to Siquinalá and change there.

El Paredón

POP UNDER 1000

El Paredón is barely more than a single street at the end of a hard earth road that can feel like a long way from anywhere, but it's a town well on the way to becoming Guatemala's surf capital. Waves here average 1.8m, with the best breaks between December and April.

There's a thriving backpacker scene here amid the tropical greenery and palm-thatched houses, and a local development NGO, La Choza Chula, that runs tours to the local mangroves, salt farms and turtle feeding grounds, as well as arranging cooking classes.

There's a laid-back atmosphere in El Paredón and it's easy to lose more than a few days doing very little. Future development plans are much discussed among locals, however, with both excitement and nervousness about what a proposed paved road might bring to such a sleepy town.

Activities

All of the guesthouses offer surfing, typically charging around Q100 per day for board hire, as well as lessons for around Q120.

★**La Choza Chula** TOURS
(www.lachozochula.org; ⏰9.30am-4.30pm) This local NGO is deeply involved in community tourism, alongside its education and environmental programs. Its most popular boat tour options are wildlife spotting and traditional fishing in the nearby mangroves (Q115), and to El Paredón's turtle feeding grounds and salt farms (Q185), as well as an introduction to local cuisine with cooking classes (Q90). All tours are minimum two people.

If you've got a minimum of three months on your hands and have some Spanish, La Choza Chula also welcomes volunteers.

Sleeping

Soul Food Kitchen & Guesthouse GUESTHOUSE $
(☎3286-6473; www.facebook.com/SoulFoodKitchenElParedon; d with/without bathroom Q250/150; 🛜) This simple guesthouse has a selection of airy whitewashed rooms with mosquito nets. It's a relaxed and quiet place, but just as much of a draw is the restaurant (noon to 3pm and 6pm to 9pm) serving up big, delicious plates of Thai and Indian curries along with big bowls of noodles (all with vegetarian options). A breakfast menu was in the planning during research.

Cocori GUESTHOUSE $
(www.cocorilodge.com; dm Q100, cabana Q250, suites with kitchen Q450; 🛜) Cocori occupies a long strip of land down to the beach. There are a couple of cute *cabañas*, and some nice family-sized suites with their own kitchen, but the absolute draw is the thatched dorm above them with 360-degree views, where the breeze keeps you cool and you sleep and wake to the sound of the waves. Heavenly.

Driftwood Surfer HOSTEL $
(☎3036-6891; www.driftwoodsurfer.com; dm Q75, d with/without bathroom Q375/250; ❄🛜) El Paredón's undisputed party hostel, the Driftwood was quick to arrive in the town and set the pace with its beachfront location and swim-up pool bar. The dorms are a bit cramped, but the air-conditioning is welcome and most guests prefer to be out with the surf breaks, on the sun deck or playing drinking games in the bar.

The restaurant's food is excellent; the fish and chips (Q60) are a fine tribute to the owner's English roots.

Hotel Pacifico HOSTEL $
(☎5788-1220; www.facebook.com/pacificelparedon; dm Q75, d Q600;) Thatched dorms are the order of the day here, with a pool to laze by and an open-sided longhouse to while away the hours when you're not surfing. Doubles (with fan) are in the rather incongruous two-story building.

Even if you're not staying here, El Tiburon restaurant has excellent wood-fired pizzas (Q55 to Q105), pasta, sandwiches and salads.

★**Hotel Paredon Surf House** BOUTIQUE HOTEL $$
(☎4994-1842; www.paredonsurf.com; dm Q205, stilt bungalow d/tr Q570/750, suites Q810-1025;) This charming beachfront guesthouse has a variety of different options, including thatched private rooms, generous dorms on stilts overlooking the ocean, and family-sized suites with open-air showers. It's well run with a relaxed, modest restraint. All prices are half-board, and beds are netted. The bar-restaurant closes early (by 9:30pm) to ensure that guests get a quiet night's sleep.

Swell BOUTIQUE HOTEL $$
(www.swellguatemala.com; d from Q450, pool suites Q750;) This 'surf and lifestyle' hotel was on the cusp of opening when we visited, and it looked a treat. Designed by the architect-owner, it has a selection of options from thatched rooms on stilts catching the ocean breeze, to achingly-cool crisp white suites facing the pool, all fitted out with great locally made wooden furniture.

A bar-restaurant is planned, along with yoga classes and an outdoor gym. Prices are approximate.

Eating

Sandra's GUATEMALAN $
(mains Q25-45; ⏱8am-8pm) Popular open-sided restaurant that serves up a bit of everything, but leans heavily toward seafood (especially ceviche). Vegetarians are well covered, and all mains come with enormous side dishes. One long-term El Paredón resident argued with us that Sandra's has the best guacamole in the country, and it's certainly worth the visit to do a taste test.

Yoli's GUATEMALAN $
(breakfast Q20, pasta Q20-35; ⏱8am-8pm) A good thatched spot near the beach for breakfasts, fruit smoothies and plates of pasta. There's usually a seafood-centered dish of the day that's worth trying.

Information

El Paredón had barely any internet access when we most recently visited, but the town was being cabled to allow it to get online properly.

There are no ATMs in El Paredón, so plan accordingly.

Getting There & Away

There are two daily tourist shuttles between El Paredón and Antigua (Q120, two hours). Tickets are sold in every travel agency in Antigua or book through your El Paredón guesthouse. Pacifico Surf Transport (p109) also runs a weekday shuttle to Santiago de Atitlán (Q150, three hours).

By public transport, take the ferry across the river (Q10) and then a *tuk-tuk* to Sipacate (Q20, 20 minutes), from where buses leave throughout the day to Guatemala City (Q45, 3½ hours) – change at La Democracía or Escuintla for onward connections.

Escuintla

POP 168,200

Surrounded by rich green foliage, Escuintla should be a tropical idyll where people swing languidly in hammocks and concoct pungent meals of readily available exotic fruits and vegetables. In fact, it's a hot, busy commercial and industrial city that's integral to the Pacific Slope's economy, but not at all important to travelers, except for making bus connections.

Escuintla was the center for relief efforts after the eruption of Volcán Fuego in 2018.

Getting There & Away

All buses from the terminal pass along 1a Av, but if you really want to get a seat, head to the main bus station in the southern part of town, just off 4a Av. The station entrance is marked by a Scott 77 fuel station. If you're heading to Monterrico and can't find a direct bus, catch one to Puerto San José or Iztapa and make a connection there.

Buses coming along the Carretera al Pacífico may drop you in the north of town, necessitating a sweaty walk through the hectic town center if you want to get to the main station.

Iztapa

POP 11,900

Iztapa, about 12km east of Puerto San José, was Guatemala's first Pacific port, used by none other than Pedro de Alvarado in the 16th century. When Puerto San José was built in 1853, Iztapa's reign as the port of the capital city came to an end, and it relaxed

WORTH A TRIP

AUTOSAFARI CHAPÍN

About 25km southeast of Escuintla, **Autosafari Chapín** (2222-5858; www.autosafarichapin.com; Carretera a Taxisco, Km 87.5; adult/child Q60/50; 9:30am-5pm Tue-Sun) is a drive-through safari park and animal conservation project. Species native to Guatemala include white-tailed deer, tapir and macaws. Around the grounds also roam non-native species such as lions, hippos and leopards. There is a restaurant and pool, and it makes a good day out if you're traveling with kids.

It's more fun if you have your own vehicle, but if not, a 20-minute cruise through the park in a minibus is included in the admission price. Various companies run buses here (Q20, 1½ hours) from the CentraSur terminal in Guatemala City. They leave every 10 minutes, from 4:30am to 5:30pm.

into a tropical torpor from which it has yet to emerge.

There's not much to do in town itself – most people look toward the sea, where you can surf, go whale-watching or go on a deep-sea fishing expedition. If you just want to relax, the best option is to get a boat across the river to the sandbar fronting the ocean, where the waves pound and a line of palm-thatched restaurants offers food and beer.

Tours

Iztapa has gained renown as one of the world's premier deep-sea fishing spots. World records have been set here, and enthusiasts can fish for marlin, shark and yellowfin tuna, among others. Trips leave from Puerto Quetzal, west across the river from Iztapa. **Buena Vista Fishing** (7880-4203; www.buenavistasportfishing.com; Puerto Quetzal) runs wallet-stretching all-inclusive deep-sea fishing tours. It is also possible to contract local boat owners for fishing trips, though equipment and comfort may be nonexistent and catch-and-release could prove a foreign concept. The boat owners hang out at the edge of the Río María Linda – bargain hard. Yellowfin tuna will likely be out of reach for the local boats, as these fish inhabit the waters some 17km from Iztapa.

Whale-watching is also possible from Puerto Quetzal, with **Productos Mundiales** (2366-1026; www.whalewatchingguatemala.com; Marina Pez Vela, Puerto Quetzal; per person Q1775; departures 7am Sat & Sun). Between December and May there's a good chance of seeing humpbacks and sperm whales; year-round species include pilot whales, bottlenose dolphins, spinner dolphins, as well as olive ridley turtles, leatherback turtles, giant manta rays and whale sharks.

Sleeping

If you're looking for a beach holiday, this isn't the place, but there's a good surf hostel for budget travelers.

Small *comedores* (cheap eateries) can be found along the main street and in the area around the market.

Surf Shack Iztapa HOTEL $$
(5680-7539; www.surfshackiztapa.wordpress.com; 3a Calle; per person Q70;) This riverside hostel is a great escape, and has simple thatched rooms for those looking for some downtime. There's a kitchen for self-caterers and free tea and coffee is always available. There are surfboards for hire (per day Q70), as well as kayaks and stand-up paddleboards – the latter being particularly useful for crossing the river to the beach.

Getting There & Away

There are direct buses between Iztapa and Guatemala City (Q35, 1½ hours), which leave about every half hour, from 5am to 6pm, traveling via Escuintla (where you can change for more destinations) and Puerto San José. The last bus heading back from Iztapa goes around 5pm.

To get to Monterrico, take a microbus to Puerto Viejo and change there.

Monterrico

POP 2400

The coastal area around Monterrico is a totally different Guatemala. Life here is steeped with a sultry, tropical flavor, with rustic wooden-slat and thatched-roof architecture and awesome volcanoes that shimmer in the hinterland. It's fast becoming popular with foreigners as a beach break from Antigua or Guatemala City. On weekdays it's relatively quiet, but on weekends and holidays it teems with Guatemalan families.

Monterrico itself is a coastal village with a few small, inexpensive hotels right on the beach, a large wildlife reserve and two centers for the hatching and release of sea turtles and caimans. The beach here is dramatic, with powerful surf crashing onto black volcanic sand at odd angles. This waveprint signals that there are rip tides; deaths have occurred at this beach, so swim with care. Behind the town is a large network of mangrove swamps and canals, part of the 190km Canal de Chiquimulilla.

Sights

Biotopo Monterrico-Hawaii WILDLIFE RESERVE
(Reserva Natural Monterrico) This reserve, administered by Cecon (Centro de Estudios Conservacionistas de la Universidad de San Carlos), is Monterrico's biggest attraction. The 20km-long nature reserve of coast and coastal mangrove swamps is bursting with avian and aquatic life. The reserve's most famous denizens are the endangered leatherback and ridley turtles, which lay their eggs on the beach in many places along the coast. The mangrove swamps are a network of 25 lagoons, all connected by mangrove canals.

Boat tours of the reserve, passing through the mangrove swamps and visiting several lagoons, take 1½ to two hours and cost Q75 to Q100 per person. It's best to go just on sunrise, when you're likely to see the most wildlife. If you have binoculars, bring them along for birdwatching; January and February are the best months. Locals will approach you on the street (some with very impressive-looking ID cards), offering tours, and you can arrange tours through hotels but if you want to support the *tortugario* arrange a tour directly through Tortugario Monterrico, which, incidentally, has the most environmentally knowledgeable guides.

Some travelers have griped about the use of motorboats because the sound of the motor scares off the wildlife. If you're under no time pressure, ask about arranging a paddled tour of the canal.

Tortugario Monterrico WILDLIFE RESERVE
(Q50; ⏲8am-1pm & 2-5pm) The Cecon-run Tortugario Monterrico is just a short walk east down the beach from the end of Calle Principal and then a block inland. Several endangered species of animals are raised here, including leatherback, olive ridley and green sea turtles, caimans and iguanas.

There's an interesting interpretative trail and a little museum with pickled displays in bottles. The staff offer lagoon trips, and night walks (Q50) from August to December to look for turtle eggs. Around sunset nightly from September to January on the beach in front of the *tortugario,* workers help release baby turtles. You're welcome to observe, but despite what everybody else is doing, please refrain from using flash cameras and flashlights.

Activities

The most popular activity in Monterrico is to take a boat tour around the mangroves of Biotopo Monterrico-Hawaii, costing Q75 to Q100 per person.

Horse-riding along the beach is popular. Expect to pay around Q100 for an hour or so – the guys with horses will find you easily enough, though you can also arrange it through your hotel.

Arcas VOLUNTEERING
(☎5039-0451; www.arcasguatemala.org; Parque Hawaii; ⏲8am-5pm) Arcas (Asociación de Rescate y Conservación de Vida Silvestre) welcome volunteers to Parque Hawaii, its nature reserve and turtle hatchery 5km west along the beach from Monterrico. The reserve is separate from the neighboring Biotopo Monterrico-Hawaii, but engages in the same line of conservation. Volunteers are welcome year-round, but the sea-turtle nesting season is from June to November, with August and September being the peak months.

Volunteers are charged Q1300 a week for food and board onsite at the project. Homestays are also available with local families. Jobs for volunteers include hatchery checks and maintenance, mangrove reforestation, basic construction and data collection. See the website for the complete lowdown on volunteering here. Most of the egg collection happens at night. It's a way out of town, but there are usually other volunteers to keep you company, and while you're here you can use the kayaks, go on village trips and go fishing in the sea and mangroves.

A bus (Q5, 30 minutes) leaves the Monterrico jetty every couple of hours during the week and every hour on weekends for the bumpy ride to the reserve. Pick-ups also operate on this route, charging Q35 per person.

Courses

Proyecto Lingüístico Monterrico LANGUAGE
(☎5475-1265; www.monterrico-guatemala.com/spanish-school.php; Calle Principal) This place, about 250m from the beach, is quite professional. Classes are generally held outdoors

OFF THE BEATEN TRACK

ISLETA DE GAIA

East down the coast from Monterrico near Las Lisas, **Isleta de Gaia** (☎7885-0044; www.isleta-de-gaia.com; Las Lisas; 2-/4-person bungalow Q600/1050;) overlooks the Pacific on one side and mangroves on the other. There are a dozen bungalows, with sea, lagoon or pool views. Each has good beds, fan, bathroom, balcony and hammock, and there's a seafront restaurant with Mediterranean-style cuisine and fresh fish naturally the star.

There are boogie boards and kayaks for rent and a boat for fishing trips. Reserve your stay in this little paradise by email a few days in advance.

A shuttle service can fetch you from Guatemala City or Antigua. From Monterrico there is no road east along the coast beyond Parque Hawaii, so you have to backtrack to Taxisco and take Carretera al Pacífico for about 35km to reach the turnoff for Las Lisas. From the turnoff it's 20km to Las Lisas, where you take a boat (Q100) to Isleta de Gaia.

in a shady garden area. You can study in the morning or afternoon, depending on your schedule. Twenty hours of study per week costs Q750, plus Q670 for a seven-night homestay.

Sleeping

Monterrico has a decent enough selection of hotels on two roads that run left and right parallel to the beach at the end of Calle Principal. Prices are on a shifting scale: weekends are more expensive than weekdays, but stays of three nights or more frequently attract discounts.

Left of Calle Principal

Johnny's Place HOTEL $

(☎5812-0409; www.johnnysplacehotel.com; dm Q45, r without bathroom Q190, r with air-con from Q320, bungalow from Q600;) Johnny's is the first place you come to turning left on the beach. It's got a decent atmosphere and attracts a mix of backpackers and family groups. The cheaper rooms are far from glamorous, but have fans and screened windows. Pay extra and things start to get very swish.

Every pair of bungalows shares a barbecue and small swimming pool. There's also a larger general swimming pool. The bar-restaurant overlooks the sea and is a popular hangout: the food is not gourmet, but there are plenty of choices and imaginative *licuados* (fresh fruit drinks) and other long cool drinks.

Brisas del Mar HOTEL $

(☎5517-1142; incl breakfast s/d with fan Q100/200, with air-con Q150/300;) One block back from the beach, this popular option offers good-sized rooms, an open-sided thatched 2nd-floor dining hall with excellent sea views and a large swimming pool.

Hotel Pez de Oro BUNGALOW $$

(☎5232-9534; s/d Q400/500;) This funky place has comfortable little huts and bungalows scattered around a palm-tree shaded property. The color scheme is a cheery blue and yellow, and the rooms have some tasteful decorations and large overhead fans. The restaurant, with big sea views, serves up great Italian cuisine and seafood dishes.

Right of Calle Principal

Hotel El Delfin HOTEL $

(☎4661-9255; www.hotel-el-delfin.com; dm Q40, s/d from Q200/300, without bathroom Q120/150;) A humble but sprawling beachside setup with a mix of dorms and rooms. Those with bathrooms also come with air-con; all beds have mosquito nets. Rooms are big and well appointed, but the place can get noisy on weekends. The beach restaurant is excellent and there's frequent live music.

Café del Sol HOTEL $$

(☎5810-0821; www.cafe-del-sol.com; s/d from Q450/650;) This hotel comes in two sections on either side of the street. On the beach side, there's the reception and the 'economy' rooms, leading down to the waves. Across the road and next to the pool (with swim-up bar) there are nicer and larger 'standard' rooms. The restaurant lets you eat on the terrace or in the big *palapa* (thatched) dining area.

Hotel Atelie del Mar HOTEL $$$

(☎5752-5528; www.hotelateliedelmar.com; s/d incl breakfast from Q415/630;) This is one of the swankiest hotels in town, with lovely landscaped grounds and spacious, simple and beautiful rooms with netted beds. It's got the best swimming pool around, along with the widest menu and an onsite art gallery.

Dos Mundos Pacific Resort RESORT **$$$**
(☎5375-9033; www.facebook.com/dosmundosmonterrico; bungalows from Q930; P ❄ 📶 🏊) The biggest complex around is pushing resort status – manicured grounds, two swimming pools and a gorgeous beachfront restaurant. The bungalows are spacious and simple, but beautifully presented, with wide shady balconies out front.

Eating & Drinking

There are many simple seafood restaurants on Calle Principal. Even better, try the simple shacks with umbrellas and tables on the beach itself and sink a cold drink over a plate of fish or garlic shrimp while watching the waves.

Most hotels have restaurants serving whatever is fresh from the sea that day.

★**Taberna El Pelicano** ITALIAN, SEAFOOD **$$**
(mains Q60-150; ⊙noon-2pm & 6-10pm Wed-Sun) This cheery thatched orange restaurant is one of the best places to eat in town, with the widest menu and most interesting food. Look for excellent salads, plenty of cleverly prepared fish and a range of jumbo shrimp dishes, as well as daily specials.

Playa Club CLUB
(⊙8am-1am) This venue, located at Johnny's Place (p174), heats up on weekends, with plenty of reggaetón, house music and drinks specials keeping the crowd moving. The food is good, too.

Information

Monterrico is very badly lit at night, and its popularity as a tourist destination has attracted the occasional mugger, tempted by a fat wallet and shiny smartphone. Ensure due diligence when going out at night.

There is a Cajero 5B ATM in the centre of Monterrico.

Getting There & Away

The quickest and easiest way to get to Monterrico is undoubtedly with a shuttle from Antigua (Q80, two hours) or Guatemala City (Q150, three hours). The shuttles fill quickly leaving Monterrico, so book the day before if you can.

There is a daily direct bus to Guatemala City, departing at 5am (Q80, three hours). This travels via Iztapa and Escuintla, from where you can change for connections to Antigua or other destinations.

CROSSING INTO EL SALVADOR: CHIQUIMULILLA

Most travellers who pass through Chiquimulilla are likely to be surfers heading to or returning from La Libertad in El Salvador. Most people shoot straight through Escuintla and Taxisco to Chiquimulilla and on to the Salvadoran border at the tiny town of Ciudad Pedro de Alvarado (Guatemala) and La Hachadura (El Salvador), from where it is about 110km along the coast of El Salvador to La Libertad.

If you need to stop for the night before crossing the border, you could do worse than the low-slung cowboy town of Chiquimulilla in the ranching country some 12km east of Taxisco. There isn't much going on here, but it's a decent enough place to take care of errands and regroup. The bus terminal is on the outskirts of town, but *tuk-tuks* will take you anywhere you want to go for Q5.

The best sleeping option in Chiquimulilla is **Hotel San Carlos** (☎7885-0817; 2a Calle, Zona 2; s/d Q120/180; P 📶). There are two serviceable *hospedajes* (guesthouses) in La Hachadura on the El Salvador side of the border, but the *hostales* (budget hotels) in Ciudad Pedro de Alvarado on the Guatemalan side are not recommended.

Buses run between either Taxisoc or Chiquimulilla and Ciudad Pedro de Alvarado all day until around 7pm. There is onward transport from La Hachadura, the El Salvador side of the border.

The other option for getting to El Salvador is to turn north from Chiquimulilla and take local buses through Cuilapa to the border at Valle Nuevo–Las Chinamas, traveling inland before veering south to La Libertad.

Chiquimulilla and the El Salvador border are served by buses from Guatemala City and those running along the Carretera al Pacífico. Buses leave Taxisco for the border every 15 minutes until 5pm.

Alternatively, it can be fun to take the 30-minute boat ride to Avellana (Q5) along the Canal de Chiquimulilla, a long mangrove canal. Boats start at 4:30am and run more or less every half hour or hour until late afternoon. There are also car ferries (Q100 per vehicle). From Avellana, there are half-hourly buses to Guatemala City via Taxisco and Escuintla. From Taxisco there are regular buses to the El Salvador border at Ciudad Pedro de Alvarado.

Cuilapa

POP 49,600

Surrounded by citrus and coffee plantations, the capital of Santa Rosa department isn't much of a tourist attraction in its own right, although the area's fame for wood carvings, pottery and leather goods may mean you'll turn up a couple of decent souvenirs.

People coming this way are usually headed for the border with El Salvador, but there are a couple of volcanoes just out of town that are easily climbed and afford some superb views.

Hotels in Cuilapa are very basic. Your best bet is in nearby Chiquimulilla or day-tripping from further afield.

Basic *comedores* (cheap eateries) can be found around the bus terminal/market area.

Sights

Volcán Cruz Quemada VOLCANO

This dormant volcano towers 1700m over the tiny village of Santa María Ixhuatán at its base. Coffee plantations reach about one third of the way up its slopes. The summit, littered with radio towers, offers excellent views of the land running down to the coast, the Cerro La Consulta mountain range and the nearby Tecuamburro volcanic complex. From Santa María it's an easy-to-moderate climb to the top that should take about three hours.

The 12km hike is possible to do on your own, asking for plenty of directions along the way. Alternatively, guides can be hired in Santa María – ask at the taxi stand on the main square.

To get to Santa María, catch a minibus (Q8, 25 minutes) from Cuilapa.

Tecuamburro VOLCANO

The Tecuamburro volcanic complex comprises various peaks, including Cerro de Miraflores (1950m), Cerro la Soledad (1850m) and Cerro Peña Blanca (1850m). This last, which has several small vents releasing steam and sulfur, provides the most interesting climb, although its forested slopes mean no views until you're almost at the top.

Buses and minibuses (Q15, 1½ hours) leave regularly for the village of Tecuamburro from Cuilapa. From there it's a two- to three-hour hike (14km) to the summit of Peña Blanca.

Getting There & Away

Cuilapa is connected by a good road with Guatemala City. Buses (Q35, 2½ hours) leave from the CentraSur bus terminal in Guatemala City.

Minibuses leave from Cuilapa's bus terminal for the El Salvador border crossing 54km away at Valle Nuevo.

Lago de Amatitlán

Lago de Amatitlán is a placid lake backed by a looming volcano, and at just 25km south of Guatemala City, it's an easy day trip from the capital. On weekends, people from Guatemala City come to row boats on the lake (its waters are too polluted for swimming) or to rent a hot tub for a dip. Many people from the capital own second homes here.

There are a few decent hotels scattered around the lake's edge, and some in the town, but most travelers come here on a day trip.

A string of *comedores* along the lakefront offers fried fish, tacos and simple meals. For something a bit more refined, follow the signs up the hill to the right to **La Rocarena** (☎6662-1400; mains Q50-120; ⏲8am-9pm), which has a decent menu, lovely grounds, good views and a couple of warm-water swimming pools.

Sights & Activities

Rowboats rent from Q30 per hour. If that seems too much effort, shared/private boat tours cost Q10/80.

Teleférico CABLE CAR

(adult/child return Q20/10; ⏲9am-5pm Fri-Sun) This cable car heads out over the lakeshore then pretty much straight up the hillside. It's a half-hour ride with some stunning views of the surrounding countryside from the top.

Getting There & Away

The lake is just off the main Escuintla–Guatemala City highway (Hwy 9). Coming in a bus from Guatemala City (Q10, one hour), just ask to be dropped at the *teleférico*. The waterfront is about half a kilometer from the signposted turnoff. Coming from Escuintla, or heading back to Guatemala City, buses stop on the main road, about 1km away. It's an easy 10- to 15-minute walk; taxis are rare.

Central & Eastern Guatemala

Includes ➡

Best Places to Eat

- Xkape Koba'n (p185)
- La Abadia (p185)
- Restaurante Buga Mama (p221)
- Sundog Café (p212)
- Kardamomuss (p185)
- El Bistrot Francés (p192)

Best Places to Stay

- Casa Tenango (p184)
- Utopia (p189)
- Candelaria Lodge (p192)
- Casa Rosada (p220)
- Casa Nostra (p220)
- Posada de Quiriguá (p200)

Why Go?

Stretching from the steamy lowland forests of El Petén to the dry tropics of the Río Motagua valley, and from the edge of the Western Highlands to the Caribbean Sea, this is Guatemala's most diverse region.

The Carretera al Atlántico (Hwy 9) shoots eastward to the sea from Guatemala City, passing the turnoffs for the wonderfully preserved ruins of Copán (Honduras), Quiriguá with its impressive stelae, and Río Dulce, a favored resting spot for Caribbean sailors and gateway to the Refugio de Vida Silvestre Bocas del Polochic (Bocas del Polochic Wildlife Reserve). While you're here, don't miss the gorgeous boat ride down the Río Dulce to Lívingston, the enclave of the Garifuna people.

The north of the region is lush and mountainous coffee-growing country. The limestone crags around Cobán attract cavers the world over, and the beautiful pools and cascades of Semuc Champey rate high on Guatemala's list of natural wonders.

When to Go

Río Dulce

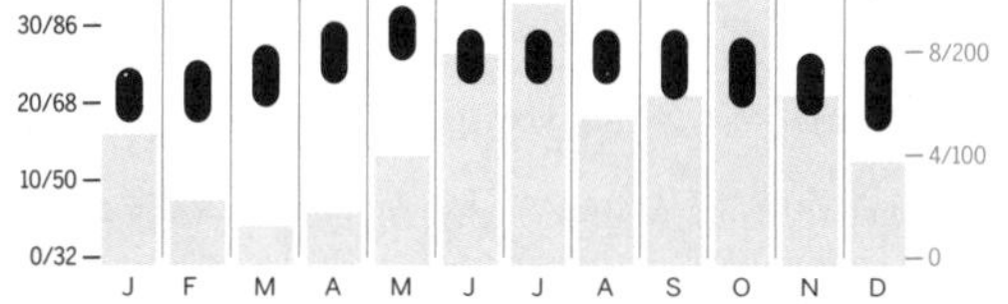

Nov Join the Garifuna in Lívingston for their national holiday at the end of November.

Mar–Jun Best time to see the Resplendent Quetzal, the bird that graces the country's currency.

Nov–Feb Cooler, good time for hiking, less good for swimming such as at Semuc Champey.

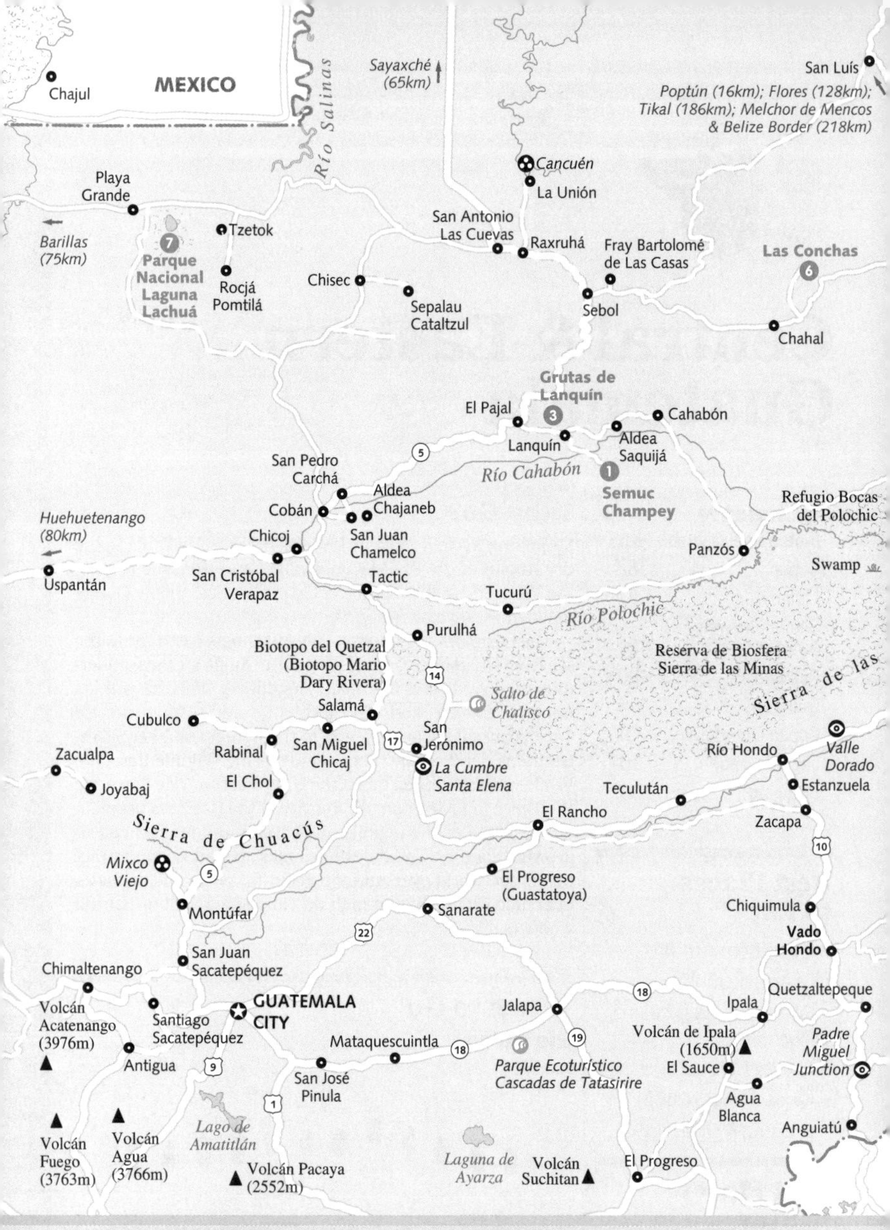
MEXICO
Chajul
Sayaxché (65km)
Río Salinas
San Luís
Poptún (16km); Flores (128km); Tikal (186km); Melchor de Mencos & Belize Border (218km)
Cancuén
La Unión
Playa Grande
Barillas (75km)
Tzetok
7
Parque Nacional Laguna Lachuá
Rocjá Pomtilá
San Antonio Las Cuevas
Raxruhá
Fray Bartolomé de Las Casas
Las Conchas
6
Chisec
Sepalau Cataltzul
Sebol
Chahal
Grutas de Lanquín
3
El Pajal
Cahabón
Lanquín
Aldea Saquijá
Río Cahabón
1
Semuc Champey
San Pedro Carchá
Aldea Chajaneb
Cobán
Huehuetenango (80km)
Chicoj
San Juan Chamelco
Refugio Bocas del Polochic
Panzós
Swamp
Uspantán
San Cristóbal Verapaz
Tactic
Tucurú
Río Polochic
Purulhá
Biotopo del Quetzal (Biotopo Mario Dary Rivera)
Reserva de Biosfera Sierra de las Minas
Salto de Chaliscó
Sierra de las
Salamá
Cubulco
San Miguel Chicaj
Rabinal
San Jerónimo
La Cumbre Santa Elena
Río Hondo
Valle Dorado
Zacualpa
Joyabaj
El Chol
Teculután
Estanzuela
El Rancho
Zacapa
Sierra de Chuacús
Mixco Viejo
El Progreso (Guastatoya)
Montúfar
Sanarate
Chiquimula
Vado Hondo
San Juan Sacatepéquez
Chimaltenango
Quetzaltepeque
Volcán Acatenango (3976m)
Santiago Sacatepéquez
GUATEMALA CITY
Jalapa
Ipala
Antigua
Mataquescuintla
Volcán de Ipala (1650m)
Padre Miguel Junction
San José Pinula
Parque Ecoturístico Cascadas de Tatasirire
El Sauce
Agua Blanca
Volcán Fuego (3763m)
Volcán Agua (3766m)
Lago de Amatitlán
Anguiatú
Volcán Pacaya (2552m)
Laguna de Ayarza
Volcán Suchitan
El Progreso

Central & Eastern Guatemala Highlights

❶ **Semuc Champey** (p189) Splashing around the turquoise waters of a series of limestone swimming pools.

❷ **Lívingston** (p217) Getting down with the Garifuna culture in this unique Caribbean town, or checking out the manatees on the Río Dulce nearby.

❸ **Grutas de Lanquín** (p187) Delving deep underground in some breathtaking caves.

❹ **Quiriguá** (p200) Admiring the impressive carvings and tallest stellae

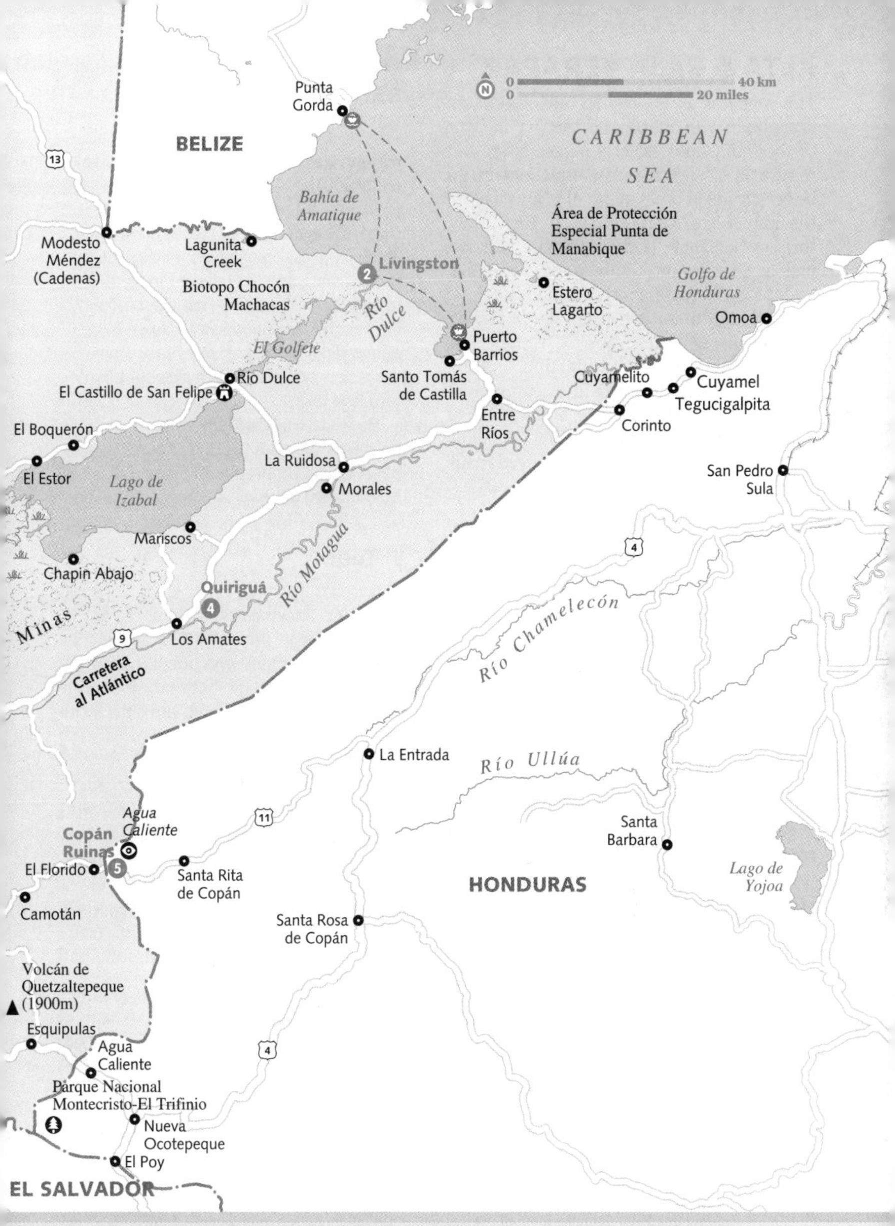

ever found in this off-the-beaten-track ruin.

5 **Copán Ruinas** (p201) Exploring a stunning long-lost civilization just across the border in Honduras.

6 **Las Conchas** (p193) Going bush in a jungle hideaway where waterfalls, jungle treks and village tours await.

7 **Parque Nacional Laguna Lachuá** (p187) Taking in the natural beauty of little-visited protected areas.

ALTA & BAJA VERAPAZ

This region is an interesting mix of local villages, often with little Spanish spoken in favor of the indigenous dialects, larger cities and some truly top-notch tourist attractions. It can be beastly hot at times, particularly just before the rainy season from February to May. Oddly, this is when some of the sights are best visited, as they are most known for swimming, spelunking, or getting wet and muddy.

Cobán is the largest urban development, with plenty of hotels, hostels, restaurants, hospitals, and even some nightlife. Outside of this city, though, you will discover quiet countryside life, kind people, and a sense of place that comes only from isolation. Many of the areas here had little or no paved roads until a few decades ago.

DON'T MISS

SALTO DE CHILASCÓ

What's claimed to be Central America's highest **waterfall** (Q35, guide Q50, horse rental Q50) lies 12km down a dirt road from a turnoff at Km 145 on Hwy 14 to Cobán. Surrounded by cloud forest, it's an impressive sight, especially if it's been raining and the fall is running at full force. Another waterfall, the **Lomo de Macho**, lies 8km away – an enjoyable walk, or you can hire a horse from the visitor booth in Chilascó (about 5km from the falls).

Buses to Chilascó leave every half hour from Salamá (Q20, 1½ hours), passing La Cumbre Santa Elena (Q10, 45 minutes) on Hwy 14.

Salamá

A wonderful introduction to Baja Verapaz' not-too-hot, not-too-cold climate, the area around Salamá hosts a wealth of attractions, both post-colonial and indigenous.

Salamá itself is known for its ornate church (complete with grisly depiction of Jesus) and bustling Sunday market. A photogenic ex-sugar-mill-turned-museum and impressive stone aqueduct can be found in the neighboring town of **San Jerónimo**.

Salamá marks the starting point for a back-roads route to Guatemala City, passing **Rabinal**, whose annual fiesta of San Pedro (January 19 to 25) is a beguiling mix of pre-Columbian and Catholic traditions, and **Cubulco**, where the *palo volador* (flying pole) tradition is still observed. There are basic, adequate *pensiones* (family-run guesthouses) in both Rabinal and Cubulco.

From there it's 100km south to Guatemala City, passing the turnoff to **Mixco Viejo**, one of the least-visited and most spectacularly situated Maya sites in the country. The former Poqomam capital, it lies wedged between deep ravines with just one way in and one way out; the Poqomam further fortified the site by constructing impressive rock walls around the city. It took Pedro de Alvarado and his troops more than a month of concerted attacks to conquer it. When they finally succeeded, they furiously laid waste to this city, which scholars believe supported close to 10,000 people at its height. There are several temples and two ball courts here.

Tours

EcoVerapaz TOURS
(☎5722-9095; ecoverapaz@hotmail.es; 8a Av 7-12, Zona 1; 1-day tour per person Q400) Mario is a local, trained naturalist who offers interesting tours throughout Baja Verapaz, including caving, birdwatching, hiking, horseback riding and orchid trips.

Sleeping & Eating

Hotel Real Legendario HOTEL $
(☎7940-0501; www.hotelreallegendario.com; 8a Av 3-57; s/d/tr Q115/160/180; P ⊖ ᯤ) You'll recognize this place, three blocks east of the plaza, by the pale yellow exterior and the stands of bamboo in the parking lot. The clean, secure rooms have fan, hot-water bathroom and cable TV.

Los Molinos HOTEL $$
(☎5762-8714; hotellosmolinos@outlook.com; Calle Los Molinos Lote 3145; s/d Q160/220; P ⊖ @ ᯤ) Brand new, spic-and-span spot on the outskirts, best for folks with cars or those who don't mind a taxi once in a while. The almost Italian chic, the eat-off-the tile floors, minimalist decor, and onsite restaurant make it a nice stop. It's a 10-minute drive from Salamá.

Antojitos Zacapanecos FAST FOOD $
(☎7954-5691; cnr 6a Calle & 8a Av; mains Q27-50; ⏲10am-9pm) For something a little different in the fast-food vein, check out the huge *gringas:* flour tortillas filled with pork, chicken or beef from this place. Better yet, grab one to go and have a picnic in the plaza.

Getting There & Away

Buses leave Salamá's downtown **bus station** frequently for Cobán (Q20, 1½ to two hours), Guatemala City (Q40, 3½ hours) and neighboring villages.

Biotopo del Quetzal

Along Hwy 14, 34km beyond the La Cumbre turnoff for Salamá, is the Biotopo Mario Dary Rivera nature reserve, commonly called **Biotopo del Quetzal** (☎4499-3236; Hwy 14, Km 160.5; Q40; ⏲7am-4pm), just east of Purulhá village.

You need a fair bit of luck to see a quetzal, as they're rare and shy, though you have the best chance of seeing them from March to June. Even so, it's well worth stopping to explore and enjoy this lush high-altitude cloud-forest ecosystem, which is the quetzal's natural habitat. Early morning or early evening are the best times to watch out for them – they're actually more prevalent around the grounds of the nearby hotels.

The reserve has a visitors center, a little shop for drinks and snacks, and a camping and BBQ area. The ruling on camping changes from time to time. Check by contacting Cecon (p62), which administers this and other biotopes.

Two excellent, well-maintained nature trails wind through the reserve: the 1800m **Sendero los Helechos** (Fern Trail) and the 3600m **Sendero los Musgos** (Moss Trail). As you wander through the dense growth, treading on the rich, spongy humus and leaf mold, you'll see many varieties of epiphytes (air plants), which thrive in the reserve's humid atmosphere.

Sleeping & Eating

★**Ranchitos del Quetzal** HOTEL **$$**
(☎4130-9456; www.ranchitosdelquetzal.com; Hwy 14, Km 160.5; s/d/tr 200/300/350; P ⊜) Carved out of the jungle on a hillside 200m away from the Biotopo del Quetzal entrance, this place has good-sized simple rooms with hot showers. Reasonably priced, simple meals are served, and there are vegetarian options. The best reason to be here is the wealth of info you'll get from the friendly staff, and the chance to be next door to the biotope.

Foxes visit in the evening, as does a host of interesting birds, which the staff will happily identify for you. The other options may be more luxurious, but if you're here for the nature (and who isn't?!), this is a perfect choice. A trail for quetzal viewing leads up into the hills. There's also a path along a gorgeous, lush river to a beautiful waterfall.

Hotel Restaurant Ram Tzul HOTEL **$$$**
(☎5908-4066; www.ramtzul.com; Hwy 14, Km 158; camping per person Q75, s/d Q422/645; P ⊜) This slightly faded place features a restaurant/sitting area in a tall, thatched-roofed structure with fire pits. The rustic, upmarket theme extends to the rooms and bungalows, which are spacious and nicely decorated. The hotel property includes waterfalls and swimming spots.

Getting There & Away

Any Monja Blanca bus (Q65 to Q85) to or from Guatemala City will set you down at the park entrance. Heading in the other direction, it's best to flag down a bus or microbus to El Rancho (Q35) and change there for your next destination.

Those with a car will find it very convenient.

COURTING THE QUETZAL

The resplendent quetzal, which gave its name to Guatemala's currency, was sacred to the Maya. Its feathers grace the plumed serpent Quetzalcóatl and killing one was a capital offense. In modern times it has enjoyed no such protection, and hunting (mostly for the male's long emerald-green tail feathers) and habitat loss have made the bird a rarity in Guatemala. You may well have a better chance of seeing one in Costa Rica or Panama.

The best place to look for a quetzal in Guatemala is in the cloud forests of the Alta Verapaz, especially in the vicinity of the Biotopo del Quetzal (p181). Look out for avocado and fruit trees as they are the preferred food of the quetzal (along with insects, snails, frogs and lizards). But you'll have to look closely – the quetzal's green plumage is dull unless it's in direct sunlight, providing perfect camouflage, and it often remains motionless for hours.

Though climate change is affecting the season year to year, females generally lay two eggs sometime from March to June, and this is the best time to go looking, as the males' tail feathers grow up to 75cm long during this period. Keep an ear out for their distinctive call – sharp cackles and a low, burbling whistle: *keeeoo-keeeoo*.

Cobán

POP 280,000 / ELEV 1320M

Once a gritty spot that tourists passed through, Cobán has become a destination in its own right and one of the best in the area (outside Guatemala City) for decent food, a range of hotels and activities. For tourists it remains a great hub for taking in the surrounding natural wonders –such as Semuc Champey (p189) – in a series of day trips.

The town was once the center of Tezulutlán (Tierra de Guerra, or 'Land of War'), a stronghold of the Rabinal Maya.

In the 19th century, when German immigrants moved in and founded vast coffee and cardamom *fincas* (plantations), Cobán took on the aspect of a German mountain town, as the *finca* owners built town residences. The era of German cultural and economic domination ended during WWII, when the USA prevailed upon the Guatemalan government to deport the powerful *finca* owners, many of whom actively supported the Nazis.

Sights

Orquigonia GARDENS

(☎4740-2224; www.orquigonia.com; Hwy 14, Km 206; Q50; ⏰7am-5pm) Orchid lovers and even the orchid-curious should not miss the wonderfully informative guided tour of this orchid sanctuary just off the highway to Cobán. The 90-minute to two-hour tour takes you through the history of orchid collecting, starting with the Maya, as you wend your way along a path in the forest. There are sweet little cabins on the grounds where you can stay for Q550 to Q750 per night, as well as campsites (Q40). The last entry is at 4pm, as people must be out by 5pm.

To get here, catch any bus (Q2) from Cobán headed for Tontem and get off when you see the sign, about 200m up the dirt road off Hwy 14.

Cobán

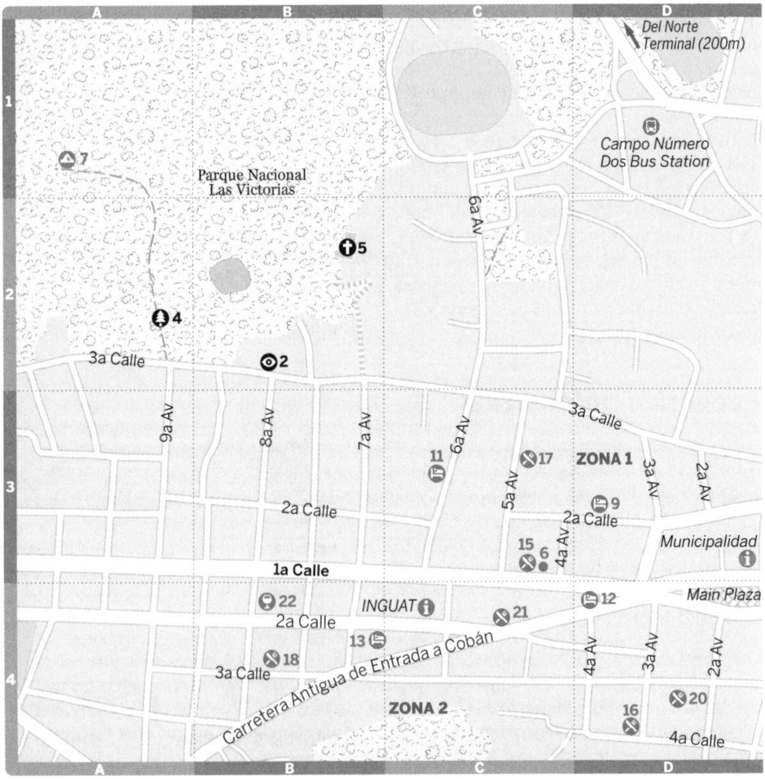

Parque Nacional Las Victorias PARK
(3a Calle, Zona 1; Q15; ⏲ 8am-4:30pm, walking trails 9am-3pm) This forested 82-hectare national park, right in town, has ponds, BBQ and picnic areas, children's play areas, a lookout point and kilometers of trails. The entrance is near the corner of 9a Av and 3a Calle. Most trails are very isolated – consider hiking in a group. You can camp (p184) here.

Templo El Calvario CHURCH
(3a Calle, Zona 1) You can get a fine view over the town from this church atop a long flight of stairs at the north end of 7a Av. Indigenous people leave offerings at outdoor shrines and crosses in front of the church, and it's an interesting stop if you have time. Don't linger here after dark, though, as muggings are not unknown in this area.

The **Ermita de Santo Domingo de Guzmán**, a chapel dedicated to Cobán's patron saint, is 150m west of the bottom of the stairs leading to El Calvario.

Catedral Santo Domingo de Coban CATHEDRAL
Cobán's majestic cathedral takes pride of place, overlooking the central plaza.

Mercado Terminal MARKET
The local market is always good for a wander, even if you're not looking to buy.

Tours

Chicoj Cooperative COFFEE TOUR
(☎ 5524-1831; www.coffeetourchicoj.com; tours Q60) Just 15 minutes out of town by bus, this is a community tourism initiative offering 2km, 45-minute tours of its coffee farm. Halfway through there's the standard stop for a canopy zipline tour. The tour winds up with a cup of coffee made from beans grown and roasted at the farm.

Cobán tour operators offer this tour for Q160, but you can easily catch a bus from the stop near the police station on 1a Calle, which goes straight to the village of Chicoj.

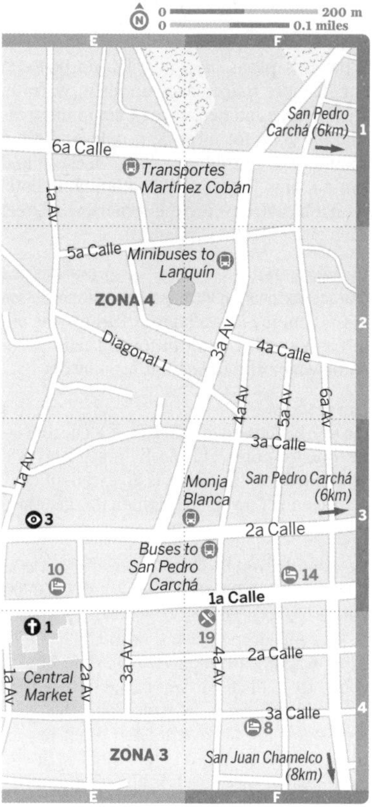

Cobán

Sights
1 Catedral Santo Domingo de Coban E4
2 Ermita de Santo Domingo de Guzmán B2
3 Mercado Terminal E3
4 Parque Nacional Las Victorias A2
5 Templo El Calvario B2

Activities, Courses & Tours
6 Aventuras Turísticas C3

Sleeping
7 Campground A1
8 Casa Duranta F4
9 Casa Tenango D3
10 Hotel Central E3
11 Hotel La Paz C3
12 Hotel La Posada D4
13 Pensión Monja Blanca B4
14 Posada de Don Antonio F3

Eating
15 Casa Chavez C3
16 Casa d'Acuña D4
17 El Peñascal C3
18 Kardamomuss B4
19 La Abadia F4
20 La Casa del Monje D4
21 Xkape Koba'n C4

Drinking & Nightlife
22 Bohemios B4

OFF THE BEATEN TRACK

AROUND COBÁN

Throughout the region around Cobán, there are scores of villages where you can experience traditional Maya culture in some of its purest extant forms. One such place is **San Cristóbal Verapaz**, a Poqomchi' Maya village set beside Laguna Chicoj, 19km west of Cobán. During **Semana Santa** (Easter Week), local artists design elaborate *alfombras* (carpets) of colored sawdust and flower petals rivaled only by those in Antigua.

San Cristóbal is also home to the Centro Communitario Educativo Pokomchi (Cecep), an organization dedicated to preserving traditional and modern ways of Poqomchi' life. Cecep inaugurated the **Museo Katinamit** (7950-4896; cecep@itelgua.com; Calle del Calvario 0-33, Zona 3, San Cristóbal Verapaz; Q10, with guide Q20; 8am-1pm & 2-5pm Mon-Sat), which recreates a typical Poqomchi' house. It also offers volunteer and ethnotourism opportunities.

Near Aldea Chajaneb, 12km east of Cobán, is the cave system **Grutas Rey Marcos** (7951-2756; Q30; 8am-5pm). It's set in the **Balneario Cecilinda** (Q10; 8am-5pm), which is a great place to go for a swim or a hike on scenic mountain trails. The caves themselves extend more than 1km under the earth, although chances are you won't get taken that far. A river runs through the cave (you have to wade through it at one point) and there are some impressive stalactites and stalagmites. Headlamps, helmets and rubber boots are included in the admission price to the cave. According to local legend, any wishes made in the cave are guaranteed to come true.

To reach the caves, take a bus or pick-up (Q3, 15 minutes) from San Juan Chamelco towards Chamil and ask the driver to let you off at the turnoff. From there it's about a 1km walk to the entrance. Alternatively, hire a taxi from Cobán (Q150).

Aventuras Turísticas TOURS
(7951-4213; www.facebook.com/aventurasturisticascoban; 1a Calle 5-34, Zona 1; prices vary; 8am-9pm) Leads tours to Laguna Lachuá, the Grutas de Lanquín, Rey Marcos and Parque Nacional Cuevas de Candelaria, as well as to Semuc Champey, Tikal, Ceibal and anywhere else you may want to go. It will customize itineraries, and prices depend on the location and number of people in the group. Guides speaking French, English or Spanish are available.

Festivals & Events

Guatemala's most impressive festival of indigenous traditions, the national folklore festival of **Rabin Ajau** (Estadio Verapaz), with its traditional dance of the Paabanc, takes place here in the latter part of July or in the first week of August. The **national orchid show** is hosted here every December.

Sleeping

When choosing a room in Cobán, you may want to ensure that the showers have hot water; it can be cold in these parts.

★ **Casa Tenango** HOSTEL $
(7952-3664; www.facebook.com/casatenango; 3a Av A 2-50, Zona 1; s/d with bathroom 80/150, dm/s/d without bathroom 45/60/110; P) What this place lacks in frills (no pool, no bar) it more than makes up for in warmth, with a large kitchen, several common areas that are good for meeting people, and clean rooms. The dorms have large lockers and some rooms feel more like a boutique hotel than a hostel. Best are the owners, who greet each guest like they're family.

Campground CAMPGROUND $
(Parque Nacional Las Victorias; campsite per person Q50) Camping is available at Parque Nacional Las Victorias, right in town. Facilities include water and toilets but no showers.

Hotel La Paz HOTEL $
(6a Av 2-19, Zona 1; s/d Q98/183; P) This cheerful budget hotel, 1½ blocks north and two blocks west of the plaza, is an excellent deal. It has many flowers to brighten up the otherwise simple decor.

Pensión Monja Blanca HOTEL $$
(7952-1712; 2a Calle 6-30, Zona 2; s/d Q200/300, without bathroom Q150/200; P) This place is peaceful despite being on busy 2a Calle. After walking through two courtyards, you come to a lush garden packed with fruit and hibiscus trees around which the spotless rooms are arranged. Each room has an old-time feel to it and is furnished with two good-quality single beds with folksy covers.

The hotel's central location and tranquil atmosphere make it a good place for solo women travelers.

Posada de Don Antonio HOTEL $$
(☎7951-1792; 5a Av 1-51, Zona 4; s/d Q265/415; P ⊜ ᯤ) MC Escher's famous *Relativity* painting could have been inspired by the multiple staircases in the lobby here, but this atmospheric two-story place provides some of the best-value accommodations in town. Rooms are spacious, have double beds, high ceilings and attention to detail. Breakfast (Q30 to Q50) in the patio area is a great way to start the day.

Casa Duranta HOTEL $$
(☎7951-4716; www.casaduranta.com; 3a Calle 4-46, Zona 3; s/d Q305/427; P ⊜ ᯤ) Some rooms at this carefully restored, eclectically decorated place are excellent value, while others are a bit cramped for the price. Tile floors grace most of the rooms, and there's a lovely courtyard. Have a look around if you can. There's also an onsite restaurant. Some rooms have street noise.

Hotel Central HOTEL $$
(☎7952-1442; 1a Calle 1-79, Zona 1; s/d Q137/260; P ᯤ) Reasonably sized rooms and lovely outdoor sitting areas make this a decent choice. Try for a room at the back for better ventilation and views out over the town.

Hotel La Posada HOTEL $$$
(☎7952-1495; www.laposadacoban.com.gt; 1a Calle 4-12, Zona 2; s/d Q480/560) Just off the plaza, this colonial-style hotel is Cobán's best, though rooms streetside suffer from traffic noise. Its colonnaded porches are dripping with tropical flowers and furnished with easy chairs and hammocks. The rooms are a bit austere, with plenty of religious relics around the place, but they have nice old furniture, fireplaces and wall hangings of local weaving.

Eating & Drinking

Most of the hotels in Cobán come with their own restaurants. In the evening, food trucks (kitchens on wheels) park around the plaza and offer some of the cheapest dining in town. As always, the one to go for has the largest crowd of locals hanging around and chomping down.

★Xkape Koba'n GUATEMALAN $
(☎7951-4152; 2a Calle 5-13, Zona 2; snacks/mains Q35/50-90; ⏲7am-8pm Mon-Fri, from 9am Sat) The perfect place to take a breather or while away a whole afternoon, this beautiful, artsy little cafe has a lush garden out back. Some interesting indigenous-inspired dishes are on the small menu. The cakes are homemade, the coffee is delectable and there are some handicrafts for sale.

★La Abadia FUSION $$
(cnr 1a Calle & 4a Av, Zona 3; mains Q90-160; ⏲6-9:30pm Mon-Sat) Cobán's dining scene has improved dramatically over the years and this is part of the finer dining scene. The surrounds are refined yet relaxed, the menu offers a great selection of local, international and fusion dishes and there's a good wine list, too.

La Casa del Monje STEAK $$
(☎7951-3845; 3a Calle 2-24, Zona 2; mains Q59-115; ⏲6:30am-10pm; ᯤ) Guarded by the 'iron friar,' Cobán's best steakhouse is set in a lovely colonial-era monastery a few blocks from the park. If you're not in the mood for big chunks of meat, local dishes like *kaq'ik* (turkey stew) are recommended.

Kardamomuss FUSION $$
(☎7952-3792; kardamomussfusioncoban@gmail.com; 3a Calle 5-34, Zona 2; mains Q60-130; ⏲7am-10pm; P ᯤ) The widest menu in town is at this chic place, which is in a location so new even the geckos haven't found it yet. Billing itself as 'fusion' food, it takes a pretty good stab at Indian, Chinese and Italian dishes, with locally grown cardamom as the featured ingredient. Creative cocktails and mocktails make it well worth the detour.

Casa Chavez INTERNATIONAL $$
(☎7951-4620; 1a Calle 4-25, Zona 1; breakfast Q25-30, lunch & dinner mains Q50-100; ⏲6am-9pm; ᯤ) Set in a lovely old house, Casa Chavez offers an ample, if uninspired, menu. Still, the location is great, and breakfast out back overlooking the garden and hills beyond is hard to beat.

Casa d'Acuña INTERNATIONAL $$
(4a Calle 3-11, Zona 2; mains Q95-161; ⏲7am-10pm) This restaurant, complete with orchids and a koi pond, offers authentic Italian and other European-style dishes served in an attractive oasis of tranquillity to a soundtrack of classical music. In addition to protein-oriented mains, there is a range of pastas (Q40 to Q65), salads, homemade breads, cakes and outstanding desserts. Service can be slow at times.

El Peñascal GUATEMALAN $$
(5a Av 2-61, Zona 1; mains Q75-160; ⏲11:30am-9pm) Probably Cobán's finest stand-alone restaurant, El Peñascal has plenty of regional specialties, Guatemalan classics, mixed-meat platters, seafood and snacks in a relaxed, upmarket setting.

Bohemios CLUB
(cnr 8a Av & 2a Calle, Zona 2; Q15-30; ⏲Thu-Sat) About as close as this town gets to a mega-disco, with balcony seating and bow-tied waitstaff.

Information

EMERGENCY

Police Station (☎7952-1225; 1a Calle; ⏲24hr)

MONEY

The banks listed here change US-dollar cash and traveler's checks.

Banco G&T (1a Calle; ⏲9am-7pm Mon-Fri, to 1pm Sat) Has a MasterCard ATM.

Banco Industrial (cnr 1a Calle & 7a Av, Zona 1; ⏲9am-6pm Mon-Fri, 10am-2pm Sat) Has a Visa ATM.

TOURIST INFORMATION

INGUAT (☎4210-9992; 2a Calle 5-12, Zona 2; ⏲9am-5pm Mon & Tue, Thu-Sat) Has an office a couple of blocks from the plaza.

Municipalidad (Town Hall; ☎7952-1305, 7951-1148; 1a Calle, Zona 1; ⏲8am-4pm Mon-Sat)

Getting There & Away

BUS

The Hwy 14 leg connecting Cobán with Guatemala City (via Hwy 9) is the most traveled route between Cobán and the outside world, though you can arrive via other routes as well. The road north through Chisec to Sayaxché and Flores is now paved all the way, providing much easier access than before to El Petén. The off-the-beaten-track routes west to Huehuetenango and northeast to Fray Bartolomé de Las Casas and Poptún are partly unpaved and still provide a bit of adventure. Always double-check bus departure times, especially for less frequently served destinations.

Buses leave from a variety of points around town, including the following:

Buses to San Pedro Carchá (cnr 4a Av & 2a Calle)

Campo Número Dos (Campo Norte; 6a Calle)

Del Norte (Hwy 9)

Minibuses to Lanquín (cnr 5a Calle & 3a Av, Zona 4)

Monja Blanca (☎7951-3571; 2a Calle 3-77, Zona 4)

Transportes Martínez Cobán (6a Calle 2-4, Zona 4)

Some early morning departures are from the market. Please be aware that the road to Uspantán and Nebaj is prone to landslides; get the latest before setting out.

Unless otherwise specified buses leave frequently – hourly, every 30 minutes, or more often – between the times shown in the table.

BUSES FROM COBÁN

DESTINATION	COST (Q)	TIME	FREQUENCY/HOURS	DEPARTURE LOCATION
Biotopo de Quetzal	15	1hr	1am-5pm	Monja Blanca
Cahabón	30	4hr	7am-4pm	Transportes Martínez
Chisec	25	2hr	6am-4pm	Del Norte
Fray Bartolomé de Las Casas	50	4hr	6am-4pm	Del Norte
Guatemala City	50-80	5hr	1am-5pm	Monja Blanca
Lanquín	25	2½hr	7am-4pm	Transportes Martínez
Nebaj	50	5hr	2 buses; 6am, 1pm	Del Norte
Playa Grande, for Laguna Lachuá	50	3½hr	6am-4pm	Del Norte
Raxruhá	35	3hr	6am-4pm	Del Norte
Salamá	20	2hr	6am-5pm	Del Norte
San Pedro Carchá	3	20min	6am-7pm	In front of Monja Blanca
Sayaxché	50	4hr	6am-4pm	Del Norte
Tactic	6	40min	6am-5pm	Campo Número Dos
Uspantán	30	3½hr	6am-5pm	Del Norte

WORTH A TRIP

PARQUE NACIONAL LAGUNA LACHUÁ

This **national park** (☎4084-1706; entry fee adult/child Q50/25, campsite per adult/child Q25/15, bunk with mosquito net Q70/35, tent hire Q25) is renowned for the perfectly round, pristine turquoise lake (220m deep) for which it was named. Until recently, this Guatemalan gem was rarely visited by travelers because it was an active, violent area during the civil war and the road was in disrepair. Now it fills up quickly on weekends and public holidays, and if you're thinking about coming at these times, it's a good idea to call and reserve a space. Overnight visitors can use the cooking facilities, so come prepared with food and drink (there is no food available to buy in the park). There is only one shower.

You can no longer rent canoes for exploring the lake, but there are about 4km of interpretative trails to explore.

A wonderfully rustic bunkhouse has been constructed on the lake's edge, but if you don't want to stay in the park, there are hotels and restaurants in nearby Playa Grande. There's also a community tourism initiative in **Rocjá Pomtilá** (☎5381-1970; rocapon@yahoo.com; r for 2 nights, incl guide & 4 meals Q350-450) on the eastern edge of the park. Contact it directly to make arrangements.

A relatively new road means you can get to the park entrance from Cobán in three to 3½ hours by bus (Q50). Take a Playa Grande (Cantabal) bus from Cobán via Chisec and ask the driver to leave you at the park entrance, from where it's about a 2km walk to the lake. From Playa Grande there are buses and pick-ups leaving for Barillas (Q50, five hours), the first stop on the back route to Huehuetenango in the Western Highlands. The Cobán tour outfits offer two-day and one-night trips out here.

CAR

Cobán has a couple of places that rent cars. If you want to go to Grutas de Lanquín or Semuc Champey, you'll want to consider a 4WD vehicle if there's a chance of rain.

Lanquín

POP 29,000

One of the best excursions to make from Cobán is to the pretty village of Lanquín, 61km to the east. People come for two reasons: to explore the wonderful cave system just out of town and as a jumping-off point for visiting the natural rock pools at Semuc Champey (p189).

Sights

Grutas de Lanquín CAVE

(adult/child 5-12yr Q30/10, tubing Q5; ⏲8am-6pm) These caves are about 1km northwest of the town, and extend for several kilometers into the earth. There is now a ticket office here. The first cave has lights, but do take a powerful flashlight (torch) anyway in case of emergencies. You'll also need shoes with good traction as inside it's slippery with moisture and bat droppings.

Though the first few hundred meters of the cavern have been equipped with a walkway and lit by diesel-powered electric lights, much of this subterranean system is untouched. If you are not an experienced spelunker, you shouldn't wander too far into the caves; the entire extent has yet to be explored, let alone mapped.

As well as featuring funky stalactites, mostly named for animals, these caves are crammed with bats. Try to time your visit to coincide with sunset (around 6pm), when hundreds of them fly out of the mouth of the cave in formations so dense they obscure the sky. For a dazzling display of navigation skills, sit at the entrance while they exit. Please be aware that bats are extremely light-sensitive, and tempting as it may be, flash photography can disorient and, in some cases, blind them.

The river here gushes from the cave in clean, cool and delicious torrents. You can swim in the river, which has some comfortably hot pockets close to shore.

Activities

Guatemala City–based Maya Expeditions (p51) offers exciting one- to five-day rafting expeditions on the Río Cahabón.

ADETES RAFTING

(☎5069-3518; www.guaterafting.com) This community tourism initiative is based in Aldea Saquijá, 12km out of Lanquín. It offers rafting trips led by well-trained community members on the Río Cahabón. Prices range from Q260 to Q360 per person for a two- to five-hour trip. To get to the headquarters, catch any bus leaving Lanquín headed toward Cahabón.

Sleeping

There are a few OK hotels in the actual town, but to get the full experience you really want to be out on the riverbanks somewhere. Accommodations tend toward the backpackers hostel end of the spectrum, but some more refined options are springing up.

Zephyr Lodge HOSTEL $$
(5168-2441; www.zephyrlodgelanquin.com; dm Q105, r Q350-500; P Wi-fi pool) Lanquín's self-admitted party hostel is all class – great rooms with spectacular views, decent dorms and some good hangout areas, including the big thatched-roof bar/restaurant. The river is a five-minute walk downhill. Wi-fi goes off at 8pm, however, meaning there's all the more reason to party with your new-found friends instead of hanging out with your computer or phone.

Viñas Hotel HOTEL $$
(4800-0061; dm Q60, r with/without bathroom Q300/250; P non-smoking air-con Wi-fi pool) On the outskirts of town, heading toward Semuc Champey, this is the best full-service hotel around. Rooms are by no means fancy (and dorms are available), but they do come with air-con and there's a big pool here, with mountains in the background. It makes great use of its hillside location, with fantastic views from the multiple balconies on offer.

El Muro HOSTEL $$
(4904-0671; www.elmurolanquin.net; dm Q50, r Q150-250; Wi-fi) By far the best option in the town itself, El Muro is a happy little hostel/bar featuring good-sized dorms and rooms. Most have attached bathrooms, fans, and all have breezy balconies overlooking the hills or garden. Hammocks are a nice way to relax. Also has a bar, a restaurant and games.

El Retiro Lodge BUNGALOW $$
(4638-3008; www.elretirolanquin.com; dm Q40, r with air-con Q350, r with fan with/without bathroom from Q225/210; P non-smoking @ Wi-fi) This sublimely located hotel is about 500m along the road just outside town on the main route west. Dorm rooms have 10 or 14 beds. Decor includes some clever use of tiles, shells, strings of beads and local fabrics. Thatched-roof huts look down over the greenest of green fields to a beautiful wide river.

Rabin Itzam HOTEL $$
(5699-1402, 4913-8927; s/d Q173/288, s/d without bathroom Q92/184) A no-frills budget hotel in the center. The beds sag a bit, but rooms upstairs at the front (without bathroom) have good valley views. Good discounts outside Semana Santa.

Eating

The food is pretty good in Lanquín – there are some good-priced *comedores* (cheap eateries) in the town, and most of the hotels offer gringo-friendly menus.

Restaurante Champey GUATEMALAN $
(3000-6130; mains Q25-60; 7:30am-11pm; P vegetarian) This large outdoor eatery halfway between town and El Retiro serves up good-sized plates of steak, eggs and rice and gets rowdy and beer-fueled at night. Vegetarian options are also available.

Information

Banrural (24hr) On Lanquín's main square. Changes US dollars and traveler's checks, and has an ATM.

Getting There & Away

Overnight tours (p184) to Grutas de Lanquín and Semuc Champey, offered in Cobán for Q400 per person, are the easiest way to visit these places, but it's really not that complicated to organize yourself. Tours take about two hours to reach Lanquín from Cobán; the price includes a packed lunch.

BUS

Buses operate several times daily between Cobán and Lanquín, stopping at the **square** before continuing to Cahabón. There are eight buses to Cobán (Q25, 2½ hours) between 6am and 5:30pm. Shuttles for Semuc Champey (Q25 one-way) leave at 9:30am (book at your hotel) and pick-ups (Q25) leave whenever they are full, half a block from the main square.

If you're heading toward Río Dulce, a back road exists, although it's unpaved for most of the way and gets washed out in heavy rains. Transportation schedules along here are flexible at best. Ask around to see what the current situation is. A daily shuttle (Q180, six hours) runs on this road and is the most reliable, easy option. Book at any of the hotels.

CAR

If it's been raining heavily and you're driving, you'll need a 4WD vehicle, as sections of the road between Lanquín and Semuc Champey are too steep for a normal vehicle to have traction. The road from San Pedro Carchá to El Pajal, where you turn off for Lanquín, is paved. The 11km from El Pajal to Lanquín is not. You can head on from Lanquín to Flores in 14 to 15 hours via El Pajal, Sebol, Raxruhá and Sayaxché. The road from El Pajal to Sebol is now paved. Or you can head from Lanquín to Sebol and Fray Bartolomé de Las Casas and on to Poptún.

Semuc Champey & Around

Eleven kilometers south of Lanquín, along a rough, bumpy, slow road, is **Semuc Champey** (Q50; 8am-5pm), famed for its great 300m-long natural limestone bridge, on top of which is a stepped series of pools with cool, flowing river water good for swimming. The water is from the Río Cahabón, and much more of it passes underground, beneath the bridge. Though this bit of paradise is difficult to reach, the beauty of its setting and the perfection of the pools, ranging from turquoise to emerald-green, make it worth it. Many people consider this the most beautiful spot in all Guatemala.

If you're visiting on a tour, some guides will take you down a rope ladder from the lowest pool to the river, which gushes out from the rocks below. Plenty of people do this and love it, though it is a bit risky.

Sights

K'anba Caves CAVE

(Q60; 8am-9pm, tours 9am, 10am, 1pm, 2:30pm & 3pm) About a kilometer before Semuc Champey, just before the large bridge crossing the river, you'll see a turnoff to the right for these caves, which many find to be much more interesting than Grutas de Lanquín (p187). Bring a flashlight for the two-hour tour or you'll be stumbling around by candlelight.

A half hour of river tubing costs an extra Q10. There have been reports of serious overcrowding on these cave tours. If you can, arrive for the 9am tour, before the tour groups start showing up. And, as always, evaluate the conditions before setting out.

Sleeping & Eating

Campground CAMPGROUND $

(camping per person Q10) It's possible to camp at Semuc Champey, but be sure to pitch a tent only in the upper areas, as flash floods are common down below. It's also risky to leave anything unattended, as it might get stolen. The place now has 24-hour security, which may reassure potential campers, but you should keep your valuables with you.

★ **Utopia** HOSTEL $$

(3135-8329; www.utopiaecohotel.com; campsites per person Q30, hammock/dm Q35/70, r with/without bathroom Q315/285;) Set on a hillside overlooking the small village of Semil, 3km from Semuc Champey, this is the most impressive setup in the area. Every type of accommodations imaginable is available, from nice riverside cabins to campsites. The restaurant/bar (serving vegetarian family-style meals) has valley views, and the stretch of river that it sits on is truly idyllic.

The turnoff to Semil is 2km before Semuc Champey. From there it's about 1km to the hotel. Call from Lanquín (or drop into the office at the crossroads where the bus arrives) for free transport out here.

El Portal HOSTEL $$

(4091-7878; dm Q60, r with/without bathroom Q250/150; P) About 100m short of the entrance to Semuc Champey, this is the obvious choice for convenient access to Semuc. There's only electricity from 6pm to 11pm, but the well-spaced wooden huts built on the bank sloping down to the river are by far the best accommodations deal in the area. Meals and tours are available.

It can arrange transport to/from all over Guatemala if you need it.

Getting There & Away

If you're into walking, the 2½-hour trip from Lanquín is a fairly pleasant one, passing through lush countryside and simple rural scenes, and if you change your mind, it's easy to flag down a ride the rest of the way.

Pick-ups run from the plaza in Lanquín to Semuc Champey – your chances of catching one are better in the early morning and on market days: Sunday, Monday and Thursday. Expect to pay somewhere between Q25. All the Lanquín hotels and hostels run shuttle services out here.

CHISEC

POP 77,000

The town of Chisec, 66km north of Cobán, is becoming a center for reaching several exciting destinations. This is thanks to the paving of the road from Cobán to Sayaxché and Flores, which runs through here, and some admirable community tourism programs aiming to help develop this long-ignored region, the population of which is almost entirely Q'eqchi' Maya. The best source of information on these programs is the office of **Puerta al Mundo Maya** (☎5978-1465, 5176-1199; www.puertamundomaya.com.gt; ⏱8am-noon, 3-5pm Thu-Sun), which administers quite a few of them.

Sights

Lagunas de Sepalau LAGOON
(lagoon/canopy/both Q60/75/150; ⏱8am-5pm) Surrounded by pristine forest, these turquoise lagoons are 8km west of Chisec. Developed as a community ecotourism project by local villagers, tours of the area include a fair bit of walking and some rowboat paddling. The obligatory zipline is also present. The area is rich in wildlife: jaguars, tapir, iguanas, toucans and howler monkeys are all in residence.

There are three lagoons, the most spectacular of which is the third on the tour, Q'ekija, which is ringed by steep walls of thick jungle. From February to June the first two lagoons dry up.

Pick-ups leave Chisec's plaza for the village of Sepalau Cataltzul throughout the day, and there's usually a bus (Q10, 45 minutes) at 10:30am. On arrival at the village, you pay the entrance fee and a guide will take you on the 3km walk to the first lagoon.

Sleeping & Eating

Chisec's not very touristy, but there is one basic hotel on the plaza and one more out on the highway.

Apart from the ubiquitous *comedores* (cheap eateries) out on the highway and the restaurant in the Hotel La Estancia de la Virgen, Chisec actually has one pretty good restaurant – the **B'omb'il Pek** (mains Q40-60; ⏱6:30am-8:30pm).

Hotel Nopales HOTEL $
(☎3231-1909; Parque Central; s/d Q80/140; 🚭📶🏊) This has large rooms (with that classic musty budget-hotel smell) set around a courtyard. The pool is usually empty.

Hotel La Estancia de la Virgen HOTEL $$
(☎5514-7444; www.hotelestanciadelavirgen.com; Calle Principal; s/d with fan Q100/160, with air-con Q150/225; P🚭❄📶🏊) Chisec's best hotel, on the main road at the northern exit from town, has neat and sensible rooms, a restaurant, and a swimming pool with some excellent waterslides in the shape of fallen tree trunks. The large display cases filled with plastic pens are perhaps the most unique decoration you will see on your trip to Guatemala.

Getting There & Away

Buses leave Chisec for Cobán (Q25, two hours) eight times daily, from 3am to 2pm. Buses or minibuses to San Antonio and Raxruhá (one hour) go hourly, from 6am to 4pm. Some of these continue to Fray Bartolomé de Las Casas. There are also regular minibuses to Playa Grande (two hours), for the Parque Nacional Laguna Lachuá. Some Cobán–Sayaxché minibuses and buses pass through Chisec.

Raxruhá

POP 40,000

A sleepy little crossroads town, Raxruhá provides a good base for exploring the nearby attractions of Cancuén and Cuevas de Candelaria.

Sleeping

Hotel Cancuén HOTEL $
(☎5764-0478; www.cuevaslosnacimientos.com; s/d Q100/140, without bathroom Q35/70; P🚭❄📶) The best hotel in town is a family-run affair on the outskirts of town (a two-minute walk from the center). Rooms are clean and well decorated (air-con is an additional Q50, hot water is Q35), and there's a little *comedor* (cheap eatery) onsite. It has good information about visiting Cancuén.

You can arrange walking/tubing tours (Q150 per person, five to six hours) of the nearby Cueva los Nacimientos, the northernmost point in the Candelaria cave complex. There's also a large peacock cage here.

Hotel El Amigo HOTEL $
(☎5900-5343; r per person Q60; P🚭❄) Large, vaguely clean rooms around an oversized parking lot. Cheap and good for a night, and nothing more.

Information

Banrural (⏱8am-5pm Mon-Fri, 9am-1pm Sat) At the main intersection. Changes cash but not traveler's checks. The nearest ATMs are in Chisec and Fray Bartolomé.

Getting There & Away

Pick-ups and the occasional bus for La Unión (to access Cancuén; Q15, one hour) leave from the **stop** one block south from the park. There are at least five scheduled departures daily to both Sayaxché (Q35, 2½ hours) and Cobán (Q35, two hours) from Raxruhá.

OFF THE BEATEN TRACK

CANCUÉN: ANOTHER TIKAL?

This large Maya **site** (Q50; ⌚8am-4pm) hit the papers when it was 'discovered' in 2000, even though it had already been 'discovered' back in 1907. Excavations are still under way, but estimates say that Cancuén may rival Tikal (p245) for size.

It's thought that Cancuén was a trading center rather than a religious center, and the usual temples and pyramids are absent. In their place is a grand palace with more than 150 rooms set around 11 courtyards.

Carvings here are impressive, particularly at the grand palace, but also along the ball courts and the two altars that have been excavated to date.

Cancuén's importance seems to stem from its geographical/tactical position. Hieroglyphs attest to alliances with Calakmul (Mexico) and Tikal, and its relative proximity to the southern highlands would have given it access to pyrite and obsidian, prized minerals of the Maya.

Artisans certainly worked here – their bodies have been discovered dressed, unusually, in royal finery. Several workshops have also been uncovered, one containing a 17kg piece of jade.

Casual visitors will need about an hour to see the main, partially excavated, sections of the site and another hour or two to see the rest, about five hours total.

Cobán tour companies make day trips to Cancuén. To get here independently, catch a pick-up (leaving hourly) from Raxruhá to La Unión (Q20, 40 minutes), from where you can hire a boat (Q350 for one to 16 people, round trip) to the site. You can also hire a guide (Q100 to Q200, depending on group size) to take you on the 4km walk to the site from La Unión, but in the rainy season this will be a very muddy affair. If walking or going by *lancha* (small motorboat), pay at the small store where the bus stops – the boat dock is an easy 1km walk from there. Pay your entrance fee at the site when you arrive.

The last pick-up leaves La Unión for Raxruhá at 3pm. Coming directly from Chisec, expect to pay Q50 for a ride to La Unión.

Parque Nacional Cuevas de Candelaria

Just west of Raxruhá, this 22km-long cave system, dug out by the subterranean Río Candelaria, features some monstrous proportions – the main chamber is 30m high, 200m wide and has stalagmites measuring up to 30m in length. Natural apertures in the roof allow sunlight in, creating magical, eerie reflections.

The caves were used by the Q'eqchi' Maya and you'll see some platforms and ladders carved into the stone.

The El Mico complex is probably the most easily accessible and spectacular of the various cave tours. Look for the sign from the highway.

A couple of kilometers west on the same highway is the turnoff to Comunidad Mucbilha'. It's 2km along a dirt road to the parking lot, then another 1km to the visitors center, where you can walk or tube through the **Venado Seco cave**.

Another couple of caves can be visited nearby at the Cuevas de Candelaria Camposanto.

Tours

El Mico CAVING
(www.cuevasdecandelaria.com; Carretera Franja Transversal del Norte Km 316.5; tubing/walking tour Q125/75; ⌚7am-5pm) Located behind – and forming part of – the Complejo Cultural de Candelaria (a community run on-again, off-again tourism project), this cave complex is probably the most easily accessible and spectacular of the various cave tours. Look for the sign from the highway. You can stay here for Q85 per person per night.

Comunidad Mucbilha' CAVING
(☎4017-4447, 5034-2056; http://cuevasdecandelariamucbilha.jimdo.com; Carretera Franja Transversal del Norte Km 315; tubing/walking tour Q100/50; ⌚8am-4pm) Look for the turnoff from the highway to this community-run tourism project. From the highway it's 2km along a dirt road to the parking lot, then another 1km to the visitor center, where you can walk or tube through the Venado Seco cave.

Cuevas de Candelaria Camposanto CAVING
(☎5996-4912, 5209-6368; Carretera Franja Transversal del Norte Km 309.5; tubing or walking tours Q60; ⌚8am-5pm) Guides can be organized

at the roadside *tienda* (store) for the short walk to the caves. With a couple of days' notice, it will put on a Maya ceremony (Q50 per person) for visitors.

Sleeping & Eating

★Candelaria Lodge HOTEL $$
(☎5352-9276; http://candelarialodge.com; Carretera Franja Transversal del Norte Km 319; s/d from Q280/350;) The Candelaria Lodge is a refined hotel so lovely it seems bizarrely out of place here in the relative nowhere of central Guatemala. The rooms are beautiful, as are the perfectly manicured grounds, which are bursting with flowers and hummingbirds. The place also has an excellent restaurant, **El Bistrot Francés** (☎5352-9276; www.candelarialodge.com; Carretera Franja Transversal del Norte Km 319; mains Q70-120; 7am-9:30am, noon-3pm, 6-7:30pm).

Getting There & Away

Any bus running between Chisec (Q10, 45 minutes) and Raxruhá can drop you at El Mico, Comunidad Mucbilha' or Cuevas de Candelaria Camposanto. Buses from Cobán cost Q30 and take about two hours.

Fray Bartolomé de Las Casas

POP 75,000

This town, often referred to simply as Fray, is a way station on the back route between the Cobán/Lanquín area and Poptún. This route is dotted with traditional Maya villages where only the patriarchs speak Spanish, and then only a little. This is a great opportunity for getting off the 'gringo trail' and into the heart of Guatemala.

Fray is substantial considering it's in the middle of nowhere, but don't let its size fool you. This is a place where the weekly soccer game is the biggest deal in town, chickens languish in the streets and siesta is taken seriously.

The town itself is fairly spread out, with the plaza – where you'll find the *municipalidad* (town hall) – and most tourist facilities at one end and the market and bus terminus at the other. Walking between the two takes about 10 minutes. Coming from Cobán, you'll want to hop out at the central plaza.

Accommodations options are very limited here. **Hotel La Cabaña** (☎7952-0097; 2a Calle 1-92, Zona 3; r per person with/without bathroom Q75/50) is about the best in town.

Eating options are few – try **Restaurante Doris** (☎3011-3396; 7am-9pm) on the main street. Otherwise, grab a steak (with tortillas and beans, Q20) at the informal BBQ shacks that open up along the main street at night.

Getting There & Away

At least two daily buses depart from the plaza for Poptún (Q40, five hours). Buses for Cobán leave hourly between 4am and 4pm. Some go via Chisec (Q50, 3½ hours). Others take the slower route via San Pedro Carchá. Buses stop at the plaza before going eastward to the stop at the other side of town. Heading west, they leave from the station but will pick up travelers at the plaza before continuing onward.

EL ORIENTE

Heading east from Guatemala City brings you into the long, flat valleys of the region Guatemalans call El Oriente (the East). It's a dry and unforgiving landscape of stunted hillsides covered in scraggly brush. It's tough out here and the cowboy hats, boots, buckles and sidearms sported by a lot of the men in the region fit well against this rugged backdrop.

Most travelers pass through on their way to Copán in Honduras or to visit the pilgrimage town of Esquipulas. Further east, the landscape becomes a lot more tropical and you'll see plenty of fruit for sale at roadside stalls. If you've got some time in this area, a quick side trip to the ruins at Quiriguá is well worth your while.

Río Hondo

POP 10,500

Río Hondo (Deep River), 50km east of El Rancho junction and 130km from Guatemala City, is a transit point – there's very little in the way of sights and attractions. The junction is where Hwy 10 to Chiquimula heads south off the Carretera al Atlántico (Hwy 9). Beyond Chiquimula are turnoffs to Copán, just across the Honduras border; to Esquipulas and on to Nueva Ocotepeque (Honduras); and the remote border crossing between Guatemala and El Salvador at Anguiatú, 12km north of Metapán (El Salvador).

The actual town of Río Hondo is northeast of the junction. Places to stay hereabouts may list their address as Río Hondo, Santa Cruz Río Hondo or Santa Cruz Teculután. Nine kilometers west of the junction are several attractive motels right on Hwy 9. By car, it's an hour from here to Quiriguá, half an hour to Chiquimula and 1½ hours to Esquipulas.

WORTH A TRIP

LAS CONCHAS

From Fray Bartolomé de Las Casas you can visit Las Conchas (Q50), a series of limestone pools and waterfalls on the Río Chiyú, which some say are better than those at Semuc Champey (p189). The pools are up to 8m deep and 20m wide and are connected by a series of spectacular waterfalls, but they're not a turquoise color like those at Semuc.

You can stay right by the pools at the rustic but charming **Oasis Chiyú** (☎4826-5247; www.oasischiyu.com; campsite per person Q60, s/d without bathroom Q180/240) – make reservations well in advance – or in nearby Chahal at the clean, family-run **Villa Santa Elena** (☎4011-6472, 4032-4053; www.hotelvse.com; Ruta 5, Km 363.5; campsite per person Q25, s/d Q150/250; P ❄ @ 📶).

Both the Oasis Chiyú and, in nearby Chahal, Villa Santa Elena have restaurants. If you're just cruising through without booking a room, the latter is much more likely to be open – you'll need to book in advance if you're planning on eating at the Oasis.

Regular minibuses (Q15, one hour) leave Fray Bartolomé de Las Casas for Chahal when full. From there you must change buses for Las Conchas (Q10, one hour). If you're in your own vehicle, look for the marked sign to Las Conchas, 15km east of Chahal. If you're coming south from El Petén, get off in Modesto Mendez (known locally as Cadenas), catch a Chahal-bound minibus to Sejux (say-whoosh) and walk or wait for another minibus to take you the remaining 3km to Las Conchas. Whichever direction you're coming from, travel connections are easiest in the morning and drop off severely in the late afternoon.

Activities

Valle Dorado WATER PARK
(☎7790-2121; www.hotelvalledorado.com; Hwy 9, Km 149; adult/child Q70/50; ⏲9am-5pm Wed-Sun) An attraction near Río Hondo is Valle Dorado, an aquatic park and tourist center. This large complex 14km east of the Hwy 10 junction includes an aquatic park with giant pools, waterslides, toboggans and other entertainment. Check the website for promotional deals and make reservations on weekends.

If you really like the place, you can stay here in large, comfortable rooms (Q580).

Parque Acuatico Longarone WATER PARK
(☎7963-8686; www.hotellongarone.com; Hwy 9, Km 126.5; adult/child Q60/45; ⏲9am-5pm Fri-Sun) Río Hondo is home to the Parque Acuatico Longarone, which has giant waterslides, an artificial river and other water-based fun.

Sleeping & Eating

For some reason Río Hondo is a favorite location for vacationing residents of Guatemala City. The upside of this is that there are some good (if somewhat overpriced) hotels around. Most have pools that nonguests can use for around Q25 per person.

All the hotels have restaurants. There are a couple of little BBQ joints set up on the main street, too, along with an impressive array of fruit vendors.

Hotel El Atlántico HOTEL $$
(☎7933-0598; Hwy 9, Km 126.5; s/d Q250/350; P ❄ 📶 🏊) The best-looking place in town has plenty of dark-wood fittings and well-spaced bungalows. The pool area is tranquil, with some shady sitting areas.

Hotel Pasabién HOTEL $$
(☎7933-0606; www.hotelpasabien.com; Hwy 9, Km 126.5; s/d Q250/300; P ⊖ ❄ 📶 🏊) On the north side of the highway, this hotel is a good choice for families – kids will enjoy the three pools with all manner of fancy slides. There's also a large onsite restaurant.

Hotel Longarone HOTEL $$$
(☎7963-8686; www.hotellongarone.com; Hwy 9, Km 126.5; s/d/tr Q500/610/885; P ⊖ ❄ @ 📶 🏊) Attached to Parque Acuatico Longarone (p193), with good-looking grounds, playgrounds for kids and a surprisingly fine Italian restaurant. Rooms are comfortable if somewhat dated.

Getting There & Away

Frequent Litegua buses traveling east–west on the Atlantic Hwy pass through Río Hondo. If you're coming from Honduras and heading east, be aware that the turnoff for Guatemala City is just west of the town – ask your driver to drop you in town as it is a much better place to wait for your onward connection. Tickets cost Q50.

DEM BONES

Most of the people you hear about who are digging stuff up in Guatemala these days are archaeologists. Or mining companies. But there's another group out there, sifting patiently through the soil in search of treasure – paleontologists.

While it's unclear whether dinosaurs ever inhabited what is now Guatemala, evidence shows that large prehistoric mammals – such as giant armadillos, 3m-tall sloths, mammoths and saber-toothed tigers – certainly did. As they migrated southward from North America they found they could not go much further than present-day Guatemala – back then the landmass stopped at northern Nicaragua, and 10 million years would pass before South and Central America joined, creating the American continents more or less as they are today.

Various theories seek to explain the disappearance of the dinosaurs and other large prehistoric mammals – the most widely accepted one being that a massive meteorite slammed into the Yucatán Peninsula, 66 million years ago, causing global climate change.

The great bulk of the fossil and bone evidence uncovered in Guatemala has been in the country's southeast corner, but giant sloth and mastodon remains have been found in what is now Guatemala City. Paleontologist Roberto Woolfolk Saravia, founder of the **Museo de Paleontología, Arqueología y Geología** (Roberto Woolfolk Saravia Archeology & Paleontology Museum; 5174-6081; Hwy 10, Estanzuela; 8am-5pm) FREE, claims to have collected more than 5000 fragments and skeletons, and he says there are a lot more out there, just that (you guessed it) the funding isn't available to dig them up.

If you have even a passing interest in prehistoric life, the museum makes for a worthy detour. On display are the remains of mastodons, giant sloths and armadillos, a prehistoric horse measuring 50cm, and two molar teeth from a mammoth.

Chiquimula

POP 106,000

Thirty-two kilometers south of Río Hondo on Hwy 10, Chiquimula is a major market town for all of eastern Guatemala. For travelers it's not a destination but a transit point. Your goal is probably the fabulous Maya ruins at Copán in Honduras, just across the border from El Florido. There are also some interesting journeys between Chiquimula and Jalapa, 78km to the west.

Sleeping

There is a range of good hotels within easy walking distance of the central plaza.

Hotel Posada Don Adan HOTEL $
(7942-3924; 8a Av 4-30, Zona 1; s/d Q120/180; P) The Don offers the best deal in this price range – neat, complete rooms with TV, fan, air-con, a couple of sticks of furniture and good, firm beds. It locks the doors at 10pm.

Hotel Hernández HOTEL $
(7942-0708; 3a Calle 7-41, Zona 1; s/d with fan Q80/120, with air-con Q120/200; P) It's hard to beat the Hernández – it's been a favorite for years and keeps going strong, with its central position, spacious, simple rooms and good-sized swimming pool.

Hotel Perla Oriental HOTEL $
(7796-9529; 2a Calle 10-07; s/d with air-con 125/180, without air-con 100/150; P) TVs are the only frill in otherwise simple but clean rooms. No breakfast is served, and some rooms, the ones on the street, have noise.

Hostal Maria Teresa HOTEL $$
(7942-0177; 6a Calle 6-21, Zona 1; s/d Q190/350; P@) Set around a gorgeous colonial courtyard with wide shady passageways, the single rooms are a bit small, but the doubles are generous and all the comforts are here: cable TV, hot showers and air-con.

Hostal Casa Vieja HOTEL $$$
(7942-7991; hostalcasaviejachiquimula@hotmail.com; 8a Av 1-60, Zona 2; s/ste Q350/600; P) A short walk from the center, Hostal Casa Vieja is the best hotel in town. Rooms are delicately decorated and the garden areas are lovely. The whole place radiates a tranquillity sorely missing in the rest of town. Laundry service and meals are also available.

Eating

There's a string of *comedores* (cheap eateries) on 8a Av behind the market. At night, snack vendors and taco carts set up along 7a Av opposite the plaza, selling the cheapest eats in town.

Casa Lú GUATEMALAN **$$**
(☎5927-2562; Parque El Calvario; mains Q30-70; ⏲10:30am-10:30pm) This chic, black-and-red restaurant has the look of a sushi shop but serves a variety of local Guatemalan dishes as well as the requisite pizzas, pastas and burgers, and some decent cocktails, too. The frozen margarita (grande) is colossal and a nice way to beat the Chiquimula heat.

Charli's INTERNATIONAL **$$**
(☎7943-8559; 7a Av 5-55, Zona 1; mains Q60-120; ⏲8am-9pm) Chiquimula option with a wide menu featuring pasta, pizza, seafood and steaks, all served up amid chilly air-con, with relaxed and friendly service.

Information

Banco G&T (7a Av 4-75, Zona 1; ⏲9am-8pm Mon-Fri, 10am-2pm Sat) Half a block south of the plaza. Changes US dollars and traveler's checks, and gives cash advances on Visa and MasterCard.

Getting There & Away

Several companies operate buses and microbuses, arriving and departing from the **bus station area** (11a Av, btwn 1a & 2a Calles). **Litegua** (☎7942-2064; www.litegua.com; 1a Calle, btwn 10a & 11a Avs), which operates buses to El Florido (the border crossing on the way to Copán) and Flores, has its own bus station a half block north. For the Honduran border crossing at Agua Caliente, take a minibus to Esquipulas and change there. If you're headed to Jalapa, you'll need to go to Ipala to make the connection. For Río Dulce, take a Flores bus or a Puerto Barrios bus to La Ruidosa junction and change there. If you're going to Esquipulas, sit on the left for the best views of the basilica (p197) housing the shrine of El Cristo Negro.

Ipala

Typical of many towns in El Oriente, Ipala is hot and dusty and holds little of interest for the average traveler. If you're not here to see the Volcán de Ipala, there's a good chance you are lost.

Sights

Volcán de Ipala VOLCANO
(☎7942-8431; Q10) The 1650m Volcán de Ipala is notable for its especially beautiful clear crater-lake measuring nearly 1km around and nestled below the summit at 1493m. The dramatic hike to the top takes you from 800m to 1650m in about two hours, though you can drive halfway up in a car (parking costs Q10). There are trails, a visitor center and a campsite on the shores of the lake.

To get there, take a bus from Chiquimula (Q20, 1½ hours) or Jalapa (two hours) to Ipala and transfer to a microbus to Agua Blanca (Q10, every 15 minutes). The trailhead is at El Sauce just before Agua Blanca; look for the blue INGUAT sign. If you're lucky, you might encounter a pick-up to Aldea Chigüiton, where the road ends, 2km from the highway, running south from Ipala. You may also be able to hire a horse in Chigüiton.

BUSES FROM CHIQUIMULA

DESTINATION	COST (Q)	TIME	FREQUENCY
Anguiatú, El Salvador border	20-30	1hr	leaves when full 5am-5:30pm, must change at Esquipulas (Q30)
El Florido, Honduras border	40	1¼hr	leaves when full 5:30am-4:30pm
Esquipulas	20-30	1hr	every 20min, 5am-9pm
Flores	75-120	7hr	2 Litegua buses daily
Guatemala City	40-50	3-4hr	every 30min, 3am-3:30pm
Ipala	20	1½hr	hourly, 5am-7pm
Puerto Barrios	50	5hr	every 30min, 3:30am-4pm
Quiriguá	50	2hr	every 30min, 3:30am-4pm
Río Hondo	20	30min	every 15min, 5am-6pm

Sleeping & Eating

Ipala has very limited sleeping options, but they're fine for a night or two.

There are fast-food joints and *churrasco* (barbecued meat) stands around the plaza.

Hotel Dorado HOTEL $
(☎7942-8334; Barrio El Rostro; s/d with fan Q100/125, with air-con Q125/150; P) If you're looking for a something a step above basic, it may be worth the 10-minute walk to this place out on the highway to Agua Blanca, which offers slightly more modern rooms.

Hotel Peña HOTEL $$
(☎7942-8064; 2a Calle 2-26; s/d without air-con Q75/125, with air-con Q125/250; P) The best hotel in the downtown area is not somewhere you'd be booking for your honeymoon, but it will do for a night, especially if you're on a budget. The rooms are clean, air-con is an option, and they have TVs.

Rosy's CAFE $
(☎7942-8086; www.facebook.com/rosyscocinacasera; mains Q20-35; 7am-9pm) Offers refreshingly tasty coffee and nice *comida típica* (regional food). Service is friendly and some staff speak excellent English. Its decor is simple, but the place is an oasis of sorts, well worth stopping in at. Note that on Saturdays it stays open till 9pm, but only for coffee and sweets.

Information

There are banks with ATMs around the plaza.

Getting There & Away

Buses pull up a block away from Ipala's plaza. There are connections to Chiquimula (Q20, 1½ hours), Jalapa (Q25, two hours) and Guatemala City (Q60, three hours).

Volcán de Quetzaltepeque

A bustling little town between Chiquimula and Esquipulas, Quetzaltepeque holds very little of interest for the visitor with the exception of the nearby **volcano** of the same name.

About 10km east of the village of Quetzaltepeque is this volcano, which tops out at 1900m. The walk to the top is tough going – through thick subtropical pine forest, with the trail disappearing in sections. But if you have a car, you can drive almost all the way to the top. From the summit there are excellent views of the nearby Ipala and Suchítan volcanoes and the surrounding countryside.

Due to the condition of the trail and some security concerns, you really need a guide to undertake this trek. Ask in the **Quetzaltepeque municipalidad** (Town Hall; ☎7944-0258; 8am-4pm Mon-Sat) on the main plaza to be put in touch with a local guide.

Sleeping & Eating

You can stay in Quetzaltepeque in the basic but functional **Hotel Vista Hermoso** (☎7944-0627; s/d Q80/160), but you're probably better off in Esquipulas or Chiquimula.

There are *comedores* (cheap eateries) and small restaurants around the plaza.

Getting There & Away

Buses running between Chiquimula (Q15, 30 minutes) and Esquipulas (Q8, 20 minutes) pass through Quetzaltepeque.

Jalapa

Jalapa is a friendly city with a small-town feel located 78km west of Chiquimula, and the route between the two is a stunning one: verdant gorges choked with banana trees alternate with fog-enveloped valleys.

While you're here, consider making a day trip to **Parque Ecoturístico Cascadas de Tatasirire** (☎5202-4150; www.alonatural.com; adult/child Q25/15; 8am-5pm), a lovely private nature reserve with waterfalls and walking trails just out of town. You can camp out here or stay in an extremely rustic 'ecolodge.'

Sleeping & Eating

Jalapa has probably the best-value accommodations in the country – it's a pity there isn't more to do around here.

Eating options are limited – a short stroll along the main street will get you up to speed. Also look around the market area, where you will find the oddly out of place yet completely welcome **Florencia** (☎7922-4557; Av Chipilapa 1-72, Zona 1; mains Q40-80; 7am-9pm).

Hotel Recinos HOTEL $
(☎7922-2580; 2a Calle 0-78, Zona 2; s/d Q60/100;) If you're just passing through, this orange-painted cheapie on the west side of the terminal/market area is a decent bet. The clean rooms with fan are a good deal, although it can get cramped when they squeeze two beds in.

Hotel y Restaurante Don José Antonio HOTEL $$
(☎7922-5751; Av Chipilapa A 0-64, Zona 2; s/d Q125/200; P ⊖ ☮) Beautifully decorated with colonial flourishes, the rooms here are huge and the bathrooms massive. There are some lovely sitting areas, a shady patio and an onsite restaurant.

Getting There & Away

Despite the construction of a **shiny terminal** at the south end of town, many buses continue to use the chaotic **market/bus terminal** area a block back from the main street.

Buses leave regularly for Chiquimula (Q28, 1½ hours) and Guatemala City (pullman/2nd class, Q35/28). For Esquipulas, change in Chiquimula.

Esquipulas

POP 66,000

From Chiquimula, Hwy 10 goes south into the mountains, where it's a bit cooler. After an hour's ride through pretty country, the highway descends into a valley ringed by mountains, where Esquipulas sits. Halfway down the slope, about 1km from the center of town, there is a *mirador* (lookout) from which you get a good view. The reason for a trip to Esquipulas is evident as soon as you catch sight of the place, dominated as it is by the towering Basílica de Esquipulas, its whiteness shimmering in the sun.

Sights

Basílica de Esquipulas BASILICA
(11a Calle) A massive structure that has resisted the power of earthquakes for almost 250 years, the basilica is approached through a pretty park and up a wide flight of steps. The impressive facade and towers are floodlit at night. And if waiting hours to view a famed 'Black Christ' is your cup of tea, this is the right place to do it.

Inside, the devout approach the surprisingly small El Cristo Negro (Black Christ; p198) with extreme reverence, many on their knees. Incense, murmured prayers and the scuffle of feet fill the air. When there are throngs of pilgrims, you must enter the church from the side to get a close view of the famous shrine. Shuffling along quickly, you may get a good glimpse or two before being shoved onward by the crowd behind you. On Sundays, religious holidays and (especially) during the **Cristo de Esquipulas festival** (January 14 to 15), the press of devotees is intense. On weekdays, you may have the place to yourself, which can be very powerful and rewarding.

Cruising the religious paraphernalia sold by the throngs of vendors around the basilica is an entertaining diversion. When you leave the church and descend the steps through the park and exit right to the market, notice the vendors selling straw hats that are decorated with artificial flowers and stitched with the name 'Esquipulas' – perfect for pilgrims who want everyone to know they've made the trip. These are very popular rearview mirror novelties for chicken-bus drivers countrywide.

Centro Turístico Cueva de las Minas CAVE
(☎4979-9086; Q30; ⊙7am-6pm) This has a 50m-deep cave (bring your own light), grassy picnic areas and the Río El Milagro, where people come for a dip and say it's miraculous. The cave and river are 500m from the entrance, which is behind the basilica's cemetery, 300m south of the turnoff into town on the road to Honduras. Refreshments are available. Note that (unlike some internet descriptions) this river does NOT go into the cave, so no tubing or wading is possible.

Sleeping

Esquipulas has an abundance of places to stay. On holidays and during the annual Cristo de Esquipulas festival (January 15), every hotel in town is filled, whatever the price; weekends are superbusy as well, with prices substantially higher. These rates reflect weekend prices. On weekdays (excluding the festival period), there are *descuentos* (discounts). For cheap rooms, look in the streets immediately north of the towering basilica.

Hotel Mahanaim HOTEL $$
(☎7943-1131; 10a Calle 1-85, Zona 1; s/d Q150/300; P ⊖ ❄ ☮ ≋) This establishment is on five levels around a covered courtyard. Rooms are comfortable but plain. It wouldn't be such a good deal if it weren't for the big covered swimming pool out back.

Hotel Monte Cristo HOTEL $$
(☎7943-1453; 3a Av 9-12, Zona 1; s/d Q220/257, without bathroom Q98/122; P ⊖ ☮) Good-sized rooms with a bit of furniture and hot showers. A policy of not letting the upstairs rooms until the downstairs ones are full might see you staying at ground level.

EL CRISTO NEGRO

Attracting more than a million pilgrims from Mexico, Central America, the US and further afield every year, the Black Christ of Esquipulas is one of Guatemala's top tourist draws.

Myths surround the sculpture's color. It was long believed that the Spaniards who commissioned it in 1594 requested a Christ with a skin tone resembling Esquipulas' Ch'ortí' natives so that they would be easier to convert. Studies have shown, though, that it is made from a light wood, possibly cedar. Some believers say it turned black mysteriously overnight – others say that it happened as a result of human contact and the amount of incense burnt in the church over the centuries.

The Black Christ first gained widespread attention when the Archbishop of Guatemala recovered miraculously from a chronic illness after visiting Esquipulas in 1737, and the town got a healthy publicity kick when Pope John Paul II visited in 1996.

But the statue's popularity has also been explained by the syncretism of pre-Christian and Christian beliefs. All throughout the Americas, when the Spanish arrived, indigenous peoples soon discovered it was less painful to appear to accept the new religion, basically retaining their traditional beliefs and renaming the old gods accordingly. In Maya culture, black was the color of warriors and associated with magic, death, violence and sacrifice. Accordingly, El Cristo Negro can be seen as a warrior Christ, defeater of death.

There are two authorized copies of Esquipulas' El Cristo Negro in the US. One in New York has come to represent the sufferings and hardships experienced by the Latino community there, while the one in Los Angeles (which was smuggled into the country, allegedly aided by bribed officials) has taken on a special significance for undocumented immigrants.

Hotel Vistana al Señor HOTEL **$$**
(7943-4294; hotelvistana@gmail.com; 1a Av 'A' 1-42; s/d Q350/450; P) By far the best deal in this price range are these sweet little rooms just south of the market. There's an attractive common balcony area with good views upstairs.

Hotel La Favorita HOTEL **$$**
(7943-1175; 2a Av 10-15, Zona 1; d Q225, s/d without bathroom Q60/120; P) A budget choice and thus nothing too special. The rooms without bathrooms are okay, but those with bathrooms are a bit nicer.

Hotel Legendario HOTEL **$$$**
(7943-1022, 7943-1824; www.hotellegendario.com; cnr 3a Av & 9a Calle, Zona 1; s/d Q200/400; P) The fanciest hotel downtown goes all out on the services, right down to a separate kids' swimming pool. Rooms are reasonable – big enough, featuring large windows opening onto a grassy courtyard, and all the comforts you'd expect for the price.

Hotel Portal de la Fe HOTEL **$$$**
(7943-4124; 11a Calle 1-70, Zona 1; s/d Q350/600; P) One of the few hotels with any real style in town and a fun spiral staircase in the main lobby. Subterranean rooms are predictably dark, but upstairs the situation improves considerably.

Eating

Restaurants are slightly more expensive here than in other parts of Guatemala. Budget restaurants are clustered at the north end of the basilica's park, where hungry pilgrims can find them readily.

Restaurante Calle Real GUATEMALAN **$**
(7943-0537; 3a Av; mains Q35-90; 7:30am-9pm Mon-Fri, 8am-10pm Sat & Sun) Typical of many restaurants here, this big eating-barn turns out cheap meals for the pilgrims. It has a wide menu, florescent lighting and lots of paintings of the basilica on the wall.

La Rotonda FAST FOOD **$$**
(7943-3038; 1a Av 'A' 10-30, Zona 1; mains Q40-180; 8am-10pm) Opposite Rutas Orientales bus station, this is a round building with chairs arranged around a circular open-air counter under a big awning. It's a welcoming place – clean and fresh. There are plenty of options to choose from, including pizza, pasta and burgers.

Restaurant El Angel CHINESE **$$**
(7943-1372; cnr 11a Calle & 2a Av, Zona 1; mains Q50-70; 8am-9pm) This main-street Chinese eatery does all the standard dishes, plus steaks and a good range of *licuados* (milkshakes). Home delivery is available, and it has daily specials on the cheap, too.

City Grill STEAK $$

(☎7943-1748; cnr 2a Av & 10a Calle, Zona 1; mains Q50-150; ⏲7:30am-9pm Mon-Fri, 7am-10pm Sat & Sun) The best steakhouse in town (featuring some of the best steaks for miles around) also serves up some decent seafood and pasta dishes. The pizza is worth a look-in, too.

Shopping

Plaza Santa Fé MARKET

(⏲7:30am-7pm Mon-Fri, to 9pm Sat, to 6pm Sun) Next to the basilica, this shopping market has all sorts of trinkets, souvenirs, clothes, textiles and more.

Information

Banco Internacional (3a Av 8-87, Zona 1; ⏲8am-6pm Mon-Fri, 9am-1pm Sat) Changes cash and traveler's checks, gives cash advances on Visa and MasterCard, is the town's American Express agent and has a Visa ATM.

Getting There & Away

Buses to Guatemala City (Q65 to Q75, four to five hours) arrive and depart hourly from 1:30am to 4pm from the **Rutas Orientales bus station** (☎7943-1366; cnr 11a Calle & 1a Av 'A', Zona 1), near the entrance to town.

Minibuses to Agua Caliente (Honduran border; Q20, 30 minutes) arrive and depart across the street, leaving every half hour from 5am to 5pm; taxis also wait here, charging the same as minibuses, once they have five passengers.

Minibuses to Chiquimula (Q15, 90 minutes, every six minutes) depart from the east end of 11a Calle (next to Plaza Pepsi).

Transportes Guerra (cnr 5a Av & 10a Calle, Zona 1) goes to Anguiatú (El Salvador border; Q15, 80 minutes, every 30 minutes, between 6am and 6pm).

There are three buses daily for Flores/Santa Elena (Q120, eight hours) from the **Transportes María Elena** (☎7943-0957; 11a Calle 0-54, Zona 1; ⏲4am-8pm) office, departing at 4:30am, 8:30am, and 1:30pm. It passes Quiriguá (Q45, two hours), Río Dulce (Q60, four hours) and Poptún (Q90, six hours).

Quiriguá

POP 4800

Quiriguá archaeological site is only 50km from Copán as the crow flies, but the lay of the land, the international border and the condition of the roads make it a journey of 175km. Quiriguá is famed for its intricately carved stelae – the gigantic brown sandstone monoliths that rise as high as 10.5m, like ancient sentinels, in a well-kept tropical park.

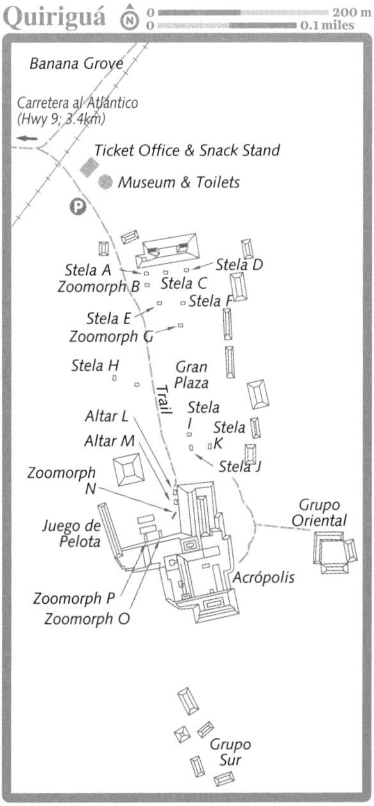

From Río Hondo junction it's 67km along Hwy 9 to the village of Los Amates, where there are a couple of hotels, a restaurant, food stalls, a bank and a small bus station. Quiriguá village is 1.5km east of Los Amates, and the turnoff to the ruins is another 1.5km to the east. The 3.4km access road leads south through banana groves.

History

Quiriguá's history parallels that of Copán, of which it was a dependency during much of the Classic period. Of the three sites in this area, only the present archaeological park is of interest.

Quiriguá's location lent itself to the carving of giant stelae. Beds of brown sandstone in the nearby Río Motagua had cleavage planes suitable for cutting large pieces. Though soft when first cut, the sandstone dried hard in the air. With Copán's expert artisans nearby for guidance, Quiriguá's stone carvers were ready for greatness. All they needed was a great leader to inspire them – and to pay for the carving of the huge stelae.

That leader was K'ak' Tiliw Chan Yo'at (Cauac Sky; r 725–84), who decided that Quiriguá should no longer be under the control of Copán. In a war with his former suzerain, Cauac Sky took Uaxaclahun Ubak K'awil (King 18 Rabbit) of Copán prisoner in 737 and later had him beheaded. Independent at last, Cauac Sky commissioned his stonecutters to go to work, and for the next 38 years they turned out giant stelae and zoomorphs dedicated to his glory.

Cauac Sky's son Sky Xul (r 784–800) lost his throne to a usurper, Jade Sky. This last great king of Quiriguá continued the building boom initiated by Cauac Sky, reconstructing Quiriguá's Acrópolis on a grander scale.

Quiriguá remained unknown to Europeans until the explorer and diplomat John L Stephens arrived in 1840. Impressed by its great monuments, Stephens lamented the world's lack of interest in them in his book *Incidents of Travel in Central America, Chiapas and Yucatan* (1841).

Stephens tried to buy the ruined city in order to have its stelae shipped to New York, but the owner, Señor Payes, assumed that Stephens (being a diplomat), was negotiating on behalf of the US government and that the government would pay. Payes quoted an extravagant price, and the deal was never made.

Between 1881 and 1894, excavations were carried out by Alfred P Maudslay. In the early 20th century all the land around Quiriguá was sold to the US-based United Fruit Company and turned into banana groves. The company is gone, but the bananas and Quiriguá remain. Restoration of the site was carried out by the University of Pennsylvania in the 1930s. In 1981 Unesco declared the ruins a World Heritage Site, one of only three in Guatemala (the others are Tikal and Antigua).

Sights

There's really only one reason to come here: the beautiful parklike archaeological site of the same name. Near the entrance, it has a *tienda* (small shop) selling cold drinks and snacks, but you'll be better off bringing your own picnic. A small **museum** just past the entrance has a few information displays and a model of how the site (much of it unexcavated) would have looked in its heyday.

On the way to the ruin, you'll pass acres and acres of banana trees, part of a United Fruit plantation. If you're lucky, the 'banana train' will be in operation and you'll see bunches being whisked along by a conveyor through the trees.

Quiriguá Archaeological Site ARCHAEOLOGICAL SITE
(Q80; 8am-4:30pm) Despite the sticky heat and (sometimes) bothersome mosquitoes, Quiriguá is a wonderful place. The giant stelae on the **Gran Plaza** (Great Plaza) are all much more worn than those at Copán. To impede further deterioration, each has been covered by a thatched roof. The roofs cast shadows that make it difficult to examine the carving closely and almost impossible to get a good photograph, but somehow this does little to inhibit one's sense of awe.

Seven of the **stelae**, designated A, C, D, E, F, H and J, were built during the reign of Cauac Sky and carved with his image. Stela E is the largest Maya stela known, standing some 8m above ground, with another 3m or so buried in the earth. It weighs almost 60,000kg. Note the exuberant, elaborate headdresses; the beards on some of the figures (an oddity in Maya art and life); the staffs of office held in the kings' hands; and the glyphs on the sides of the stela.

At the far end of the plaza is the Acrópolis, far less impressive than the one at Copán. At its base are several **zoomorphs**, blocks of stone carved to resemble real and mythic creatures. Frogs, tortoises, jaguars and serpents were favorite subjects. The low zoomorphs can't compete with the towering stelae in impressiveness, but as works of art, imagination and mythic significance, the zoomorphs are superb.

Sleeping & Eating

Hotel y Restaurante Royal HOTEL $
(7934-2624; s/d Q80/150; P) Of the budget options in town, this is by far the better choice, with spacious clean rooms and a restaurant serving simple, filling meals (Q40 to Q60). Room prices are heavily negotiable.

Posada de Quiriguá BOUTIQUE HOTEL $$
(5349-5817; www.facebook.com/posadadequirigua; s/d Q160/300; P) This *posada* gets high marks, not only for lovely rooms and a gracious owner, but for delicious Japanese food that's served there. There are only a few rooms, and when the owner is traveling it is closed, so advance reservations are essential.

Getting There & Away

Buses running Guatemala City–Puerto Barrios, Guatemala City–Flores, Esquipulas–Flores or Chiquimula–Flores will drop you off or pick you up here. If you're heading for the hotel (p200), make sure you get dropped at the *pasarela de Quiriguá* (the pedestrian overpass). Buses will also drop you at the turnoff to the archaeological site (p200) if you ask.

From the highway it's 3.4km to the archaeological site – Q5 to Q10 by *tuk-tuk* (three-wheeled motor taxi), but if one doesn't come, don't fret: it's a pleasant walk (without luggage) through banana plantations to get there.

If you're staying in Quiriguá village or Los Amates and walking to the archaeological site, you can take a shortcut along the railroad that goes from the village through the banana fields, crossing the access road very near the entrance to the archaeological site. A *tuk-tuk* from Quiriguá village to the site should cost around Q20.

Out on the main highway buses pass frequently for Río Dulce (Q35, two hours), Chiquimula (Q35, two hours) and Puerto Barrios (Q25).

COPÁN (HONDURAS)

Copán Ruinas

POP 39,490

The town of Copán Ruinas, often simply called Copán, is a beautiful place, paved with cobblestones and lined with white adobe buildings with red-tiled roofs. It's also one of the most charming and traveler-oriented places in Honduras, with a friendly local population, widely spoken English and some great hotels and restaurants. Many people come here just to see the famous nearby Maya ruins, but with plenty of other attractions in the town and nearby, there's reason enough to linger.

Sights

Though the archaeological site is the main attraction of the Copán region, there are other fine places to visit in the area, including several museums in and around town.

Macaw Mountain Bird Park ZOO

(2651-4245; www.macawmountain.org; L230; 9am-5pm) Around 2.5km outside Copán Ruinas is an extensive private reserve aimed at saving Central American macaws. There are plenty of them here, along with toucans, motmots, parrots, kingfishers and orioles, all flying around in spacious, humanely constructed cages. In the 'Encounter Center' uncaged birds fly onto your shoulders or hands and you can pose for photos with them.

If caged birds upset you, bear in mind that nearly all of these birds have been donated to the park by owners who didn't want them anymore, or were confiscated from bird smugglers. It's a lovely place to wander around, with plenty of walking trails weaving through the lush forest and over boardwalks to lookout points and swimming holes; there's also a cafe-restaurant on the property. The entrance ticket – which includes a guided tour in English – is valid for three days. To get here, catch a *mototaxi* (three-wheeled motor taxi) for L20 per person.

Museo de Arqueología Maya MUSEUM

(2651-4437; Parque Central; L69; 2-9pm) The Museo de Arqueología Maya is worth a visit. The exhibits include some of the best excavated ceramics, fragments from the altars and the supports of the Maya ruins, an insight into the Maya's sophisticated use of calendars and a re-creation of a female shaman's tomb. Some descriptions have English translations.

Tea & Chocolate Place AGRICULTURAL CENTER

(2651-4087; 4-6pm Mon-Sat) This charming place is a research center that doubles as a tea and gift shop every afternoon to support the important reforestation work carried out by its environmental charity. Enjoying a cup of tea (try the cacao and spice) on the wonderful veranda is something of a rite of passage in Copán Ruinas. Take a *mototaxi* to get here or walk the kilometer uphill from town.

Museo Digital de Copán MUSEUM

(Parque Central; L69; 1-9pm) This museum opened in late 2015 as a gift to the people of Copán from Japan and contains some interesting old photographs. The main reason to visit, though, is to watch the excellent 12-minute video on demand that's a great primer before you visit the Copán Archaeological Site.

Memorias Frágiles GALLERY

(2651-3900; Palacio Municipal, Parque Central; 8am-5pm Mon-Fri) FREE This fascinating photo exhibition was a gift from Boston's Peabody Museum; it features a collection of rare photos detailing the first archaeological expeditions to Copán at the turn of the 20th century. Many of these proved essential in later restoration work, as the photos showed the site decades beforehand and offered clues to how the various stone hieroglyphs had lain.

Copán Ruinas

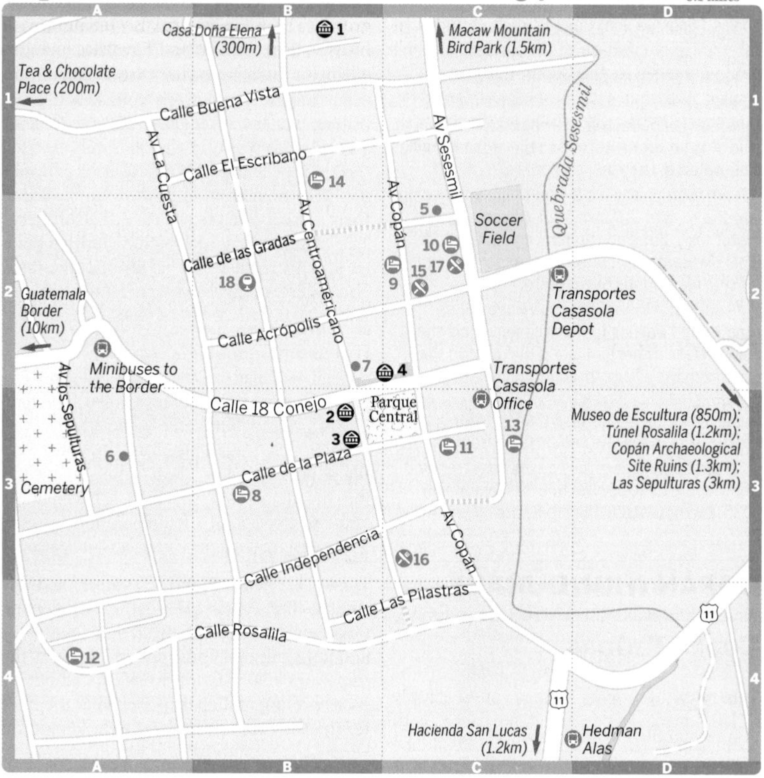

Copán Ruinas

Sights

1 Casa K'inich.......B1
2 Memorias Frágiles.......B3
Mirador El Cuartel.......(see 1)
3 Museo de Arqueología Maya.......B3
4 Museo Digital de Copán.......C2

Activities, Courses & Tours

Basecamp Tours.......(see 8)
5 Guacamaya Spanish Academy.......C2
6 Ixbalanque Spanish School.......A3
7 Welchez Copan Coffee Tours.......B2
Yaragua Tours.......(see 11)

Sleeping

8 Café ViaVia.......B3
Hostel Iguana Azul.......(see 12)
9 Hotel & Hostal Berakah.......C2
10 Hotel Mary.......C2
11 Hotel Yaragua.......C3
12 La Casa de Café.......A4
13 Madrugada Copan.......C3
14 Terramaya.......B1

Eating

15 Asados Copán.......C2
Cafe at La Casa de Cafe.......(see 12)
16 Café San Rafael.......C3
Café ViaVia.......(see 8)
17 Casa Ixchel.......C2
Comedor Mary.......(see 10)

Drinking & Nightlife

Café ViaVia.......(see 8)
18 Sol de Copán.......B2

Casa K'inich MUSEUM
(☎2651-4105; off Av Centroaméricano; L30; ⊙8am-noon & 1-5pm Tue-Sun) Casa K'inich includes an interactive re-creation of the ancient football game practiced by the Copán residents more than a millennia ago. Displays are in three languages: English, Spanish and Ch'orti'. Kids might get a kick out of the stela with a cutout hole to poke their heads through.

Mirador El Cuartel VIEWPOINT
(off Av Centroaméricana) The atmospheric ruins of the old town jail have a fine view of the town and surrounding countryside, making it worth the steep walk uphill to get here.

Courses

Guacamaya Spanish Academy LANGUAGE
(☎2651-4360; www.guacamaya.com; Calle de las Gradas, off Av Copán) Offers a package of 20 hours of one-on-one tuition for L3840. For L2400 more you can have full board and lodging with a local family.

Ixbalanque Spanish School LANGUAGE
(☎2651-4432; www.ixbalanquespanish.com; Av los Jaguares) Offers 20 hours of one-on-one instruction in Spanish for L6240 per week, including a homestay with a local family that provides three meals a day.

Tours

A huge number of tours can be organized from Copán Ruinas; local companies promote these widely. You can go caving, tube a river, visit a Maya village, make tortillas, manufacture ceramics, plunge into hot springs, visit a coffee plantation or head off into the wilds of Honduras.

Birdwatching tours are very popular in the area around Copán – it's said that there are more quetzals in the surrounding cloud forest than there are in the whole of Guatemala (where it's the national bird). One recommended English-speaking birdwatching guide is **Alexander Alvarado** (☎9751-1680; alexander.alvarado469@gmail.com).

Horseback riding can be arranged by any of the town's tour companies and most hotels. You can ride to the ruins or make other, lengthier excursions. Three- to five-hour rides out of Café ViaVia visit the hot springs, Hacienda San Lucas, Los Sapos and the small Ch'orti' village of La Pintada.

Welchez Copan Coffee Tours ECOTOUR
(www.cafehonduras.com; half-day tours L960) These morning or afternoon tours take guests to Finca Santa Isabel where some of the finest coffee beans in the region are grown. The hillsides are also teeming with birds so bring binoculars! The price includes a delicious meal at a charming ranch.

Basecamp Tours ADVENTURE
(☎2651-4695; www.basecamphonduras.com; Calle de la Plaza) Located inside Café ViaVia, this outfit offers a range of original and adventurous tours around the local area on foot (L230 to L460) and horseback (L345, three hours). The highly recommended two-hour 'Alternative Copán' walking tour (L230) delves beneath the glossy surface of the town and investigates the reality of life for many Hondurans.

Yaragua Tours ADVENTURE
(☎2651-4147; www.yaragua.com; cnr Calle de la Plaza & Av Copán; tours L230-1050) Leads recommended hikes, horseback-riding trips, coffee tours, ceramic tours where you can try making your own and outings to nearby caves.

Sleeping

There's a great deal of accommodations choices in Copán Ruinas, from some of the best hostels in Honduras to fine boutique hotels and lots in between.

Madrugada Copan HOSTAL $
(www.madrugadacopan.com; dm/s/d from L240/360/480; 📶) Situated in a colonial-style hacienda next to a bougainvillea-lined creek and near the town center, this place opened in late 2017 and is oriented specifically to backpackers. Rooms are simple but tastefully furnished and are cooled with overhead fans. There's a hammock-strewn terrace to chill on and a kitchen for guests' use, and there's a friendly vibe.

Café ViaVia HOTEL $
(☎2651-4652; www.viaviacafe.com/en/copan/hotel; Calle de la Plaza; r L230; 📶) This small, Belgian-run, European-style hotel has five very simple, spotless rooms with hot-water bathrooms, tiled floors and good beds. There are hammocks, a small garden and enough space to chill out. It's a great place to come for tourist information, and also has a lively bar attached, which – be aware – can get noisy. Overall it's an amazing deal.

Hostel Iguana Azul HOSTEL $
(☎2651-4620; www.iguanaazulcopan.com; Calle Rosalila; dm/s/d L200/400/450; 📶) This colonial-style home has eight comfy bunk beds in

two rooms and a shared bathroom with hot water; four private rooms sleep two. There's also a pretty back garden. The communal area has books and lots of travel information, and there's a fridge but no kitchen. This is backpacking elegance at its finest: even a room-cleaning service is included.

Hotel & Hostal Berakah HOSTEL $
(☎ 9951-4288, 2651-4771; www.hotelberakahcopan.hostel.com; Av Copán; dm/d/tw L174/400/450) One of the few true hostels in Copán Ruinas, Berakah is very well set up for backpackers, with a range of different rooms and clean, modern bathrooms. Dorms are rather cramped but a great deal, while the house next-door that functions as the hostel's second site has a well-equipped kitchen, a pool table and more dorms.

Hotel Yaragua HOTEL $
(☎ 2651-4147; www.yaragua.com; cnr Av Copán & Calle de la Plaza; s/d with air-con L600/800, without air-con L400/500; ❄ 📶) The bright-yellow paint job and jungly patio area give this place a local feel. Rooms are small and very basic but the staff are super helpful, speak English and you can't beat the central location. There's hot water and a shared balcony.

★ **La Casa de Café** B&B $$
(☎ 2651-4620; www.casadecafecopan.com; Calle Rosalila; s/d incl breakfast L1275/1512; ❄ 📶) This impeccably decorated B&B has rooms adorned with carved wooden doors and Guatemalan masks. The setting is stunning – the view from the lawn over the copious and delicious breakfast service is of morning mists rising around the Guatemalan mountains in the distance. North American owner Howard is a mine of local information and staying here feels like being his personal guest.

La Casa de Café operates an excellent restaurant, open all day. There's also an upscale house called La Casa de Don Santiago (L2880), townhouse called Casa Jaguar (L2400) and apartment named Studio 22 (L960) available across the street with prices dropping for long stays.

Casa Doña Elena GUESTHOUSE $$
(☎ 2651-4029; www.casadonaelena.com; Av Centro américano; s/d/tr incl breakfast L700/1200/1440; ❄ 📶) This lovely, family-run hilltop place enjoys some great views of the town and surrounding valley and has a beautifully tended garden shared by its seven individually named rooms. The rooms themselves are simple, but spacious and clean and a good breakfast is included in the price. It's a 10-minute sturdy uphill walk from the center of town.

Hotel Mary HOTEL $$
(☎ 2651-4673; www.comedormary.com; Av Sesesmiles; s/d L1050/1180; ❄ 📶) This nicely presented place has very sweet rooms that are brightly painted and well maintained. There's hot water, ceiling fans, attractive traditional bed covers and a pretty garden to boot. Air-conditioning costs an extra L230 per night.

★ **Terramaya** BOUTIQUE HOTEL $$$
(☎ 2651-4623; www.terramayacopan.com; Av Centroaméricano; s/d incl breakfast from L2090/2280; ❄ 📶) This ultra-comfortable, flawlessly run, stylish gem hovers somewhere between a B&B and boutique hotel, offering six terra-cotta–tiled, cream linen-draped rooms, a flowery backyard garden and a candlelit terrace with misty-eyed mountain views. Upstairs rooms offer spectacular balconies with vistas out to the mountains beyond – room number six is to die for. It's fantastic value and a worthy splurge.

Eating

There are some excellent eating options in Copán Ruinas, with new places opening all the time.

★ **Cafe at La Casa de Cafe** INTERNATIONAL $$
(☎ 2651-4620; www.casadecafecopan.com; mains L50-175; ⏰ 7am-8pm) Inspired by trips the owners have taken around the world, you'll find homemade, healthy and fresh delights here from tamales to perfectly spiced curries. The pancakes, egg dishes and smoothies at breakfast are superb as are the lunchtime sandwiches on bread sometimes still warm from the oven. Chefs use plenty of vegetables, herbs, spreads and delicious fillings like pan-fried tilapia.

Everything is served in a cosy garden patio bursting with flowers.

Casa Ixchel CAFE $$
(Av Sesesmiles; mains L90-250; ⏰ 7am-6pm; 📶) There's a friendly welcome at this serious coffee lover's place, where locally grown Casa Ixchel Arabica coffee is the fuel of choice and the espresso machine is rarely out of use. There's a great little back patio for eating and drinking in the sunshine, and a brunchy menu for tasty breakfasts and light lunches.

Comedor Mary HONDURAN **$$**
(Av Sesesmiles, Hotel Mary; mains L88-250; ⏲7am-9pm; 📶) This charming space comprises a garden for alfresco dining and a dining room full of dark wood furniture where excellent *pupusas* (L12 to L25 each) are served up. *Comida típica* is also redefined here (try the *lomito de res a la plancha*, a grilled beef tenderloin); service is uncharacteristically friendly and the atmosphere is upscale. Don't miss it.

Café ViaVia INTERNATIONAL **$$**
(www.viaviacafe.com/en/copan; Calle de la Plaza; breakfast L60-95, mains L95-150; ⏲7am-10pm; 📶🌿) This terrific restaurant serves breakfast, lunch and dinner in a hip, convivial atmosphere, with tables next to a garden courtyard or overlooking the street. The organically grown coffee it prepares is excellent, the bread is homemade and there's always a good selection of vegetarian and meat-based dishes on offer.

Asados Copán STEAK **$$**
(cnr Calle Acrópolis & Av Copán; mains L120-250; ⏲8am-10pm) With one of the best settings in town, this large, open-air steakhouse is popular with tourists and locals alike. The menu's simple but effective – a variety of beef and chicken dishes, flame-grilled to perfection.

★**Café San Rafael** CAFE, DELI **$$$**
(Av Centroaméricano; sandwiches L160-200; ⏲11am-11pm Tue-Sat, 8am-6pm Sun & Mon; 📶) This smart cafe serves organic coffee grown at its *finca* (ranch), though it's mostly known for its delicious cheeses (platters L150 to L700). Breakfasts (L100 to L200) are a filling splurge, while the toasted sandwiches (try the excellent steak and provolone) are a great lunch option. Half the place is in a beautiful garden patio and the other is indoors and very modern.

Drinking & Nightlife

★**Sol de Copán** BREWERY
(Av Mirador; mains L130-180; ⏲2-10pm Tue-Sat; 📶) A terrific, German-owned microbrewery in a basement pub. The owner, Thomas, is friendly and makes sure everyone's regularly topped up with pilsner or lager. Delicious German sausages are served, and there's live music some nights, too. If you're lucky, Thomas might show you his fermenting vats out the back. Sit at a big table to meet locals and other travelers.

Café ViaVia BAR
(www.viaviacafe.com/en/copan; Calle de la Plaza; ⏲7am-10pm; 📶) The bar here has a sociable vibe, with drink specials and occasional gigs and DJs playing Latin and pop tunes on weekends. Definitely a good place to meet both locals and backpackers.

Information

US dollars can be changed at most banks, though Guatemalan quetzals can at present only be changed on the black market. The following banks have ATMs that accept foreign cards.

BAC (Parque Central; ⏲9am-5pm Mon-Fri, to noon Sat) Exchanges US dollars and has a 24-hour ATM.

Banco Atlántida (cnr Calle Independencia & Av Copán) Changes US dollars and has an ATM.

Banco de Occidente (cnr Calle 18 Conejo & Av Copán) On the plaza; changes US dollars and gives cash advances on Visa and MasterCard.

Getting There & Away

An airport opened here in 2015, but it has never received commercial flights and no one expects it to in the near future.

Casasola (☎2651-4078; Av Sesesmiles) buses arrive and depart from an open-air **bus depot** (☎2651-4078) at the entrance to town, where destinations include San Pedro Sula (L140, three hours, five daily) and Santa Rosa de Copán (L100, three hours, hourly), from where you can connect easily to Tegucigalpa.

Minibuses to/from the **Guatemalan border** (L25, 20 minutes, every 20 minutes) run between 6am and 5pm from near the town's cemetery at the end of Calle 18 Conejo. On the Guatemala side, buses to Esquipulas and Chiquimula leave the border regularly until about 5pm.

You can book popular shuttle buses at either Basecamp Tours (p203) and Hotel & Hostal Berakah (p204) to Antigua (L600, six hours), Guatemala City (L600, five hours), El Salvador, stopping at Santa Ana or Tunco (both L960, 4½ hours) and San Salvador (L880, five hours); there's one shuttle to Leon and Managua in Nicaragua (L2040, 12 hours) and also one to La Ceiba (L960, seven hours), Lago de Yojoa (L480, six hours) and to the San Pedro Sula airport (L480, four hours). Note that many shuttles only run when there are enough people.

Hedman Alas (☎2651-4037; Km 62 Carretera a San Lucas) has a modern terminal just south of town, where you can get daily 1st-class buses to San Pedro Sula and the airport (L395, three hours), Tegucigalpa (L790, eight hours), Lago Yajoa (L790, six hours), La Ceiba (L731, seven hours) and Tela (L731, six hours).

Copán Site

One of the most important of all Maya civilizations lived, prospered, then mysteriously crumbled around the Copán archaeological site, a Unesco World Heritage Site. During the Classic period (AD 250–900), the city at Copán Ruinas culturally dominated the region. The architecture is not as grand as that across the border in Tikal, but the city produced remarkable sculptures and hieroglyphs, and these days you'll often be virtually alone at the site, which makes it all the more haunting.

The booklet *History Carved in Stone: A Guide to the Archaeological Park of the Ruins of Copán*, by William L Fash and Ricardo Agurcia Fasquelle, is usually available at the site. For further reading see *Scribes, Warriors and Kings* by William Fash (2001), a comprehensible overview of Copán.

History

Maya Copán

People have been living in the Copán Valley since at least 1200 BC; ceramic evidence has been found from around that date. Copán must have had significant commercial activity since early times, as graves showing marked Olmec influence have been dated to around 900 to 600 BC.

In the 5th century AD one royal family came to rule Copán, led by a mysterious king named Mah K'ina Yax K'uk' Mo' (Great Sun Lord Quetzal Macaw), who ruled from AD 426 to 435. Archaeological evidence indicates that he was a great shaman, and later kings revered him as the semidivine founder of the city. The dynasty ruled throughout Copán's florescence during the Classic period (AD 250 to 900).

We know little about the subsequent kings who ruled before AD 628. Only some of their names have been deciphered: Mat Head, the second king; Cu Ix, the fourth king; Waterlily Jaguar, the seventh; Moon Jaguar, the 10th; and Butz' Chan, the 11th.

Among the greatest of Copán's kings was Smoke Imix (Smoke Jaguar; r 628–95), the 12th king. Smoke Imix built Copán into a major military and commercial power in the region. He may have taken over the nearby princedom of Quiriguá, as one of the famous stelae at that site bears his name and image. By the time he died in 695, Copán's population had grown substantially.

Smoke Imix was succeeded by Uaxaclahun Ubak K'awil (18 Rabbit; r 695–738), the 13th king, who willingly took the reins of power and pursued further military conquest. In a war with King Cauac Sky, his neighbor from Quiriguá, 18 Rabbit was captured and beheaded. He was succeeded by K'ak' Joplaj Chan K'awiil (Smoke Monkey; r 738–49), the 14th king, whose short reign left little mark on Copán. Smoke Monkey's son, K'ak' Yipyaj Chan K'awiil (Smoke Shell; r 749–63), was, however, one of Copán's greatest builders. He commissioned the city's most famous and important monument, the great Escalinata de los Jeroglíficos (Hieroglyphic Stairway), which immortalizes the achievements of the dynasty from its establishment until 755, when the stairway was dedicated. It is the longest inscription ever discovered in the Maya lands.

Yax Pasaj Chan Yopaat (Sunrise or First Dawn; r 763–820; also known as Yax Pac, Yax Pasaj Chan Yoaat and Yax Pasah), Smoke Shell's successor and the 16th king, continued the beautification of Copán. The final occupant of the throne, U Cit Tok', became ruler in 822, but it's not known when he died.

Until recently, the collapse of the civilization at Copán had been a mystery. Now, archaeologists have begun to surmise that near the end of Copán's heyday the population grew at an unprecedented rate, straining agricultural resources. In the end, Copán was no longer agriculturally self-sufficient and had to import food from other areas. The urban core expanded into the fertile lowlands in the center of the valley, forcing both agricultural and residential areas to spread onto the steep slopes surrounding the valley. Wide areas were deforested, resulting in massive erosion that further decimated food production and brought flooding during rainy seasons. Interestingly, this environmental damage of old is not too different from what is happening today – a disturbing trend, but one that meshes with the Maya belief that life is cyclical and history repeats itself. Skeletal remains of people who died during Copán's final years show marked evidence of malnutrition and infectious diseases, as well as decreased life spans.

The Copán Valley was not abandoned overnight – agriculturists probably continued to live in the ecologically devastated valley for maybe another one or two hundred years. But by the year 1200 or thereabouts even the farmers had departed, and the royal city of Copán was reclaimed by the jungle.

Copán Area

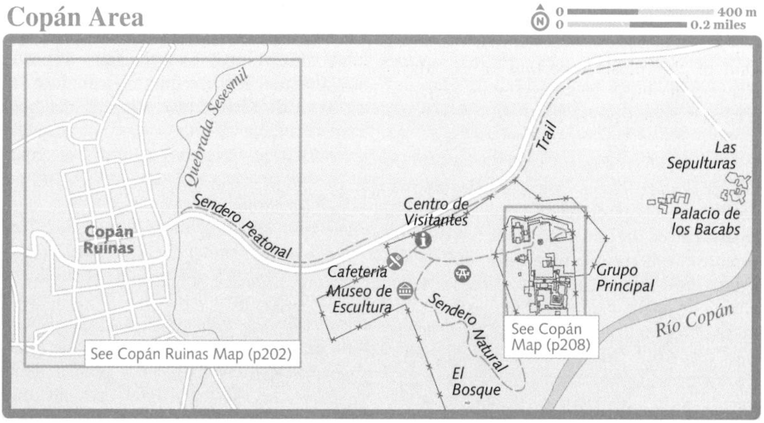
0 400 m
0 0.2 miles
Quebrada Sesesmil
Sendero Peatonal
Copán Ruinas
Trail
Centro de Visitantes
Cafetería
Museo de Escultura
Sendero Natural
El Bosque
Grupo Principal
Las Sepulturas
Palacio de los Bacabs
Río Copán
See Copán Ruinas Map (p202)
See Copán Map (p208)

European Discovery

The first known European to see the ruins was a representative of Spanish King Felipe II, Diego García de Palacios, who lived in Guatemala and traveled through the region. On March 8, 1576, he wrote to the king about the ruins he found here. Only about five families were living here at the time, and they knew nothing of the history of the ruins. The discovery was not pursued, and almost three centuries went by before another Spaniard, Colonel Juan Galindo, visited the ruins and made the first map of them.

It was Galindo's report that stimulated John L Stephens and Frederick Catherwood to come to Copán on their Central American journey in 1839. When Stephens published the book *Incidents of Travel in Central America, Chiapas and Yucatan* in 1841, illustrated by Catherwood, the ruins first became known to the world at large.

Copán Today

The history of Copán continues to unfold today. The remains of 3450 structures have been found in the 27 sq km surrounding the Grupo Principal, most of them within about half a kilometer of it. In a wider zone, 4509 structures have been detected in 1420 sites within 135 sq km of the ruins. These discoveries indicate that at the peak of civilization here, around the end of the 8th century AD, the valley of Copán had more than 27,500 inhabitants – a population figure not reached again until the 1980s.

In addition to examining the area surrounding the Grupo Principal, archaeologists continue to make new discoveries in the Grupo Principal itself. Five separate phases of building on this site have been identified; the final phase, dating from AD 650 to 820, is what we see today. But buried underneath the visible ruins are layers of other ruins, which archaeologists are exploring by means of underground tunnels. This is how they found the Templo Rosalila (Rosalila Temple), a replica of which is now in the Museo de Escultura. Below Rosalila is yet another, earlier temple, Margarita, and below that, Hunal, which contains the tomb of the founder of the dynasty, Yax K'uk' Mo' (Great Sun Lord Quetzal Macaw). Two of the excavation tunnels, including Rosalila, are open to the public, though you'll need to pay a second entry fee to access them.

Sights

If you're short on time or money, plan on seeing the **Archaeological Park** (Principal Group) only. Entry to this portion costs US$15 per person and includes entry to Las Sepultras two kilometers away. Adding access to Tunel Rosalila and Tunel de los Jaguares – which are certainly cool but contain only a few carvings behind glass – costs another US$15 per person; admission to the Museo de Esculturas (which houses many of the original sculptures from the site and is worth visiting) is US$7.

To really bring the ruins to life, hire a guide from the excellent **Asociación de Guías Copán** (☎2651-4018; guiascopan@yahoo.com; Archaeological Park US$30, tunnels US$15, Sepulturas US$18) who will approach you when you buy your ticket. Prices are for groups of up to five people.

Copán

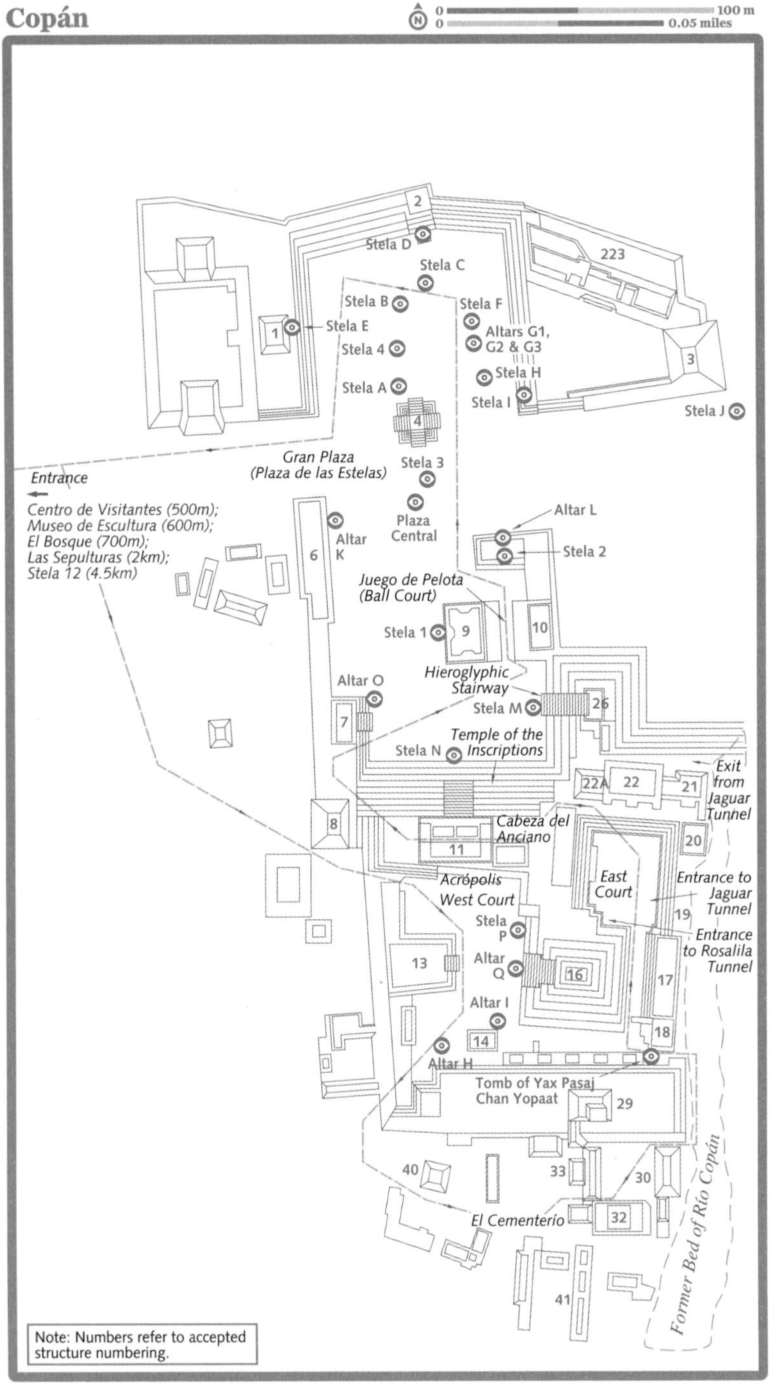
0
100 m
0
0.05 miles
N
2
Stela D
223
Stela C
Stela B
Stela F
1
Stela E
Altars G1, G2 & G3
Stela 4
3
Stela H
Stela A
Stela I
Stela J
4
Gran Plaza (Plaza de las Estelas)
Stela 3
Entrance
Centro de Visitantes (500m); Museo de Escultura (600m); El Bosque (700m); Las Sepulturas (2km); Stela 12 (4.5km)
Plaza Central
Altar L
Altar K
6
Stela 2
Juego de Pelota (Ball Court)
Stela 1
9
10
Hieroglyphic Stairway
Altar O
Stela M
26
7
Temple of the Inscriptions
Stela N
Exit from Jaguar Tunnel
22A
22
21
8
Cabeza del Anciano
11
20
Acrópolis West Court
East Court
Entrance to Jaguar Tunnel
19
Stela P
Entrance to Rosalila Tunnel
13
Altar Q
16
17
Altar I
14
18
Altar H
Tomb of Yax Pasaj Chan Yopaat
29
40
33
30
El Cementerío
32
Former Bed of Río Copán
41
Note: Numbers refer to accepted structure numbering.

Count on 90 minutes to see the main site with a guide, or three to four hours to see the site, tunnels, Las Sepultras and the museum.

Grupo Principal

The Principal Group of ruins is about 400m beyond the visitors center across well-kept lawns, through a gate in a fence and down shady avenues of trees. A group of resident macaws loiter along here and bird houses have been built high in the trees for their nesting. The ruins themselves have been numbered for easy identification and a well-worn path circumscribes the site.

Stelae of the Gran Plaza

The path leads to the **Gran Plaza** (Great Plaza; Plaza de las Estelas) and the huge, intricately carved stelae portraying the rulers of Copán. Most of Copán's best stelae date from AD 613 to 738. All seem to have originally been painted; a few traces of red paint survive on Stela C. Many stelae had vaults beneath or beside them in which sacrifices and offerings could be placed.

Many of the stelae on the Gran Plaza portray King 18 Rabbit, including stelae A, B, C, D, F, H and 4. Perhaps the most beautiful stela in the Gran Plaza is **Stela A** (AD 731); the original has been moved inside the Museo de Escultura, and the one outdoors, like many here, is a reproduction. Nearby and almost equal in beauty are **Stela 4** (AD 731); **Stela B** (AD 731), depicting 18 Rabbit upon his accession to the throne; and **Stela C** (AD 782), with a turtle-shaped altar in front. This last stela has figures on both sides. **Stela E** (AD 614), erected on top of Estructura 1 (Structure 1) on the west side of the Gran Plaza, is among the oldest.

At the northern end of the Gran Plaza at the base of Estructura 2, **Stela D** (AD 736) also portrays King 18 Rabbit. On its back are two columns of hieroglyphs; at its base is an altar with fearsome representations of Chac, the rain god. In front of the altar is the **burial place of Dr John Owen**, an archaeologist with an expedition from Harvard's Peabody Museum who died during excavation work in 1893.

On the east side of the plaza is **Stela F** (AD 721), which has a more lyrical design than other stelae here, with the robes of the main figure flowing around to the other side of the stone, where there are glyphs. **Altar G** (AD 800), showing twin serpent heads, is among the last monuments carved at Copán. **Stela H** (AD 730) may depict a queen or princess rather than a king. **Stela I** (AD 692), on the structure that runs along the east side of the plaza, is of a person wearing a mask. **Stela J** (AD 702), further off to the east, resembles the stelae of Quiriguá in that it is covered in glyphs, not human figures.

Juego de Pelota

South of the Gran Plaza, across what is known as the Plaza Central, is the Juego de Pelota (Ball Court; AD 731), the second largest in Central America. The one you see is the third one on this site; the two smaller courts were buried by this construction. Note the macaw heads carved atop the sloping walls. The central marker in the court is the work of King 18 Rabbit.

Escalinata de los Jeroglificos

South of the Juego de Pelota is Copán's most famous monument, the Escalinata de los Jeroglíficos (Hieroglyphic Stairway; AD 743), the work of King Smoke Shell. Today it's protected from the elements by a canvas roof. The flight of 63 steps bears a history (in several thousand glyphs) of the royal house of Copán; the steps are bordered by ramps inscribed with more reliefs and glyphs. The story told on the inscribed steps is still not completely understood because the stairway was partially ruined and the stones jumbled, but archaeologists are using 3D-scanning technology to make a digital version of the original, with the hope of one day reading it in its entirety.

At the base of the Hieroglyphic Stairway is **Stela M** (AD 756), bearing a figure (probably King Smoke Shell) dressed in a feathered cloak; glyphs tell of the solar eclipse in that year. The altar in front shows a plumed serpent with a human head emerging from its jaws.

Beside the stairway, a tunnel leads to the **tomb of a nobleman**, a royal scribe who may have been the son of King Smoke Imix. The tomb, discovered in June 1989, held a treasure trove of painted pottery and beautiful carved-jade objects that are now in Honduran museums.

Acrópolis

The lofty flight of steps to the south of the Hieroglyphic Stairway mounts the **Templo de las Inscripciones** (Temple of the Inscriptions). On top of the stairway, the walls are carved with groups of hieroglyphs. On the south side of the Temple of the Inscriptions is the **Patio Occidental** (West Court), with the **Patio Oriental** (East Court), also called the **Patio de los Jaguares** (Court of the Jaguars) to its east. In the West Court, check out **Altar Q** (AD 776), among the most famous sculptures here; the original is inside the Museo de Escultura. Around its sides, carved in superb relief, are the 16 great kings of Copán, ending with its creator, Yax Pasaj Chan Yopaat. Behind the altar is a sacrificial vault in which archaeologists discovered the bones of 15 jaguars and several macaws that were probably sacrificed to the glory of Yax Pasaj Chan Yopaat and his ancestors.

This group of temples, known as the Acrópolis, was the spiritual and political core of the site – reserved for royalty and nobles, a place where ceremonies were enacted and kings buried.

The East Court also contains evidence of Yax Pasaj Chan Yopaat – his **tomb**, beneath Estructura 18. Unfortunately, the tomb was discovered and looted long before archaeologists arrived. Both the East and West Courts hold a variety of fascinating stelae and sculptured heads of humans and animals. To see the most elaborate relief carving, climb Estructura 22 on the northern side of the East Court. This was the **Templo de Meditación** (Temple of Meditation) and has been heavily restored over recent years.

Túnel Rosalilia & Túnel de los Jaguares

In 1999 archaeologists opened up the **Túnel Rosalila and Túnel de los Jaguares** (Copan Archaeological Site; US$15; ⏲8am-6pm), which allow visitors to get a glimpse of pre-existing structures below the visible surface structures. The first tunnel, **Rosalila**, is very short and takes only a few visitors at a time. The famous **Temple Rosalila** is only barely exposed, and is behind thick glass. The other tunnel, Los Jaguares, running along the foundations of Temple 22, was originally 700m in length, but a large section has been closed, reducing it to about 80m. This tunnel exits on the outside of the main site, so you must walk around the base and rear of the main site to get back in again. While fascinating, it's hard to justify the additional entry fee.

Museo de Escultura

While Tikal is celebrated for its tall temple pyramids and Palenque is renowned for its limestone relief panels, Copán is unique in the Maya world for its sculpture. Some of the finest examples are on display at this impressive **museum** (Museum of Sculpture; Copan Archaeological Site; US$7; ⏲8am-6pm), which is fully signed in English. Entering the museum is an experience in itself: you go through the mouth of a serpent and wind through the entrails of the beast before suddenly emerging into a fantastic world of sculpture and light.

The highlight of the museum is a full-scale replica of the **Rosalila Temple**, which was discovered in nearly perfect condition by archaeologists in 1989 by means of a tunnel dug into Structure 16, the central building of the Acrópolis. Rosalila, dedicated in AD 571 by Copán's 10th ruler, Moon Jaguar, was apparently so sacred that when Structure 16 was built over it, Rosalila was not destroyed but was left completely intact. The original Rosalila Temple is inside the core of Structure 16.

El Bosque & Las Sepulturas

Excavations at El Bosque and Las Sepulturas have shed light on the daily life of the Maya in Copán during its golden age. Las Sepulturas, once connected to the Gran Plaza by a causeway, may have been the residential area where rich and powerful nobles lived. One huge, luxurious residential compound seems to have housed some 250 people in 40 or 50 buildings arranged around 11 courtyards. The principal structure, called the **Palacio de los Bacabs** (Palace of the Officials), had outer walls carved with the full-sized figures of 10 men in fancy feathered headdresses; inside was a huge hieroglyphic bench. To get to Las Sepulturas you have to go back to the main road, turn right, then right again at the sign (2km from the Gran Plaza).

The walk to get to **El Bosque** is the real reason for visiting it, as it's removed from the main ruins. It's a 5km (one hour) walk on a well-maintained path through foliage dense with birds, though there isn't much of note at the site itself save for a small ball court. Still, it's a powerful experience to have an hour-long walk on the thoroughfares of an ancient Maya city all to yourself. To get to El Bosque, go right at the hut where your ticket is stamped. Be sure to slather on the insect repellent before you set off and it's advised not to go alone.

Getting There & Away

The Copán archaeological site is a kilometer from Copán Ruinas proper and can be walked easily enough. An alternative is to take a *mototaxi* from the town (per person L20). To get between the Archaeological Park and Sepulturas you can walk the two kilometers or hire a *mototaxi* (per person L20 each way).

CARIBBEAN COAST

This is a very different Guatemala – a lush and sultry landscape dotted with palm trees and inhabited by international sailors (around the yachtie haven of Río Dulce and the working port of Puerto Barrios) and one of the country's lesser-known ethnic groups, the Garifuna (around Lívingston).

A boat ride down the Río Dulce is pretty much mandatory for any visit to this region, and many visitors find a few days in Lívingston to be a worthwhile detour. Dedicated naturalists will want to check out the huge wetlands reserves at Bocas del Polochic and Punta de Manabique, which take some effort to get to.

Lago de Izabal

Guatemala's largest lake, to the north of Hwy 9, is starting to earn its place on travelers' itineraries. Most visitors checking out the lake stay at Río Dulce town, by the long, tall bridge where Hwy 13, heading north to Flores and Tikal, crosses the Río Dulce, which empties out of the east end of the lake. Downstream, the beautiful river broadens into a lake called El Golfete before meeting the Caribbean at Lívingston. River trips are a highlight of a visit to eastern Guatemala. If you're looking for lakeside ambience minus the Río Dulce congestion and pace, head to Chapin Abajo, west of Mariscos or El Estor near the west end of the lake, both of which give access to the rich wildlife of the Bocas del Polochic river delta. There are many undiscovered spots in this area waiting to be explored, so don't limit yourself.

Río Dulce

POP 7200

At the east end of the Lago de Izabal, this town still gets referred to as Fronteras – a hangover from the days when the only way across the river was by ferry, and this was the last piece of civilization before embarking on the long, difficult journey into El Petén.

Times have changed. A huge bridge now spans the water and the Petén region's roads are some of the best in the country. The town sees most tourist traffic from yachties – the US Coast Guard says this is the safest place on the western Caribbean for boats during hurricane season. The rest of the foreigners here are either coming or going on the spectacular river trip between here and Lívingston.

Ask around at any of the marinas for the latest on which sailboats are offering charter tours.

Sleeping

There are several places to stay just out of town on the water, which is the best place to be. You can call or radio them and they'll come and pick you up. Among these, Mansión del Río (p213) provides all-inclusive resort-style accommodations for those seeking some pampering downtime.

Hotel Kangaroo HOTEL **$**
(☎5363-6716, in English 4513-9602; www.hotelkangaroo.com; dm Q60, r Q160-180, bungalow Q220-250; @ 📶) On the Río La Colocha, just across the water from El Castillo de San Felipe, this beautiful, simple Australian/Mexican-run place is built on stilts in the mangroves. Its restaurant's beguiling menu (mains Q50 to Q100) features some Aussie classics and probably the best Mexican food you're likely to find outside of Mexico.

The whole place is constructed from wood, with thatched roofs, and windows are mosquito-netted – there's not a pane of glass in sight.

Wildlife is particularly abundant around here, with blue warblers, pelicans, a 2-metre iguana and turtles making the surrounds their home. There's also a bar-restaurant. Drinks on the deck overlooking the river are a great way to start, finish or while away the day. Call from Río Dulce or San Felipe, and it'll arrange a free pick up, even if you're just dropping in for lunch.

Hacienda Tijax HOTEL **$$**
(☎7930-5505; www.tijax.com; s/d from Q339/439, without bathroom Q123/223; P ⊖ ❄ 📶 🏊) This 500-acre hacienda, a two-minute boat ride across the cove from Bruno's (p212), is a special place to stay. Activities include horseback riding, hiking, birdwatching, and walking and canopy tours around the rubber plantation and private nature reserve. Accommodations in lovely little cabins are connected by boardwalks. The pricier ones have kitchens and are well set up for families.

Most cabins face the water and there's a very relaxing pool/bar area. Access is by boat or by a road that turns off the highway

WORTH A TRIP

TURICENTRO EL PARAÍSO

On the north side of the lake, between Río Dulce and El Estor, is **Turicentro El Paraíso** (☎7949-7122, 4069-8095; Q15, parking Q10) in an incredibly beautiful jungle setting. Here, a wide, hot waterfall drops about 12m into a clear, deep pool. You can bathe in the hot water, swim in the cool pool or duck under an overhanging promontory and enjoy a jungle-style sauna.

To reach the waterfall, head north (away from the lake) where the bus drops you off – you pay the admission fee there, from where it's about a 2km walk to the falls.

You can also stay at **Finca El Paraíso** (☎5349-7564; cabins fan/air-con Q390/500; P ⊖ ❄), a collection of simple little cabins located along the lakefront. This place can get rowdy on weekends.

This spot is on the Río Dulce–El Estor bus route, about one hour (Q15) from Río Dulce and 30 minutes (Q10) from El Estor. The last bus in either direction passes at around 4:30pm to 5pm.

about 1km north of the village. The folks here speak Spanish, English and French, and they'll pick you up from across the river.

Bruno's HOTEL **$$**
(☎7930-5721; www.brunoshotel.com; camping per person Q25, dm Q50, s Q100-220, d Q200-500; P ❄ ☜ ≋) A path leads down from the northwest end of the bridge to this riverside hangout for yachties needing to get some land under their feet. The dorms are clean and spacious and the building offers some of the most comfortable rooms in town, with air-con and balconies overlooking the river. It's well set up for families.

Bruno's also serves good breakfasts and gringo comfort food and has a full bar. The restaurant is open 7am to 10pm daily.

Casa Perico HOSTEL **$$**
(☎7930-5666; www.casa-perico.com; dm Q60, s/d without bathroom from Q110/160, cabins Q220; ☜) One of the more low-key options in the area, this place is set on a lovely little inlet about 200m from the main river. Cabins are well built and connected by boardwalks. It offers tours all up and down the river and puts on an à la carte dinner (mains Q40 to Q90).

If you want the one cabin with a bathroom, make sure you book ahead.

El Tortugal BUNGALOW **$$**
(☎7742-8847; www.tortugal.com; r from Q420, bungalow from Q513; ☜) The best-looking bungalows on the river are located here, a five-minute *lancha* (small motorboat) ride south from town. There are a few rooms, too. There are plenty of hammocks, the showers are seriously hot and kayaks are free in the morning for guest use.

Hotel Backpackers HOSTEL **$$**
(☎7930-5168, 7930-5480; www.hotelbackpackers.com; dm Q30-50, r with/without bathroom from Q250/120; @ ☜) Across the bridge from Río Dulce town, this is an old backpacker favorite, set in a rickety, waterside building with basic rooms and dorms. The bar kicks on here at night. Visitors are warned to avoid having food in their backpacks as it may be nibbled at night by rats.

If you're coming by *lancha* (small motorboat) or bus, ask the driver to let you off here to spare yourself the walk across the bridge.

Eating

Most of the hotels in town have restaurants. Bruno's serves good breakfasts and gringo comfort food and has a full bar. Hacienda Tijax (p211) is a popular lunch spot – give it a call and it'll arrange to have you picked up.

★ **Sundog Café** INTERNATIONAL **$**
(☎4999-6972; sandwiches Q50, mains Q35-115; ⊙noon-9pm, bar to 11pm) Down a laneway opposite the Litegua bus office (200m up the main street past the end of the bridge), this open-air riverfront bar-restaurant makes sandwiches and offers a few vegetarian dishes, brick-oven pizzas and fresh juices, as well as great views. It's also the place to come for unbiased information about the area.

Cafe Paris CRÊPES **$**
(☎7930-5038; crepes Q25-55; ⊙7am-9pm) This cafe/hotel offers very tasty coffee and espresso drinks, plus passable French croissants. While its crepes might not quite pass muster at a bistro on the Champs-Élysées, they're a decent respite from the Guatamalan breakfast norm. Wi-fi is spotty.

Orientation

Unless you're staying at Hotel Backpackers, get off the bus on the north side of the bridge. Otherwise, you'll find yourself trudging over what is believed to be the longest bridge in Central America – it's a very hot 3.5km walk.

The main dock is now under the bridge on the opposite side of the main road from Bruno's – you'll see a side road leading down to it.

Information

The local online newspaper **Chisme Vindicator** (www.riodulcechisme.com) has loads of information about Río Dulce.

If you need to change cash or traveler's checks, visit one of the banks in town, all on the main road. **Banco Industrial** (9am-4pm Mon-Fri) has a Visa ATM. There's also a trustworthy Visa/MasterCard ATM inside the **Dispensa Familiar** (CA-13; 8am-8pm) supermarket, also on the main street.

Getting There & Away

BOAT

From the main dock, shared *lanchas* (small motorboats; per person one-way/round trip Q125/250) go down the Río Dulce to Lívingston, usually requiring eight to 10 people. The trip is a beautiful one, making a 'tour' of it, with several stops along the way. Boats usually leave from 9am to about 2pm. There are regular, scheduled departures at 9:30am and 2pm. Pretty much everyone in town can organize a *lancha* service to Lívingston and most other places you'd care to go, but they charge more.

BUS

The **Litegua bus office** (7930-5251; 5am-8pm) is on the north side of the bridge. Seven buses depart for Guatemala City daily (Q80 to Q100).

Minibuses leave for Puerto Barrios (Q25, two hours) when full, near the Litegua bus station.

There's a daily shuttle to Lanquín (Q180, five hours), leaving from in front of the Sundog Café (p212) at 1:30pm.

Minibuses leave for El Estor (Q20, 1½ hours, 7am to 6pm hourly) from the San Felipe and El Estor turnoff in the middle of town.

San Felipe

The small village now known as San Felipe (de Lara, if we want to get technical) was once a fortress and castle, El Castillo de San Felipe. Today the castle is protected as a park and is one of the Lago de Izabal's principal tourist attractions. There's not much else to do here, though the spot is pretty and far quieter than noisy Rio Dulce nearby.

In addition to the fort itself, there are grassy grounds, BBQ and picnic areas, and the opportunity to swim in the lake. The place rocks during the **Feria de San Felipe** (April 30 to May 4).

Sights

El Castillo de San Felipe FORT

(Q25; 8am-5pm) The fortress and castle of San Felipe de Lara, El Castillo de San Felipe, about 3km west of Río Dulce town, was built in 1652 to keep pirates from looting the villages and commercial caravans of Izabal. Though the fortress somewhat deterred the buccaneers, a pirate force captured and burned it in 1686. By the end of the next century, pirates had disappeared from the Caribbean, and the fort's sturdy walls served as a prison.

Sleeping & Eating

There's a surprising range of hotels in the little township around the castle.

A few places to eat are located on the street leading down to the entrance to the castle. All the hotels in town have restaurants, too.

Hotel Don Humberto HOTEL $

(7930-5051; s/d Q48/86;) Near El Castillo, offering basic rooms with big beds and good mosquito netting. It's nothing fancy, but is more than adequate for a cheap sleep.

Hotel Monte Verde HOTEL $$

(4858-5805; hotelrestaurantemv@gmail.com; s/d with fan Q100/180, with air-con Q140/225;) One of the best deals for miles around – generously sized rooms, a huge pool set in a lush garden and an onsite bar-restaurant.

Mansión del Río RESORT $$$

(7930-5020; www.mansiondelrio.com.gt; r Q1455;) For those seeking some downtime and resort-style pampering, this place is the only standard 'resort' in town, with two pools, a Jacuzzi, a restaurant, bar, gym, and somewhat plain rooms with garden or lake views. Dedicated kiddie pools, animal statues and a waterslide make for family fun.

Getting There & Away

San Felipe is on the lakeshore, 3km south of Río Dulce. It's a beautiful 45-minute walk between the two towns, or take a minivan (Q15, every 30 minutes). In Río Dulce it stops on the corner of the highway and road to El Estor; in San Felipe it stops at the entrance to El Castillo.

Boats coming from Lívingston will drop you in San Felipe if you ask. The Río Dulce river tours usually come to El Castillo, allowing you to get out and visit the castle if you like, or you can come over from Río Dulce by private *lancha* (small motorboat).

El Estor

POP 21,100

The major settlement on the northern shore of Lago de Izabal is El Estor, a friendly, quiet town with a lovely setting, which provides an easy jumping-off point for Bocas del Polochic, a highly biodiverse wildlife reserve at the west end of the lake. The town is also a staging post on a possible route between Río Dulce and Lanquín.

Sights

El Boquerón CANYON

(per person Q30) This beautiful, lushly vegetated canyon abutting the tiny Maya settlement of the same name is about 6km east of El Estor. Pay your Q10 entry fee, and for around Q20 per person, villagers will paddle you 15 minutes up the Río Sauce through the canyon, drop you at a small beach – where you can swim and, if you like, scramble up the rocks – and wait or return for you at an agreed time.

Río Dulce–bound buses from El Estor will drop you at El Boquerón (Q10, 15 minutes), as will El Estor–bound buses from Río Dulce.

Sleeping & Eating

There are no upscale hotels here, but there are solid options in the budget and midrange brackets.

Restaurante Típico Chaabil HOTEL $

(7949-7666, 7949-7272; 3a Calle; s/d Q75/150; P) Although they go a bit heavy on the log-cabin feel, the rooms at this place, at the west end of the street, are the best deal in town. Get one upstairs for plenty of light and good views. The restaurant here, on a lovely lakeside terrace, cooks up delicious food, such as *tapado* (Garifuna casserole).

The water here is crystal clear and you can swim right off the hotel's dock.

Hotel Vista al Lago HOTEL $$

(7949-7205, 7949-7658; 6a Av 1-13; s/d/tr Q150/225/300) Set in a classic historic building down on the waterfront, this place has plenty of style, although the rooms themselves are fairly ordinary. Views 'of the world's largest swimming pool,' from the upstairs balcony are superb. Rooms with fans have negotiable prices, always lower than those with air-con.

Hotel Villela HOTEL $$

(4930-5043; 6a Av 2-06; s/d/tr Q130/255/380; P) The rooms are less attractive than the neat lawn and trees they're set around, but some are airier and brighter than others. All have fan and bathroom. Significant discounts in the off season.

Gardenia's Café MEXICAN $

(5359-2694; 4a Calle, Barrio El Centro, Zona 1; mains Q25-60; 9am-9:30pm) A simple, no frills (except the parquet floor) kind of place, serving a variety of tasty Mexican dishes as well as hot dogs, sandwiches and the like. Coffee and espresso are options, too.

Information

Banrural (cnr 3a Calle & 5a Av; 8:30am-5pm Mon-Fri, 9am-1pm Sat) Changes US dollars and Amex traveler's checks and has an ATM.

Getting There & Away

El Estor is most easily reached from Río Dulce via a new paved road. Combis cost Q20 and run between 5am and 7pm.

You can get to Lanquín by taking the truck that leaves El Estor's Parque Central at 10:30am for Cahabón (Q40, four to five hours), and then a bus or pick-up straight on from Cahabón to Lanquín the same day. Coming the other way involves changing in Cahabón, sometimes meaning an overnight there.

Refugio Bocas del Polochic & Reserva de Biosfera Sierra de las Minas

The Refugio de Vida Silvestre Bocas del Polochic (Bocas del Polochic Wildlife Reserve) covers the delta of the Río Polochic, which provides most of Lago de Izabal's water. A visit here affords great birdwatching and howler-monkey observation. The reserve supports more than 300 species of birds – the migration seasons, September to October and April to May, are reportedly fantastic – and many varieties of butterflies and fish. You may well see alligators and, if you're lucky, glimpse a manatee. Ask in El Estor for boat guides. The reserve is managed by the **Fundación Defensores de la Naturaleza** (3011-7575, 7949-7237; https://defensores.org.gt; cnr 5a Av & 2a Calle; varies), whose research station, the Estación Científica Selempim, just to the south in

Reserva de Biosfera Sierra de las Minas, is open for ecotourism visits. Contact Defensores' El Estor office for bookings and further information.

To explore the reserves, you can use canoes free of charge, take boat trips (Q250 to Q400) or walk any of the three well-established trails.

Sleeping & Eating

There's no restaurant, but you can bring food and use the kitchen at Estación Científica.

Estación Científica Selempim CABIN, CAMPGROUND $
(☎3011-7507; https://defensores.org.gt; camping/dm per person Q20/50) Accommodations are available in a rustic wood-and-thatch cabin or in the campground. Note that the facility itself does not have any contact info. All arrangements must be made either through the website or by contacting staff at Fundación Defensores de la Naturaleza in El Estor.

Getting There & Away

You can get to the Estación Científica Selempim by special hire (Q600 for a boatload of up to 12 people).

Puerto Barrios

POP 117,000

Port towns have always had a reputation for being slightly dodgy, and those acting as international borders doubly so. Puerto Barrios has an edgy feel; for foreign visitors, it's mainly a jumping-off point for boats to Punta Gorda (Belize) or Lívingston, and you probably won't be hanging around.

The town's favorite landmark and monument is **El Muñecón** (intersection 8a Av, 14a Calle & Calz Justo Rufino Barrios), a statue of a dockworker.

Sleeping

Mostly used as a one-night stopover, Puerto Barrios has a range of decent but unexciting hotels.

Hotel Ensenada HOTEL $
(☎7948-0861; hotelensenadapuertobarrios@hotmail.com; 4a Av btwn Calles 10a & 11a; s/d Q120/180; P ⊖ ❄) Offers tidy little rooms with good bathrooms and OK beds. Get one upstairs to catch a breeze.

Hotel Lee HOTEL $
(☎7948-0830; 5a Av btwn Calles 9a & 10a; s/d with fan Q57/100, d with air-con Q180; P ⊖ ❄ ☎) This is a friendly, family-owned place, close to the bus terminals. Typical of Puerto Barrios' budget hotels, it offers straightforward, vaguely clean rooms. The little balcony out front catches the odd breeze.

Puerto Bello HOTEL $$
(☎7948-0525; 8a Av btwn Calles 18 & 19; s/d Q255/440; P ⊖ ❄ @ ☎ ≋) By far the best-looking hotel in town, marred only by its slightly out-of-the-way location. The rooms are spacious and modern and the lovely garden and pool (with waterslide!) area is a blessing year-round.

Hotel del Norte HOTEL $$
(☎7948-0087; cnr 7a Calle & 1a Av; s/d with fan Q90/160, with air-con Q165/280; P ❄ @ ☎ ≋) A classically tropical wooden building with mosquito-screened corridors, the century-old Hotel del Norte is in a class by itself. Its weathered and warped frame is redolent of history, and the floorboards go off at crazy angles. Pick a room carefully – some are little more than a wooden box; others have great ocean views and catch good breezes.

Rooms with air-conditioning are in the newer, less atmospheric building, but are still an excellent deal. There's a swimming pool beside the sea.

Hotel El Reformador HOTEL $$
(☎7948-0533; www.hotelelreformador.com; cnr 7a Av & 16a Calle; s/d breakfast incl with fan Q150/250, with air-con Q180/320; P ⊖ ❄ ☎) Like a little haven away from the hot busy streets outside, El Reformador offers big, cool rooms set around leafy patios. Air-con rooms lead onto wide interior balconies. There is a restaurant here. Breakfast is included.

Hotel Europa HOTEL $$
(☎7948-1292; 3a Av btwn Calles 11a & 12a; s/d with fan Q87/170, with air-con Q145/290; P ⊖ ❄ ☎) Near the public dock and thus convenient, this spot has clean rooms with TV, arranged around a parking courtyard, but check that the rate you're given isn't higher than the prices the hotel lists in the lobby.

Eating

The eating scene in Puerto Barrios is surprisingly varied, and most restaurants are within easy walking distance of where you're likely to be staying.

Kaffa CAFE $

(☎7942-9175; 8a Av btwn Calles 7a & 8a; sandwiches & breakfast Q25-40; ⊙8am-9:30pm Tue-Sun) A hip coffee shop in Puerto Barrios? Who would have guessed! The coffee and the breezy deck overlooking the park are both excellent.

★ **Restaurante Safari** SEAFOOD $$

(☎7948-0563; cnr 1a Calle & 5a Av; seafood Q45-125; ⊙10am-9pm; P) The town's most enjoyable restaurant is on a thatch-roofed, open-air platform right over the water about 1km north of the town center. Locals and visitors alike love to eat and catch the sea breezes here. Excellent seafood of all kinds, including the specialty *tapado* – that great Garifuna soup (Q110).

Chicken and meat dishes are less expensive than seafood. If the Safari is full, the Cangrejo Azul next door offers pretty much the same deal, in a more relaxed environment.

La Habana Vieja CUBAN $$

(13 Calle btwn Avs 6a & 7a; mains Q60-125; ⊙11am-1pm) A good, wide selection of Cuban classics (including *ropa vieja* – a shredded beef stew) and some straightforward sandwiches. Also has a good bar if you're looking for a quiet drink.

Restaurante Morano Calabro MEDITERRANEAN $$

(☎7947-2278; 4a Av & 19a Calle; mains Q80-160; ⊙11am-9pm Tue-Sun) Located right on the water. The nearby mangrove trees and views are lovely. Service is friendly, but the food is slow to arrive, and the menu is mainly so-so pizzas with a few other options.

Orientation

Because of its spacious layout, you must walk or ride further in Puerto Barrios to get from place to place. For instance, it's 800m from the bus terminals by the market in the town center to the Muelle Municipal at the end of 12a Calle, from which passenger boats depart. Very few businesses use street numbers – most just label which street it's on, and the cross streets it's in between.

Information

Immigration Office (cnr 12a Calle & 3a Av; ⊙7am-6pm) A block from the Muelle Municipal. Come here for your entry or exit stamp if you're arriving from or leaving for Belize. If you're leaving by sea, there is a Q80 departure tax to pay. If you are heading to Honduras, you can get your exit stamp at another immigration office on the road to the border at Corinto.

GETTING TO HONDURAS

Minibuses leave for the Honduran frontier (Q30, 1½ hours) every 20 minutes from 5am to 5pm, from 6a Av outside the market in Puerto Barrios. They stop en route to the border at Guatemalan immigration, where you may be required to pay Q10 for an exit stamp. Honduran entry formalities will leave you around L60 lighter.

One semi-express minibus per day departs at 7am (Q75), from the Muelle Municipal (city dock).

Banco Industrial (7a Av; ⊙9am-6pm Mon-Fri, to 1pm Sat) Changes US dollars and traveler's checks, and has an ATM.

Getting There & Away

BOAT

Boats depart from the Muelle Municipal (city dock) at the end of 12a Calle.

Regular *lanchas* (small motorboats) depart for Lívingston (Q35, 30 minutes, eight daily) between 5:30am and 5:30pm. Buy your ticket as early as you can on the day (you can't book before your day of departure) – spaces are limited and sometimes sell out.

Outside these regular times, *lanchas* depart whenever they have six people ready to go and cost Q50 per person.

Most of the movement from Lívingston to Puerto Barrios is in the morning, returning in the afternoon. From Lívingston, your last chance of the day may be the 5pm *lancha*, especially during the low season when fewer travelers are shuttling back and forth.

Lanchas also depart from the Muelle Municipal three times daily for Punta Gorda in Belize (Q200, one hour) at 10am, 1pm, and 2pm. The 10am departure arrives in time for the noon bus from Punta Gorda to Belize City. Tickets are sold at the dock. Before boarding you also need to get your exit stamp at the nearby immigration office and pay Q80 in departure tax (US$10).

If you want to leave a car in Puerto Barrios while you visit Lívingston for a day or two, there are plenty of *parqueos* (parking lots) around the dock area that charge around Q50 per 24 hours. Many of the hotels offer this service, too.

BUS

Minibuses for Chiquimula & Río Dulce (cnr 6a Av & 9a Calle) Buses to Chiquimula (Q45, 4½ hours), also via Quiriguá, leave every half hour from 3am to 4pm. Minibuses to Río Dulce (Q25, two hours) leave from the same location.

Transportes Litegua (☎7948-1172; cnr 6a Av & 9a Calle) Frequent services to Guatemala City (Q100 to Q150, five to six hours), via Quiriguá and Río Hondo. *Directo* services avoid a half-hour detour into Morales.

Lívingston

POP 7000

Lívingston is unlike anywhere else in Guatemala. Its Garifuna people, their colors, culture, rhythms, flavors, and disposition, are the best reason to visit – nowhere else in Guatemala will you find such a friendly, fun and relaxed vibe. But it's not just the people: good beaches are nearby and the slow-and-easy take on life is enchanting. Here boats lie derelict in picturesque decay; people paddleboard or kayak lazily amid refreshing ocean breezes; and pelicans soar overhead as happy hour starts in late afternoon. It's just lovely.

Though the town is most easily and cheaply visited from nearby Puerto Barrios, the approach along the Río Dulce is worth the extra time: it's so wild it was used as the location for the television series *The New Adventures of Tarzan*. The river's mist-shrouded cliffs, thick jungle, jade-colored water (which hides numerous manatees) make arriving in this quirky Caribbean town all the more memorable.

Sights

Beaches in Lívingston itself are disappointing, as buildings or vegetation come right down to the water's edge in most places. Those beaches that do exist are often contaminated; however, there are better beaches within a few kilometers to the northwest. You can reach Playa Quehueche near the mouth of the Río Quehueche by taxi (Q30) in about 10 minutes. The best beach in the area is **Playa Blanca** (Q20), around 12km from Lívingston. This is privately owned and you need a boat to get there.

Los Siete Altares WATERFALL

(The Seven Altars; Q20) About 5km (1½ hour walk) northwest of Lívingston along the shore of Bahía de Amatique is Los Siete Altares, a series of freshwater falls and pools. It's a pleasant goal for a beach walk and is a good place for a picnic and swim. Food here costs Q70 to Q80, drinks Q10 to Q20.

Follow the shore northward to the river mouth and walk along the beach until it meets the path into the woods (about 30 minutes). Follow this path all the way to the falls. Boat trips go to Los Siete Altares, but if you're a walker it's better to go by foot to experience the natural beauty and the Garifuna people along the way. About halfway along, just past the rope bridge, is Hotel Salvador Gaviota (p219), serving decent food and ice-cold beers and soft drinks. You can stay out here, too.

Rasta Mesa CULTURAL CENTRE

(☎4459-6106; www.rastamesa.com; Barrio Nevago; ⏲9am-2pm, cooking class 6pm) This is a friendly, informal, enthusiastic cultural center where you can drop in for classes in Garifuna cooking (per person Q125, fish stew Q150), drumming (per person Q125) and dancing (Q125), or even get a massage (from Q250). It also offers volunteering opportunities.

Tours

A few outfits in Lívingston offer tours that let you get out and experience the natural wonders of the area. Happy Fish Travel (p222) is one of the standbys, but you can get excellent information and arrange tours with your hotel or hostel, and in some cases, they're more reliable.

The popular ecological tour/jungle trip (Q70) takes you for a walk through town, out west up to a lookout spot and on to the Río Quehueche, where you take a half-hour canoe trip down the river to Playa Quehueche. Then you walk through the jungle to Los Siete Altares, hang out there for a while, then walk back down the beach to Lívingston. This is a great way to see the area, and the friendly local guides can also give you a good introduction to the Garifuna people who live here.

The Playa Blanca tour goes by boat first to Los Siete Altares and then on to Playa Blanca, the best beach in the area, for two or three hours. This trip goes with a minimum of two people and costs Q100 per person.

Happy Fish (p222) offers a return boat trip (Q220) just along the canyon section of Río Dulce (the most interesting and picturesque part), which gives you more time to enjoy the trails, birdwatching and so on than the 'tour' given on the public *lanchas* (small motorboats). It also runs tours to **Cueva del Tigre**, a community-run tourism project 8km from Lívingston (Q175 for a tour, or staff will tell you how to get there on your own).

Also popular are day/overnight trips to the **Cayos Sapodillas** (or Zapotillas), well

Lívingston

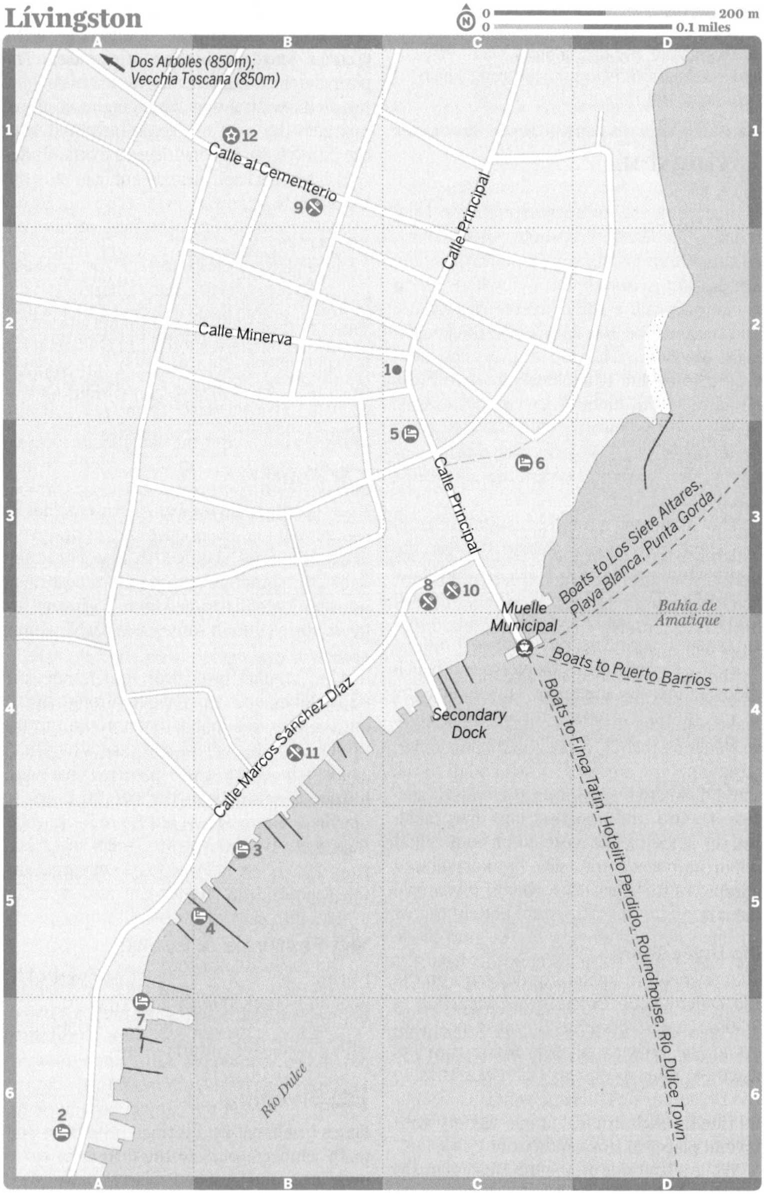

0 200 m
0 0.1 miles
Dos Arboles (850m); Vecchia Toscana (850m)
12
Calle al Cementerio
9
Calle Principal
Calle Minerva
1
5
6
Calle Principal
8
10
Muelle Municipal
Boats to Los Siete Altares, Playa Blanca, Punta Gorda
Bahía de Amatique
Boats to Puerto Barrios
Secondary Dock
Calle Marcos Sánchez Díaz
11
Boats to Finca Tatin, Hotelito Perdido, Roundhouse, Río Dulce Town
3
4
7
Río Dulce
2

off the coast of southern Belize, where there is great snorkeling (Q560/1200 for one/two days). A minimum of eight people is required and exit taxes and national-park fees (US$30 in total) are separate.

Manatee Tours WILDLIFE WATCHING

(☎5807-4474; 1-5 people for 3hr Q500) Captain Daniel Bó Dardón does private tours at reasonable prices to any of the local sights and attractions. He can bring you to Playa Blanca, Puerto Barrios, or up into the Rio Dulce.

Lívingston

Activities, Courses & Tours

One of his best tours is manatee watching, which leaves early in the morning and goes up the river into the lagoon. Along the way, you'll see egrets, herons, jacaras and other birds. If you're lucky (luck is required!), manatees will surface close by.

Manatees, despite their size, are not like whales: they don't breach, and they don't make sounding dives with flukes that wave, so watching them is more about being quiet, observant, and creeping close enough to see some distinctive ripples on the water's surface. The tip of a manatee's nose may be all you see in the turbid water. But it's a thrilling opportunity for anyone who has longed for a glimpse of the elusive sea cow in its natural habitat.

Río Dulce Tours

Tour agencies in town offer day trips up the Río Dulce to Río Dulce town (departing at 9:30am and 2:30pm), as do most local sailors at the Lívingston dock. Many travelers use these tours as one-way transportation to Río Dulce, paying Q125 one-way. It's a beautiful ride through tropical jungle scenery, with several places to stop on the way.

While a boat ride on the Río Dulce is not to be missed, if you're coming from Guatemala City or Puerto Barrios it makes much more sense to catch a boat from Puerto Barrios to Lívingston and do the tour on your way out.

Shortly after you leave Lívingston, you pass the tributary Río Tatin on the right, then will probably stop at an **indigenous arts museum** set up by **Asociación Ak' Tenamit** (☎5908-3392; www.aktenamit.org), an NGO working to improve conditions for the Q'eqchi' Maya population of the area. The river enters a gorge called **La Cueva de la Vaca**, its walls hung with great tangles of jungle foliage and the humid air noisy with the cries of tropical birds. Just beyond that is **La Pintada**, a rock escarpment covered with graffiti. Further on, a **thermal spring** forces sulfurous water out of the base of the cliff, providing a chance for a warm swim. The river widens into **El Golfete**, a lakelike body of water that presages the even more vast expanse of Lago de Izabal further upstream.

On the northern shore of El Golfete is the **Biotopo Chocón Machacas**, a troubled 72-sq-km reserve established within the Parque Nacional Río Dulce to protect the beautiful river landscape, the valuable forests and mangrove swamps and their wildlife, which includes such rare creatures as the tapir and above all the manatee. A network of 'water trails' (boat routes around several jungle lagoons) provides ways to see other bird, animal and plant life of the reserve. You can stay here, at the community-run lodge Q'ana Itz'am in **Lagunita Salvador**, but you will have to arrange transportation separately.

Boats will probably visit **Islas de Pájaros**, a pair of islands where thousands of waterbirds live, in the middle of El Golfete. From El Golfete you continue upriver, passing increasing numbers of expensive villas and boathouses, to the town of Río Dulce, where the soaring Hwy 13 road bridge crosses the river, and on to El Castillo de San Felipe on Lago de Izabal. You can also do this trip starting from Río Dulce.

Festivals & Events

During **Semana Santa** (Easter week) Lívingston is packed with merrymakers. **Garifuna National Day** (Nov 26) is celebrated with a variety of cultural events.

Sleeping

Prices in Lívingston hit their peak from July to December – outside these months many midrange and top-end places halve their rates.

Lívingston Town

Hotel Salvador Gaviota BUNGALOW $
(☎7947-0874; www.hotelsalvadorgaviota.com; Playa Quehueche; r per person with bathroom & air-con Q550, without air-con & bathroom Q80-250; @)

CATCH THE RHYTHM OF THE GARIFUNA

Lívingston is the heartland of Guatemala's Garifuna community, and it won't take too long before you hear some of their distinctive music. A Garifuna band generally consists of three drums (the *primera* takes the bass part, the other two play more melodic functions), a shaker or maraca, a turtle shell (hit like a cowbell) and a conch shell (blown like a flute).

The lyrics are often call and response – most often sung in Garifuna (a language with influences from Arawak, French and West African languages) but sometimes in Spanish. Most songs deal with themes from village life – planting time, harvests, things that happen in the village, honoring the dead and folktales of bad sons made good. Sometimes they simply sing about the beauty of the village.

Traditional Garifuna music has given birth to an almost bewildering array of musical styles, among them Punta Rock, *jugujugu, calachumba, jajankanu, chumba, saranda, sambé* and *parranda*.

Punta Rock is by far the most widely known adaptation of traditional Garifuna rhythms, and you can hear 'Punta' in most discos throughout Central America. The dance that accompanies it (also called *punta*) is a frenzied sort of affair, following the nature of the percussion. The left foot swivels back and forth while the right foot taps out the rhythm. Perhaps coincidentally, this movement causes the hips to shake wildly, leading some observers to comment on the sexual nature of the dance.

If you're interested in learning more about Garifuna culture or want drumming lessons, drop in to Rasta Mesa (p217).

Beautiful simple wood and bamboo rooms set back 200m from a reasonably clean beach. Day-trippers going to and from Los Siete Altares (p217) drop in for meals (Q50 to Q100) and drinks here – otherwise you may have the place to yourself.

It's 500m from the swing bridge where the road ends – a *tuk-tuk* will charge about Q5 to get you there, a taxi Q10.

Casa de la Iguana HOSTEL **$**
(☎7947-0064; www.casadelaiguana.com; Calle Marcos Sánchez Díaz; hammocks/dm Q25/50, cabins with/without bathroom Q200/120;) A five-minute walk from the main dock, this happy-to-admit-it party hostel offers good-value cabins, camping and hammocks. The cabins are wooden affairs, with simple decoration. Happy hour here leads, hours later, to beer pong…which comes with a roulette wheel of fates that befall the losers: most involve drunkenness, nudity, or a combination. So don't come planning on going to sleep at nine.

★ **Casa Rosada** HOSTEL **$$**
(☎7947-0303; www.restaurantcasarosada.com; Calle Marco Sánchez Días; dm/bungalow Q80/200;) Casa Rosada is a one-stop spot that manages somehow to do it all, and do it well. The owner, Ismael, is a wealth of knowledge about the area and can arrange tours, set up performances and offer advice or suggestions, as well as handle issues that come up. Bungalows (all with clean shared bathrooms) are delightful, as is the food.

You need to order up to two hours early to have dinner, but the restaurant is open the rest of the day for walk-ins, and has great coffee, good breakfasts and tasty margaritas. The dock and hammocks make it easy to jump on boats or just lounge the day away.

★ **Casa Nostra** BOUTIQUE HOTEL **$$**
(☎7947-0842; www.livingstoncasanostra.com; Calle Marcos Sánchez Díaz; d without bathroom Q200, ste Q450;) A lovely spot right on the water with (on a good day) views of Honduras from the upper floor, the Casa Nostra is a place that feels like home. Owner Stuart makes incredible food, the staff are friendly, the spot exudes just the right balance of casualness and style. Pick-ups and drop-offs are available from the dock.

Dos Arboles HOSTEL **$$**
(☎7947-0530; www.dosarbolesguate.com; dm/r/bungalow Q85/250/350;) A relative newcomer in what was the Vecchia Toscana, Dos Arboles is a fun, hip hostel and more, with live-music shows, a lovely pool with hummingbirds, and experienced owners who know what makes a place tick. Any closer to the water and you'll be wading. Good mosquito nets mean that you'll actually get some sleep here, too.

Hotel Ríos Tropicales HOTEL $$

(☎7947-0158; Calle Principal; s/d/tr 100/200/300; ⊖ 📶) The Ríos Tropicales has a variety of big, well-screened rooms facing a central patio with plenty of hammocks and chill-out space in the 2nd-floor lounge. Rooms have private bathrooms but no air-con.

Posada El Delfín HOTEL $$$

(☎7947-0056; www.posadaeldelfin.com; Calle Marcos Sánchez Díaz; s/d from Q580/760; ⊖ ❄ 📶 🏊) Down by the waterfront, this is a big modern construction with reasonably sized, spotless rooms and a great swimming pool overlooking the river. Don't expect views from your room – the (recommended) 2nd-floor restaurant steals them all.

Hotel Villa Caribe HOTEL $$$

(☎7947-0072; www.villasdeguatemala.com; Calle Principal; s/d/bungalow Q788/927/1064; P ⊖ ❄ 📶 🏊) The 45-room Villa Caribe is a luxurious anomaly among Lívingston's laid-back, low-priced lodgings. Modern but still Caribbean in style, it has many conveniences and comforts, including extensive tropical gardens, a restaurant, a big swimming pool and two bars, one (appropriately) next to the pool.

Rooms are fan-cooled with modern bathrooms; little balconies overlook the gardens and river mouth. The bungalows are air-conditioned.

Around Lívingston

Lanchas traveling between Río Dulce and Lívingston (or vice versa) will drop you at the Roundhouse, Finca Tatin or Hotelito Perdido. These places can also pick you up, charging around Q40 per person from Lívingston, more from Puerto Barrios or Río Dulce.

Roundhouse HOSTEL $

(☎4294-9730; www.roundhouseguatemala.com; dm/d without bathroom Q50/120) This medium-sized hostel, 20 minutes by boat from Lívingston, has a 1st floor with a pleasant riverfront bar/restaurant/hammock area. On the 2nd floor there's a spacious dorm and some good, simple private rooms.

Snorkeling and sailing tours are usually on offer, and there's a launch service to Lívingston (Q40) at 12:30pm and 4pm.

Finca Tatin BUNGALOW $$

(☎4148-3332; www.fincatatin.com; dm/s/d Q60/250/300, s/d without bathroom Q80/150; 📶) Experience the forest at this rustic B&B at the confluence of Ríos Dulce and Tatin, 10km from Lívingston. Four-hour guided walks and kayak trips, some visiting local Q'eqchi' villages, are offered. Accommodations are in funky wood-and-thatch cabins scattered through the jungle and spiffy riverfront cabins (double Q350 to Q400, depending on room layout and beds) with balconies overlooking the water.

There are trails, waterfalls and endless river tributaries that you can explore with one of the *cayucos* (indigenous fishing dugouts) available for guest use (per day Q80). Guided night walks through the jungle offer views of elusive nightlife, and cave tours are good for swimming and soaking in a natural sauna. You can walk to Lívingston from here in about four hours or take your kayak. Alternatively, staff from Finca Tatin will come pick you up. A temescal sauna is a new addition for those needing a good purifying sweat.

Hotelito Perdido HOTEL $$

(☎5725-1576; www.hotelitoperdido.com; dm Q70, s/d bungalow Q200/250, without bathroom Q150/200; 📶) This beautiful, secluded hideout is a five-minute boat ride from Finca Tatin. The ambience is superb – relaxed and friendly. The whole place is solar powered and constructed in such a way as to cause minimal impact on the environment.

The two-story bungalows are gorgeous: simple yet well decorated, with a sleeping area upstairs and a small sitting area downstairs. It's a small, intimate place, so it's a good idea to book ahead. You can organize many of the activities available at Finca Tatin from here as well.

Eating

Food here is relatively expensive because most of it must be brought in by boat. There's fine seafood, though, and some unusual flavors for Guatemala, including coconut and curry. *Tapado,* a rich stew made from fish, shellfish, and coconut milk, spiced with coriander, is the delicious local specialty.

Open-air eateries dot Calle Principal, and many hotels' restaurants are also delicious.

Mama Norma GARIFUNA $

(plate Q20; ⏲noon-midnight) This simple eatery run by a town matron is your best spot for cheap eats, with a big plate of rice, beans, tortillas, and main (such as chicken, beef, or pork) costing only Q20.

★**Restaurante Buga Mama** SEAFOOD $$

(☎7947-0198; Calle Marcos Sánchez Díaz; mains Q70-120; ⏲6am-9pm Tue-Sun; 📶) This place enjoys the best location of any restaurant in town, and profits go to the Asociación Ak' Tenamit (p219), an NGO with several projects in the area. There's a wide range of seafood, homemade pasta, curries and other dishes on the menu, including a very good *tapado* (fish stew; Q110).

Most of the waiters here are trainees in a community sustainable-tourism scheme, so be forgiving if the service is lacking.

Margoth GARIFUNA **$$**
(☎7947-0019; Calle al Cementerio; mains Q65-100; ⏲8am-9:30pm) A clean spot with polished wood decor, Margoth is a decent place with a decent selection at decent prices. The mix of mains runs the gamut from burgers to pasta, but there's even chow mein and some Garifuna options as well.

Restaurante Gaby GUATEMALAN **$$**
(☎7947-0858; Calle Marcos Sánchez Díaz; mains Q35-180; ⏲7am-9pm) For a good honest feed in humble surrounds, you can't go past Gaby's. She serves up the good stuff: lobster, *tapado* (Q80), rice and beans, and good breakfasts at good prices. The *telenovelas* (soap operas) come free.

Happy Fish SEAFOOD **$$**
(☎7947-0661; www.happyfishtravel.com; Calle Principal; mains Q75-165; ⏲7am-10pm; 📶) One of the bustling main-street spots, Happy Fish will try to sell you tours as well as something to eat. There's a slick, marketed, inauthentic feel, but the spot remains popular. The requisite *tapado* (Q100) is here, plus a good range of other options.

Drinking & Nightlife

A handful of bars down on the beach to the left of the end of Calle Principal pulls in travelers and locals at night. It's very dark down here, so take care. Music ranges from *punta* (a Garifuna dance) to salsa, merengue, even electronica. Saturday is the party night.

Happy hour is an institution. Every restaurant has discounts on something.

Adventurous drinkers should try *guifiti*, a local concoction made from coconut rum, often infused with herbs. It's said to have medicinal properties.

Entertainment

You may get lucky and find a roaming band playing songs for diners along the Calle Principal around dinnertime. If you like the music, make sure to sling them a few bucks. Several places around town have live Garifuna music, although this tends to happen only once or twice a week. Currently it's Thursdays and Sundays, but this may change.

Café-Bar Ubafu LIVE MUSIC
(☎5469-1785; Calle al Cementerio; ⏲8am-11pm) Probably the most dependable nightlife option in town; it's liveliest on weekends.

Information

For more on Lívingston, check out its community website (www.livingston.com.gt).

Lívingston has a few hustlers who are famous for asking you for money 'to fund a Garifuna school or orphanage,' which they quickly pocket. Sometimes this involves a visit to a 'school, destroyed by hurricane', which is really just a derelict house. Don't be sucked in.

Use mosquito repellent, especially if you go out into the jungle; mosquitoes here carry both malaria and dengue fever.

Banrural (Calle Principal; ⏲9am-5pm Mon-Fri, to 1pm Sat) Changes US dollars and traveler's checks, and has an ATM.

Immigration Office (Calle Principal; ⏲6am-7pm) Issues entry and exit stamps for travelers arriving direct from or going direct to Belize or Honduras, charging Q80 for exit stamps. Crossing in via Corinto (Honduras) is Q30. Outside business hours, you can knock for attention at any time.

Getting There & Away

Frequent boats come downriver from Río Dulce and across the bay from Puerto Barrios. There are also international boats from Honduras and Belize.

Those coming from Guatemala City or Antigua will likely want to take a Litegua express bus to Puerto Barrios (Q125), then take a boat to Lívingston (Q35), which is the cheapest and fastest way to arrive.

Happy Fish (☎7947-0661; www.happyfishtravel.com; Calle Principal, Happy Fish restaurant; ⏲7am-10pm) operates combined boat and bus shuttles to the Honduran city of La Ceiba (the cheapest gateway to Honduras' Bay Islands) for around Q550 per person, with a minimum of four people. Leaving Lívingston at 6am or earlier will get you to La Ceiba in time for the boat to the islands, making it a one-day trip, which is nearly impossible to do independently.

There's also a boat that goes direct to Punta Gorda (Belize) daily at 7am (Q250, 1½ hours), leaving from the **public dock**. In Punta Gorda, the boat connects with a bus to Placencia and Belize City. The boat waits for this bus to arrive from Placencia before it sets off back for Lívingston from Punta Gorda at about 10:30am.

If you are taking one of these early international departures, get your exit stamp from immigration in Lívingston the day before.

El Petén

Includes ➡

Best Places to Eat

- Las Orquídeas (p244)
- Terrazzo (p236)
- Mon Ami (p244)
- Maple y Tocino (p235)
- Antojitos Mexicanos (p236)
- Finca Ixobel (p230)

Best Places to Stay

- Finca Ixobel (p230)
- Private Reserve Ni'tun (p241)
- Chiminos Island Lodge (p231)
- Estación Biológica Las Guacamayas (p258)
- Alice Guesthouse (p243)

Why Go?

Vast, sparsely populated and jungle-covered, Guatemala's largest and northernmost department is a wonderland of exploration. Whether it's the mysteries of the Classic Maya, the bounty of the jungle, or the chance to lounge lakeside that inspires you, it's all here in abundance. How deeply you choose to delve into the Maya legacy will depend on your willingness to get your feet muddy. The towering temples of Tikal can be reached by tour from just about anywhere, while more remote sites such as El Mirador and Piedras Negras require days of planning and further days of jungle trekking. The Reserva de Biósfera Maya (Maya Biosphere Reserve) covers virtually the entire northern third of El Petén, and together with its counterparts in Mexico and Belize forms a multinational wildlife haven that spans more than 30,000 sq km.

When to Go

El Petén

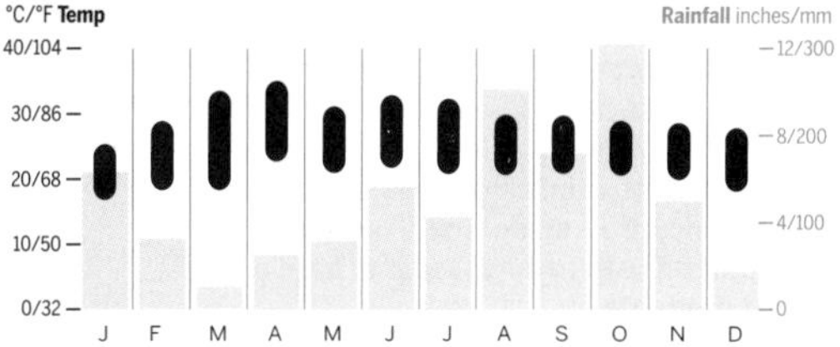

Feb–May Drier, less boggy, less mud, though May gets humid.

Jun–Aug Rainy season. Cooler but bring bug spray (and a mosquito net) for any outdoor activities.

Dec–Feb Cool nights and mornings, with temperatures moderate during the day.

El Petén Highlights

1. **Tikal** (p245) Exploring this vast ancient city at sunset, sunrise, or any time in between.
2. **El Mirador** (p259) Trekking through the jungle to this huge, though still scarcely excavated, Maya ruin.
3. **Laguna Petexbatún** (p230) Awakening to the sound of howler monkeys and herons in this idyllic reserve.
4. **Crater Azul** (p228) Swimming in pristine spring-fed waters that are unbelievably clear and making the birdlife-filled trip to get here.
5. **Flores** (p231) Lounging lakeside over evening cocktails on the *malecón* of this picturesque island town.
6. **Yaxhá** (p255) Viewing the lagoons from its highest pyramid is hard to beat.
7. **Finca Ixobel** (p230) Breaking bread with fellow travelers at this rural retreat.
8. **Aguateca** (p228) Going up a tributary of the Río de la Pasión to this remote riverside ruin defended by steep cliffs.

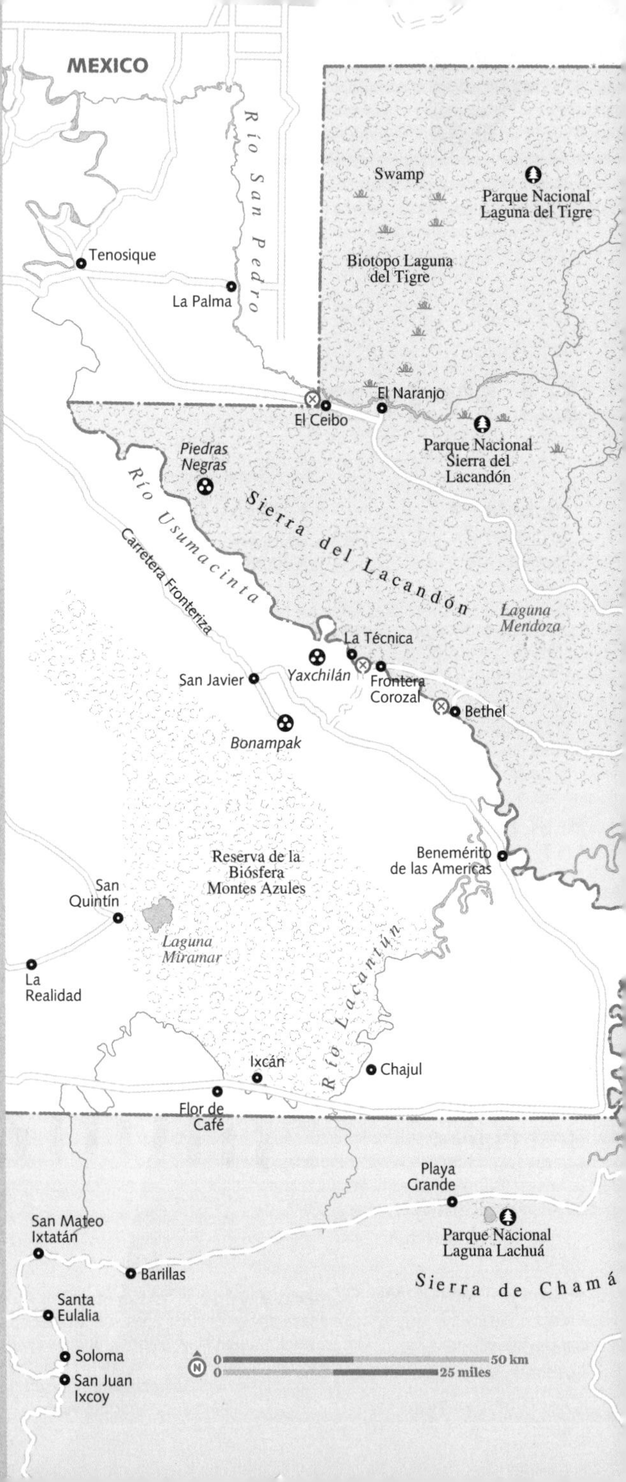

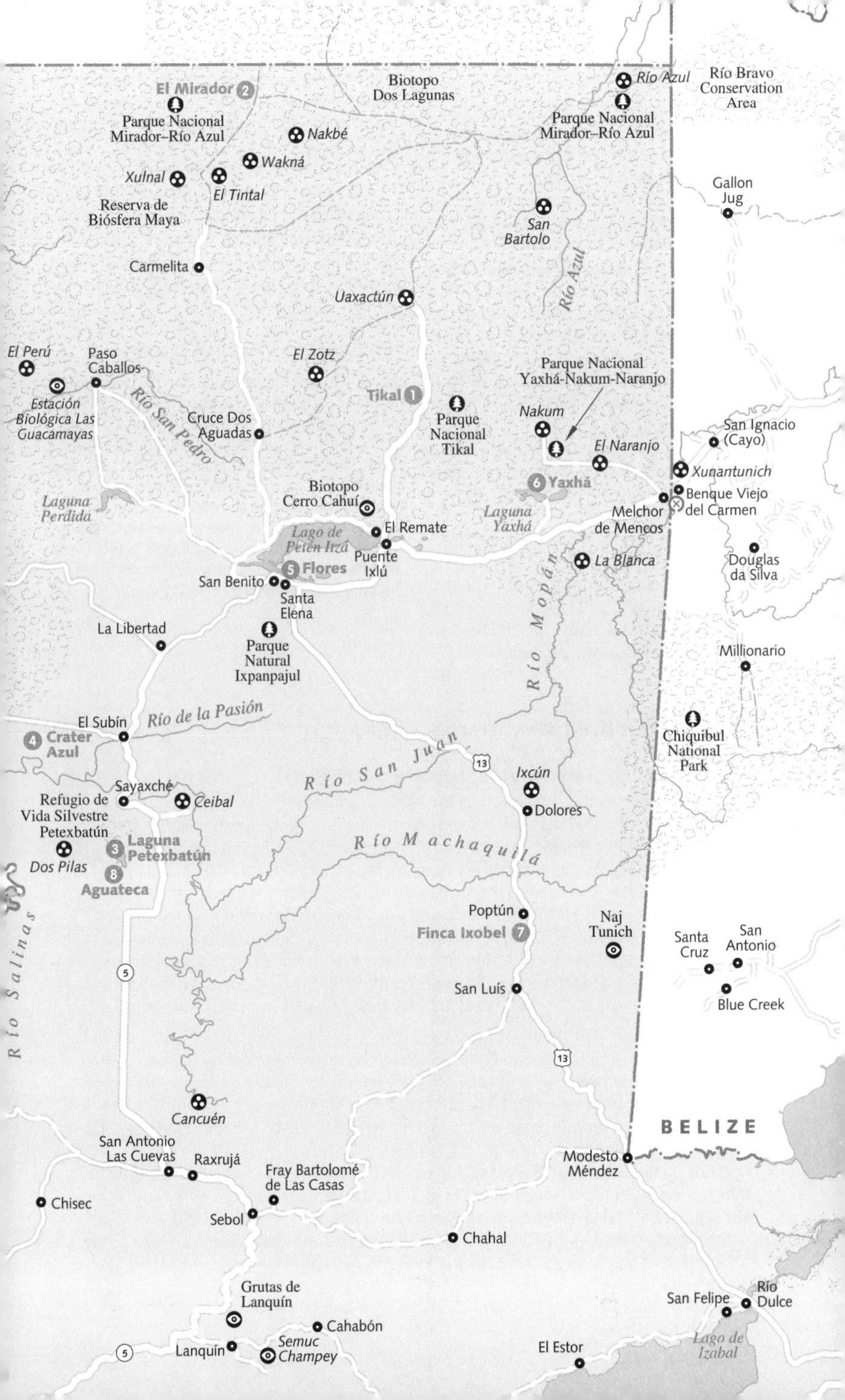
El Mirador 2
Parque Nacional Mirador–Río Azul
Biotopo Dos Lagunas
Río Azul
Río Bravo Conservation Area
Parque Nacional Mirador–Río Azul
Nakbé
Wakná
Xulnal
El Tintal
Reserva de Biósfera Maya
Gallon Jug
San Bartolo
Carmelita
Río Azul
Uaxactún
El Perú
Paso Caballos
El Zotz
Parque Nacional Yaxhá-Nakum-Naranjo
Estación Biológica Las Guacamayas
Río San Pedro
Tikal 1
Parque Nacional Tikal
Nakum
Cruce Dos Aguadas
San Ignacio (Cayo)
El Naranjo
Xunantunich
Biotopo Cerro Cahuí
6 Yaxhá
Benque Viejo del Carmen
Laguna Perdida
Melchor de Mencos
Laguna Yaxhá
El Remate
Lago de Petén Itzá
Puente Ixlú
5 Flores
La Blanca
Douglas da Silva
San Benito
Santa Elena
Río Mopán
La Libertad
Parque Natural Ixpanpajul
Millionario
Río de la Pasión
El Subín
4 Crater Azul
Chiquibul National Park
Río San Juan
13
Ixcún
Sayaxché
Ceibal
Dolores
Refugio de Vida Silvestre Petexbatún
Río Machaquilá
3 Laguna Petexbatún
Dos Pilas
8 Aguateca
Poptún
Finca Ixobel 7
Naj Tunich
Santa Cruz
San Antonio
5
San Luís
Blue Creek
Río Salinas
13
Cancuén
BELIZE
San Antonio Las Cuevas
Raxrujá
Modesto Méndez
Fray Bartolomé de Las Casas
Chisec
Sebol
Chahal
Grutas de Lanquín
Río Dulce
San Felipe
Cahabón
Semuc Champey
5
Lanquín
El Estor
Lago de Izabal

History

Often referred to as the cradle of Maya civilization, El Petén has historically been isolated from the rest of present-day Guatemala, a situation that continued until quite recently. The major Maya population centers – Tikal and El Mirador – had more contact with neighboring settlements in Belize and Mexico than with those down south.

The arrival of the Spanish changed little in this regard. The Itzá, who lived on the island now known as Flores, earned a reputation for cruelty and ferocity. Along with El Petén's impenetrable jungles and fierce wildlife, this kept the Spanish at a distance until 1697, about 150 years after the rest of the country had been conquered.

Even after conquest, the Spanish had no great love for El Petén. The island of Flores was a penal colony before a small city was founded, mostly to facilitate the trade in chicle, hardwood, sugarcane and rubber that had been planted in the region.

The big change came in 1970, when the Guatemalan government saw the opportunity to market Tikal as a tourist destination and work began on a decent road network.

El Petén's population boom – largely a result of government incentives for farmers to relocate – has seen the population increase from 15,000 to a staggering 660,000 in the last 50 years.

Some of the new neighbors are not entirely welcome, however – large tracts of land, particularly in the northwest corner and in the Parque Nacional Laguna del Tigre, have been taken over by drug traffickers and people smugglers, capitalizing on the unpatrolled border with Mexico.

Getting There & Away

El Petén's main tourism node is at the twin towns of Flores and Santa Elena, about 60km southwest of Tikal. The main roads to Flores (from Río Dulce to the southeast, from Cobán and Chisec to the southwest, from the Belize border to the east, and from the Mexican border to the northwest) are now all paved and in good condition, though conditions may change. Frequent buses and minibuses carry travelers along these routes. Santa Elena also has the only functioning civil airport in the country aside from Guatemala City.

MEXICAN BORDER: CHIAPAS & TABASCO

Via Bethel & La Técnica and Frontera Corozal

Regular transportation service reaches the Mexican border at Bethel or La Técnica, on the eastern bank of the Río Usumacinta, from where there is a regular ferry service to Frontera Corozal on the Mexican bank. Guatemalan immigration is in Bethel, but the crossing is quicker and much cheaper from La Técnica (Q10 per person). Microbus drivers will normally stop and wait for you to do the formalities in Bethel before proceeding to La Técnica.

Autotransporte Chamoán vans run hourly from Frontera Corozal *embarcadero* (wharf) to Palenque (M$120, 2½ to three hours), with the last departure at 2:55pm.

To visit the Maya ruins at Yaxchilán on the Mexican side of the river, Escudo Jaguar runs boats from M$950 (one to four people) to M$1300 (five to 10 people), round trip, with a two-hour wait at the ruins. You must also pay the park entry of Q70 per person.

Via El Ceibo & La Palma

Travelers may enter the Mexican state of Tabasco via the border post by El Ceibo, a village on the Río San Pedro. Microbuses run from Santa Elena to El Ceibo, more frequently to El Naranjo, which let you off at 'El Cruce' to catch a shuttle the additional 15 minutes to the border. (In the reverse direction, the last micro from El Ceibo to Santa Elena departs at 5pm.)

A tiny immigration post operates 24 hours on the Guatemalan side, while a facility on the Mexican side is open from 9am to 6pm. From the Mexican side, *tuk-tuks* shuttle travelers around 600m to a little terminal for vans to Tenosique, Tabasco (M$40, one hour, hourly till 6pm). Arriving in Tenosique, get off by the bus terminal to catch an ADO bus to Villahermosa (3½ hours); or get a *tuk-tuk* to where vans leave for Palenque (M$50, 1½ hours) until 7pm.

Sayaxché

POP 147,000 / ELEV 133M

Sayaxché, on the south bank of the Río de la Pasión, 61km southwest of Flores, is the closest town to around 10 scattered Maya archaeological sites, including Ceibal, Aguateca, Dos Pilas, Tamarindito and Altar de Sacrificios. You could stay here for weeks exploring all of them, but most travelers opt for just a few, and many skip the town proper entirely for the lovely riverside hotels an hour or so away by *lancha* (small motorboat).

Besides its strategic position between Flores and the Cobán area, Sayaxché has a riverside appeal all its own, with rickety motorboats and funky barges floating trucks across the broad waterway. If you want to explore a part of Guatemala that most tourists overlook, stop here for a night or a week and see what you can see.

The ferry across the river operates round the clock (pedestrian Q2; car Q15 5am to 10pm, and Q20 10pm to 5am).

Sleeping

Though the lodges around nearby Laguna Petexbatún make a far more appealing option, Sayaxché has a few laid-back guesthouses by the riverside and one or two nicer hotels.

Hospedaje Yaxkín BUNGALOW $

(☎4913-4879; Barrio La Esperanza; bungalow per person with/without bathroom Q50/35) East of the center are these 15 rustic cabins scattered around a wooded tract. A big open-air restaurant serves pastas, tacos and river fish (Q50). It's two blocks south and three blocks east of the church. A taxi will zip you from the ferry to the hotel for Q25 to Q80 depending on the time of day.

Hotel Villa Aquazul HOTEL $$

(☎7928-6811; www.facebook.com/hotelvillaaquazul; cnr 1a Calle & 7a Avenida B; s/d Q280/480, suite s/d Q380/580; P ⊖ ❄ ☜ ≋) This modern hotel has all the comforts a family traveling through might want: wi-fi, a restaurant and spare but clean tile-floor rooms. The pool even has a waterslide for the kiddos. The only downside is it's on the outskirts of town – a five-minute *tuk-tuk* or taxi ride, but still walkable for those who don't mind the extra exercise.

Hotel Del Río HOTEL $$

(☎7928-6138; hoteldelriosayaxche@hotmail.com; s/d Q125/200, with air-con Q175/250; P ⊖ ❄ @ ☜) A few steps to the right of the wharf (with your back to the river) is this modern hotel. It's the cushy choice, with sparkling rooms alongside and above an airy lobby.

Eating

Decent options are limited to the Café Maya and the cook shack at Hospedaje Yaxkín. River fish may not be available due to unacceptable pollution levels.

Bold travelers might venture into the you'll-be-the-only-tourist-they've-seen-in-years bars near the ferry launch; otherwise nightlife here is limited to strolling the dusty streets.

Café Maya GUATEMALAN $$

(☎4641-9753; Calle del Ferry; mains Q45-95; ⏲7am-9pm) About the best bet for grub in town is this casual, open-air hall, a popular gathering place both morning and evening. Aside from the usual eggs-and-beans, it does *pinchos* (brochettes), served with abundant portions of salad, beans and rice, and fries, and the papaya smoothies are heavenly. Chicken, fish and pasta are the lunch/dinner options.

Information

Banrural (⏲8:30am-5pm Mon-Fri, 9am-1pm Sat) Just downhill from the church toward the river. Changes dollars and euros; a nearby branch has a Cajero 5B ATM.

Getting There & Away

Southbound from Sayaxché, several microbuses head for Cobán (Q55, four hours) between 5am and 3pm. Every 25 minutes or so, Raxruhá-bound microbuses go to the San Antonio junction (Q35, 1½ hours), from where there are frequent departures for Cobán. Vehicles depart from a lot near the ferry dock. From the north side of the Río de la Pasión, microbuses leave for Santa Elena every 15 minutes from 5:45am to 6:30pm (Q25, 1½ hours).

For river transportation, contact **Viajes Don Pedro** (☎4580-9389; servlanchasdonpedro@hotmail.com; ⏲8am-5pm).

Around Sayaxché

Of the archaeological sites reached from Sayaxché, Ceibal and Aguateca are the most interesting to the amateur visitor. Both are impressively restored and can be reached by boat trips along jungle-fringed waterways followed by forest walks. Most people arrive as part of a tour, but it is possible to make arrangements independently.

Getting to any of the archaeological sites around Sayaxché involves making arrangements with boat operators in Sayaxché, or taking a tour. Viajes Don Pedro (p227) offers a straightforward half-day return trip from Sayaxché to Aguateca, charging Q700 for up to five people. You could, for example, arrange to be dropped at one of the lodges afterward and be picked up the next afternoon after making a trip to Dos Pilas. Outfits in Flores offer one-day tours to Aguateca, including lunch and guide.

There's no cafe or snack bar at Ceibal; most tours to the site include lunch; otherwise pack a picnic in Sayaxché.

Sights

Crater Azul SPRING

This stunning spring-fed tributary lies just a 90-minute boat ride from Sayaxché, during which you pass birdlife and a mix of farms, fields and forests. The last few hundred meters are too shallow for the engine, and your guide will row the rest of the way. At the source, the water clarity is unsurpassed, allowing for stunning underwater photography and swimming. A small dock is the only facility, so you will need to bring all sunscreen, food and beverages, and carry out your trash.

Dos Pilas RUINS

If you have the time, it's well worth visiting this ruin. It has fine carvings on display, particularly the hieroglyphic staircase, with five 6m-wide steps, each with two rows of superbly preserved glyphs, climbing to the base of the royal palace near the main plaza. (But find out if it's currently visible as archaeologists may cover it up.) In addition, a number of stelae standing here are in excellent shape with clear inscriptions. The best way to reach Dos Pilas is by tour (boat Q500, 4x4 Q800) from Sayaxché or by staying at the Posada Caribe (p231) and organizing a tour there, possibly by horseback.

Aguateca ARCHAEOLOGICAL SITE

(8am-4:30pm) FREE The ruins of Aguateca stand on a hilltop at the far south end of Laguna Petexbatún. Defended by cliffs and split by a ravine, the city enjoyed military successes (including one over nearby Ceibal) up until about AD 735, according to data gleaned from carved stelae. Of the sites within reach of Sayaxché, this is the most accessible and most immediately impressive.

It's fairly certain that rulers from Dos Pilas abandoned that city for the better-fortified Aguateca around AD 761, and that the city was finally overrun by unknown attackers around 790 – a wealth of arrowheads and skeletons have been found dating back to that time. It was abandoned shortly afterwards.

The visitor center is a short walk from the dock. Rangers can guide you round the site in about 1½ hours (a small tip is in order). Two main groups feature well-restored structures: the **Grupo del Palacio**, where the ruler lived, and the **Plaza Mayor** (Main Plaza) to its south, where fiberglass copies of stelae showing finely attired rulers stand beside the fallen originals. The two groups are connected by a causeway over the ravine.

From the visitor center, you can skirt the cliff wall north to reach a **mirador** (lookout) with views over the rivers and swampland toward the east. The trail then turns left and descends into the ravine, continuing 100m between two sheer limestone walls, then climbs back up to emerge onto the Grupo del Palacio. Proceed through the palatial complex back toward the entrance. At the lower end, turn right to take the causeway over the ravine (70m deep here) to reach the Main Plaza.

Aguateca is a 1¾-hour *lancha* (small motorboat) trip direct from Sayaxché, via the mangrove-fringed Río Petexbatún.

Ceibal

With its strategic position along the west bank of the Río de la Pasión, the independent kingdom of **Ceibal** (Q60; 8am-4pm) amassed considerable power controlling commerce along this key stretch of the waterway. Though Ceibal is architecturally less amazing than some other sites, the river journey to access it is among the most memorable, as is hiking below the jungle canopy with monkeys howling overhead.

There's a large scale model of the site by the entrance. The ceremonial core of the city covers three hills, connected over steep ravines by the original causeways. Smallish temples, many of them covered with jungle, surround two principal groups, A and D. In front of some temples, and standing seemingly alone on paths, are magnificent stelae, their intricate carvings still in excellent condition.

Ceibal

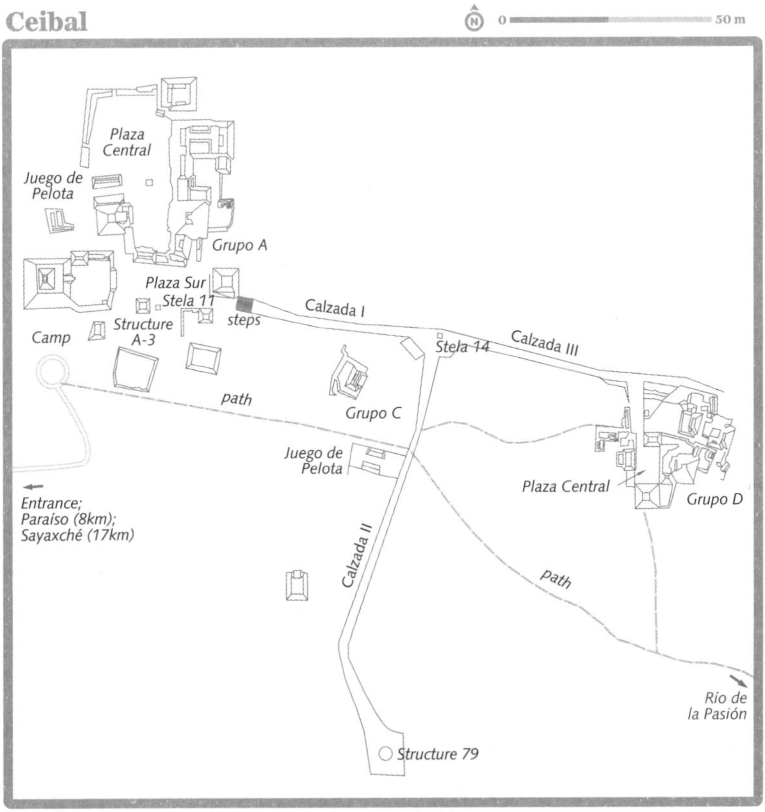

It takes about two hours to explore the site. Bring mosquito repellent and snacks and water.

Sights

Most of the stelae appear at Grupo A, made up of three plazas at the site's highest point. At the best excavated of these, Plaza Sur, stands **Structure A-3**, a pyramidal platform with a stela on each side and one at the top. Some of the characters depicted here have distinctly non-Maya features and dress, which has led to speculation that foreigners once inhabited the area. According to one hotly debated theory, the city was invaded by Putun Maya, a race of merchant-warriors from the Tabasco area of Mexico, around the mid-9th century. This might account for the 'foreign' look of the moustachioed warrior on **stele 11**, for example, who stands on the east side of the platform.

Calzada I leads east to Grupo D, a more compact series of temples that backs up against a precipitous gorge. About midway is a turnoff south for Calzada II, just beyond which is the fantastically preserved **stela 14**, which may depict a tax collector. Proceeding down Calzada II to the south, you reach the intriguing **Structure 79**. Three stone steps surround the unusual ring-shaped structure, which stands alone in a clearing with a small altar in the shape of a jaguar's head. It is believed to have served as an astronomical observatory, from which the inhabitants studied planetary movements.

Getting There & Away

Viajes Don Pedro (p227) in Sayaxché, on the south side of the river, runs *lanchas* here (Q700 for up to five passengers). The fee should include a guide, who may actually be the boat operator. In high season, ask the *lancheros* about joining a tour group.

WORTH A TRIP

FINCA IXOBEL

The **Finca Ixobel** (5410-4307; www.fincaixobel.com; campsite Q40, dm Q55, private room s/d Q205/355, without bathroom Q100/155, treehouse from Q150/275; P @) is a solitary standout in an area with little tourism overall, an oasis of class and relaxation a few kilometers south of the small town of Poptún.

Everything at Finca Ixobel works on the honor system: guests keep an account of what they eat and drink and the services they use.

If this place suits your style, and you want to help/hang out for six weeks minimum, ask about volunteering.

Among the numerous options for bedding down at Finca Ixobel are *palapas* (thatched palm-leaf shelters) for hanging hammocks, bungalows and 'treehouses' – most of which are actually cabins on stilts. The large, grassy camping area has good bathrooms and plenty of shade. Assorted other accommodations include a couple of dormitories and rooms with shared and private bathroom, all with fan, mosquito nets and screened windows.

Swimming, horsebackriding (from two hours to four days), cave trips and rainy-season inner-tubing on the Río Machaquilá can be organized. The caves of **Naj Tunich** (5034-7317; 8am-6pm) FREE, with their replica galleries of Maya paintings, are a popular excursion; including admission, guide and lunch, it's Q550 per person for a group of two (prices drop with additional group members).

Finca Ixobel is 5km south of the regional commercial center of Poptún, from where you can take a taxi (Q50) or *tuk-tuk* (Q20-30). Otherwise, any bus or minibus along Hwy 13 can drop you at the turnoff, from where it's a 15-minute walk to the lodge. Departing, most buses will stop on the highway to pick you up, but not after dark.

The best way to get to Poptún from Flores/Santa Elena is to take a minibus from the main terminal (Q30, every 10 minutes, 5am to 7pm); tell the driver where you're heading and they'll drop you at the lodge. Coming from Guatemala City or Río Dulce, all Santa Elena–bound buses make a stop in Poptún.

The one-hour boat ride up the Río de la Pasión brings you to a primitive dock. After landing, you clamber up a narrow, rocky path beneath gigantic ceiba trees and jumbles of jungle vines to reach the archaeological zone, perched about 100m above the river.

Alternatively, Ceibal can be reached overland: get any bus, minibus or pick-up heading south from Sayaxché on Hwy 5 (toward Raxruhá and Chisec) and get off after 9km at Paraíso, from where it's an 8km walk east down a dirt track to Ceibal. About 2km in, where the road bends left by a small farmhouse, continue straight uphill to enter the park – there's no sign. In the rainy season check first with locals that this stretch is passable.

Laguna Petexbatún

Laguna Petexbatún is a shallow, turbid 6km-long lake southwest of Sayaxché, approached by an hour's *lancha* ride up the Río Petexbatún, a tributary of the Río de la Pasión. The lake, river and surrounding forests harbor many birds, including kingfishers, egrets, vultures, eagles, cormorants and herons. Though rare, the occasional crocodile sighting happens according to boat operators. It's a lovely spot made more lovely by its remoteness and the Amazon-like boat ride to get here from Sayaxché.

Within reach of the waterways are five significant archaeological sites and a pair of jungle-hideaway accommodations. The island of Chiminos (once a peninsula) was also significant in Maya times and now houses a beautiful ecolodge.

What we know of the history of Dos Pilas, Aguateca and Chiminos has mostly been unraveled by archaeologists since the late 1980s. Dos Pilas was founded about AD 640 by a prince who left Tikal and later defeated it in two wars, capturing its ruler Nuun Ujol Chaak (Shield Skull) in 679, according to inscriptions at the site. Dos Pilas' second and third rulers carried out monumental building programs, waged wars of conquest and came to dominate most of the territory between the Pasión and Chixoy rivers, but in AD 761 their vassal Tamarindito rebelled and killed the fourth ruler, causing the Dos Pilas nobility to relocate to the naturally fortified site of Aguateca, which was already functioning as a twin capital. Aguateca in turn was abandoned in the early 9th century, around the same time as three defensive moats were cut across the neck of the Chiminos peninsula on the edge of Laguna Petexbatún. Archaeologists surmise that Punta de Chiminos was the last refuge of the Petexbatún dynasty founded at Dos Pilas.

Sleeping & Eating

Both of the ecolodges at Laguna Petexbatún prepare meals; otherwise there's nowhere to eat around the principal archaeological sites.

Posada Caribe BUNGALOW **$$**
(5304-1745, 4376-1736; www.posadacaribe.com; bungalow Q380) Located on a lazy stretch of the river about halfway between Sayaxché and Laguna Petexbatún is this appealingly remote encampment managed by the ebullient don Julián and family. Seven humble, thatched bungalows with wood-plank floors and lacy curtains are set back from the riverbank. Meals are served for around Q100 each.

From here you can arrange tours to the archaeological site of Dos Pilas. You'll travel by pick-up truck to the village of El Nacimiento, from where it's a 30-minute hike to the site.

★ **Chiminos Island Lodge** LODGE **$$$**
(4008-6840; www.chiminosisland.com; r adult/child under 13yr incl 3 meals Q1144/572) Jutting out from the western shore of Laguna Petexbatún, this magical lodge shares its promontory with a largely unexcavated Maya citadel that includes a ballcourt and stellae. Five spare but elegantly furnished bungalows, with private bathroom, fan and porch, are spaced well apart from one another and reached along trails through the forest.

Built of natural hardwoods and equipped with wraparound screened windows, they give the feeling of sleeping in the jungle without all those nasty bugs and bats. Naturally prepared food is served in an open-air restaurant/clubhouse, and folders full of absorbing archaeological information and articles about the area are available to peruse.

Getting There & Away

Laguna Petexbatún is most conveniently reached by motorboat. Most visitors are brought here by one of the lodges in the vicinity or by tour operators in Flores. To arrive independently, try any of the boat operators in Sayaxché, who charge around Q600 for a half-day tour of the lake, including a visit to Aguateca (p228).

Flores & Santa Elena

POP 73,000 / ELEV 117M

With its pastel houses cascading down from a central plaza to the emerald waters of Lago de Petén Itzá, the island town of Flores evokes Venice or something Mediterranean. A 500m causeway connects Flores to its humbler sister town of Santa Elena on the mainland, which then merges into the community of San Benito to the west. The three towns actually form one large settlement, often referred to simply as Flores.

Flores proper is by far the more attractive base. Small hotels and restaurants line the streets, many featuring rooftop terraces with lake views. Residents take great pride in their island-town's gorgeousness, and a promenade (partly submerged now due to lake levels rising) runs around its perimeter.

Santa Elena is where you'll find banks, buses and a major shopping mall.

History

Flores was founded on a *petén* (island) by the Itzáes, who came here after being expelled from Chichén Itzá on Mexico's Yucatán Peninsula, probably in the mid-15th century. They called it Tah Itzá (place of the Itzá), which the Spanish later corrupted to Tayasal. Hernán Cortés dropped in on King Canek of Tayasal in 1525 on his way to Honduras, and the meeting was, amazingly, peaceable. Cortés left behind a lame horse, which the Itzáes fed on flowers and turkey stew. When it died, the Itzáes made a statue of it, which, by the time a couple of Spanish

DON'T MISS

CUEVAS DE AK'TUN KAN

Try spelunking at the impressive limestone **Cuevas de Ak'tun Kan** (Q35; 7am-5pm), which translates from Q'eqchi' Maya as 'Cave of the Serpent.' The cave-keeper provides the authorized interpretation of the weirdly shaped stalagmite and stalactite formations, including the Frozen Falls, the Whale's Tail, and the Gate of Heaven, the last within a great hall where bats flutter in the crevices.

The provided helmets have a small light inside them. Explorations take 30 to 45 minutes. It's 2km south of Flores; take a *tuk-tuk* there (Q15).

friars visited in 1618, was being worshipped as a manifestation of the rain god Chac. It was not until 1697 that the Spaniards brought the Itzáes of Tayasal – by some distance the last surviving independent Maya kingdom – forcibly under their control. The Spanish soldiers destroyed its many pyramids, temples and statues, and today you won't see a trace of them, although the modern town is doubtless built on the ruins and foundations of Maya Tayasal.

Sights

Flores is great for strolling, especially now that the lakefront promenade that rings the islet is complete – though rising lake levels have submerged much of the northern section. In the center, atop a rise, is the Parque Central, with its double-domed cathedral, **Nuestra Señora de los Remedios**. Mostly the sights are just the vistas of the lake, its birdlife and the streets themselves.

Museo Santa Bárbara MUSEUM
(7926-2813; www.radiopeten.com.gt; Isle of Santa Bárbara; Q25; 8am-5pm) On an islet to the west of Flores, this little museum holds a grab bag of Maya artifacts from nearby archaeological sites, plus some old broadcasting equipment from Radio Petén (88.5 FM), which still broadcasts from an adjacent building. Phone ahead to get picked up (Q10 per person) at the dock behind **Hotel Santana** (7867-5123; www.santanapeten.com.gt; Calle 30 de Junio, Flores; d/tr Q600/700;).

Activities

Arcas VOLUNTEERING
(Asociación de Rescate y Conservación de Vida Silvestre; 7830-1374, volunteer coordinator 5690-6762; www.arcasguatemala.org/volunteering; initial week US$250, per week after US$200) This Guatemalan NGO has a rescue and rehabilitation center for wildlife on the mainland northeast of Flores, where volunteers can assist in feeding animals, such as macaws, parrots, jaguars and coatis, that have been rescued from smugglers and the illegal pet trade. The fee covers food and accommodations.

Tours

Various travel agencies in Flores offer day tours to archaeological sites such as Tikal, Uaxactún, Yaxhá and Ceibal. Prices, with a guide and lunch, range from Q150 for a basic Tikal tour, by Hostel Los Amigos, to Q2175 for a Ceibal excursion.

More demanding hiking-and-camping experiences to remote archaeological sites such as Nakum, El Perú, El Zotz, El Mirador, Nakbé and Wakná/El Perú are also offered by local tour operators.

Maya Expeditions (p51), based in Guatemala City, offers mild (ie good for families or inexperienced rafters) one- to 10-day rafting expeditions on the Río Chiquibul, with options to visit lesser-known sites such as Yaxhá, Nakum and Topoxte.

Explore TOURS
(7926-2375; www.exploreguate.com; 2a Calle 4-68, Santa Elena; 7am-6pm Mon-Fri, to noon Sat) Professionally managed agency offering custom-designed tours and its own accommodations in Santa Elena.

Lake Tours

Boats can be hired for lake tours at the *embarcaderos* (wharfs) opposite **Hotel Petenchel** and beside the **Hotel Santana** in Flores, and in the middle of the Flores–Santa Elena causeway. Prices are negotiable. An hour-long jaunt runs around Q150. A three-hour tour, which might include the Petencito Zoo, the isle of Santa Bárbara and its museum, and the ruins of Tayazal should cost Q350, with stops and waiting time included.

TOURS TO LOCAL ARCHAEOLOGICAL SITES

The sample prices are per person for two or more people, normally including food, water, sleeping gear and Spanish-speaking guide, and are dependent on the current exchange rate.

LOCATION	DURATION (DAYS)	COST (Q)
El Zotz & Tikal	3	2625
El Perú & Estación Biológica Las Guacamayas	3	3000
El Mirador–Nakbé–Wakná	7	2250 (shared group tour)
Yaxhá & Nakum	2	2250

Sleeping

Except for a few upscale properties along Santa Elena's waterfront, Flores is by far the more desirable place to stay, though the former's hotels are often good value.

Hostel Los Amigos HOSTEL $
(☎4495-2399, 7867-5075; www.amigoshostel.com; Calle Central, Flores; dm Q100-120, r Q220; @) Far and away the most popular backpackers' haven in El Petén, this hostel has grown organically in its 15 years of existence and now includes various sleeping options, from six- and 10-bed dorms to a treehouse (Q200). An annex around the corner is quieter, with seven originally designed rooms.

All the global traveler's perks are here in abundance: herbal steam bath, massage, pool table, hammocks, heaping helpings of food, yoga and cut-rate jungle tours. It also offers bike tours around the area.

Despite the good-time atmosphere, it's lights out after 10pm, but the fun goes on in an ingeniously soundproofed night lounge upstairs.

La Posada de Don José HOTEL $$
(☎7867-5298; cnr Calle del Malecón & Calle Fraternidad, Flores; dm Q75, r with/without air-con Q250/175;) Near the northern tip of the island, this is an old-fashioned establishment (check the lobby for a portrait of the founder) with rocking chairs scattered around a plant-laden patio and a friendly family that knows your name. The lake level has reclaimed the *malecón* (jetty) here, making the rear terrace infinitely more peaceful than further down. Besides the neat little rooms, there's a spacious fan-cooled dorm in back.

Hotel Quinta Maya HOTEL $$
(☎7926-4976; www.hotelquintamaya.com; 6a Av & 4a Calle; s/d/tr Q275/390/490; P) Newly rebranded, this comfortable hotel offers large rooms arranged around a pleasant courtyard. There's a restaurant, airport transfers and a travel agent onsite.

Hostel Yaxha HOSTEL $$
(☎7867-5055; www.cafeyaxha.com; Calle 15 de Septiembre, Flores; dm/d/apt Q70/220/400;) A haven for archaeologists, historians and fans of pre-Hispanic cuisine, Café Arqueológico Yaxha (p236) now offers a clean and simple place to lay your head. There are four, six-, and nine-bed dorms, private rooms with bathroom, and an apartment – all with quality mattresses and ceiling fans. Air-con adds to the price.

Casazul BOUTIQUE HOTEL $$
(☎7867-5451; www.hotelesdepeten.com; Calle Unión, Flores; s/d/tr Q400/450/650;) As the name suggests, it's blue all over, from the plantation-style balconies to the nine individually decorated, spacious and comfortable rooms. A couple have their own balconies and everyone can enjoy the beautiful top-floor terrace.

Hotel La Mesa de los Mayas HOTEL $$
(☎7867-5268; mesamayas@hotmail.com; Av La Reforma, Flores; s/d Q125/200, with air-con Q150/250;) Standing alongside a narrow alley, the Mesa is terrific value. Its 19 rooms are neatly furnished, with pyramidal headboards, checkered bedspreads and reading lamps; some feature plant-laden balconies. There's a restaurant on the 1st floor.

Casa Amelia BOUTIQUE HOTEL $$
(☎7867-5430; www.hotelcasamelia.com; Calle Unión, Flores; s/d Q350/450;) Standing tall along Flores' western shore, the Amelia offers bright, stylish chambers with excellent lake views; rooms 301 and 302 are best, opening onto the superb balustraded roof terrace.

Hotel Villa del Lago HOTEL $$
(☎7867-5131; www.hotelvilladelago.com.gt; Calle 15 de Septiembre, Flores; r 545;) Behind the odd Grecian columns there's a cool, breezy interior that's long on potted plants and patio furniture. Comfortable, airy rooms have bright decor and big ceiling fans. Breakfast (not included) is served on the delightful upper terrace.

Hotel Petenchel HOTEL $$
(☎7867-5450; escalofrio_puga@hotmail.com; Calle Playa Sur, Flores; s/d Q150/230, with air-con Q200/270;) Just off the causeway, this comfy hideaway has six spacious rooms, all with firm beds and high arched ceilings, set around a lush garden. Get breakfast burritos at the attached cafe, called Escalofrío ('chill').

Hotel El Peregrino HOTEL $$
(☎7867-5701; peregrino@itelgua.com; Av La Reforma, Flores; s/d/tr Q175/320/420, without bathroom Q80/150/220;) El Peregrino is an older, family-run place with home cooking in the front *comedor* (basic, cheap eatery). Large rooms with tile floors and powerful overhead fans line up along plant-festooned corridors – no views here.

Hotel Posada de la Jungla HOTEL $$
(☎7867-5185; Calle Centroamérica 30, Flores; s/d Q150/220, with air-con Q210/320;) Worth

Flores

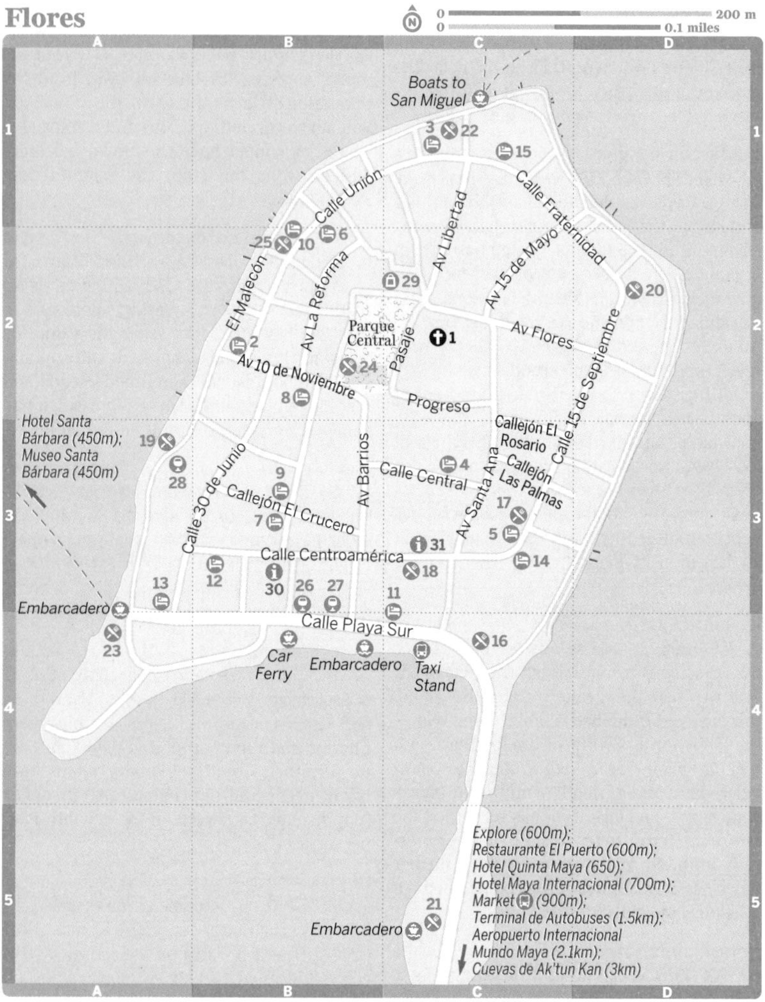
0 200 m
0 0.1 miles
Boats to San Miguel
Calle Unión
Calle Fraternidad
Av Libertad
Av 15 de Mayo
El Malecón
Av La Reforma
Parque Central
Pasaje
Av Flores
Calle 15 de Septiembre
Av 10 de Noviembre
Progreso
Callejón El Rosario
Callejón Las Palmas
Calle Central
Av Barrios
Av Santa Ana
Calle 30 de Junio
Callejón El Crucero
Calle Centroamérica
Calle Playa Sur
Hotel Santa Bárbara (450m); Museo Santa Bárbara (450m)
Embarcadero
Car Ferry
Embarcadero
Taxi Stand
Embarcadero
Explore (600m); Restaurante El Puerto (600m); Hotel Quinta Maya (650); Hotel Maya Internacional (700m); Market (900m); Terminal de Autobuses (1.5km); Aeropuerto Internacional Mundo Maya (2.1km); Cuevas de Ak'tun Kan (3km)

considering is this slender, three-story building with front balconies. Though a bit on the small side, rooms are comfortably arranged, with quality beds.

Hotel Aurora HOTEL **$$**
(7867-5516; aldeamaya@gmail.com; Calle Unión, Flores; dm/s/d Q45/100/200;) This backpacker spot's got banisters made to look like climbing vines. Rooms are plain, airy and well scrubbed, with screened windows, and most have some kind of view. A super roof terrace is popular for hanging out. Guest kitchen available.

Hotel La Unión HOTEL **$$**
(7867-5531; launionhotel2013@gmail.com; Calle Unión, Flores; s/d Q183/244; @) Considering its location on the waterfront, this family-run property is quite a deal, with cozy decor, quality beds and nicely tiled bathrooms, and there's a superb rear terrace. The drawback is that the waterfront promenade turns into a cruising zone each evening with the attendant noise and exhaust.

The hotel doubles as an agency for reliable shuttle service, does laundry, and even has a book exchange.

Flores

Sights
1 Nuestra Señora de los Remedios......... C2

Activities, Courses & Tours
Mayan Adventure .... (see 17)

Sleeping
2 Casa Amelia.. B2
3 Casazul...C1
4 Hostel Los Amigos................................ C3
5 Hostel Yaxha... C3
6 Hotel Aurora B2
7 Hotel El Peregrino.................................. B3
8 Hotel Isla de Flores B2
9 Hotel La Mesa de los Mayas................. B3
10 Hotel La Unión....................................... B2
11 Hotel Petenchel...................................... C3
12 Hotel Posada de la Jungla B3
13 Hotel Santana... A3
14 Hotel Villa del Lago C3
15 La Posada de Don José..........................C1

Eating
16 Antojitos Mexicanos.............................. C4
17 Café Arqueológico Yaxha......................C3
18 Cafe Uka C3
19 Café/Bar Doña Goya A3
20 Cool Beans D2
21 Las Mesitas C5
22 Maple y Tocino.. C1
23 Raíces...A4
24 Restaurante El Mirador B2
Restaurante El Peregrino .... (see 7)
25 Terrazzo...B2

Drinking & Nightlife
26 El Trópico...B3
27 Jamming...B3
28 Qué Pachanga..A3

Shopping
29 Castillo de Arizmendi.............................C2

Information
30 Comisión de Turismo Cooperativa Carmelita Agency...............................B3
31 INGUAT..C3

Hotel Santa Bárbara HOTEL $$$
(7926-2813; http://radiopeten.com.gt; cabins incl breakfast Q750;) Part of a trio that includes a museum (p232) and a cafe, this is a perfect retreat from the hubbub of Flores on an islet just five minutes west by *lancha* (small motorboat; included in price). Three comfy cabins with big beds and tile floors overlook the lake past a garden brimming with coconut palms and a ceiba tree.

Hotel Isla de Flores HOTEL $$$
(2476-8775; www.hotelisladeflores.com; Av La Reforma, Flores; s/d Q570/663; @) This island hotel sports an understated tropical style that's highly appealing. Hardwood beams frame bone-white walls with floral motifs that are echoed on cool stone floors, and large firm beds back up on painted headboards. Though it doesn't stand on the lakeshore, the plank-deck roof terrace, with a small pool, commands fantastic views over the whole island.

Enjoy mojitos and fusion cuisine in the equally stylish street-level restaurant-bar.

Hotel Maya Internacional HOTEL $$$
(7926-2083; www.villasdeguatemala.com; 1a Calle, Santa Elena; s/d/tr Q738/927/1064; P) One of the best reasons to stay in Santa Elena is this tropical-chic resort spreading over a landscaped marsh by the waterfront. The big-top dining room is the center of activity; an adjacent wooden deck with a small infinity pool is great for sunset daiquiris. A boardwalk snakes through tropical gardens to reach the 26 thatch-and-teak rooms. Rooms 49 to 54 have the best lake views.

Eating

Flores has loads of pizza, pasta and burger options, often unimpressive. Nevertheless, a few local gems rise above the pack, and the scene seems to be changing for the better... and tastier.

★ **Maple y Tocino** CAFE $
(7867-5294; www.facebook.com/mapleytocino; btwn Calle La Union & El Malecón; mains Q29-54; 7am-9pm Sun-Thu, to 10pm Fri & Sat) Amazing spot for breakfasts and lunches, ranging from smoothies and frappés (some topped with a fresh donut!) to waffles, pizza, sandwiches and wraps. Tasty coffee and espresso drinks and, to top it all, a view of the lake (and the now submerged *malecón*).

Cafe Uka CAFE $
(www.facebook.com/cafeukapeten; Calle Centroamérica; breakfast mains Q25-35; 7am-3pm Mon-Sat) Cheap, clean and tasty, the cheery turquoise- and peach-painted Cafe Uka won't win awards for fanciness, but the service is friendly and the food (a mix of Guatemalan and Western dishes) is fine.

Restaurante El Mirador GUATEMALAN $
(7867-5246; Parque Central, Flores; set menu Q25; 7am-10pm Mon-Sat) Refreshingly not aimed at foreign travelers, this traditional eatery does toothsome home cookin'. You'll find such hearty options as *caldo de res* (beef stew, only on Mondays), served with all the trimmings, and *fresco* (fruit drink) in the bright lunch hall that looks over the treetops. It's next to the basketball court on the Parque Central.

Restaurante El Peregrino GUATEMALAN $
(7867-5701; Av La Reforma, Flores; mains Q35-60; 7am-10pm) Part of the hotel of the same name, this humble *comedor* serves heaping helpings of home-cooked fare such as *caldo de panza* (beef belly stew, Q40) and breaded tongue. Ask for the daily lunch specials (Q30).

Cool Beans CAFE $
(5571-9240, cell phone 7867-5400; Calle 15 de Septiembre, Flores; breakfast Q25-35; 7am-10pm Mon-Sat;) Also known as Café Chilero, this laid-back place is more clubhouse with snacks than proper restaurant, featuring salons for chatting, watching videos or laptop browsing. The lush garden with glimpses of the lake makes a *tranquilo* spot for breakfast or veggie burgers. Be warned – the kitchen closes at 9pm sharp.

Las Mesitas GUATEMALAN $
(El Malecón, Flores; mains Q10-20; 2-10pm) Every afternoon and evening the midpoint of the bridge to Flores turns into a cheap-eats paradise, as local families fix enchiladas (actually *tostadas* topped with guacamole, chicken salad and so on), tacos and tamales, and dispense fruity drinks from giant jugs. All kinds of cakes and puddings are served, too. Everyone sits on plastic chairs or low barrier walls.

★ **Terrazzo** ITALIAN $$
(7867-5479; Calle Unión, Flores; pasta Q70-90; 11am-10pm) Inspired by a chef from Bologna, this Italian gourmet restaurant covers a romantic rooftop terrace. The fettuccine is produced in house, the pizzas (made of seasoned dough) are grilled rather than baked, and the fresh mint lemonade is incredible. All this, and the service is the most attentive in town.

★ **Antojitos Mexicanos** STEAK $$
(Don Fredy; 3130-5702; Calle Playa Sur, Flores; grilled meats Q60-70; 7-10:30pm; P) Every evening at the foot of the causeway these characters fire up the grill and char steak, chicken and pork ribs of exceptional quality. Their specialty is *puyazo* (sirloin) swathed with garlic sauce. Sit outside facing the twinkly lights on the lake or, if it's raining, inside under a tin roof. Staff behave with all the formality of an elegant restaurant.

Note that this can be a slow spot when they're just starting the grill.

Café/Bar Doña Goya CAFE $$
(7867-5774; El Malecón, Flores; mains breakfast Q40-50, lunch or dinner Q50-100; 6:30am-10pm;) Doña Goya's is good for an early breakfast or sunset snack, with a pretty terrace facing the lake. Toward the weekend, it blends into the nightlife scene along this stretch of the promenade.

Raíces STEAK $$
(7867-5743; Calle Playa Sur, Flores; mains Q90-270, pizzas Q70-160; 7am-10pm;) A broad deck and a flaming grill are the main ingredients at this lakefront restaurant/bar, possibly the prettiest setting in Flores for dinner. Chargrilled meats and seafood are the specialty; it also does wood-oven pizzas. The food is tasty and the view sublime, but despite the multitude of waiters, it's often hard to get service when needed.

Café Arqueológico Yaxha CAFE $$
(7867-5055; www.cafeyaxha.com; Calle 15 de Septiembre, Flores; mains Q45-80; 6:30am-10pm) Part of the Hostel Yaxha (p233), this spot offers the usual egg-and-bean breakfasts, but what's special here are the pre-Hispanic and Itzá items – pancakes with *ramón* seeds (Q30), yucca scrambled with *mora* herbs (Q38), chicken in *chaya* sauce (Q60). There's also a 'Tight Ass Traveler' special that ranges from Q15 to Q35.

Restaurante El Puerto SEAFOOD $$
(4211-8668, 5510-5023; 1a Calle 2-15, Santa Elena; mains Q90-130; 11am-11pm) Seafood is the star attraction at this breezy, open-air hall by the lakefront in Santa Elena, with a well-stocked bar at the front. It's an ideal setting to enjoy shellfish stews, popular *ceviches* or the famous *pescado blanco* – white fish from the lake.

Drinking & Nightlife

Flores' little Zona Viva is traditionally the strip of bars along Calle Playa Sur, but there's also action around the bend, along the lakefront promenade north of Hotel Santana.

OFF THE BEATEN TRACK

EXPLORE MORE OF EL PETÉN

The Petén region is full of archaeological sites in various stages of excavation. Some are harder than others to get to; tour operators in Flores and El Remate can help you reach them, but they require advance planning. Here are a few of the more intriguing ones that you might want to check out:

San Bartolo Discovered in 2003, this site features one of the best-preserved Maya murals with a depiction of the creation myth from the Popul Vuh (the Maya 'Bible'). It's approximately 40km northeast of Uaxactún, near the Río Azul.

Piedras Negras On the banks of the Río Usumacinta amid black cliffs, these remote ruins have impressive carvings and a sizable acropolis complex. It was here that part-time archaeologist Tatiana Proskouriakoff deciphered the Maya hieroglyphic system. She requested to be buried here after her death in 1985, but due to the civil war that did not happen. Finally, 10 years later, her remains were placed beneath a simple gravestone at the top of Structure J23.

La Blanca Located along the Río Mopan near the Belize border, this palatial complex may have flourished as a trading center in the Late Classic Period. The acropolis is notable for its remarkably preserved stone walls and an abundance of graffiti. Excavation was done by a Spanish team. The **Mayan Adventure** (☎5830-2060; www.the-mayan-adventure.com; Calle 15 de Septiembre, Flores; ⏲bookings Mon-Fri), based in Flores, leads tours here.

El Zotz This sprawling site occupies its own biotope abutting Tikal National Park. Of the three barely excavated temples, one, the Pirámide del Diablo, can be scaled for views all the way to Tikal. Stick around till dusk to see how the place gets its name – 'The Bat' in Maya. Researchers from the University of Southern California uncovered 23 masks within the tombs of the largest pyramid. INGUAT-authorized guides from the community of **Cruce Dos Aguadas** (☎5039-1188), 42km north of Flores, lead tours here, a 24km hike east through the jungle.

Río Azul Located up near the corner where the Belize, Guatemala and Mexico borders meet, this medium-sized site fell under the domain of Tikal in the Early Classic Period and became a key trading post for cacao from the Caribbean. Most notable are the tombs with vibrant painted glyphs inside. Campamento El Chiclero (p255) in Uaxactún leads a recommended excursion.

El Naranjo Major excavations and restorations are happening at this immense site 12km from the Belize border. In the process archaeologists have ascertained that the city was more densely populated than Tikal and possibly larger. Ruled by Princess Six Sky, daughter to a Dos Pilas governor, Naranjo conquered neighboring kingdoms and produced some of the most refined art in the Maya world. Contact Río Mopán Lodge (p244) about visiting the site.

Qué Pachanga CLUB

(El Malecón, Flores; ⏲2pm-1am) One of a pair of lively nightspots round the west side of the island, this room gets heavy most evenings, when young Guatemalans decked out in their tightest possible jeans gyrate to a continuous barrage of throbbing reggaetón and *cumbia* (Colombian dance tunes).

El Trópico BAR

(Calle Playa Sur, Flores; ⏲5pm-1am Mon-Sat) Longest running of the bars along the southern bank, El Trópico supplies tacos and *cerveza* (beer) to a mostly older Guatemalan clientele. It's quiet at sunset, but many *gallos* (tortilla sandwiches) later, the pulse picks up and DJs work the crowd.

Jamming BAR

(Calle Playa Sur, Flores; ⏲5pm-1am) One of several nightlife venues along the southern bank, Jamming sports a reggae theme, though there's more beer guzzling than ganja smoking. It attracts a younger set of middle-class Guatemalans, and by 8pm you can expect at least a few to be twerking to appreciative onlookers.

Shopping

Castillo de Arizmendi ARTS & CRAFTS
(Parque Central, Flores; 9am-6pm) This market is a monument to Martín de Ursúa Arizmendi y Aguirre, who snatched the island from the Maya in 1697. The castle on the main plaza's north side houses a series of shops with local handicrafts, particularly wood carvings by artists from El Remate, who work in mahogany, cedar and *chicozapote*. It was closed for remodeling at the time of research.

Information

DANGERS & ANNOYANCES

Unscrupulous salespeople often ride the buses, offering fake tickets to tourist sites such as Tikal, claiming bus services won't go to Flores and trying to get you to take an expensive shuttle there, or getting you to book next-day tours from your hotel that never arrive. While it may seem convenient to grab tickets from a friendly or official-looking guy on the bus, don't be sucked in. Instead, make reservations at your hotel or from one of the services listed here. If in doubt, see what people are saying online before you buy.

MEDICAL

Regional Hospital de San Benito Petén (7932-1111; San Benito; 24hr) One of the largest hospitals in the region. Emergency service available.

MONEY

Many travel agencies and places to stay will change cash US dollars and sometimes traveler's checks, though at poorer rates than the banks. There are plenty of banks with ATMs along 4a Calle in Santa Elena.

5B Cajero ATM (7am-8:30pm) In Marlin Espadas tour agency, opposite the Ramada Tikal.

Banco G&T Continental (Maya Mall Petén, 1a Calle 6-17, Santa Elena; 10am-7pm Mon-Sat, to 6pm Sun) Has an ATM.

Banco Industrial (Metroplaza Mundo Maya, 1a Calle, Santa Elena; 9am-4pm Mon-Fri, 10am-2pm Sat) This reliable ATM is in the shopping mall opposite the airport.

Super Fotomart (Calle 30 de Junio, Flores; 6am-1am) Convenience store with an ATM, opposite Hotel Casona de la Isla.

TOURIST INFORMATION

Comisión de Turismo Cooperativa Carmelita Agency (4836-9423, 7867-5629; Calle Centroamérica, Flores; Tikal tour per person Q150, El Mirador 5-day/4-night per person Q1925; 8am-8pm) Flores agency for this Carmelita-based cooperative of trekking guides.

INGUAT (3128-6906; info-ciudadflores@inguat.gob.gt; Calle Centroamérica, Flores; 8am-4pm Mon-Fri, sometimes Sat & Sun) The official INGUAT office provides basic information. There's another **branch** (3128-6905, 7926-0533; info-mundomaya@inguat.gob.gt; Aeropuerto Internacional Mundo Maya; 7am-7pm Tue-Thu, 7-11am & 3-7pm Fri-Mon) at the airport.

Getting There & Away

AIR

Aeropuerto Internacional Mundo Maya is on the eastern outskirts of Santa Elena, 2km from the causeway connecting Santa Elena and Flores. **Avianca** (www.avianca.com) has two flights daily between here and Guatemala City. The Belizean airline **Tropic Air** (7926-0348; www.tropicair.com) flies once a day to/from Belize City.

BUS

Long-distance buses use the Terminal Nuevo de Autobuses in Santa Elena, located 1.5km south of the causeway along 6a Av. It is also used by a slew of *aka expresos* (microbuses), with frequent services to numerous destinations. Second-class buses and some micros make an additional stop at 5a Calle, in the **market area** (the 'old' terminal) before heading out. You can reduce your trip time by 15 minutes by going straight to the market, though the vehicle may be full by then.

CAR

Several car-rental companies have desks at the airport.

Hertz (3724-4424; www.hertz.com; per day from Q461; 7am-6pm)

Tabarini (7926-0253; www.tabarini.com; per day from Q300; 7am-6pm)

SHUTTLE MINIBUS

Most hotels and travel agencies can book shuttles, and they will pick you up from where you're staying. Returns leave Tikal at 12:30pm, 3pm and 5pm. If you know which roundtrip you plan to be on, ask your driver to hold a seat for you or arrange one in another minibus. If you stay overnight in Tikal and want to return to Flores by minibus, it's a good idea to reserve a seat with a driver when they arrive in the morning.

Getting Around

A taxi from the airport to Santa Elena or Flores costs Q60 (or Q20 per person in a shared ride). There's a **taxi stand** on Calle Playa Sur in Flores. *Tuk-tuks* will take you anywhere between or within Flores and Santa Elena for Q20; the *tuk-tuk* service stops after 7pm. For lake travel, catch a **boat** (1-way Q5-20; 6am-midnight) from Flores, or (if you need it) the **car ferry** (car & driver Q15, per additional passenger Q2; 5am-9:30pm).

BUSES FROM SANTA ELENA

DESTINATION	COST	DURATION	FREQUENCY	CONNECTIONS
Belize City	Q160	4½-5hr	Línea Dorada leaves at 7am, returning from Belize City at 1pm.	Connects with boats to Caye Caulker & Ambergris Caye.
Bethel/La Técnica (Mexican border)	Q50	4-4½hr	Fuente del Norte also departs at 6am.	
Carmelita	Q80	4½hr	Microbus transport possible, but unreliable.	Private transport best, usually arranged via your tour operator.
Cobán	Q80-125			Take a bus or minibus to Sayaxché, from where connecting microbuses leave for Cobán.
El Ceibo/La Palma (Mexican border)	Q50	4hr	El Naranjo–bound microbuses depart every 20min, 4am-6pm, stopping at the El Ceibo junction, from where there are shuttles to the border (Q15, 15min). Some go all the way to El Ceibo..	At La Palma, on the Mexican side, you can find transport to Tenosique, Tabasco (1hr), & onward to Palenque or Villahermosa.
El Remate	Q20	45min	ATIM (p239) microbuses leave every 30min (p244)	Buses & minibuses to/from Melchor de Mencos will drop you at Puente Ixlú junction, 2km south of El Remate.
Guatemala City	Q130-205	8-9hr	Línea Dorada runs 1st-class buses at 8am, 8pm & 9pm (Q205). Autobuses del Norte has buses at 9pm & 10pm (Q180). Fuente del Norte runs at least 11 buses between 4am & 10pm (Q130), including 5 deluxe buses (Q180).	
Melchor de Mencos (Belizean border)	Q30-50	2hr	Microbuses go about every hr 5am-6pm. Fuente del Norte leaves at 2:30am, 5am, 6am & 4:30pm.	
Puerto Barrios	Q270	6hr	No direct buses.	Take a Guatemala City–bound Fuente del Norte bus & change at La Ruidosa junction (Q90-150), south of Río Dulce.
Río Dulce	Q140	4hr		Take a Guatemala City–bound bus with Fuente del Norte or Línea Dorada.
San Andrés/San José	Q8-10	35-40min	Microbuses depart around every 15min 5am-6:40pm, from the left side of the terminal entrance.	
Sayaxché	Q23	1½hr	Microbuses depart about every 15min 5:35am-6pm.	
Tikal	Q30-80	1¼hr	8 microbuses by ATIM btwn 6am & 3:20pm, the last returning at 5pm.	You could also take the slower Uaxactún-bound bus (Q40) at 2:15pm or 3:40pm.

San Miguel & Tayazal

San Miguel itself is a quiet, slow-moving place. A short boat ride from busy cosmopolitan Flores, it has a far more idyllic vibe, especially along the waterfront promenade. Steps from the dock stands a stone horse, dedicated in 2014 to the 'wisdom and bravery of the indomitable Itzá people.'

There's really little to do here other than relax or visit the nearby ruin of the same name. But that's the joy of coming here…to get away from it all.

Sights

San Miguel & Tayazal ARCHAEOLOGICAL SITE

(Q5; 8am-5pm) Covering the western end of the San Miguel peninsula are the remains of Tayazal, among the last of the Maya capitals. The chiefly Classic-era mounds are overgrown by vegetation, and a few pockmarked stelae have been recovered. The real draw, though, is the chance to wander the forested spine of the peninsula, taking in panoramic views of the lake.

Tayazal was settled by the Itzáes, refugees from the destroyed city of Chichén Itzá in Yucatán, who held out against the Spanish until 1697.

Lanchas (small motorboats; Q5 per person) make the five-minute crossing to San Miguel village from the north side of Flores whenever they have a boatload. To reach the ruins, walk 250m to the left along the shore from where the boat drops you, then turn up the paved street to the right. After 300m, turn left at the 'Playa' sign, passing a football field on your right. About another 600m on, a trail on the right leads to **Playa El Chechenal**, a swimming beach with a dock extending over turquoise waters and a few picnic tables (admission Q5). Continue west another 300m to reach the main entrance to the site. From here it's a precipitous climb up the hillside – actually one of the pyramids of ancient Tayazal – to reach **El Mirador del Rey Canek**, an observation point with 360-degree views around Lago de Petén Itzá. The archaeological site can be visited by circling round the base of the tower and skirting the lake back toward the village. Around 800m further, go left up a hill (past a building foundation), then follow a dirt road left to reach the Gran Plaza, where you'll find some weathered **stelae** dating from the Late Classic Period.

Sleeping & Eating

The one shoreline hotel here prepares *pescado blanco* (white fish) from the lake and other local specialties.

Posada San Miguel HOTEL $

(7867-5312; http://laposadasanmiguel.com; s/d Q98/195;) This amiably managed little lakefront hotel is on the incredibly idyllic Peninsula San Miguel, just a five-minute passage over from Flores by *lancha* (Q15, or free if you call 24 hours in advance). There's a section of rooms with orthopedic beds along a fabulous terrace with painted-wood lounge chairs. From the dock, head left and go round the bend.

A café prepares *pescado blanco* (whitefish) from the lake and other local specialties.

Lago de Petén Itzá

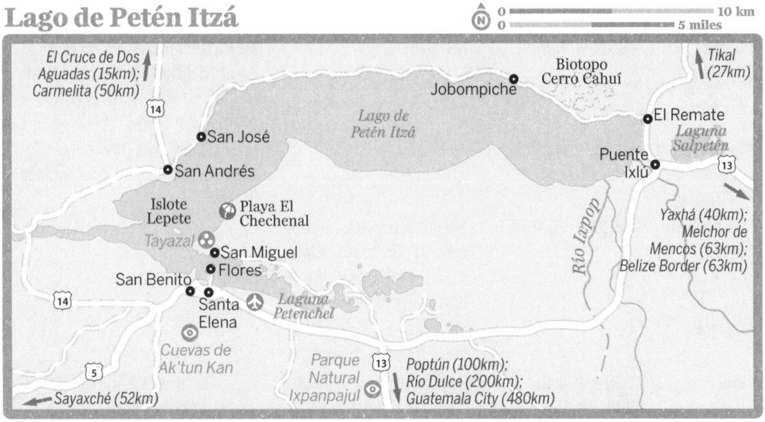

Getting There & Away

Lanchas (Q15 per person, or free if made with the hotel) make the five-minute crossing to San Miguel village from the north side of Flores whenever they have a boatload. You can also access by car, either with a **car ferry** (car with driver Q15, per additional passenger Q2; ⏲ 5am-9:30pm) or on land.

San José & San Andrés

POP 9340 / ELEV 202M

San Andrés and San José, a pair of similarly sized, small towns at the northwest corner of Lago de Petén Itzá, are just a few kilometers apart but are distinct in character.

In San Andrés, a jumble of mismatched houses covers a precipitous hillside interwoven with lushly overgrown paths, all imbued with the calming presence of the lake.

San José is peopled by Itzá Maya, descendants of the area's pre-Hispanic inhabitants. The extraordinarily neat and orderly village descends steeply from its little blue church to the lakefront, site of a waterslide park and a couple of seafood shacks.

Sleeping & Eating

Most visitors to the area stay at one of two lakefront lodges.

Hotel Bahía Taitzá HOTEL **$$**
(☎7928-8125; www.taitza.com; d/tr Q300/400; P ⊖ ❄ ☎ ≋) West of San José, this is an elaborate spread where you can truly unwind. Twenty-four well-designed rooms with tropical hardwood furnishings and lovely porches are in three buildings facing the lake across a lawn dotted with ficus and almond trees. The 16 new units in a row on a rise are less exotic, but are more spacious and have air-con.

Wood-fired pizzas, vegetarian curries and such are served under a beachfront *palapa*, and kids will love the trampoline, pool and playground.

★**Private Reserve Ni'tun** RESORT **$$$**
(☎5201-0759; www.nitun.com; s/d incl breakfast from Q1100/1770; P ⊖ @ ☎) West of San Andrés and down a gravel road, Ni'tun is set on a 35-acre patch of protected secondary forest where six species of hummingbird nest year-round. Four spacious huts built from indigenous materials feature handcrafted furniture and wraparound screened windows. Superb meals are prepared in the open-air clubhouse with a lounge on the upper deck.

> **NIGHT OF THE SKULLS**
>
> San José is a special place to be on the night of October 31, when perfectly preserved human skulls, normally housed in the church, are paraded around town on a velvet pillow followed by devotees in traditional dress, carrying candles. Throughout the night, the skulls make visits to predetermined houses, where blessings are sought, offerings made and a feast eaten.

Bernie and Lorena, Guatemalan conservationists, built and operate the lodge and coordinate adventure excursions through their affiliated company, **Monkey Eco Tours** (☎5201-0759, 5414-5780; www.nitun.com; San Andrés).

Getting There & Away

Microbuses depart around every 15 minutes from 5am to 6:40pm from the left side of the main terminal in Santa Elena, stopping in San Andrés (Q10, 35 minutes) and continuing another five minutes along the shore to San José.

El Remate

This peaceful spot at the eastern end of Lago de Petén Itzá makes a good alternative base for Tikal-bound travelers – it's more relaxed than Flores and closer to the site, and its lakeside living has a ramshackle vibe all of its own. People come here to bask in life-affirming slowness, so don't expect pumping discos or craft cocktails. This is all about the *cerveza* (beer) and the view.

El Remate begins 1km north of Puente Ixlú, where the road to the Belize border diverges from the Tikal road. The village strings along the Tikal road for 1km to another junction, where a branch heads west along the north shore of the lake.

El Remate is known for its wood carving, which you can buy from stalls along the main road.

Activities

Most El Remate accommodations can book two-hour boat trips for **birdwatching** or nocturnal **crocodile spotting** (each Q150 per person). Try Hotel Mon Ami (p243), which also offers sunset lake tours with detours up the Ixlú and Ixpop rivers (Q200 per person).

Biotopo Cerro Cahuí NATURE RESERVE
(Q40; ⌚7am-4pm) Comprising a 7.3-sq-km swath of subtropical forest rising up from the lake over limestone terrain, this nature reserve offers mildly strenuous hiking and excellent wildlife-watching, with paths to some brilliant lookout points. As a bonus, there's an adjacent lakeside park with diving docks for a refreshing conclusion to the tour.

More than 20 mammal species roam the reserve, including spider and howler monkeys, white-tailed deer and even the elusive Mesoamerican tapir, though sightings are rare. Birdlife is rich and varied, with the opportunity to spot toucans, woodpeckers and the famous ocellated turkey, a big bird resembling a peacock. Trees include mahogany, cedar, *ramón* and cohune palm, along with many types of bromeliads, ferns and orchids.

A network of loop trails ascends the hill to three lookout points, affording views of the whole lake and of Laguna Salpetén to the east. The trail called Los Escobos (4km long, about 2¼ hours), through secondary growth forest, is good for spotting monkeys.

The admission fee includes the right to camp or sling your hammock under small thatch shelters inside the entrance. There are toilets and showers. The reserve is 1.75km west along Jobompiche Rd from El Remate.

Project Ix-Canaan VOLUNTEERING
(☎5804-8639; www.ixcanaan.com) This group supports the improvement of health, education and opportunities for rainforest inhabitants. Operating here since 1996, it runs a community clinic, women's center, library and research center. Volunteers work in the clinic, build and maintain infrastructure, and assist in various other ways.

Tours

La Casa de Don David offers tours to Yaxhá (US$60 per person, minimum two people, US$40 for four or more), and Tikal (US$120). Prices include transport, an English-speaking guide and lunch, but not admission to the site. Horizontes Mayas (p244) has slightly cheaper tours and runs by reservation only. Most other hotels will also do their best to arrange tours, as this is a key reason people come. Do *not* purchase tours or tickets from anyone who boards your bus, as these are usually scams.

Sleeping

Hotels here range from budget hostels to fairly fancy resorts, with most falling into the category of clean and economical family-run spots. Most are set up for swimming in – and watching the sun set over – the lake.

Along the Main Road

Hotel Las Gardenias HOTEL $
(☎5923-4338; www.hotelasgardenias.com; Ruta a Tikal; s/d Q80/160, with air-con Q150/250; P ⊖ ❄ @ 📶) Right at the junction with the north-shore road, this cordial hotel/restaurant/shuttle operator has two sections: the wood-paneled rooms at the front are bigger, while those in the rear are appealingly removed from the road. All feature comfortable beds with woven spreads, attractively tiled showers and some porches with hammocks. There's also an on-site restaurant.

Posada Ixchel HOTEL $
(☎3044-5379; hotelixchel@yahoo.com; s/d/tr Q90/140/190) This family-owned place near the village's main junction is a superior deal, with spotless, wood-fragrant rooms featuring fans and handcrafted mosquito nets. The cobbled courtyard has inviting little nooks with tree-log seats.

Hostal Hermano Pedro HOSTEL $
(☎5164-6485; www.hhpedro.com; Calle Camino Biblico 8055; dm/s/d incl breakfast Q80/80/160; P ⊖ 📶) About 150m from the north-shore junction, this two-level wooden structure has a relaxed environment, with plenty of hammocks in the patio and along the verandas. Recycled elements are cleverly incorporated into the decor of the spacious rooms, which feature big fans and lacy curtains. Guests can use the kitchen. Q50 for a dorm without breakfast.

Hotel Sun Breeze HOTEL $$
(☎5898-2665; infosunbreezehotel@gmail.com; Main Rd; s/d Q150/200, with air-con Q200/250; P ⊖ ❄ 📶) The nearest place to the junction, this excellent-value homey guesthouse has neatly kept and well-ventilated rooms with TVs, screened windows, and porches. Rear units at the back of a pleasant patio are best. It's a short stroll to the public beach.

Hotel Palomino Ranch HOTEL $$
(☎3075-4189; hotelpalominorancho@gmail.com; Jobompiche Rd; s/d Q300/488; P ⊖ ❄ 📶 🏊)

An incongruous slice of the old west in El Remate, this hotel has air-conditioned rooms with a cowpoke motif. It has a swimming pool and a stable: guests are allowed to ride around the grounds for free from 7am to 4pm, and trail rides can be arranged as well. Food and beverages are served from 7am to 9pm in the vintage saloon/restaurant.

Along the North Shore Road

Casa de Doña Tonita HOSTEL **$**

(5767-4065; dm/r Q50/150) This friendly family-run place has seven basic, adequately ventilated rooms, each with two single beds and screened windows, in a two-story clapboard *rancho* (small house), plus a dorm situated over a restaurant that serves tasty, reasonably priced meals. There's just one shower. Across the road at the end of a pier is a hut for sunset gazing.

★ **Alice Guesthouse** BUNGALOW **$$**

(3087-0654; www.facebook.com/aliceguesthouse guatemala; dm Q70, bungalow with/without bathroom Q230/200;) As in Wonderland, that is. Fruit of the budding imaginations of a Franco-Belgian pair, this slightly remote spread looks not at the lake but at a swath of jungle. Free-form, friendly and fun, it has dorms in fanciful huts with conical thatch roofs, a pair of neat colorful cabins and a tropical shower in a roundhouse, all connected by pebbly paths.

An open-air kitchen is the domain of a chef imported from Nantes. To reach Alice, go down the Jobompiche road about 1.5km; a signed track on the right angles uphill. The lake is a short walk away.

★ **Posada del Cerro** BUNGALOW **$$**

(5376-8722; www.posadadelcerro.com; Jobompiche Rd; dm/s/d/tr/apt Q100/220/330/450/550;) This ecologically sound option blends into the jungle, close enough to Biotopo Cerro Cahuí to hear monkeys howl the evening in. Ten thoughtfully furnished rooms occupy stone-and-hardwood houses and solitary huts scattered over the hillside; one is open to the woods with its own lake-view deck. It also has an eight-bed hut and an apartment that sleeps four to five.

Gringo Perdido Ecological Inn RESORT **$$**

(2334-2305; www.hotelgringoperdido.com; Jobompiche Rd; campsite Q50, s/d with breakfast & dinner Q360/700;) Ensconced in a paradisaical lakefront setting within the Cerro Cahuí biosphere reserve, this jungle-style lodge offers a bank of rooms with full-wall roll-up blinds to give you the sensation of sleeping in the open air. A few lakeside bungalows offer a bit more seclusion. It also has a grassy campground with thatched-roof shelters for slinging hammocks, and a large bookcase lending library.

The Gringo Perdido is 3km along the north shore from the main Tikal road.

La Casa de Don David HOTEL **$$**

(5949-2164; www.lacasadedondavid.com; Jobompiche Rd; s/d incl breakfast or dinner from Q248/468; restaurant 6:30am-9pm;) Just west of the junction, this full-service outfit has spotless, modern rooms decorated with Maya textiles. All feature verandas and hammocks facing the broad garden that's been cultivated into an incredible aviary. Whether or not you're staying here, don't miss the ceiba tree and Maya calendar arrangement in the rear garden designed by owner David Kuhn (the original Gringo Perdido).

Those needing liquid refreshment need look no further than the 'Toucan Express,' a handmade beverage robot that zips your drinks out from the restaurant to the deck, several hundred yards away. Birders will enjoy the multiple feeders, with easy sightings of orioles and hummingbirds.

Substantial discounts in the slower seasons after Semana Santa.

Hotel Mon Ami HOTEL **$$**

(3010-0284; Jobompiche Rd; dm/s/d Q75/150/200, s/d without bathroom Q100/150;) A 15-minute walk from the Tikal road, Santiago's place maintains a good balance between jungle wildness and Euro sophistication. Quirkily furnished cabins and dorms with hammocks are reached along candlelit paths through gardens bursting with local plant life. And the pier opposite is a delight. Fans of French cuisine will appreciate the open-air restaurant.

Pirámide Paraiso HOTEL **$$$**

(2334-1967; www.hotelgringoperdido.com; Jobompiche Rd; s/d Q488/975;) Built in time for the dawn of the new *baktún* (a *baktún* equals about four centuries) of the Maya calendar (in 2012) is this glitzy addition to the Gringo Perdido Ecological Inn, a smooth white structure that rises surreally from the forest like a Maya temple. Each of the eight huge, luxuriously decorated suites features its own exterior Jacuzzi.

Eating

Most hotels have their own restaurants, which are open to non-guests, and there are simple *comedores* (cheap eateries) scattered along the main road.

Desayunos El Árbol CAFE $
(5950-2367; breakfast mains Q30-40, dinner mains 40-60; 6am-2pm, 5-9pm Thu-Tue) This gringo-friendly shack sports a lovely, lake-view terrace, a fine setting for healthy breakfasts, including granola, pancakes and omelets. Sandwiches come with a side of salad, and the smoothies are just grand. It's 50m south of the crossroads.

La Casa de Don David INTERNATIONAL $
(5949-2164; mains Q45; 7am-8:30pm;) This splendid open-air dining hall serves a good breakfast, including banana pancakes (Q30), fruit and granola, and has a collection of *National Geographic* articles on Maya sites to browse over coffee. Nightly *prix fixe* specials include vegetarian fare – reserve your meal by 4pm.

★ **Mon Ami** FRENCH $$
(3010-0284, 5805-4868; Jobompiche Rd; mains Q35-85; 6am-10pm) On Jobompiche Rd, this peaceful palm-thatched affair is the French jungle bistro you've dreamed of. Try the lake white fish or the big *ensalada francesa* (French salad). Specials usually run Q35 to Q45, and change frequently.

★ **Las Orquídeas** ITALIAN $$
(5701-9022; Jobompiche Rd; pastas Q55-120; noon-9pm Tue-Sun; P) Almost hidden in the forest, a 10-minute walk along the north shore from the Tikal junction, is this marvelous open-air dining hall. The genial Italian owner-chef blends *chaya,* a local herb, into his own tagliatelle and *panzarotti* (smaller version of calzones).

Information

You can change US dollars and euros or check your email at **Horizontes Mayas** (5773-6193; www.horizontesmayas.com; Ruta a Tikal), near the junction.

Getting There & Away

El Remate is linked to Santa Elena by frequent minibus service (Q25) from 5:30am to 6pm daily.

For Tikal, a collective shuttle departs at 5:30am, starting back at 2pm (one-way/round trip Q30/50). Any El Remate accommodations can make reservations. Or catch one of the **ATIM** (ATIM; 5905-0089) or other shuttles passing through from Santa Elena to Tikal from 5am to 3:30pm.

For taxis, ask at Hotel Sun Breeze (p242). A one-way ride to Flores costs about Q250; a round trip to Tikal costs Q350.

For Melchor de Mencos on the Belizean border, get a minibus or bus from Puente Ixlú, 1km south of El Remate (Q60, 1¼ hours). Additionally, Horizontes Mayas (p244) offers private departures to Belize City (Q400) via Melchor.

Melchor de Mencos

POP 10,299

It's 100km from Flores to Melchor de Mencos, the Guatemalan town on the border with Belize. From the Tikal junction at Puente Ixlú, 27km from Flores, the good paved road continues to the border with a brief stretch of rough rutted surface.

Most travelers pass through Melchor, though there is an actual town across the Río Mopán, with hotels, banks and businesses. There's little reason to linger.

Sleeping & Eating

You'll find a handful of places to stay in workaday central Melchor, from basic guesthouses to a business-class hotel, but far and away the most appealing option is the one that's secluded by the river, the Río Mopán Lodge. It's between the bridge and Guatemalan immigration.

Beyond the immigration post, you can get decent tacos, burgers and meals at the stores and shacks on either side of the river. In town try the restaurant at the main business hotel.

Río Mopán Lodge LODGE $
(7926-5196; avinsa@yahoo.com; r with/without air-con Q188/150; P) Set back from the road in lush, jungle grounds, this spot is so tranquil that you'll find it hard to comprehend you're just 50m from the immigration booth. It's between the bridge and Guatemalan immigration. The rooms are big and cool, with Maya decor and balconies overlooking the still river. Some units have air-con.

Swiss owner Marco is an expert on Maya history and archaeology.

Information

There are money changers at the border for changing quetzals to Belize dollars, an exchange that is not performed by banks. Rates are better on the Guatemalan side.

In Melchor, there are several Cajero 5B ATMs.

Getting There & Away

The Guatemalan immigration post is open 6am to 9pm. Officially there are no fees at the border for entering or leaving Guatemala, but in reality immigration officials on the Guatemalan side charge a Q20 fee to enter or leave the country. Get around this by saying you don't have cash and need to pay by credit card – they will likely let it slide, since they won't be able to pocket any cash.

No fee is charged to enter Belize, but travelers leaving that country have to pay B$40 for the departure tax and protected-areas conservation fee (in Belizean or US dollars), though only if they've spent a night there.

Taxis run between the border and the nearest town in Belize, Benque Viejo del Carmen, 3km away, for B$6. Authorized rates are posted for other destinations, including Belize International Airport (B$200). Buses run from Benque to Belize City (B$10, three hours) about every hour from 3:30am to 6pm.

Coming in the other direction, travelers bound for Flores or Tikal, after clearing immigration, should cross the bridge, then continue two streets until the military post on the left. Turn left there to find a **microbus terminal** with departures to Santa Elena at least once an hour until 5:30pm (Q50, two hours). Red Asetur vans provide a shuttle service to Yaxhá, Tikal and Flores with highly negotiable rates.

Tikal

The most striking feature of **Tikal** (☎2367-2837; www.tikalnationalpark.org; Q150; ⏲6am-6pm) is its towering, steep-sided temples, rising to heights of more than 44m, but what distinguishes it is its jungle setting. Its many plazas have been cleared of trees and vines, its temples uncovered and partially restored, but as you walk from one building to another you pass beneath a dense canopy of rainforest amid the rich, loamy aromas of earth and vegetation. Much of the delight of touring the site comes from strolling the broad causeways, originally built from packed limestone to accommodate traffic between temple complexes. By stepping softly you're more likely to spot monkeys, agoutis, foxes and ocellated turkeys.

Tikal is a popular day trip from Flores or El Remate, so it is much quieter in the late afternoon and early morning, which makes an overnight stay an attractive option.

History

Tikal is set on a low hill, which becomes evident as you ascend to the Gran Plaza from the entry road. Affording relief from the surrounding swampy ground, this high terrain may explain why the Maya settled here around 700 BC. Another reason was the abundance of flint, used by the ancients to make clubs, spear points, arrowheads and knives. The wealth of this valuable stone meant good tools could be made, and flint could be traded for other goods. Within 200 years the Maya of Tikal had begun to build stone ceremonial structures, and by 200 BC there was a complex of buildings on the site of the Acrópolis del Norte.

Classic Period

The Gran Plaza was beginning to assume its present shape and extent by the time of Christ. By the dawn of the Early Classic Period, around AD 250, Tikal had become an important religious, cultural and commercial city with a large population. King Yax Ehb' Xooc, in power about AD 230, is looked upon as the founder of the dynasty that ruled Tikal thereafter.

Under Chak Tok Ich'aak I (King Great Jaguar Paw), who ruled in the mid-4th century, Tikal adopted a brutal method of warfare, used by the rulers of Teotihuacán in central Mexico. Rather than meeting their adversaries on the battlfield in hand-to-hand combat, the army of Tikal used auxiliary units to encircle the enemy and throw spears to kill them from a distance. This first use of 'air power' among the Maya of Petén enabled Siyah K'ak' (Smoking Frog), the Tikal general, to conquer the army of Uaxactún; thus Tikal became the dominant kingdom in El Petén.

By the middle of the Classic Period, in the mid-6th century, Tikal's military prowess and its association with Teotihuacán allowed it to grow until it sprawled over 30 sq km and had a population of perhaps 100,000. But in 553, Yajaw Te' K'inich II (Lord Water) came to the throne of Caracol (in southwestern Belize), and within a decade had conquered Tikal and sacrificed its king. Tikal and other Petén kingdoms suffered under Caracol's rule until the late 7th century when, under new leadership, it apparently cast off its oppressor and rose again.

BIRDWATCHING AT TIKAL

As well as howler and spider monkeys romping through the trees of Tikal, the plethora of birds flitting through the canopy and across the green expanses of the plazas is impressive. The ruined temple complexes present ideal viewing platforms for this activity, often providing the ability to look down upon the treetops to observe examples of the 300 or so bird species (migratory and resident) that have been recorded here. Bring binoculars and a copy of *The Birds of Tikal: An Annotated Checklist*, by Randell A Beavers, available at the visitor center (p252) shop. Tread quietly and be patient, and you'll probably see some of the following birds in the areas specified:

Templo de las Inscripciones Tody motmots, four trogon species and royal flycatchers

El Mundo Perdido Two oriole species, keel-billed toucans and collared aracaris

Complejo P Great curassows, three species of woodpecker, crested guans, plain chachalacas and three tanager species

Aguada Tikal (Tikal Reservoir) Three kingfisher species, jacanas, blue herons, two species of sandpiper, and great kiskadees

Entrance path Tiger herons sometimes nest in the huge ceiba tree located here

Complejo Q Red-capped and white-collared manakins

Complejo R Emerald toucanets

Tikal's Renaissance

A powerful king named Ha Sawa Chaan K'awil (682–734, also called Ah Cacao or Moon Double Comb), 26th successor of Yax Ehb' Xooc, restored not only Tikal's military strength but also its primacy in the Maya world. He conquered the greatest rival Maya state, Calakmul in Mexico, in 695, and his successors were responsible for building most of the great temples around the Gran Plaza that survive today. King Ah Cacao was buried beneath the staggering height of Templo I.

Tikal's greatness waned around 900, but it was not alone in its downfall, which was part of the mysterious general collapse of lowland Maya civilization.

Rediscovery

No doubt the Itzáes, who occupied Tayazal (now Flores), knew of Tikal in the Late Postclassic Period. Perhaps they even came here to worship at the shrines of old gods. Spanish missionary friars who moved through El Petén after the conquest left brief references to these jungle-bound structures, but their writings moldered in libraries for centuries.

It wasn't until 1848 that the Guatemalan government sent out an expedition, under the leadership of Modesto Méndez and Ambrosio Tut, to visit the site. This may have been inspired by John L Stephens' bestselling accounts of fabulous Maya ruins, published in 1841 and 1843 (though Stephens never visited Tikal). Like Stephens, Méndez and Tut took an artist, Eusebio Lara, to record their archaeological discoveries. An account of their findings was published by the Berlin Academy of Science.

In 1877 the Swiss Dr Gustav Bernoulli visited Tikal. His explorations resulted in the removal of carved wooden lintels from Templos I and IV and their shipment to Basel, where they are still on view in the Museum für Völkerkunde.

Scientific exploration of Tikal began with the arrival of English archaeologist Alfred P Maudslay in 1881. Others continued his work, Teobert Maler, Alfred M Tozzer and RE Merwin among them. Tozzer worked at Tikal on and off from the beginning of the 20th century until his death in 1954. The inscriptions at Tikal were studied and deciphered by Sylvanus G Morley.

Archaeological research and restoration was carried on by the University of Pennsylvania and the Guatemalan Instituto de Antropología e Historia until 1969. Since 1991, a joint Guatemalan–Spanish project has worked on conserving and restoring Templos I and V. The Parque Nacional Tikal (Tikal National Park) was declared a Unesco World Heritage Site in 1979.

LIDAR, A New Era

This process of rediscovery is continuing, and improvements in LIDAR scanning have made it possible to map and identify ever more sections of the Yucatán's forests and swamps. This has led to spectacular discoveries and scientists are currently estimating that the Tikal complex, once estimated at 6000 structures, may exceed 10,000. Even more fascinating, newly discovered structures indicate that people may have occupied areas considered far too swampy to live in today.

These recent and ongoing rediscoveries make it impossible to speak with absolute authority of the real size and scope of cities such as Tikal. What's unequivocal is that this is without a doubt the most important ruin in Guatemala and a must-see on many tourists' lists.

Sights

Gran Plaza

The entry path comes into the Gran Plaza around the **Templo I**, the Templo del Gran Jaguar (Temple of the Grand Jaguar). This was built to honor – and bury – Ah Cacao. The king may have worked out the plans for the building himself, but it was actually erected above his tomb by his son, who succeeded him to the throne in AD 734. The king's rich burial goods included stingray spines, which were used for ritual bloodletting, 180 jade objects, pearls and 90 pieces of bone carved with hieroglyphs. At the top of the 44m-high temple is a small enclosure of three rooms covered by a corbeled arch. The sapodilla-wood lintels over the doors were richly carved; one of them was removed and is now in the Basel Museum für Völkerkunde. The lofty roofcomb that crowned the temple was originally adorned with reliefs and bright paint. When it's illuminated by the afternoon sun, it is still possible to make out the figure of a seated dignitary.

Although climbing to the top of Templo I is prohibited, the views from **Templo II** just across the way are nearly as awe-inspiring. Templo II, also known as the Temple of the Masks, was at one time almost as high as Templo I, but it now measures only 38m without its roofcomb.

Nearby, the **Acrópolis del Norte** (North Acropolis) significantly predates the two great temples. Archaeologists have uncovered about 100 different structures, the oldest of which dates from before the time of Christ, with evidence of occupation as far back as 600 BC. The Maya built and rebuilt on top of older structures, and the many layers, combined with the elaborate burials of Tikal's early rulers, added sanctity and power to their temples. The final version of the acropolis, as it stood around AD 800, had more than 12 temples atop a vast platform, many of them the work of King Ah Cacao. Look especially for the two huge, powerful wall masks, uncovered from an earlier structure and now protected by roofs. On the plaza side of the North Acropolis are two rows of stelae. These served to record the great deeds of the kings, to sanctify their memory and to add power to the temples and plazas that surrounded them.

Acrópolis Central

South and east of the Gran Plaza, this maze of courtyards, little rooms and small temples is thought by many to have been a palace where Tikal's nobles lived. Others think the tiny rooms may have been used for sacred rites and ceremonies, as graffiti found within them suggest. Over the centuries the configuration of the rooms was repeatedly changed, suggesting that perhaps this 'palace' was in fact a noble or royal family's residence and alterations were made to accommodate groups of relatives. One part of the acropolis provided lodgings for archaeologist Teobert Maler (1842–1917) when he worked at Tikal.

Templo III

West of the Gran Plaza, across the Calzada Tozzer (Tozzer Causeway) stands **Templo III**, still undergoing restoration. Only its upper reaches have been cleared. A scene carved into the lintel at its summit, 55m high, depicts a figure in an elaborate jaguar suit, believed to be the ruler Dark Sun. In front of it stands Stela 24, which marks the date of its construction, AD 810. From this point, you can continue west to Templo IV along the Calzada Tozzer, one of several sacred byways between the temple complexes of Tikal.

Templo V & Acrópolis del Sur

Due south of the Gran Plaza, **Templo V** is a remarkably steep structure (57m high) that was built sometime between the 7th and 8th centuries AD. It consists of seven stepped platforms and, unlike the other great temples, has slightly rounded corners. A recent excavation of the temple revealed a group of embedded structures, some with Maya calendars on their walls. Tempting as it may seem, you are not allowed to scale the broad central staircase.

Tikal

SURVEYING THE CLASSIC MAYA KINGDOM

Constructed in successive waves over a period of at least 800 years, Tikal is a vast, complicated site with hundreds of temples, pyramids and stelae. There's no way you'll get to it all in a day, but by following this itinerary you'll see many of the highlights. Before setting out be sure to stop by the visitor center and examine the scale model of the site. The small ❶ **Museo Sylvanus G Morley** usually houses a wealth of artefacts, although the majority of its contents (other than Stela 31) are currently located in the CCIT research center while the museum is indefinitely under restoration. Present your ticket at the nearby ticket booth and when you reach the posted map, take a left. It's a 20-minute walk to the solitary ❷ **Templo VI**. From here it's a blissful stroll up the broad Calzada Méndez to the ❸ **Gran Plaza**, Tikal's ceremonial core, where you may examine the ancient precinct of the ❹ **North Acropolis**. Exit the plaza west, and take the first left, along a winding path, to ❺ **Templo V**. Round the rear to the right, a trail encircles the largely unexcavated South Acropolis to the ❻ **Plaza de los Siete Templos**. Immediately west stands the great pyramid of the ❼ **Mundo Perdido**. From here it's a quick stroll and a rather strenuous climb to the summit of ❽ **Temple IV**, Tikal's tallest structure.

TOP TIPS

- Bring food and water.
- All tickets, including sunrise/sunset, must be purchased in advance or at the entry gate. No tickets are sold inside the park.
- If you enter after 3pm, your ticket is good for the next day.
- Stay at one of the onsite hotels to catch the sunset/sunrise.
- To watch the sunset/sunrise from Temple IV, you'll need to purchase an additional ticket (Q100).
- Bring mosquito repellent.

ZAI ARAGON/SHUTTERSTOCK ©

Templo IV
Arrive in the late afternoon to get magically tinted photos of Temples I, II and III poking through the jungle canopy. Sunrise tours offer mystical mists tha

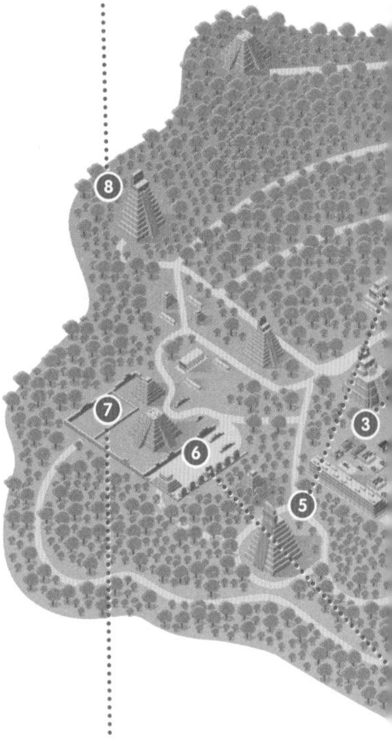

Mundo Perdido
This 'Lost World' features two impressive pyramids and some smaller structures, and the *talud-tablero* design hints at influences from distant Teotihuacán.

RALF BROSKVAR/GETTY IMAGES ©

FRANCISCO SANDOVAL GUATE/

KOBBY DAGAN/SHUTTERSTOCK ©

MICHAEL ZYSMAN/SHUTTERSTOCK ©

Templo V
As steep as it is massive, Tikal's second tallest temple (52m) has unusual rounded corners. Tempting as it may seem to climb, the broad front staircase is off-limits.

Gran Plaza
Though the surreally tall Templo I, a mausoleum to the Late Classic ruler Ah Cacao, is off-limits to climbers, you're welcome to ascend the almost-as-tall Templo II across the plaza.

North Acropolis
Amid the stack of smaller and much older temples that rise up the hillside north of the plaza, take a peek beneath the two thatched shelters on a ledge to find a pair of fearsome masks.

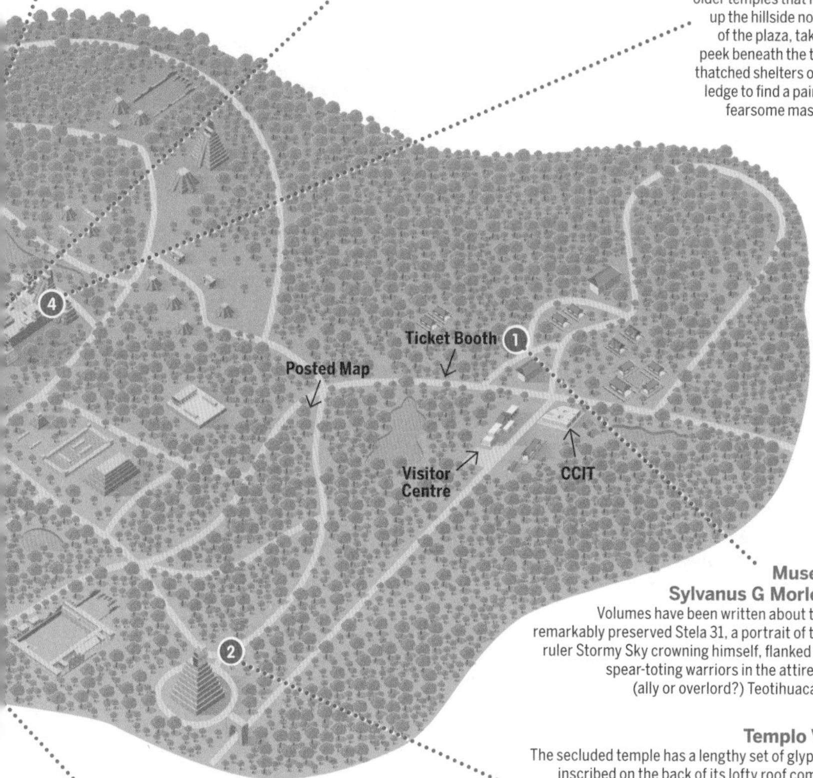

Museo Sylvanus G Morley
Volumes have been written about the remarkably preserved Stela 31, a portrait of the ruler Stormy Sky crowning himself, flanked by spear-toting warriors in the attire of (ally or overlord?) Teotihuacán.

Templo VI
The secluded temple has a lengthy set of glyphs inscribed on the back of its lofty roof comb, recording the lineage of successive kingdoms. Be patient: the contents of the weathered slab may take some effort to discern.

FRANCISCO SANDOVAL GUATE/SHUTTERSTOCK ©

Plaza de los Siete Templos
Seven miniature temples line up along the east side of this grassy courtyard. Climb the larger 'palace' at the south end to get a sightline along the septet.

MATYAS REHAK/SHUTTERSTOCK ©

Excavation is slow to progress on the mass of masonry just west of the temple, known collectively as the **Acrópolis del Sur** (South Acropolis). The palaces on top are from the Late Classic Period (the time of King Moon Double Comb), but earlier constructions probably go back 1000 years.

Plaza de los Siete Templos

To the west of the Acrópolis del Sur is this broad grassy plaza, reached via a path to its southern edge. Built in the Late Classic Period, the seven **temples** with their stout roofcombs line up along the east side of the plaza. On the south end stand three larger '**palaces**'; on the opposite end is an unusual **triple ballcourt**.

El Mundo Perdido

About 400m southwest of the Gran Plaza is **El Mundo Perdido** (Lost World), a complex of 38 structures with a huge pyramid in its midst, thought to be essentially Preclassic (with some later repairs and renovations). The pyramid, 32m high and 80m along the base, is surrounded by four much-eroded stairways, with huge masks flanking each one. The stairway facing eastward is thought to have functioned as a platform for viewing the sun's trajectory against a trio of structures on a raised platform to the east, a similar arrangement to the astronomical observatory at Uaxactún. Tunnels dug into the pyramid by archaeologists reveal four similar pyramids beneath the outer face; the earliest (Structure 5C-54 Sub 2B) dates from 700 BC, making this pyramid the oldest Maya structure at Tikal.

A smaller **temple** to the west, dating from the Early Classic Period, demonstrates Teotihuacán's influence, with its *talud-tablero* (stepped building) style of architecture.

Templo IV & Complejo N

Templo IV, at 65m, is the highest building at Tikal and the second-highest pre-Columbian building known in the western hemisphere, after La Danta at El Mirador. It was completed about AD 741, probably by order of Ah Cacao's son, Yax Kin, who was depicted on the carved lintel over the middle doorway (now in a museum in Basel, Switzerland), as the western boundary of the ceremonial precinct. A steep wooden staircase leads to the top. The view east is almost as good as from a helicopter – a panorama across the jungle canopy, with (from left to right) the temples of the Gran Plaza, Temple III, Temple V (just the top bit) and the great pyramid of the Mundo Perdido poking through.

Between Templo IV and Templo III is **Complejo N**, an example of the 'twin-temple' complexes erected during the Late Classic Period. This one was built in AD 711 by Ah Cacao to mark the 14th *katun*, or 20-year cycle, of *baktún* 9. The king himself is portrayed on the remarkably preserved Stela 16 in an enclosure just across the path. Beside the stelae is Altar 5, a circular stone depicting the same king accompanied by a priestly figure in the process of exhuming the skeleton of a female ruler.

Templo de las Inscripciones (Templo VI)

Templo VI is one of the few temples at Tikal to bear written records. On the rear of its 12m-high roofcomb is a long inscription – though it will take some effort to discern it in the bright sunlight – giving us the date AD 766. The sides and cornice of the roofcomb bear glyphs as well. Its secluded position, about a 25-minute walk southeast of the Gran Plaza along the Calzada Méndez, makes it a good spot for observing wildlife. From here, it's a 20-minute hike back to the main entrance.

Northern Complexes

About 1km north of the Gran Plaza is **Complejo P**. Like Complejo N, it's a Late Classic twin-temple complex that probably commemorated the end of a *katun*. **Complejo M**, next to it, was partially torn down by the Late Classic Maya to provide building materials for a causeway, now named after Alfred P Maudslay, which runs southwest to Templo IV. **Grupo H**, northeast of Complexes P and M, with one tall, cleared temple, had some interesting graffiti within its temples.

Complejo Q and **Complejo R**, about 300m north of the Gran Plaza, are very Late Classic twin-pyramid complexes with stelae and altars standing before the temples. Complex Q is perhaps the best example of the twin-temple type, as it has been partly restored. Stela 22 and Altar 10 are excellent examples of Late Classic Tikal relief carving, dated to AD 771.

Museums

Museo Sylvanus G Morley MUSEUM
(Museo Cerámico; Museum of Ceramics; Q30, also valid for Museo Lítico; 8am-4pm) This museum exhibits a number of superb ceramic pieces from excavations, including incense burners and vases, with descriptions of their uses and significance (in Spanish). The usual museum building is under restoration indefinitely, during which time the ceramics are displayed at the CCIT.

Two of the most highly prized items, the elaborately carved Stela 31 dedicated to the ruler Stormy Sky-Double Comb, and the simulated tomb of King Moon Double Comb with the precious items unearthed from his burial site beneath Temple I, remain inside the museum, and the guard can show them to you on request.

CCIT MUSEUM
(Centro de Conservación e Investigación de Tikal; 8am-4pm) FREE This Japanese-funded research center is devoted to the identification and restoration of pieces unearthed at the site. The 1300-sq-meter facility has a huge cache of items to sort through, and you can watch the restorers at work. Though not strictly a museum per se, it features an excellent gallery on the different materials used by Maya craftspeople.

The center is home to the Museo Sylvanus G Morley for an indefinite period while that museum is under restoration.

Museo Lítico MUSEUM
(Stone Museum; Q30, also valid for Museo Sylvanus G Morley; 8am-4pm) The larger of Tikal's two museums is in the visitor center. It houses a number of carved stones from the ruins. The photographs taken by pioneer archaeologists Alfred P Maudslay and Teobert Maler of the jungle-covered temples in various stages of discovery are particularly striking. Outside is a model showing how Tikal would have looked around AD 800.

Tours

Family-owned, local **Gem Trips** (4051-3805, USA (530) 853-4329, cell 4214-9514; www.gemtrips.com; Tikal sunrise US$150) offers excellent sunrise tours as well as guided trips to Tikal and other Maya sites, while archaeologist **Roxy Ortiz** (5197-5173; www.tikalroxy.blogspot.com) has years of experience trekking throughout the Maya world.

Multilingual guides are available at the information kiosk. These authorized guides display their accreditation card, listing the languages they speak. Before 7am the charge for a half-day tour is Q100 per person for three to six people. After that you pay for a group tour (Q600).

Canopy Tours Tikal ADVENTURE
(5615-4988; www.tikalcanopy.com; tours Q240; 7am-5pm) By the national-park entrance, this outfit offers a one-hour tour through the forest canopy, with the chance to ride a harness along a series of cables linking trees up to 300m apart, and to cross several hanging bridges. The fee does not include transport from Tikal or El Remate.

Sleeping

Staying overnight enables you to relax and savor the dawn and dusk, when most of the jungle birds and animals can be seen and heard (especially the howler monkeys). Other than camping, there are only three places to stay, and tour groups often have many of the rooms reserved. Almost any travel agency in Guatemala offers Tikal tours, including lodging, a meal or two, a guided tour and transportation.

Campground CAMPGROUND $
(campsite per person Q50, hammock with mosquito net Q85) Located across the road from the visitor center, the campground covers a large, grassy area and has a clean bathroom block and thatched shelters for hanging hammocks. Pay for your campsite at the main ticket booth. You don't need a reservation.

Tikal Inn HOTEL $$$
(7861-2444; www.tikalinn.com; s/d/bungalow Q500/730/720; P) Built in the late '60s, this resort-style lodging offers rooms in the main building and thatched bungalows alongside the pool and rear lawn, with little porches out front. All are simple, spacious and quite comfortable. The most secluded accommodations are the least expensive, in a handful of cabins at the end of a sawdust trail through the forest.

Jungle Lodge HOTEL $$$
(7861-0446; www.junglelodgetikal.com; s/d Q680/772, without bathroom Q359/423; P) Nearest of the hotels to the site entrance, this was originally built to house archaeologists working at Tikal. Self-contained bungalows, plus a bank of cheaper units, are well spaced

throughout rambling, jungle grounds. Some newer suites feature jungle-chic decor and outdoor rain-showers. The restaurant-bar serves veggie pastas, crepes and other international dishes in a tropical ambience.

Wi-fi is in the pool area and lobby only.

Jaguar Inn HOTEL **$$$**
(☎7926-2411; www.jaguartikal.com; campsite per person Q50, with tent Q115, s/d/tr Q532/639/852; P❄@📶) The inn of choice for youthful, independent travelers has duplex and quad bungalows with thatched roofs and hammocks on the porches, plus a smart little restaurant with a popular terrace out front. For those on a tight budget there are tents for rent on a platform.

Eating

Along the right-hand side of the access road stands a series of little *comedores* (eateries). All are open from about 6:30am to 8:30pm daily. Another restaurant is in the visitor center, with pastas and hamburgers among the offerings. If you want to spend all day at the ruins without having to make the 20- to 30-minute walk back to the *comedores,* carry food and water with you.

Comedor Tikal COMEDOR **$$**
(mains Q50-70; ⏱6:30am-8:30pm) This is one of a series of little open-air *comedores* along the right-hand side of the access road to Tikal.

Orientation

The archaeological site is at the center of the 550-sq-km Parque Nacional Tikal. The road from Flores enters the park 19km south of the ruins. From the parking lot at the site, it's a short walk back to the junction where there's an information kiosk. Immediately south of this junction, a **visitor center** (⏱8am-4pm) sells books, maps, souvenirs, hats, insect repellent, sun block and other necessities; it also houses a restaurant and museum (p251). Near the visitor center are Tikal's hotels, a campground, a few small *comedores* and a modern research center containing a second museum (p251).

It's a five-minute walk from the ticket control booth to the entry gate. Just beyond, there's a large map posted. From here, it's a 1.5km walk (20 minutes) southwest to the Gran Plaza. From the Gran Plaza west to Templo IV, it's more than 600m.

Information

Everyone (even those staying inside the park at one of the hotels) must purchase an entry ticket *in advance* at the initial gate on the road in (or at Banrural locations such as Flores or Guatemala City). Note that *tickets are no longer available anywhere inside the entry gate* – that includes sunrise tour tickets. You purchase in advance and then use them as needed at the time/day of your choice.

Seeing the sunrise from Templo IV at the west end of the main site is possible from about October to March, but to enter the park before or after visiting hours you must purchase an additional ticket for Q100, as this is not covered in the normal park entry. You must also have a guide.

The core of the ancient city takes up about 16 sq km, with more than 6000 structures, to which an additional 4000 have recently been identified by LIDAR technology, making this one of the largest Maya cities ever discovered. To visit all the major building complexes, you must walk at least 10km, so wear comfortable shoes with good rubber treads that grip well. The ruins here can be slick from rain and organic material, especially during the wet season. Bring plenty of water, as you'll be walking around all day in the heat.

Please don't feed the coatis (pisotes) that wander about the site.

MONEY

Jaguar Inn exchanges US dollars cash and traveler's checks.

Getting There & Away

Eight ATIM (p244) microbuses depart Flores between 6:30am and 3pm (Q30 to Q80, 1¼ hours). They return from Tikal at noon, 1:30pm, 3pm and 6pm. You could also take the Uaxactún-bound bus from the market of Santa Elena at 3:30pm, which goes a bit slower.

From El Remate, a collective shuttle departs at 5:30am for Tikal, starting back at 2pm (one-way/round trip Q30/50). Any El Remate accommodations can make reservations.

If traveling from Belize, get a Santa Elena–bound microbus to Puente Ixlú, sometimes called El Cruce, and switch there to a northbound microbus for the remaining 36km to Tikal. Heading from Tikal to Belize, start early and get off at Puente Ixlú to catch a bus or microbus eastward. Be wary of shuttles to Belize advertised at Tikal: these have been known to detour to Flores to pick up passengers! And do not purchase any tickets for ruins (or anything else) from so-called vendors on the bus.

Uaxactún

POP 700 / ELEV 175M

Uaxactún (wah-shahk-*toon*), 23km north of Tikal along an unpaved road through the jungle, was Tikal's political and military rival in Late Preclassic times. It was conquered by Tikal's Chak Tok Ich'aak I (King Great Jaguar

Paw) in the 4th century, and was subservient to its great sister to the south for centuries thereafter, though it experienced an apparent resurgence during the Terminal Classic, after Tikal went into decline.

Villagers make an income from collecting chicle, *pimienta* (allspice) and *xate* (low-growing palm, exported to Holland for floral arrangements) in the surrounding forest. In the *xate* warehouse at the west end of town, women put together bunches of the plants for export.

Much of the attraction here is the absolute stillness and isolation. Few visitors make it up this way.

Sights

Research performed by the Carnegie Institute in the 1920s and '30s laid the groundwork for much of the archaeological study that followed in the region, including the excavations at Tikal.

The fee of Q50 to enter Uaxactún is collected at the gate to Tikal National Park, though there is no ticket control at the site itself.

Colección Dr Juan Antonio Valdés MUSEUM (Campamento El Chiclero) FREE The collection on display here, on the north side of the airstrip, holds a remarkable wealth of Maya pottery from Uaxactún, Yaxhá and as far away as Oaxaca, Mexico. There are vases, cups, plates, bowls, incense burners and tall vessels for drinking chocolate. Caretaker Neria can tell you the history, origin, meaning and use of each one.

A case contains some of the most precious finds: stone earrings, arrowheads and three plates showing the dance of the corn god.

Although there's no admission fee, donations are appreciated.

Grupo E

The buildings here are grouped on five low hills. From the airstrip find the sign pointing to Grupo E between the Catholic and Evangelical churches on the right side, from where it's a 10- to 15-minute walk. The most significant temple here is **Templo E-VII-Sub**, among the earliest intact temples excavated, with foundations going back perhaps to 2000 BC. The pyramid is part of a group with astronomical significance: seen from it, the sun rises behind **Templo E-I** on the longest day of the year and behind **Templo E-III** on the shortest day. The four jaguar and serpent masks affixed to the main temple's staircase were painstakingly restored in 2014 by a group of Slovak archaeologists, but then covered up again for conservation. Viewed from Templo E-VII-Sub, the sun sets behind **Templo E-II** at the start of spring and autumn. **Templo E-V** is part of a complex of unexcavated temples at Grupo E. **Templo E-X** is the tallest and possibly the oldest of a set of temples at Grupo E.

Grupos B & A

About a 20-minute walk to the northwest of the airstrip are Grupo B and Grupo A, the latter featuring the more formidable structures around the city's main square. **Palacio V**, on the east side of the square, is considered a model for Tikal's North Acropolis. In 1916 the American archaeologist Sylvanus Morley uncovered a stelae dating from the 8th *baktún* at Grupo A. Thus the site was called Uaxactún, meaning 'eight stone.' Behind Palacio V, along a path back toward the village, is the imposing **Palacio A-XVIII**, affording the most panoramic view of the site from its summit.

Stela 5, at Grupo B, displays Tikal's signature glyph, from which archaeologists deduced that Uaxactún was under that city's sway by the date inscribed, 358.

Tours

Tours to Uaxactún can be arranged in Flores or at the hotels in El Remate and Tikal.

In Uaxactún, Hector Aldana Nuñez from Aldana's Lodge is an English-speaking guide specializing in nature-oriented tours of the region. He leads three-day treks to El Zotz and Tikal for around Q3000 per person. He also offers survival training (Q2000 per day), in which participants learn to find sustenance and shelter in the jungle; machetes are provided. He can also guide to El Mirador.

Campamento El Chiclero (p255) can also organize trips to more remote sites such as El Mirador, Río Azul (three days), Xultún, Nakbé and San Bartolo.

Sleeping & Eating

If you arrive here by public bus, you'll need to spend the night, since the only return trip is early in the morning. There are two places to stay, one basic, the other rustic.

A few basic cookshacks provide food, including **Comedor Uaxactún** (mains Q35-50; 8am-8pm) and **Comedor Imperial Okan Arin** (4132-5709; mains Q25-40; 7am-10pm), and the village's main lodging prepares all meals.

Uaxactún

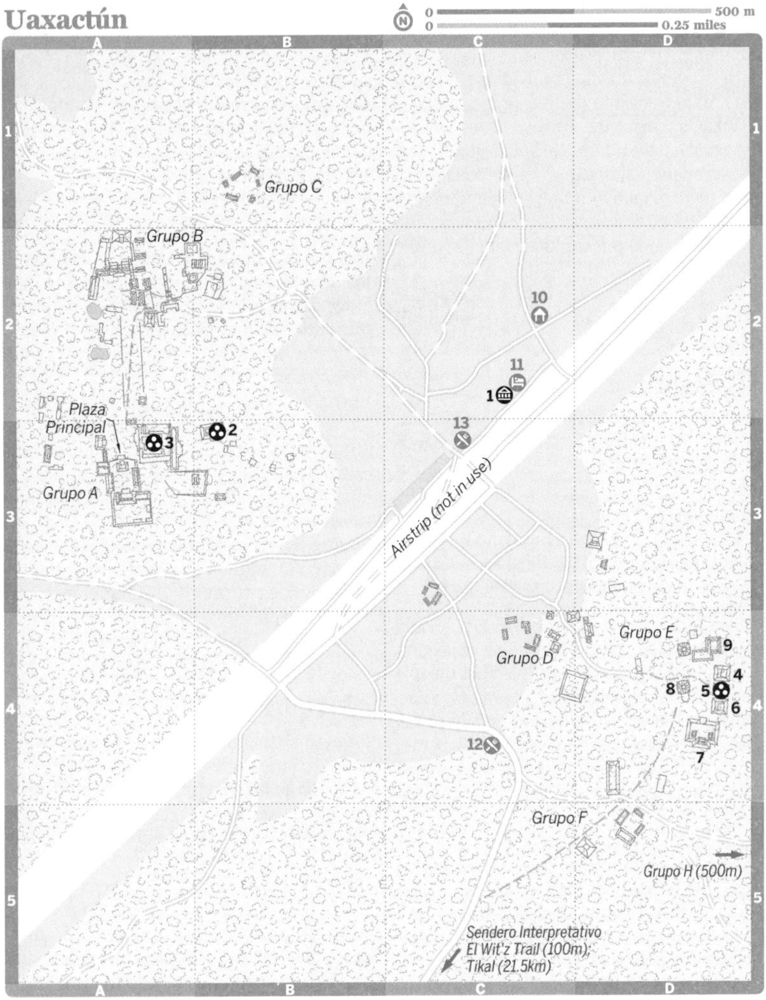

Uaxactún

Sights

1 Colección Dr Juan Antonio Valdés C2
2 Palacio A-XVIII B3
3 Palacio V A3
4 Templo E-I D4
5 Templo E-II D4
6 Templo E-III D4
7 Templo E-V D4
8 Templo E-VII-Sub D4
9 Templo E-X D4

Sleeping

10 Aldana's Lodge C2
11 Posada & Restaurante Campamento El Chiclero C2

Eating

12 Comedor Imperial Okan Arin C4
13 Comedor Uaxactún C3

Posada & Restaurante Campamento El Chiclero HOTEL $
(campamentochiclero@gmail.com; campsite/r per person Q30/75) On the north side of the airstrip, this place has 10 spartan, institutional green rooms underneath a thatched roof, with decent mattresses and mosquito-netted ceilings and windows. Clean showers and toilets are in an adjacent outbuilding; lights out at 9pm. Perky owner Neria does the best food in town (Q75 for soup and a main course with rice).

Aldana's Lodge HUT $
(☎7783-3931; posadaaldana@gmail.com; campsite/r per person Q20/40) To the right off the street leading to Grupos B and A, the Aldana family offers seven clapboard cabins, with thin mattresses on pallets. Father and son Alfido and Héctor Aldana lead tours to jungle sites such as El Zotz (Q3000) or El Mirador (Q2000), and Amparo prepares good meals.

You will need to be in good physical condition for any of the jungle tours, as extended walking in intense heat is required.

Orientation

Uaxactún village lies either side of a disused airstrip, a remnant of the age when planes were the only way to reach this inaccessible spot. The strip now serves as pasture and a football field. About halfway along the airstrip, roads go both left and right to the ruins. Village boys will want to guide you: you don't need a guide to find the ruins, but you might want to let one or two of them earn a small tip.

Information

At the time of writing there is still no cell-phone coverage and just one public phone, in an **office** (⏲varies to 6pm) on the south side of the airstrip. The phone is there, but only useful if someone is there to answer, which they sometimes aren't.

Internet access is available Monday to Friday via satellite signal next to the phone office.

Getting There & Away

A Pinita bus leaves the main terminal of Santa Elena for Uaxactún (Q40) at 2pm, then migrates to the market terminal, finally leaving town at 2:30pm. This bus passes through El Remate around 3:30pm and Tikal by 5pm. The following day it starts back for Santa Elena from Uaxactún at 7am. This means you'll need to spend two nights in Uaxactún to see the ruins. Otherwise, private tours from El Remate to Uaxactún and back by Casa de Don David (p243) can be arranged on a case-by-case basis.

If you're driving, the last chance to fill your fuel tank as you come from the south is at Puente Ixlú, just south of El Remate. During the rainy season (from May to October, sometimes extending into November), the road from Tikal to Uaxactún can become pretty muddy. From Uaxactún, unpaved roads lead to other ruins at El Zotz (about 30km southwest), Xultún (35km northeast) and Río Azul (100km northeast).

Yaxhá

The Classic Maya sites of Yaxhá, Nakum and El Naranjo form a triangle that is the basis for a national park covering more than 370 sq km and bordering the Parque Nacional Tikal to the west. Yaxhá, the most visited of the trio, stands on a hill between two sizable lakes, Lago Yaxhá and Lago Sacnab. The setting, the sheer size of the site, the number of excellently restored buildings and the abundant jungle flora and fauna all make it particularly worth visiting. There are also some stunning views from the tallest pyramid, which looks out over the lagoons. Not surprisingly, the foot traffic here is far less than at more popular, easy-to-reach sites.

The site is 11km north of the Puente Ixlú–Melchor de Mencos road, accessed via an unpaved road from a turnoff 32km from Puente Ixlú and 33km from Melchor de Mencos.

Sights

Occupied as early as 600 BC, Yaxhá (translated as 'blue-green water') achieved its cultural apex in the 8th century AD, when it counted some 20,000 inhabitants and 500 buildings, including temples, palaces and residential complexes.

It takes about two hours to wander round the main groups of ruins, which have been extensively excavated and reconstructed. Pick up an excellent map/information guide (Q20; in English) at the ticket booth. One approach is to cover the site in a clockwise fashion, traversing the original road network. The first group of buildings you come to, the **Lesser Astronomical Complex (Plaza C)**, is one of a pair of astronomical observatories. Take the Calzada de las Canteras to the **South Acropolis**, a complex of palatial structures from which Yaxhá's aristocracy could watch the games going on in the **Palace Ball Court** below. To the northwest stands one of Yaxhá's most ancient constructions, the **Greater Astronomical Complex (Plaza F)**. The arrangement is similar to the one at Uaxactún's Grupo E,

Yaxhá

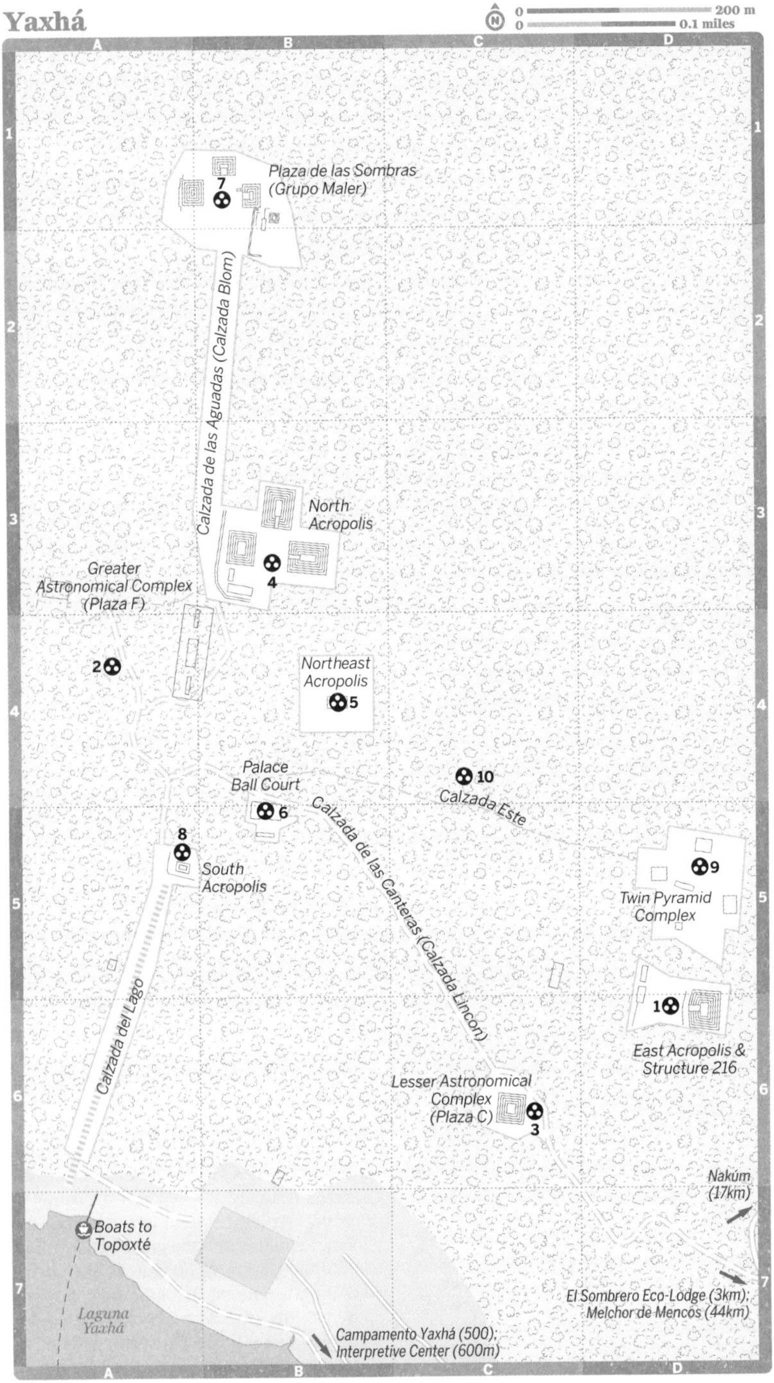
0 200 m
0 0.1 miles
Plaza de las Sombras
(Grupo Maler)
Calzada de las Aguadas (Calzada Blom)
North
Acropolis
Greater
Astronomical Complex
(Plaza F)
Northeast
Acropolis
Palace
Ball Court
Calzada Este
Calzada de las Canteras (Calzada Lincon)
South
Acropolis
Twin Pyramid
Complex
East Acropolis &
Structure 216
Calzada del Lago
Lesser Astronomical
Complex
(Plaza C)
Nakúm
(17km)
Boats to
Topoxté
Laguna
Yaxhá
El Sombrero Eco-Lodge (3km);
Melchor de Mencos (44km)
Campamento Yaxhá (500);
Interpretive Center (600m)

Yaxhá

Sights

1	East Acropolis & Structure 216	D6
2	Greater Astronomical Complex (Plaza F)	A4
3	Lesser Astronomical Complex (Plaza C)	C6
4	North Acropolis	B3
5	Northeast Acropolis	B4
6	Palace Ball Court	B5
7	Plaza de las Sombras (Grupo Maler)	B1
8	South Acropolis	A5
9	Twin Pyramid Complex	D5
10	Yaxhá	C4

with an observation tower (unexcavated) facing a three-part platform for tracking the sun's trajectory through the year. You can ascend the pyramidal tower (there's a wooden staircase alongside) for jaw-dropping views of the **North Acropolis** to the northeast, with a formidable temple rising above the jungle foliage. Far less impressive is the **Northeast Acropolis**, nearby. From here, take the Calzada de las Aguadas north to reach the **Plaza de las Sombras (Grupo Maler)**, where archaeologists believe throngs of citizens once gathered for religious ceremonies. Return toward the entrance along the Calzada Este to reach the high point of the tour (literally), **Structure 216** in the East Acropolis. Also called the Temple of the Red Hands, because red handprints were discovered there, it towers over 30m high, affording views in every direction. Though mostly unexcavated, the **Twin Pyramid Complex** is similar to a structure at Tikal.

A trail from the boat landing leads along the lake shore to an **Interpretive Center**, which displays ceramic pieces, musical instruments and jewelry unearthed from the site, along with descriptions of its discovery and excavation.

On an island near the far (south) shore of Laguna Yaxhá is a Late Postclassic archaeological site, **Topoxté**, where the dense covering of ruined temples and dwellings harbor some 100 structures. Evidence shows two distinct periods of occupation here: the latter, as late as AD 1450, by a migrant group from the Yucatán Peninsula. At the bottom of the Calzada del Lago in Yaxhá is the **boat landing**, from where a boat operator might be willing to take you to Topoxté for around Q250.

Sleeping

Campamento Yaxhá CAMPGROUND

FREE On the lakeshore below the Yaxhá ruins is Campamento Yaxhá, where you can camp for free on raised platforms with thatched roofs. Outbuildings have showers and toilets. Drinking water can be purchased at a store, but you must bring food. There's no need to purchase another admission ticket if you'd like to stay another day or two.

El Sombrero Eco-Lodge BUNGALOW $$$

(☎4147-6380, 5460-2934; www.ecolodgeelsombrero.com; s/d/tr Q380/750/940; P⊖🛜) In a lovely setting on the Laguna Yaxhá, El Sombrero features solar-powered, mosquito-netted bungalows with wraparound screened windows, most with lake views, scattered around the woods. A pleasant thatched clubhouse/dining room is attached to the kitchen. El Sombrero can pick up guests (call ahead) on the main road.

You could also camp here or sling a hammock for Q80. *Lancha* (small motorboat) tours to Topoxté are offered (Q200) as well as night crocodile observation tours, horseback riding (Q75 per hour) and overnight trips to Nakum (p258; one/two persons US$250/400), El Naranjo, Holmul and other lesser-known Maya sites in the vicinity. Bikes cost Q50 to rent for a half day.

Getting There & Away

Agencies in Flores and El Remate offer organized trips to Yaxhá, some combined with Nakum and/or Tikal. Horizontes Mayas (p244) in El Remate runs tours (Q125 per person, minimum three people), including guide and entrance fee, at 7am and 1pm, returning at 1pm and 6:30pm. Otherwise, take a Melchor de Mencos–bound microbus and get off at Restaurante El Portal de Yaxhá, opposite the Yaxhá turnoff; it can arrange transport to the site by pick-up truck or motorcycle (Q200 return). *Colectivos* from Flores charge Q200 as well.

Parque Nacional Laguna del Tigre

A vast expanse of seasonally flooded forest cut through by slow-moving rivers, this 3340-sq-km park in the northwest corner of El Petén forms the largest protected wetlands area in Mesoamerica. For many, this kind of deep jungle, middle-of-nowhere experience is Guatemala at its very best.

OFF THE BEATEN TRACK

NAKUM

Nakum is an impressive sight that is also impressively hard to get to, requiring 4WD or horses. Nakum was a significant port on the Holmul river, a waterway that linked Tikal with the Caribbean coast, though it reached its cultural peak in the Late Classic Period, well past Tikal's prime. It's 17km north of Yaxhá, a 1½-hour drive over a rough road that's impassable from August to January. It's at its best between March and May.

Remote as this spot is, it's particularly exciting to find such a formidable group of structures here. The excavated section is not huge, but it packs a lot in. Major excavations of the site have recently been completed. Archaeological research focused on the predominance of *talud-tablero*-type structures (stepped building style, with alternating vertical and sloping sections) in the south section, suggests a connection with Teotihuacán in Mexico. The question remains why Nakum flourished during the Terminal Classic at a time when its contemporaries were collapsing all around it.

The site features two major architectural groups, the North and South Sectors, connected by a causeway; most of the excavated structures are in the latter. The most interesting of these, in the part dubbed the **Plaza Central**, features an unusually well-preserved roofcomb with a clearly visible mask. In tandem with the pyramidal structure opposite, it presumably served as some kind of astronomical observatory.

Moving south from the Plaza Central, you enter the **South Acropolis**, a walled compound on a raised platform comprising 12 courtyards surrounded by 33 buildings that housed palatial residences. This arrangement was in place around AD 900, though there is evidence that the site had been occupied for the previous 14 centuries. What's unique about some of the courtyards here, like **Patio 1**, is that they were completely enclosed by buildings, a layout not found elsewhere in the Maya world. Outside the South Acropolis to the east are **stelae** bearing dates from the 9th century, among the latest recorded dates in the Maya lowlands.

Birders, nature-lovers, and those looking to bask in the simple things will love it here.

Though its northwestern reaches are threatened by petroleum extraction operations and drug-running activities, it remains a haven for endemic wildlife.

The obvious (and really, the only!) choice for accommodations are the semi-luxurious cabins above the Río San Pedro at Estación Biológica Las Guacamayas. Otherwise, it is possible to camp by the ranger station at El Perú (Waká) archaeological site.

Sights

Estación Biológica Las Guacamayas — WILDLIFE RESERVE

(Scarlet Macaw Biological Station; ☎5699-3735, 5699-3669; www.lasguacamayas.org; d 2-day/1-night Q4800, 3-day/2-night Q6660) A scientific research center within the Parque Nacional Laguna del Tigre, Scarlet Macaw Biological Station offers wildlife-watching/archaeology tours and the chance to tag along with researchers as they monitor macaws and butterflies. Overlooking the broad lazy river, it's a splendidly isolated spot and there is comfortable, ecofriendly accommodations in several thatched-roof houses.

One-day birding tours are devoted to spotting and photographing not just macaws but more than 300 other avian species found in and around the reserve, including red-capped manakin, red-legged honeycreeper and long-tailed hermit. Two- to three-day tours consist of some combination of a visit to the archaeological site of El Perú, 20 minutes west down the Río San Pedro, and nighttime observation of the endemic Morelet's crocodile, along with the chance to fish for the renowned *pescado blanco* (white fish).

The 15 rooms are semi-luxurious jungle affairs featuring bamboo-frame beds, mahogany furniture, screened picture windows and porches overlooking the river. A separate building contains the *comedor* (dining hall), where healthy meals are prepared.

Volunteering is also possible, with the chance to contribute to infrastructure, maintain trails, cultivate the butterfly garden or support environmental education projects among the Q'eqchi' community in Paso Caballos. There's a minimum two-week commitment, and volunteers pay Q750 per week for accommodations, food and transport to the site.

El Perú RUINS

(Waká) This ruin, deep in the jungles of Laguna del Tigre, has several important Classic-period structures and stelae. Carvings here have led archaeologists to believe it may have been allied with Calakmul, Tikal's great rival to the north.

Though there are no excavated buildings here, a number of stelae, in various states of deterioration, occupy four plazas. Stela number 16 in plaza 3 (the original lies under a thatched roof next to a fiberglass replica) portrays Siyaj K'ak', aka Smoking Frog, a warrior from Teotihuacán who arrived here in 378 and apparently allied with El Perú in a campaign to overthrow Tikal.

A visit to this ruin offers fantastic birding opportunities as well, both in the jungle and on the river trip to get there. Either arrange for a visit via Estación Biológica Las Guacamayas or in the nearby community of Paso Caballos.

Getting There & Away

Most visitors are shuttled here from Santa Elena as part of a tour by Estación Biológica Las Guacamayas. However, it is possible to get to the national park independently by taking the bus to Paso Caballos (Q30, 2½ hours), which leaves Santa Elena terminal at approximately 1:30pm, then hiring a boat down the Río San Pedro. This same bus returns to Santa Elena at 5am. Access is also possible by 4WD vehicle.

El Mirador

Buried within the furthest reaches of the Petén jungle, just 7km south of the Mexican border, the Late Preclassic metropolis at **El Mirador** (Lookout; www.miradorbasin.com; 24hr) contains possibly the largest cluster of buildings of any single Maya site, among them the biggest pyramid ever built in the Maya world. Ongoing excavations have only scratched the surface.

El Mirador was so-named by local *chicheros* (chicle harvesters) for the excellent views provided by some of the pyramids. **La Danta** (the Tapir) looms 70m above the forest floor. **El Tigre** is 55m high with a base covering 18,000 sq meters. At its height, the city spread over 16 sq km and supported tens of thousands of citizens. It was certainly one of the greatest Maya cities of the Preclassic era.

The temples erected here display an unusual 'triadic' style, in which three pyramids crown a large platform, with the one in the middle dominating the other two, which face each other at a lower level. The facades of these buildings were once embellished with carved masks.

Scholars are still figuring out why and how El Mirador thrived (there are few natural resources and no water sources save for the reservoirs built by ingenious, ancient engineers) and what led to its abandonment in 150 AD. Some five centuries after that date, El Mirador appears to have been resettled, as suggested by the existence of Classic architecture among the older structures. Pottery unearthed from this era displays the highly refined codex-style of decoration, in which calligraphic lines are painted on a cream-colored surface, with designs believed to resemble Maya codices.

Richard Hansen, a professor from Idaho State University, is leading the effort to map the Mirador basin, a vast swath of northern El Petén comprising dozens of interconnected cities, with funding from an assortment of international and Guatemalan foundations and private sources. In March 2009, Dr Hansen and his crew made a significant discovery when they excavated a 4m frieze at the base of La Danta, dating from 300 BC, which they surmise decorated a royal pool. The carved images upon it depict the twin heroes Hunahpú and Ixbalnqué swimming through the underworld domain of Xibalbá, a tale that is related in the Popol Vuh (the Maya 'Bible'). The finding underlines the importance of El Mirador in establishing the belief system of Classic-era civilizations.

Sleeping & Eating

If arriving at the site by tour, your guides will set up camp with mosquito netting at Tintal, El Mirador and Nakbe. In Carmelita (launching point for the trek), local families offer beds.

Trekking guides prepare snacks along the trail and meals at campsites, though it's a good idea to pack a few of your preferences. Neria from Posada del Campamento El Chiclero (p255) is known for her culinary skills.

Getting There & Away

A visit to El Mirador involves an arduous jungle trek of at least five days and four nights (it's about 60km each way), with no facilities or amenities aside from what you carry in and what can be rustled from the forest. During the rainy season, especially September to December, the mud can make it extremely difficult; February to June is the best period to attempt a trek. Alternatively, you can go by helicopter.

THE MIRADOR BASIN

The 2169 sq km of tropical forest surrounding El Mirador harbors dozens of substantial cities that flourished during the Middle and Late Preclassic eras. At least six major causeways connected El Mirador to these satellites, an engineering feat that enabled it to become what was possibly the New World's first political state. The four largest cities in the vicinity are all within a day's walk of El Mirador.

El Tintal (23km southwest of El Mirador) One of the largest and most important Preclassic cities, with a moat surrounding the civic center both to defend the city and ensure a year-round water supply.

Wakná (15km south) Built around what is possibly the largest astronomical observatory in the Maya world, with Preclassic murals and a series of internal causeways.

Nakbé (13km southeast) Established around 1200 BC, it grew to be one of the most important Preclassic sites. El Mirador was probably modeled upon this predecessor. All the characteristic features of Maya civilization – monumental architecture, palaces, causeways and ballcourts – had appeared here by 600 BC.

Xulnal (7km west of El Tintal) Discovered in 2001. Pottery found here is evidence of some of the earliest occupation in the Mirador Basin.

TREKKING

The trip usually departs from a cluster of houses called Carmelita, 82km up the road from Flores. The **Comisión de Turismo Cooperativa Carmelita** (☎7867-5629; www.turismocooperativacarmelita.com), a group of INGUAT-authorized guides, can make all arrangements for a trek to El Mirador, with optional visits to the Preclassic sites of Nakbé, El Tintal, Wakná and Xulnal. Travelers who participate in these treks should be in good physical shape, able to withstand high temperatures (average of nearly 38°C) and humidity (average 85%) and be prepared to hike or ride long distances (up to 30km per day).

On the first day of a typical itinerary, you'll hike six hours to El Tintal, where you'd camp for the night. On the second day, after a look around El Tintal, you proceed through denser forests to El Mirador and set up camp there. The next day is reserved for exploring El Mirador. Five-day hikers will simply return the way they came. Those with six or more days will hike southeast to arrive at Nakbé and camp there. The next day the expedition begins the return, possibly stopping for the night at the site of La Florida. On day six, you head back to Carmelita.

For a five-/six-day trip, the cooperative charges Q1925/2240 per person in a group of at least three people. The fee includes tents, hammocks and mosquito netting; all meals and drinking water; Spanish-speaking guide; mules and muleskinners; and first-aid supplies. An English-speaking guide is available for an extra charge.

Two buses daily travel from Flores to Carmelita, at 5am and 1pm (Q80). Generally you'd take the morning bus and start hiking straight away if your guide hasn't arranged private transportation.

It's also possible to get El Mirador from Uaxactún, a longer but gentler approach since there are fewer *bajos* (seasonal swamps) and it's less affected by agricultural clearing, so you're underneath the jungle canopy from the outset. Going this route has become very unusual, so you'll need to plan things yourself well ahead of time rather than depending on catching a group tour. Posada Campamento del Chiclero (p255) or Aldana's Lodge (p255) will be your best chance of getting solid info on what is available and costs (currently Q2000 per person). On the first leg of the journey you're driven in a monster truck to a campground at the former *chichero* camp of Yucatán, a five-hour journey. The next morning the group is outfitted with mules and proceeds to another camp, La Leontina, a four-hour tramp through the jungle. The following day it's a three-hour walk to Nakbé. After visiting that site, the expedition continues to El Mirador. The journey back follows the same route in reverse.

HELICOPTER

If hiking, camping, and mosquito-swatting isn't for you, you can go by helicopter. During selected periods throughout the year, **TAG Airlines** (☎4218-5485, Guatemala City office 2380-9494; www.tag.com.gt; Aeropuerto Internacional Mundo Maya) offers chopper packages from Flores to El Mirador for as low as US$399 per person. Prices and availability fluctuate constantly, so contact the airline ahead of time to find out about the current schedule. Going by air means a short visit of only four to five hours, so there's far less chance to explore the ruin, but (weather permitting) you will have time to hike up to La Danta and El Tigre as well. The chopper leaves early in the morning and returns to Flores around 3:30pm. Water and snacks are provided, but bring sunscreen and repellent.

Understand Guatemala

Guatemala Today

Guatemala is a nation with a bright tourism scene, but one that continues to struggle economically and politically. More than half its population is under the age of 25, with a similar proportion living below the poverty line. Gang violence and the still unresolved aftermath of the civil war are countered by the boundless energy (if limited resources) of Guatemala's grass-roots organizations. Successive governments may continue to make promises, but Guatemalans rely on each other to deliver solutions.

Best in Print

Men of Maize (Miguel Ángel Asturias; 1949) Nobel Prize–winning Guatemalan author reaches deep into history for this novel of Maya magic realism.

A Mayan Life (Gaspar Pedro Gonzáles; 1995) The first published novel by a Maya author is an excellent study of rural Guatemalan life.

Time Among the Maya (Ronald Wright; 1989) Masterful travelogue covering Maya Central America but centered on Guatemala.

The Art of Political Murder (Francisco Goldman; 2008) Meticulously researched account of the assassination of Bishop Gerardi.

Best on Film

Aquí me Quedo (Rodolfo Espinoza; 2010) Subtle political commentary, black comedy and satire abound in this story of a kidnapping.

When the Mountains Tremble (Pamela Yates & Newton Thomas Sigel; 1983) Documentary featuring Rigoberta Menchú, telling the story of the civil war.

Capsulas (Verónica Riedel; 2011) A look at greed, corruption and the drug trade from one of Guatemala's few female directors.

Ixcanúl (Jayro Bustamante; 2015) Multi-award winning film (and Guatemala's first entry at the Academy Awards) about a young Kaqchiquel girl's coming of age.

Neither Corrupt Nor a Thief?

Guatemala was ahead of the American curve when Jimmy Morales, a popular television personality, was inaugurated as president in January 2016. He swept into power after the impeachment of former president Otto Pérez Molina on corruption charges, running on the slogan 'Ni corrupto, ni ladrón' (neither corrupt nor a thief).

The country has found the reality of the Morales government rather more sobering than its early promise. The evangelical president's close ties to the military – the core of Guatemala's political elite – has led to stagnation on human rights issues, including the paring back of the country's human rights commission and an unsuccessful attempt to expel the UN's top representative. After concerns about his own presidential campaign funding, Morales pushed Congress into passing a law granting him immunity from prosecution, and has proposed further amnesties for those convicted of illegal spending.

A Political Eruption

The national conversation dramatically switched its focus on June 3 2018 when Fuego earthquake erupted south of Antigua. In the country's deadliest eruption since 1929, around 160 people were killed and thousands were left homeless. Across Guatemala, communities pulled together to collect supplies to help the victims, but foreign aid groups were only allowed restricted access to help. Protests later broke out over alleged mismanagement of relief funds as well as the wider governmental response to the eruption, further tarnishing the Morales administration in the eyes of many Guatemalans. Continued delays over the resettling of those displaced mean that Fuego is likely to cast a long shadow into the 2019 election season.

The Global Picture

Global policy continues to affect Guatemala, not least in its relationship with the USA. Jimmy Morales was the first international leader to follow Donald Trump's recognition of Jerusalem as the capital of Israel, announcing that the country would move its embassy from Tel Aviv to the city. Guatemala-Israeli ties have always been close, but the plan provoked condemnation from Arab states. The Middle East is an important market for Guatemala's cardamom exports, and threats of a boycott still hang in the air.

A sensitive subject in rural Guatemala has to do with large (often foreign-administered) projects such as hydroelectric dams and mineral mines. Local indigenous organizations are currently campaigning against the International Development Bank-Funded Pojom II and San Andres hydroelectric dams in northern Huehuetenango province, saying that it threatens local livelihoods as well as water supplies.

The Slow Road to Recovery

Despite the promise of the 1996 peace accords, the road to recovery from the civil war has been a slow and painful one. Official recognition of some atrocities has been an important step in the recovery process, however reluctant it appeared to some observers. Though President Morales has stated he does not believe the genocide in the Ixil Triangle ever took place, the exhumation of clandestine cemeteries used by the military to bury 'disappeared' dissidents continues, and in December 2017 172 newly identified victims were reburied in the area. More than 35,000 people remain missing, and the mandated reparation measures have never been fully put in place.

Some war criminals have been brought to book. So far the heftiest penalty to be handed down was to ex-Military Commissioner Lucas Tecún, who was sentenced to 7710 years in prison. Former dictator Efraín Ríos Montt was tried and convicted of genocide, but a later court ruling overturned the verdict. Despite his alleged senility, he is currently being retried.

Grass Roots Movement

In the face of official indifference and/or inability to deal with the country's myriad problems, many community-based organizations and NGOs are moving in to fill the void. Large segments of the Guatemalan population have become active in volunteer work, focusing on everything from neighborhood watch–type programs in areas unpatrolled by police to larger efforts focusing on food security and housing for the poor.

The mass protests against the old Pérez Molina government and now the Jimmy Morales presidency, mainly non-politically aligned and organized chiefly through social media, have sparked a continued interest in politics among young Guatemalans, with alliances being formed from previously disparate groups, and a strengthening of civil society.

POPULATION: **17,303,000**

AREA: **108,889 SQ KM**

GDP: **US$68.76 BILLION**

INFLATION: **4.4%**

POPULATION BELOW POVERTY LINE: **59%**

if Guatemala were 100 people

59 would be *Ladino* (person of mixed ancestry)
40 would be Maya
1 would be other

Guatemalan diaspora

(% of migrating population)

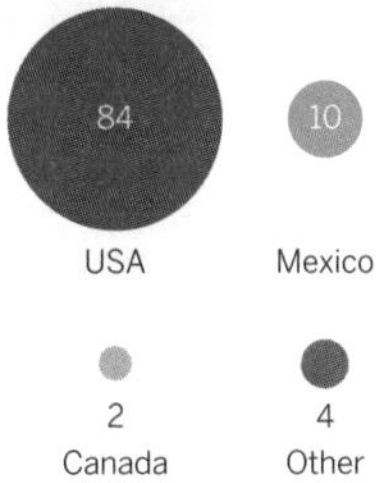
84
10
USA
Mexico
2
Canada
4
Other

population per sq km

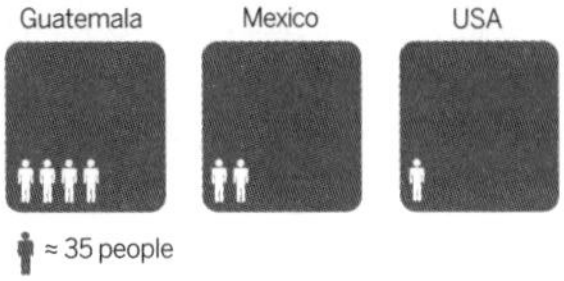
Guatemala
Mexico
USA
≈ 35 people

History

Tumultuous barely begins to describe the series of events that this small piece of land has seen over the past few millennia. Great empires have risen and fallen, conquerors have come and gone, and the population has repeatedly found itself trapped in the crossfire of war. From the ancient Maya to the Spanish Empire and the modern civil war, a tour of Guatemala's history will deepen your experience while traveling in the country.

Preclassic Period (2000 BC–AD 250)

Maya history before the arrival of Europeans is divided into three broad periods: the Preclassic, the Classic and the Postclassic.

The Preclassic Period is generally thought to have coincided with the emergence of stable social structures and early forms of agriculture, pottery and tool-making in what is now Mexico and Guatemala. The improvement in the food supply led to an increase in population, a higher standard of living, and developments in agricultural and artistic techniques. Decorative pots and healthier, fatter corn strains were produced. Even at the beginning of the Preclassic period, people in Guatemala spoke an early form of the Maya language.

By the middle Preclassic period (800–300 BC) there were rich villages in the Copán Valley, and villages had been founded at what would become the majestic city of Tikal, amid the jungles of El Petén. Trade routes developed, with coastal peoples exchanging salt and seashells for highland tribes' tool-grade obsidian.

As the Maya honed their agricultural techniques, including the use of fertilizer and elevated fields, a noble class emerged, constructing temples that consisted of raised platforms of earth topped by thatch-roofed shelters. The local potentate was buried beneath the shelter, increasing the site's sacred power. Such temples have been found at Uaxactún, Tikal and El Mirador. Kaminaljuyú, in Guatemala City, reached its peak from about 400 BC to AD 100; it was home to thousands of inhabitants, and had scores of temples built on earth mounds.

In El Petén, where limestone was abundant, the Maya began to build platform temples from stone. As each succeeding local potentate

TIMELINE

3114 BC

The Maya creation story says that the world was created on August 13 of this year, which corresponds to the first date on the Maya Long Count Calendar.

1100 BC

Proto-Maya settlements begin to appear in the Copán Valley. By 1000 BC settlements on the Guatemalan Pacific coast show early signs of developing a hierarchical society.

c 250 BC

Early Maya cities El Mirador and Kaminaljuyú flourish between 250 BC and AD 100 due to tactical and commercial advantages. Agricultural techniques are refined as the trade in obsidian and jade booms.

demanded a bigger temple, larger and larger platforms were built over existing platforms, eventually forming huge pyramids. The potentate was buried deep within the stack of platforms. El Tigre pyramid at El Mirador, 18 stories high, is believed to be the largest ever built by the Maya. More and more pyramids were built around large plazas. The stage was set for the flowering of Classic Maya civilization.

Classic Period (AD 250–900)

The Classic Maya were organized into numerous city-states. While Tikal began to assume a primary role around AD 250, El Mirador had been mysteriously abandoned about a century earlier. Some scholars believe a severe drought hastened this great city's demise.

Each city-state had its noble house, headed by a priestly king who placated the gods by shedding his blood by piercing his tongue, penis or ears with sharp objects. As sacred head of his community, the king also led his soldiers into battle against rival cities, capturing prisoners for use in human sacrifices.

A typical Maya city functioned as the religious, political and market hub for the surrounding farming hamlets. Its ceremonial center focused on plazas surrounded by tall temple pyramids and lower buildings with warrens of small rooms. Stelae and altars were carved with dates, histories and elaborate human and divine figures.

In the first part of the Classic period, most of the city-states were probably grouped into two loose military alliances centered on Calakmul, in Mexico's Campeche state, and Tikal.

In the late 8th century, trade between Maya states waned and conflict grew. By the early 10th century the cities of Tikal, Yaxchilán, Copán, Quiriguá and Piedras Negras had reverted to minor towns or even villages, and much of El Petén was abandoned. Many explanations, including population pressure, drought and ecological damage, have been offered for the collapse of the Classic Maya period.

The Blood of Kings: Dynasty & Ritual in Maya Art, by Linda Schele and Mary Ellen Miller, is a heavily and fascinatingly illustrated guide to the art and culture of the ancient Maya.

LIDAR – a type of laser radar – is creating the biggest revolution in Maya archaeology in decades, revealing thousands of previously unknown buildings and structures.

Postclassic Period (900–1524)

Some of the Maya who abandoned El Petén must have moved southwest into the highlands of Guatemala. In the 13th and 14th centuries they were joined by Maya-Toltecs from the Tabasco or Yucatán areas of Mexico. Groups of these newcomers set up a series of rival states in the Guatemalan highlands: the most prominent were the K'iche' (or Quiché; capital: K'um'arkaj, near modern Santa Cruz del Quiché), the Kaqchiquels

AD 230

El Mirador begins to decline in importance. King Yax Ehb' Xooc of Tikal establishes the dynasty that will make Tikal the dominant city of the southern Maya world.

682

King Moon Double Comb, or Lord Chocolate, ascends Tikal's throne and begins remodeling and reconstructing Tikal's grand plazas and temples that had been destroyed by Caracol and Calakmul.

900

The collapse of Classic Maya civilization begins, and the Postclassic era starts. A century-long exodus from Tikal commences, after which the city will never be inhabited again.

c 13th century

Ruthlessly organized Toltec-Maya migrants from southeast Mexico establish kingdoms in Guatemala. Highlands Maya organize into competing kingdoms, establishing language and cultural groupings that survive today.

(capital: Iximché, near Tecpán), the Mam (capital: Zaculeu, near Huehuetenango), the Tz'utujil (capital: Chuitinamit, near Santiago Atitlán) and the Poqomam (capital: Mixco Viejo, north of Guatemala City). Another group from the Yucatán, the Itzáes, wound up at Lago de Petén Itzá in El Petén, settling in part on the island that is today called Flores.

Spanish Conquest

Spaniards under Hernán Cortés defeated the Aztec Empire based at Tenochtitlán (modern Mexico City) in 1521. It only took a couple of years for the conquistadors to turn to Guatemala in their search for wealth. Pedro de Alvarado, one of Cortés' most brutal lieutenants, entered Guatemala from the Pacific coast in 1524, forging temporary alliances with local Maya groups while murdering and subjugating their rivals. And then laying waste to them.

Archaeologists estimate that less than 10% of Tikal – Guatemala's biggest and most famous Maya site – has so far been uncovered.

And so it went throughout Guatemala as Alvarado sought fortune and renown. The one notable exception was the Rabinal of present-day Baja Verapaz, who survived with their preconquest identity intact and remain one of Guatemala's most traditional groups to this day.

Alvarado moved his base to Santiago de los Caballeros (now called Ciudad Vieja) in 1527, but, shortly after his death in 1541, Ciudad Vieja was destroyed by a flood. The Spanish capital was relocated under the same name to a new site nearby, known today as Antigua.

After the first contacts between Europe and America, the following crops all travelled from the New World to the Old: tomatoes, sweet potatoes, squash, potatoes, avocados, corn (maize), cocoa and tobacco.

Colonial Period (1524–1821)

The Spanish effectively enslaved Guatemala's indigenous people to work what had been their own land for the benefit of the Spanish, just as they did throughout the hemisphere. Refusal to work meant death. The colonists believed themselves omnipotent and behaved accordingly.

Enter the Antigua-based Dominican friar Bartolomé de Las Casas. Las Casas had been in the Caribbean and Latin America since 1502 and had witnessed firsthand the near complete genocide of the indigenous populations of Cuba and Hispaniola. Horrified by what he had seen, Las Casas managed to convince Carlos V of Spain to enact the New Laws of 1542, which technically ended the system of forced labor. In reality, forced labor continued, but wanton waste of Maya lives ceased. Las Casas and other friars went about converting the Maya to Christianity.

Part of the Church's conversion success can be attributed to the education provided in indigenous languages and the relative respect extended to traditional beliefs. The latter often enabled Maya beliefs to persist under a veneer of Christianity, as they do to this day.

1523

Spaniard Pedro de Alvarado begins the conquest of Guatemala. Alvarado quickly conquers much of the country, although parts of the highlands hold out for years and El Petén is not subdued for another 170 years.

1542

Spain enacts the New Laws, officially banning forced labor in its colonies. Catholic influence becomes more institutionalized and traditional Maya social structures are transformed.

1609–1821

The Captaincy General of Guatemala comprises what are now Costa Rica, Nicaragua, Honduras, El Salvador, Guatemala and the Mexican state of Chiapas, with its capital at Antigua, then at Guatemala City.

1697

The Spanish conquest of Guatemala is completed as the island of Tayasal (present-day Flores) – home of the Itza, the last remaining unconquered tribe – is defeated.

Independence

By the time thoughts of independence from Spain began stirring among Guatemalans, society was rigidly stratified. The European-born Spaniards held the real power, followed by the *criollos* (Guatemalan-born Spaniards) who lorded it over the *ladinos* (of mixed Spanish and Maya blood), who in turn exploited the indigenous population who still remained on the bottom rung of the socioeconomic ladder.

Angered at being repeatedly passed over for advancement, Guatemalan *criollos* successfully rose in revolt in 1821. Independence changed little for Guatemala's indigenous communities, who remained under the control of the Church and the landowning elite.

Mexico, which had recently become independent, quickly annexed Guatemala, but in 1823 Guatemala reasserted its independence and led the formation of the United Provinces of Central America (July 1, 1823), along with El Salvador, Nicaragua, Honduras and Costa Rica. Their union lasted only until 1840 before breaking up into its constituent states. This era brought prosperity to the *criollos,* but worsened the lot of the Guatemalan Maya. The end of Spanish rule meant that the Crown's few liberal safeguards, which had afforded the Maya a minimal protection, were abandoned. The Maya, though technically and legally free, were reduced to debt peonage to the big landowners.

To translate a date using the Maya calendar, visit the Maya Date Calculator at www.mayan-calendar.com/calc.html. Try it on your birth date.

The Liberals & Carrera

Guatemala's ruling classes split into two camps: the elite conservatives, including the Catholic Church and the large landowners, and the liberals, who had been the first to advocate independence and who opposed the vested interests of the conservatives.

A short succession of liberal leaders ended when unpopular economic policies and a cholera epidemic led to an indigenous uprising that brought a conservative *ladino* pig farmer, Rafael Carrera, to power. Carrera held power from 1844 to 1865, undoing many liberal reforms and ceding control of Belize to Britain in exchange for construction of a road between Guatemala City and Belize City, a road that was never built.

Liberal Reforms of Barrios

The liberals returned to power in the 1870s. Justo Rufino Barrios, a rich, young, coffee-plantation owner held the title of president, but ruled as a dictator (1873–79). Barrios modernized Guatemala's roads, railways, schools and banking system and expanded the burgeoning coffee industry. Under Barrios' successors a small group of landowning and commercial families came to control the economy, while foreign companies were given generous concessions, and political opponents were censored, imprisoned or exiled.

1773

Antigua, a jewel in the colonial crown, complete with a university, a printing press, schools, hospitals and churches, is destroyed by an earthquake. The new capital is founded at present-day Guatemala City.

1823–40

Guatemala, El Salvador, Honduras, Nicaragua and Costa Rica form the United Provinces of Central America. Liberal reforms are enacted, and vehemently opposed by conservative groups and the Catholic Church.

1838

Much of southwestern Guatemala declares independence, becoming the sixth member of the United Provinces. The new state, called Los Altos, has its capital at Quetzaltenango. It will secede, briefly, in 1844, 1848 and 1849.

1844

Rafael Carrera seizes power and declares Guatemala fully independent and reincorporates Los Altos into Guatemala. He sets about dismantling many of the liberal reforms of the United Provinces.

Estrada Cabrera

Manuel Estrada Cabrera ruled from 1898 to 1920, bringing progress in technical matters, but placing a heavy burden on all but the ruling oligarchy. He fancied himself a bringer of light and culture to a backward land, styling himself the 'Teacher and Protector of Guatemalan Youth.'

In reaction to Cabrera's doublespeak, the *Huelga de Dolores* (Strike of Sorrows) began around this time. Students from Guatemala City's San Carlos University took to the streets during Lent – wearing hoods to avoid reprisals – to protest against injustice and corruption. The tradition caught on in university towns across the country, culminating with a parade through the main streets on the Friday before Good Friday, a tradition that continues to this day (Desfile de Bufos – The Parade of Fools; p23).

Jorge Ubico

Estrada Cabrera was overthrown in 1920 and Guatemala entered a period of instability, ending in 1931 with the election of General Jorge Ubico as president. Ubico insisted on honesty in government, and modernized the country's health and social welfare infrastructure. His reign ended when he was forced into exile in 1944.

Arévalo & Arbenz

Just when it appeared that Guatemala was doomed to a succession of harsh dictators, the elections of 1945 brought a philosopher – Juan José Arévalo – to the presidency. Arévalo, in power from 1945 to 1951 (despite 25 coup attempts by conservative military forces) established the nation's social security system, a bureau of indigenous affairs, a modern public health system and liberal labor laws – as well as finally granting women the right to vote in 1946.

Arévalo was succeeded by Colonel Jacobo Arbenz, who continued Arévalo's policies, instituting agrarian reforms designed to break up the large estates and foster productivity on small, individually owned farms. He also expropriated vast, unused lands conceded to the United Fruit Company during the Estrada Cabrera and Ubico years. Compensation was paid at the value declared for tax purposes (far below its real value), and Arbenz announced that the lands were to be redistributed to peasants and put into cultivation for food. The announcement set off alarms in Washington, and in 1954 the US, in one of the earliest documented covert operations by the CIA, orchestrated an invasion from Honduras. Arbenz stepped down, and the land reform never took place.

Arbenz was succeeded by a series of military presidents. More covert (but well documented) support came from the US government, in the form of money and counterinsurgency training. Violence became a staple

1870s

Liberal governments modernize Guatemala, but turn indigenous lands over to coffee plantations. European newcomers are given preferential treatment, further disenfranchising the Maya.

1901

President Manuel Estrada Cabrera courts the US-owned United Fruit Company to set up shop in Guatemala. United Fruit soon takes on a dominant role in national politics.

1940s

Bowing to pressure from the US (buyers of 90% of Guatemala's exports at the time), President Jorge Ubico expels German landowners from the country. Their lands are redistributed to political and military allies.

1945–54

Juan José Arévalo, elected with 85% of the popular vote, comes to power, ushering in an era of enlightened, progressive government that is continued by his successor Jacobo Arbenz.

of political life, land reforms were reversed, voting was made dependent on literacy (disenfranchising around 75% of the population), the secret police force was revived and military repression was common.

In response left-wing guerrilla groups began to form in the 1960s.

Seeds of Repression

Guatemalan industry developed fast, but the social fabric became increasingly stressed as most profits flowed upwards. Labor unions organized, and migration to the cities, especially the capital, produced urban sprawl and slums. Protests were met with violent repression led by government-sanctioned death squads, kicking off a cycle of extreme violence that would last another two decades. Amnesty International estimated that 50,000 to 60,000 people had been killed during the political violence of the 1970s alone. Rural Maya struggling for enfranchisement were particularly targeted, but students, unionists, journalists and academics were all in the firing line.

Guatemala's troubles were exacerbated by a severe earthquake in 1976 that killed about 22,000 people and left around one million homeless. Most of the aid sent for those in need never reached them.

The 1980s: A Decade of Civil War

In the early 1980s four disparate, mainly indigenous, guerrilla groups united to form the URNG (the Guatemalan National Revolutionary Unity) and military suppression of antigovernment elements in the countryside peaked, especially under the presidency of General Efraín Ríos Montt, an Evangelical Christian who came to power by coup in March 1982. Huge numbers of people – mainly indigenous men – from more than 400 villages were murdered in the name of anti-insurgency, stabilization and anticommunism.

It was later estimated that 15,000 civilian deaths occurred as a result of counterinsurgency operations during Ríos Montt's term of office alone, not to mention the estimated 100,000 refugees (again, mostly Maya) who fled to Mexico. The government forced villagers to form Patrullas de Autodefensa Civil (PACs; Civil Defense Patrols), who were later accused of some of the worst human rights atrocities committed during Ríos Montt's rule.

In August 1983 Ríos Montt was deposed by General Oscar Humberto Mejía Victores, but the abuses continued. Survivors were herded into remote 'model villages' surrounded by army encampments. The ongoing reports of human rights violations and civilian massacres led the US to cut off military assistance to Guatemala, which in turn resulted in the 1986 election of a civilian president, Marco Vinicio Cerezo Arévalo of the Christian Democratic Party.

1954

Effecting the country's first serious attempt at land reform, Arbenz appropriates Guatemalan lands of the US-owned United Fruit Company. He is soon deposed in a US-orchestrated coup.

1950s–1960s

Military dictators rule the country, reversing liberal reforms of previous governments. Crackdowns lead to the formation of left-wing guerrilla groups. The civil war begins.

1967

Guatemalan writer and diplomat Miguel Ángel Asturias, credited as a pioneer of modernist Latin American literature, is awarded the Nobel Prize for Literature for his political novel *El Señor Presidente*.

1976

Earthquake kills 22,000 in Guatemala. Reconstruction efforts help to consolidate leftist opposition groups, who are met with fierce military reprisals. The Carter administration bans military aid to Guatemala.

There was hope that Cerezo Arévalo's administration would temper the excesses of the powerful elite and the military, and establish a basis for true democracy. But armed conflict festered in remote areas and when Cerezo Arévalo's term ended in 1990, many people wondered whether any real progress had been made. Tens of thousands of indigenous Guatemalans fled into Mexico as refugees.

Early 1990s

President Jorge Serrano (1990–93) from the conservative Movimiento de Acción Solidaria (Solidarity Action Movement) reopened a dialogue with the URNG, hoping to bring the decades-long civil war to an end. When the talks collapsed, the mediator from the Catholic Church blamed both sides for intransigence.

Human-rights abuses continued during this period despite the country's return to democratic rule. In one dramatic case in 1990, Guatemalan anthropologist Myrna Mack, who had documented army violence against the rural Maya, was fatally wounded after being stabbed dozens of times. Former head of the Presidential Guard, Colonel Juan Valencia Osorio, was found guilty of masterminding the assassination and sentenced to 30 years' imprisonment, but went into hiding before he could be arrested.

In *Silence on the Mountain*, Daniel Wilkinson uncovers in microcosm the social background to the civil war as he delves into the reasons for the burning of a coffee estate by guerrillas.

Serrano's presidency came to depend more on the army for support. In 1993 he tried to seize absolute power, but after a tense few days was forced to flee into exile. Congress elected Ramiro de León Carpio, an outspoken critic of the army's strong-arm tactics, as president, to complete Serrano's term.

Peace Accords

President de León Carpio's elected successor, Álvaro Arzú of the center-right Partido de Avanzada Nacional (PAN; National Advancement Party), took office in 1996. Arzú continued negotiations with the URNG and, finally, on December 29, 1996, the 'Firm and Lasting Peace Agreement' was signed. During the 36 years of civil war, an estimated 200,000 Guatemalans had been killed, a million made homeless, and untold thousands had disappeared.

La Hija del Puma (The Daughter of the Puma, 1994), directed by Ulf Hultberg, is a powerful film, based on a true story, about a K'iche' Maya girl who survives the army massacre of her fellow villagers and sees her brother captured. She escapes to Mexico, but then returns to Guatemala in search of her sibling.

1982
Four powerful guerrilla organizations unite to form the URNG (Guatemalan National Revolutionary Unity). An estimated half a million people actively support the guerrilla movement.

1982–83
State terror against rural indigenous communities peaks during the rule of General Efraín Ríos Montt. Peasants, particularly in the highlands, begin an exodus to Mexico to escape violence from both sides.

1992
Indigenous rights and peace activist Rigoberta Menchú is awarded the Nobel Prize for Peace. Menchú receives the award while living in exile in Mexico, returning to Guatemala two years later.

1996
After nearly a decade of talks, the Peace Accords are signed, bringing to an end the 36-year civil war in which an estimated 200,000 Guatemalans died.

Guatemala After the Peace Accords

Hopes for a truly just and democratic society have been regularly frayed in the years since 1996. International organizations regularly criticize the state of human rights in the country and Guatemalan human rights campaigners are threatened or simply disappear on a regular basis. The major problems – poverty, illiteracy, lack of education and poor medical facilities (all much more common in rural areas, where the Maya population is concentrated) – remain a long way from being resolved.

The 1999 presidential elections were won by Alfonso Portillo of the conservative Frente Republicano Guatemalteco (FRG). Portillo was seen as a front man for FRG leader, ex-president General Efraín Ríos Montt. At the end of his presidency Portillo fled the country in the face of allegations that he had diverted US$500 million from the treasury to personal and family bank accounts. Having evaded prosecution for years, Portillo was finally charged by the US for laundering money using US banks, and looks set to be extradited and put on trial there.

Ríos Montt was granted permission by Guatemala's constitutional court to stand in the 2003 elections, despite the fact that the constitution banned presidents who had taken power by coup in the past, as Ríos Montt had in 1982.

Guatemala: Nunca Mas (1998), published by ODHAG (Human Rights Office of the Archbishopric of Guatemala) and REMHI (Recovery of Historical Memory), details many of the human-rights abuses committed during Guatemala's civil war, and includes moving testimonials.

The 'New' Guatemala

In the end Guatemala's voters dealt Ríos Montt a resounding defeat, electing Oscar Berger of the moderately conservative Gran Alianza Nacional (GANA) as president. Berger managed to stay relatively untouched by political scandal, critics saying this was because he didn't really do anything, let alone anything bad.

The Central America Free Trade Agreement (CAFTA; TLC or Tratado de Libre Comercio, in Spanish) was ratified by Guatemala in 2006. Supporters claim it frees the country up for greater participation in foreign markets, while detractors state that the agreement is a bad deal for the already disenfranchised rural poor.

Another round of elections was held in late 2007, bringing to power Álvaro Colom of the center-leftist Unidad Nacional de la Esperanza (UNE). Colom followed Berger's example of steady, minimalist governance and spearheaded some much-needed improvements to the country's infrastructure. However, his entire presidency was dogged by corruption claims, from straight-out vote buying to back-room deals granting contracts to companies who had contributed to his campaign fund.

But probably the most bizarre twist of the Colom presidency happened as he was leaving office. The Guatemalan constitution prohibits members of the president's family from running for the subsequent presidency

1998
The true nature of peace is questioned as Bishop Gerardi, author of a paper blaming the army for the overwhelming amount of civil-war deaths, is found bludgeoned to death in his home.

2000–2004
Presidency of Alfonso Portillo of the FRG party, led by Efraín Ríos Montt. Portillo begins by prosecuting those responsible for the death of Bishop Gerardi, but is soon mired in corruption allegations.

2006
Guatemala ratifies CAFTA, a free-trade agreement between the US and Central America. Massive street protests and seemingly endless media discussion have little effect on the final document.

Jan 2012
Ex–civil war general Otto Perez Molina takes office as president, having won the election promising a reign of '*mano dura*' (iron fist) as a solution to Guatemala's burgeoning crime problems.

(supposedly an anti-dictatorship measure), so Colom and his wife filed for divorce in the lead-up to the 2011 elections in an attempt to make her a valid candidate. The Constitutional Court banned her candidature anyway, leaving the door open for hard-line, ex-civil war general Otto Pérez Molina to take office in early 2012.

Pérez Molina's election was always going to be controversial – he was a general in Ríos Montt's army in the period when the worst atrocities occurred, in the regions where they occurred. Guatemalans had grown tired of the growing lawlessness in their country, though, and turned a blind eye to history in the hope that Molina would deliver on his two campaign promises – jobs and security.

Despite some heavy-handed reactions to protesters (the army killed seven and wounded 40 in one incident at an anti-dam and anti-mining protest), Pérez Molina did little to combat real crime, and his early presidency was plagued by vague rumors of corruption in the administration. In April 2015, the UN anti-corruption agency CICIG issued a report and things got a whole lot less vague.

Granito: How to Nail a Dictator (2011) is a gripping documentary by Pamela Yates following the attempts by human rights groups to bring Guatemala's leaders to book for civil-war abuses.

The report claimed several senior members of the Pérez Molina administration were involved in taking bribes from importers in return for reduced customs fees. Within days, mass protests were organized over social media and tens of thousands turned out in downtown Guatemala City. Vice president Roxana Baldetti was the first to go – she resigned in early May, unable to explain how she paid for her US$13 million helicopter, among other things.

In the following months more than 20 officials resigned and many were arrested as the scandal snaked its way to the top. Mass protests continued as more findings were released. Baldetti was arrested in August amid calls for Pérez Molina's impeachment. The president hung on for a few weeks more, then resigned in the face of impending impeachment. He was arrested in early September.

Guatemala finally recognized Belizean independence in 1992, but the exact border remains in dispute. An agreement for both countries to hold referendums on taking the matter to the International Court of Justice for resolution was signed in 2008, but the matter has remained largely in limbo ever since.

For the latest on human rights in Guatemala, visit the Guatemala Human Rights Commission/USA website (www.ghrc-usa.org) or click the Guatemala reports from Human Rights Watch (www.hrw.org/americas/guatemala).

Dec 21, 2012

Despite lurid end-of-the-world predictions from non-Maya, Baktun 13 ends without major incidents and a new Great Cycle of the Maya Long Count calendar begins.

2015

President Pérez Molina and Vice president Baldetti resign following mass anti-corruption protests.

2016

Former comedian Jimmy Morales, an evangelical Christian who has publicly opposed same-sex marriage, is elected president.

2018

Volcán Fuego, near Antigua, erupts on June 3, killing around 160 people and leaving thousands homeless.

Guatemalan Way of Life

The usual socioeconomic dividers aside, the *way* you live in Guatemala depends largely on where you live – the differences between the coast and the highlands, big cities and small villages are so marked that sometimes it feels like that one-hour bus ride has taken you into another country. Some things are common to all Guatemalans, though – a set of national characteristics that when taken together largely define the essence of *ser Chapín* (being Guatemalan).

Life in the Big City

Around half of all Guatemalans live in what are classified as 'urban environments,' but it's important to remember that by international standards, Guatemala City is the country's only really big city: while the capital has 3.5 million inhabitants, Quetzaltenango (the second-largest city) is yet to hit 200,000.

Life in the capital (and even in the larger cities) resembles life in any big city in many ways. There are slums, middle-class neighborhoods and exclusive gated communities. Overcrowding and an ever-growing car culture make for traffic jams that wouldn't be out of place in London or New York. Guatemala City, in particular, has a bad reputation for street crime and it's rare to see people out walking at night. The capital is also where you'll see the most fortified homes, with razor wire, barred windows and closed-circuit camera surveillance – people tend to take as many measures as they can afford to guard against burglars and home invasion.

That the standard of living in Guatemala City has slowly improved is thanks largely to the efforts of ex-President and five-time mayor Álvaro Arzú, whose initiatives to open up public spaces and create pedestrian-only streets earned him the nickname 'El Jardinero' (the Gardener) from critics.

While many rural houses now have running water, the village *pila* (communal laundry trough) remains a place to get together and exchange gossip.

Home in the Mountains

Guatemala's mountainous regions also happen to be the most indigenous. As a result, Maya culture and tradition is much stronger in the mountains than on the coastal plain and in the capital. Even in larger cities you'll see many more women (and even some men) dressed in traditional Maya clothing, and no doubt you'll hear locals speaking in their dialect. Many people from these regions, particularly from older generations, speak Spanish as a second language, and some don't speak it at all.

The cold is a factor in the mountains – towns like Quetzaltenango and Todos Santos regularly register below-freezing temperatures in December. Another sight you're likely to see is men chopping and hauling firewood, which is used for both heating and cooking in many traditional homes.

The highlands' rich volcanic soil makes for some of the best farmland in the country. Vegetables grown in the Western Highlands are exported as far away as Belize, while the Cobán region has become a leading exporter of cardamom – much of it going as far away as India and the Middle East. Many mountain dwellers work in agriculture, either tending small subsistence plots or working on larger commercial farms.

Down on the Coast

The pace of life on the coast – where midday temperatures regularly hit 40°C (104°F) – slows right down. There's very little industry in these parts, and economic opportunities are few. The big employers on the coast are the sugar cane, chicle and African palm farms, which provide seasonal work. It's hardly cushy employment (imagine cutting cane with a machete in 40°C heat) and many coastal dwellers migrate to the cities in search of better opportunities.

Fishing is another income source. There are a few large industrial operations, but the bulk of fishermen (Guatemalan fisherwomen are extremely rare) either work independently, selling the day's catch at market, or in small cooperatives.

Housing on the coast is radically different to the rest of the country. Due to the extreme heat, cinderblock is not the popular construction material it is elsewhere, nor is corrugated iron for roofing. The classic coastal house will be open plan, often with wooden walls and a thatched roof. Doors will always be open and windows often lack glass, instead just having wooden shutters to keep out the monsoonal downpours of the rainy season.

Village Life

Guatemala's rural areas, while undoubtedly the country's most picturesque, are the epicenter for many of the country's persistent problems. Life in many villages has barely changed over the last hundred years, as subsistence farmers eke out a daily existence on tiny plots of land. The precariousness of this life is emphasized with every flood, drought, plague or crop failure – the smallest of any of these being enough to place entire families in danger of starvation.

THE BASICS OF GUATEMALAN CUISINE

Guatemalan cuisine reflects both the old foodstuffs of the Maya – corn (maize), beans, squash, potatoes, avocados, chilies and turkey – and the influence of the Spanish – bread, greater amounts of meat, rice and European vegetables.

The fundamental staple is the tortilla – a thin, round patty of corn meal cooked on a griddle called a *comal*. Many Guatemalans complain that they don't feel full without putting down at least three or four of these with a meal. In restaurants, tortillas accompanying meals are unlimited – in the unlikely event that you run out, just ask for more (the international symbol for this being waving the empty tortilla basket at your server).

The second staple is *frijoles* (fri-hoh-les), or black beans. These can be eaten boiled, fried, refried, in soups, spread on tortillas or accompanying eggs. They may come served in their own dark sauce, as a runny mass or a thick black paste. However they come, they are usually tasty and always nutritious.

The third Mayan staple is the squash. Many people complain that it is a flavorless vegetable, and is best served in soups or else combined with other strongly flavored ingredients.

On the coast, seafood is the go (although many coastal-dwellers will prefer a good chunk of steak, possibly for variety). Generally, your fish will come fried in oil, but for a little more flavor you can always specify *con ajo* (with garlic). These plates come with salad, fries and tortillas. Also good is *caldo de mariscos*, a seafood stew that generally contains fish, shrimp and mussels.

Guatemalan governments have ignored villages, and infrastructure levels can be dire. Many children have to travel for hours to attend the local school and what they call a school may not be something that you recognize as such. Access to health care is equally limited – at best a village will have a small medical clinic, capable of dealing with minor complaints. Patients requiring hospitalization may need to be transported several hours away. Many smaller villages don't even have a doctor, and medical care is provided by *curanderas* (healing women), *comadres* (midwives) and maybe a pharmacist.

Despite all of these drawbacks, Guatemalan villages are often stunningly beautiful – surrounded by lush countryside, with dirt roads winding between adobe huts, an old colonial church on the plaza and chickens and horses roaming about, as barefoot children play in the streets in a carefree way unseen in the rest of the country.

To understand more about Guatemala's place in the current American migrant crisis, see the 2016 Unicef report *Broken Dreams: Central American children's dangerous journey to the United States* (PDF available online).

Being Guatemalan

Despite the huge regional differences, there is such a thing as *ser Chapín*. With a few unfortunate exceptions, you'll be amazed when you first reach Guatemala by just how helpful, polite and unhurried Guatemalans are. Everyone has time to stop and chat and explain what you want to know. This is apparent even if you've just crossed the border from Mexico, where things aren't exactly rushed either. Most Guatemalans like to get to know other people without haste, feeling for common ground and things to agree on, rather than making blunt assertions and engaging in adversarial dialectic.

What goes on behind this outward politeness is harder to encapsulate. Few Guatemalans exhibit the stress, worry and hurry of the 'developed' nations, but this obviously isn't because they don't have to worry about money or employment. They're a long-suffering people who don't expect wealth or good government, but make the best of what comes their way – friendship, family, a good meal, a bit of good company.

The tales of violence – domestic violence, civil-war violence, criminal violence – that one inevitably hears in Guatemala sit strangely with the mild-mannered approach you will encounter from nearly everybody. Whatever the explanation, it helps to show why a little caution is in order when strangers meet.

Religion

Guatemalans are a religious bunch – atheists and agnostics are very thin on the ground. People will often ask what religion you are quite early in a conversation.

Orthodox Catholicism is gradually giving way to Evangelical Protestantism among the *ladinos* (people of mixed indigenous and European parentage), with the animist-Catholic syncretism of the traditional Maya always present. The number of new Evangelical churches, especially in indigenous Maya villages, is astonishing. Since the 1980s, Evangelical Protestant sects, around 60% of them Pentecostal, have surged in popularity and it is estimated that up to 45% of Guatemalans are now Evangelicals, and as this number grows higher, Guatemala is on course to become the world's first majority-Evangelical country in a couple of decades.

To get a handle on Maximón and shamanism around Lago de Atitlán, check out *Scandals in the House of Birds: Shamans and Priests on Lake Atitlán*, by anthropologist and poet Nathaniel Tarn.

During the civil war, many priests gave outspoken support to the Maya and their struggle for self-determination. This defence of human rights attracted persecution (and worse) from dictators at the time, especially from the Evangelical Ríos Montt.

Catholicism in the Maya areas has never been exactly orthodox. The missionaries who brought Catholicism to the Maya in the 16th century wisely permitted aspects of the existing animistic, shamanistic Maya religion to continue alongside Christian rites and beliefs. Syncretism was aided by the identification of certain Maya deities with certain Christian saints, and survives to this day. A notable example is the deity known as Maximón in Santiago Atitlán, San Simón in Zunil and Rilaj Maam in San Andrés Itzapa near Antigua, who seems to be a volatile combination of Maya gods, the Spanish conquistador Pedro de Alvarado and Judas Iscariot.

Guatemala's most venerated local Christian figure, the 17th-century Antigua-hospital-founder Hermano Pedro de San José de Bethancourt, was canonized in 2002 when Pope John Paul II visited Guatemala.

Family Life

Despite modernizing influences - education, cable TV, contact with foreign travelers, international popular music, time spent as migrant workers in the USA - traditional family ties remain strong at all levels of society. Large extended-family groups gather for weekend meals and holidays. Old-fashioned gender roles are strong, too: many women have jobs to increase the family income, but relatively few have positions of much responsibility.

Cynics say that much of this closeness has more to do with economics than sentiment - that it's hard to be distant when there are three generations living under the same roof. But this doesn't really play out. You see the strong bonds of family among middle- and upper-class Guatemalans, and one of the questions you're bound to get asked at least once (and possibly many more times) while on your travels is whether you miss your mother.

Despite this closeness, it's rare to meet a family who doesn't have at least one member who has emigrated to the US to work - the couple of hundred dollars that these emigrants send back per month is the sole income for some families, and, when tallied up, equals around half of what Guatemala earns from exports.

Women in Guatemala

One of the goals of the 1996 Peace Accords was to improve women's rights in Guatemala. By 2003, the Inter-American Commission on Human Rights had to report that laws discriminating against women had yet to be repealed. Women got the vote and the right to stand for election in 1946, but in 2015 only 13% of congressional deputies were women. Women's rights leaders repeatedly criticize Guatemala's *machista* culture,

MINDING YOUR MANNERS IN GUATEMALA

While Guatemalans tend to give foreigners a fair amount of leeway, at least trying to adapt to local ways is bound to make your travels run more smoothly.

- Even in such routine situations as entering a store or taking a bus seat, a simple greeting is often exchanged: *buenos días* or *buenas tardes* and a smile is all that's needed.
- When leaving a restaurant, it is common to wish other diners *buen provecho (bon appétit)*.
- In general, the Maya are a fairly private people and some communities are still recovering from the nightmare of the civil war. People may be willing to share their war stories, but don't dig for information – let your hosts offer it.
- Referring to a Maya person as *indio* (Indian) is considered racist. The preferred term is *indígena*.
- When dealing with officialdom (police, border officials, immigration officers), try to appear as conservative and respectable as possible.
- Dress modestly when entering churches or attending family gatherings.

which believes a woman's place is in the home. The situation is, if anything, worse for indigenous women in rural areas, who also have to live with most of the country's direst poverty.

The international organization Human Rights Watch reported in 2002 that women working in private households were persistently discriminated against. Domestic workers, many of whom are from Maya communities, lack certain basic rights, including the rights to be paid the minimum wage and to work an eight-hour day and a 48-hour week. Many domestic workers begin working as young adolescents, but Guatemalan labor laws do not provide adequate protection for domestic workers under the age of 18 years.

For information on Guatemalan women's organizations including volunteer opportunities and background on rights issues, visit the website of Quetzaltenango-based Entre Mundos (www.entremundos.org).

Probably of greatest concern is the high incidence of violence against women, accompanied by Guatemala's steadily rising murder rate. These victims were once brushed off as being part of a bad crowd, but it is now clear that murder, rape and kidnapping of women is a serious issue. The international community has begun to put pressure on Guatemala to act, but the realities of *machista* society mean that even with the passing of legislation specifically aimed at protecting women, crimes against women are seldom investigated and rarely solved.

Education in Guatemala

Education is free and, in theory, compulsory between the ages of seven and 14. Primary education lasts for six years, but the average school-leaving age is 11 years, according to UN statistics. Secondary school begins at age 13 and comprises two cycles of three years each, called *básico* and *magisterio*. Not all secondary education is free – a major deterrent for many. Some people continue studying for their *magisterio* well into adulthood. Completing *magisterio* qualifies you to become a school teacher yourself. It's estimated that only about 56% of children of the 13-to-18 age group are in secondary school. Guatemala has five universities.

Overall, adult literacy is around 81% in Guatemala, but it's lower among women (76%) and rural people. Maya children who do seasonal migrant work with their families are least likely to get an education, as the time the families go away to work falls during the school year. It is estimated that 21% of Guatemalans between the ages of five and 14 work instead of attending school.

A limited amount of school teaching is done in Maya languages – chiefly the big four, K'iche', Mam, Kaqchiquel and Q'eqchi' – but this rarely goes beyond the first couple of years of primary school. Spanish remains the necessary tongue for anyone who wants to get ahead in life.

Sport (aka Futból)

If there's one thing that unites almost all Guatemalans, it is their passion and enthusiasm for *fútbol* (soccer). If you'd like a universal talking point, you could do worse than brush up on your soccer teams. Many Guatemalans keep a keen eye on their local team and at least one European team (Barcelona being by far the most popular Spanish side).

For the best up-to-the-minute news on the football scene in Guatemala, including results, fixtures and league tables, log on to www.guatefutbol.com.

The national squad has never qualified for a major international tournament, and Guatemala's football federation was suspended from FIFA between 2017 and 2018 following corruption allegations.

The 10-club Liga Mayor (Major League) national competition is keenly followed by reasonably large crowds. Two seasons are played each year: the Torneo de Apertura (Opening Tournament), from July to November, and the Torneo de Clausura (Closing Tournament), from January to May. The two big clubs are Municipal and Comunicaciones, both from Guatemala City. The 'Classico Gringo' is when teams from Quetzaltenango and Antigua (the two big tourist towns) play.

Maya Heritage

The ancient Maya constructed a civilization that was vastly impressive, complex and fruitful. While some legacies, such as the archaeological sites, are obvious, scholars are still working to put together the various pieces of how Maya society worked. The Maya didn't disappear with the arrival of the conquistadors, however, and traditional rituals and beliefs still carry on into 21st-century Guatemala.

Ancient Maya Beliefs

The date of creation that appears in inscriptions throughout the Maya world is 13.0.0.0.0, 4 Ahaw, 8 Kumk'u, or August 13, 3114 BCE on our calendar.

On that day the creator gods set three stones in the dark waters that covered the primordial world. These formed a cosmic hearth at the center of the universe. They then struck divine fire by means of lightning, charging the world with life.

The gods made three attempts at creating people before getting it right. First they made deer and other animals, but as they were unable to speak and honor the gods, the animals were condemned to be eaten.

Next was a person made from mud. At first, the mud person spoke, 'but without knowledge and understanding,' and he soon dissolved back into the mire.

The Maya, by Michael D Coe, is probably the best single-volume, not-too-long telling of the ancient Maya story. Coe's *Breaking the Maya Code* recounts the modern decipherment of ancient Maya writing, and his *Reading the Maya Glyphs* will help you read ancient inscriptions.

The gods' third attempt was people carved from wood. These too were imperfect and also destroyed. The Popol Vuh, a book compiled by members of the Maya nobility soon after the Spanish conquest, says that the survivors of these wooden people are the monkeys that inhabit the forests.

The gods finally got it right when they discovered maize, and made humankind from the yellow ears and white ears of this indispensable grain.

The Maya Cosmovision

For the ancient Maya, the world, the heavens and the mysterious underworld called Xibalbá were one great, unified structure that operated according to the laws of astrology, cyclical time and ancestor worship.

The towering, sacred ceiba tree symbolized the world-tree, which united the heavens (represented by the tree's branches and foliage), the earth (the trunk) and the nine levels of Xibalbá (the roots). The world-tree had a sort of cruciform shape, so when the Franciscan friars came bearing a cross and required the Maya to venerate it, the symbolism meshed easily with established Maya beliefs.

Each point of the compass had a color and a special religious significance. Everything in the Maya world was seen in relation to these cardinal points, with the world-tree at the center.

Blood-letting ceremonies were the most important religious ceremonies for the Maya – a way for humans to link themselves to the underworld – and the blood of kings was seen as the most acceptable for these rituals. Maya kings often initiated blood-letting rites to heighten the responsiveness of the gods.

THE LIDAR REVOLUTION

Archaeologists' understanding of the ancient Maya is currently undergoing a revolution, thanks to the development of LIDAR technology. LIDAR (Light Detection And Ranging) is best described as radar but using lasers. Lasers sent from a survey plane to the ground penetrate even the thickest of jungle cover and bounce back to a recorder to give a detailed 3D image of the terrain.

Our picture of the Maya has been transformed as a result. To date, over 2000 sq km of northern Guatemala has been surveyed and more than 60,000 previously hidden structures revealed. Not least among these are the complex series of elevated causeways linking cities; a more intensive system of farming and irrigation canals, dykes and reservoirs than previously imagined; and whole networks of defensive walls and forts. Where population estimates for the Maya civilization at the height of the Classic period previously hovered around 5 million people, the new data suggests that the region could have supported between 10 and 15 million instead.

There are plans to survey around 5000 sq miles of the Guatemalan lowlands, but already the results are revealing a culture larger and more complex than even the experts have previously imagined.

Maya ceremonies were performed in natural sacred places as well as their human-made equivalents. Mountains, caves, lakes, cenotes (natural limestone cavern pools), rivers and fields were – and still are – sacred. Pyramids and temples were thought of as stylized mountains. A cave was the mouth of the creature that represented Xibalbá, and to enter it was to enter the spirit of the secret world. This is why some Maya temples have doorways surrounded by huge masks: as you enter the door of this 'cave' you are entering the mouth of Xibalbá.

Ancestor worship was very important to the ancient Maya, and when they buried a king beneath a pyramid or a commoner beneath the floor or courtyard of a *na* (thatched Maya hut), the sacredness of the location was increased.

Maya Writing

The Maya developed a sophisticated hieroglyphic script that formed the most advanced writing system in the Americas. The script was developed in the Preclassic period, with the earliest surviving texts dating from the 3rd century BC. It's thought that its use persisted until at least a century after the Spanish conquest.

The script is partly phonetic (glyphs representing sounds) and partly logographic (glyphs representing words). Over 1000 glyphs are known, and around 80% of these have their meanings known. Scholars have suggested that the written language throughout the Maya world was a form of Chol, the language group of the Eastern Highlands.

Each heiroglyph is actually a block consisting of a main sign with one or two smaller signs affixed to it to assign it further meaning. The script itself is read left to right and top to bottom. To learn more on the script, and the battle to decipher it, watch the documentary *Cracking the Mayan Code*, widely available online.

Mayan Folktales, edited by James D Sexton, brings together the myths and legends of the Lago de Atitlán area, translated into English.

The Maya Calendar

The ancient Maya's astronomical observations and calculations were uncannily accurate and time was, in fact, the basis of the Maya religion. Perhaps the best analogy to the Maya calendar is the gears of a mechanical watch, where small wheels mesh with larger wheels, which in turn mesh with other sets of wheels to record the passage of time.

The Maya Solar Year

The two smallest 'wheels' were two cycles: one of 13 days and another of 20 days. As these two wheels meshed, the passing days received unique names. The two small wheels thus created a larger wheel of 260 days, called a *tzolkin, cholq'ij* or *tonalamatl.*

Another set of wheels in the Maya calendar comprised 18 'months' of 20 days each, which formed the basis of the solar year or *haab* (or *ab'*). Eighteen months, each of 20 days, equals 360 days, a period known as a *tun;* the Maya added a special omen-filled five-day period called the *uayeb* at the end of this cycle in order to produce a solar calendar of 365 days.

The Long Count

The huge wheels of the *tzolkin* and the *haab* also meshed and repeated every 52 solar years, a period called the Calendar Round. The Calendar Round was the dating system used not only by the Maya, but also by the Olmecs, Aztecs and Zapotecs of ancient Mexico.

Mary Ellen Miller's well-illustrated *Maya Art and Architecture* paints the full picture from gigantic temples to intricately painted ceramics.

The Calendar Round has one serious limitation: it only lasts 52 years. Hence the Long Count, which the Maya developed around the start of the Classic period.

The Long Count uses the *tun*, but ignores the *uayeb*. Twenty *tuns* make a *katun* and 20 *katuns* make a *baktun*. Curiously for us today, 13 *baktuns* (1,872,000 days, or 5125 Gregorian solar years) form something called a Great Cycle, and the first Great Cycle began on August 11, 3114 BC, which means it ended on December 23 (or 25), AD 2012. The end of a Great Cycle was a time charged with great significance – you may have noticed a little (non-Maya) end-of-the-world panic around Christmas 2012.

Maya Architecture

Ancient Maya architecture is a mixed bag of incredible accomplishments achieved despite severe limitations. The Maya's great buildings are both awesome and beautiful, with their aesthetic attention to intricately patterned facades, delicate 'combs' on temple roofs, and sinuous carvings. These magnificent structures, such as the ones found in the sophisticated urban centers of Tikal, El Mirador and Copán, were created without beasts of burden (except for humans) or the luxury of the wheel. Once structures were completed, experts hypothesize, they were covered with stucco and painted red with a mixture of hematite and most probably water.

Although formal studies and excavations of Maya sites in Guatemala have been ongoing for more than a century, much of their architectural how and why remains a mystery. For example, the purpose of *chultunes,*

COLORS OF THE MAYA

The Maya put great stock in the significance of different colors, something that can still be seen today in the choosing of colored candles for traditional religious ceremonies.

The four basic Maya colors are red, white, black and yellow, which correspond to the cardinal points, and the four branches of the Maya tree of life. Red represents the sun rising in the sacred east. White represents north, for the North Star and the heavens. Black is west for the dying sun at the end of the day, while yellow is south, and the sun itself. Red, white, black and yellow are also the four colors of traditional maize kernels – humanity itself was created out of yellow and white maize.

A fifth color, blue-green, is associated with religious sacrifice. Maya Blue, as it is known, was a locally created mix of indigo and clay minerals, whose composition made it resistant to age and sunlight – a uniquely Maya piece of chemistry.

THE MAYA BURY THEIR DEAD

It is the night before the funeral, and the shaman is in the house of the deceased, washing candles in holy water. If he misses one, a family member could go blind or deaf. He has counted off the days, and divined that tomorrow will be propitious for the burial.

He prays to the ancestral spirits, asking for the health of the family and the absence of disaster. The list is long and detailed. Personal objects are placed in the coffin; if they're not, the deceased's spirit might return home looking for them.

Members of the *cofradía* (fraternity) bear the coffin to the cemetery, a trail of mourners following. Four stops are made on leaving the house: at the doorway, in the yard, on entering the street, and at the first street corner. At each stop, mourners place coins on the coffin – in reality to buy candles, symbolically so that the spirit can buy its way out of purgatory and into heaven.

As the coffin is lowered into the ground, mourners kiss handfuls of dirt before throwing them on top. Once the coffin is buried, women sprinkle water on top, packing down the soil and protecting the corpse from werewolves and other dark spirits.

Every All Souls' Day (November 2) the family will come to the cemetery to honor their dead. Sometimes this will stretch over three days (beginning on November 1). They will come to clean and decorate the grave, and set out food such as roasted corn, sweet potatoes, vegetable pears (*chayote* or chokos), and other fresh-picked fruit of the field. The church bells will ring at midday to summon the spirits, who feast on the smells of the food.

underground chambers carved from bedrock and filled with offerings, continues to baffle scholars. And while we know that the Maya habitually built one temple on top of another to bury successive leaders, we have little idea how they actually erected these symbols of power. All the limestone used to erect the great Maya cities had to be moved and set in place by hand – an engineering feat that must have demanded astronomical amounts of human labor.

Modern Maya Rituals

Many sites of ancient Maya ruins – among them Tikal, Kaminaljuyú and K'umarcaaj – still have altars where prayers, offerings and ceremonies continue to take place today. Fertility rites, healing ceremonies and sacred observances to ring in the various Maya new years are still practiced with gusto. These types of ceremony are directed or overseen by a Maya priest known as a *tzahorín* and usually involve burning candles and copal (a natural incense from the bark of various tropical trees), making offerings to the gods and praying for whatever the desired outcome may be – a good harvest, a healthy child or a prosperous new year, for example. Some ceremonies involve chicken sacrifices as well. Each place has its own set of gods – or at least different names for similar gods.

Maya priests used a variety of drugs during divination rituals – ranging from fermented maize and wild tobacco to hallucinogenic mushrooms.

Visitors may also be able to observe traditional Maya ceremonies in places such as the Pascual Abaj shrine at Chichicastenango, the altars on the shore of Laguna Chicabal outside Quetzaltenango, or El Baúl near Santa Lucía Cotzumalguapa, but a lot of traditional rites are off-limits to foreigners.

Arts & Architecture

Guatemala's rich cultural heritage stretches back centuries and the country has produced more than its share of important artists and groundbreaking artistic achievements. The enduring legacy of Maya architecture and weaving cannot be denied, and the country has produced writers and musicians who have attained international fame. Many traditional crafts survive as well, with handicrafts manufactured both as everyday items and for sale as souvenirs.

Literature

Literature in Guatemala begins with the creation of the Maya script, the most sophisticated writing system in the Americas. The *Popul Vuh*, the creation story of the K'iche' Maya is the country's first great literary epic, a centuries-old oral tradition first transcribed in the 16th century.

Colonial Guatemala's first great literary figure was poet and Jesuit priest Rafael Landívar, whose collection of poetry *Rusticatio Mexicana*, containing 5348 verses in Latin, was published in 1781.

A great source of national pride is the Nobel Prize for Literature that was bestowed on Guatemalan Miguel Ángel Asturias (1899–1974) in 1967. Best known for *Men of Maize*, his magical-realist epic on the theme of European conquest and the Maya, and for his thinly veiled vilification of Latin American dictators in *The President*, Asturias also wrote poetry. He served in various diplomatic capacities for the Guatemalan government.

Other celebrated Guatemalan authors include short-story master Augusto Monterroso (1921–2003), who is credited as having written the shortest story in published literature, *El Dinosaurio*. Look also for his published work *The Black Sheep and Other Fables*. Luis Cardoza y Aragón (1901–92) is principally known for his poetry and for fighting in the revolutionary movement that deposed dictator Jorge Ubico in 1944. Gaspar Pedro Gonzáles' *A Mayan Life* is claimed to be the first novel written by a Maya author.

Guatemalan-born Arturo Arias is an author and professor of Spanish-American literature at the University of Texas. His most famous works include *Itzam Na* (1981), *Jaguar en llamas* (1990) and *The Rigoberta Menchú Controversy* (2001), in which he examines the heated debate that ensued after Menchú won the Nobel Prize.

Born in the US to a Guatemalan mother, Francisco Goldman is probably the most famous author writing about Guatemala in modern times. Primarily a novelist, Goldman has also written a nonfiction account of the assassination of Bishop Gerardi, *The Art of Political Murder*, that won him international and critical acclaim and a good selection of enemies from within Guatemala's power structure.

One of Central America's largest literary competitions, the Juegos Florales Hispanoamericanos, is held in Quetzaltenango – the nation's literary capital – in September to coincide with Independence Day celebrations.

Painting

Precolonial

No discussion of painting in Guatemala would be complete without a mention of the fabulous mural work that the Maya created long before the Spanish arrived. Most have been severely worn by time and vandals, but a few archaeological sites such as San Bartolo and Río Azul have paintings that remain surprisingly vivid. The tradition continues with large modern Maya murals such as that in Chichicastengo, using the Maya Popul Vuh to narrate an account of the civil war.

Early Postcolonial

One of the earliest postcolonial painters of note was Tomás de Merlo, widely credited as the father of the 'Antigua Baroque' movement. You can see many of his works in the National Museum of Colonial Art, in Antigua, and hanging on church walls in Antigua, too.

Nan Cuz, a Maya painter of mixed German–K'iche' heritage grew up in Nazi Germany and found international fame with her bright, sometimes surreal landscapes of her Lago de Atitlán home. La Galería in Panajechel celebrates her life and work.

Modern Maya Painting

One truly Guatemalan genre of painting, dubbed 'Maya naïve art' was spearheaded by Andrés Curruchich, a native of San Juan Comalapa near Lago de Atitlán. Curruchich's works depicted the simple rural scenes of the Guatemalan countryside you can still see today. There is a permanent exhibition of Curruchich's work in the Museo Ixchel in Guatemala City. While the artist died in 1969, his legacy continues – there are an estimated 500 artists working in San Juan Comalapa today, many of them trained by Curruchich himself. Juan Sisay was another Maya primitivist painter from the Atitlán region to gain international fame.

Contemporary Artists

Of all modern Guatemalan artists, the architect, muralist, painter and sculptor Efraín Recinos is probably the most famous. His murals grace Guatemala City's National Music Conservatory and he is also responsible for the facade of the National Library and the design of the Centro Cultural Miguel Ángel Asturias, both also in Guatemala City. Recinos was awarded Guatemala's highest honor, the Order of the Quetzal, in 1999, and the country went into mourning when he died in 2011.

Music

Folk Music

Guatemalan festivals provide great opportunities to hear traditional music featuring instruments such as cane flutes, square drums and the *chirimía,* a reed instrument of Moorish roots related to the oboe.

The other popular form of 'folk' music is made by the Garifuna people who live around the country's Caribbean coast. Completely different from traditional Maya music, the Garifuna's most popular style is Punta Rock, variants of which you can hear in dance clubs around the country.

Contemporary Music

Guatemalan tastes in pop music are greatly influenced by the products of other Latin American countries. Reggaetón and Latin Pop are huge.

The only record label seriously promoting new Guatemalan artists (mostly in the urban/hip-hop vein) is Guatemala City–based Outstanding Productions.

Guatemalan rock went through its golden age in the 1980s and early '90s. Bands from this era such as Razones de Cambio, Bohemia Suburbana and Viernes Verde still have their die-hard fans. The most famous Guatemalan-born musician is the Latin Pop superstar Ricardo Arjona.

Architecture

For most visitors, Guatemala's built heritage is typified by either monumental Maya temples or ornate Spanish colonial buildings. The country does have one architectural star, however, in the late Efraín Recinos, who blended modernism with traditional Maya themes to try to create a distinctive Guatemalan style. His most famous building is the Centro Cultural Miguel Ángel Asturias in Guatemala City.

Outside this, and a few flashy bank and office buildings along Av La Reforma in Guatemala City, Guatemala's built environment is chiefly characterized by expanses of drab concrete. Some humbler rural dwellings still use a traditional wall construction known as *bajareque*, where a core of stones is held in place by poles of bamboo or other wood, which is faced with stucco or mud. If you see a flashy house in a poor town, it will often be a *remisas* building – built by money sent home from Guatemalans working abroad.

Colonial Architecture

During the colonial period (the early 16th to early 19th centuries), churches, convents, mansions and palaces were all built in the Spanish styles of the day, chiefly Renaissance, baroque and neoclassical. But while the architectural concepts were European-inspired, the labor used to realize them was strictly indigenous. Thus, Maya embellishments – such as the lily blossoms and vegetable motifs that adorn Antigua's La Merced – can be found on many colonial buildings, serving as testament to the countless laborers forced to make the architectural dreams of Guatemala's newcomers a reality.

Not all of Antigua's colonial masterpieces were built by Spanish architects. Its iconic 17th-century cathedral was designed by Joseph de Porres, who was of mixed African–Mayan descent.

Guatemala does not have the great colonial architectural heritage of neighboring Mexico, partly because earthquakes destroyed many of its finest buildings. But the architecture of Antigua is particularly striking, as new styles and engineering techniques developed following each successive earthquake. Columns became lower and thicker to provide more stability. Some Antigua buildings, including the Palacio de los Capitanes and Palacio del Ayuntamiento on the central plaza, were given a double-arch construction to strengthen them. With so many colonial buildings in different states of grandeur and decay, Antigua was designated a World Heritage Site by Unesco in 1979.

After the 1773 earthquake, which prompted the relocation of the capital from Antigua to Guatemala City, the neoclassical architecture of the day came to emphasize durability. Decorative flourishes were saved for the interiors of buildings, with elaborate altars and furniture adorning churches and homes. By this time Guatemalan architects were hell-bent on seeing their buildings stay upright, no matter how powerful the next earthquake. Even though several serious quakes have hit Guatemala City since then, many colonial buildings (such as the city's cathedral) have survived. The same cannot be said for the humble abodes of the city's residents, who suffered terribly from the devastating quake of 1976.

Handicrafts

Guatemalans make many traditional handicrafts, both for everyday use and to sell to tourists and collectors. Crafts include basketry, ceramics and wood carving, but the most prominent are weaving, embroidery and other textile arts practiced by Maya women. The beautiful, handmade *traje* (traditional clothing) worn by local women is one of the most awe-inspiring expressions of Maya culture.

Weaving

The most arresting feature of Maya traditional clothing is the highly colorful weaving and embroidery, which makes many garments true works of art. It's the women's *huipil,* a long, sleeveless tunic, that receives the most painstaking, loving care in its creation. Often entire *huipiles* are covered in a multicolored web of stylized animal, human, plant and mythological shapes, which can take months to complete. Each garment identifies the village from which its wearer hails (the Spanish colonists allotted each village a different design in order to distinguish the inhabitants from each other) and within the village style there can be variations according to social status, as well as the creative individual touches that make each garment unique.

Well-illustrated books on Maya textiles will help you to start identifying the wearers' villages. Two fine works are *The Maya of Guatemala – Life and Dress,* by Carmen L Pettersen, and *The Maya Textile Tradition,* edited by Margot Blum Schevill.

Maya men now generally wear Western clothing, except in places such as Sololá and Todos Santos Cuchumatán, where they still sport colorful *trajes*.

Materials and techniques are changing, but the pre-Hispanic backstrap loom is still widely used. The warp (long) threads are stretched between two horizontal bars, one of which is fixed to a post or tree, while the other is attached to a strap that goes round the weaver's lower back. The weft (cross) threads are then woven in. Throughout the highlands you can see women weaving in this manner outside the entrance to their homes. Nowadays, some *huipiles* and other garments are machine made, as this method is faster and easier than weaving by hand.

Yarn is still hand-spun in many villages. For the well-to-do, silk threads are used to embroider bridal *huipiles* and other important garments. Vegetable dyes are not yet totally out of use, and red dye from cochineal insects and natural indigo are employed in several areas. Modern luminescent dyes go down very well with the Maya, who are happily addicted to bright colors, as you will see.

The colorful traditional dress is still generally most in evidence in the highlands, which are heavily populated by Maya, though you will see it in all parts of the country. The variety of techniques, materials, styles and designs is bewildering to the newcomer, but you'll see some of the most colorful, intricate, eye-catching and widely worn designs in Sololá and Santiago Atitlán, near Lago de Atitlán; Nebaj, in the Ixil Triangle; Zunil, near Quetzaltenango; and Todos Santos and San Mateo Ixtatán in the Cuchumatanes mountains.

You can learn the art of backstrap weaving at weaving schools in Quetzaltenango, Santiago de Atitlán and other towns. To see large collections of fine weaving, don't miss Museo Ixchel (p49) in Guatemala City or the shop Nim Po't (p85) in Antigua.

Other Handicrafts

The Maya, particularly in the highlands, have a long tradition of skilled artistry, products of which you can see in nearly every market in the country. The small town of Totonicapán has dozens of tiny workshops that are open to visitors where you can see tinsmiths, potters, wood carvers and instrument makers at work.

If you are looking for a traditional blanket made from home-spun wool, make your way to Momostenango, near Quetzaltenango.

Jade was a sacred stone to the Maya and remains a popular material for jewelers. To see the finest pieces you can tour the workshops and showrooms in Antigua.

Some of the most popular Guatemalan souvenirs are the wooden masks used for village festivals. Many display a curious mixture of pre- and post-Columbian influences, such as the very devilish-looking masks used to depict the Spanish colonizers. Again, masks are in markets everywhere, but to see the best selection, go to Chichicastenango, and for the best prices, head to Panajachel or Antigua.

Land & Wildlife

Even 'city people' will have to admit that some of the best parts of Guatemala are in the countryside. The ever-changing terrain takes in the balmy coast, the harsh highlands, cool cloud forest, lush jungle and desert-like savannah. The birdlife is rich wherever you go, and there are enough exotic four-legged creatures around to keep most wildlife-spotters happy.

The Land

Guatemala covers an area of 108,889 sq km – a little less than the US state of Louisiana, a little more than England. Geologically, most of the country lies atop the North American tectonic plate, but this abuts the Cocos plate along Guatemala's Pacific coast and the Caribbean plate in the far south of the country. When any of these plates gets frisky, earthquakes and volcanic eruptions ensue. Hence the major quakes of 1917, 1918 and 1976 and the spectacular chain of 30 volcanoes – some of them active – running parallel to the Pacific coast from the Mexican border to the Salvadoran border. North of the volcanic chain rises the Cuchumatanes range.

Tajumulco (4220m), northwest of Quetzaltenango, is the highest peak in Central America. La Torre (3837m), north of Huehuetenango, is the highest nonvolcanic peak in Central America.

North of Guatemala City, the highlands of Alta Verapaz gradually decline to the lowland of El Petén, occupying northern Guatemala. El Petén is hot and humid or hot and dry, depending on the season. Central America's largest tracts of virgin rainforest straddle El Petén's borders with Mexico and Belize, although this may cease to be true if conservation efforts are not successful.

Northeast of Guatemala City, the valley of the Río Motagua (dry in some areas, moist in others) runs down to Guatemala's short, very hot Caribbean coast. Bananas and sugarcane thrive in the Motagua valley.

Between the volcanic chain and the Pacific Ocean is the Pacific Slope, with rich coffee, cotton, rubber, fruit and sugar plantations, cattle ranches, beaches of black volcanic sand and a sweltering climate.

Guatemala's unique geology also includes tremendous systems of caves. Water coursing for eons over a limestone base created aquifers and conduits that eventually gave way to subterranean caves, rivers and sinkholes when the surface water drained into underground caverns and streams. This type of terrain (known as karst) is found throughout the Verapaces region and makes Guatemala a killer spelunking destination.

Wildlife

Guatemala's natural beauty, from volcanoes and lakes to jungles and wetlands, is one of its great attractions. With an astonishing range of different ecosystems, the variety of fauna and flora is great – and if you know where to go, opportunities for seeing exciting species are plentiful.

Animals

Estimates point to 250 species of mammals, 600 species of birds, 200 species of reptiles and amphibians, and many species of butterflies and other insects.

The national bird, the resplendent quetzal (for which the national currency is named), is small but exceptionally beautiful. The male sports a bright-red breast, brilliant blue-green neck, head, back and wings, and a blue-green tail several times as long as the body, which stands only around 15cm tall. The female has far duller plumage. The quetzal's main habitat is the cloud forests of Alta Verapaz.

Exotic birds of the lowland jungles include toucans, macaws and parrots. If you visit Tikal, you can't miss the ocellated turkey (also called the Petén turkey), a large, multicolored bird reminiscent of a peacock. Tikal is an all-round wildlife hot spot: you stand a good chance of spotting howler and spider monkeys, coatis (locally called *pisotes*) and other mammals, plus toucans, parrots and many other birds. Some 300 endemic and migratory bird species have been recorded at Tikal, among them nine hummingbirds and four trogons.

Good areas for sighting waterfowl – including the jabiru stork, the biggest flying bird in the western hemisphere – are Laguna Petexbatún and the lakes near Yaxhá ruins, both in El Petén, and the Río Dulce between Lago de Izabal and Lívingston.

Guatemala's forests still host many mammal and reptile species. Petén residents include jaguars, ocelots, pumas, two species of peccary, opossums, tapirs, kinkajous, agoutis (*tepescuintles;* rodents 60cm to 70cm long), white-tailed and red brocket deer, and armadillos. Guatemala is home to at least five species of sea turtle (the loggerhead, hawksbill and green ridley on the Caribbean coast, and the leatherback and olive ridley on the Pacific) and at least two species of crocodile (one found in El Petén, the other in the Río Dulce). Manatees exist in the Río Dulce, though they're notoriously hard to spot.

Bird lovers must get hold of either *The Birds of Tikal: An Annotated Checklist,* by Randell A Beavers, or *The Birds of Tikal,* by Frank B Smithe. If you can't find them elsewhere, at least one should be on sale at Tikal itself, and both are useful much further afield.

When Fuego volcano erupted on June 3, 2018, its ash plume reached more than 14.5km into the atmosphere, killing around 160 people and leaving thousands homeless.

EARTHQUAKES, HURRICANES & VOLCANOES

We don't want to worry you, but Guatemala, along with being the Land of the Eternal Spring, the Land of Smiles and the Land of the Trees also seems to be the Land of the Natural Disaster. Don't panic – there are really only three biggies you have to worry about:

Earthquakes Sitting on top of three tectonic plates hasn't really worked out that well for Guatemala. The present-day capital was founded after Antigua got flattened, but Guatemala City still got pummeled in 1917, 1918 and 1976. This last one left 23,000 people dead.

Hurricanes Nobody likes a hurricane. They're windy and noisy and get mud and water everywhere. Guatemala has two coastlines so theoretically the hit could come from either angle, although it's statistically more likely to come from the Pacific side. Hurricane Stan in 2005 was the worst the country's seen, killing more than 1500 and affecting nearly half a million people. Hurricane season runs June to November – for the latest news, you can check with the National Hurricane Center & Tropical Prediction Center (www.nhc.noaa.gov).

Volcanoes Great to look at, fun to climb, scary when they erupt. Guatemala has four active volcanoes: Pacaya, Fuego, Santiaguito and Tacaná. The nastiest event to date was back in 1902 when Santa María erupted taking 6000 lives. In recent years Pacaya and Fuego (both outside of Antigua) have been acting up, with increased lava flow and ash. When Fuego erupted in June 2018, over 160 people were killed by the resulting ash flow. If you need to keep an eye on it, log on to the Smithsonian's volcano page (www.volcano.si.edu).

Endangered Species

Guatemala's wildlife faces two major threats. The first is the loss of habitat, as more land is turned over to farming. The second threat is hunting, which is mostly done for food, but also takes place for the collection of skins and other products, as is the case for deer, turtles and some reptiles. Endangered mammals include jaguars, howler monkeys, manatees, several species of mice and bats, and the Guatemalan vole.

More than 25 bird species native to the region are listed as endangered, including the Atitlán grebe (found only in Guatemala) and the national bird, the resplendent quetzal. Many reptiles, including the Morelet's crocodile, are likewise disappearing.

Jonathon Maslow's *Bird of Life, Bird of Death* begins as a story about a naturalist's search for the quetzal, but quickly develops into a terrifying portrait of Guatemala during the civil war.

Plants

Guatemala has more than 8000 species of plants in 19 different ecosystems that range from mangrove forests and wetlands on both coasts to the tropical rainforest of El Petén, and the pine forests, open grasslands and cloud forests of the mountains. The cloud forests, with their epiphytes, bromeliads and dangling old-man's-beard, are most abundant in Alta Verapaz. Trees of El Petén include the sapodilla, wild rubber trees, mahogany, several useful palms and Guatemala's national tree for its manifold symbolism to the Maya, the ceiba (also called the kapok or silk-cotton tree in English). Cities such as Antigua become glorious with the lilac blooms of jacaranda trees in the early months of the year.

The Pacunam foundation (www.pacunam.org) ties together work and research on conservation issues with Maya archaeology and sustainable tourism.

The national flower, the *monja blanca* (white nun orchid), is said to have been picked so much that it's now rarely seen in the wild; nevertheless, with 550 species of orchid (one third of them endemic to Guatemala), you shouldn't have any trouble spotting some. If you're interested in orchids, be sure to visit the Vivero Verapaz orchid nursery at Cobán and try to land in town for its annual orchid festival, held every December.

Domesticated plants, of course, contribute at least as much to the landscape as wild ones. The *milpa* (maize field) is the backbone of agricultural subsistence everywhere. *Milpas* are, however, usually cleared by the slash-and-burn method, which has been an important factor in the diminution of Guatemala's forests.

Parks & Protected Areas

Guatemala has more than 90 protected areas, including *reservas de biosfera* (biosphere reserves), *parques nacionales* (national parks), *biotopos protegidos* (protected biotopes), *refugios de vida silvestre* (wildlife refuges) and *reservas naturales privadas* (private nature reserves). Even though some areas are contained within other, larger ones, they amount to 28% of the national territory. The Parque Nacional Tikal is the only such area on the Unesco World Heritage list in Guatemala, and owes half its listing to the archaeological site found within.

Many of the protected areas are remote and hard to access for the independent traveler.

Environmental Issues

Environmental consciousness is not enormously developed in Guatemala, as the vast amounts of garbage strewn across the country and the choking clouds of diesel gas pumped out by its buses and trucks will quickly tell you. Despite the impressive list of parks and protected areas, genuine protection for those areas is harder to achieve, partly because of official collusion to ignore the regulations and partly because of pressure from poor Guatemalans in need of land.

NATIONAL PARKS & PROTECTED AREAS

PROTECTED AREA	FEATURES	ACTIVITIES	BEST TIME TO VISIT
Área de Protección Especial Punta de Manabique	large Caribbean wetland reserve; beaches, mangroves, lagoons, birds, crocodiles, possible manatee sightings	boat trips, wildlife observation, fishing, beach	any
Biotopo Cerro Cahuí (p242)	forest reserve beside Lago de Petén Itzá; Petén wildlife including monkeys	walking trails	any
Biotopo del Quetzal (Biotopo Mario Dary Rivera; p181)	easy-access cloud-forest reserve; howler monkeys, birds	nature trails, birdwatching, possible quetzal sightings	any
Biotopo San Miguel La Palotada	within Reserva de Biosfera Maya, adjoins Parque Nacional Tikal; dense Petén forest with millions of bats	jungle walks, visits to El Zotz archaeological site and bat caves	any, drier Nov-May
Parque Nacional Grutas de Lanquín	large cave system 61km from Cobán	bat-watching; observation of the nearby Semuc Champey lagoons and waterfalls	any
Parque Nacional Laguna del Tigre (p257)	remote, large park within Reserva de Biosfera Maya; freshwater wetlands, Petén flora and fauna	wildlife-spotting, including scarlet macaws, monkeys, crocodiles; visiting El Perú archaeological site	any, drier Nov-May
Parque Nacional Laguna Lachuá (p187)	circular, jungle-surrounded, turquoise lake, 220m deep; many fish, occasional jaguars and tapir	camping, swimming	any
Parque Nacional Mirador–Río Azul	national park within Reserva de Biosfera Maya; Petén flora and fauna	jungle treks to El Mirador archaeological site	any, drier Nov-May
Parque Nacional Río Dulce	beautiful jungle-lined lower Río Dulce between Lago de Izabal and the Caribbean; manatee refuge	boat trips	any
Parque Nacional Tikal	diverse jungle wildlife among Guatemala's most magnificent Maya ruins	wildlife-spotting, seeing spectacular Maya city	any, drier Nov-May
Refugio Bocas del Polochic (p214)	delta of Río Polochic at western end of Lago de Izabal; Guatemala's second-largest freshwater wetlands	birdwatching (more than 300 species), howler monkey observation	any
Refugio de Vida Silvestre Petexbatún	lake near Sayaxché; water birds	boat trips, fishing, visiting several archaeological sites	any
Reserva de Biosfera Maya	vast 21,000-sq-km area stretching across northern Petén; includes four national parks	jungle treks, wildlife-spotting	any, drier Nov-May
Reserva de Biosfera Sierra de las Minas (p214)	cloud-forest reserve of great biodiversity; key quetzal habitat	hiking, wildlife-spotting	any
Biotopo Monterrico-Hawaii (p173)	Pacific beaches and wetlands; birdlife, turtles	boat tours, birdwatching and turtle-watching	Jun-Nov (turtle nesting)

Guatemala's popularity as a tourist destination leads to a few environmental problems – the question of sewerage and trash disposal around Lago de Atitlán being a major one, and some inappropriate development in the rainforests of El Petén being another. Infrastructure development in Guatemala is moving at such a pace, though, that these problems seem minor compared to some of the other challenges that environmentalists face.

Deforestation is a problem in many areas, especially El Petén, where jungle is being felled not just for timber but also to make way for cattle ranches, oil pipelines, clandestine airstrips, new settlements and new maize fields cleared using the slash-and-burn method.

Oil exploration is a concern all over the country – Guatemalans are scrambling to start drilling in El Petén, as the Mexicans have been doing for years, tapping into a vast subterranean reserve that runs across the border. In his short stint in office, then-president Alfonso Portillo proposed drilling for oil in the middle of Lago de Izabal. The plan was shelved after massive outcry from international and local environmental agencies and some not too subtle pressure from Guatemala's trading partners. It's a project that's gone, but not forgotten.

Large-scale infrastructure projects are being announced with regularity, often in environmentally sensitive areas. The most controversial of these was the Northern Transversal, a strip of highway consolidating existing roads stretching from the Mexican border at Gracias a Dios, past Playa Grande and connecting with Modesto Méndez on the Belize border. Concerns with the project are many, as the road passes through sites of archaeological, environmental and cultural significance. Local environmental groups fear the new road will facilitate oil exploration in the Ixcán. One component of the plan is the construction of the Xalalá dam, a hydroelectric project. Despite claims that the dam will produce 886GWh of hydroelectric energy per year, thus reducing the country's energy deficit and reliance on fossil fuels, the project has run into stiff opposition as detractors claim that construction will displace local communities, affect water quality downstream and alter the ecology of the area through habitat loss.

Guatemala lost 17% of its forest between 1990 and 2005, but despite continued deforestation, still has 52% tree cover.

Transnational mining companies are moving in, most notably in San Marcos in the Western Highlands and the Sierra de las Minas in the southeast. Without the proper community consultation called for by law, the government has granted these companies license to operate open-cut mines in search of silver and gold. Chemical runoff, deforestation, eviction of local communities and water pollution are the main issues here. Police have been used to forcibly evict residents and quash community groups' peaceful protests.

Enviromental Organizations

Despite such a dire-sounding list of obstacles, a number of Guatemalan organizations are doing valiant work to protect their country's environment and biodiversity. The following are good sources of information for finding out more about Guatemala's natural and protected areas:

Arcas (www.arcasguatemala.com) NGO working with volunteers in sea-turtle conservation and rehabilitation of Petén wildlife.

Asociación Ak' Tenamit (www.aktenamit.org) Maya-run NGO working to reduce poverty and promote conservation and ecotourism in the rainforests of eastern Guatemala.

Cecon (www.cecon.usac.edu.gt) Manages six public *biotopos* and one *reserva natural*.

Fundación Defensores de la Naturaleza (www.defensores.org.gt) NGO that owns and administers several protected areas.

Survival Guide

Directory A–Z

Accessible Travel

Guatemala is not the easiest country to negotiate for travelers with a disability. Although many sidewalks in Antigua have ramps and cute little inlaid tiles depicting a wheelchair, the streets are cobblestone, so the ramps are anything but smooth and the streets worse.

Many hotels in Guatemala are old converted houses with rooms around a courtyard; such rooms are wheelchair accessible, but the bathrooms may not be. The most expensive hotels have facilities such as ramps, elevators and accessible toilets. Transportation is the biggest hurdle for travelers with limited mobility: travelers in a wheelchair may consider renting a car and driver as the buses will prove especially challenging due to lack of space.

Antigua-based **Transitions** (www.transitionsfoundation.org) is an organization aiming to increase awareness and access for people with disabilities in Guatemala.

Download Lonely Planet's free Accessible Travel guides from http://lptravel.to/AccessibleTravel.

Accommodations

Hotels From desperate dives out by the bus terminal to fancy-pants boutique numbers, there is no shortage of options.

Hostels Starting to make a dent in the budget accommodations scene, especially in backpacker-favored destinations such as Antigua, Quetzaltenango and around Lago de Atitlán.

Homestays Generally organized through Spanish schools, these are a great way to connect with local culture. Expect to pay between Q300 and Q600 a week on top of your tuition for your own room, a shared bathroom, and three meals a day except Sunday. It's important to find a homestay that gels with your goals – some families host several students at a time, creating more of an international hostel atmosphere than a family environment.

BOOK YOUR STAY ONLINE

For more accommodations reviews by Lonely Planet authors, check out http://lonelyplanet.com/hotels/. You'll find independent reviews, as well as recommendations on the best places to stay. Best of all, you can book online.

SLEEPING PRICES

The following price ranges refer to a double room with bathroom in high (but not absolute peak) season. Unless otherwise stated, taxes of 22% are included in the price.

$ less than Q200

$$ Q200–Q550

$$$ more than Q550

Camping Can be a hit-or-miss affair as there are few designated campgrounds and safety is rarely guaranteed. Where campsites are available, expect to pay from Q20 to Q50 per person per night.

Auto Hotels Anonymous drive-in hotels usually found on the edge of towns. Don't expect a quiet night if you stay in one; rooms are usually rented by the hour.

Children

Young children are highly regarded in Guatemala and can often break down barriers and open doors to local hospitality.

However, Guatemala is so culturally dense, with such an emphasis on history and archaeology, it's easy to overwhelm kids. That said, the ruins at Tikal (p245) should inspire all ages – if scrambling over ruins that aren't just home to an ancient civilization but also featured in several *Star Wars* movies isn't enough, there are also plenty of howler and spider monkeys to spot.

To keep kids entertained, try to make a point of breaking up the trip with visits to places such as Guatemala City's **Museo de los Niños** (Children's Museum; Map p52; ☎2475-5076; www.museodelosninos.com.gt; 5a Calle 10-00, Zona 13; Q40; ⏰8:30am-noon & 1-4:30pm Tue-Fri, 9:30am-1:30pm & 2:30-6pm Sat & Sun) and **Museo de Historia Natural** (Natural History Museum; Map p52; ☎2334-6065; Calle Mariscal Cruz 1-56, Zona 10; Q10; ⏰8am-3pm Mon-Fri), **Autosafari Chapín** (☎2222-5858; www.autosafarichapin.com; Carretera a Taxisco, Km 87.5; adult/child Q60/50; ⏰9:30am-5pm Tue-Sun), and Retalhuleu's **Xocomil** (☎7772-9400; www.irtra.org.gt; Carretera CITO, Km 180.5; adult/child Q100/50; ⏰9am-5pm Thu-Sun) water park and **Xetulul** (☎7722-9450; www.irtra.org.gt; Carretera CITO, Km 180.5; adult/child Q100/50; ⏰10am-5pm Fri-Sun) theme park. Most Spanish schools are open to kids, too, and many older children will enjoy activities such as ziplining, kayaking and horseback riding.

For general information on traveling with children, have a look at Lonely Planet's *Travel with Children*.

Practicalities

➡ Facilities such as safety seats in hired cars are rare, but nearly every restaurant can rustle up something resembling a high chair.

➡ If you are particular about specific brands of diapers and creams, bring what you can with you and stock up in supermarkets.

➡ If your child has to have some particular tinned or packaged food, bring supplies with you.

➡ Fresh milk is rare and may not be pasteurized – again, supermarkets are your best bet. Packet UHT milk and milk powder are much more common.

➡ Public breastfeeding is not common among urban, non-indigenous women and, when done, is done discreetly

Electricity

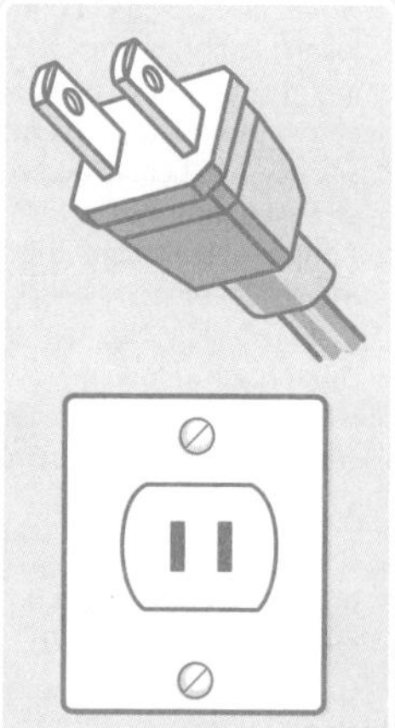

Type A
120V/60Hz

Type B
120V/60Hz

Embassies & Consulates

Australia, New Zealand and Ireland do not have diplomatic representation in Guatemala; their nearest embassies are in Mexico City.

Belizean Embassy (☎2367-3883; www.embajadadebelize.org; 5a Av 5-55, Europlaza 2, Office 1502, Zona 14, Guatemala City; ⏰9am-noon & 2-4pm Mon-Fri)

Canadian Embassy (☎2363-4348; www.guatemala.gc.ca; 13a Calle 8-44, 8th fl, Edificio Edyma Plaza, Zona 10, Guatemala City; ⏰8am-12:30pm & 1-4:30pm Mon-Thu, 8am-1:30pm Fri)

French Embassy (☎2421-7370; www.ambafrance-gt.org; 5a Av 8-59, Zona 14, Guatemala City; ⏰9am-noon Mon-Fri & by appt)

German Embassy (☎2364-6700; http://guatemala.diplo.de; Av La Reforma 9-55, Edificio Reforma 10, 10th fl, Zona 10, Guatemala City; ⏰9am-noon Mon-Fri)

Honduran Consulate (☎2332-6281; embhond@intelnet.net.gt; Av La Reforma 6-64, Zona 9, Guatemala City; ⏰9am-1pm Mon-Fri)

Mexican Embassy (☎2420-3400; https://embamex.sre.gob.mx/guatemala; 2a Av 7-57, Zona 10, Guatemala City; ⏰8am-12:30pm Mon-Fri)

Netherlands Consulate (☎2296-1490; guatemala@nlconsulate.com; Carretera a El Salvador Km 14.5, Santa Catarina Pinula; ⏰9am-1pm Mon-Fri)

Salvadoran Embassy (☎2245-7272; http://embajadaguatemala.rree.gob.sv; 15a Av 12-01, Zona 13, Guatemala City; ⏰8:30am-12:30pm & 1:15-3:30pm Mon-Fri)

UK Embassy (☎2380-7300; www.gov.uk/world/guatemala; 16a Calle 0-55, 11th fl, Torre Internacional, Zona 10, Guatemala City; ⏰7:30am-12:30pm & 1:30-4:30pm Mon-Thu, to 11:30am Fri)

US Embassy (☎2326-4000; http://guatemala.usembassy.gov; Av La Reforma 7-01, Zona 10, Guatemala City; ⌚7am-3:30 Mon-Thu, to noon Fri)

Food

What you eat in Guatemala will be a mixture of Guatemalan food, which is nutritious and filling without sending your taste buds into ecstasy, and international traveler-and-tourist food, which is available wherever travelers and tourists hang out. Your most satisfying meals in both cases will probably be in smaller eateries where the boss is in the kitchen themselves.

Essentials

Frijoles Beans, served refried or whole.

Tortillas A Guatemalan meal is naked without a serving of corn tortillas.

Tamal Steamed corn dough served a dozen ways with a dozen names.

Rellenitos Fried plantain meal served sweet as a finger-licking dessert.

Breakfast

Desayuno Chapín (Guatemalan breakfast) is a large affair consisting of (at least) eggs, tortillas, beans, fried plantains and coffee. If that's not enough, you can add steak, fresh fruit, cream and oatmeal to your order. Anywhere tourists are, you'll probably have the option of *desayuno Americano* (American breakfast), which will include some combination of bacon, pancakes, cereal, eggs, fruit juice and coffee.

EATING PRICES

The following price ranges refer to a standard main course, including taxes but not including tip.

$ less than Q50

$$ Q50–Q150

$$$ more than Q150

FANCY A BREW?

Traditionally, if you fancied a beer in Guatemala you had two choices – either Gallo or Cabro, with both of them made by Cerveceria Nacional, the country's monopolistic brewer. Things have started to change in recent years, however, and Guatemala has a small but growing craft-beer scene.

The arrival of Brahva, made by the world's biggest brewing company, in 2012 started to prise open the doors. Brahva is about as un-crafty as you can get, but while Gallo slugged it out with the new player, several local microbreweries sprang up to try their luck. Working in a grey legal area and short on technical supplies, innovators like Quetzaltenango's much-missed Xelita brewery showed what could be accomplished with a bit of vision.

Today, players like El Principe Gris in Guatemala City, Antigua Cerveza and the Antigua Brewing Company are broadening the beer palates of the country – often literally bar-by-bar, as they help install CO_2 supplies and other hard-to-locally-obtain equipment. And if imitation is the best form of flattery, then even the Cerveceria Nacional has finally got in on the act, producing dark ale under the Moza brand.

Lunch

Lunch is the biggest meal of the day. Many small eateries offer a set meal, which will consist of soup, a plate with some sort of meat, vegetables and rice, and potatoes. If you're on a budget, this *almuerzo del día* is often a good, filling option. In more expensive restaurants, the menu will be wider.

Dinner

La cena is, for Guatemalans, a lighter version of lunch, usually eaten between 7pm and 9pm. Even in cities, few restaurants will serve you after 10pm. In smaller villages, dinner will look very similar to breakfast – tortillas, beans, eggs and plantains. In restaurants catering to tourists, it could be anything from pepper steak to Thai curry.

Vegetarians & Vegans

Given that meat is a bit of a luxury for Guatemalans, it's not hard to get by without it. The basic Maya combination of vegetables, beans and tortillas is fairly nutritious. If you request a set lunch without the meat you'll still get soup, rice, vegetables or salad, cheese and tortillas. Be aware that some beans can be cooked in lard. There are a few dedicated vegetarian restaurants, mostly in bigger cities and tourist haunts. Chinese restaurants are always a good bet, and sometimes offer tofu dishes. Plenty of fruit, vegetables and nuts are always available in markets and supermarkets.

Drinking

While the bigger cities obviously have the higher concentration of places to drink, you can pretty much get a drink anywhere – restaurants are almost always licensed, as are gas stations and corner stores (unless run by Evangelicals, in which case there will be no alcohol whatsoever). While alcohol consumption is certainly not frowned upon, public drunkenness is.

Health

Staying healthy in Guatemala involves some common-sense precautions and a few destination-specific ones.

Before You Go

HEALTH INSURANCE

Despite relatively low costs for health care, it is strongly recommended that travelers to Guatemala take out travel insurance, covering medical costs. Check your policy carefully to see what is and is not covered before buying. Emergency medical evacuation is a recommended inclusion.

VACCINATIONS

Discuss your requirements with your doctor, but the vaccines that are usually recommended for travel to Central America are hepatitis A and B and typhoid. If you are planning to spend time handling animals or exploring caves, consider getting vaccinated for rabies.

In Guatemala

AVAILABILITY & COST OF HEALTHCARE

Larger towns have both public (cheap, with long waiting times) and private (expensive, but faster) hospitals, often with doctors who speak at least a little English. In smaller towns there will be a health clinic, and in villages there is usually a doctor. Guatemala City naturally has the best range of health services in the country.

Health care is relatively cheap in Guatemala (around Q30 for a standard doctor's consultation).

While 'medical tourism' is taking off in Guatemala (dentistry, for example, is a serious bargain compared to what you will pay elsewhere), if you have a serious complaint that does not require immediate attention, consider returning to your home country for treatment.

PRACTICALITIES

Smoking Forbidden in any enclosed space in Guatemala. Many businesses prohibit smoking anywhere on the premises (even in open-air patios). There are, of course, exceptions.

Weights & Measures Metric system for weights and distances; some food items such as meat, sugar and coffee sold in pounds; gasoline sold by the *galón* (US gallon).

HEALTHY EATING

By far the most common health issues that travelers to Guatemala experience are stomach-related. This can range from serious diseases such as cholera to simple cases of diarrhea. Watch what you eat, drink and generally put in your mouth. The following are a few simple guidelines to keep you out of the bathroom and on the road:

- Wash your hands thoroughly before eating or touching your face. Carry anti-bacterial hand gel.
- Eat only in places that appear to be clean (conditions in the dining room are sometimes a good indicator of what's going on in the kitchen).
- To ensure the food you eat is fresh and freshly cooked, eat only in busy places around mealtimes.
- Peel, cook or disinfect fruits and vegetables.
- Be very selective when it comes to street food.
- If you do get sick and it lasts longer than a few days, take a stool sample to a medical laboratory (even the smallest towns have them) for analysis. Any pharmacist will be able to use the readout to prescribe the appropriate medicine.

WATER

While many Guatemalans drink the tap water (often through necessity rather than choice), it is not recommended that foreigners do so.

- Tap water needs to be boiled thoroughly or disinfected.
- Purified water is cheap and readily available in tourist areas and many backcountry regions as well.
- Ice in more expensive restaurants is made from purified water, but order drinks without it if you want to be really cautious.

MOSQUITOES

Mosquitoes can transmit several serious diseases, including malaria, dengue fever and zika virus. Malaria tablets are available and recommended if you are planning to travel in rural areas at altitudes lower than 1500m, especially in the rainy season (June to November). It's worth noting that there is no malaria risk in Antigua or around Lago de Atitlán. The best prevention against mosquito-borne diseases is to avoid getting bitten. In high-risk areas this means a DEET–based insect repellent (bring one from home), long sleeves and pant legs, avoiding being outside around sunrise and sunset, and checking window screens and mosquito nets in hotel rooms for holes.

SEXUAL HEALTH

Guatemala's backpacker scene has a strong 'party hostel' element. Condoms are widely sold and responsible hostels should have information about local clinics where you can get tested for sexually transmitted diseases – strongly recommended for both your own health and that of potential partners.

Insurance

Getting travel insurance to cover theft, loss and medical problems is strongly recommended. Some policies specifically exclude dangerous activities, which can include scuba diving, motorcycling and even trekking.

You may prefer a policy that pays doctors or hospitals directly, rather than you having to pay on the spot and claim later. If you have to claim later, ensure you keep all documentation.

Check that the policy covers ambulances or an emergency flight home.

Worldwide travel insurance is available at www.lonelyplanet.com/travel-insurance. You can buy, extend and claim online anytime – even if you're already on the road.

Internet Access

Wi-fi is becoming readily available across the country, but can only really be counted on in large and/or tourist towns. Most (but not all) hostels and hotels offer wi-fi, as do many restaurants. If you have trouble finding a signal, try a Pollo Campero fast-food restaurant – they're in pretty much every town of any size and all offer free, unsecured access.

Internet cafes typically charge between Q5 and Q10 an hour – they're less common than they used to be but most towns still have one.

Language Courses

Guatemala is justly celebrated for its language schools. A spot of study here is a great way not only to learn Spanish, but also to meet locals and get an inside angle on the culture. Many travelers heading south through Central America to South America make Guatemala an early stop so they can pick up the Spanish skills they need for their trip.

Guatemalan language schools are some of the cheapest in the world, but few people go away disappointed. There are so many schools to choose from that it's essential to check out a few before deciding on one.

You can start any day at most schools, and study for as long as you like. If you're coming in peak season and hoping to get into one of the more popular schools, it's a good idea to book ahead. All decent schools offer a variety of elective activities, from salsa classes to movies to volcano hikes. Many schools offer classes in Maya languages as well as Spanish.

Where to Study

Antigua (p73) is the most popular place to study. Quetzaltenango (p134) is second, perhaps attracting a more serious type of student; Lago de Atitlan is another popular option. Antigua has a livelier students' and travelers' social scene. Outside of these areas, there are Spanish schools scattered across the country. Schools typically charge from Q900 to Q1200 per week for four hours of one-on-one classes five days a week. Homestays with a local family are a key draw for many, allowing you to further practice your Spanish – expect to pay roughly the same again for this as you do for your course.

Studying in a small town has its pros and cons. On the upside, you may be the only foreigner around, so you won't be speaking any English. On the downside, Spanish may be the second language of the inhabitants of the village (including your teacher), meaning that you could pick up all sorts of bad habits.

Choosing a School

Choosing between the mass of Spanish schools in Guatemala can be tough. Many schools don't have in-house teacher-training programs, so there aren't so many 'good schools' as there are 'good teachers.' It's best to pay for as little time as possible (a week, usually) so you can change if you're really unhappy. You should be completely up-front about what your goals are when starting (conversation, grammar, vocabulary etc), as well as any specialized interests that you have (politics, medical, legal etc) so the school can design a curriculum and assign you a teacher to best suit your needs. If you end up liking the school, but not the teacher, ask for a new teacher as soon as possible – personality conflicts occur, and four or five hours of one-on-one with someone you don't like can soon turn into hard work.

Here are some questions to think about when you're looking at schools. Some you can find out just by turning up, some you should ask the school, others you'll have to talk to current and ex-students to get a feel for.

- Where do the classes take place – on a quiet, shaded patio or in hot classrooms with buses roaring along the street outside?
- What experience and qualifications do the teachers have in teaching a second language?
- Is Spanish your teacher's first language?
- What afternoon and evening activities are available?
- What is the general atmosphere of the school? Serious students probably won't fit in at a school whose activities include all-night bar crawls, and party animals may feel out of place at schools with names like the Christian Spanish Academy.
- If the school claims to be involved in community or volunteer projects, is it a serious commitment, or just a marketing ploy?
- Many schools also offer further remote lessons by Skype.

Legal Matters

You may find that police officers in Guatemala are, at times, somewhat unhelpful. Generally speaking, the less you have to do with the law, the better.

Whatever you do, don't get involved in any way with illegal drugs – even if the locals seem to do so freely. As a foreigner you are at a distinct disadvantage and you may be set up by others. Drug laws in Guatemala are strict, and though enforcement may be uneven, penalties are severe. If you do get caught doing something you shouldn't, your best line of defense is to apologize, stay calm and proceed from there.

While many commentators claim that corruption is rife in Guatemala, don't take this to mean you can buy your way out of any situation. If it does seem that you can 'make everything go away' by handing over some cash, proceed cautiously and tactfully.

LGBT+ Travelers

Few places in Latin America are outwardly gay-friendly and Guatemala is no different. Technically, homosexuality is legal for persons over 18 years, but the reality can be another story, with harassment and violence against gays too often poisoning the plot. Don't even consider testing the tolerance for homosexual public displays of affection here.

Though Antigua and Guatemala City have palatable – if subdued – scenes, affection and action are still kept largely behind closed doors. Keep your eye out for Pride events in these cities, as well as Quetzaltenango. Mostly, though, LGBT travelers in Guatemala will find themselves keeping it low-key.

The best information site, Gay Guatemala (www.gayguatemala.com), is in Spanish.

Money

Guatemala's currency, the quetzal (ket-sahl, abbreviated to Q), has been fairly stable at around Q7.5 = US$1 for years. The quetzal is divided into 100 centavos.

ATMs

You'll find ATMs (cash machines, *cajeros automáticos*) for Visa/Plus System cards in all but the smallest towns, and there are MasterCard/Cirrus ATMs in many places, too, so one of these cards is the best basis for your supply of cash in Guatemala. The 5B network is widespread and particularly useful, as it works with both Visa and MasterCard cards.

Be aware that card skimming is a problem in Guatemala. Avoid ATMs that are left unguarded at night (ie those in the small room out front of the bank) and look for one that is in a secure environment (such as those inside supermarkets or shopping malls). Failing that, keep your hand covered when entering your PIN and check your balance online.

Cash

Cash is king in Guatemala, although carrying too much of it makes getting robbed a bigger pain than it would otherwise be. Some towns suffer from change shortages: always try to carry a stash of small bills. Keep a small supply of low-denomination US dollars (which are accepted pretty much anywhere, at various rates of exchange) as an emergency fund.

While everybody accepts dollars, you will almost always get a better deal by paying in quetzals.

Currencies other than the US dollar are virtually useless, although a small handful of places now change cash euros.

Credit Cards

Many banks give cash advances on Visa cards, and some on MasterCard. You can pay for many purchases with these cards or with American Express (Amex) cards – particularly in higher-end hotels and restaurants. Paying with credit card can attract service charges of up to 5% – be sure to ask if there is a *recargo* (transaction fee).

Traveler's Checks

If you're not packing plastic, a combination of Amex US-dollar traveler's checks and some cash US dollars is the way to go. Take some of these as a backup even if you do have a card. Many banks change US-dollar traveler's checks, and tend to give the best rates. Amex is easily the most recognized traveler's check brand. Few businesses will accept traveler's checks as payment or change them for cash.

Photography

Photography is a sensitive subject in Guatemala. Always ask permission before taking portraits, especially of Maya women and children. Don't be surprised if your request is denied. Children often request payment (usually Q1) in return for posing.

➡ In certain places, such as the church of Santo Tomás in Chichicastenango, photography is forbidden.

➡ Maya ceremonies (should you be so lucky to witness one) are off-limits for photography unless you are given explicit permission to take pictures.

➡ If local people make any sign of being offended, put your camera away and apologize immediately, both out of decency and for your own safety.

➡ Never take photos of army installations, men with guns or other sensitive military subjects.

Post

The privatised Guatemalan postal service is currently suspended, due to a years-long contract dispute with the government. For the time being, the only option for sending or receiving mail/packages is through an international courier. FedEx, UPS and DHL all operate in Guatemala.

Public Holidays

Guatemalan public holidays include the following:

New Year's Day (Año Nuevo) January 1

Easter (Semana Santa; Holy Thursday to Easter Sunday inclusive) March/April

Labor Day (Día del Trabajo) May 1

Army Day (Día del Ejército) June 30

Assumption Day (Día de la Asunción) August 15

Independence Day (Día de la Independencia) September 15

Revolution Day (Día de la Revolución) October 20

All Saints' Day (Día de Todos los Santos) November 1

Christmas Eve afternoon (Víspera Navidad) December 24

Christmas Day (Navidad) December 25

New Year's Eve afternoon (Víspera de Año Nuevo) December 31

Safe Travel

Guatemala is a mostly safe destination but crime can happen.

➡ The most frequently reported type of nasty incident involves robbery on walking trails.

➡ The days of robbers targeting tourist buses out on the open highway seem to be thankfully in the past, although some tourists in rental cars have been targeted.

➡ The crime you're most likely to become a victim of involves pickpocketing, bag-snatching, bag-slitting and the like in crowded streets, markets, bus stations and on buses, but also in empty, dark city streets.

➡ There are dedicated tourist police in Guatemala City and Antigua. Elsewhere, **Proatur** (☎in English 1500; http://proatur.visitguatemala.com) offers 24-hour assistance to tourists and is a good initial point of contact if you get into difficulty.

Tips

➡ It's best to travel and arrive in daylight hours. If that's not possible, travel at night using 1st-class buses and catch a taxi to your hotel once you arrive.

➡ Only carry the money, cards, checks and valuables that you need. Leave the rest in a sealed, signed envelope in your hotel's safe, and obtain a receipt for the envelope.

➡ Don't flaunt jewelry, cameras, smart phones or valuable-looking watches. Keep your wallet or purse out of view.

➡ On buses keep your important valuables with you, and keep a tight hold on them.

➡ Try to use ATMs in secure environments such as inside banks, shops or hotels, and be aware that card skimming is a reality here.

➡ Hiking in large groups and/or with a police escort reduces the risk of robbery.

➡ Resisting or trying to flee from robbers usually makes the situation worse – hand over what's asked for.

➡ Hiking on active volcanoes obviously has an element of risk. Get the latest story before you head out. In the wet season, hike in the morning before rain and possible thunderstorms set in.

➡ Be careful, especially in rural areas, when talking to small children: always ask permission to take photographs, and generally try not to put yourself in any situation that might be misinterpreted.

Scams

➡ A not uncommon scenario is for someone to spray ketchup or some other sticky liquid on your clothes. An

REPORTING A CRIME

Reporting a crime is always a toss-up in Guatemala. If you're the victim of something really serious, of course you should take it to the police – the phrase you're looking for here is '*Yo quisiera denunciar un crimen*' (I'd like to report a crime). If you've been robbed, get a statement filed so you can show your insurance company.

If it's a minor thing, on the other hand, you might want to decide whether or not it's really worth your while reporting it to the police.

Specially trained tourist police (often English speaking) operate in some major tourist areas – you can call them in Antigua (p86) and Guatemala City (p61).

Outside of those areas (and normal office hours) your best bet is to call **Proatur** (☎in English 1500; http://proatur.visitguatemala.com), which operates a 24-hour nationwide toll-free hotline in English and Spanish. It can give you information and assistance, help deal with the police and even arrange a lawyer if need be.

accomplice then appears to help you clean up the mess and robs you in the process. Other methods of distraction, such as dropping a purse or coins, or someone appearing to faint, are also used by pickpockets and bag snatchers.

➡ At bus stations, a 'priest' dashes up and on establishing that you speak English, tells you that he needs money as his wife has urgent medical needs and he can't even afford the bus ticket home.

➡ ATM card cloning happens in Guatemala. Card reading devices attach to the ATM (often inside the slot where you insert your card) and once they have your data, proceed to drain your account. The only way to avoid it is to use ATMs that cannot be tampered with easily (inside supermarkets or shopping malls). The ATMs most prone to tampering are the ones in the little unlocked room at the front of a bank. You should *never* have to enter your PIN number to gain access to an ATM room.

➡ In Lívingston, you might be approached by someone asking for donations to fund a Garifuna school or orphanage, that exists only in the story the scammer is spinning you.

Government Travel Advice

The following government websites offer travel advisories and information on current hot spots. Bear in mind that these sites are updated occasionally and are obliged to err on the side of caution – the vast majority of travelers visit Guatemala and don't experience any of the reported problems.

Australian Department of Foreign Affairs (www.smartraveller.gov.au)

Canadian Department of Foreign Affairs (https://travel.gc.ca/travelling)

New Zealand Ministry of Foreign Affairs (www.safetravel.govt.nz)

UK Foreign Office (www.gov.uk/foreign-travel-advice)

US State Department (http://travel.state.gov)

Shopping

Souvenirs are available all over the country, but you'll find the best range in the markets in Guatemala City, Antigua and Chichicastenango. The last of these is Guatemala's largest handicrafts market and a tourist attraction in its own right.

Coffee

Although most of Guatemala's finest beans are exported, some are (thankfully) held back for the local market. To get the finest, freshest beans available, visit a coffee farm and/or roaster and buy from them directly. Cobán, Quetzaltenango, Huehuetenango and Antigua produce some of the world's greatest coffee and support growers and roasters.

Jade

Beloved of the ancient Maya, jade is mined in Guatemala today and you'll find it both as jewelry and as miniature sculpture. Colors vary from light cream to the deep green traditionally associated with the stone. Antigua has some good shops where you can see the stone being worked on-site.

Leather Goods

Guatemala has some terrific leather goods. Fine briefcases, duffel bags, backpacks and belts are sold in most handicrafts markets. Cowboy boots and hats are a specialty in some areas, and custom work is welcome – head for the village of Pastores just outside Antigua for the best work. The artisanship of these items is usually phenomenal, and the prices astoundingly reasonable.

Textiles

Guatemala's intricate, brilliantly colored textiles are world famous. Weaving is a traditional and thriving art of the local Maya people. Clothing – especially the beautiful embroidered *huipiles* (tunics), *cortes* (skirts) and *fajas* (sashes) of the Maya women – as well as purses, tablecloths, blankets and many other woven items, are ubiquitous and good value, some for practical use, some more for souvenirs.

The largest craft markets are in Chichicastenango, the Mercado Central and Mercado de Artesanías in Guatemala City, and the Mercado de Artesanías in Antigua. Fine textiles of an infinite variety are also available in Antigua's shops. Elsewhere, in places such as Nebaj, Sololá, Santa Catarina Palopó, Santiago Atitlán and Todos Santos Cuchumatán, you can obtain local textiles at weekly markets or a few permanent stalls.

Telephone

Guatemala has no area or city codes. Calling within Guatemala, just dial the eight-digit local number. Calling from other countries, dial the international access code (☎00 in most countries), then the Guatemala country code (☎502), then the eight-digit local number. The international access code from Guatemala is ☎00.

Cell phones

Roaming is expensive in Guatemala. Most travelers buy a local SIM card (if you have an unlocked phone) or a local prepaid phone on arrival. ID is required to buy both. 4G is increasingly available.

There are three cell companies in the country. Tigo (www.tigo.com.gt) and Claro (www.claro.com.gt) have the best coverage; Movistar (www.movistar.com.gt) tends to be cheaper but has poor coverage outside major towns.

Phonecards

Telgua public phones are common, and require a phone card *(tarjeta telefónica de Telgua)*, bought from shops, kiosks and the like. Card sales points may advertise the fact with red signs saying *'Ladatel de Venta Aquí.'* The cards come in denominations of Q20, Q30 and Q50: you slot them into a Telgua phone, dial your number, and the display will tell you how much time you have left.

Time

Guatemala runs on North American Central Standard Time (GMT/UTC minus six hours). The 24-hour clock is often used, so 1pm may be written as 13 or 1300.

Toilets

- You cannot throw *anything* into Guatemalan toilets, including toilet paper, because of poor sewage drains. Bathrooms are equipped with some sort of receptacle (usually a small wastebasket) for soiled paper.
- Toilet paper is not always provided, so always carry some. If you don't have any and need some, asking a restaurant worker for *un rollo de papel* (a roll of paper), accompanied by a panicked facial expression, usually produces fast results.
- Public toilets are rare. Use the ones at cafes, restaurants, your hotel and archaeological sites. Buses rarely have toilets on board and if they do, don't count on them working.

Tourist Information

Guatemala's national tourism institute, INGUAT (El Instituto Guatemalteco de Turismo; www.visitguatemala.com), has information offices in major tourist areas. A few towns have departmental, municipal or private-enterprise tourist information offices. **Proatur** (☎in English 1500; http://proatur.visitguatemala.com), a joint private-government initiative, operates a useful 24-hour toll-free advice and assistance hotline.

Volunteering

Volunteer programs abound in Guatemala, but not all are created equal. If you're interested in giving something back, remember that the best schemes should be designed with their beneficiaries in mind, not just to make their participants feel good about themselves, and volunteers shouldn't join programs to do something they're not qualified for back home.

Most volunteer posts require basic or better Spanish skills and a minimum time commitment. Depending on the organization, you may have to pay for room and board for the duration of your stay. Before making a commitment, read the fine print and ask lots of questions.

Short-term placements in orphanages have been a staple of Guatemalan volunteering for years. Unicef and other child-protection organizations have pointed out the damage that can be done to children's welfare by such programs, and no reputable scheme should allow volunteers such access to children.

Lonely Planet strongly encourages those considering volunteering to do research and make informed, responsible choices. One source of information on trusted volunteer opportunities is Quetzaltenango-based **EntreMundos** (Map p136; ☎7761-2179; www.entremundos.org; 6a Calle 7-31, Zona 1; ⏲2-4pm Mon-Thu), which works with a large variety of local NGOs that welcome skilled volunteers.

Women Travelers

Women should encounter no special problems traveling in Guatemala. The primary thing you can do to make it easy for yourself while traveling here is to dress modestly. Modesty in dress is highly regarded, and if you practice it, you will usually be treated with respect.

Shorts should really be worn only at the beach, not in town, and especially not in the highlands. Skirts should be at or below the knee. Going braless is considered provocative. Many local women swim with T-shirts over their swimsuits.

Women traveling alone can expect plenty of attention from talkative men. Often they're just curious and not out for a foreign conquest. It is, of course, up to you how to respond, but there's no need to be intimidated. Consider the situation and circumstances, and stay confident. Try to sit next to women or children on the bus. Local women rarely initiate conversations, but usually have lots of interesting things to say once the ball is rolling.

While there's no need to be paranoid, the possibility of rape and assault does exist. Use your normal traveler's caution – avoid walking alone in isolated places or through city streets late at night, and skip hitchhiking.

Work

Some travelers find work in bars, restaurants and places to stay in Antigua, Panajachel or Quetzaltenango, but wages are usually barely above survival pay. If you're looking to crew a yacht, there's always work being offered around the Río Dulce area, sometimes for short trips, sometimes to the US and further afield. Check noticeboards and online forums for details.

Transportation

GETTING THERE & AWAY

With land borders on three sides, river- and sea-port entries and two international airports, it's not hard to get into or out of Guatemala. Flights, cars and tours can be booked online at lonelyplanet.com/bookings.

Air

There are direct flights from the US with most major US airlines. AeroMexico (www.aeromexico.com) and Interjet (www.interjet.com) fly direct from Mexico City. Avianca (www.avianca.com/gt) has flights to Guatemala City from most Central American capitals. If you are coming from elsewhere, you will almost certainly be changing planes in the US, Mexico or elsewhere in Central America.

Land

Where possible, cross borders as early in the day as possible. Onward transportation tends to wind down in the afternoon and border areas are not always the most salubrious places to hang around late. There is no departure tax when you leave Guatemala by land, although many border officials will ask for an illicit Q10.

Border Crossings

Guatemala has official border crossings with all of its neighboring countries. Check visa requirements (p16) before arrival.

BELIZE

- Melchor de Mencos (GUA) – Benque Viejo del Carmen (BZE)

EL SALVADOR

- Ciudad Pedro de Alvarado (GUA) – La Hachadura (ES)
- Valle Nuevo (GUA) – Las Chinamas (ES)
- San Cristóbal Frontera (GUA) – San Cristóbal (ES)
- Anguiatú (GUA) – Anguiatú (ES)

HONDURAS

- Agua Caliente (GUA) – Agua Caliente (HND)
- El Florido (GUA) – Copán Ruinas (HND)
- Corinto (GUA) – Corinto (HND)

MEXICO

The busiest and most useful border crossings:

- Ciudad Tecún Umán (GUA) – Ciudad Hidalgo (MEX)
- El Carmen (GUA) – Talisman (MEX)
- La Mesilla (GUA) – Ciudad Cuauhtémoc (MEX)

Bus

Bus is the most common way to enter Guatemala by land. Most first-class international buses run nonstop from

CLIMATE CHANGE & TRAVEL

Every form of transport that relies on carbon-based fuel generates CO_2, the main cause of human-induced climate change. Modern travel is dependent on aeroplanes, which might use less fuel per kilometre per person than most cars but travel much greater distances. The altitude at which aircraft emit gases (including CO_2) and particles also contributes to their climate change impact. Many websites offer 'carbon calculators' that allow people to estimate the carbon emissions generated by their journey and, for those who wish to do so, to offset the impact of the greenhouse gases emitted with contributions to portfolios of climate-friendly initiatives throughout the world. Lonely Planet offsets the carbon footprint of all staff and author travel.

DEPARTURE TAX

Guatemala levies a departure tax of US$30 on outbound air passengers, which should be included in your fare. If it's not, it has to be paid in cash US dollars or quetzals at the airline check-in desk.

Guatemala City to their destinations. First-class buses for Belize also depart from Flores/Santa Elena. On first-class buses (particularly to Honduras and El Salvador) the driver may take your passport and complete border formalities for you. Going to Belize or Mexico, you will be required to do them yourself. Whatever border fees (official or otherwise) there are will not be included in the ticket price.

Popular tourist shuttles from Guatemala and Antigua include to San Cristobál de las Casas (Mexico), Flores (Belize) and Copán (Honduras).

Second-class buses tend not to cross the border.

Car & Motorcycle

The mountain of paperwork and liability involved with driving into Guatemala deters many travelers. You will need the following documents, all clear and consistent, to enter Guatemala with a car:

- current and valid registration
- proof of ownership (if you don't own the car, you'll need a notarized letter of authorization from the owner that you are allowed to take it)
- your current and valid driver's license or an International Driving Permit (IDP), issued by the automobile association in your home country
- temporary import permit (available free at the border and good for a maximum 90 days).

Insurance from foreign countries is not recognized by Guatemala, forcing you to purchase a policy locally. Most border posts and nearby towns have offices selling liability policies. To deter foreigners from selling cars in Guatemala, the authorities make you exit the country with the vehicle you used to enter it. Do not be the designated driver when crossing borders if you don't own the car, because you and it will not be allowed to leave Guatemala without each other.

Gasoline is readily available in all but the tiniest of villages. If you see a young kid waving a funnel at you, it means he is selling cheap contraband Mexican gas – some people swear by it, others claim that its high sediment content ruins engines.

Mechanics are also everywhere. Authorized agencies can only be found in the larger cities. Generic parts are easy to come by, but if you're looking for originals, Toyota is by far the most popular make in the country, followed (distantly) by Mazda and Ford.

River

There are two possible crossings from Mexico's Chiapas State to El Petén – the most commonly used one crosses at the Mexican town of Frontera Corozal by boat to either La Técnica or Bethel in Guatemala. Frontera Corozal has good transport connections to Palenque in Mexico and there are regular buses from La Técnica and Bethel to Flores/Santa Elena, Guatemala.

The other theoretical river route from Mexico into Guatemala's Petén department is up the Río de la Pasión from Benemérito de las Américas, south of Frontera Corozal, to Sayaxché, but there are currently no immigration facilities or reliable passenger services along this route.

Sea

Three daily public boats connect Punta Gorda in Belize with Lívingston (p222) and Puerto Barrios (p216) in Guatemala. The boats connect with bus services to/from Belize City.

There is a Q80 departure tax when leaving Guatemala by sea.

GETTING AROUND

Air

At the time of writing the only scheduled internal flights were between Guatemala City and Flores, a route operated daily by Avianca (www.avianca.com) and TAG (www.tag.com.gt).

Bicycle

Guatemala's mountainous terrain and occasionally terrifying road conditions make for hard going when it comes to intercity pedaling. That said, if you have your wits about you, cycling is a great way to get around smaller towns – Antigua, Quetzaltenango and San Pedro La Laguna are among the towns where you can rent reasonable mountain bikes (you don't want skinny wheels here) by the hour, day, week or longer. There are bike shops in almost every town where you can buy a new bike starting from around Q800.

Boat

The Caribbean town of Lívingston is only reachable by boat, across the Bahía de Amatique from Puerto Barrios or down the Río Dulce from the town of Río Dulce – both great trips. In Lago de Atitlán fast fiberglass *lanchas* (launches) zip across the waters between villages – by far the best way to get around.

Bus

Buses go almost everywhere in Guatemala, and the buses will leave you with some of your most vivid memories of the country. Most of them are ancient school buses from the US and Canada. Many travelers know these vehicles as chicken buses, after the live cargo accompanying many passengers. They are frequent, crowded and cheap. Expect to pay around Q10 to Q15 for an hour of travel.

Chicken buses will stop anywhere, for anyone. Helpers will yell '*hay lugares!*' (eye loo-*gar*-ays), which literally means 'there are places.' The space they refer to may be no more than a sliver of air between hundreds of locals mashed against one another. These same helpers will also yell their bus's destination in voices of varying hilarity and cadence; just listen for the song of your town. Tall travelers will be especially challenged on these buses. To catch a chicken bus, simply stand beside the road with your arm out parallel to the ground.

Some routes, especially between big cities, are served by more comfortable buses with the luxury of one seat per person. The best buses are labeled 'Pullman,' '*especial*' or '*primera clase.*' Occasionally these may have bathrooms (but don't count on them working), televisions and even food service.

Pullman routes always originate or end in Guatemala City.

In general, more buses leave in the morning (some leave as early as 2am) than the afternoon. Bus traffic drops off precipitously after about 4pm; night buses are rare and not generally recommended.

Distances in Guatemala are not huge and, apart from the Guatemala City–Flores run, you won't often ride for more than four hours at a time. On a typical four-hour bus trip you'll cover 175km to 200km for Q60 to Q100.

For a few of the better services you can buy tickets in advance, and this is generally worth doing as it ensures that you get a place.

On some shorter routes, minibuses, usually called 'microbuses,' are replacing chicken buses. These are operated with the same cram-'em-all-in principle and can be even more uncomfortable because they have less leg room. Where neither buses nor minibuses roam, *picop* (pick-up) trucks serve as de facto buses; you hail them and pay for them as if they were the genuine article.

At least a couple of times a month, a chicken bus plunges over a cliff or rounds a blind bend into a head-on collision. Newspapers are full of gory details and diagrams of the latest wreck, which doesn't foster affectionate feelings toward Guatemalan public transportation.

Shuttle Minibus

Heavily advertised shuttle minibuses run by travel agencies provide comfortable and quick transport along all the main routes plied by tourists. They're much more expensive than buses but a lot more convenient – they usually offer a door-to-door service from your hotel, with scheduled meal and bathroom breaks. The most popular shuttle routes include Guatemala City airport–Antigua, Antigua–Panajachel, Panajachel–Chichicastenango and Lanquín–Antigua.

Note that you'll sometimes be asked to swap vehicles halfway through a journey so individual shuttles can quickly return to their city of origin. It's a way of keeping costs down, but a bit of a surprise the first time the driver leaves you at a gas station waiting for your onward connection.

A CHICKEN BUS IS HATCHED

If you rode the bus to school 10 years ago or more in the US, you might just end up meeting an old friend in Guatemala, resurrected and given new life as a 'chicken bus.' Love 'em or hate 'em, chicken buses (*camionetas* or *parrillas* to Guatemalans) are a fact of life in traveling around Guatemala. A lot of times there is no alternative.

In the US, once school buses reach the ripe old age of 10 years or do 150,000 miles, they're auctioned off. They then get towed through the States and Mexico, taken to a workshop where they are refitted (bigger engine, six-speed gearbox, roof rack, destination board, luggage rack, longer seats) and fancied up with a paint job, stereo and chrome detailing. Drivers then add their individual touches – anything from religious paraphernalia to stuffed toys and Christmas lights dangling around the dashboard area.

If you've got a choice of buses to go with, looks are important – chances are if the paint is fresh and the chrome gleaming, the owner also has the cash to spend on new brakes and regular maintenance. And, with a conservative estimate of an average of one chicken-bus accident per week in Guatemala, this is something you may want to keep in mind.

Car & Motorcycle

You can drive in Guatemala with your home-country driver's license or with an International Driving Permit (IDP). Guatemalan driving etiquette will probably be very different from what you're used to back home: passing on blind curves, ceding the right of way to vehicles coming uphill on narrow passes and deafening honking for no apparent reason are just the start. Expect few road signs and no indication from other drivers of what they are about to do. Do not pay any attention to turn signals – they are rarely used and even more rarely used to indicate a turn in the direction they would seem to be. Hazard lights generally mean that the driver is about to do something foolish and/or illegal.

A vehicle coming uphill always has the right of way. *Túmulos* are speed bumps that are generously (sometimes oddly) placed throughout the country, usually on the main drag through a town. Use of seat belts is obligatory, but generally not practiced.

Navigating colonial-era street plans, which often control traffic with devilish one-way systems, can be a nightmare.

In Guatemala driving at night is a bad idea for many reasons, not the least of which are armed bandits, drunk drivers and decreased visibility.

Every driver involved in an accident that results in injury or death is taken into custody until a judge determines responsibility.

If someone's car breaks down on the highway (particularly on curvy mountain roads), they'll warn other drivers by putting shrubs or small branches on the road for a few hundred meters beforehand. Annoyingly, they rarely pick them up afterwards, but if you're driving and you see these, it's best to be cautious and slow down.

Rental

While car hire is certainly possible, if you're sticking to the main sights, logistically it is rarely a good idea – Antigua is best seen on foot, the villages around Lago de Atitlán are best visited by boat, and the distance from either of those to Tikal makes it a much better idea to catch a bus or fly. That said, for freedom and comfort, nothing beats having your own wheels.

There are car-hire places in all the major tourist cities. To rent a car or motorcycle you need to show your passport, driver's license and a major credit card. Usually, the person renting the vehicle must be 25 years or older. Insurance policies accompanying rental cars may not protect you from loss or theft, in which case you could be liable for hundreds or even thousands of dollars in damages. Be careful where you park, especially in Guatemala City and at night. Even if your hotel does not have parking, they will know of a secure garage somewhere nearby. Red-painted kerbs mean no parking.

Motorcycles are available for rent in Antigua and around Lago de Atitlán. Bringing safety gear is highly recommended.

Hitchhiking

Hitchhiking in the strict sense of the word is generally not practiced in Guatemala because it is not safe. However, where the bus service is sporadic or nonexistent, pick-up trucks and other vehicles may serve as public transport. If you stand beside the road with your arm out, someone will stop. You are expected to pay the driver as if you were traveling on a bus and the fare will be similar. This is a reliable system used by locals and travelers, and the only inconvenience you're likely to encounter is full-to-overflowing vehicles – get used to it.

Any other form of hitching is never entirely safe, and we don't recommend it. Travelers who hitch should understand that they are taking a small but potentially serious risk.

Local Transportation

Bus & Minibus

Public transportation within towns and cities outside of Guatemala City is chiefly provided by newish, crowded minibuses. They're useful to travelers mainly in the more spread-out cities such as Quetzaltenango and Huehuetenango. Guatemala City has its own forms of bus services – the old red buses that are not recommended for safety reasons and the newer fleets of TransMetro and TransUrbano buses.

Taxi

Taxis are fairly plentiful in most significant towns. A 10-minute ride can cost about Q60, which is relatively expensive – expect to hear plenty of woeful tales from taxi drivers about the price of gasoline. Except for some taxis in Guatemala City, they don't use meters: you must agree upon the fare before you set off – best before you get in, in fact. Uber is available in Guatemala City and Antigua.

If you feel reluctant to take on the Guatemalan roads, an interesting alternative to car hire can be to hire a taxi driver for an extended time. This often works out only slightly more expensive than renting and gives you all the freedom and comfort without the stress of having to drive.

Tuk-tuk

If you've spent any time in Asia, you'll be very familiar with the *tuk-tuk*, a three-wheeled minitaxi nominally seating three passengers and a driver, but obviously capable of carrying twice that amount.

Language

There are around 20 Maya indigenous languages used in Guatemala, but Spanish is the most commonly spoken language.

SPANISH

Latin American Spanish pronunciation is easy, as most sounds have equivalents in English. Note that kh is a throaty sound (like the 'ch' in the Scottish *loch*), v and b are like a soft English 'v' (between a 'v' and a 'b'), and r is strongly rolled. There are some variations in spoken Spanish across Latin America, the most notable being the pronunciation of the letters *ll* and *y*. In our pronunciation guides they are represented with y because they are pronounced as the 'y' in 'yes' in most of Latin America. Note, however, that in some parts of the continent they sound like the 'lli' in 'million'. If you read our colored pronunciation guides as if they were English, you'll be understood. The stressed syllables are indicated with italics in our pronunciation guides.

The polite form is used in this chapter; where both polite and informal options are given, they are indicated by the abbreviations 'pol' and 'inf'. Where necessary, both masculine and feminine forms of words are included, separated by a slash and with the masculine form first, eg *perdido/a* (m/f).

Basics

Hello.	*Hola.*	o·la
Goodbye.	*Adiós.*	a·*dyos*
How are you?	*¿Qué tal?*	ke tal
Fine, thanks.	*Bien, gracias.*	byen *gra*·syas
Excuse me.	*Perdón.*	per·*don*
Sorry.	*Lo siento.*	lo *syen*·to
Please.	*Por favor.*	por fa·*vor*
Thank you.	*Gracias.*	*gra*·syas
You are welcome.	*De nada.*	de *na*·da
Yes./No.	*Sí./No.*	see/no

WANT MORE?

For in-depth language information and handy phrases, check out Lonely Planet's *Latin American Spanish Phrasebook*. You'll find it at **shop.lonelyplanet.com**, or you can buy Lonely Planet's iPhone phrasebooks at the Apple App Store.

My name is ...
Me llamo ... — me *ya*·mo ...

What's your name?
¿Cómo se llama Usted? — *ko*·mo se *ya*·ma oo·*ste* (pol)
¿Cómo te llamas? — *ko*·mo te *ya*·mas (inf)

Do you speak English?
¿Habla inglés? — *a*·bla een·*gles* (pol)
¿Hablas inglés? — *a*·blas een·*gles* (inf)

I don't understand.
Yo no entiendo. — yo no en·*tyen*·do

Accommodations

I'd like a single/double room.
Quisiera una habitación individual/doble. — kee·*sye*·ra *oo*·na a·bee·ta·*syon* een·dee·vee·*dwal*/*do*·ble

How much is it per night/person?
¿Cuánto cuesta por noche/persona? — *kwan*·to *kwes*·ta por *no*·che/per·*so*·na

Does it include breakfast?
¿Incluye el desayuno? — een·*kloo*·ye el de·sa·*yoo*·no

campsite	*terreno de cámping*	te·*re*·no de *kam*·peeng
guesthouse	*pensión*	pen·*syon*
hotel	*hotel*	o·*tel*
youth hostel	*albergue juvenil*	al·*ber*·ge khoo·ve·*neel*

air-con	*aire acondicionado*	*ai*·re a·kon·dee·syo·*na*·do
bathroom	*baño*	*ba*·nyo
bed	*cama*	*ka*·ma
window	*ventana*	ven·*ta*·na

Directions

Where's ...?
¿Dónde está ...? — *don*·de es·*ta* ...

What's the address?
¿Cuál es la dirección? — kwal es la dee·rek·*syon*

Could you please write it down?
¿Puede escribirlo, por favor? — *pwe*·de es·kree·*beer*·lo por fa·*vor*

Can you show me (on the map)?
¿Me lo puede indicar (en el mapa)? — me lo *pwe*·de een·dee·*kar* (en el *ma*·pa)

at the corner	*en la esquina*	en la es·*kee*·na
at the traffic lights	*en el semáforo*	en el se·*ma*·fo·ro
behind ...	*detrás de ...*	de·*tras* de ...
in front of ...	*enfrente de ...*	en·*fren*·te de ...
left	*izquierda*	ees·*kyer*·da
next to ...	*al lado de ...*	al *la*·do de ...
opposite ...	*frente a ...*	*fren*·te a ...
right	*derecha*	de·*re*·cha
straight ahead	*todo recto*	*to*·do *rek*·to

Eating & Drinking

Can I see the menu, please?
¿Puedo ver el menú, por favor? — *pwe*·do ver el me·*noo* por fa·*vor*

What would you recommend?
¿Qué recomienda? — ke re·ko·*myen*·da

Do you have vegetarian food?
¿Tienen comida vegetariana? — *tye*·nen ko·*mee*·da ve·khe·ta·*rya*·na

I don't eat (red meat).
No como (carne roja). — no *ko*·mo (*kar*·ne *ro*·kha)

QUESTION WORDS

How?	*¿Cómo?*	*ko*·mo
What?	*¿Qué?*	ke
When?	*¿Cuándo?*	*kwan*·do
Where?	*¿Dónde?*	*don*·de
Who?	*¿Quién?*	kyen
Why?	*¿Por qué?*	por ke

That was delicious!
¡Estaba buenísimo! — es·*ta*·ba bwe·*nee*·see·mo

Cheers!
¡Salud! — sa·*loo*

The bill, please.
La cuenta, por favor. — la *kwen*·ta por fa·*vor*

I'd like a table for ...	*Quisiera una mesa para ...*	kee·*sye*·ra *oo*·na *me*·sa *pa*·ra ...
(eight) o'clock	*las (ocho)*	las (*o*·cho)
(two) people	*(dos) personas*	(dos) per·*so*·nas

Key Words

bottle	*botella*	bo·*te*·ya
breakfast	*desayuno*	de·sa·*yoo*·no
(too) cold	*(muy) frío*	(mooy) *free*·o
dinner	*cena*	*se*·na
fork	*tenedor*	te·ne·*dor*
glass	*vaso*	*va*·so
hot (warm)	*caliente*	kal·*yen*·te
knife	*cuchillo*	koo·*chee*·yo
lunch	*comida*	ko·*mee*·da
plate	*plato*	*pla*·to
spoon	*cuchara*	koo·*cha*·ra

Meat & Fish

beef	*carne de vaca*	*kar*·ne de *va*·ka
chicken	*pollo*	*po*·yo
duck	*pato*	*pa*·to
lamb	*cordero*	kor·*de*·ro
pork	*cerdo*	*ser*·do
prawn	*langostino*	lan·gos·*tee*·no
salmon	*salmón*	sal·*mon*
tuna	*atún*	a·*toon*
turkey	*pavo*	*pa*·vo
veal	*ternera*	ter·*ne*·ra

Fruit & Vegetables

apple	*manzana*	man·*sa*·na
banana	*plátano*	*pla*·ta·no
beans	*judías*	khoo·*dee*·as
cabbage	*col*	kol
capsicum	*pimiento*	pee·*myen*·to
carrot	*zanahoria*	sa·na·*o*·rya
cherry	*cereza*	se·*re*·sa
corn	*maíz*	ma·*ees*
cucumber	*pepino*	pe·*pee*·no
grape	*uvas*	*oo*·vas
lemon	*limón*	lee·*mon*
lettuce	*lechuga*	le·*choo*·ga

SIGNS

Abierto	Open
Cerrado	Closed
Entrada	Entrance
Hombres/Varones	Men
Mujeres/Damas	Women
Prohibido	Prohibited
Salida	Exit
Servicios/Baños	Toilets

mushroom	*champiñón*	cham·pee·*nyon*
nuts	*nueces*	*nwe*·ses
onion	*cebolla*	se·*bo*·ya
orange	*naranja*	na·*ran*·kha
peach	*melocotón*	me·lo·ko·*ton*
peas	*guisantes*	gee·*san*·tes
pineapple	*piña*	*pee*·nya
plum	*ciruela*	seer·*we*·la
potato	*patata*	pa·*ta*·ta
spinach	*espinacas*	es·pee·*na*·kas
strawberry	*fresa*	*fre*·sa
tomato	*tomate*	to·*ma*·te
watermelon	*sandía*	san·*dee*·a

Other

bread	*pan*	pan
butter	*mantequilla*	man·te·*kee*·ya
cheese	*queso*	*ke*·so
egg	*huevo*	*we*·vo
honey	*miel*	myel
jam	*mermelada*	mer·me·*la*·da
pepper	*pimienta*	pee·*myen*·ta
rice	*arroz*	a·*ros*
salt	*sal*	sal
sugar	*azúcar*	a·*soo*·kar

Drinks

beer	*cerveza*	ser·*ve*·sa
coffee	*café*	ka·*fe*
(orange) juice	*zumo (de naranja)*	*soo*·mo (de na·*ran*·kha)
milk	*leche*	*le*·che
red wine	*vino tinto*	*vee*·no *teen*·to
tea	*té*	te
(mineral) water	*agua (mineral)*	*a*·gwa (mee·ne·*ral*)
white wine	*vino blanco*	*vee*·no *blan*·ko

Emergencies

Help!	*¡Socorro!*	so·*ko*·ro
Go away!	*¡Vete!*	*ve*·te

Call ...!	*¡Llame a ...!*	*ya*·me a ...
a doctor	*un médico*	oon *me*·dee·ko
the police	*la policía*	la po·lee·*see*·a

I'm lost.
Estoy perdido/a. — es·*toy* per·*dee*·do/a (m/f)

I'm ill.
Estoy enfermo/a. — es·*toy* en·*fer*·mo/a (m/f)

I'm allergic to (antibiotics).
Soy alérgico/a a (los antibióticos). — soy a·*ler*·khee·ko/a a (los an·tee·*byo*·tee·kos) (m/f)

Where are the toilets?
¿Dónde están los baños? — *don*·de es·*tan* los *ba*·nyos

Shopping & Services

I'd like to buy ...
Quisiera comprar ... — kee·*sye*·ra kom·*prar* ...

I'm just looking.
Sólo estoy mirando. — *so*·lo es·*toy* mee·*ran*·do

Can I look at it?
¿Puedo verlo? — *pwe*·do *ver*·lo

I don't like it.
No me gusta. — no me *goos*·ta

How much is it?
¿Cuánto cuesta? — *kwan*·to *kwes*·ta

That's too expensive.
Es muy caro. — es mooy *ka*·ro

There's a mistake in the bill.
Hay un error en la cuenta. — ai oon e·*ror* en la *kwen*·ta

ATM	*cajero automático*	ka·*khe*·ro ow·to·*ma*·tee·ko
internet cafe	*cibercafé*	see·ber·ka·*fe*
market	*mercado*	mer·*ka*·do
post office	*correos*	ko·*re*·os
tourist office	*oficina de turismo*	o·fee·*see*·na de too·*rees*·mo

Time, Dates & Numbers

What time is it?	*¿Qué hora es?*	ke *o*·ra es
It's (10) o'clock.	*Son (las diez).*	son (las dyes)
It's half past (one).	*Es (la una) y media.*	es (la *oo*·na) ee *me*·dya

morning	*mañana*	ma·nya·na
afternoon	*tarde*	tar·de
evening	*noche*	no·che
yesterday	*ayer*	a·yer
today	*hoy*	oy
tomorrow	*mañana*	ma·nya·na

Monday	*lunes*	loo·nes
Tuesday	*martes*	mar·tes
Wednesday	*miércoles*	myer·ko·les
Thursday	*jueves*	khwe·ves
Friday	*viernes*	vyer·nes
Saturday	*sábado*	sa·ba·do
Sunday	*domingo*	do·meen·go

1	*uno*	oo·no
2	*dos*	dos
3	*tres*	tres
4	*cuatro*	kwa·tro
5	*cinco*	seen·ko
6	*seis*	seys
7	*siete*	sye·te
8	*ocho*	o·cho
9	*nueve*	nwe·ve
10	*diez*	dyes
20	*veinte*	veyn·te
30	*treinta*	treyn·ta
40	*cuarenta*	kwa·ren·ta
50	*cincuenta*	seen·kwen·ta
60	*sesenta*	se·sen·ta
70	*setenta*	se·ten·ta
80	*ochenta*	o·chen·ta
90	*noventa*	no·ven·ta
100	*cien*	syen
1000	*mil*	meel

Transportation

boat	*barco*	bar·ko
bus	*autobús*	ow·to·boos
plane	*avión*	a·vyon
train	*tren*	tren

A … ticket, please.	*Un billete de …, por favor.*	oon bee·ye·te de … por fa·vor
1st-class	*primera clase*	pree·me·ra kla·se
2nd-class	*segunda clase*	se·goon·da kla·se
one-way	*ida*	ee·da
return	*ida y vuelta*	ee·da ee vwel·ta

first	*primero*	pree·me·ro
last	*último*	ool·tee·mo
next	*próximo*	prok·see·mo

bus stop	*parada de autobuses*	pa·ra·da de ow·to·boo·ses
cancelled	*cancelado*	kan·se·la·do
delayed	*retrasado*	re·tra·sa·do
ticket office	*taquilla*	ta·kee·ya
timetable	*horario*	o·ra·ryo
train station	*estación de trenes*	es·ta·syon de tre·nes

I want to go to …
Quisiera ir a … kee·sye·ra eer a …

Does it stop at …?
¿Para en …? pa·ra en …

What stop is this?
¿Cuál es esta parada? kwal es es·ta pa·ra·da

What time does it arrive/leave?
¿A qué hora llega/sale? a ke o·ra ye·ga/sa·le

Please tell me when we get to …
¿Puede avisarme cuando lleguemos a …? pwe·de a·vee·sar·me kwan·do ye·ge·mos a …

I want to get off here.
Quiero bajarme aquí. kye·ro ba·khar·me a·kee

I'd like to hire a …	*Quisiera alquilar …*	kee·sye·ra al·kee·lar …
bicycle	*una bicicleta*	oo·na bee·see·kle·ta
car	*un coche*	oon ko·che
motorcycle	*una moto*	oo·na mo·to

helmet	*casco*	kas·ko
mechanic	*mecánico*	me·ka·nee·ko
petrol/gas	*gasolina*	ga·so·lee·na
service station	*gasolinera*	ga·so·lee·ne·ra

Is this the road to …?
¿Se va a … por esta carretera? se va a … por es·ta ka·re·te·ra

(How long) Can I park here?
¿(Cuánto tiempo) Puedo aparcar aquí? (kwan·to tyem·po) pwe·do a·par·kar a·kee

The car has broken down (at …).
El coche se ha averiado (en …). el ko·che se a a·ve·rya·do (en …)

I have a flat tyre.
Tengo un pinchazo. ten·go oon peen·*cha*·so

I've run out of petrol.
Me he quedado sin gasolina. me e ke·*da*·do seen ga·so·*lee*·na

MODERN MAYA

Since the pre-Columbian period, the two ancient Maya languages, Yucatec and Cholan, have subdivided into more than 20 separate Maya languages (such as Yucatec, Chol, Ch'orti', Tzeltal, Tzotzil, Lacandón, Mam, K'iche' and Kakchiquel). Indigenous languages are seldom written, but when they are, the Roman alphabet is used. Most Maya speakers will only read and write Spanish – they may not be literate in Maya.

Maya pronunciation is pretty straightforward. There are just a few rules to keep in mind: **c** is always a hard 'k' sound, as in 'cat'; **j** is similar to the 'h' in 'half'; **u** is pronounced as in 'prune', but at the beginning or end of a word, it's like English 'w'; and **x** is pronounced like the 'sh' in 'shoes'. The consonants followed by an apostrophe (**b'**, **ch'**, **k'**, **p'**, **t'**) are pronounced more forcefully and explosively. Vowels followed by an apostrophe (') indicate a glottal stop (like the sound between the two syllables in 'uh-oh'.) Stress usually falls on the last syllable.

K'iche'

K'iche' is spoken throughout the Guatemalan highlands, from around Santa Cruz del Quiché to the area around Lago de Atitlán and Quetzaltenango. There are around two million K'iche' Maya in Guatemala.

Good morning.	*Saqarik.*
Good afternoon.	*Xb'eqij.*
Good evening/night.	*Xokaq'ab'.*
Goodbye.	*Chab'ej.*
See you soon.	*Kimpetik ri.*
Excuse me.	*Kyunala.*
Thank you.	*Uts awech.*
What's your name?	*Su ra'b'i?*
My name is ...	*Nu b'i ...*
Where are you from?	*Ja kat pewi?*
I'm from ...	*Ch'qap ja'kin pewi ...*

Where is a/the ...?	*Ja k'uichi' ri ...?*
bathroom	*b'anb'al chulu*
bus stop	*tek'lib'al*
doctor	*ajkun*
hotel	*jun worib'al*

Do you have ...?	*K'olik ...?*
boiled water	*saq'li*
coffee	*kab'e*
rooms	*k'plib'al*

bad	*itzel*
blanket	*k'ul*
closed	*tzapilik*
cold	*joron*
good	*utz*
hard	*ko*
hot	*miq'in*
open	*teb'am*
sick	*yiwab'*
soft	*ch'uch'uj*
vegetables	*ichaj*

north (white)	*saq*
south (yellow)	*k'an*
east (red)	*kaq*
west (black)	*k'eq*

1	*jun*
2	*keb'*
3	*oxib'*
4	*kijeb'*
5	*job'*
6	*waq'ib'*
7	*wuqub'*
8	*wajxakib'*
9	*b'elejeb'*
10	*lajuj*

Mam

Mam is spoken in the department of Huehuetenango. This is the language you'll hear in Todos Santos Cuchumatán. Note that many Mam words have been in disuse for so long that the Spanish equivalent is used almost exclusively. The numbers from one to 10 are the same as in K'iche', and for numbers higher than 10, Spanish words are used.

Good morning/ afternoon/evening.	*Chin q'olb'el teya.* (sg inf) *Chin q'olb'el kyeyea.* (pl inf)
Goodbye.	*Chi nej.*
See you soon.	*Ak qli qib'.*
Excuse me.	*Naq samy.*
Thank you.	*Chonte teya.*
How are you?	*Tzen ta'ya?*
What's your name?	*Tit biya?*

My name is ...	*Luan bi ...*
Where are you from?	*Jaa'tzajnia?*
I'm from ...	*Ac tzajni ...*
Where is a/the ...?	*Ja at ...?*
bathroom	*bano*
doctor	*medico/doctor*
hotel	*hospedaje*
Is there somewhere we can sleep?	*Ja tun kqta'n?*
Where is the bus stop?	*Ja nue camioneta?*
How much are the fruit and vegetables?	*Je te ti lobj?*
Do you have ...?	*At ...?*
boiled water	*kqa'*
coffee	*café*
rooms	*cuartos*
I'm cold.	*At xb'a'j/choj.*
I'm sick.	*At yab'.*
bad	*k'ab'ex/nia g'lan*
closed	*jpu'n*
good	*banex/g'lan*
hard	*kuj*
hot	*kyaq*
open	*jqo'n*
soft	*xb'une*

north (white)	*okan*
south (yellow)	*eln*
east (red)	*jawl*
west (black)	*kub'el*

GLOSSARY

Apartado Postal – post-office box; abbreviated Apdo Postal

Ayuntamiento – often seen as H Ayuntamiento (Honorable Ayuntamiento) on the front of town hall buildings; translates as 'Municipal Government'

barrio – district, neighborhood

billete – bank note

boleto – ticket (bus, train, museum etc)

bolo – colloquial term for drunk (noun)

cabañas – cabins

cacique – Maya chief; also used to describe provincial warlord or strongman

caféteria – literally 'coffee-shop,' but refers to any informal restaurant with waiter service; not usually a cafeteria in the North American sense of a self-service restaurant

cajero automático – automated teller machine(ATM)

callejón – alley or narrow or very short street

camión – truck or bus

camioneta – bus or pickup truck

cardamomo – cardamom; a spice grown extensively in the Verapaces and used as a flavor enhancer for coffee and tea

casa de cambio – currency exchange office; offers exchange rates comparable to those of banks and is much faster to use, though uncommon in Guatemala

cenote – large, natural limestone cave used for water storage (or ceremonial purposes)

cerveza – beer

Chac – Maya god of rain

chac-mool – Maya sacrificial stone sculpture

chapín – slang term for citizen of Guatemala

charro – cowboy

chicle – sap of the sapodilla tree; used to manufacture chewing gum

chicleros – men who collect chicle

Chinka' – small, non-Maya indigenous group living on the Pacific Slope

chuchkajau – Maya prayer leader

chuj – traditional Maya sauna; also known as *tuj*

chultún – artificial Maya cistern

cigarro – cigarette

cocina – kitchen; also used for a small, basic one-woman place to eat, often located in or near a municipal market, and in the phrases *cocina económica* (economical kitchen) or a *cocina familiar* (family kitchen)

cofradía – religious brotherhood, most often found in the highlands

colectivo – jitney taxi or minibus that picks up and drops off passengers along its route

comal – hot griddle or surface used to cook tortillas

comedor – basic and cheap eatery, usually with a limited menu

completo – full; a sign you may see on hotel desks in crowded cities

conquistador – explorer-conqueror of Latin America from Spain

copal – tree resin used as incense in Maya ceremonies

correos – post office

corte – Maya wraparound skirt

costumbre – traditional Maya rites

criollos – people born in Guatemala of Spanish blood

cruce – crossroads, usually where you make bus connections; also known as *entronque*

cuadra – a city block

curandero – traditional indigenous healer

damas – ladies; the usual sign on toilet doors

dzul, dzules – Maya for foreigners or 'townsfolk'

faja – Maya waist sash or belt

ferrocarril – railroad

finca – plantation, farm

galón, galones – US gallons; fluid measure of 3.79L

glyph – symbolic character or figure; usually engraved or carved in relief

gringo/a – a mildly pejorative term applied to a male/female North American visitor; sometimes applied to any visitor of European heritage

gruta – cave

guayabera – man's thin fabric shirt with pockets and appliquéd designs on the front, over the shoulders and down the back; often worn in place of a jacket and tie on formal occasions

hacienda – estate; also 'treasury,' as in Departamento de Hacienda, Treasury Department

hay – pronounced like 'eye,' meaning 'there is' or 'there are'; you're equally likely to hear no hay, meaning 'there isn't' or 'there aren't'

hombre/s – man/men

huipil – Maya woman's woven tunic; often very colorful and elaborately embroidered

IVA – *impuesto al valor agregado* or value-added tax; on hotel rooms it is 12%

juego de pelota – ball game

kaperraj – Maya woman's all-purpose cloth; used as a head covering, baby sling, produce sack, shawl and more

Kukulcán – Maya name for the Aztec-Toltec plumed serpent Quetzalcóatl

ladino – person of mixed indigenous and European race; a more common term in Guatemala than *mestizo*

lancha – motorboat used to transport passengers; driven by a *lanchero*

larga distancia – long-distance telephone

lavandería – laundry; a *lavandería automática* is a coin-operated laundry

leng – in the highlands, a colloquial Maya term for coins

libra – pound; weight measurement of 0.45kg

lleno – full (fuel tank)

machismo – maleness, masculine virility

malecón – waterfront boulevard

manglar – mangrove

manzana – apple

mariachi – small group of street musicians featuring stringed instruments, trumpets and often an accordion; sometimes plays in restaurants

marimba – Guatemala's xylophone-like national instrument

mestizo – person of mixed indigenous and European blood; the word *ladino* is more common in Guatemala

metate – flattish stone on which corn is ground with a cylindrical stone roller

milla – mile; distance of 1.6km

milpa – maize field

mirador – lookout, vista point

mochilero – backpacker

mordida – 'bite'; small bribe paid to keep the wheels of bureaucracy turning

mudéjar – Moorish architectural style

mujer/es – woman/women

na – thatched Maya hut

onza – ounce; weight of 28g

palacio de gobierno – building housing the executive offices of a state or regional government

palacio municipal – city hall; seat of the corporation or municipal government

palapa – thatched shelter with a palm-leaf roof and open sides

panza verde – literally 'green belly,' a nickname given to Antigua residents who are said to eat lots of avocados

parada – bus stop; usually for city buses

picop – pickup truck

pie – foot; measure of 0.30m

pisto – colloquial Maya term for money, quetzals

posada – guesthouse

propino, propina – a tip, different from a *mordida*, which is really a bribe

punta – sexually suggestive dance enjoyed by the Garífuna of the Caribbean coast

puro – cigar

Quetzalcóatl – plumed serpent god of the Aztecs and Toltecs; see also Kukulcán

rebozo – long woolen or linen scarf covering the head or shoulders

refago – Maya wraparound skirt

retablo – ornate, often gilded altarpiece

retorno – 'return'; used on traffic signs to signify a U-turn or turnaround

sacbé, sacbeob – ceremonial limestone avenue or path between great Maya cities

sacerdote – priest

sanatorio – hospital, particularly a small private one

sanitario – literally 'sanitary'; usually means toilet

secadora – clothes dryer

stela, stelae – standing stone monument(s); usually carved

supermercado – supermarket; anything from a corner store to a large, US-style supermarket

taller – shop or workshop

taller mecánico – mechanic's shop, usually for cars

teléfono comunitario – community telephone; found in the smallest towns

tepezcuintle – edible jungle rodent the size of a rabbit

tienda – small store that may sell anything from candles and chickens to aspirin and bread

típico – typical or characteristic of a region; particularly used to describe food

tocoyal – Maya head covering

traje – traditional clothing worn by the Maya

tzut – Maya man's equivalent of a *kaperraj*

viajero – traveler

vulcanizadora – automobile tire repair shop

zonas – zones

zotz – bat (the mammal) in many Maya languages

Behind the Scenes

SEND US YOUR FEEDBACK

We love to hear from travelers – your comments keep us on our toes and help make our books better. Our well-traveled team reads every word on what you loved or loathed about this book. Although we cannot reply individually to your submissions, we always guarantee that your feedback goes straight to the appropriate authors, in time for the next edition. Each person who sends us information is thanked in the next edition – the most useful submissions are rewarded with a selection of digital PDF chapters.

Visit **lonelyplanet.com/contact** to submit your updates and suggestions or to ask for help. Our award-winning website also features inspirational travel stories, news and discussions.

Note: We may edit, reproduce and incorporate your comments in Lonely Planet products such as guidebooks, websites and digital products, so let us know if you don't want your comments reproduced or your name acknowledged. For a copy of our privacy policy visit lonelyplanet.com/privacy.

OUR READERS

Many thanks to the travelers who used the last edition and wrote to us with helpful hints, useful advice and interesting anecdotes: Colette Campbell Stuart, C Stephen Murray, Shane McCarthy, Lucy Berry, Judith Cooper Haden, Michael Miller, Scott Barnwell, Nathalie Van Den Bosch

WRITER THANKS

Paul Clammer

Muchas gracias to Valeria Ayerdi in Xela for friendship and advice on everything important, and to Natalia Pedermo Ayerdi, the coolest David Bowie fan in Guatemala. On the lake, thanks to Deedle and Dave Ratcliffe for the reassuring pots of tea. In Xela, cheers to Bryan Seibel, Mark Peacock and Josh Wood, in El Paredón to Sonal Amin of La Choza Chula, and in Antigua to Sunny Flores. In the Cuchumatanes, I could have had no better guide than Carlos Tucuxlopez – *gracias*. At LP, thanks to Alicia Johnson, not least for the understanding when I was moving house (and country). Finally, thanks and love above all to Robyn, no matter which continent we end up on.

Ray Bartlett

Thanks first and always to my family and amazing friends, for letting me go on these adventures and still remembering me when I get back. To the incredible Alicia J, for the editorial wisdom and for speedy answers when I needed them. To all the people I met or who helped along the way, especially Virginia, Mereja, Nathalie, Valerie, Peggy, Marlon, Ismael, Jane, Kelsey, Stuart, Rachna, Flor, and so many others. Thanks so much. Can't wait to be back again soon.

ACKNOWLEDGEMENTS

Climate map data adapted from Peel MC, Finlayson BL & McMahon TA (2007) 'Updated World Map of the Köppen-Geiger Climate Classification', *Hydrology and Earth System Sciences*, 11, 163344.

Illustrations p248-9 by Michael Weldon.

Cover photograph: Textile from Chichicastenango, Robert Fried/Alamy ©

THIS BOOK

This 7th edition of Lonely Planet's *Guatemala* guidebook was curated by Paul Clammer who also researched and wrote it along with Ray Bartlett, with contributions by Celeste Brash. The previous edition was written by Daniel C Schechter and Lucas Vidgen.

This guidebook was produced by the following:

Destination Editor Alicia Johnson

Senior Product Editors Grace Dobell, Saralinda Turner

Regional Senior Cartographer Corey Hutchison

Product Editor Jenna Myers

Book Designer Jessica Rose

Assisting Editors Michelle Coxall, Carly Hall, Victoria Harrison, Fionnuala Twomey, Simon Williamson

Assisting Cartographer Michael Garrett

Cover Researcher Naomi Parker

Thanks to Bailey Freeman, Anne Mason, Kathryn Rowan

Index

Map Pages **000**
Photo Pages 000

Map Pages **000**
Photo Pages 000

Map Legend

Sights

- Beach
- Bird Sanctuary
- Buddhist
- Castle/Palace
- Christian
- Confucian
- Hindu
- Islamic
- Jain
- Jewish
- Monument
- Museum/Gallery/Historic Building
- Ruin
- Shinto
- Sikh
- Taoist
- Winery/Vineyard
- Zoo/Wildlife Sanctuary
- Other Sight

Activities, Courses & Tours

- Bodysurfing
- Diving
- Canoeing/Kayaking
- Course/Tour
- Sento Hot Baths/Onsen
- Skiing
- Snorkeling
- Surfing
- Swimming/Pool
- Walking
- Windsurfing
- Other Activity

Sleeping

- Sleeping
- Camping
- Hut/Shelter

Eating

- Eating

Drinking & Nightlife

- Drinking & Nightlife
- Cafe

Entertainment

- Entertainment

Shopping

- Shopping

Information

- Bank
- Embassy/Consulate
- Hospital/Medical
- Internet
- Police
- Post Office
- Telephone
- Toilet
- Tourist Information
- Other Information

Geographic

- Beach
- Gate
- Hut/Shelter
- Lighthouse
- Lookout
- Mountain/Volcano
- Oasis
- Park
- Pass
- Picnic Area
- Waterfall

Population

- Capital (National)
- Capital (State/Province)
- City/Large Town
- Town/Village

Transport

- Airport
- Border crossing
- Bus
- Cable car/Funicular
- Cycling
- Ferry
- Metro station
- Monorail
- Parking
- Petrol station
- Subway/Subte station
- Taxi
- Train station/Railway
- Tram
- Underground station
- Other Transport

Routes

- Tollway
- Freeway
- Primary
- Secondary
- Tertiary
- Lane
- Unsealed road
- Road under construction
- Plaza/Mall
- Steps
- Tunnel
- Pedestrian overpass
- Walking Tour
- Walking Tour detour
- Path/Walking Trail

Boundaries

- International
- State/Province
- Disputed
- Regional/Suburb
- Marine Park
- Cliff
- Wall

Hydrography

- River, Creek
- Intermittent River
- Canal
- Water
- Dry/Salt/Intermittent Lake
- Reef

Areas

- Airport/Runway
- Beach/Desert
- Cemetery (Christian)
- Cemetery (Other)
- Glacier
- Mudflat
- Park/Forest
- Sight (Building)
- Sportsground
- Swamp/Mangrove

Note: Not all symbols displayed above appear on the maps in this book

OUR STORY

A beat-up old car, a few dollars in the pocket and a sense of adventure. In 1972 that's all Tony and Maureen Wheeler needed for the trip of a lifetime – across Europe and Asia overland to Australia. It took several months, and at the end – broke but inspired – they sat at their kitchen table writing and stapling together their first travel guide, *Across Asia on the Cheap*. Within a week they'd sold 1500 copies. Lonely Planet was born.

Today, Lonely Planet has offices in Franklin, London, Melbourne, Oakland, Dublin, Beijing and Delhi, with more than 600 staff and writers. We share Tony's belief that 'a great guidebook should do three things: inform, educate and amuse'.

OUR WRITERS

Paul Clammer

Antigua, The Highlands, The Pacific Slope Paul has worked as a molecular biologist, tour leader and travel writer. Since 2003 he has worked as a guidebook author for Lonely Planet, contributing to over 25 LP titles, covering destination swathes of South and Central Asia, West and North Africa, and the Caribbean. In recent years he's lived in Morocco, Jordan, Haiti and Fiji, as well as his native England. Paul also wrote the Plan chapters.

Ray Bartlett

Central & Eastern Guatemala, El Petén, Guatemala City Ray has been travel writing for nearly two decades, bringing Japan, Korea, Mexico, Tanzania, Guatemala, Indonesia, and many parts of the United States to life in rich detail for top industry publishers, newspapers, and magazines. His acclaimed debut novel, *Sunsets of Tulum*, set in Yucatán, was a Midwest Book Review 2016 Fiction pick. Among other pursuits, he surfs regularly and is an accomplished Argentine tango dancer.

Contributing Writer: Celeste Brash (Copán, Honduras)

Published by Lonely Planet Global Limited
CRN 554153
7th edition – Jul 2019
ISBN 978 1 78657 490 9

10 9 8 7 6 5 4 3 2 1
Printed in China